PRAISE FOR

⊷ SCALIA ⊷

"[A] sweeping new intellectual biography. . . . [Murphy's] biography of Justice Scalia is patient and thorough, alive both intellectually and morally, and written in fluid, unshowy prose. . . . [It] functions as an M.R.I. scan of one of the most influential conservative thinkers of the 20th century."

—Dwight Garner, *The New York Times*

"[A] fair-minded biography. . . . Murphy's deeper and more scholarly focus on Scalia offers . . . an opportunity to study one justice's progress from the Reagan administration's great right hope to the more problematic character he's become."

—Paul M. Barrett, *San Francisco Chronicle*

"May be the most exhaustive treatment of a sitting justice ever written. . . . *Scalia* is a skeptical, often critical look at its subject, but free of snark; it does its readers the service of taking Scalia's ideas seriously."

—Jeff Shesol, *The New York Times Book Review*

"An intellectual biography of one of [the Supreme Court's] most colorful members. . . . A lucid account of a wide variety of topics through the lens of judicial biography."

—Alexander Tsesis, *The Chicago Tribune*

"A compelling biography of one of the most conservative, combative, and bombastic Supreme Court Justices in our nation's history. . . . A terrific start to understanding Justice Scalia and his impact on American constitutional law."

—Kevin J. Hamilton, *The Seattle Times*

"Endlessly fascinating . . . *Scalia* offers a deep examination of the man and his work, one certain to ignite the passions of partisans in our increasingly polarized nation."

—Jay Strafford, *Richmond Times-Dispatch*

"In Bruce Allen Murphy, Scalia has met a timely and unintimidated biographer ready to probe. . . . Murphy does not shrink from adjudicating Scalia's dueling public claims: that separating faith from public life is impossible and, at the same time, that he himself has done just that on the Court."

—Dahlia Lithwick, *The Atlantic*

"Murphy does Scalia the unwarranted honor of treating originalism seriously but does not flinch when he gets to the bottom line: At least in Scalia's hands, originalism is not a method of judicial interpretation, it is a device to import his values into the Constitution."

—Jim Newton, *Los Angeles Times*

"A deeply probing biography of the controversial Supreme Court justice. . . . Murphy moves case by case in an evenhanded, thoroughgoing study."

—*Kirkus Reviews*

"A highly engaged, well-researched analysis of a brash justice whose single-mindedness may ultimately reduce his legacy."

—*Booklist* (starred review)

"Murphy gives Scalia's intellect and influence its due. . . . What is strong in *Scalia*—and what probably irks so many fans of Scalia—is that Murphy does a good job poking holes in Scalia's strict textual interpretation of the Constitution."

—Tom Deignan, *Newark Star-Ledger*

"Comprehensively researched, accessible, and fascinating. . . . Recommended for friend and foe alike of Nino to understand just what the Supreme Court is up to."

—*Library Journal* (starred review)

ALSO BY BRUCE ALLEN MURPHY

Wild Bill: The Legend and Life of William O. Douglas

Fortas: The Rise and Ruin of a Supreme Court Justice

The Brandeis/Frankfurter Connection:
The Secret Political Activities of Two Supreme Court Justices

SCALIA

⤙⤙ A COURT OF ONE ⤚⤚

BRUCE ALLEN MURPHY

SIMON & SCHUSTER PAPERBACKS

NEW YORK   LONDON   TORONTO   SYDNEY   NEW DELHI

Simon & Schuster Paperbacks
An Imprint of Simon & Schuster, Inc.
1230 Avenue of the Americas
New York, NY 10020

First Simon & Schuster trade paperback edition June 2015

SIMON & SCHUSTER PAPERBACKS and colophon are
registered trademarks of Simon & Schuster, Inc.

For information about special discounts for bulk purchases,
please contact Simon & Schuster Special Sales at
1-866-506-1949 or business@simonandschuster.com.

The Simon & Schuster Speakers Bureau can bring authors to your live event.
For more information or to book an event contact the Simon & Schuster Speakers
Bureau at 1-866-248-3049 or visit our website at www.simonspeakers.com.

Interior design by Joy O'Meara

Manufactured in the United States of America

10   9   8   7   6   5   4   3   2   1

The Library of Congress has cataloged the hardcover edition as follows:
Murphy, Bruce Allen, author.
    Scalia : a court of one / Bruce Allen Murphy.
       p.   cm.
    Includes bibliographical references and index.
1. Scalia, Antonin.   2. Judges—United States—Biography.   3. United States.
Supreme Court—Biography.   4. Constitutional law—United States.   I. Title.
    KF8745.S33M87   2014
    347.73'2634—dc23
    [B]   2013042971

978-0-7432-9649-6
978-0-7432-9650-2 (pbk)
978-1-4516-1146-5 (ebook)

For my world
Carol, Emily, Geoff, and Adam

and

In memory of
Patricia Gebhard Wright

and

John T. McCartney

"Anyway, that's my view. And it happens to be correct."

Justice Antonin Scalia
2008

CONTENTS

Scalia in Winter

It was a bitterly cold day in Washington, D.C., on Monday, January 21, 2013, as roughly a million people gathered on the National Mall in front of the United States Capitol to celebrate the second inaugural of President Barack Hussein Obama. One man, though, was not in such a celebratory mood. A stocky, balding, distinguished-looking gentleman in a black judicial gown trudged slowly behind Chief Justice John Roberts to his prime seat in the front of the platform, immediately to the left of where Obama would swear his oath of office.[1]

Surrounding the man on the inaugural platform was a veritable who's who of current and past American politics, including members of the cabinet, senators, members of Congress, former presidents, and other dignitaries. Usually on occasions such as this, except for the president being sworn into office, everyone else is just a face in the crowd. But, as he usually did on such occasions, this man in a judicial gown found a way to make himself the center of attention.

United States Supreme Court Associate Justice Antonin Gregory Scalia, then less than two months shy of his seventy-seventh birthday, had become the most recognizable and most controversial member of the Court. He had become famous for his "originalism" theory for deciding cases, believing that the Constitution and its amendments should be interpreted according to the meaning of the words as people understood them at the time they were written. But he was just as famous for his provocative speeches and public statements, as well as the controversies that always seemed to swirl around him.

Today Scalia turned heads with his strange headwear, which appeared to be a billowing, puffy, black velvet hat with peaked corners, which the New York *Daily News* would later describe as a "beret on steroids."[2] Before long the Twitterverse buzzed with comments under the hashtag

#Scaliaweirdhat, initially created by Democratic senator Claire McCaskill of Missouri, when she tweeted her photo of the justice wearing his hat.

"How 16th Century German/Northern Italian of him!" read one of the earliest tweets.

"He thinks he's at the Trial of Emile Zola," tweeted snarky liberal television commentator Keith Olbermann.

"Looking like the antagonist from a Dan Brown novel," tweeted someone whose twitter handle was "The Opportunity."

"Scalia in that hat: the mad medieval monk, fresh from illuminating a biblical manuscript and torturing heretics," tweeted another.[3]

Soon, Scalia's headwear was getting so much attention in the Twitterverse that he was, in the parlance of the technology, "trending."

In time, various Internet news sites contributed to the exchange, e-blasting the photo through the rest of the press corps. "What's the deal with Justice Scalia's weird hat?" posted Microsoft's MSN News in the "What's Trending" column of its website. "It makes him look like a grumpy cardinal from a thousand years ago."

"If you're looking for truly weird, once-every-four-years head gear, look no further than the justices of the Supreme Court," wrote Russell Goldman of ABC News.[4]

Whether or not Scalia had intended for his choice of headwear to cause such a sensation, or whether he just wore it because it was a cold day and he really liked the hat, he could not have been unhappy with the result. On such occasions, he was usually most pleased if the focus was on him. And it often was. Nearly everyone in the press and public had an opinion about him—either positive or negative. The new army of legal bloggers on the Internet had long ago made him and his views one of their main topics of conversation. As a result, on a Court comprised of nine members, he was always the most visible and most discussed. Surely, at Obama's second inaugural, having everyone discussing him must have been the way Antonin Scalia liked it.

After much discussion in cyberspace about Scalia's haberdashery, former Scalia law clerk Kevin Walsh, a professor of law at the University of Richmond Law School, posted on his blog site, *Walshslaw*: "The twitterverse is alive with tweets about Justice Scalia's headgear for today's inauguration. At the risk of putting all the fun speculation to an end. . . . The hat is a custom-made replica of the hat depicted in [the younger Hans] Holbein's famous portrait of St. Thomas More. It was a gift from the St. Thomas More Society [a nonprofit, socially conservative public interest law center] of Richmond,

Virginia. We presented it to him in November 2010 as a memento of his participation in our 27th annual Red Mass and dinner."[5] Scalia, according to the St. Thomas More Society, was "over the moon" about the gift, and said that he would wear it to future academic occasions.[6]

Far from ending the speculation, though, this news only fueled it. Scalia had repeatedly commented over the years on his reverence for St. Thomas More, the patron saint of lawyers. More was the devout lord chancellor for King Henry VIII of England. In his early career, he had sentenced heretics and religious dissenters to death. Later, when the king asked for More's acquiescence to remove the English church from the authority of Pope Clement VII, and to the annulment of his marriage to Catherine of Aragon in order to marry Anne Boleyn, More refused. Standing on his principles led to More's beheading for high treason, making him a religious martyr. Some Catholic analysts on the internet wondered whether Scalia saw himself in a similar battle over principles on the Supreme Court and with the Democratic president.

On January 23, *The Christian Post* put on its internet blog, "CP Politics," a column bearing the headline, "Was Scalia's Inauguration Hat a Birth Control Mandate Protest?" The piece speculated about a reference by the justice to a recent political battle over whether Obama's new national health care law could require companies and organizations with religious affiliations to fund birth control, even if they had a religious objection to it. The piece argued: "Some observers speculate that the hat symbolized religious conscience protections and was worn to protest efforts by the Obama administration to enforce a birth control mandate on religious groups."[7] Agreeing with this view, Matthew Schmitz, the new deputy editor of the "First Thoughts" blog on the Catholic *First Things* blog site, posted a piece titled "Scalia Wears Martyr's Cap to Inauguration," saying, "Wearing the cap of a statesman who defended liberty of church and integrity of Christian conscience to the inauguration of a president whose policies have imperiled both: Make of it what you will."[8]

• • •

The chatter over Scalia's presumed reaction to Barack Obama's second term continued when three weeks later, on Tuesday, February 12, two hours before President Obama was to deliver the State of the Union address, Scalia attracted attention by *not* attending a presidential affair. Instead of attending the State of the Union address, Scalia explained to National Public Radio's longtime Supreme Court reporter Nina Totenberg: "I haven't gone for a long time. . . . It has become a very political, very political event. And I just don't think it's appropriate for justices to be there. . . . I think it's turned into a rather silly, silly affair in which there are applause lines for one side, and that side of the house jumps up and cheers and then applauds, then the other side jumps up and cheers, and the Supreme Court justices always look at the chief justice to see whether he's—whether he's clapping or not, you know. . . . So I just think it's a—has turned into a childish spectacle, and I do not think I want to be there to lend dignity to it."[9]

Sensing an opening to raise the larger issue of objections to the Obama administration, Totenberg asked the justice to explain his decision to wear a replica of St. Thomas More's hat to the president's second inaugural. As he frequently did when faced with an uncomfortable question, Scalia went for a laugh while shifting the direction of the question, explaining that it was "a replica of the hat that you see Thomas More wearing in the famous Holbein portrait. . . . I would have thought it would have been recognized immediately, but apparently the press is . . . ignorant of both art and religion."

Unwilling to be derailed, Totenberg pressed, using the language from the *First Things* blog to ask whether he had worn "the cap of a statesman who defended liberty of church and integrity of Christian conscience to the inauguration of a president whose policies have imperiled both?"

Scalia scoffed at the idea: "Oh, no, that—come on. . . . [I w]as not at all that subtle. . . . I'm not that—I like Thomas More. I wore his hat. He was Lord Chancellor of England. How can it be improper to wear that kind of a hat to a—to a legal event?"[10]

Whatever his intentions, Scalia had spent a lifetime being noticed—as the only child of learned parents, the valedictorian of his high school, one of the top students in his class at Georgetown University, a law review editor at Harvard Law School, the head of the Office of Legal Counsel for President Gerald R. Ford, a federal Court of Appeals judge for the District of Columbia Circuit, and one of the most brilliant, vocal, and controversial justices ever to serve on the U.S. Supreme Court.

But it was not just excelling in his work that satisfied Scalia's ambitions. He possessed two traits that defined him at every stage of his life. One was his unwavering adherence to the traditional Roman Catholic faith he had learned from his Italian American parents during his childhood. Contrary to the Vatican II reforms to Catholic faith, Scalia remained true to the Latin Mass and conservative Catholic views of his parents. The other trait, he explained to PBS interviewer Charlie Rose, was, "I like to argue. It's one reason I like the law, I think. I like to figure out where the truth lies between two— two different assertions. I don't know. It's just who I am." [11]

It's just who I am. Scalia's revealing self-description of his love for arguing, and his unwavering steadfastness in doing so, could not have surprised those who knew him, for he had always been that way.

Throughout his early years, his intellectual talents, his charismatic personality, his unchanging nature, indeed, even his consummate ability to argue, together with all of the accomplishments that resulted from them, led him to the Supreme Court. But once he got there, those traits, combined with his need for attention, turned him from becoming the consensus builder so many observers had expected him to be on a court of nine into a court of one.

CHAPTER 1

Pride of the Scalias

The Scalia family of Trenton, New Jersey, produced just one heir, but Antonin Gregory Scalia would one day make his family's name famous. He was born on March 11, 1936, to Salvatore Eugene and Catherine Panaro Scalia. Following Sicilian tradition, they named him in honor of his paternal grandfather, Antonino, and as he grew everyone called him "Nino."[1]

The nine siblings in the Scalia and Panaro clans collectively produced only this one child, little Nino, who was treated by his aunts and uncles as special. The impact of that exalted status had a profound effect. "I was spoiled," Scalia once said. "I had a very secure feeling. So many people who loved me and who would look out for me."[2] Being the center of attention for so many people shaped his ego.

Antonin's father, Salvatore, was born on December 1, 1903, in Somma-tino, Sicily. Salvatore's father, Antonino, was a mechanic in Palermo; his mother, Maria Di Pietra Scalia, was only twenty years old when Salvatore was born.[3] He was reasonably well educated in the Italian system and in his youth he became something of a radical socialist activist.[4] Years later, by then a traditional, "deeply religious" Roman Catholic and cultural conservative, Salvatore enjoyed telling colleagues the story of how he and several other teenagers had organized a demonstration on behalf of a socialist cause one day only to be thrown in the town jail for a few hours.[5] "Anyone who knew him in his mature years," wrote Professor Joseph F. DeSimone of Brooklyn College, "could easily see how poorly the term 'radical' suited him."[6]

At age seventeen, Salvatore stood just four foot, ten inches tall when he arrived at Ellis Island with his family just before Christmas of 1920. Like his parents and sister Carmela, he was recorded as reading and writing Italian (although he also knew French and Spanish)[7], and was described by the immigration officer as having a "dark" complexion with brown hair and eyes. His "calling or occupation" was listed as "labour," while his father's was listed as a "meccanic." With those skills and their life savings of $400, the Scalia family set forth to build a new life.[8]

Despite the description of the immigration officials, "Sam," as Salvatore was first called by bureaucrats at Ellis Island and later by his friends, set his sights on using his intellectual gifts more than his physical talents.[9] After learning the language and culture of his new country, Sam became an outstanding student at Rutgers University.

He fell in love with Catherine Panaro, a public school teacher two years his junior. Catherine was a first-generation Italian American from Trenton. After a suitably long courtship, they married in 1929. Three years later, in 1932, with his bachelor's degree in hand, Sam matriculated as a graduate student in Romance Languages at Columbia University.[10] His excellent work there marked him as a man with a future career in academia.

In 1936 they were blessed with their only child. During the first few years of young Antonin's life, he and his parents lived with the Panaro family in a series of row houses in Ewing Township, New Jersey, in what they called "the family homestead."[11] Surrounded by extended family, young Nino had an aunt as a baby-sitter, a lawyer uncle who let him visit his law office, and a grandfather who taught him to shoot his prized L. C. Smith shotgun. He later remembered how he "would sit on the porch and aim at passing rabbits," shooting the ones that were eating his vegetable garden.[12]

During this time, Scalia's father established himself in the academic community. To complete his master's degree in Romance Languages, Sam wrote an impressive thesis on nineteenth-century Italian poet and Nobel laureate Giosuè Carducci. Carducci was considered "the greatest Italian literary figure in the latter part of the nineteenth century."[13] Yet the translations of his work into English, Sam believed, were unfaithful to the text and style of the original. In his thesis, Sam retranslated Carducci for an American audience. The resulting work, *Carducci: His Critics and Translators in England and America, 1881–1932*, quickly found a publisher.[14]

It was in this volume that Sam, whose professional name became S. Eugene Scalia, first outlined his philosophy of "literalness." He explained that an 1881 translation done by Francis Hueffer, a German music critic, "exhibit[ed] most of the mistaken criteria of aesthetic judgment" by writers who were translating Carducci's work.[15] S. Eugene's facility with his new English language was evident in his summation of the errors made by Hueffer: "This introduction of Carducci to English readers [by Hueffer] is topped by the statement that he 'is not a lyrical poet, and seldom touches the heart,' which is not unlike saying that red is not a color and seldom ravishes the color-blind."[16]

S. Eugene explained how his "literal" translation technique allowed him to reveal both the "lyricist" and "romantic" in Carducci. "A poem is a poem, not this plus that. It is begot, not built," he argued. "A poet is not a cross between a lexicographer or encyclopedist and a metrician, hence the merit of his art cannot lie in the richness of his vocabulary or the vastness of his knowledge, nor in the variety of his meters. Words and meters he uses, but they form an integral part of his poem, just as body and soul are an integral part of man's individuality and personality."[17] The trick, he argues, is in finding "a good translator" or one "who is a poet in his own right." The task is to capture the meaning of the poet, in his own time, in his own geographical region, and observing the purpose of the poet: "[The translator's] most eminent quality is the rare faculty of reproducing the lyric vision of a poet; he must always seek to transfer bodily the image from one language into another without sacrifice of glow or warmth, and not attempt to *reconstruct* it with dictionary in hand."[18] In other words, the images that the words convey to readers of the original poem should be conveyed to readers of the translation.[19] For the elder Scalia, "The translator, far from being a literary hack, is a man of great poetic qualities," meaning that for him a German music critic such as Hueffer was not qualified to translate the work.[20]

Scalia then went on to describe in more detail the literal philosophy that guided his translation. "Literalness is, for us, one of the chief merits of a translation. . . . Literalness, in a work which purports . . . to be a guide to Carducci's verse, is essential. Otherwise the translator, instead of aiding, hinders the reader not sufficiently familiar with Italian."[21]

Scalia's *Carducci* soon gained him a seat in Columbia graduate school to study for his Ph.D. While he took his classes there, Scalia worked with Professor Giuseppe Prezzolini to amass a bibliography of Italian literature and literary criticism between 1902 and 1942. This book, *Repertorio Bibliografico Della Storia e Della Critica Della Litteratura Italiana*, was later published in four massive volumes and became a staple for scholars. For his dissertation, which is designed to make an original contribution to one's academic field, Scalia produced an impressive biography of Luigi Capuana, a prominent Italian novelist of the late nineteenth and early twentieth centuries. Capuana was one of the most prominent leaders of the iconoclastic verist literary movement in Italy, which sought to replace classical approaches to the arts with a more contemporary approach. Once more, Scalia relied on his "literalness" approach to produce a work of excellent scholarship, carefully analyzing Capuana's life and work in order to assess his importance in the field. "For my part," Scalia argued at the end of his work, "I have spared no effort in this work to avoid going down the easy path of vacuous generalities and pointless idealities."[22] Once again, the dissertation was so good that it was published as a book in 1952. Those published works, together with the large number of articles on literary criticism and his excellent teaching, assured S. Eugene Scalia's academic career.

In 1939, Scalia moved his family to a middle-class immigrant neighborhood in Elmhurst in the borough of Queens, New York, where they lived in a second-floor apartment.[23] Unlike in Trenton, young Antonin now saw the world through the eyes of the wide variety of other immigrant families then trying to move into American society: "Queens in the neighborhood I grew up in was a fairly, very integrated community. I mean it wasn't just an Italian neighborhood at all. It was Italian, Irish, Puerto Rican, [and] Germans. It was a wonderful sort of cosmopolitan, middle class, I guess lower-middle class community. I thoroughly enjoyed it."[24] Scalia would later say of his childhood world, "It was a really mish-mosh sort of a New York . . . cosmopolitan neighborhood."[25]

Young Nino was very much a child of New York City. Years later, he would still recall with a shudder being in his room on the second floor "with the windows open, and you'd listen to the trolley going by and just lie there and sweat in the heat."[26] Neighbors would later recall of Scalia that he came from a "very generous family" and he "knew his place . . . we never had a word out of tune."[27]

S. Eugene Scalia became a well-respected professor in the Italian division of the Department of Romance Languages at Brooklyn College.[28] He was described by his office mate, Joseph DeSimone, as "an excellent teacher, severe yet fair, pleasant in his dealings with students and colleagues, and . . . well liked by both. He was always available outside of the classroom for advice to students."[29] Scalia was such a "dedicated teacher," with a "strict sense of morality and decency," his colleague recalled, that he almost never missed class, once having to walk for three or four hours from his home to his classroom in Brooklyn because a transit strike had shut down public transportation.[30]

Despite the success of an immigrant Italian who could not speak a word of English when he arrived in America, but who rose to become a college professor, the teaching responsibilities of his job failed to fulfill S. Eugene's intellectual needs. His son remembered, "He taught these Romance languages in the day when you had to have a foreign language to graduate, and he was quite exasperated to have to teach to a class that didn't really care. They didn't—they didn't have the intellectual curiosity or any real—most of them—any real desire to learn—learn the language. So, you know, he would teach to the few students there that really were interested."[31] But there was another disappointment for the elder Scalia when he failed to be named the chairman of the Romance Languages Department, which he believed was due to his immigrant status.[32]

Professor Scalia's students never knew about his reservations and regrets. Rather, he became so respected and popular in his three decades of teaching that, after his retirement in 1969, the S. Eugene Scalia Memorial Library was established, consisting of more than nine hundred reference volumes, begun with the donation of his own personal library, and housed in the Center for Italian American Studies in Boylan Hall on the Brooklyn College campus.[33]

Late in his life, in 1980, he would coauthor a masterful translation of the autobiography of Philip Mazzei, a close friend of many of the American Founding Fathers, including Washington, Jefferson, and Madison. A Renaissance man and something of a cultural diplomat, Mazzei traveled the world and cross-pollinated the American and European continents with the ideas of the other.[34] Through his literary translations and analyses, Professor Scalia had done the same.

But in those early years there was a price to be paid for the labor-intensive work required of a rising scholar to master his field. He could not spend as much time as he wished with his only son. Much later, Antonin Scalia would tell audiences that he had "a mother who was doting and a father who was stern."[35] Scalia has always been careful to say that he was not some poor son of an immigrant who had to "lif[t] myself up by my bootstraps."[36] To be sure, Professor Scalia was an immigrant, but his son made clear that the family's life was not a prolonged economic struggle. "My father was very intellectual, a more intellectual man than I am," Scalia would recall. "I mean, he always had a book in front of his face. He was always reading something in French, or Spanish, or Italian."[37] Besides the importance of scholarship, the elder Scalia always stressed ethics and honor, frequently telling his son, "Bear in mind that brains and learning, like muscle and physical skill, are articles of commerce. They are bought and sold. You can hire them by the year or by the hour. The only thing in the world not for sale is character."[38]

Most of Antonin's life lessons, however, came from his mother. "[My mother made] sure I did the right things, hung out with the right people, joined the right organizations . . . [and] associated with young people that would not get me into trouble, but rather would make me a better person," he recalled. "She made it her job to know who I was hanging out with. We had them over to my house and she was a den mother for the Cub Scouts, things of that sort."[39] Eventually he would join the Boy Scouts and he attended Boy Scout camp every summer. His mother was the one who attended his softball games, not his father. In the end, Scalia concluded, it was his mother who had more influence over him: "She devoted a lot of attention to raising her son. . . . Certainly more than my father did overall."[40] All in all, Scalia admits that as the only child of his family he was "spoiled rotten," but it was "a pretty normal childhood."[41]

Since both Sam and Catherine Scalia loved music and the opera, they passed on to their only son their knowledge of, and affection for, high culture. Sam taught his son to play the piano until he was in junior high school, making sure that by that point he had become a very competent musician.[42] Years later, Nino would rely on those lessons to entertain friends in the legal and political world at parties and gatherings. While they could not afford to take their son to the professional opera, Sam did take Nino to Brooklyn College's productions. Years later, a smiling Justice Scalia would tell a *New York Times* reporter, "I loved 'Gianni Schicchi,' and I still love it."[43]

Father and son would occasionally talk politics, but they agreed on nothing beyond the importance of American patriotism. Like many immigrant Italians of that era who were devoted to the new inclusiveness of Franklin Delano Roosevelt's New Deal programs, both mother and father were staunch Democrats. But, like many children of intelligent parents, from the beginning, Antonin went the opposite way, becoming a dedicated conservative.[44]

Like his father before him, Scalia's future would revolve around the world of competitive academia. He began by attending elementary and junior high school at P.S. 13, where he was a star student, missing very few days of class, never arriving late, and receiving all As every year. Bringing a report card with anything less to his father was unthinkable, so he never did. Being educated in the general population of the New York City public schools gave him a chance to interact with many other kinds of students. It was a "polyglot," Scalia would later recall. "There were Greeks—one of the girls in the class was named Eurydice. We didn't even know how to say it: we called her 'you're-a-dice.' There were Irish, German, Jewish, Italian. . . . It was the face of New York."[45] Years later, looking at a photo from May 1947 showing him seated at his old school desk in the second row of Consuela Goin's sixth-grade class, Scalia recalled that "my first crush was a girl in this class whose name was Theresa," and "Hugh McGee was generally the class troublemaker. . . . He was a really smart student, but was always getting into trouble."[46] Late in his life, Scalia still had fond memories of his early education: "Great school, and I had a wonderful education. It was a diverse student body, terrific teachers. Every silver lining has a cloud. It was in the days when not very many jobs were open to women. For really bright women, your choices were to be a schoolteacher, or a secretary, or a nurse, and that was very unfair. But one of the consequences was that we had some wonderful, wonderful women as schoolteachers who today would be CEOs or something, or doing something different."[47]

But it was not all work and no play for Scalia during his public school years: "I spent a lot of time in the schoolyard at Public School (P.S.) 13. The police used to cordon off streets—they were called play streets—and we used to play street hockey on roller skates with a regular hockey puck. There were a lot of vacant lots around in those days in Queens and Elmhurst, and we used to have campfires and camped out, if you can imagine that, in pup tents. We would go sled riding in a cemetery that was known as Dead Man's Hill. It was pretty much devise your own amusement."[48]

Beyond the academics and play life in P.S. 13, Scalia's earliest memories of his public school education had to do with his experiences as a Catholic in those schools, which some in their faith complained was Protestant-oriented in its approach. Perhaps to help their young son better assimilate into the country, the Scalias chose not to start him in parochial school as many other devout Catholic families did.[49] But in the 1950s, public schools had a "released time" program to allow Catholic students to leave the school during school hours on Wednesdays in order to receive religious training in the neighborhood church.[50] "It was a good deal," Scalia later told a religious group. "You got out early; the rest of the kids had to stay in school. You took your time getting there, you kicked cans in the gutters or what not."[51] But what he later appreciated, because of a decision by the Supreme Court in upholding the program, was the support that the Court showed for religion.[52]

• • •

Growing up in the conservative Roman Catholic tradition in a devoutly religious Italian immigrant family had a profound effect on young Antonin Scalia.[53] Catholics, his father taught him, believed that they were "born" to the Catholic faith, which was viewed as *the* Church."[54] The Church was a hierarchy, from the pope to his cardinals and bishops, then to the parish priest, and finally to the parishioners. The priest, who received the teachings and instructions of the Church from above, shepherded his parishioners, whom he guided and instructed in the ways of the Church. Young Scalia could see that the relationship of priest to parishioners was just like the relationship of his father to him.

"We grew up different," writes Garry Wills, the Pulitzer Prize–winning author, who once entered the Jesuit order. Growing up as a young Catholic in that pre–Vatican II era, one experienced a world of obscure religious ceremony.[55] One took comfort in the changelessness of those words and ceremonies, explains Wills, because they were "what *always* was . . . eternal, unchangeable, like the church" and there was "eternity in those Latin prayers."[56] There was no reason to know the history of the Church, because it never changed, Wills adds; "it was easier to pretend the church *had* no past, only an eternal present."[57] The fixed nature of the Catholic Church guided its followers to chart their lives.

For Catholics in America at that time, there was an emphasis on the power of words and an appreciation for the rhythm of religious phrases that had, in Wills's words, "hypnotic power." That "hypnotic power" extended to the Latin responses required of the congregation during Sunday Mass.[58] Days of the week and frequent holy days had religious meaning, helping to organize one's life. One did not eat meat on Fridays; on Saturdays, one confessed one's sins to the priest; on Sundays, one attended Mass. Children came to recognize the passage of time by the changing colors of the vestments worn by the priests during religious holidays. Parents encouraged their sons to become altar boys. Having a priest or nun in the family was a source of pride.

Because of their religious identity, Wills explains, Catholic children came to see themselves as "a chosen people," adding quickly that they were "chosen, it seemed, to be second rate." They lived "outside time altogether," observing "an unanchored, anachronistic style" and possessing a hidden "superior moral tone, obvious to us, concealed from others, a secret excellence, our last joke on the World."[59]

This was the early life of Antonin Scalia. He came of age in the timeless changelessness of his church, while the clergy in his neighborhood and later the religious teachers in his high school battled against challenges to their views. Beyond the literalism of the Catholic faith, what also made an impression on a devoutly Catholic child like Antonin Scalia was the timeless source of the Church's teachings. The Catholic religion at the time, says Father John W. O'Malley in his book *What Happened at Vatican II,* was based on the French notion of *ressourcement,* meaning "return to the sources." Like Scalia's father, who argued that fully understanding the subjects of his books and their literary works came only when one returned to the original sources and read them in a manner consonant with their times, the Catholic faith was governed by earlier religious texts in interpreting the Bible and understanding religious teachings. Explains Father O'Malley, "It entails a return to the sources with a view not to confirming the present but to making changes in it to conform it to a more authentic or more appropriate past, to what advocates of *ressourcement* considered a more profound tradition."[60]

• • •

In order to give him a proper Catholic training, Scalia's parents took him out of the public school system in high school. It was here that Scalia suffered one of the very few failures in his early life. Seeking a top-flight parochial education, he took the entrance exam for the elite Jesuit-run Regis High School, on the Upper East Side of Manhattan, where every student attends on scholarship. However, for reasons that he could not later explain, Scalia failed the exam.[61]

In a pattern that would be repeated throughout Scalia's life, though, this failure became only a temporary setback leading to what was, for him, a better opportunity. He won a full scholarship to another Jesuit prep school called Xavier High School, named for the Jesuit missionary St. Francis Xavier, and located on West 16th Street, near Union Square.[62] There he could stand out in ways he might not have at Regis. Every day, he rode the subway from his home in Queens to Xavier, whose motto, like that of the Jesuits, is *Ad Maiorem Dei Gloriam,* "for the greater glory of God." Xavier was both a Jesuit school, teaching both "loving" discipline and devout Catholicism, and a military prep school.[63] The students, most of whom came from working-class families, all became part of the Xavier High School regiment of the Junior Reserve Officers' Training Corps. They wore military-style uniforms, and saluted both senior classmen and faculty members. Students attended Mass at the adjacent church and were known as "Sons of Xavier." The school's mission stressing leadership skills was so strong that it became, in the words of one of its graduates, "the place where boys were made men and where men were made leaders."[64]

It was there that the only child of the Scalia and Panaro families would be taught how to lead and inspire others by his example. The school was as strict and severe as Antonin's father. Any violation of the school's lengthy list of conduct rules would result in detention, or JUG—"Judgment Under God." Unlike public school, though, where such punishment would consist of sitting quietly in detention after school, at Xavier students were sent to the quadrangle between the school and the adjoining Church of St. Francis Xavier shouldering a fifteen-pound rifle and spent the afternoon following school marching the four sides of the inner square using perfect military 90-degree corners, never allowing the elbow supporting the weapon to drop.[65]

Scalia, though, was not one to worry about the harshness of such rules, because he never broke them. Instead, he studied constantly and participated in every activity available to him. As a member of the school's junior varsity rifle team, Scalia and his classmates competed in shooting competitions against West Point plebes.[66] Years later, Scalia liked to recall how he and his fellow students rode the subway from Queens to Manhattan carrying their .22 carbine rifles so that they could shoot in the school's basement rifle range and drill at the armory on 14th Street in order to compete for the junior ROTC rifle and drill teams. "I grew up at a time when people were not afraid of people with firearms. Could you imagine doing that today?" Scalia asked various audiences in a post-9/11 world.[67]

Xavier students received, recalled one of Scalia's classmates, a "very, very classical education" consisting of training in languages, including three years of Greek, reading Homer, and four years of Latin, where they read classics such as Caesar's *Gallic Wars,* Cicero's *Orations*, and Virgil's *Aeneid*, together with intensive training in analyzing English literature and learning to write.[68] Former classmate William Stern recalls, "There was no time for girl friends at Xavier. You were expected to do three or four hours of homework a night and if you were involved in activities, you went to school, came home, studied, and went to bed."[69]

Years later, though, Justice Scalia repeatedly told audiences one tale illustrating the impact that this rigorous academic training had on him:

> One of the things I learned there I call the Shakespeare Principle, which I think applies to the Court's ignoring our traditions and mak-

ing up its own notion. . . . The Shakespeare Principle was explained to me by an elderly and quite crusty Jesuit in a class where we were studying Shakespeare. One of my classmates, I remember his name for some reason, John Antonelli, he was a real wise guy. He interjected the comment, some critical comment about the play we were reading, I don't remember which one we were reading, *Hamlet* or whatever. It was a sophomoric stupid thing. Father Tom Matthews looked down at him, and said with his Boston accent, "Mister, when you read Shakespeare, Shakespeare's not on trial—YOU ARE!" I have always thought that's a very good prescription for life.[70]

From the moment he stepped into Xavier, everyone could see that Antonin Scalia would be a success. Good grades could have come easily to a boy of Scalia's intelligence, but that suited neither his temperament nor what his father would permit. "I was a greasy grind. I studied real hard," he liked to tell audiences. "I worked really hard. My father, my mother put me to that. And I—well, I enjoyed that. I don't like doing anything badly."[71] He was first in his class every year, receiving As in every class.[72] The school newspaper, *Xavier Review*, wrote of him in his senior year, in its "Presenting" column, which featured the finest students: "The honor cord about his shoulder is with him a permanent mark of distinction. For the past three years he has compiled one of the most enviable records at Xavier. To date 19 First Honor awards, one for each marking period, have been won by him. Needless to say, he has also received each year the Gold Medal for class excellence."[73] Classmate William Stern later recalled, "People just competed for second, he was so superior academically."[74] With no grade on his transcript below a 90, Scalia's faculty adviser described him as "The gold medal winner. A very outstanding boy. By far the best in his class in every way."[75]

Beyond just academics, Scalia was a member of as many extracurricular activities as he could fit into his busy schedule, so many in fact that the school's yearbook looked like his own personal photo album. In each group, he rose to a position of leadership. He played the French horn, and he was made the commander of the school band. He rose to become one of the five lieutenant colonels in the elite Xavier Regiment, often marching in parades in Manhattan streets.[76] He loved what those marches showed him about his city. Years later he would recall for CBS's Lesley Stahl the difference he noticed when his school's band went to play in Washington, D.C.: "These people just stood there and looked at us, you know? In New York, people say, 'Hey, play something for us, you know? You bums, why don't you play something?' They were—they were alive, they were confrontational."[77] Scalia loved his early life in New York City, and could see later how it had helped to shape his personality. "It was a wonderful place. You had the subway; the world was your oyster. There was just enough responsibility that was put on young people that any New Yorker would acquire a certain cockiness."[78]

Scalia discovered that he was a born theatrical performer and public speaker. He became president of the dramatic society and starred in various school plays, even taking the lead in *Macbeth*, an effort that won praise from the school yearbook as "display[ing] extraordinary ability." It was "probably the most significant thing I've done in my life," Scalia, as a Supreme Court justice, later told a group of honors students from Virginia. "You know how many lines there are in *Macbeth*?"[79] Unlike other actors who were concerned only with themselves, classmates saw that the student they held in such awe academically could also be a good and supportive friend. Upon seeing that one of the cast members in the all-male group, John Gallagher, was upset at being teased by his classmates for having to wear a dress to play Lady Macbeth, Scalia pulled him aside and said: "Look, I know you're going through a tough time, but don't let them see it's bothering you—they'll just do it more. And think of the part; it's really a masculine part because she's so domineering."[80] An appreciative Gallagher later recalled, he "took me under his wing, and counseled me not to feel badly. He was very kindhearted and low key, a special young man."[81]

Scalia also learned that he had a natural talent for debate, an intellectually competitive activity that is taken very seriously at Jesuit educational institutions. Rising to the top of that group with his quick intelligence and mastery of the language, he enjoyed the chance to display his argumentative skills against his fellow students and those at other schools.[82] But Scalia always relished more the opportunity to perform for the general public. As a junior, he represented his school as a panel member on a Sunday television show filmed in New York City called *Mind Your Manners*. The teenage panelists were questioned about the etiquette for certain events in their lives, such as going on dates. Young Scalia's skill in answering the questions was such that his school newspaper reported, "His keen, sensible answers, well seasoned with a bit of humor, stole the show again and again."[83] Years later, Scalia would remember his participation in this show with great fondness: "Oh, it was great. We would—I would go from Queens, where I lived, take the subway on—the show was Sunday morning. Saturday night we'd go—

they would put us up at the Algonquin Hotel, which was a—which was a, you know, theatrical kind of hotel. We stayed there in the night, and they'd slip us 50 bucks too. I'm not sure they were supposed to, but anyway, it was— it was wonderful. Really enjoyed it."[84]

Early in his senior year, in October 1952, he was selected to be one of three boys on a six-student debate panel from around the city for a *New York Times* debate forum on the issue "Will a Democratic Victory Secure Our Future?," which was broadcast on both television and radio. While the plan was to have three girls represent the Democrats and the boys the Republicans, the debate evolved into a policy discussion with the girls arguing that "the average man" had benefited from the Democrats' domestic programs, while the boys countered with the argument that the Democrats' foreign policy had lost much of the world to communism. Not surprisingly, the judge, Democrat Averell Harriman, voted for the girls' position, but likely had this same debate taken place the following week, when former Republican presidential candidate Thomas Dewey was the judge, Scalia and his team would have won with the same arguments.[85] Proving how well he was liked by his classmates, Scalia was voted the treasurer of the Senior Sodality group, a religious organization devoted to the Blessed Virgin, which "conduct[ed] spiritual and apostolic projects" as well as the school's three "elaborate dances."[86]

As his years progressed at Xavier, Scalia's classmates could see that he was more than just a political conservative, he was also a very conservative Catholic. Classmate Stern recalled, "This kid was a conservative when he was 17 years old. An archconservative Catholic. He could have been a member of the [Catholic] Curia," the governing officials in the Vatican.[87] The school newspaper wrote of his religious dedication: "It might be said that the fine Catholic education given him by his parents and the continuation of that education by his teachers at Xavier gave [Scalia] the foundation of his beliefs and the means to win graces to keep him continually strong in his Faith. Antonin in short has been leading among us a full Catholic life and we know him as a man who can truly be called an 'exemplary Catholic.'"[88]

No one was surprised when Scalia was named valedictorian in the class of 1953. Later he would be described by a school publication, "National Leadership," as "one of the best students ever to attend Xavier."[89] With such a record of success, and accustomed to being close to home, Scalia thought seriously of getting an Ivy League education.

Princeton was the school he set his sights on, and learned for the first time that there might be something in his background that could hold him back. When this proud son of an intellectual Italian immigrant and a first-generation Italian American schoolteacher went to his admissions interview for Princeton, he did not feel welcome. Asked years later whether his Italian heritage ever caused him to feel any "injustice," Scalia said: "Only once did I feel that I couldn't make the grade because of my Italian background. And that was when I interviewed to get into Princeton and I sort of felt, Princeton was still a very, what we used to call a 'white shoe place' in those days and I sort of felt the interviewers, who were alumni of Princeton, sort of felt that this kid was not the Princeton sort."[90]

As it turned out, the elitist Ivy League interviewers did Scalia a favor. Guided by the Jesuits at Xavier High School, Scalia decided to attend Georgetown, the elite Catholic school in America's political power center. Once more his brilliance won him another full tuition scholarship.[91] And so, while his parents moved to a house in Ewing Township near Trenton to live close to the Panaro family homestead, young Antonin journeyed to Georgetown, where he would discover his mission, both spiritual and vocational.[92]

CHAPTER 2

The Chosen Few

In late summer of 1953, Nino Scalia bid farewell to his parents and the ethnic diversity of his Queens neighborhood and traveled to the manicured streets of the Georgetown section of Washington, D.C. He carried with him his love of learning and of family, devoutly conservative Catholic beliefs, and strong sense of patriotism. What he would learn in his new school and do in the coming four years would influence his philosophy and behavior for the rest of his life.

For a young man imbued with the conservative, text-oriented Catholicism of his father, Georgetown University, "an American, Catholic, Jesuit Institution of higher learning," seemed a good fit.[1] The school dated back to either 1788 or 1789, depending on whose history one read, and housed seven magnificent chapels with sixteen altars, where one could pray. Daily Mass was celebrated in the 1950s, compulsory classes in the Catholic faith were taught, and Catholic students were required to "attend all the religious exercises of the college," "approach the Sacraments" at least once a month, and go on a three-day religious retreat at the beginning of the school year.[2] Like his high school in Manhattan, Georgetown was a school steeped in the Jesuit educational tradition. He would learn that the mission of the Jesuits was a three-legged stool consisting of "intellectualism, scholarship, and activism."[3]

While many of the students, like Scalia, were conservative Catholics, they found that their Jesuit professors often followed a different path. In the mid-1950s, the only Catholics who veered away from the timelessness of their religion were the intellectuals, most of whom could be found in the nation's Jesuit colleges and universities. Students at Jesuit colleges of that era were struck by the contradiction between the strict, inward-looking, church of their upbringing and the missionary intellectualism of their college education, which preached the need to look beyond their religion to participate in service to mankind.[4] The unchanging, rigid teachings of the American Catholic Church were also being challenged by a more liberal, and critical, worldview coming from Europe, where many of these Jesuits had been educated and had served.

As for many other Catholic college students in the 1950s, the challenge for Scalia was how to resolve his traditional religious views with the more liberal, activist views of his Jesuit college teachers. This emerging liberal philosophy did not please the Vatican. In 1957, Egidio Vagnozzi, the apostolic delegate sent by the Vatican to observe the American Church, condemned the "false aestheticism" and "cult of intellect" he observed.[5]

Scalia joined the History and Government Department, which in his second semester would split into two distinct departments. Scalia stayed in the History Department[6] under the leadership of Hungarian Tibor Kerekes. Kerekes, who lost an arm in World War I, was a former tutor for the Hapsburg imperial family and an expert in modern European history.[7] Despite the split with the Government Department, some History Department courses still had a distinctly political focus. The initial twenty-five course offerings in the department expanded to forty-four. They were wide-ranging, from histories of Greece, Rome, Europe, Russia, the Middle East, and America to English and American constitutional history and American foreign policy. Yet another set of courses investigated the history of the Catholic Church, and "Church and State."[8] The rest of the required curriculum at Georgetown was traditional, with required courses in English composition and literature, foreign languages, mathematics, and science.[9] Fellow Georgetown graduate and friend Richard Coleman says that Scalia "had a European education—a classical education." Coleman thinks "Scalia's training, which included six years of Latin and five years of Greek, gave him 'a long-range viewpoint,' one that allows him to see contemporary issues in a far-reaching historical and philosophical context."[10]

• • •

Loving a good argument, Scalia gravitated toward the Philodemic Society, the oldest collegiate debating society in the country.[11] The Philodemic Society became Scalia's new intellectual home, and college debate shaped who he later became. The goal of this society was to produce students with a "faculty for thinking clearly and speaking effectively." Over the decades, the Philodemic Society produced influential alumni such as Supreme Court Chief Justice Edward Douglass White and one of the nation's most prominent attorneys of the late nineteenth century, Richard T. Merrick. The society became a national powerhouse beginning in 1911 under the direction of Father John J. Toohey. The debaters from that team were so skilled that for an eighteen-year period in the 1920s and 1930s, they never lost a single debate.[12]

Scalia competed in policy debate, where two-person teams argue about the same broad public policy topic for an entire year, alternately taking the affirmative side, supporting the proposition and proposing a policy to address it, and the negative side, disagreeing with the proposition and critiquing the affirmative plan. Each speaker gives a ten-minute opening "constructive" speech, beginning with the affirmative plan to solve the issue, and then each speaker offers a five-minute rebuttal, ending with an affirmative side speaker summarizing the issues. Since each team might have its unique approach to the topic, a successful debater must be able to adapt quickly to new arguments. Indeed, the better teams, like Georgetown, brought several proposals to tournaments, adjusting their strategy according to the teams they faced. Judges decided the winning team, and ranked the four speakers in the round.[13]

College debaters become a special breed, developing a verbally aggressive, almost narcissistically arrogant personality that helps them survive intellectual battles. To the outside world debaters frequently appeared to be nerdy, intellectually analytical individuals. But to win they had to be highly disciplined and rigorously organized intellectuals who could turn their verbal attack 180 degrees, if need be, to win a point. Debaters are often abrasive, caustic, even at times mean, calling each other by their last names and looking for the perfect insult to weaken their opponents. Done properly, these critical comments might bring a laugh from the judge (often a former debater who appreciates such attacks). The point is not to anger the target of the attack. In the debate world, arguments were not personal; what mattered was *who had the unanswerable argument* and was able to score points. Success required four skills: a razor-sharp wit to cut through arguments under great pressure, a sharper tongue to deliver penetrating and concise attacks, an unflappable nature to deal with a barrage of attacks, and the ability to organize and deliver swift persuasive extemporaneous orations.

This became the new intellectual world, and persona, of Nino Scalia. He both reveled and excelled in it. His time in the Philodemic Society rewarded him for the ego-centered argumentation skills that he brought with him to Georgetown, and for honing those skills into a dominating and confident personality.

Beyond the historical tradition of the Philodemic Society, the George-town team had some advantages over other schools. First, the sheer size of the team, roughly 160 students, allowed it to gather more evidence, partici-pate in more competitions, and share the workload preparing for the cases and arguments they would see on the circuit. The research process proceeded by bringing government officials and experts to the Philodemic Room to ex-plain the nuances of policy topics dealing with economic and foreign policy issues. Finally, there was a nearly unlimited pool of new, skilled policy de-baters coming to Georgetown each year from the network of Jesuit high schools, like Xavier. So skilled were Georgetown's teams, and so respected and feared were its debaters, that others on the national circuit considered it an accomplishment to beat any of their teams.[14]

The topic for 1953, "Resolved: That the United States should adopt a policy of free trade," could well have posed problems for a history major not well versed in economics. But it did not seem to bother Scalia in the least. In the annual intramural competition between his freshman Gaston team and the sophomore White team, Scalia debated so skillfully that he won the Edward Douglass White Memorial Medal, awarded to the best debater in the tournament. And in an extraordinary recognition of his talent, Scalia was elected president of the White Debating Society for his sophomore year.[15]

But Scalia had a rival for leading young debater. One of his classmates, Peter G. Schmidt from New Rochelle, New York, came from a more upscale background.[16] Schmidt was also the son of a college professor, but unlike Salvatore Eugene Scalia, an immigrant who taught Romance languages at Brooklyn College, Godfrey Schmidt taught labor and malpractice law at Fordham University, and represented among others the New York Catholic leader, Francis Cardinal Spellman.[17] Schmidt attended the Fordham Pre-paratory School on Fordham University's campus in the Bronx, won the New York State debate championship, and placed third in the nation in 1953. Owing to these accomplishments, Schmidt was offered a full debate scholarship to Georgetown.[18] Beyond his commanding, stentorian voice, argumentative brilliance, highly persuasive oratorical skills, and ability to think creatively, on a personal level Schmidt was so charming and funny that he was later described by one journalist as having a "roguish panache" that enabled him to become everyone's best friend. Everyone, that is, except for the student who was competing with him for the star position on the Georgetown debating team, Scalia. "There was an aura about him," said one of Schmidt's business associates years later. "He made everyone feel you were his closest friend. Peter had 50 'closest friends.'"[19]

It surprised no one when the talented and likable Schmidt was elected the president of the Gaston Debating Society for his freshman year, was chosen for a special individual debate against the Georgetown School of Foreign Service, and won the contest.[20] By the fall of 1954 the varsity team was able to hire a full-time debate coach, John Fitzmaurice. With the school's resources at a premium, Fitzmaurice decided to institute a "star" system, allocating travel funds for only twelve elite debaters from among the many hopefuls. Normally, that would mean that the juniors and seniors in the Philodemic Society would get the travel funds, with the sophomores in the White Society and the freshmen in the Gaston Society left to participate in intramural debates on campus.[21]

But the new debate coach had no favorites, and in this new meritocracy, the most skillful, not necessarily the most senior, competitors would be funded to carry the school's banner to national tournaments. For Coach Fitzmaurice, Nino Scalia and his new partner, Peter Schmidt, were too good to ignore. So the promising young team of "Scalia and Schmidt" was born. This team of first-term sophomores quickly established itself as one of the top debate teams in the country. The topic that year was much easier for the history major with an interest in political science, "Resolved: That the United States should extend diplomatic recognition to the communist government of China." Arguing in a practice tournament in Vermont for the affirmative position, certainly not the conservative Scalia's personal view, he and Schmidt were remarkably successful.[22] By the end of the term the Philodemic Society had won over 80 percent of its debates, with the college newspaper reporting that "Nino Scalia and Pete Schmidt head the Philodemic record."[23]

In recognition of this fact, Scalia and Schmidt were sent to the prestigious Hall of Fame Tournament at New York University. This was, in the words of the team's annual report, "one of the nation's truly important debating events."[24] The Georgetown team tied with two other schools for the top honors. With no final round, it was left to a totaling of the individual speaker points awarded to each competitor after each round to break the tie. Georgetown won. The Philodemic Society had its best start in years.[25]

Debate was not the only extracurricular activity for Scalia. While "Nino" Scalia was making his reputation in debate, a different Scalia also became very well known to the campus as an actor in the college acting troupe, the Mask and Bauble. Georgetown students became aware of Scalia, billed under the name "Tony," because of his sterling performance as Max Levene, a boxing manager in *Heaven Can Wait*.[26] Scalia had two personas in the campus press. As "Nino," the championship Philodemic Society debater, he was ruthlessly competitive and argumentative, interested only in winning, while as "Tony," in the Mask and Bauble, he was witty, charming, and entertaining, seeking applause and approval.

Owing to his impressive performances and friendly personality in the school's dramatic society, Scalia was elected the president of the Mask and Bauble club in the middle of his sophomore year. His most important duty was to supervise the preparation for the club's entry into the Jesuit One-Act Play Contest, which was to be held on the Georgetown campus. The Mask and Bauble decided to perform Stephen Vincent Benet's "The Devil and Daniel Webster." Scalia's performance as "The Fiddler" in the play helped the Mask and Bauble take second place in the competition to Loyola of Baltimore.[27]

Between obligations for the debate team and the acting club on top of his heavy load of classwork, Scalia had much to do. "These extracurricular activities, plus my studies, left me with little time for anything else," recalled Scalia of those years.[28] But during his third year at college, Scalia took a dramatic break for a year of study abroad. He attended a Georgetown program at the Swiss Jesuit University of Fribourg—a program that had just become available to Georgetown students in 1954.[29]

The sixteen students in Scalia's group, including his debate partner, Peter Schmidt, took courses taught almost entirely in French at the bilingual French/German school. Beyond the courses, though, this program gave the product of Queens, New York, the opportunity to see Spain, Portugal, and Gibraltar on the Italian ocean liner *Conte Biancamano* on the way there, and to tour the historic sights of Europe during breaks, with bus trips to Rome, Venice, Genoa, Palermo, and Naples and train trips throughout Europe.[30] He toured Spain for Christmas vacation, Austria for Easter vacation, and traveled up the Rhine after school ended. At the end of their year, they toured England before boarding their ship back home. Perhaps the highlight for all of the students was their two general audiences with Pope Pius XII.[31]

Scalia and Schmidt returned for their senior year to find a new coach at the helm of the Philodemic Society, Father J. William Hunt. The two debaters began the year as part of a four-man team, this time with Schmidt working with another student for the affirmative and Scalia and his new partner working on the negative. They bested forty-four other schools to garner an undefeated record and once again win New York University's top-flight Hall of Fame Tournament. Scalia and his four-man team were the best collegiate debating team in the nation that fall, winning thirty-six of their forty debates and two other tournaments that semester.[32]

Everything was going well for the team during the second semester, when disaster struck. With Georgetown's annual Cherry Blossom tournament approaching, the University Administration changed the date of the capstone oral examinations for the seniors, advancing them by a full five weeks, in order to allow more time for students to prepare for the required written comprehensive exams in each academic department. This change left only a couple of weeks for the seniors on the debate team to prepare for the "graduate-or-not" exams.[33] Both Scalia and Schmidt felt compelled to drop out of the Cherry Blossom tournament, leaving a much less experienced, freshman team to compete, and ultimately fail, in their place.

With the full resources of the school and the team behind him, Scalia and Schmidt had helped to bring Georgetown debate back to national prominence. However, Father Hunt's "star system" in backing his top team had left the school almost bereft of experienced debaters for the following year. And the team paid a price for that decision, winning no tournaments and significantly fewer debates.[34]

More than fifty years later Scalia would tell television interviewer Tim Russert how little he remembered of his debate experience: "The only advice I remember from my debate coach when I was in college, he taught me to button my jacket. It's the only thing I took away from it—button your jacket."[35] It was hardly true. His absolute certainty in the merits of his positions, his love of attention, the abrasiveness of his attacks against opponents, his magnetic speaking persona, and more than all of that, his sheer love of winning, are all hallmarks of his background as a championship collegiate debater. By combining this legacy with the influence of the school's evangelistic Jesuit Catholicism with his traditionalist Catholic upbringing, these four years helped shape Antonin Gregory Scalia.

• • •

Scalia's college journey ended, along with that for Georgetown's class of 1957, just before 8:30 P.M. on June 9. The class gathered in a driving rainstorm on that night before graduation for the annual Tropaia Awards ceremony in the Healy Quadrangle, a basketball-floor-sized, parquet-brick outdoor courtyard bordered by a rectangle of the school's oldest buildings. They were there to see a short class play, hear the class poem, and listen to the university president, but mostly to hear the class's most decorated student, Antonin Gregory Scalia. He had been selected to give the Cohonguroton Address, regarded as the school's valedictory speech, although it was not always given by the student with the highest four-year grade-point average. No one questioned the selection of Scalia after all that he had accomplished at Georgetown.

Scalia had drawn the theme for his speech from the lesson he learned at Georgetown during that spring's senior class final oral exams. After easily acing all the early questions from the panel of three faculty members, Scalia later told journalist and biographer Joan Biskupic, one of the professors closed with: "Very good, Mr. Scalia. I have one last question. If you look back over all the history that you've studied here over the last four years, if you had to pick one event that you thought was the most significant, what would it be?" Whatever it was that Scalia offered, the professor shook his head and said, "No, Mr. Scalia. The Incarnation, Mr. Scalia." From this exchange, Scalia explained: "It was the last lesson I learned at Georgetown: not to separate your religious life from your intellectual life. They're not separate." Scalia took that advice to heart. And in his Cohonguroton Address he imparted that advice to his classmates.[36]

In his speech Scalia told his fellow graduates that their future mission was quite simple: "If we will not be leaders of a real, a true, a Catholic intellectual life, no one will! We cannot shift responsibility to some vague 'chosen few.' *We are the chosen few.* The responsibility rests upon all of us, whatever our future professions. . . . It is our task to carry and advance into all sections of our society this distinctively human life, of reason learned and faith believed." Failure to fulfill this mission, he argued, would mean that they had "betrayed ourselves, our society, our race." And, Scalia made clear, the beacon guiding them should be their Catholic faith: "If we really love the truth, we will believe that we have been shown a marvelous pathway, that we must brace ourselves at once to follow it, that life will not be worth living if we do otherwise! The prize is great. The risk is glorious."[37] It was a magnificently eloquent speech. Only twelve minutes in length, it was much shorter than usual, but it made a powerful impact on Scalia's fellow students. Months afterward, the college newspaper, *The Hoya*, was still writing about it, describing it as being "widely acclaimed" and "an extremely easily read and meaningful speech."[38]

The life mission Scalia laid out for his classmates could not have been clearer. His four years at Georgetown had led him far beyond the individualistic, conservative faith of his father and mother, and layered over it the activism and public service mission of the Jesuits. Scalia in turn charged his classmates to become lay leaders for Christ and lay representatives for their Catholic faith. He, and Scalia hoped they, would spread "the truth" as they understood it, the tenets of their Catholic faith, throughout America.

Decades later, when Scalia was nominated for the Supreme Court, some members of the national press searched for copies of the speech in the university archives only to find that unlike the other Cohonguroton speech and graduation files that were filled with drafts of speeches and other material, the Scalia speech files were empty.[39] But a copy of the text survived because it had been reproduced in *The Journal*, the school's literary magazine, and remained available on the bookshelves of the college's Lauinger Library.[40]

Scalia never forgot what Georgetown University had done for him, and done to him. In 2002, he returned to his alma mater for its annual weeklong religious celebration to sum up what the school had meant to his personal and intellectual development. In a speech to the undergraduates, Scalia said that "protecting one's Catholic identity" was a key part of what he had learned at the school. Reflecting on the national movement toward nondenominational education in major colleges and universities, Scalia told the group that the movement to separate religion from American public life and government had been "distorted by social beliefs." It was clear to the audience that this was a movement that Scalia was prepared to resist, partly because of what he had learned at Georgetown. "I would be a different person if not for my years here," Scalia concluded.[41]

• • •

At twenty-one years old and graduating from college, Scalia had to choose a career path to fulfill the religious mission that he set for himself and his classmates. He "gave some thought" to the idea of becoming a priest, but then rejected it because "I . . . decided He was not calling me."[42] He considered also becoming a college professor like his father. But Scalia recalled his father's dissatisfaction with unmotivated students and the administrators who had blocked his career path. His father counseled that if he had a chance to do it all over again and had had other career options, he would have gone in a different direction. The advice had a considerable impact on his son: "I remember him saying to me . . . he wouldn't want me to be an undergraduate professor. I ended up being a professor at graduate [law] school, where you do have people who [want to be there learning]."[43]

Scalia acted, he told a group of high school students years later, according to the French phrase "pour l'absence de n'importe quoi mieux," or "for the absence of anything better."[44] As he recalled: "when I got out of college, I didn't have the slightest idea of what I wanted to do with my life. And in those days, if you were going to go to graduate school, unlike today, you did it right away. You went right from college to graduate school. You didn't take off a couple of years to work somewhere to learn who you were. You were considered a goof-off if you did that." So, wondering where to turn at this pivotal moment in his life, Scalia turned to one of his accomplished relatives. "I had an Uncle Vince. Okay, most Italians have an Uncle Vince. . . . Vince was a lawyer and I used to visit his law offices in downtown Trenton now and then. He seemed to have a good life, so I thought I'd give it a shot. As it turned out, it was what I loved." But the idea of becoming a Supreme Court justice, the first Italian one at that, never once crossed his mind in those early days.[45]

In deciding where to attend law school, though, despite his disappointment in applying to Princeton, Scalia sought the best law school he could find to test whether his intellect and skills would allow him to compete and succeed against the best in the country. As he put it years later:

> Well, you want to get into the best law school you can, and generally speaking, [Harvard] is the most prestigious law school. Some of them I would pass, but they generally will have the best professors and the professors teach themselves rather than the law. The law is just like chewing gum. It's what they use to develop your mental jaws, and you spit it out because the law will probably change by the time you're in practice for 20 years. It's important to have good teachers. Now some law schools are better teaching law schools than others, and the best thing to get is a school that both has very intelligent professors and professors who place a premium on teaching.[46]

He decided to apply to Harvard Law, and was accepted. Meanwhile, Scalia's longtime debate partner, Peter Schmidt, had won the prestigious Elihu

Root–Samuel J. Tilden Scholarship underwriting three years of study at the New York University School of Law.[47] While Scalia had won no such scholarship, he had earned the right to learn from, and compete against, some of the best legal minds in the country. It was a challenge he would relish facing.

But Scalia's and Schmidt's lives would follow different paths after law school. Just sixteen months after Antonin Scalia took his seat on the United States Supreme Court, Peter Schmidt, then a prominent Park Avenue attorney, entrepreneur, and financial adviser, became an international fugitive. On February 29, 1989, he boarded a plane in Miami and vanished, leaving behind a trail of broken promises, forged documents, and missing funds.[48] Scalia's decision to attend Harvard Law School proved to be a very wise choice and set him on a very different path. Langdell Hall was filled not only with many of the best law teachers in the country in the latter part of the 1950s, but because of the fault lines of American Constitutional law at the time, it was also the epicenter of the legal universe. In a legal world dominated on the United States Supreme Court by the battles between former Harvard Law professor Felix Frankfurter on the conservative side, and former Yale Law professor William O. Douglas, as well as former U.S. Senator Hugo Black, on the left, it was the perfect place to study law.

CHAPTER 3

The Harvard Hit Parade of the 1950s

Students in the audience for the opening day of Harvard Law School in mid-September 1957 quickly realized when Dean Erwin Griswold rose to speak that they were in a new academic world. The class, consisting of about five hundred students, including twelve women, was told, "We have no glee clubs here. This is hard work. I know you are all high-achieving students, and you are used to being at the top of your class. But I want to tell you everybody here was at the top of their class. We have 300 Phi Beta Kappas in this class, 200 *Magna Cum Laudes*, and 100 *Summa Cum Laudes*. We have a Doctorate in Philosophy from Budapest and a Doctorate in Economics from Oxford. And . . ." Griswold said after a short pause, "we also have Miss Apple Dessert Queen from Virginia." The men in the audience "hoot[ed] and whistl[ed] and cheer[ed]," scanning the room for a beauty queen, while Zona F. Hostetler, a distinguished graduate from the College of William and Mary who would go on to become a highly respected advocate for civil rights and the rights of the poor, sank in her chair. "I was the Apple Dessert Queen of Virginia all right," Hostetler later recalled, "but it was a 4-H title, not a beauty queen title." It would be years later before she would learn that her two recommending professors had put that tidbit in their letters because, they told her, "We were afraid you wouldn't get in and so we figured we better spice up your record." [1]

Scalia, who later described himself as a "greasy grind" student in those days, fit in well. The buttoned-down students always wore suit jackets and ties and worked constantly, developing a disciplined approach to the study of law. Frank Michelman, a law review editor with Scalia who later taught at Harvard, recalled that law students at that time were "very much anchored in the fifties," taking "the attitude that there was truth, and method, and enlightenment to be gathered from this educational experience." Fellow classmate Daniel Mayers, later a Washington corporate attorney, explained that Harvard Law students at the time "were a very traditionalist group of people. Many of us had done two years of military service before going to graduate school."[2]

Harvard Law students, who were divided into four sections of about 125, were very much individual scholars, sometimes banding together in study groups. "In those days, you really didn't know your professors outside of the classroom, and the classes were large," Zona Hostetler later recalled.[3] All first-year students took the same classes: Agency, Civil Procedure, Contracts, Criminal Law, Property I, Torts, and a "Group Work" session of sixteen or seventeen students, led by teaching fellows, to consider legal problems applying the theory they had learned to real-world situations.[4] In the second year, students took Administrative Law, Commercial Law, Corporations, Taxation, Trusts, Accounting, Constitutional Law, and a course exploring the links between law and such subjects as legal philosophy, history, legislation, international organization, and comparative law in order to provide more context for their case work.[5] For their third year, students were left to choose from a series of electives as well as one of the third-year legal seminars in which students would concentrate on one field of law and apply all that they had learned toward solving some of the major problems in that area of study.[6]

Classes were "a fearsome thing," recalls Scalia classmate Charles Tighe. This was the era of the Socratic "case method," in which students were assigned heavy reading loads and professors called on individual students to stand and answer a series of increasingly difficult legal hypothetical questions, applying the reading assignments to other cases and situations. "There was a lot of interchange," recalled Tighe of those classes. "The professor would expect you to be prepared. Every single one of the people in the class were expected to be prepared on the cases they had to read the previous night. They were called on to recite the facts of the case or to explain the rationale and that sort of thing. If you didn't know it, it could be quite embarrassing. It was edifying for everybody."[7] This helped students learn how a slight change in facts could change the outcome of a case, and enabled them to analyze the law under pressure, just as they would have to do in a courtroom.

The intellectual and personal challenges of the school were great, but by applying his well-honed work ethic to his Harvard classes, Scalia thrived. He ranked in the top 5 percent of his class after the first-year grades were computed. In recognition of this achievement, he was invited to join the staff of the prestigious *Harvard Law Review*. The publication put out eight issues per academic year, comprising more than sixteen hundred pages of articles and notes of interest to those in the legal world. Staff members prepared several editions at once, selecting, writing, or editing articles for future editions, while checking citations and proofreading galleys or page proofs for editions about to be published. Students worked in the law review's office in Gannett House for over forty hours per week, making it almost impossible to remain current with their daily classwork. But since law review membership was considered a mark of success, ensuring a better job after law school, it was a task worth undertaking.[8]

While being on the staff of the law review was good, being elected an editor was even better. By his third year, Scalia was Notes coeditor for Volume 73, making him responsible for writing or coauthoring several unsigned law notes and for editing other students' comments and critiques of current Supreme Court cases, some running up to fifteen pages long. The job of an editor was even more demanding. As the Harvard Law yearbook put it, an editor "has two full-time jobs—and time for only one."[9]

Life for the *Law Review* staff was always lively, and Scalia helped to make it so. The Harvard class was predominantly liberal. There were many conservatives sprinkled among the student body, but Scalia was the only one who served on the law review. That never intimidated him; he loved to argue with his fellow classmates on any issue. "He has those bushy eyebrows that furrow up when he's concentrating," said fellow law review member and Harvard law professor Philip Heymann, "and for 45 minutes on end, he had that furrowed look."[10] "If you didn't feel like having a good debate about something," Heymann continues, "you'd better avoid him."[11] Frank Michelman, who served as Notes coeditor on the law review with Scalia, remembered him "as having delighted in chiding [Adlai] Stevenson liberals about the excesses of government regulation. . . . I don't remember anyone I thought was more fun to be with and argue with."[12]

Friends noticed that Scalia did not have any sympathy at the time for the plight of the poor people in the country, whom John F. Kennedy would later call "the forgotten Americans." Daniel Mayers, who served on the law review with Scalia, recalled "conversations with him—not intellectual conversation, more like what you'd talk about drinking beer at night—where it was clear that he believed there were more important things in life than to go out and struggle on behalf of the poor, and that God or somebody had ordained there were inevitably going to be a lot of poor people in the world, and there wasn't much to do about it." [13]

Scalia did find time, though, to explore the links between his religion and his new profession during his years at Harvard. He was a member of the St. Thomas More Society all three years. According to the 1958 yearbook, the club "aspires to offer Catholic students at the Law School a community in which they can develop an appreciation of the relevance of Christian philosophy and values to the law and to contemporary society. It recognizes that the vocation of the Christian lawyer is to further the process of development by which the law responds to human needs." [14] The group met each month, had an annual banquet with a speaker from the Boston legal community, and participated in Communion breakfasts, which enabled them to interact with local legal experts and academics on "matters of interest linking the legal and spiritual realms." [15] For Scalia, pursuing this interconnection between religion and law became a lifelong mission.

•   •   •

The school's faculty and philosophy of the day were dominated by one universal theme: follow the principles of the school's former faculty member and leading conservative on the Supreme Court, Associate Justice Felix Frankfurter. Peter Edelman, whose time at the school coincided with two of Scalia's years there, remembered, "Felix Frankfurter was God." Observing Frankfurter's work, Edelman recalled, "We . . . were taught judicial restraint and neutral principles. We were taught that if one used the right method, it would yield the right answer. If it happened that one side tended to win fairly routinely, this was incidental, merely the product of the methodology." [16] William Wiecek, who also attended Harvard during Scalia's time there, recalls the affection held during that time for "Our Felix" by the faculty, and their moniker for him, "Teacher of the Law," which was invented by their beloved Dean Griswold. [17]

The curriculum at that time was shaped largely by two casebooks. The first was *The Legal Process: Basic Problems in the Making and Application of Law*, coauthored by Henry M. Hart Jr., a former assistant to and coauthor with Frankfurter when he taught at Harvard Law School, and Albert M. Sacks, a former Frankfurter Supreme Court law clerk, both of whom were self-restraint advocates who taught at Harvard. It outlined a Frankfurter-style theory of judging by an adherence to a clear set of decision-making rules rather than ideology. As Wiecek explained, "Where there are no controlling precedents that would dispose of the case on the basis of its authority alone, judges had to articulate the reasons for their result and lay out that reasoning in a coherent manner. This was meant to avoid arbitrary or irrational bases of judging, such as the judge's hostility to a party's counsel."[18]

The other influential casebook was *The Federal Courts and the Federal System*, written by Professor Hart and another of Frankfurter's disciples, Professor Herbert Wechsler of Columbia Law School. This book was described by William Wiecek as "the single most influential casebook in American legal education."[19] Students in the third year used the book in an advanced course in public law and judicial administration in which the principal emphasis was on "the central problems of legal statesmanship in the delimitation of the powers of the government with which the federal courts have been and are confronted."[20]

Proponents of Frankfurter's view heard a clear, straightforward explanation of that philosophy in the Oliver Wendell Holmes Lecture on April 7, 1959, near the end of Scalia's second year at the school. The speech, "Toward Neutral Principles of Constitutional Law," was given by the casebook coauthor Herbert Wechsler. Frank Michelman later wrote of the importance of this occasion: "In those days, the Holmes Lectures were truly festival events for which everyone turned out, and in fact two of the most famous lecturers in the series occurred on our watch as students: Learned Hand's probing and eloquent 'The Bill of Rights' in 1958, and Herbert Wechsler's daring 'Toward Neutral Principles of Constitutional Law' in 1959."[21]

Michelman recalled that in theorizing about "the role of courts in general and the Supreme Court in particular in our constitutional tradition,"[22] Wechsler offered a disciplined critique of the Supreme Court's decision making. He argued that while the Supreme Court "cannot escape the duty of deciding whether actions of the other branches of the government are consistent with the Constitution, when a case is properly before them," that what mattered most was "the standards to be followed in [the] interpretation" of the Constitution.[23] Rather than seeking to right an individual wrong, a correctly decided case is "one that rests on reasons with respect to all the issues in the case, reasons that in their generality and their neutrality transcend any immediate result that is involved."[24] Using this approach, Wechsler critiqued the Supreme Court's liberal ruling five years earlier in *Brown v. Board of Education* that segregation in public schools was unconstitutional. Despite the fact that Wechsler favored the result in this case, he made clear that only a neutral, "principled decision" should allow the Court to consider extending the desegregation decision to other areas of public life, such as public transportation, hotels, and recreation businesses. And for him, *Brown*, with its reliance on data dealing with the self-esteem of children in segregated schools rather than legal precedents, was more politically motivated than principled.[25]

As Wechsler saw it, the *Brown* case "rested on the view that racial segregation is, in principle, a denial of equality to the minority against whom it is directed; that is, the group that is not dominant politically and, therefore, does not make the choice involved."[26] For Wechsler, this was not a neutral principle, as "the question posed by state-enforced segregation is not one of discrimination at all." Rather, he posited that the more neutral principle was "the denial by the state of freedom to associate," as the denial of this right "impinges in the same way on any groups or races that may be involved." For Wechsler, the more principled way to resolve the school segregation cases was to answer the following question: "Given a situation where the state must practically choose between denying the association to those individuals who wish it or imposing it on those who would avoid it, is there a basis in neutral principles for holding that the Constitution demands that the claims for association should prevail?"[27] Lending credence to Wechsler's argument was the fact that Frankfurter, the self-proclaimed wearer of the judicial self-restraint mantle passed down by his judicial heroes and mentors, Louis D. Brandeis and Oliver Wendell Holmes, was reluctant to join Chief Justice Warren's opinion, though he ultimately supported it.[28]

It was a powerful argument, and it had a significant effect on the entire Harvard Law community. Michelman recalled: "It was stunning. Professor Wechsler had stood before us declaring himself unable to explain the legitimacy of *Brown*. He had done so by way of illustrating . . . what he called 'neutral principles' and their bearing on adjudicative legitimacy. The aptness of the illustration was later to be very sharply questioned, but no one can doubt its having been good for memorability. From personal knowledge I can say the illustration was well chosen to leave the neutral-principles thesis deeply imprinted in the minds and memories of those in attendance."[29] Scalia classmate Mayers recalls of that speech: "We were all very struck by this argument that there were neutral principles of law which, if you really disciplined yourself, you could apply without regard to your own political preferences."[30] In Michelman's words, the "core of the lesson" for the judicial process was clear: "The adjudicative act earns its legitimacy by contracting a debt to the future, for which its author signs in the script of neutral principle. In that signature lies 'the very essence' of the judicial (as opposed to the political) method of decision-making."[31]

Scalia later claimed that he did not attend the lecture, a claim that many questioned. Michelman conceded, "I cannot today claim eyewitness recall of . . . Nino attending the lectures, but I'd lay odds that [he] attended. . . . Everybody did. It was *de rigueur*."[32] Regardless of his attendance, Scalia certainly would have been familiar with Wechsler's message since the law review board edited his speech for its first article in the following year's issue.[33]

While Georgetown shaped Scalia's view of his religious mission, Harvard Law School layered over that foundation both a refinement of his political conservatism and an understanding of his legal mission to realize it. The conservatism and judicial self-restraint theories of Felix Frankfurter, the "legal process" lessons of Frankfurter's acolytes on the Harvard Law faculty, and the "search for neutral principles" of Wechsler laid the cornerstone for Scalia's theories for working in the law. As Peter Edelman put it:

> Reading Justice Scalia's opinions thirty years later, there is a sense of *déjà vu*. Harvard may have moved on to Critical Legal Studies and other postmodern curiosities, but much of Justice Scalia's work reads like the Harvard Hit Parade of the 1950s. Justice Scalia is no doubt a product of many influences; one, most assuredly, is the Harvard Law School of the 1950s. Like Justice Frankfurter, Justice Scalia seems to believe that methodology is a significant part of the message. He spends a great deal of time defending his method of reading the Constitution, to the point where it sometimes means to tell us that the results on the merits are incidental.[34]

The raw materials were there for Scalia to exercise his affinity for using a textual analysis and historical originalism when considering his decisions. What made it so perfect, though, was the harmony between this approach and his earlier experiences. Like the close, textual analysis taught him by his father, and the literal biblical tradition favored by his faith, this conservative legal approach could reach his desired policy goals by relying on a careful reading and application of ancient legal sources.

• • •

In his final year of Harvard Law School, Scalia met another person who would have a lasting influence on his life: a senior student in English at Radcliffe (Harvard's women's college) named Maureen McCarthy. They met on a blind date, and had a seven-month courtship before marrying on September 10, 1960. They jokingly referred to it as a "mixed marriage" because he was of Italian descent while her ancestors were Irish. After Scalia's *magna cum laude* graduation from Harvard Law they spent their first year out of school traveling in Europe. Years later, Scalia would say, "Actually, the main reason she married me was that, after graduation, I had a Sheldon Fellowship. Under this traveling fellowship, Harvard gives you money to travel with virtually no strings attached, with one exception. You cannot enroll for a degree in any university, which, after seven years of college and law school, was the farthest thing from my mind!"[35] This fellowship allowed Scalia to take his new wife to many of the locales he had seen while studying at the University of Fribourg during his Georgetown years.

Maureen was a devout Catholic, like her new husband. When it came to the family plans, Scalia explained, "We're just old-fashioned Catholics, you know, playing what used to be known as Vatican Roulette."[36] Indeed, practicing no birth control, the Scalias would welcome their first child into the world, a daughter they named Ann Forrest, a year after they were married, on September 2, 1961. In time, they would have nine children, born over a nineteen-year span, and by 2012 the only child of his extended family's generation would be a grandfather to thirty-three children.

Maureen Scalia filled the same role with their children that Scalia's own mother had with him. "She went to all the [kids'] games," he said, to which Maureen Scalia added, "I would get five minutes at each on a Saturday."[37] While Scalia became engrossed in his legal work, his wife remained fixed in the real world. Noting the disparity, she would call her husband "Mr. Clueless."[38]

After the year of travel, Scalia's first job out of law school was in the prominent Cleveland, Ohio, law firm of Jones, Day, Cockley & Reavis. Partner James Lynn loved to tell the story of how he hired one of Harvard's finest students to join his firm. Lynn happened to be on Harvard's campus late one Saturday night looking for future law graduates to interview. Knowing that the best people might be found working on the law review, Lynn made his way to the publication's office in the library on the top floor of Gannett House. There he spied a heavyset, bushy-eyebrowed, black-haired law student who happened to be the law review's notes coeditor. The young man was buried in law books editing a manuscript. This was hardly an unusual situation. As classmate Daniel Mayers recalled, Scalia "would bring cannoli from a Cambridge bakery to the office and eat them hunched over his desk" while doing his work.[39] Even though Scalia made clear to the man interrupting him that Cleveland was hardly where he envisioned moving, Lynn finally persuaded the earnest student to join him for a late night meal of bacon and eggs at a restaurant on Harvard Square.

Lynn pursued Scalia for two months, and was certain he had found the right man for the job when he observed Scalia on a trip to interview with the firm. Holding a drink in his hand and leaning against the fireplace mantel in the senior partner's Shaker Heights home, Scalia held his own in an argument with eight other senior members of the firm over the merits of a *Harvard Law Review* article he had edited on the Supreme Court's decisions dealing with Sunday blue laws forcing businesses to close for the day. Lynn recalled later: "He already had that habit of getting intensely serious with those heavy black eyebrows of his scrunching up and his jaw setting so that he spoke without moving his jaw much. We were shouting at each other saying things like, 'How did you ever make law review?' It didn't seem to bother him that everyone was on the other side." Scalia gave no quarter and, job or no job, he was still arguing until three in the morning with the men who would vote on his hiring. "It was one against eight," one partner, Richard Pogue, said later. "He was so intense and enthusiastic. I tell you, it was the best recruiting session I have ever been to."[40]

When he was offered the job, Scalia accepted. Scalia later told a gathering of law students and recent law graduates at a Philadelphia meeting of the Federalist Society, "I worked for my first job in Cleveland. Cleveland! The New York law firms were already sweat shops, but [the lawyers working at] Jones Day, did not work nights, or weekends, unless it was an emergency." By working there, Scalia added, it allowed him to "fulfill his other responsibilities to his family, to his church, and to his community."[41] For the next six years Scalia worked in Cleveland, continuing to impress every member of the firm.

While his personal and professional lives improved dramatically, the course of his religious life took an unexpected turn. Scalia's faith was tested, first by the nature of American politics, and later by Pope John XXIII's religious reforms. Like many Catholics in 1960, Scalia, eligible for the first time to vote in a presidential election, was delighted to see a Catholic from Boston,

Senator John F. Kennedy, run for president. With a chance to become the first member of his faith to win the office, Kennedy found himself in a difficult religious situation in the West Virginia Democratic primary. Faced with the latent and open bigotry of the heavily Protestant electorate in the state, fueled by Senator Hubert Humphrey's campaign song, "Give Me That Old Time Religion," Kennedy had to deemphasize his religious background.[42] Speaking to the national convention of the American Society of Newspaper Editors in Washington, D.C., on April 21, 1960, Kennedy assured everyone that the Catholic Church "has no claim over my conduct as a public officer sworn to do the public interest." For him, this meant that, "I do not speak for the Catholic Church on issues of public policy—and no one in that church speaks for me."[43] The argument was persuasive enough to the West Virginia voters that Kennedy won the state easily, taking more than 60 percent of the vote, and Humphrey was forced to withdraw from the race for the presidential nomination.

During the general election campaign, Kennedy, whose religious views were not especially devout, told a gathering of Protestant ministers at the Greater Houston Ministerial Association on September 12, 1960, "what kind of church I believe in . . . should matter only to me." As he explained: "I believe in an America where the separation of church and state is absolute— where no Catholic prelate would tell the President (should he be Catholic) how to act, and no Protestant minister would tell his parishioners for whom to vote—where no church or church school is granted any public funds or political preference—and where no man is denied public office merely because his religion differs from the President who might appoint him or the people who might elect him."[44] Creating a separation between his personal faith and his public duties, Kennedy added: "I believe in a President whose religious views are his own private affair, neither imposed by him upon the nation or imposed by the nation upon him as a condition to holding that office." Later in the speech, Kennedy seemed ready to construct, in the words of Thomas Jefferson and James Madison, his own personal "high wall of separation" between his religion and his political obligations: "I am not the Catholic candidate for president. I am the Democratic Party's candidate for president, who happens also to be a Catholic." Then, repeating his line from the West Virginia primary speech, he added: "I do not speak for my church on public matters, and the church does not speak for me. Whatever issue may come before me as president—on birth control, divorce, censorship, gambling or any other subject—I will make my decision in accordance with these views, in accordance with what my conscience tells me to be the national interest, and without regard to outside religious pressures or dictates. And no power or threat of punishment could cause me to decide otherwise."[45] Michael Sean Winters, a journalist who covered the Catholic Church, correctly described Kennedy's view of the relationship between religion and politics this way: "For Kennedy, religion was private . . . denying the public consequences of his faith."[46] As a result, Kennedy "was a candidate first, and a Catholic second. . . . He was trying to lay to rest the fear of overt papal intrusions in a Catholic presidency as well as the fear that, as a Catholic, he was of a certain cast of mind attuned to obedience, mystery, and dogma."[47]

Like so many of Kennedy's legendary speeches, these words contained the perfect pitch and tone to secure his election, but they cost him the support of conservative Catholics like Antonin Scalia. The notion that Kennedy would disregard his Catholic roots in the Oval Office was distasteful to Scalia. "I was offended by John F. Kennedy when he was running for president and said he hoped no one would vote against him because of his religious affiliation," Scalia later recalled, noting that the views of the abolitionists and many public decency laws, such as those against bigamy and public nudity, all had their basis in religion.[48] When Scalia later faced a similar choice serving on the United States Supreme Court, blogged Catholic law professor Rick Garnett, he would not "put aside" his religious views and teaching in the performance of his duties.[49] He explained his views as a federal judge: "A religious person cannot divide his view of man. He can't separate religion from his own natural inclinations. Catholicism is not some superficial overlay. . . . It is who I am and how I see [the world]." For Scalia, "religiously motivated work is *not* un-American. . . . Official public expression of God and God's law distinguish us from most Western countries."[50]

Years later, Scalia would use these arguments to try to persuade an audience that religion did not drive his judicial decision making. But few would believe him because, when put in a situation similar to that of Kennedy, Scalia reached the opposite conclusion, and pursued a different course.

This debate over the role of religion in the White House was a precursor of what was to come for the followers of the Catholic faith. On October 11, 1962, Pope John XXIII convened the 21st Ecumenical Council of the Catholic Church. Called the Second Vatican Council, or Vatican II, because for only the second time the council met at St. Peter's Basilica in the Vatican, over the next four years, up to 2,300 Catholic religious figures from around the world met to determine the direction of the Church in the modern world. The participants reviewed all of the religion's teachings, finishing under Pope John's successor, Pope Paul VI. The sixteen documents that they promulgated changed the face of Roman Catholicism. Perhaps the biggest change coming from Vatican II, and the one that had the greatest impact on the thinking of Catholics such as Scalia, was in the baseline philosophy governing these changes. The existing approach of a "return to the sources," promulgated in Vatican I nearly a century earlier was abandoned in favor of "updating and modernizing." This new approach went "beyond the sources" in a process sometimes called the "new theology."[51]

No longer was the Catholic faith to be governed vertically by monarchical, hierarchical relationships within the religious bureaucracy or between the priests and their congregations. The new model was more open, with equal participation between the priests and their parishioners. Masses would be said in the congregants' native language, meaning a switch from Latin to English in the United States, and with the priest facing the congregation (instead of away from them toward an altar) and inviting all to participate fully in the liturgy. Religion would be more inclusive, even to visitors from other religions, with readings being made available in new English translations. Worshippers were taught and encouraged to think for themselves, to interpret the Bible and their religion themselves, and work side by side with their priest and others in the congregation, sharing their new understanding. As a result of this change, many American Catholics would begin to drift away from the strict observance of the past to develop their own form of the religion, with many, possibly even a majority, choosing to take an "à la carte" approach, picking and choosing those parts of the religion that they wanted to follow.

The precise text of the old Catholic sources no longer mattered as much as what was called "the spirit of the [Vatican II] council." As church historian Father John W. O'Malley explains: " 'Spirit' here meant an overriding vision that transcended the particulars of the documents and had to be taken into account in interpreting the council. The vagueness of the 'spirit' is brought down to earth and made verifiable when we pay attention to the *style* of the council, to its unique literary form and vocabulary, and draw out their implications. Through an examination of 'the letter' (form and vocabulary) it is possible to arrive at 'the spirit.' "[52] This was certainly not the textual, historical approach taught to Scalia by his father, using his theory of "literalness." Said David Snow, a partner in the Jones Day firm who knew Scalia at the time, "In the sixties, I can recall him being perturbed by the liberalizations in the Catholic Church."[53] From the moment that Vatican II took hold in America, Antonin Gregory Scalia was a man out of tune with his time and his religion. He now realized that he was a member of a religious minority even within his Catholic faith, which itself was a minority in America. The double-sided nature of that identity as a minority would help to shape his later views and actions.

CHAPTER 4

Building a Résumé

After touring Europe with his new wife on the Sheldon Fellowship, and having learned legal theory in Cambridge, Scalia learned how to practice law in Cleveland. Traveling as though he were on a mountain train chugging its way to the top, Scalia began moving through a series of career stations. With each stop, he searched for the place that would occupy his prodigious intellect, and afford him the chance to use his argumentative skills in exploring issues that appealed to him, all the while offering him the power, public visibility, and upward mobility that he craved.

Operating out of the Huntington Bank Building in downtown Cleveland, the Jones, Day, Cockley & Reavis law firm was the perfect place for a young attorney to learn diverse aspects of a legal career, well outside the high-pressure world of New York firms. The firm was the most prominent one in Cleveland, with around seventy-five attorneys, large for that time. It would grow even larger over the next half-dozen years, adding another thirty attorneys.[1] In addition, it had an office in Washington, D.C.

Once there, Scalia was pressed into service in a round-robin approach to training associates, and was thus able to experience the full range of the practice, including litigation, antitrust, real estate, tax law, labor law, commercial law, wills, contracts, and even private international law. "He was one of the last of the real generalists in the sense that he wanted to do as much of everything as he possibly could," remembers Herbert Hansell, a Jones Day partner from that time. "And he did damn near everything and he did it well."[2] Most of his cases were, in Scalia's words, "settled before trial, defaulted, or were already at the appellate stage."[3] The only downside, another partner from that era, James Lynn, recalls, was that "he wanted to spend more time on a problem than you might like in a practice. But that's part of what drove him to teach and later drove him to be a judge."[4]

Like those who knew him during the Harvard Law School years, the lawyers at Jones Day saw Scalia as one of the most conservative, brilliant, and fun-loving members of the firm. Daniel Elliott Jr., who overlapped with Scalia at Jones Day, said, "I remember the guy vividly. He was a real hard-core [Barry] Goldwater person. I interviewed [with Scalia, among others] in the fall of 1963, before Goldwater had a head of steam, and he was a very articulate advocate [of that point of view]." Another partner, David Snow, added, "He was one of the first Bill Buckley–type conservatives and was a big *National Review* fan."[5] Always included in a group of young associates who met regularly for luncheon discussions on constitutional law at Chef Hector's, a downtown Italian restaurant, Scalia stood out. "Those were exciting times," recalled Jones Day attorney Robert Nelson. "All points of view were represented. Nino's, of course, was one of the most conservative."[6] To which Richard Pogue, the firm's managing partner, added, Scalia had a "superb ability to express himself."[7]

Scalia loved to be the life of the party for the law firm gatherings. At the annual Christmas party, William Reale recalled, "the lawyers would get up and do skits and sing and Nino was always prominent at those events."[8] Pogue told reporters that he found Scalia to have "a great sense of humor" and a lovely tenor voice that he used at office parties to sing operas and show tunes to entertain the guests.[9] "I wouldn't say he's terribly good at [playing the piano]," recalled James Lynn. "But he likes to hammer."[10] James Courtney, a former partner at Jones Day, liked to recall how Scalia arrived at his home in Cleveland Heights for a Christmas party, slipping into the basement window well outside the house as he tried to press his face against a first-floor window to make a funny face at the guests inside.[11]

As a junior associate in Jones Day, Scalia learned his craft by doing grunt work, assisting senior members develop cases for a range of state and federal courts. Even though he was a new attorney, they entrusted him with work for their major clients, a veritable who's who of corporations in Cleveland, including: Sears, Roebuck, Ohio Bell, East Ohio Gas Company, Cleveland Cliffs Iron Ore, Ohio Brass, Clark Controller, Firestone Tire & Rubber, McGraw-Edison, and Chrysler.

During the summer of 1961, Scalia and another young associate, William Reale, helped prepare the defense in an antitrust case for some of Jones Day's corporate clients.[12] It was a massive class action lawsuit involving over 25,000 claims that came to be known as the Electrical Equipment Antitrust Cases. The plaintiffs alleged over eighteen hundred price-fixing arrangements, in violation of the Clayton Act, by nineteen different electrical equipment product lines spread over thirty-five federal judicial districts. The Jones Day clients were Ohio Brass and the Clark Controller, which were municipally and investor-owned electrical utilities, in addition to some Rural Electrification Administration (REA) cooperatives also represented by the firm. Scalia recalled that his duties provided many lessons: "My participation was an intensive education in pre-trial practice, including pleadings, motions, interrogatories and depositions. I prepared our clients' answers and objections to the complaints, requests for admissions, and interrogatories, and prepared interrogatories, requests for admissions, motions of various sorts and briefs in support of and opposition to motions. I assisted in preparing our clients' witnesses for deposition and in preparing for deposition of the plaintiffs." [13] Over time, Scalia took on more and more responsibility in the case, even being put in charge of running a meeting when the senior attorney was unable to attend. William Reale recalls of the performance, "I think he did a superb job—I was quite impressed." [14] Scalia did not appear at trial for this case, as all but one of the cases were settled before going to trial.

The following year, in June 1962, Scalia got a chance to develop the legal theory behind the firm's litigation strategy when he was asked by another senior partner, James Sennett, to help prepare a case for Sears, Roebuck. Sears filed a civil suit for damages as a result of the collapse of the plaster ceiling of a Cleveland Sears store on June 29, 1960, that injured people, damaged goods, and impaired the ability of the store to operate while repairs were made. The Cleveland Trust, which had leased the store to Sears since 1935, was named as the defendant. It was determined that the plaster from the ceiling had given way because the diamond-mesh lath, which held it to the wood frame, had been fastened with smaller and thinner nails than were recommended by the standard construction practices of the time. Sears alleged that there had been a "violation of the covenant to deliver and keep the building in good condition and repair," and that there had been negligence in maintaining the property during the tenure of the lease. The case went to a jury trial in April 1964. Judge James Connell threw out the negligence aspects of the suit, leaving the jury to decide only whether Cleveland Trust had upheld its part of the lease to "deliver the building in good condition and repair." When Sears won the suit, receiving damages of just over $29,000, Cleveland Trust appealed.

It was during the appeal that Scalia was given more responsibility than a young associate usually received, being charged with fashioning the legal theory for the appellate briefs in support of the judgment. It would be a tricky case to win, since the Cleveland Trust attorneys, Michael Gallagher and Edward Cass, from another prominent Cleveland law firm, Hauxhurst, Sharp, Cull & Kellogg, argued that the statute of limitations had expired. Their argument seemed to be a persuasive one, since the negligence portion of the case was no longer relevant and the lease dated back to the construction of the building nearly thirty years before. Ohio law required that such a suit, based on a contract or written promise, had to be filed within fifteen years of the completion of that agreement *and* within two years of the incident causing bodily injury.

Scalia's argument in response was ingenious. He argued that since the lease was renewed several times since 1935, the building had been "constructively redelivered" within the statute of limitations. This meant that Cleveland Trust was still obligated to deliver and "keep [the building] in good condition and repair." It was a persuasive argument and a three-judge panel of the United States Court of Appeals for the Sixth Circuit agreed with Scalia's position and held for Sears, which allowed the company to settle all of the other personal injury lawsuits relating to this incident on very favorable terms.[15]

Though he was well on his way to making partner, in 1967 Scalia decided that, having built up a sufficiently long résumé in private legal practice to get a law school teaching position, the time had come for him to leave the practice of law. He accepted a position on the faculty of the University of Virginia School of Law. "I had intended to go into teaching," Scalia, the son of a college professor, later told an interviewer. "Then, the first thing I knew, nearly seven years had passed."[16]

Scalia and Maureen packed up their five young children, and moved to historic and scenic Charlottesville, Virginia. The school's original campus, or "the Grounds," was designed and built by Thomas Jefferson, but the law school was in Clark Hall, on the western part of campus. The university was very traditional, still three years away from admitting women into its undergraduate program and abolishing its school uniform of men's orange blazers and blue ties.[17] The law school was not yet in the top ten of America's 134 accredited law schools (as it later would be), but the students were so valued by the nation's elite corporate law firms and government agencies in Washington that the graduates had no trouble getting good jobs.[18]

Scalia was still a generalist, teaching contracts, commercial code, and comparative law, and while he did not teach administrative law, he wrote extensively on the subject. He quickly amassed an impressive publication list.[19] Typical of the fine quality of his work was an article about a crisis in the Virginia appellate court, in which Scalia studied the state's response to the problem of court congestion and the burgeoning number of case dockets. While Virginia had created eight new trial court systems, it had done nothing to increase the size of the appellate court structure. With what would become a trademark skill with language, Scalia wrote: "These external symptoms strongly suggest that the Commonwealth's body judicial may be suffering from a disease that is extraordinarily (and some would say regrettably) rare among modern governmental institutions—microcephalia. Perhaps moved by fear of this malady, the General Assembly has prescribed a complete internal examination, the results of which it is now awaiting." After proving through an impressive use of statistical charts that the caseload for the appellate courts had increased exponentially, the article argued for the creation of a lower appellate court.[20] But that did not happen.

While Scalia published, a time-honored requirement for gaining tenure, he decided that he did not want to remain at UVA long enough to become a candidate. With the election of Republican president Richard Nixon in 1968, he discovered that living in the city of Charlottesville made possible an even more attractive career path. With daily train service on Norfolk Southern's Crescent Route to Washington, he could commute the 112 miles into the city frequently and develop contacts in the conservative Nixon administration. Soon, he was taking a leave of absence from the Virginia law school faculty to work in Washington full time.

By now, some of Scalia's friends from Harvard and Jones Day had found their way into the Nixon administration, and in 1970 those contacts paid off when the new Office of Telecommunications Policy (OTP) was established. The OTP was charged with regulating the newly emerging cable television industry and was answerable to the president, its authority juxtaposed between the quasi-independent Federal Communications Commission (FCC) and the Office of Management and Budget (OMB). Clay T. "Tom" Whitehead, an unpretentious man in his early thirties, became the agency's first director. Whitehead had been searching for months without success for a general counsel. When he mentioned the problem to former Jones Day partner James Lynn, then general counsel for the Department of Commerce, Lynn suggested Scalia. In January 1971, Scalia got the appointment.[21] It was in his capacity as general counsel for the Office of Telecommunications Policy that he began his political education, learning how to negotiate among competing people and interests and how to deal with both the White House and the executive branch to help form regulatory policy in the communications field.[22]

Scalia's first foray into the creation of executive branch policy was a challenging one. In the early years of television, most Americans received programs for free over one of the twelve Very High Frequency, or VHF, channels or the many Ultra High Frequency, or UHF, channels. But broadcast networks did not serve remote rural areas, and since signals traveled only in straight lines, those who lived in mountainous regions often could not receive a signal even from stations in their vicinity. Then, in 1948, John Walson of Mahanoy City, Pennsylvania, constructed the first cable television service, receiving broadcast signals using a mountaintop antenna and delivering the programming by cable to his customers. Soon others followed, and a new industry was born.[23] But the networks and eventually the FCC complained that this amounted to a rebroadcast of copyrighted programs.

Eventually, cable services began to encroach on areas served by broadcast television, and in 1966 the FCC put a freeze on cable television, preventing it from competing with the major networks in the largest hundred markets, mostly major cities and their environs. In addition, the FCC ruled that cable could not use copyrighted programming from the networks without paying the networks substantial royalties that the small companies could ill afford. The only way for cable systems to overcome the freeze was to apply for FCC approval, presenting evidence that their enterprise was in "the public interest" and that it was "consistent with the establishment and sound maintenance of UHF television broadcast service."[24]

The success of the cable industry depended on the resolution of these two issues, one concerning turf and the other money. After the cable industry won a Supreme Court case, *Fortnightly Corp. v. United Artists Television, Inc.*, in 1968, allowing it to broadcast copyright-protected material into distant rural regions, Congress tried but failed to legislate a framework that would regulate that process.[25]

In 1971, it became Scalia's task to broker a "consensus agreement" among cable operators, broadcast networks, movie producers, and the FCC, in order to get the freeze lifted and allow cable television to serve not just rural areas, but to compete in major markets as well. The process took six months. Sol Schildhause, who negotiated the agreement for the FCC, recalled Scalia's effort with admiration. "Let me tell you, that thing was hammered out. That was not written, that was blacksmithed. I mean there was blood on every word of that thing, there honestly was."[26] Schildhause explained that the FCC was ready "to permit the importation of two distant signals into one of the major markets on the theory that you couldn't make cable go without having at least that—something new to offer." The problem was that successfully negotiating the agreement required secrecy, an ingredient that Scalia learned was in very short supply in Washington. Every time a draft agreement was proposed, it would be presented to a member of the Senate and the next day it would be leaked to all of the concerned parties in Washington. Says Schildhause, "That word was out. You couldn't keep a secret because by that time we must have had twenty-five drafts and lots of meetings and you know how that goes. If it didn't leak out, one way or another somebody was going to find out about it. Anyway, it was all over the place."[27]

Once they were ready to issue a letter of intent from the FCC regarding the new regulation, Whitehead of the OTP stepped in to argue for the rights of the movie and television producers who held the copyrights to programming that would be broadcast by cable companies. Sol Schildhause recalled: "The first thing you know there were a bunch of meetings set up . . . representing Clay Whitehead, and . . . running interference for the producers, was, believe it or not, Antonin Scalia."[28] And so, four people, Schildhause, representing the FCC, Scalia, representing the OTP, Henry Goldberg, a lawyer representing the Nixon administration and its backers in the movie producing world, and Henry Geller, a lawyer representing the broadcast networks, "hammered out a compromise."[29] Scalia's work drew nothing but praise from those around him. Whitehead later told a reporter that the consensus agreement negotiations "brought out Nino's ability to deal with real people and real situations that are inherently messy." To which Henry Goldberg, whose interests were aligned with Scalia's, added: "Something that impressed me was that despite his academic outlook he was able to hammer out this sort of compromise. . . . Some people doubted that Nino could mix it up at this level, but he could."[30]

The consensus agreement, known as the Cable Compromise of 1971, called on Congress and the courts to deal with the copyright exclusivity issues, presented a request by all parties concerned that legislation be passed, and offered a complicated formula using three concepts, "mandatory service," "minimum service," and "additional service" to determine when cable stations could operate in the largest hundred regions. It was this consensus agreement, agreed to by cable companies under pressure, that allowed the cable industry to develop and grow while protecting broadcast television's copyrights. Eventually, it was incorporated into new copyright regulations in 1976.[31]

Since the Office of Telecommunications Policy was also charged with dealing with the newly created Corporation for Public Broadcasting (CPB), this became part of Scalia's portfolio as well. Although Nixon was initially a supporter of public broadcasting, by the time Scalia came to OTP at the beginning of 1971, the increasingly paranoid president had become convinced that the national news and public affairs division of the Public Broadcasting Service (PBS), which depended on the government for funding, was an "enemy" group staffed by relentless liberal journalists.[32] Nixon decided to try to take control of this agency, or, if he could not, to destroy it by cutting off its funding. Because the OTP was charged with preserving and protecting the PBS system, it meant that conservatives such as OTP head Tom Whitehead and Scalia, whose conservative political views were obvious to everyone around him, had to find a way to oppose the Nixon policy in order to preserve their agency, without destroying their own future political careers. "We were on the hot seat," Whitehead told a reporter. "Assistants to President Nixon [H. R.] Haldeman, [John] Ehrlichman, and crew were yammering at us to try to get the [broadcasting] board to do this or that."[33]

When Whitehead got what he interpreted as "a rather incredible memo from the White House" ordering him to get a particular PBS station off the air, he turned the matter over to his general counsel. Recalls Whitehead: "Nino said, 'hell, write back a memo that says it's illegal.'" While Scalia acknowledged that that was not true, he added, "Hell, they don't know that." Whitehead told a reporter that he did precisely what Scalia had recommended and the White House soon dropped the issue.[34]

In early 1971, the OTP was asked to prepare a long-promised legislative proposal for financing of the Corporation for Public Broadcasting for the president to submit to Congress.[35] Sensing that the support of the Nixon White House for funding the CPB was waning as the publicly funded network aired programs critical of administration policies, Scalia wrote a memo urging that since legislation to solidify the federal government's financial support for CPB had long been promised, "an apparent change of heart at this point would be alleged to be politically motivated." Rather than starving the network for funds, Scalia argued: "The best possibility for White House influence over the Corporation is through the Presidential appointees to the Board of Directors."[36] On June 18, Scalia and Whitehead crafted another memorandum for the president, pointing out that "four more vacancies [on the CPB board] will also be filled [in 1972], giving us clear control of the Board." They also recommended replacing CPB president John W. Macy Jr. with "a professional, apolitical President of our choosing as soon as discretion permits."[37]

Seeking to guide the White House in this direction, Scalia wrote several memos opposing the centralized control of the Corporation for Public Broadcasting, favoring instead funding to individual, local stations. The final version of Whitehead and Scalia's proposal seemed ready for distribution by September 23. It recommended, among other things, "to induce CPB to change its orientation and emphasis on public affairs programming," and to support the efforts of the new conservative appointees to the Board of Directors by replacing Macy and Chairman Frank Pace, while the White House worked to "keep a rein on the full-time CPB and PBS staffs."[38]

But Nixon wanted the entire funding for public television to be eliminated. The president had learned that PBS reporters Robert MacNeil and Sander Vanocur were going to launch a new weekly public affairs program that promised, in their words, to "try to reverse the usual focus of political reporting from the politician down to the people." Said Vanocur: "We have taken an institutional view of politics in the past . . . in a sense [we] will be doing psychological reporting." OTP staff secretary Jon M. Huntsman wrote, "The above report greatly disturbed the President who considered this the last straw. It was requested that all funds for Public Broadcasting be cut immediately."[39]

While the OTP was instructed to relay this instruction to the House Appropriations Committee, Whitehead showed courage in resisting. Instead, drawing on his planning with Scalia, in a memo to the president he argued: "We have identified several options for dealing with the public affairs programming of public broadcasting. In the short run, there does not appear to be any way to cut off Federal funds." The problem, he explained, was that federal funds had already been transferred to the CPB, and any cutback of funds would spill over into educational and cultural programs.[40] After offering a variety of options for cutting back on PBS funding and shifting the money to local stations, Whitehead recommended instead that the tax laws be changed to prevent corporations and other foundations from supporting the political programs on public television.[41] Recognizing that such a change in the tax laws would inevitably result in controversy, Whitehead offered to open the administration's attack with a speech on October 20 to a convention of the local public television stations. The memo circulated around the administration, but by mid-October the more moderate and long-range OTP proposals of Scalia and Whitehead were not winning.[42]

On October 20, Whitehead became the point man for the Nixon administration's attack on public broadcasting with his blistering speech at the annual convention of the National Association of Educational Broadcasters in Miami.[43] Whitehead was in the middle of negotiating between the public broadcasting industry and the government. When a frustrated Scalia saw that the White House was advocating the removal of public affairs broadcasting from the CPB portfolio, he decided that it was time to risk his political career by opposing the White House in order to protect the future of his agency and his boss. Just two days before Christmas, Scalia sent an "EYES ONLY" memorandum to Whitehead, declaring that the administration's plan for the CPB Board of Directors was a loser and that the OTP—and Whitehead—should "dissociate yourself from this particular 'initiative.'"[44]

Whitehead did not follow Scalia's advice, continuing to privately recommend to members of Congress how the CPB might be moved in a new, conservative direction. As Scalia predicted, the effort by the White House to take control of public broadcasting soon was made public and became the subject of controversy, with the American Civil Liberties Union, on February 20, 1972, issuing a fifty-five-page report charging that the White House had tried to "intimidate" and "starve" the industry.[45] When Congress ignored the White House and authorized funding for public broadcasting in 1972, Nixon vetoed the bill. It was not until a year later, after considerable negotiations among the CPB, PBS, and the White House, with the help of several new Nixon appointments to the CPB governing board, that Nixon, without any conditions involving public affairs broadcasting, signed a new two-year congressional reauthorization of public television.

Nixon's attack on public broadcasting never ended, but his presidency did. On August 9, 1974, just two days after he finally took full control of the governing board of the CPB with five new appointments, he resigned from office as a result of the Watergate scandal.

• • •

While Scalia could not save the administration from political damage on the telecommunications issue, he once more displayed remarkable skill working behind the scenes, cutting through to the central issues in political disputes. And in doing so, he not only saved his career, but also won new admirers and supporters. Years later, a review of the telecommunications policy of the Nixon administration written for the Jimmy Carter White House concluded: "Scalia actually comes off looking very good. He's about the only one."[46]

In each of these disputes Scalia learned how to master historical and government policy material, craft his summary, analyze and recommend policy in concise and clear memos, and adjust his recommendations as the developing disputes required. These were skills that would later serve him well in his next stop in the White House bureaucracy and later on the federal judiciary. But beyond that, Scalia learned how to deal within a governmental bureaucracy with sharply competing, partisan groups, remain in the middle of these combatants without being seen as an ally of either side, sometimes win his arguments, and develop theories that would allow him to take the high ground in the dispute. Once having survived and even won those battles, Scalia learned the best lesson of all—when to leave for another job so as not to make permanent enemies of people who might impede his future career. His next opportunity came when Professor Roger Crampton resigned as the chairman of the Administrative Conference of the United States, an independent research agency charged with analyzing the efficiency and fairness of federal agencies' procedures and making recommendations to Congress and the White House for their improvement.

Scalia had never resigned his faculty position at the University of Virginia, so when the conference vacancy occurred, which was to be filled by an academic, he was well positioned. Unaffected by, or unaware of, Scalia's opposition in the PBS funding dispute, President Nixon nominated him as the agency's third chairman, and he took office after the Senate confirmed him on September 19, 1972. The Administrative Conference consisted of a chairman drawn from academia, a council of ten additional presidential appointees that acted like a "corporate board of members," and an assembly of seventy-five to ninety-one members drawn from any agency that would be affected by the conference's deliberations, plus scholars and members of the private bar who were experts in administrative law. As Scalia later explained: "[The conference's] purpose was to identify the causes of inefficiency, delay, and unfairness in administrative proceedings affecting public rights, and to recommend improvements to the President, the agencies, the Congress and the Courts."[47]

For Scalia, it was the perfect job. The conference was a government research think tank that allowed him to develop contacts with federal officials throughout the government and prominent attorneys in administrative law, and to organize and solve academic-style governmental problems with little risk of making political enemies in the process. Even better, the position involved discussions with members of Congress as well as key executive officials who could become instrumental in his next career move. Scalia later explained that he "had the authority to call plenary sessions of the Conference and to fix their agenda, to recommend subjects for study, to receive and consider reports and recommendations before the assembly considered them, and to exercise general budgetary and policy supervision."[48] As the chairman of the conference, Scalia was back in the familiar role of negotiating among competing parties: the White House, Congress, the courts, and various federal agencies. Years later, he explained his central goal in those years: "Most of my energy was devoted to the development and implementation of administrative procedures, throughout the government, that would ensure fairer treatment of all persons by federal agencies. . . . In all of my professional activities, I have regarded it as the supreme rule of our system that each individual is of equivalent worth, and must be treated by the government accordingly. In my personal life, my religious beliefs impose the same view."[49]

During Scalia's time as chairman of the Administrative Conference a number of changes were successfully recommended for specific agencies in specific situations. Congress passed the conference's recommendation abolishing the doctrine of sovereign immunity for lawsuits in which courts were reviewing actions by federal agencies. Congress also adopted verbatim the conference's recommendations for improvements to the new Freedom of Information Act, including the imposition of civil monetary penalties against uncooperative agencies. The conference in those years was also instrumental in changing the Civil Service procedures dealing with "adverse actions against Federal Employees," changing federal parole procedures to allow for a right to counsel and other guarantees, changing the procedures for certifying immigrant aliens for work, regulating publicity that could harm private individuals as part of the regulatory process of federal agencies, and regulating various environmental issues.

As part of his job, Scalia also became well known to Congress as he testified before them on a wide variety of legislative proposals. Not all of his recommendations were calls for change. As Scalia later explained: "Some recommendations were framed not in terms of what to do, but rather in terms of what to avoid—for example, the recommendation cautioning against Congress's imposition of complex rulemaking procedures, which has been followed with few exceptions."[50] For Scalia, these years from 1972 to 1974 were perfect for applying his interest in administrative law to governmental policy making. He was able to further develop his personal contacts in Washington in order to take the next step in his career.

After two years of work on the Administrative Conference, Scalia was ready to get back into the political fray in the hopes that it would propel his career even higher. And, as luck would have it, the perfect position opened up, but at exactly the wrong time for the man appointing him.

CHAPTER 5

The President's Legal Adviser

Fourteen years had passed since his graduation from Harvard Law School before Antonin Scalia was appointed to what he thought was his dream job: assistant attorney general and the head of the Office of Legal Counsel in President Richard M. Nixon's Department of Justice. But within days of his nomination on July 30, 1974, he learned that it had the potential to become a political nightmare that could wreck his career in government. As Scalia later recalled about his life in the disintegrating Nixon administration: "It was a sad time. It was very depressing. Every day, *The Washington Post* would come out with something new—it trickled out bit by bit. Originally, you thought, *It couldn't be,* but it obviously was. As a young man, you're dazzled by the power of the White House and all that. But power tends to corrupt."[1]

With members of the executive branch deserting the Nixon administration or being purged from their positions by an administration obsessed with loyalty, the Office of Legal Counsel job opened up. The previous occupant, Robert Dixon Jr., appointed by then–Attorney General Elliot Richardson, had not endeared himself to the Nixon crowd when he wrote a cautionary memo warning that any effort by a sitting president to withhold evidence from an investigation of possible impeachment would provoke "a constitutional confrontation of the highest magnitude."[2] When Dixon left, Associate Deputy Attorney General Jonathan Rose, a former partner at Jones Day, recommended Scalia.

Deputy Attorney General Laurence H. Silberman, who in time would become one of Scalia's closest friends in Washington, received the recommendation with pleasure. Silberman liked the tough Italian American attorney from New York City, but, more than that, he liked the talent that Scalia had shown in his Office of Telecommunications Policy and Administrative

Conference work. Silberman would later say, "There was a range of potentially serious constitutional issues, and it was absolutely imperative to have a first-class legal mind and a man of courage."[3] There was something in the position for both sides. For the Nixonians, the selection of the conservative Scalia would provide them with a more supportive legal voice, and for Scalia, it was a promotion to a new position with responsibilities on a full range of issues.

The head of the Office of Legal Counsel assists the attorney general in rendering formal written and informal verbal opinions, and offers legal advice on all manner of domestic and international legal issues for the president, the cabinet, and executive agencies. The official governmental description for the post makes clear the wide-ranging nature of the responsibilities: the office drafts legal opinions of the attorney general and also provides its own written opinions and oral advice in response to requests from the Counsel to the President, the various agencies of the executive branch and offices within the department. Such requests typically deal with legal issues of particular complexity and importance or about which two or more agencies are in disagreement.[4] Another feature of the position that might not have escaped Scalia's attention was that this was the position from which William Rehnquist had been selected to become a Supreme Court justice in 1971.

As Scalia saw it, his real position was to help his many clients stay out of legal trouble in the performance of their political tasks. Because of the wide-ranging executive branch responsibilities of the position, some people called it the "government lawyers' lawyer," but those familiar with the importance of the position for keeping the White House out of legal trouble, such as Justice Felix Frankfurter, liked to call the position by a much simpler title, the president's legal adviser.[5]

One attraction of the new job to the academic-minded Scalia was the wide-ranging and unpredictable nature of the research tasks associated with it, changing as often as the daily news. But it soon became clear to him that it would also give him something that his other governmental positions had lacked: constant access to higher officials who could advance his career. Since part of the job involved advising the attorney general and the White House, it would give Scalia the opportunity to work directly with Nixon's attorney general, William Saxbe, and with the Nixon White House as well.

But days after Scalia's nomination, Richard Nixon resigned from the presidency, on August 9, 1974, rather than endure possible impeachment due to the Watergate scandal. For the nation, it marked the end of a nightmare. For Scalia, though, it meant his job was now at risk. He served at the pleasure of the president, meaning that Gerald R. Ford, were he so inclined, could withdraw the nomination and fill the slot with one of his own people. Fortunately for Scalia, the new administration wanted him. He would now have the chance to work alongside President Ford's energetic staff. Led by chief of staff Donald Rumsfeld and his deputy, Dick Cheney, both advocates of strong presidential power, Scalia would be in a position to assist them in restoring the luster to the office that Nixon had tarnished. Now satisfied with his governmental position, Scalia resigned his faculty position at the University of Virginia.

The timing for advocates of presidential power was not optimal as members of Congress and the press, fueled by public anger over the Nixon scandal, sought to dismantle the power of the Nixon White House. Scalia would later describe the challenges of his tenure of office in the new Ford administration this way: "It was a terrible time, not for the Republican Party, but for the presidency. It was such a wounded and enfeebled presidency, and Congress was just eating us alive. I mean, we had a president who had never been elected to anything except . . . what? A district in Michigan? Everything was in chaos. It was a time when people were talking about 'the imperial presidency.' I knew very well that the 900-pound gorilla in Washington is not the presidency. It's Congress. If Congress can get its act together, it can roll over the president. That's what the framers thought. They said you have to enlist your jealousy against the legislature in a democracy—*that* will be the source of tyranny."[6] For the members of the Ford Justice Department, it would be, in Scalia's words, a "struggle to maintain the sphere of independence accorded to the Executive."[7]

Scalia realized this when he was asked by Attorney General Saxbe to generate a legal opinion as to whether Richard Nixon owned, and thus controlled the release of, or possible destruction of, all the papers and materials from his administration deposited with the administrator of general services. In addition, the attorney general was asked to advise on the question of "the obligations of the government with respect to subpoenas or court orders issued against the government or its officials pertaining to them."[8] There is little doubt that the departed Robert Dixon, fearing the "misplacing" or destruction of key documents, would have held that Nixon had no rights to ownership of his White House papers. While Scalia had a duty to the new president, and a professional obligation to give his best legal judgment, he knew that his answer would determine how Republican political operatives who could help or hurt his career would view him.

Scalia's memo to Attorney General Saxbe on the ownership and control of the Nixon papers was a textbook defense of an expansive presidential power. "Beginning with George Washington," Scalia began his memo, "every President of the United States has regarded all the papers and historical materials which accumulated in the White House during his administration, of a private or official nature, as his own property."[9] Scalia argued that the basis for his belief in a former president's total control of his official White House papers came from the theory of former president William Howard Taft: "The office of the President is not a recording office. The vast amount of correspondence that goes through it, signed either by the President or his secretaries, does not become the property or a record of the government unless it goes on to the official files of the department to which it may be addressed. The President takes with him all the correspondence, original and copies, carried on during his administration." Scalia cited section 507 of the Federal Records Act of 1950, a 1951 memorandum from the assistant solicitor general, and a 1955 joint resolution of Congress that set up the presidential library system to argue that it is impossible to differentiate between personal and official papers of the president. Accordingly, "a President has title to all the documents and historical materials—whether personal or official—which accumulate in the White House during his incumbency."[10]

Scalia supported his view by pointing out that the previous three presidents "have had to make special provisions through the means of the presidential library to take care of *their* papers." To which Scalia added, "So far as we are aware, no members of Congress disagreed." All in all, Scalia concluded, "the historical precedents, taken together with the provisions of the Presidential Libraries Act, indicated that the papers of President Nixon should be considered his personal property."

Despite this conclusion, there was also something in this opinion for Nixon's opponents, as Scalia determined that such materials could be reached by subpoenas. As he argued, since "the government is merely the custodian and not the owner of the subject materials," it meant "that those portions of the documents and materials in question which are the subject of court orders or subpoenas issued before August 9 and addressed to the United States or to Richard M. Nixon, President of the United States, must be treated and disposed of in accordance with the terms of those orders or subpoenas. Such obligation would supersede any demand by President Nixon for return of the materials subject to those orders or subpoenas." In conclusion, Scalia argued that, with respect to "those portions of the materials which are not subject to court order or subpoena, being the property of former President Nixon, should generally speaking be disposed of according to his instructions. These materials are, however, affected by public interest which may justify subjecting the absolute ownership rights of the ex-President to certain limitations directly related to the character of the documents as records of government activity."

What was interesting about Scalia's memo was what he chose not to include. There was no consultation with Special Prosecutor Leon Jaworski, who was investigating the Watergate cover-up, or mention of the latter's position strongly opposing Nixon's custody and control of the White House materials.[11] Later Scalia would say of his role as head of the Office of Legal Counsel: "We must call it down the middle. If we told our client only what he wants to hear, we wouldn't be doing our job effectively."[12] The episode served as Scalia's executive branch calling card with the new Ford administration and the Nixon conservatives who were trying to protect themselves. "It was a baptism under fire," former associate deputy attorney general James Wilderotter later recalled. "It certainly was not a popular decision."[13]

On the basis of this memo, Saxbe was able to advise Ford on the day that he pardoned Nixon: "To conclude that such materials are not the property of former President Nixon would be to reverse what has apparently been the almost unvaried understanding of all three branches of the Government since the beginning of the Republic, and to call into question the practices of our Presidents since the earliest times."[14] When Ford gave Nixon complete control over the papers as part of his September 8 pardon, the former president wrote Arthur Sampson, the director of the General Services Administration, that he would be donating "a substantial portion of my Presidential materials which are of historical value to our Country" and depositing them in a temporary archival facility in College Park, Maryland.[15] Then, citing a provision that he would use for years thereafter to prevent White House tapes and documents from being released, Nixon said that he would make this donation only after a "meticulous, thorough, time-consuming" review to determine whether the materials should be released under federal law.[16] Saxbe would say that he "had no advance warning" of the deal giving Nixon the "sole right and power of access" to the materials. White House counsel Philip Buchen claimed that this arrangement was made to keep the Ford administration from being "caught in the middle of trying on a case-by-case basis to resolve each dispute over the right of access or disclosure."[17] But Special Prosecutor Jaworski and Congress were not buying it. Three months later, Congress reversed the Ford administration's position and passed a law compelling the federal government to take permanent custody of the Nixon papers and keep them in the District of Columbia area. When Ford signed the bill on December 19, the issue was heading to the Supreme Court.[18]

The Supreme Court ruled against Nixon's ownership of the papers in the case of *Nixon v. Administrator of General Services* in 1977. Speaking through Justice William Brennan, the Court ruled that removing control of the White House papers from former President Nixon was not a violation of the constitutional separation of powers, did not undermine presidential powers, did not intrude into the confidentiality of the presidential position, and did not diminish either Nixon's right to privacy or his First Amendment free speech rights.[19] While eight members of the Court were against Nixon, the sole dissenter, sounding very much like OLC head Antonin Scalia, was William Rehnquist, who argued that making Nixon the sole president without control over his papers violated his constitutional rights and represented "a clear violation of the constitutional principle of separation of powers."[20]

• • •

Next, Scalia happily waded into the fight to preserve the secrets of the Ford administration. In doing so, he would earn his stripes as the legal lieutenant of chief of staff Rumsfeld and deputy chief Cheney.

After the rapid collapse of the Nixon administration, members of Congress were hastily organizing all manner of investigations to unearth its excesses. The American public was demanding the dismantling of the imperial presidency and the creation of congressional limits that would prevent it from returning. For his part, though, Scalia studied Article II of the Constitution, which created the presidency, and his law books, to lay the legal groundwork for defending the power of the president.

President Ford was the former minority leader of the House of Representatives who, in taking the presidential oath of office, promised to "follow my instincts of openness and candor with full confidence that honesty is always the best policy in the end." It was ironic that his first battle with the legislative branch would be over Congress's effort to improve the Freedom of Information Act, or FOIA, with new amendments.

Spurred by the axiom of Justice Louis D. Brandeis that "sunlight is said to be the best of disinfectants; electric light the most efficient policeman," the Freedom of Information Act was originally passed by Congress in 1966 with the intention of making government more open and thus keeping it honest.[21] The original law was so expensive for those seeking to use it, so bureaucratically hard to implement, and so routinely evaded and even ignored by government officials, that it had virtually no impact on the government. Having seen the power of the disclosures that led to the downfall of the Nixon administration, and the difficulty of getting key materials such as the White House tapes, Congress was determined to pass a series of amendments that would make it easier to gain access to governmental documents.

The new bill, under consideration in September 1974, sought to increase access to papers, to diminish secrecy within government, and to allow both the people and the press access to information that they could use to hold the government accountable. Not surprisingly, governmental agencies, including the CIA and FBI, allied to oppose the bill. And their legal point man was the newly installed head of the Office of Legal Counsel.

Ford did not support the bill, but wrote on the legislative briefing book, "a veto presents problems. How serious are our objections?"[22] Scalia believed that power could be maintained only by secrecy, which meant that he was determined to scuttle the Freedom of Information Act. So he helped to plan a strategy to do just that.

The administration's opening assault on FOIA came on September 23, 1974, when CIA general counsel John Warner began trolling for the administration's response to the bill. When he received confirmation that "Justice will recommend [a] veto," and after learning that deputy attorney general Laurence Silberman was also "firmly in opposition," Warner expressed the view that the Justice Department would recommend a presidential veto and "prepare a Presidential message which would indicate the President's willingness to approve a bill from which the objectionable provisions have been deleted."[23]

One day later, on September 24, while FOIA was being debated in the White House and the Department of Justice, Scalia, who was already inclined to back the presidency at every turn, learned how important it was for the Ford administration to derail FOIA. Consumer advocate Ralph Nader had sent a letter to the White House two weeks before, on September 11, requesting the release of all information relating to "the negotiating or communicating process between [President Ford's] office (as Vice President and President) and Richard M. Nixon and his agents and representatives" leading to the controversial "full and absolute" presidential pardon issued by Ford for Nixon's Watergate-related and other offenses on September 8. Nader argued that the Ford administration violated existing Department of Justice regulations dating back to 1962 requiring that a presidential pardon could be issued only "to anyone found guilty of a 'violation of public trust involving personal dishonesty' if there had been a conviction for a crime and a five-year waiting period had passed since that time." [24]

Given the explosive nature of this controversy, the information sought was hardly something that the White House wanted to release. Scalia wrote a detailed memo to Phillip Areeda, counsel to President Ford, offering what would become his standard advice on all FOIA issues: stonewall and deny. Scalia put forward every conceivable argument he could construct to avoid granting Nader's request. First, he argued, "There is some problem involved in determining the scope of the information request involved." Second, since FOIA applies only to government agencies in seeking information release, Scalia advised that the White House was not such an agency and thus would not be covered, saying that "there are obvious constitutional questions as to whether it could be." [25] Scalia added that this argument had another advantage, "It should be noted that this conclusion would protect from disclosure President Ford's Vice Presidential materials, as well as his Presidential materials, if they are now located in the White House office." [26] The message could not have been clearer: if there were any sensitive materials relating to the Nixon pardon, have them collected, ship them to the White House immediately, and let Nader try to argue against that position in federal court. This argument found favor with others in the administration. In the end, the White House did not release the materials to Nader.

On September 26, as a compromise FOIA bill forged in a congressional conference committee was readied for the president, Scalia began to rally the opposition to it. In a meeting on other issues with director of the CIA William Colby, the CIA's general counsel, John Warner, and Attorney General Saxbe, Scalia raised the issue of the new FOIA measure, asking the CIA officials for the agency's view. When the CIA officials insisted that the measure must be vetoed by the president, Scalia said that "if [they] wanted to have any impact, [they] should move quickly to make [their] views known directly to the President." The advice seemed all the more pressing when Scalia added that neither the Department of State nor the Department of Defense would be recommending that the president veto the measure. Later that day, Scalia called the CIA, "urging" them to contact the White House regarding their opposition to the FOIA law, even providing the name of the White House staff member in charge of the legislation.[27]

Inside the White House, aides were telling the president that vetoing the pending legislation was sure to cause a political firestorm. Newly released documents from the Ford administration, some made public as a result of FOIA requests, round out the picture of how Scalia tried to derail the new FOIA legislation. The FOIA amendments were sent to Ford on October 8, so close to the upcoming October 18 recess that some in the administration gave thought to the idea of rejecting the measure using a pocket veto, that is, allowing the time needed for a presidential signature to expire. But there was never any doubt what the president would do.

Ford vetoed the bill on October 17, issuing a message that relied on many of the arguments made by Scalia and the Department of Justice to explain why it was "unconstitutional and unworkable." He urged Congress to recraft the law with "more flexible criteria" and "additional latitude" in its timetable for responding to requests for declassification.[28] Congress had a different response, finding the votes in each house to override Ford's veto.

After the FOIA law was passed, Scalia searched for ways to direct a rearguard action undercutting its implementation by preventing the release of new documents in order to limit what he viewed as potential damage to the administration. As the head of the OLC, he directed a subcommittee of the Interagency Classification Review Committee (ICRC), a group of representatives of the various agencies that was charged with devising policies for dealing with FOIA requests. Scalia met with the subcommittee to plan ways to subvert the new law by moving to the federal court system as their next line of defense. The downside to this strategy, they all realized, was that such cases could be lost. Seeking to avoid the consequences of such a result, Scalia and his ICRC group searched for a mechanism to prevent the release of information. It was agreed that the ICRC did not have the necessary expertise and ability to take appropriate action.[29]

Scalia then turned his attention to devising ways to prevent FOIA from reaching into the White House. In this effort he showed how much he had learned about the necessary political maneuvering from the earlier OTP negotiations. First he wanted to present the appearance that the administration would be implementing the new legislation to the letter of the law. Charged with recommending guidelines for the implementation of the new FOIA amendments, Scalia wrote, "The President has asked me, in issuing these guidelines, to emphasize on his behalf that it is not only the duty but the mission of every agency to make these Amendments effective in achieving the important purposes for which they were designed." Scalia sent a copy to counsel to the president Phillip Areeda. With that, the president followed Scalia's suggestions that he orally instruct the attorney general on this issue in a meeting the following day.[30]

With the political cover established, Scalia used the White House's request that he "consider which entities within the Executive Office of the President are 'agencies' for the purposes of the FOIA, as amended," and thus covered by the law, to determine ways to limit the oversight power of the new legislation.[31] Having publicly promised to observe the new FOIA amendments, Scalia devised every possible means to shield the Ford administration from being subjected to the new law. After his review, Scalia concluded that FOIA covered only some in the Executive Office based on four factors: "functional proximity to the President," concluding that the more direct the reporting lines to the president the less likely that FOIA could reach it; the "authority to make dispositive determinations," or agencies that make decisions rather than just recommendations would be covered; "constitutional basis for the functions performed," or agencies performing presidential functions would not be covered; and "manner of creation," or agencies created by law are more likely to be covered than ones established under the inherent executive power or executive orders. While the definition of the "White House Office" was not entirely clear, Scalia concluded, "It is clear from the legislative history that the FIA [sic] does not embrace the President's immediate personal staff.... Presumably, it means that records maintained in the President's own offices or maintained by his closest aides are beyond the scope of the FIA."[32] Since he performed "staff functions" for the president, did not have "independent functions," and was "advising and assisting" the president, Scalia believed that *he* was not covered by the new act, either.

It is here that Scalia developed an ingenious means to exempt the White House from FOIA throughout the executive branch. He recommended that any group within an agency that might be subject to FOIA, but was in fact "advising and assisting" the White House, should be re-created as "a segregable subunit of the White House Office," so that it would not be subject to FOIA. Implementing this "concept of a separate 'White House Office'" throughout the executive branch agencies, Scalia explained, "should be fostered and strengthened in as many ways as possible," using such devices as revised organizational charts displaying the new advisory subunit.

As he saw it: "Judicial acceptance of such a functional division can greatly simplify our FIA [*sic*] problems with respect to the Executive Office." For Scalia, this plan, which was circulated throughout the White House, would achieve his and their goal of placing the administration beyond the reach of the new FOIA while appearing to favor the new reforms.[33] In advising this way, Scalia was, to turn Will Rogers's aphorism on its head, a man who never saw a FOIA request that he liked. Throughout his tenure in office, indeed throughout his life, he would continue to oppose that act.

The FOIA fight revealed just how far Scalia had come in his early professional career and just how talented he was. He demonstrated to all around him an extraordinary legal skill, fully capable of finding the central components of very complicated issues and explaining them in the way most favorable to the administration. His memos were well-written models of comprehensiveness, clarity, and persuasiveness. Reading them, one had full confidence that the recommendations were complete and correct. Beyond this, though, there was a signature style now evident in every Scalia memo. Time after time, he knew the results that he wanted to achieve on an issue, and he demonstrated an ability to manipulate the information and recommendations that he offered to achieve those results.

• • •

In January 1975, Attorney General William Saxbe resigned to become ambassador to India and was replaced by Edward Levi, a former dean of the University of Chicago Law School. Levi was universally respected for his intellect and integrity, reminding one of an Ivory Tower intellectual. Once, while driving the attorney general home because his regular driver was unavailable, Scalia asked his boss where he lived. Levi responded that "he didn't have the slightest idea; the driver just let him off every night, and he went in."[34] An unpretentious man, Levi appreciated it when Scalia invited him, Solicitor General Robert Bork, and *Washington Post* publisher Katharine Graham to dinner. After taking their drink orders, Scalia went to the locked liquor cabinet only to discover that the key that had been there moments before had disappeared, thanks to one of their toddlers. As Scalia later recalled, "I will never forget the image of the Attorney General, the Solicitor General, and I—and I think Kate joined us—crawling around on our hands and knees on the living room oriental rug, feeling for the missing key."[35]

By that time, the Democratic-controlled Congress was launching a series of investigations into the Nixon and Ford administrations' misuse of undercover and electronic surveillance by the FBI and the CIA against American citizens who were suspected of opposing government policymaking. Three investigative committees were formed in 1975. Senator Frank Church of Idaho chaired a Select Committee to Study Governmental Operations with Respect to Intelligence Activities, popularly known as the Church Committee. Congresswoman Bella Abzug of New York chaired the Subcommittee on Government Information and Individual Rights, and the House Select Committee on Intelligence, led by Otis Pike of New York, the so-called Pike Committee, simultaneously launched investigations into various government intelligence programs allegedly spying on organizations believed to be radical.[36]

While one congressional agency after another sought to investigate the government, OLC head Antonin Scalia became the legal point man in the Ford administration determined to keep government files closed. Scalia's stock response to congressional committees was to stonewall by claiming "executive privilege." Executive privilege is a concept implied in the "inherent powers" of the president, Article II, Section 1, of the Constitution. One of these powers is that the chief executive can preserve the candor of advice to the office by maintaining its secrecy from the other branches of government. There are limitations. In 1974, in *United States v. Nixon,* a unanimous Supreme Court upheld the existence of executive privilege but said that it could not be used for personal gain by, or the protection of, the president to avoid criminal prosecution, or to frustrate legitimate congressional or judicial inquiry into possible wrongdoing by the chief executive. To preserve the right, the president must show that executive privilege was needed to preserve military, diplomatic, or national security secrets.[37]

Scalia was asked for his opinion on the White House's obligation to respond to requests for information from the chairman of the House Committee on Government Operations issued to the FBI, the National Security Agency, and Western Union. Scalia was persuaded by the FBI and the NSA that "disclosure of this information would severely hamper the foreign intelligence and counterintelligence efforts of the United States and would result in serious diplomatic repercussions. While the material subpoenaed may include information which is not, in itself, sensitive, the disclosure of even this material could reveal to other nations the techniques now utilized to obtain foreign intelligence, thus hampering our intelligence efforts," as he put it. He recommended making a claim of executive privilege denying the information to the committee. And, fine attorney that he was, he added that even if all of these pro–presidential power arguments failed, a "systematic review of the quantity of information sought . . . would be impossible prior to the return date of the subpoena."[38] When Attorney General Levi also sent a memo to the White House advising that executive privilege be invoked to avoid releasing the information to Congress, the president agreed.

Eventually, in 1976, President Ford chose to support congressional legislation limiting the electronic surveillance program. The president issued an executive order restricting the activities of the CIA by limiting the physical and electronic surveillance of United States citizens and resident aliens, and the infiltration of domestic organizations to situations where there was a suspicion that the individuals or groups were working on behalf of a foreign government against the United States. Two years later the Foreign Intelligence Surveillance Act (FISA) was passed by Congress, forbidding the government's intelligence agencies from domestic spying on American citizens, and requiring judicial supervision of other investigations using a special, secret FISA Court, to assess the legality of search warrants.

It was in the area of foreign policy that Scalia learned the most about the power of the presidency, and demonstrated the lengths to which he would go to protect that power. Scalia's journey into foreign policy was a result of Levi's membership on the Intelligence Coordinating Group, which oversaw American covert operations around the world. Frequently Levi would send deputies such as Scalia or the assistant attorney general of the Civil Division, Rex Lee, to represent him. In time, this interagency group broke up into task forces on which both Levi and Scalia represented the Department of Justice. More than a dozen times through 1975 and 1976, Scalia attended meetings to participate in the approval process for covert operations.[39]

Years later, in a speech in Ottawa, Canada, Scalia described how he came to be the Ford administration's point man for the CIA's "black box" covert international operations:

> During part of this [Office of Legal Counsel] period I attended a daily
> morning meeting in the Situation Room of the White House at which
> Bill Colby, the Director of Central Intelligence . . . Mitchell Rogovin,
> a special counsel, outside counsel hired by the CIA, and a number of
> other high-level figures decided which of the nation's most highly
> guarded secrets would be turned over that day to Congress. There
> was scant chance in those days that they would not appear in *The
> Washington Post* the next morning. One of the consequences of these

investigations was an agreement by the CIA that all covert actions would be cleared through the Justice Department. So believe it or not, for a brief period of time, all covert actions had to be approved by me. Needless to say I did not feel that this was an area in which I possessed a whole lot of expertise. Nor did I feel that the Department of Justice had a security apparatus necessary to protect against a penetration by foreign operatives. We had enough security procedures to frustrate *la Cosa Nostra* [organized crime] but not the KGB.[40]

• • •

A newly declassified memo written by Scalia and now in the Ford Library makes it possible to recount a typical instance of covert operations oversight from 1976. The issue concerned the fate of the Meo tribesmen in Laos, a country that had fallen to the communists in May 1975. The Meo had been working with American forces in a series of paramilitary operations throughout Southeast Asia since 1961. The CIA sought to spend unregulated "black box" money on the resettlement of these allies, even though there was no presidential finding that the "operation was 'important to the national security of the United States,'" and there had been no "timely report to the appropriate committee of the Congress," as required by federal law. Since the communist takeover, the Meo had fled to Thailand and had been supported by State Department money, United Nations aid, and covert CIA money.[41] The problem was how to provide "socio-economic aid to the Meos to aid their recovery from war and resist communist political challenges." An advisory memo to the president on this issue said that while "several arguments can be made that a finding and report were not required" by federal law, it did concede that "this matter raises serious questions of legality and demonstrates the need for better guidelines within the Executive Branch on compliance with this statute."[42] Even the general counsel for the CIA conceded that a presidential finding and congressional reporting should have been done here.

As with many of these vexing legal-political problems heading for the attorney general's and the president's desks, this one first ended up in the hands of OLC head Antonin Scalia for a shaping of the legal argument. Scalia knew his task: find a way to retroactively, legally support the argument for funding the resettlement of the Meo tribesmen even though the administration was in technical violation of Congress's Hughes-Ryan Amendment. As nearly always happened in such circumstances, Scalia found a way to shape the argument that no one else saw, while still achieving the desired effect of preserving presidential power. After a lengthy legal analysis, Scalia recommended that President Ford retroactively either make a finding of the need to spend this resettlement money or state clearly that an Omnibus Finding on ongoing covert operations around the world made on January 10, 1975, did include this operation, and then designate someone to report formally to Congress.

Then, Scalia went beyond the executive mea culpas to offer helpful advice to future administrations in order to avoid legal oversights. In the future, Scalia argued, the Office of the Attorney General should "assure strict compliance with legal requirements" and in doing so oversee "all matters sufficiently distinct to require a separate Presidential finding or separate reporting." To do this, "approval guidelines" should be drafted containing a "standard statement in each OAG recommendation to the President to the effect that a finding and report are or are not necessary."[43] Scalia's advice was followed to the letter, with President Ford arguing in a memo to CIA director George H. W. Bush that under his "general finding" this was "the result of a long continuing program by the CIA to support non-Communist elements in Laos." In making this report, the president adopted Scalia's argument as to why his Omnibus Finding had implied this support: "Inherent in the conduct of any operations of this sort is the possibility of having to withdraw from positive endeavors and to protect the human and physical assets which had been committed to the operation."[44]

Thinking back on these experiences, Scalia marveled at the dangers of the reach of his responsibilities and powers in the OLC:

Nothing in the professional training of the lawyer and hence of the judge gives him [the ability] to call on the experience and the requisite skill to answer many of the questions presented. If the law says "thou shalt not assassinate foreign leaders" I can readily decide that a scheme to blow up the El Cigar is unlawful. But short of such absolute proscriptions, what makes me as lawyer or as judge capable of doing the necessary balancing and threat assessment in national interests inherent in the review of covert actions? And the same for the evaluation of the necessity for . . . wiretapping and physical entry. In the last analysis the judge is at the mercy of the executive officials who give them their judgment but are subject neither to his appointment nor to his discipline. . . . These officers will follow the rules, if rules there are. The problem before, for the regularization of national security and intelligence activities, is simply that there were no rules.[45]

Such arguments in favor of deferring to presidential power in the areas of foreign policy and national security would shape Scalia's views for decades to come.

• • •

Among Scalia's many duties in the Office of Legal Counsel was defending the president by testifying before Congress on various bills seeking to limit the powers of his office. It was here that Scalia displayed his considerable talent for dueling with senators and members of Congress. He did so by writing opening statements assessing the constitutionality and merits of the legislation, impressive for both their clarity of logic and expression, and then appearing before the committee to face questioning by its members. With Congress now feeling its ascendancy over a crippled presidency, sometimes this meant that Scalia would have to fence verbally with Democratic Party members of the Senate and House. One of the most interesting such episodes came when the Senate Subcommittee on Intergovernmental Relations of the Committee on Government Operations, chaired by Maine's Democratic senator Edmund Muskie, considered Senate Bill 2170 in late 1975. This bill proposed adding a Part 4 to the Legislative Reorganization Act of 1970, titled "Keeping the Congress Informed," to codify and limit the president's use of the power of executive privilege to keep matters secret from Congress. It was this power that Nixon had tried unsuccessfully to use to prevent Congress and the federal judiciary from gaining access to the Oval Office audio recordings that would end his presidency, and which Scalia had later urged President Ford to use against the FOIA law and to protect foreign policy operations. This bill proposed that the executive branch be legally required to "keep each Congressional Committee and Subcommittee 'fully and currently informed' with respect to all matters within its jurisdiction." To accomplish this goal, the head of a federal agency would be required to respond to the heads of the relevant committee or subcommittee, or a two-fifths minority of the members of those committees. Provisions were also made for a congressional subpoena power to request information, implemented if necessary by the appropriate forms of judicial enforcement power.

For Senator Muskie, a likable former champion debater for Bates College and country-smart Yankee lawyer who was the vice presidential candidate with Hubert Humphrey in 1968 and failed presidential aspirant in 1972, this legislation was simply a matter of the prerogative of Congress to seek the information necessary for exerting its constitutional legislative powers and oversight power over the executive branch. However, for Scalia this was a matter of defending the president's powers in a separation of powers system against congressional investigative incursions and preventing the president's secrets from being leaked to the newspapers by those same legislators. Scalia was the ideal man to do battle with the Senate on behalf of President Ford's control over the secrets of his administration. With the stage thus set, the result was a spirited verbal battle between two skilled advocates.

As with all of his presentations, for this testimony on October 23, 1975, Scalia had prepared a powerful opening statement. As written, it was a powerful document, defending vigorously the inherent powers of the presidency in the face of an ascendant Congress's repeated assertions of its own constitutional powers to gather information for its investigations and legislative purposes. In concluding, Scalia took a moment to demonstrate what would become his trademark imagery in acknowledging the untimely nature of his appeal, coming so soon after the misuse of this presidential secrecy power by that office's previous occupant: "I realize that anyone saying a few kind words about Executive privilege after the events of the last few years is in a position somewhat akin to the man preaching the virtues of water after the Johnstown flood, or the utility of fire after the burning of Chicago. But fire and water are, for all that, essential elements of human existence. And Executive privilege is indispensable to the functioning of our system of checks and balances and separation of powers. I hope that, whatever action your Committee takes with respect to the present legislative proposals, you will not seek to eliminate a vital element of our system merely because it may sometimes have been abused."[46]

This was the statement that Scalia came prepared to read to the subcommittee. Normally a speaker gets to read the entire prepared statement before the committee, but Chairman Muskie had come to the hearing room ready to do battle over language in the prepared text that he found offensive, hyperbolic, and lacking in appreciation for congressional authority. Unwilling to accord this speaker the usual Senate courtesy, Muskie interrupted Scalia's reading before he could finish. The first verbal fireworks began as soon as Muskie heard Scalia call the bill's allowance of a "two-fifths" minority of a committee to request information "surely extraordinary."

"Do you find it even more extraordinary for one Senator to ask for information? If it is extraordinary for two-fifths of the committee to ask for it, is it even more extraordinary for a single Senator to ask for information," Muskie asked.[47]

"Single Senators are usually accommodated," responded Scalia. "But what I find extraordinary is that the Congress, if this section is adopted, would make it unlawful for the executive not to reply to a particular request when a majority of the subcommittee in question doesn't think the request should be made. I just find that extraordinary."

With the verbal battle now joined, Muskie said: "That logic suggests that a single Senator ought not to ask for information, except as a matter of grace on the part of the executive, without getting the support of the majority of some committee."

"I would find it extraordinary if the President should be placed in violation of the law by a statute which says if any Senator asks for the information, despite the fact that the rest of the Senate doesn't think it should be sought—" said Scalia, before Muskie interjected, "You are suggesting that Congress would be in violation of the Constitution to ask for information?"

"No sir. Let me make it clear. I have no objection to the asking at all. As I say, in the Justice Department and elsewhere we receive numerous requests from individual Senators and Congressmen which are complied with promptly."

"As a matter of grace, not as a matter of our right for information," complained Muskie. "It is interesting that you . . . engage in a logic that leaves me astounded. The whole thrust of the issue is that we get information from the executive branch, in your view, only as a matter of grace. The notion that the Congress has as a matter of constitutional right the power to inquire into anything that happens in the executive branch is challenged by your logic. . . . I will listen to the rest of your statement, but I have listened for 10 pages here to this logic that is the most incredible exposition of this point of view that I have been exposed to in all of the time I have been in the Senate. With that why don't you proceed and give your argument whatever credibility you can."

"May I just reply to the last point?" said Scalia.

"Of course you may," responded Muskie.

Scalia began: "Let us assume at this point in my testimony that Congress has an absolute right to all of the information. Let's assume, further, that Congress can delegate that right of obtaining information to a single Senator. I would nevertheless find it extraordinary that they should delegate it to him even if the rest of the Congress does not want him to obtain it, and that is the effect of this provision. A minority of the subcommittee, the majority of which is opposed to the request, is being delegated the congressional power to demand information."

Muskie said: "The scheme of this bill, I don't think, is that mystical or that unreasonable and what it undertakes to do is, first, to establish the Congress' general right to information of what is going on in the executive branch. That is an established congressional right. It is a constitutional right. . . . For you to find it necessary to attack that kind of a statement of the general congressional right to information about what is going on in the executive branch, I find extraordinary. If you don't challenge the existence of the right, why do you go to such pains to challenge the provision in this legislation which simply sets the stage for the mechanism of the bill? I find that extraordinary." After going on for quite some time about this provision, Muskie questioned the bureaucratic line that Scalia was drawing here: "I don't see anything extraordinary about a Senator asking you in the Department of Justice for information, and I don't find you challenging my letters when I send them down to ask for information. Why are you going through all the business of challenging that kind of routine providing of information by the executive? I find that extraordinary. But go ahead. I apologize for interrupting your testimony. But I find myself just getting wound up and you haven't gotten half through."

"If we now fail to reply to a letter of yours adequately, we are not in violation of a statute—which is the effect of this provision," responded Scalia. "Maybe I am wrong on this point, and you certainly know all of the congressional procedures better than I, but I don't know of any other instance in which subcommittee action or committee action can be taken by a minority rather than the majority. That is the only reason I called this procedure 'extraordinary.'"

"Let me tell you this," said Muskie: "Without this statute, without this statute here, committees in the Senate have considered the possibility of going to the full Senate to seek contempt proceedings for refusal on the part of somebody in the executive branch to provide information. That is without this statute. It can be done by a majority of the committee. The committee goes to the floor. The action can be initiated by a subcommittee of that committee, so the subcommittee initiates the action. You are quarreling with the internal operations of a committee which undertakes to initiate the contempt proceedings—which can be authorized only by the full Senate. Before

I know it, you are going to be challenging my right as an individual Senator to bring up the question in subcommittee. How petty can you get? That is extraordinary."

"Yes Senator. But I consider it extraordinary. As a matter of logic, I would find it more logical if the power were delegated to individual Senators," responded Scalia. "But when power is delegated to committees and subcommittees, which is the case here, the normal procedure is for that exercise of power to be by majority vote."

"If minorities in the Congress had no rights," said Muskie, "the Republicans would have very little power to act in this Congress. Suppose you had a Democratic administration and a Republican minority in committee wanted to initiate an inquiry, are you saying they should not have the right to do so? What kind of constitutional theory is that?"

"If that is a desirable practice, it perhaps should have broader application," explained Scalia. "All I am suggesting is that its application here is extraordinary. Perhaps it is desirable and it should be made more widespread."

"All I really wanted to indicate to you at this point in your testimony is that you have developed an incredulous listener," concluded Muskie.

That said, Scalia conceded: "Let me skip the rest of that section. I think we have spent more time on it than I intended to. It is a relatively technical point."

Back and forth the two men continued to debate the wording of the proposed legislation and over whether only the president himself can assert executive privilege, and if not, just how far down the executive bureaucracy that power extended. Only after Scalia was at last given the opportunity to finish reading his statement did Senator Muskie say, "I think it is obvious that neither you nor I are going to change the view of the other to persuade the other. I am more confirmed than I was at 8 o'clock this morning on the need for legislation we have before us, or something like it. So you have achieved the reverse of what I am sure you have tried." But Scalia gave not an inch in this discussion. Several minutes later, while the two men fenced over the power of Congress to use the contempt power to compel the president to reveal military and diplomatic secrets that the legislators requested, Muskie asked, "Does Congress have the power to use contempt to insist upon information which the President refuses to give?" Scalia harked back to his theatrical work in high school for an answer, "Of course it has. There is a line in *Macbeth* where one of the persons says, 'This man has the power to command the sea.' And another says, 'Oh, yes, but will it obey him?'"

The two men may have debated to a draw in the hearing room, but Scalia had played his role in successfully defending his president and the executive branch as a whole, because Congress failed to pass any new legislation to codify and limit the use of executive privilege. And once more he had learned that he could hold his own in a debate among the best, even in Washington, D.C.

• • •

By early 1976, Scalia had become so visible in his work at the Office of Legal Counsel that he was considered for a promotion to become the chairman of the Federal Trade Commission. When White House counsel Philip Buchen learned of the prospect, he argued strenuously that Scalia was too valuable in his current position to be transferred elsewhere. It was clear that Scalia was going to remain in the OLC for as long as he wished to be in the Ford administration.[48]

With the election of Jimmy Carter in November 1976, Scalia along with everyone else in the administration knew that their time in this cycle of government had come to an end. Like a good soldier he remained until the very last days of the term, offering his resignation on January 14, 1977, to take effect on inauguration day.[49]

Scalia would be left to wonder just how far he would have ascended had there been another term of office for Ford. He started in the job as the perfect attorney for the president, defending the powers of the office with gusto and legal brilliance. But by the end of his two years, it was clear that Scalia had become a devoted and remarkably effective advocate for presidential power. After seeing what could happen to a presidency crippled by forces beyond the president's control, Scalia stood ready to help rebuild the office to the point that it would be able to defend itself against incursions by Congress and the press. A willing president needed to grab more power rather than concede it to Congress as Ford had done and oftentimes was forced to do. This was the lesson that Scalia would remember for the rest of his life. He knew, two months away from turning forty-one years old, his return to government was just a Republican presidential election victory away.

CHAPTER 6

Wildflowers Among the Weeds

January 20, 1977, inauguration day for President Jimmy Carter, saw a tide of Republican conservative operatives who had worked in the Nixon and Ford administrations since 1969 leaving office. Like thousands of other conservatives, Antonin Scalia needed to find a new job. After sampling private legal practice, teaching law school, and government service, he looked to augment his résumé to be in a prime position for a better job when the Republicans returned to the White House. Now on the outside of the revolving door of Beltway politics, he sought a place in private life that would allow him to earn a living and, most importantly, make new and broader contacts among conservatives.

Normally, political activists remain in Washington at lobbying firms or think tanks in order to continue to position themselves for their next opportunity. But the ever-confident and capable Scalia was not one to follow the normal path, and he was still uncertain where his interests would take him. Initially, he took an offer of a temporary teaching position for the spring term at the Georgetown University Law Center. This allowed him to determine whether, after the adrenaline rush of government service, the more sedate world of academia would hold enough interest for him while providing the school's administration time to consider whether to offer him a long-term appointment. In order to maintain his public service contacts, Scalia also accepted a position as a resident scholar in the American Enterprise Institute, a conservative think tank headed by William J. Baroody Jr., an Office of Public Liaison official for Gerald Ford. This position not only afforded Scalia maximum flexibility to study whatever conservative political issues interested him, but also to discuss them with the institute's renowned conservatives, including political émigrés from the Nixon and Ford administrations.

As a consequence of this new association, in July 1977 Scalia joined the editorial board of the institute's new bimonthly *Regulation* magazine, featuring articles on government regulation, antitrust issues, and trade restrictions.[1] Scalia's conservative bent fit well with the magazine's basic philosophy that government "regulation could be sensible, cost-efficient, and as unburdensome as the nature of its objectives will allow."[2]

Scalia described his work on *Regulation*: "I participated to varying degrees in the writing for the *Perspectives* portion of the publication, which consists of four or five unsigned pieces. In most cases it would be difficult to say which of those pieces were 'mine,' and to what degree."[3] The editorial board at that time consisted of many of the leading conservative legal and political thinkers, including Yale professor Robert Bork, journalist Irving Kristol, future U.S. ambassador to the United Nations Jeane Kirkpatrick, and conservative political scholar Austin Ranney. In time, legal thinker Laurence Silberman was added to the board. This editorial group began to function as a conservative public policy incubator, generating a wide range of ideas for advancing the small government philosophy that would guide the next Republican administration. In time Scalia would become a coeditor of the magazine, along with Murray Weidenbaum, later the chairman of the Council of Economic Advisers, and then the sole editor of *Regulation,* affording him total control over the publication.

By the fall of 1977, Scalia decided to return to the relatively peaceful life of the Midwest, accepting a teaching post at the University of Chicago Law School. The law school was becoming the home of a coterie of conservative legal economics thinkers who argued that the law was best understood by applying the same cost-benefit analysis used by economists. For Scalia, who had already begun to establish his credentials as a conservative legal scholar, the University of Chicago Law School was the perfect place to hone his views and network in the academic world. And his continued work with *Regulation* and the American Enterprise Institute allowed him to maintain his contacts in Washington.

There was an additional personal advantage to academic life that could not be ignored: the Scalias then had eight children, and the two oldest, Ann and Eugene, were sixteen and fourteen. Chicago offered college tuition assistance for children of faculty members. The large Scalia family moved into a former fraternity house just off campus in Hyde Park. Over the next five years, Chicago would become his academic home, interrupted only by a one-year visiting professorship at Stanford Law School from 1980 to 1981.[4]

At that time, the law school was filled with academic luminaries—many of whom were at one point or another considered for the Supreme Court, including Constitutional Law professor Philip Kurland, a former law clerk to Justice Felix Frankfurter; Jurisprudence professor Edward Levi, Scalia's boss in President Ford's Justice Department; and Torts professor Richard Posner, later to become one of the nation's most visible Court of Appeals judges, serving on the Seventh Circuit. There were also many promising junior professors, including conservative law and economics theorist Richard Epstein, who taught Torts and Corporate Tax, and the equally impressive Geoffrey Stone, then teaching Evidence but who would later become one of the nation's leading scholars on constitutional law and the First Amendment. Scalia taught a full load of courses, including the first-year Contracts course, and second- and third-year courses in Administrative Law, Constitutional Law I, Constitutional Law II: Freedom of Expression, Regulated Industries, as well as seminars of twenty students or fewer in both Federal Communications Law and Federal Regulatory Reform.[5] Of Scalia's early teaching, his student and later federal Court of Appeals judge Michael McConnell said, "[Scalia] gave of his time very generously and was very good one on one with students. But at the time he did not have much of a classroom presence."[6]

Scalia came to Chicago just a few years after the death of that school's highly influential conservative political philosopher Leo Strauss. Strauss had preached to his growing band of devoted academic followers the need for strict adherence to a careful textual reading of philosophical works, bolstered by rigorous historical analysis, in an effort to deconstruct texts to uncover what they argued were their hidden meanings within. One of Strauss's most influential lessons dealt with the "idea of the perfect speech," or the notion that a certain kind of speech, if understood properly, can be perfectly revealing of a political reality.[7] With the proper examination of text, driven by the right kind of intelligence applied to the correct set of analytical materials, Strauss explained, a deeper meaning can be revealed to the careful reader. Strauss's teaching, which spawned generations of conservative political scientists, was still alive at Chicago during that period.

The rigorous rules of intellectual and verbal engagement at the University of Chicago Law School were a bit different from other law schools. Both in and out of class, discussions operated on what Professor Richard Epstein called an "invisible set of legal rules that would have made the Marquess of Queensbury proud." Under highly democratic, but inevitably Darwinian, discussion rules known as the "first possession rule," people who got the floor, regardless of age or rank, were "allowed to keep it. The shy [had] to remain silent on the sidelines. But keeping the floor [was] not simply a matter of moving one's jaw. You had to say something that was worth hearing, or else you found yourself quieted under our local version of the gong show." The result was a "cultural feature [that] liberates debate by creating, as we Chicagoans like to say, the right kind of incentive structure. Senior faculty members are kept on their toes because they know that rank has few if any privileges. Junior faculty members get on their toes because they know that they can participate from the get-go in the life of the community."[8] The process taught everyone the value of successful argument, but it also bred in the more junior people an antiestablishment iconoclasm that fit well with Scalia's world view. The result was what Epstein described as "a laboratory for Social Darwinism, red in tooth and claw."

For Scalia, who had been schooled in Georgetown college debate, and then again in the rigorous Socratic argumentation of his law school colleagues at Harvard Law, the adjustment from the more respectful, hierarchical world of governmental service had taken little time. Scalia was fully prepared for the effect of the iconoclastic classroom that this culture encouraged. His performance in class "brought a sense of lightness and humor to the classroom—at first," one of his students remembered. He "seemed intent on making Contracts fun, or at least comprehensible. He was an energetic teacher and anxious to succeed, just as we were, so we viewed him sympathetically."[9] As he proposed hypothetical twists on the day's legal concepts, Scalia tried to make them entertaining, referring to everyman as "John Q. Public" and "Joe Six-Pack," representatives of the average American blue-collar person.[10] The hypothetical contracts always seemed to involve some kind of bizarre sale situation for the legendary Albemarle Pippins, a tasty apple that was discovered by George Washington and Benjamin Franklin and became the favorite of Thomas Jefferson. The students loved it: "His choice of the humble apple for his hypotheticals seemed a brilliant stroke. What better way to introduce students to legal complexities than through easily understood examples involving apples?"[11]

One of the stories from Scalia's early years of teaching said much about who he was in the classroom and who he would become. Fueled by Chicago Law's cultural lack of hierarchy, Scalia's class members decided to play a prank on him to relieve some of the stress of this educational pressure cooker.

One day, as Scalia was conducting his class, someone began banging on the door. When it was opened, a tall, blond, second-year female student, her hair in braids, marched into the room outfitted in "farmer's overalls and a red-checked shirt" with "a hayseed between her teeth." Only the teacher seemed perplexed by the scene. "Antonin Scalia?" the farm girl shouted in a down-home drawl. "We got yer shipment for ya. C'mon boys, bring 'em in." As the confusion on Scalia's face became more apparent, students dressed as farmers brought bushel after bushel of ripe apples and placed them in front of the room. "These here are yer Albemarle Pippins," one of the "farmers" said. Scalia smiled as the students began to laugh heartily.

But the mood changed a few moments later. One student recalled:

> For a few minutes we enjoyed the pleasant delirium of group partici-pation in a shared joke. Then Scalia stopped . . . smiling. He didn't merely stop—his entire demeanor changed. Perhaps he suddenly felt we were laughing *at* him, not *with* him. That perception couldn't have been further from the truth, but it might explain the transfor-mation that took place. One moment, Scalia was the jovial teacher, absolutely certain of his abilities and completely secure in the admira-tion of his students. In an instant, his entire affect changed. "That's enough," he said angrily, dismissing the farmer actors. Our laughter died down in a hurry as we returned to the case at hand.[12]

And from that day on, Scalia's demeanor in class changed, as John Q. Public and Joe Six-Pack took their Albemarle Pippins and left the teacher's world. Scalia became a stern taskmaster and "never recovered his prior avuncular manner, preferring instead to grill students harshly about legal issues. No more cheerful repartee in class." Rather than seeing the class prank as evi-dence that his students "liked him so much," their teacher seemed to take offense.[13] In following years, Scalia "regained his equilibrium and once again displayed a spirited and brilliant teaching style," but some of the students in the apple-incident class wondered whether the teacher who came "across as self-assured" was in fact much more "thin-skinned."[14]

As he closed many of his classes, Scalia drew from the lesson he had learned from his undergraduate days at Georgetown that it was not pos-sible "to separate your religious life from your intellectual life. They're not separate." Using his dramatic reading skills, Scalia would read a passage from Robert Bolt's play *A Man for all Seasons,* detailing the religious and legal battles between Britain's lord chancellor Sir Thomas More and King Henry VIII. Standing on religious and legal principles, More dared to refuse to sanction an annulment of the king's marriage to Catherine of Aragon, the first of his six wives, in order for the king to marry Anne Boleyn. More paid for his beliefs with his life. Scalia read from a powerful passage in which More refuses to order the arrest of the man who would commit perjury against him, telling his future son-in-law, William Roper, "Whoever hunts for me, Roper, God or Devil, will find me hiding in the thickets of the law! And I'll hide my daughter with me! Not hoist her up to the mainmast of your seagoing principles! They put about too nimbly!"[15] Later, Scalia would explain his use of this passage to close his classes to his biographer Joan Biskupic: "It's such a beautiful expression of the importance of law."[16] Left unsaid, though, was the fact that More's life resonated so well with Scalia because it also represents such a "beautiful expression" of the importance of religion in law, as More sought to defend his faith and the power of the pope against Henry's claim of religious supremacy.

Beyond the formal classes, Scalia helped to organize and lead what would become an army of young legal conservatives. Law school faculty members in the late 1970s, many having been educated during the liberal, activist, Warren Court years, were predominantly liberal. The comparative handful of conservative faculty members and law students found themselves vastly outnumbered and unorganized. Change began as a result of a report by Michael Horowitz to the conservative Scaife Foundation in 1979 analyzing the nonprofit, public interest legal reform prospects for conservative law students. The widely distributed report argued there was a need for a network of conservative legal scholars and students. It took three years before the idea began to take hold.[17]

Early in the 1981–82 academic year, coincident with the start of Ronald Reagan's presidency, a small group of conservative students at Yale Law School, led by a second-year law student named Steven Calabresi and advised by their antitrust professor, University of Chicago alumnus Robert Bork, launched a debating society through which conservative law students and faculty could discuss constitutional and legal ideas. That same year, two conservative law students at the University of Chicago, Lee Liberman Otis and David McIntosh, both of whom had known Calabresi when they were undergraduates at Yale, approached Scalia and persuaded him to become the faculty adviser for a chapter of the Yale group at Chicago. The students named their group the Federalist Society for Law and Public Policy Studies, or more commonly the Federalist Society. Rallying around a silhouette profile of James Madison, they sought to limit what they saw as the liberal, activist excesses of the federal judiciary in expanding federal rights. Instead, they favored returning to a strict adherence to the text of the Constitution and the Bill of Rights. Eventually, the group would offer as its mission statement: "[The Federalist Society] is founded on the principles that the state exists to preserve freedom, that the separation of governmental powers is central to our Constitution, and that it is emphatically the province and duty of the judiciary to say what the law is, not what it should be. The Society seeks both to promote an awareness of these principles and to further their application through its activities."[18]

Professors Scalia and Bork played an indispensable role in developing their new student organizations, meeting with students, teaching them about conservative legal philosophy, and speaking at their events. Despite Bork's nomination to the federal Court of Appeals for the District of Columbia in December 1981, his contribution was enormous. The students' early efforts were hampered by people taking down their meeting announcements or scrawling graffiti such as "fascist" on them.[19] Rather than striking back, Bork convinced Calabresi to focus on developing a national organization through which they could institutionalize their discussions, and plan for a national symposium on law, while also plotting strategy for undermining the liberal control over the federal judiciary. Years later, Calabresi would say of Bork's guidance that he "did more than anyone else . . . to help create, nourish, and legitimize the Federalist Society. . . . Judge Bork had faith in us when we were a small handful of law students, and he spent hours teaching us, setting an example for us, speaking at our events and helping us get started. Without Judge Robert H. Bork there would be no Federalist Society today. He was, and is, our inspiration, our teacher, and our hero."[20]

With Bork leaving for the Court of Appeals after his Senate confirmation on February 8, 1982, Scalia's role became even more important to the development of the new Federalist Society. He helped to raise funds and used his contacts at Harvard and Stanford law schools to help organize a national group by inviting prominent conservative law faculty and their students to Chicago to speak to his students, even, at times, hosting them at his home. Because of these institution-building efforts, Steven Teles, in his definitive history of the origins of the conservative legal movement, describes Scalia as "the most important elite sponsor of the [Federalist] Society in its early years."[21]

Buoyed by a $25,000 grant from the conservative Institute for Educational Affairs, directed by journalist Irving Kristol and William Simon, secretary of the Treasury under Presidents Nixon and Ford, along with support from the conservative Olin Foundation and Intercollegiate Studies Institute, the Yale and Chicago Federalist Society chapters decided to hold their first national symposium in New Haven in April 1982. They invited two other conservative law student organizations from Harvard and Stanford. All of these groups used the occasion to organize debates about law, presenting all points of view in the belief that the conservative views would win out. They were joined in this effort by E. Spencer Abraham, founder of Harvard Law School's *Journal of Law and Public Policy,* which would serve as the journal for the society.

Seventy-five students gathered at Yale Law School on April 24–25 for the group's first national symposium, on the topic "Federalism: Legal and Political Ramifications." Judge Robert Bork was the keynote speaker, with Scalia also giving a prominent address.[22] Calabresi recalled that Bork, by reason of his new appointment to the prestigious D.C. Court of Appeals, "was the marquee name who everyone else came to our conference to see."[23]

As they heard Bork speak, everyone in the room believed that with Ronald Reagan in control of Supreme Court appointments, and the Republicans in control of the Senate, it was only a matter of time before he would be elevated to the High Court. Having already been considered twice before for the Supreme Court vacancies in 1975 and 1981, first and foremost among the names on any list of people who should be considered by the Reagan administration for the next vacancy on the United States Supreme Court was Robert Bork.[24] Bork's visibility in this race was well earned. He had served as solicitor general of the United States from June 1973 through January 1977. On October 20, 1973, with Richard Nixon under fire as a result of the Watergate break-in controversy, the president ordered his attorney general, Elliot Richardson, to fire the Watergate special prosecutor, Archibald Cox. Richardson refused and resigned, as did his deputy, William Ruckelshaus, who was then fired. Nixon then made Bork the acting attorney general, from which position he did the president's bidding in firing Cox in what became known as the "Saturday Night Massacre." While the action enraged liberals, it delighted conservatives in both the Ford and Reagan administrations, who considered Bork among their leading legal intellects.

Bork's seminal book *The Antitrust Paradox: A Policy at War with Itself,* published in 1978, helped to cement his scholarly reputation. In it he argued against the nation's antitrust laws, relying on both "original intent" evidence, that is, the intent of the Constitution's or other laws' drafters, and a "law and economics" public policy argument in positing that the corporate mergers resulting from governmental deregulation would promote economic competition as well as consumer welfare.[25]

While the goal of the young legal conservatives in the new Federalist Society was to establish a national conservative legal organization, the society served another important function. As described by Yale law professor Owen Fiss: "[it was] less a philosophic society than a mutual support group, a therapeutic community in which people who feel aggrieved and alienated can find comfort and support from those with similar feelings."[26] Almost immediately after the first national symposium, bolstered by coverage in William F. Buckley's conservative *National Review* magazine, law students at fifteen other law schools contacted Calabresi about forming their own chapters. Over time a web of conservative lawyers was spun nationwide, as Federalist Society historian Steven Teles explains: "The nascent Federalist Society was beginning to connect conservative law students from across the country, and the involvement of Scalia [among others] connected the society to the conservative legal establishment."[27] From there, the value of these contacts became apparent. Otis, Calabresi, and McIntosh would be hired by Reagan attorney general Edwin Meese and given the mandate as assistant attorneys general to build a Federalist Society network within the Justice Department, which in turn would develop lists of conservative lawyers to be appointed to the federal judiciary. New law school chapters formed around the country along with companion lawyer divisions of alumni. In the beginning the chapters were small. Justice Samuel Alito recalled that when he was a member of Reagan's Justice Department, the Washington chapter was so small that its monthly meetings were held in a Chinese restaurant called the Empress. The meetings were so secretive, with few admitting they attended. Alito later recalled bumping into another Justice Department official at one of the gatherings. "Well you're here," the fellow said to Alito. "This is like meeting a friend at a bordello."[28]

In time, though, the number and size of these chapters grew so rapidly that by the fall of 1985, political journalist Sidney Blumenthal wrote about the society's rising power in *The Washington Post*. It became clear that membership, and leadership, in the Federalist Society was now considered a requirement for seeking a legal position in the Reagan administration.[29] In time, journalists would call the movement the "Conservative Elite."[30] By 1986, Otis and McIntosh would tell journalists that half of the 150 political appointees in the Justice Department were former members of the society.[31] Society members became the group to look to for conservative federal clerkships and other political positions during the presidencies of Reagan and George H. W. Bush, as well as for a network of influential conservative legal scholars. Even after Bork and Scalia had left their academic appointments to serve in the federal judiciary, both men continued to travel to speak at Federalist Society chapters around the country to foster the organization's growth.

This organization that Scalia, Bork, and their law students launched in the early 1980s never stopped growing. Twenty-five years after their first national convention, there would be chapters in nearly two hundred law schools, bolstered by so many burgeoning companion lawyer chapters that the group that once met in a Chinese restaurant now drew enough attendees in 2007 from its national membership of forty thousand to fill Union Station's massive lobby in Washington for its twenty-fifth anniversary convention.[32] And among the many dignitaries praising the founders' vision and the courage was one of those early faculty supporters. Antonin Scalia, by then a Supreme Court justice, would boast from the podium, "We thought we were just planting a wildflower among the weeds of academic liberalism and it turned out to be an oak."[33]

Once more, a lucky star seemed to hang over Scalia's career. As one of the founding faculty leaders of the new conservative network of Federalist Society law students and lawyers, Scalia would enjoy the organization's support in all of his future career moves. It would provide sustenance for him in facing his liberal critics.

But in 1982 Robert Bork was the more visible of these two conservative legal scholars. With Bork on the Court of Appeals, though, Scalia would continue working to build his résumé.

• • •

Beyond all of his accomplishments at the University of Chicago, Scalia took on considerable work with the Chicago-based American Bar Association. Launched by his service in the Ford administration, Scalia moved through the administrative ranks in the ABA's maze of committees. He became the chairman of the Committee on Judicial Review from 1979 to 1980, then chairman-elect of the Section of Administrative Law and Regulatory Practice, becoming its chairman in 1981. This position gave Scalia an opportunity to write a "Chairman's Message" for the ABA's *Administrative Law Review* and to give speeches on many of his favorite administrative law bêtes noires, including administrative oversight of congressional legislation, the Freedom of Information Act, and the constitutionality of the legislative veto.[34]

He maintained his contacts in Washington. Continuing his work with the American Enterprise Institute, Scalia built up his publication record, writing many essays articulating his conservative philosophy. His first article for the maiden issue of *Regulation* in July 1977, titled "Two Wrongs Make a Right: The Judicialization of Standardless Rulemaking," was exactly what the Nixon and Ford administration officials had seen in his work for the Office of Legal Counsel and the Office of Telecommunications Policy.[35] It was a learned piece of scholarly research and analysis, targeting his conservative audience's cherished anti-regulation views while also offering some of his trademark phrasemaking and metaphorical imagery.[36] Following that article, Scalia made full use of his new platform on the *Regulation* magazine Board of Editors by commenting on all manner of public policy issues, frequently attacking those government policies that most vexed him. He did not spare the federal courts either, writing, "We live in an age of 'hair-trigger unconstitutionality,' and almost no result produced or about to be produced by the democratic process at any level of government seems immune from attack by some Scribe or Pharisee with a law degree on the ground that it contravenes the Basic Charter of our Liberties."[37]

In 1983, Scalia had a chance to take aim at one of his favorite targets, the legislative veto. The case involved Jagdish Rai Chadha, a student from Kenya who had overstayed his visa. Ordinarily he would have been deported, but the attorney general had suspended deportations under the existing federal immigration law. Under the legislative veto provision of that law, the House of Representatives vetoed the suspension, thus dooming Chadha to deportation. After the U.S. Court of Appeals for the Ninth Circuit ruled that legislative vetoes were unconstitutional, and the Supreme Court indicated that it would review the appeal, the American Bar Association decided to submit an *amicus curiae* brief in support of the Ninth Circuit's decision. As chairman for the ABA's Section of Administrative Law and Regulatory Practice, Scalia wrote most of the first draft of the brief to be presented to the

Supreme Court. Taking the strong pro–presidential power approach that he had developed in Ford's Office of Legal Counsel, Scalia argued that such vetoes were unconstitutional "because they permitted legislative inteference in executive functions and purported to authorize the legislature to take acts of legislative character and effect without following the procedures mandated by the Constitution."[38] The Supreme Court largely adopted Scalia's position by ruling that the blending of the constitutional legislative and executive powers in the legislative veto provisions of dozens of federal laws made them unconstitutional.[39]

Scalia had made clear in his work in the Office of Legal Counsel his opposition to the Freedom of Information Act. One of Scalia's most visible and quoted *Regulation* commentaries came on this topic in 1982, in a piece titled "The Freedom of Information Act Has No Clothes."[40] Scalia termed the FOIA "the Taj Mahal of the Doctrine of Unanticipated Consequences, the Sistine Chapel of Cost-Benefit Analysis Ignored."[41] Scalia's real target was not the original act in 1966, which he termed "a relatively toothless beast," but the 1974 amendments that he had unsuccessfully tried to undo in Ford's Office of Legal Counsel. To him, while these were "promoted as a boon to the press, the public interest group, the little guy; they have been used most frequently by corporate lawyers."[42] Noting that any effort to reform the FOIA process "take[s] on an Alice-in-Wonderland air," Scalia concluded, "The defects of the Freedom of Information Act cannot be cured as long as we are dominated by the obsession that gave them birth—that the first line of defense against an arbitrary executive is do-it-yourself oversight by the public and its surrogate, the press." Instead, once more pressing for greater democracy, Scalia pointed out that all of the recent revelations of presidential excesses during the Watergate investigation, and the revelations in the 1970s about the excesses of the CIA and the FBI, which he had fought during the Ford years, resulted not from FOIA investigations but instead were "primarily the product of the institutionalized checks and balances within our system of representative democracy."[43] While he admitted that FOIA was "probably part of the permanent legacy of Watergate," Scalia pleaded, "We need not, however, admire the emperor's clothes."[44]

Scalia also found the opportunity to increase his visibility and make his views known in testifying before Congress. In early 1978, he took time out from his first year of teaching at Chicago to return to Washington to testify in support of a plan to create federal college tuition tax credits. This proposal was designed in Congress as a response to President Carter's plan to create college scholarships designed to benefit middle-class college students. Scalia was particularly distressed that the Carter Office of Legal Counsel was arguing that the congressional tuition tax credit legislation was unconstitutional and would be struck down by the Supreme Court. Scalia took issue with that reading, arguing that Congress's plan would, and should, constitutionally benefit religious education at the college level. In reviewing what he described as "the utter confusion of Supreme Court pronouncements in the church-state area," Scalia argued that the constitutionality of such tuition tax credit programs "has not been resolved by any holding, or even by any consistent line of dictum, from the Supreme Court." Scalia urged Congress to take responsibility for this measure because it was expressing the democratic will: "In approving or disapproving the present proposal on constitutional grounds, you will not be following—and cannot pretend to be following—any dictate of the Supreme Court, but will rather be expressing your sense, and the sense of the society, as to what our most profound national convictions require. Your expression, in turn, can be expected to influence the course which the Supreme Court will steer in the future." [45]

That said, the man who, during his time in the Office of Legal Counsel had routinely opposed Congress in order to protect President Ford, now placed the issue squarely in their hands. "I urge you, then, to approach this issue as a question of what the constitutional law 'should be,' rather than vainly seeking to determine what it 'is' under the decisions of the Court. For me, the answer to that question seems quite clear. There is no doubt, of course, that the tuition tax relief provided by this legislation is constitutional as applied to parents and students paying tuition to *non*religious private schools. . . . You must ask yourselves whether the special solicitude for religion contained in the Constitution was meant to produce such a distinctively anti-religious result." [46] Three years later, Scalia recrafted these remarks into a policy article, writing that "these issues should be discussed in Congress at a principled level. They should not be foreclosed by lawyerly hair-splitting of selected hairs and brash judicial entrail-reading of the sort represented by the Justice Department opinions." [47]

Scalia used some of his most impassioned rhetoric when discussing governmental affirmative action programs that had been flourishing since the Supreme Court's endorsement of that policy in the 1978 *Regents of the University of California v. Bakke* decision. [48] Affirmative action programs sought to balance results by including race as a factor in decision making when all other factors were equal in order to increase diversity.

In a law review article titled "The Disease as Cure," this son of an Italian immigrant who had made his living in academia during xenophobic times had no tolerance for governmental programs that gave advantages to people based on their race or gender. In a scathing piece mocking the Supreme Court's logic and decisions, Scalia argued that "tak[ing] account of race," as Harry Blackmun argued in the *Bakke* case, in order to give some people a "plus factor" in programs distributing benefits of some kind, was itself a racist policy. In what was becoming his trademark hyperbolic style, Scalia criticized the Court's work in race cases as "an embarrassment to teach" and "an historic trivialization of the Constitution," creating an "utterly confused field." The program was, Scalia explained, "based upon concepts of racial indebtedness and racial entitlement rather than individual worth and individual need." People who had never discriminated were compelled to suffer in order for others of a different race or gender to benefit.[49] He argued instead on behalf of a merit-based system, allowing for success based only on individual achievement.[50] In considering federal Court of Appeals judge John Minor Wisdom's opposing concept of "restorative justice" in the form of affirmative action programs, Scalia turned to his own family history. "My father came to this country when he was a teenager. Not only had he never profited from the sweat of any black man's brow, I don't think he had ever seen a black man. There are, of course, many white ethnic groups that came to this country in great numbers relatively late in its history—Italians, Jews, Irish, Poles—who not only took no part in, and derived no profit from, the major historic suppression of the currently acknowledged minority groups, but were, in fact, themselves the object of discrimination by the dominant Anglo-Saxon majority." As for Scalia himself, "I owe no man anything, nor he me, because of the blood that flows in our veins."[51] Seeking to ridicule the Court's decisions, Scalia offered a satirical "modest proposal" for an affirmative action program called "RJHS—the Restorative Justice Handicapping System" by which "each individual in society would be assigned at birth Restorative Justice Handicapping Points, determined on the basis of his or her ancestry."[52]

• • •

With his conservative credentials renewed inside the Beltway by all of these efforts, his legal credentials were bolstered with each passing year that he taught his law classes at the University of Chicago. And with his effect on future generations of young conservative attorneys expanding every time the

Federalist Society met, Scalia knew that if he had any interest in moving into the federal judiciary, whereupon the American Bar Association would review his résumé upon his nomination, he would have to find a way to renew his credentials as a practicing attorney. For that, he would have to demonstrate that he could handle himself in a courtroom. He decided to demonstrate his legal credentials and bolster his conservative intellectual bona fides, not to mention at times his finances, by joining various legal teams arguing cases in front of appellate court panels.

The range of cases that he joined was impressive. In the spring of 1977 he became of counsel to the prominent Chicago law firm Baker & McKenzie to plan strategy and draft the petitions and legal briefs for Dresser Industries in its fight against the Securities and Exchange Commission. The issue concerned the so-called Voluntary Disclosure Program created by the agency in 1975 to encourage industries to disclose any bribery payments to people in other countries in order to further the American firm's business, even though such activity was not illegal in the other country. The Dresser firm's leadership was concerned that such revelations would endanger the careers or even the lives of those foreign nationals who had agreed to assist their business. When the Department of Justice began to investigate, arguing that the corporation had paid "extortionate" amounts to foreign nationals, Dresser Industries sought to block its subpoenas for a grand jury. Scalia's work on the appeal before the District of Columbia federal appellate court was initially successful in keeping the company's files from the Justice Department.[53]

In another case, the attorneys for the drug company Merck hired Scalia to write a legal brief in a controversial class action tort case called *Payton v. Abbott Labs*. The case involved a suit in Massachusetts state court against Merck for the use of a drug called DES, which was designed to prevent miscarriages. However, DES was alleged to cause abnormalities in pregnant women's reproductive organs. The issue was that the complainants were often unable to say which company had produced the drug they had used. Under the legal theory known as "market share liability" the plaintiffs argued that each company producing the drug, among them Merck, should be liable for its share of the product sold, regardless of whether it had been used by the plaintiffs or whether it could be demonstrated to have caused the physical problems. Merck hired Scalia in an effort to avoid being subjected to market share liability, knowing that if it were adopted by the court the company might have to pay damages for harms it had not committed and would be barred from proving lack of responsibility in the case. In the end, Scalia's argument in the legal brief helped to persuade the Massachusetts Supreme Judicial Court to reject this general shared liability theory, arguing that it might compel some companies to pay more in damages than their products had actually caused.[54]

• • •

With all of these efforts Scalia had made himself one of a handful of the most visible legal academics in the United States. But he and his wife were ready to leave Chicago to return to the East Coast—so much so that he began exploring other law school positions. He was hoping to be appointed Reagan's solicitor general. This position was everything that Scalia could wish for. Being charged with briefing and arguing cases before the United States Supreme Court gave one the kind of visibility and access to key officials in the Department of Justice and the White House that could lead to an important federal judicial appointment.

Few doubted that Scalia had the necessary credentials for the position. He had demonstrated the kind of legal acumen and political insight required to solve the most perplexing legal problems for the administration. In the competition for the solicitor generalship as well as other administrative positions, Scalia benefited both from his legal experience and his national heritage. The Scalia appointment file, being developed by Pendleton James, the director of personnel management for the Reagan transition team, bulged with letters solicited and unsolicited from conservative allies supporting Scalia and sent both to James and Attorney General–designate William French Smith.[55] As well, the National Italian American Foundation launched an orchestrated lobbying effort for him.[56]

As the months dragged on into early 1981, Scalia's main competition for the solicitor generalship became Rex Lee, who had been the assistant attorney general in the Civil Division of the Department of Justice in the Ford administration and was then the dean of the law school at Brigham Young University in Provo, Utah. In the spring of 1981, both Scalia and Lee were asked to come to Washington for an interview with Attorney General Smith. For the first time in his professional life, however, Scalia came out second best, with the appointment going to Lee on May 22, 1981. Devastated, Scalia met with Ernest Gellhorn, the managing partner of Scalia's old Jones Day law firm's Los Angeles office. Gellhorn tried to console him by pointing out that this failure might "be a blessing in disguise." When a vacancy occurred on the Supreme Court, Gellhorn told Scalia, he would be considered for selection "without the dangerous baggage that solicitors general carry from all the briefs they sign in controversial cases."[57]

Scalia was again reminded that he had not yet made it to the A List of appointees later that year when the new administration passed over him for vacancies on the federal Court of Appeals. Scalia saw well-respected conservatives Ralph Winter and Richard Posner receive appointments for the Second Circuit and the Seventh Circuit, respectively. When a vacancy occurred on the Circuit Court for the District of Columbia in late 1981, that seat went instead to Robert Bork.[58] For Scalia, these disappointments were an indication that as of early 1982 in any competition for a vacancy for the Supreme Court, which was occurring less and less often as justices served longer and longer, he would be no better than third in line behind Bork and Lee, and without a Court of Appeals seat on his résumé, likely not even that high.

Despite his fears, the Reagan people had not forgotten Scalia. In the spring of 1982, he was offered a seat on the federal Court of Appeals for the Seventh Circuit, based in Chicago. But Chicago was no longer where he and his family wanted to be, and the Seventh Circuit held no attraction for him. It was not considered a springboard to the Supreme Court, Justice John Paul Stevens's appointment in 1975 aside, and that bench did not hear the administrative law cases well known to him and most advantageous to his future career prospects. Those were reviewed in the D.C. Circuit. With seven of the eleven members on the D.C. Circuit having been appointed before 1971, four of them before the mid-1960s, the likelihood of vacancies on the rapidly aging Court seemed great. After considering his options, the forty-six-year-old Scalia decided, "Hell, I'll wait."[59]

It was the career gamble of a confident man, but it was also the decision of a man who knew that, the solicitor generalship position aside, these choices had almost always worked out in his favor. And this was no different. For, unknown to him, the wheels had already been set in motion for his next career move.

CHAPTER 7

It Isn't Easy to Be Right

Life changed for the forty-six-year-old Antonin Scalia in early April 1982 when Judge Roger Robb of the Court of Appeals for the District of Columbia Circuit announced that he would retire on June 1. With that announcement, *The Washington Post* speculated that the "leading contender" for the position would be Scalia.[1] The rumor was well founded. The Reagan Justice Department had been building its list for possible federal judicial appointments since before inauguration day, and, given his wide contacts in the conservative community since 1974, as well as his refusal of the Seventh Circuit Court appointment, Scalia was now positioned for selection. Washington attorney Theodore Olson, who then headed the Office of Legal Counsel, later said, "[Scalia] was a very obvious choice. There were very few people who had the expertise he had in administrative law issues that come before the D.C. Circuit."[2]

Once again at this career turning point, Scalia's connection to the Jones Day law firm in Cleveland paid dividends. The head of Reagan's screening committee for judicial appointments in the Office of Legal Policy at the Department of Justice was Jonathan Rose, the former Jones Day partner who had first recommended Scalia to head the Office of Legal Counsel in the Ford administration. Nothing that Rose had observed in their work together for Ford and Nixon had changed his mind about his former associate. The truth was, though, Scalia was so well known in conservative Washington circles that he needed only a nod from Rose to advance: "We were looking for outstanding academics [for the D.C. Circuit] who shared the president's political philosophy. He came up on every list." While the Justice Department and the White House quickly settled on Scalia for the vacancy, the American Bar Association, where he was so well known, was not so sure.[3]

The ABA's Standing Committee on the Federal Judiciary, charged with evaluating potential federal court nominees, gave him only a "qualified" rating rather than the expected "well qualified." The problem with his résumé, some members of the committee privately told reporters, was that Scalia lacked sufficient courtroom experience.[4] The lower ranking in no way fazed Rose, who later explained: "This was the continuing argument we had with the ABA panel. They have a rather inflexible view. They said that we will consider [nonlitigators] up to the point of being labeled qualified but anyone who would get highly or extremely qualified would have to have substantial litigation experience."[5] Scalia was nonetheless nominated by Reagan, and his name was forwarded to the Senate for confirmation in late July 1982.

For Scalia, taking this position would come at a significant financial cost. Court of Appeals judges at the time were paid $77,300, and the financial disclosure forms filed by Scalia for the period prior to his taking his judicial seat indicated that in addition to his nearly $50,000 salary at the University of Chicago, he had earned roughly $70,000 more in editing, consulting, speaking, and legal fees.[6] As a federal judge, Scalia would have to abstain from those moneymaking opportunities.

But the appointment could also yield a benefit. Scalia well knew that the most likely sources for the next Supreme Court appointment, other than the solicitor general's position, were the federal Courts of Appeals. And, of these courts, the District of Columbia Circuit was the most likely bullpen from which Reagan would choose his next Supreme Court nominee. Robert H. Bork, who had joined the court two months before Judge Robb announced his retirement, was already at the top of nearly everyone's list for the High Court. Scalia knew if he were on the same court as Bork, he could show off his talents side by side with the front-runner.

The Senate confirmation hearings for Scalia were routine. Conservative South Carolina Republican Strom Thurmond chaired the Judiciary Committee. After some jocularity during the introduction of the candidate's large family, all sitting in the front row, Thurmond offered Scalia a chance to express his well-known views on the problems posed by the Freedom of Information Act. After repeating many of his criticisms of the "excesses" of the bill, and the accelerated nature of the judicial appeals in FOIA cases, Scalia was careful to reset his posture relative to congressional acts: "Let me make it clear at the outset, Mr. Chairman, that the article came from the days which, if I am confirmed, would be bygone days—days in which as a private citizen

I could comment on the wisdom of laws that the Congress had enacted. Needless to say, my views on the wisdom would have nothing to do with my interpretation of it were I sitting as a judge."[7]

Would Scalia recuse himself from a case in which he had a conflict of interest, he was asked. On those occasions, the candidate responded, he would be guided by the Code of Judicial Conduct. "As far as my own personal soul search is concerned, I would disqualify myself in any case in which I believed my connection with one of the litigants or any other circumstances would cause my judgment to be distorted in favor of or against one of the parties. I would furthermore disqualify myself if a situation arose in which, even though my judgment would not be distorted, a reasonable person would believe that my judgment would be distorted. That does not mean anybody in the world, but a reasonable person." No federal judge would be expected to do less.[8]

The states'-rights oriented Thurmond closed this session by asking his pet question about the Tenth Amendment, "The powers not delegated to the United States by the Constitution, nor prohibited by it to the States, are reserved to the States respectively, or to the people." He wanted to know whether it represented "an affirmative grant of authority to the states." Scalia cited in response a theory from conservative legal analysts, including Bork, about the meaning of the "original Constitution," arguing that "the States did not need a grant of authority," making the Tenth Amendment, by the Supreme Court's rulings, "redundant" because "it is clear under the original Constitution that the Federal Government is a government of specified powers, and that unless those powers have been affirmatively granted to the Federal Government, they automatically remain with the States."[9] This was exactly what Thurmond and other Republicans wanted to hear. Confirmation came easily on August 9 with the plan that Scalia would be sworn in eight days later and sit for the first time with the court after Labor Day.[10]

Scalia's addition to the eleven-member court allowed the administration to continue its effort to assemble a more conservative, self-restrained court. The court then consisted of seven Democratic appointees and four Republicans. The liberal imbalance made garnering a conservative majority a challenge. Over the next four years, though, while Scalia served on the bench, Reagan would get five more appointments to the D.C. Circuit, allowing him to turn it into a conservative bastion.

Once on the Court of Appeals, Scalia learned quickly that life as a federal judge was vastly different from his earlier life. Fellow jurist Robert Bork explained, "They lock you away in this room. . . . It's like a life sentence to the Law Review. . . . You sit all day in chambers by yourself working on these things and then you go home and talk to the dog at night. It's a very isolated lifestyle." [11] There was little personal interaction among the judges. As Bork explains: "Everybody's busy and you don't drop in on a judge to kick around a legal question because the judging has become much too much of an assembly line process—get the stuff out. And it was regarded as an imposition on somebody to drop in to talk over a case, particularly if they weren't involved in it. Even if they were involved in it, they communicate by sending drafts back and forth—memoranda and dissents and so forth. Rarely do you get together. We'd get together right after the argument for discussion and a vote. But typically that's the last time you are face-to-face about the case." [12]

Cases were generally heard by panels of three judges. However, for some of the most important issues, all eleven judges would hear a case in what was known as an *en banc* hearing. Beyond that, in some cases in which one of the litigants was not satisfied with the decision of the three-judge panel, they could appeal for a full *en banc* hearing. Judge Patricia Wald explained how this possibility acted as a check on the minority jurists: "There was a period in the mid-80s, when Bork and Scalia and [Kenneth] Starr were here, when there [were] still a lot of questions about where the Court stood. Either side could still win. I remember winning or at least getting *en banc* on a couple of Nino Scalia's decisions in the early 80s because we still had enough votes which we [Carter liberal judges] never had later. . . . When you're a minority, and you're much more vulnerable to being *en banced,* I think you begin to write your decisions much more cautiously." [13] The Court of Appeals was usually not one where junior judges in a minority position were anxious to speak for themselves in dissent, so Scalia was expected to be cautious, at least while there were few conservative judges on the court. As Judge Wald explains: "You have to pick your shots. There's no point in dissenting on everything that you would have liked to come out differently. If it's a close call, and you realize that your judgment may be on the other side of the line from your colleagues, most of the time you let it go. Mostly, you reserve a dissent for the things you feel really strongly about." [14]

Scalia, though, was not like the other judges. He had strong views and was utterly certain in their correctness. Moreover, he had always been willing to make his views known. Now, with the chance to display his skills vis-à-vis Robert Bork, he was not willing to delay his opportunity to show the differences between them. Scalia made sure in his very first case on the

Court of Appeals to establish his identity as a vocal, determined opponent to the overwhelming liberal majority controlling his circuit.

The case of *The Washington Post v. United States Department of State* raised the issue of the reach of the Freedom of Information Act, the legal thorn in Scalia's side since his days in Ford's Office of Legal Counsel. The *Post* was seeking information from the Department of State using the FOIA to uncover information about an "emergency fund" for the diplomatic and consular service. The State Department claimed that it need not reveal information because of Exemption 3 of the FOIA, which "excludes from the coverage of the Freedom of Information Act matters specifically exempted from disclosure by statute, provided that such statute (A) requires that the matters be withheld from the public in such a manner as to leave no discretion on the issue, or (B) establishes particular criteria for withholding or refers to particular types of matters to be withheld."[15] A three-judge panel explored the intent of Congress in drafting the Freedom of Information Act and its legislative history to determine the limits of Exemption 3. After coming to the conclusion that under the exemption the court did not have the power to bar the disclosure of the information, the judges remanded the request to the district court to consider the possible applicability of other exemptions to the request.

When the full circuit denied a rehearing for an *en banc* appeal, meaning that there would be no reconsideration, Scalia dissented, along with Bork and George MacKinnon, also a Republican appointee. The three dissenters saw a conflict between this interpretation of the 1976 FOIA amendments limiting the State Department's rights to keep its funding secret and a 1980 General Accounting Office act that authorized the GAO to audit any expenditure to determine whether the spending was legally authorized while keeping that information confidential.[16] Seeing the conflict between the panel's interpretation of this 1976 FOIA and the 1980 General Accounting Office, Scalia and his two colleagues argued that the case should be reheard *en banc*. Scalia described the liberal judges' pro-disclosure opinion as "a perverse result," containing "legislative construction [that] lays traps for the unwary, in Congress and the Executive branch as well as among the general public, and impedes the development of a coherent body of law in this field." For him, this result "may be harmful to the national interest," which, by narrowing exemptions to FOIA, will "swell unnecessarily the list of FOIA filings."[17]

In several other cases over the next three months, Scalia dispensed with the notion of learning his job slowly in favor of using a series of sharp dissents to establish his conservative judicial identity.[18] Of these early Scalia dissents, the one that best demonstrated his early judicial technique and philosophy came in March 1983, in a case called *Community for Creative Non-Violence v. Watt,* when he sought to unravel the unlikely constitutional puzzle posed by the issue of whether sleeping on national park land could be considered protected freedom of expression under the First Amendment. As a symbolic-speech act of protest against Reagan policies that were allegedly harming the homeless, the Community for Creative Non-Violence (CCNV) sought permits from the National Park Service to build tent cities on the National Mall and Lafayette Park in Washington on the first day of winter. The Park Service would not issue a permit because it would violate existing anti-camping regulations. The CCNV challenged this ruling, arguing that sleeping at the sites was exactly the symbolic message it was trying to convey about the plight of the homeless. After the federal district court upheld the Park Service's ruling, an *en banc* hearing of the then liberal-dominated Court of Appeals overturned the regulation, arguing that "the Park Service cannot be upheld in its decision that tenting is all right, lying down is all right, maintaining a twenty-four-hour presence is all right, but sleeping is impermissible."[19]

Scalia dissented, seeking "to deny that sleeping is or can ever be speech for First Amendment purposes." For him, the majority's position was "a commentary upon how far judicial and scholarly discussion of this basic constitutional guarantee has strayed from common and common-sense understanding." To support his argument, Scalia demonstrated a new judicial theory of "textualism," going to his dictionary for a textual meaning of the limits of speech in the Constitution's First Amendment: "I start from the premise that when the Constitution said 'speech' it meant speech and not all forms of expression. Otherwise, it would have been unnecessary to address 'freedom of the press' separately—or, for that matter, 'freedom of assembly,' which was obviously directed at facilitating expression. . . . But to extend equivalent protection against laws that affect actions which happen to be conducted for the purpose of 'making a point' is to stretch the Constitution not only beyond its meaning but beyond reason, and beyond the capacity of any legal system to accommodate."[20]

In the usually dry world of Court of Appeals decision making, Scalia vehemently expressed just how unhappy he was with the majority's decision: "I dissent from this decision, which seems to me to endanger the great right of free speech by making it ridiculous and obnoxious, more than the

Park Service regulation in question menaces free speech by proscribing sleep."[21]

Despite the feisty nature of these initial dissenting opinions, Scalia established himself as a genial member of the D.C. Court of Appeals. *Washington Post* reporters Ruth Marcus and Susan Schmidt wrote that Scalia was "a gregarious, back-slapping host who enjoys sitting down at the piano after a cocktail party and leading a group in belting out tunes from the 1940s and 1950s." One of Scalia's liberal colleagues on the Court of Appeals, Abner Mikva, said that he was "not what you think of as a typical conservative . . . who scowls at the world."[22] Even when he disagreed with his liberal colleagues, they forgave him. One friend, Daniel Mayers, a Washington attorney at the time, told a reporter: "He is a very politic person, as opposed to political . . . a hail-fellow-well-met, and an extrovert."[23]

Scalia's minority position on the D.C. Court of Appeals seemed to test his patience a bit by the fall of 1983, when he found himself in dissent against what he viewed to be an unsupportable reading of the Eighth Amendment in an unusual death penalty case. Several death row inmates in five states argued that the so-called cocktail mix of drugs in a lethal injection violated the Food and Drug Administration's guidelines, because it was legally unapproved, and thus had been illegally shipped through interstate commerce, making its use for the imposition of the death penalty unconstitutionally "arbitrary and capricious." The three-judge panel of the Court of Appeals for this case pitted Scalia against liberal J. Skelly Wright, with the tie-breaking vote supporting the inmates' claim cast by visiting Senior District Court Judge Stanley Alexander Weigel from the Northern District of California, a liberal Democrat appointed by John F. Kennedy. The liberal judges joined in an opinion penned by Judge Wright holding for the inmates and sending the case back to the lower court "with instructions to order the FDA to fulfill its statutory function," which they expected would be to ban the lethal injection. Judge Wright argued that the "Appellants have presented substantial and uncontroverted evidence to support their claim that execution by lethal injection poses a serious risk of cruel, protracted death. . . . In light of these risks . . . [it] may also implicate the Eighth Amendment's prohibition of cruel and unusual punishment."[24]

Scalia, a devoted supporter of biblical retributive justice and the death penalty, had already endured enough of the liberalism of judicial colleagues such as Judge Wright. He attacked much more aggressively than he had to this point what he saw as the majority's "implausible result" and its "rewriting the law with regard to . . . FDA jurisdiction," which to him represented "a clear intrusion upon powers that belong to Congress, the Executive Branch and the states." Scalia accused the majority of misinterpreting the FDA regulations and labeled the majority's reading of the regulations as "the height of irrationality." Scalia had little patience for this end-around attempt at undermining the death penalty: "Without belittling the humane concerns associated with the present complaint, it must be acknowledged that the public health interest at issue is not widespread death or permanent disability, but (at most) a risk of temporary pain to a relatively small number of individuals (200, which the majority swells to 1,100 by including prisoners under sentence of death in states that have not adopted lethal injection statutes)." For him, the notion that lethal injections "pose a 'serious danger to the public health'" was "fanciful."[25]

When the majority said in a footnote that Scalia's statement in his dissent based on a Court of Appeals precedent from nine years earlier that the "agency enforcement discretion is 'generally unreviewable'" had "an anachronistic ring," he returned the fire with considerable disdain for his colleagues' position: "As for the 'anachronistic ring' which the majority hears in all this. . . . The sound which the majority heard was not an anachronistic ring at all, but the stifled cry of smothered *stare decisis*, or perhaps the far-off shattering of well established barriers separating the proper business of the executive and judicial branches."[26] For him, the FDA had acted properly in refusing to deal with this appeal, adding, "This court should have done the same. It is our embroilment, rather than the FDA's abstention, that is remarkable."

• • •

Scalia had developed a reputation as an exacting jurist who was willing to go to war with his senior colleagues. He was a hands-on judge, who, unlike some of his colleagues, mastered the early version of the word processor in order to draft many of his own opinions without the assistance of his law clerk.

Scalia also developed a unique manner of preparing for the oral arguments of the attorneys presenting their cases. He read all of the written legal briefs himself and instructed his law clerks to do the same and prepare their own oral argument to debate with him before the actual hearing. By the time the attorneys presented their case, Scalia was so well prepared that he could easily probe the weaknesses of the case, often focusing on the essence of an argument. "Scalia comes across as a knife-fighter, but a friendly knife-fighter," said one of those attorneys. Adds Judge Harry Edwards, a liberal on that court who became one of Scalia's favorite judicial targets, "He thinks as do I that if you are going to have oral argument, it should have a purpose."[27]

In the circulation of opinions before their publication, Scalia had also become a demanding presence for his fellow judges. Unlike his colleagues, who often let one of their fellow judges' draft opinions go by without substantial change, Scalia "pore[d] over other judges' drafts, covering them with detailed and often critical marginal comments, even if he [wasn't] on the panel deciding a case."[28] A fellow judge would later recall that he would "send back a memo praising [your draft] opinion, and then say, 'I will join if you make the following 19 changes.'"[29] As time went on, he would demand so many changes from his liberal colleagues, and challenge their opinions so regularly, personally, and vituperatively, that the law clerks for those judges developed a nickname for Scalia—"The Ninopath." This title was their shorthand version for his "almost pathological unwillingness to bend."[30]

Scalia's demanding nature also made life challenging for those around him, including his law clerks. Scalia's good friend federal Court of Appeals for the Ninth Circuit Judge Alex Kozinski said, "Apparently his law clerks kept complaining that it was hard to come up with some grand theory in which to fit every case; it was much easier, they argued, to decide each case as it came—by the seat of the pants."[31] Years later, some of his assistants would recount how they labored on his opinions only to be castigated for making a mistake. "He'd catch a mistake that we had made and he'd say, 'Well, it's hard to get it right.' He wanted everything perfect," recalls former law clerk Paul Cassell. His law clerks had a calligrapher make a plaque reading "It isn't easy to be right."—Antonin Scalia, 1985.[32] For the judge whose textualist decision-making theory depended upon the precise interpretation of words, this phrase had an interesting double meaning. It was hard to get these judgments correct, and sometimes it was also hard to reach the conservative side of a political decision that he sought.

Scalia rarely disagreed with Bork, but one epic battle between them did occur in December 1984, in the case of *Ollman v. Evans*, when an *en banc* court considered the libel suit by a Marxist political science professor named Bertell Ollman. After Ollman was named the chairman for the Department of Political Science at the University of Maryland, columnists Rowland Evans and Robert Novak wrote about him in *The Washington Post*, speculating about what they viewed as his ultra-left-wing "intentions" in teaching. Would he "use the classroom as an instrument for preparing what he calls 'the revolution'?" they asked. They also quoted an anonymous "political scientist in a major eastern university, whose scholarship and reputation as a liberal are well known," as saying, "Ollman has no status within the profession, but is a pure and simple activist." After Ollman filed a libel suit alleging that the reporters had impugned his academic reputation, and the district court issued a summary judgment dismissing the suit, a three-judge Court of Appeals panel wrote an unsigned, unanimous, *per curiam* opinion in the professor's favor, sending it back to the district court for further review. The Court of Appeals argued that the article "tended to suggest that Ollman regards the classroom as a forum for winning adherents to Marxism." [33]

When the case returned to the Court of Appeals for an *en banc* review a year later, a majority reversed the decision and held for the journalists under the theory that in expressing opinion, the two reporters were entitled to total First Amendment protection. In the words of Kenneth Starr's majority opinion:

> We cannot forget that the public has an interest in receiving information on issues of public importance even if the trustworthiness of the information is not absolutely certain. . . . By giving weight on the opinion side of the scale to cautionary and interrogative language, courts provide greater leeway to journalists and other writers and commentators in bringing issues of public importance to the public's attention and scrutiny. [34]

Robert Bork wrote a concurring opinion, agreeing with the court's pro–freedom of the press position, but arguing that it had not gone far enough. Bork did not entirely accept the rigid dichotomy between protected opinion and less protected alleged factual content. Thus, Bork argued, he was ready to take his expansive reading of the First Amendment's freedom of speech further, to protect "all of the allegedly libelous statements at issue here [that] can be immunized as expressions of opinion. . . . In my view, the law as enunciated by the Supreme Court imposes no such sharp dichotomy." Seeking greater protection for the exchange of free expression by the press, Bork argued that the *Ollman* case "arouses concern that a freshening stream of libel actions, which often seem as much designed to punish writers and publications as to recover damages for real injuries, [and] may threaten the public and constitutional interest in free, and frequently rough, discussion. Those who step into areas of public dispute, who choose the pleasures and distractions of controversy, must be willing to bear criticism, disparagement, and even wounding assessments." Bork conceded:

> Perhaps it would be better if disputation were conducted in measured phrases and calibrated assessments, and with strict avoidance of the ad hominem; better, that is, if the opinion and editorial pages of the public press were modeled on The Federalist Papers. But that is not the world in which we live, ever have lived, or are ever likely to know, and the law of the First Amendment must not try to make public dispute safe and comfortable for all the participants. That would only stifle the debate.[35]

This opinion was typical of Bork, who approached the law and these cases from a more academic point of view, taking his decision wherever his intellectual analysis of the issue directed, regardless of its effect on his ideological position. He was a conservative, to be sure, but if his original intent and public policy analysis meant taking a more pro–Bill of Rights defense position from time to time, so be it.

Scalia approached his work on the Court of Appeals differently. He wrote from a more ideological point of view, concerned by the result he sought in the case, then bolstering it with his textualism and other decision-making tools. In this case, while he approached the issue as no supporter of the press, he also could identify with Professor Ollman's situation on the other end of the political spectrum. He wrote in dissent as part of an unlikely trio with liberals Patricia Wald and Harry Edwards, usually two of his favorite targets. All of them were unwilling to extend either the majority's or Bork's protection for journalistic opinion columns. In Scalia's judgment, Evans and Novak had gone too far in their "disparagement of Ollman's professional reputation," venturing beyond protected opinion into actionable factual statements.[36] Then, Scalia took on Bork's more pro-press position and his judicial technique for reaching that result:

> The [Bork] concurrence perceives a "modern problem" consisting of "the freshening stream of libel actions, which . . . may threaten the public and constitutional interest in free, and frequently rough, discussion," and of claims for damages that are "quite capable of silenc-

ing political commentators forever." . . . I do not know the answers to these questions, but I do know that it is frightening to think that the existence or nonexistence of a constitutional rule (the willfully false disparagement of professional reputation in the context of political commentary cannot be actionable) is to depend upon our ongoing personal assessments of such sociological factors. And not only is our cloistered capacity to identify "modern problems" suspect, but our ability to provide condign solutions through the rude means of con-stitutional prohibition is nonexistent.[37]

The argument here was politely put, but Scalia was charging Bork with being an activist, sociologically oriented "legal realist" judge in the First Amendment area, more protective of the journalists' rights than a self-re-strained textualist like himself who was willing to limit the press and thus protect reputations.

Bork was not willing to let Scalia's characterization of his judicial work stand. In the body of his opinion he turned to his "original intent" theory to respond:

Judge Scalia's dissent implies that the idea of evolving constitutional doctrine should be anathema to judges who adhere to a philosophy of judicial restraint. But most doctrine is merely the judge-made super-structure that implements basic constitutional principles. . . . There would be little need for judges—and certainly no office for a philoso-phy of judging—if the boundaries of every constitutional provision were self-evident. They are not. In a case like this, it is the task of the judge in this generation to discern how the framers' values, defined in the context of the world they knew, apply to the world we know.

After offering two specific historical examples, drawn from the search and seizure and interstate commerce clause areas, to demonstrate his notion of the acceptability of judges updating the Constitution, Bork added: "The First Amendment's guarantee of freedom of the press was written by men who had not the remotest idea of modern forms of communication. But that does not make it wrong for a judge to find the values of the First Amend-ment relevant to radio and television broadcasting."[38]

Unwilling to concede the last word to Bork, Scalia responded in a footnote to his opinion:

In opposing such unguided "evolution," I am not in need of the concurrence's reminder that the Fourth Amendment must be applied to
modern electronic surveillance, the Commerce Clause to trucks and
the First Amendment to broadcasting. . . . What is under discussion
here is not application of pre-existing principles to new phenomena,
but rather alteration of pre-existing principles in their application to
pre-existing phenomena on the basis of judicial perception of changed
social circumstances. The principle that the First Amendment does
not protect the deliberate impugning of character or reputation, in its
application to the pre-existing phenomenon of political controversy,
is to be revised to permit "bumping" of some imprecisable degree
because we perceive that libel suits are now too common and too successful.[39]

By adding in the body of his dissent the veiled charge that Bork was using
his theory to "legislate" from the bench, Scalia saw the opening to separate
himself from Bork on the political right, demonstrating that he was the
purer conservative. This single verbal duel would prove to have enormous
ramifications.

• • •

After deciding cases based on textualism, the dictionary meaning of the
words in a law or constitutional provision, in September of 1985 Scalia
turned for the first time to evaluating a case by relying on a wider historical
lens. The court considered a case dealing with a request from the Reporters Committee for Freedom of the Press and four reporters for access to the
court records and documents secured from Mobil Oil Corporation during a
libel trial while it was still under way. The issue was whether there existed
within the First Amendment a "public right to know" this material. Never
an advocate for the unlimited freedom of either the press or the public's
"right to know," Scalia used his reading of text and "historical tradition" to
undercut such a claim: "In deciding whether the public has a First Amendment right of access to judicial proceedings . . . an historical tradition of at
least some duration is obviously necessary." Otherwise, he argued, "With
neither the constraint of text nor the constraint of historical practice, nothing would separate the judicial task of constitutional interpretation from the
political task of enacting laws currently deemed essential."[40] Only by using

this textual and historical decision-making technique, Scalia argued, could he, a judge, avoid legislating from the bench.

After reviewing the case law on libel, Scalia concluded on the basis of historical tradition: "We take it as a given that there is a tradition of public access to court records, and that that right is not absolute. The factor most obviously distinguishing the request for records in the present case from the requests at issue in the vast majority of reported cases . . . was the pendency of the litigation at the time the request was made." Scalia concluded that there was no right of public access to these court records and materials. "Because of their sparseness, the authorities discussed above are perhaps weak support for a general common law rule of non-access to pre-judgment records in private civil cases. But when laid beside our inability to find any historical authority, holding or dictum, to the contrary, they are more than enough to rule out a general tradition of access to such records."[41] By thus adding an inquiry into the historical tradition of a case to his textual approach, Scalia assumed more freedom to explore evidence beyond dictionary definitions in order to decide as he saw fit.

Now three years into his tenure on the Court of Appeals, in the fall of 1985 Scalia missed the back-and-forth contact with audiences that he had enjoyed while teaching in law school. Having learned firsthand how federal judges made, rather than interpreted, law, he was anxious to reveal that lesson beyond the court's chambers. More than that, with at least three other possible candidates for elevation to the Supreme Court on his own Court of Appeals panel, not to mention many others throughout the country, Scalia needed a way to separate himself from the others in the minds of those politicians who would be selecting future justices. The opportunity to increase his visibility and resume to some extent his academic lifestyle came in the form of a stack of invitations from law schools and other venues around the country for speaking engagements between the fall of 1985 and the spring of 1986. Scalia decided to write a stock speech for these occasions, much like the stump speech that a politician running for office would deliver, and present it to each of these audiences. Since the speeches were not televised, and Scalia's addresses were not enough of a public event to gain newspaper coverage, audiences were not aware of the overlap in content. The fun came after the speech, when a lively question-and-answer period allowed Scalia to interact with his audience and speak more freely on a wider range of topics.[42]

Searching for an interesting topic for the speech, Scalia used the same technique that Herbert Wechsler had employed in crafting the "neutral principles" for judicial decision making address that he gave when Scalia attended Harvard Law School in 1957. He would seek in his own way to answer Wechsler's powerful legal puzzle: how can one decide cases in a disciplined fashion by resorting to "neutral principles." Scalia searched here not for a phrase, such as the "Freedom of Association" that Wechsler had used, but rather an interpretative process or technique designed to reach an answer while also limiting the discretion of judicial power. Scalia's "neutral principle" would be to use both textual interpretation and an extended historical examination to anchor a judge's power to find the precise meaning of a law or constitutional phrase. By preaching the strict examination of the meaning of the text, Scalia was adhering to the philosophy in which he had been raised. And, even better, this process allowed him to find a way to arrive at a result that was consistent with his political conservatism.[43]

Scalia decided to craft his speech as an attack on the practice of the liberals on his Court of Appeals and elsewhere of deciding cases based on "legislative history," that is, determining the expressed intent of the legislature when passing a law. He had seen enough in his own work and his three years on the bench to know how judges could bolster their judgments by referring to the language in a committee report or statements made by members of Congress during floor debates.

As with all of Scalia's Court of Appeals opinions, his new speech was a model of legal scholarship. After announcing that his topic would explore a "relatively new development" in judicial decision making, the use of "legislative history," Scalia began with a surefire joke line: "Some creatures that seem pleasant and tractable in their infancy—tiger cubs, for example—are better abandoned when they reach their full natural development. Now that legislative history has reached its adulthood, perhaps it is time to reconsider whether we want to live with it."[44] Pointing out that the great English legal theorist William Blackstone never mentioned "legislative history" in interpreting laws, Scalia proved that this technique for interpreting statutory construction had become an increasingly prevalent practice in early-twentieth-century American law. Scalia recounted that when he was the head of the Office of Legal Counsel in the Ford administration, nearly "60 percent of the research time of my staff attorneys was devoted to legislative history." By the 1981–82 term, Scalia quoted his Court of Appeals colleague Patricia Wald, legislative history was being used "in fully half of the cases—and in *all* of the cases where the meaning of a statutory text was at issue." Yet, Scalia argued, a true legislative intent cannot be determined because these legislative histories, especially in the form of committee reports, were being written for the purpose of "affecting the courts rather than informing the Congress." In other words, while many read these documents as legislative histories, hoping to glean the reasons for supporting or opposing the law, Scalia argued that they were written as legal advocacy with an eye toward influencing future judges' interpretations of legislation when it ended up in court.

Scalia argued that the use of legislative history should never be the goal of judges because the task of a judge is "to 'fill in' those elements of the legal scheme which the legislature in fact never considered." For him, judges cannot accurately determine, and should not even attempt to discern, legislative intent because, "To ask what a reasonable legislature would have meant by existing language is not the same as asking what a reasonable legislature *would have done*—but a degree of discretion and judgment is still involved."

He argued that the manipulative use of legislative history skewed the role of judges, in effect turning them into legislators. Those judges who favor the use of legislative intent, Scalia argued, do so "to abandon this judicial role—this responsibility for making a harmonious whole out of the system of laws—in favor of obeisance to a conclusory statement inserted in a committee report." This process was for him "a great mistake," which he explained as "the equivalent of looking over the faces of the crowd at a large cocktail party and picking out your friends." Despite this powerful verbal assault, Scalia confessed that as a judge on a federal appellate court, from time to time he could "hardly ignore legislative history when [he] knew it will be used by the Supreme Court."

Scalia concluded his speech by proposing the replacement of the legislative history approach with his "textualism" and "historical tradition" theory by which a judge can "asses[s] the meaning that would reasonably have been 'conveyed to a citizen' at 'the time the law was enacted,' as modified by the relationship of the statute to later enactments similarly interpreted."

This was not yet a fully formed theory, but just the kernel of an idea. Scalia was proposing a new decision-making approach that differed from that of Bork, whose "original intent" relied solely on the understanding of the Framers of the Constitution in determining its meaning. Scalia was now proposing that judges rely on his version of the "public meaning" of the Constitution, interpreting laws according to the meaning of the words in the minds of the people at the time of the creation of that charter. Scalia argued that by using this approach a law would be interpreted "according to its most plausible objective import," rather than "according to the unlegislative 'intent' of those who enacted it."[45] Just how one objectively determines the meaning of a law that would be "conveyed to a citizen at the time the law was enacted," though, was a topic for another day.[46]

With this stump speech, Scalia staked a claim to a new conservative judicial paradigm. If this technique gained attention and adherents, Scalia could distinguish himself from others on the list of conservative federal judges who might be considered for promotion. In addition, by going on the road for the next nine months to deliver such speeches, Scalia would be able to satisfy his desire to continue teaching, recruit new followers for his cause, and increase his professional visibility. It was a way for him to fight his judicial wars in the guise of legal education, while still appearing to maintain his posture as a neutral federal judge.

By 1985 the ideological balance of the D.C. Circuit Court was in transition. When Reagan appointed Laurence Silberman to fill a newly created twelfth seat on the court in October, the liberal dominance was narrowed to a 7–5 majority of Democratic appointees. Two months later, in December, former Republican senator James Buckley was confirmed to fill another vacancy.[47] The addition of young, conservative Republicans to the court significantly affected the working environment. As Bork recalled:

> I think that insofar as there were tensions about ideologies, I think they grew as the number of Reagan appointees grew. At first there wasn't many [sic]. They were friendly, but I think over time as the number of Reagan appointees grew and then became a majority, I think there were tensions between the groups. . . . People were a little less jolly with each other. Mostly in conferences, but there was nothing horrible about it. . . . I think it was just a little less happy when the division became really strong and the blocs were roughly equal and finally the Reagan appointees became the majority.

The conservatives also began to press their numerical advantages as they "began *en bancing* a lot," in Bork's words.[48]

• • •

By February 1986, Scalia was just a few weeks from turning fifty and stood at a turning point. He lost both of his parents, each in their early eighties, within a two-week span around the previous Christmas and New Year's holidays. His mother died in December of a heart attack after discovering her husband had suffered a stroke; Sam lingered for several days before his death in early January.[49] In addition to the personal loss, Scalia suddenly entered a new season of his life. He was the sole member of his generation in the Scalia family. For the first time, he had no parents to share the pride of his success.

Given the increasingly geriatric Supreme Court, then averaging nearly seventy-two years of age, he believed there would soon be one or more openings on that body. He hoped that it would come before the 1988 election, after which Reagan would leave the White House. Scalia had served roughly six months less on the Court of Appeals than Bork, and while both had similarly conservative credentials, Bork had to be considered the front-runner for any Supreme Court vacancy based on his having made the long list of candidates considered for the openings in 1975 and 1981.[50] Now, though, there were two other competitors on the same D.C. Court of Appeals: Kenneth Starr, who was appointed in 1983, and Scalia's good friend Laurence Silberman, appointed in 1985. Both were developing the kind of conservative judicial résumé that made them serious candidates. To have any chance of being selected, Scalia had to separate himself from the others.

Just at this point, Scalia faced a pivotal case, called *Synar v. United States*, involving the Reagan administration's economic policies. Recent budget cuts of New Deal and Great Society entitlement programs did not keep pace with tax cuts for the wealthy, causing the federal deficit to grow exponentially. In reaction, Texas senator Phil Gramm, fiscally moderate New Hampshire senator Warren Rudman, and South Carolina conservative senator Ernest Hollings combined to shepherd passage of the Balanced Budget and Emergency Deficit Control Act of 1985. Popularly known as Gramm-Rudman-Hollings, this law set a series of budgetary spending targets for Congress and created a system of automatic budget cuts if those targets were not met. But the law's political as well as constitutional challenges were legion. Who would enforce those targets? Who would oversee the budgetary enforcers? And what assurance was there that all money being budgeted and spent would be included in the calculations?

The law worked this way. Congress set a "maximum deficit amount" for each of the years from 1986 to 1991, as determined by the Office of Management and Budget (OMB) and the Congressional Budget Office (CBO), with the goal of balancing the federal budget in 1991. The OMB and the comptroller general, the latter of which is a nonpartisan official within the legislative branch, would then determine whether the planned spending by the federal government in various programs exceeded these targets, and if so, automatic deficit reduction spending cuts, called "sequestrations," could be imposed on the president according to the calculations of the comptroller general.[51] This was despite the Constitutional power of the executive branch to implement the budget. If any part of this process were to be declared unconstitutional by the federal courts, a "fallback" procedure was established under which Congress, operating under the spending cut recommendations of the OMB and CBO, would report those adjustments to a joint committee of Congress, which was required to pass the spending bill within five days in the form of a joint resolution that would be presented to the president for a budget-cutting sequestration order.

Whether this law represented a constitutional delegation of Congress's spending power, whether these statutory limitations on the governmental budgetary process were proper, and just how the law would affect the constitutional separation of powers made the law destined for a judicial review. When Congressman Mike Synar of Oklahoma and several other members of Congress, the comptroller general, and members of the National Treasury Employees Union who faced losing their annual cost-of-living allowances all sued in federal court in the District of Columbia to challenge the constitutionality of the law, the legal bombshell landed in the laps of that circuit's judiciary. Did these litigants have standing to raise these issues, could Congress delegate these budgetary powers to other executive or semi-executive agencies, and did the budgetary decisions by the comptroller general as constituted and operated under the provisions of this act violate the separation of powers?

Since the legislation provided for an expedited hearing if the constitutionality of the bill was challenged, the case was to be heard by a special three-judge court comprised of members of both the Court of Appeals and the lower-level, federal district court, with the guarantee of an immediate appeal to the Supreme Court. Given the controversial nature of the issue, and the certainty of an immediate Supreme Court review, not to mention the intense press coverage, this was the kind of case that could make or break a judicial career, depending on how it was handled.

To hear and rule on the case, the chief judge of the Court of Appeals, Spottswood W. Robinson III, a Democrat from the Lyndon Johnson era, assigned Scalia from his court and added two district court judges, Oliver

Gasch and Norma Holloway Johnson. For an ambitious judge like Scalia, this assignment carried as many risks as possible benefits. Getting the decision correct, and doing so without offending anyone, was a challenging task indeed.

Despite all of these inherent career dangers, this was just the sort of question that Scalia had untangled as the head of the Office of Legal Counsel for President Ford: how much power should the president have, and how could that power be preserved against congressional assaults designed to control the office? Scalia's colleague Patricia Wald could see that this case was right up his alley: "I credit people like Scalia with a consistency of belief that will transcend changes in administrations. I think he honestly believes in a separation of powers theory and this attitude toward statutory interpretation is part of his separation of powers theory, but it really does give a lot more power to the executive. . . . I think it is a theory of government, sometimes jokingly I say, it is a theory of 'OLC' (Office of Legal Counsel). All the principal advocates of executive power came out of the OLC school—from [then Associate Justice William] Rehnquist to Scalia. It's something they teach at OLC, regardless of who's running it."[52] Scalia realized that he would have to harness his normally unwavering instincts to defend and expand executive power from congressional encroachment, which would endear him to the Reagan administration but might simultaneously offend members of Congress who could also affect his future.

As it turned out, the result in this case was largely going to be what Scalia decided it would be. Judge Johnson was then involved in "a protracted criminal case" and, Judge Gasch recalled later, they "didn't have many conferences in which she was present but . . . Scalia and I did confer a number of times before the argument."[53] Gasch and Scalia quickly realized after the oral arguments by the numerous attorneys in the case where their opinion would center: "Right away we recognized the principal issue was [the] separation of power since the Comptroller General is a functionary of the legislative branch and this legislation called upon him to make [the budget-cutting] decision more properly within the scope of the duties of the Executive."[54]

Knowing the power of writing the first draft, not to mention the career benefits of being seen as the principal author of the joint opinion, Scalia immediately got to work. Judge Gasch recalls: "I shall always remember going up to confer with Nino Scalia after we heard argument—Norma Johnson was again involved in some criminal case—and here he was in front of his computer banging out things he wanted to say and erasing lines and restoring some lines with some changes. It was the first time I had ever seen a judge work at a computer."[55] Searching from among the many decision-making approaches that he had utilized over the past three-plus years, Scalia relied this time on more of a public policy/separation of powers approach. He argued for the unanimous three-judge panel that the law was unconstitutional because it vested the presidential budget-cutting power in the comptroller general, an agency whose head official could be removed by Congress, thus violating the Constitution's Article II powers of the presidency. As Scalia wrote for the panel: "It is . . . unthinkable that Congress could constitutionally provide for veto of those [budgetary] determinations by an officer removable by Congress—the Comptroller General, for example. . . . We hold, therefore, that since the powers conferred upon the Comptroller General as part of the automatic deficit reduction process are executive powers, which cannot constitutionally be exercised by an officer removable by Congress, those powers cannot be exercised and therefore the automatic deficit reduction process to which they are central cannot be implemented."[56]

To support his decision, Scalia analyzed the "text and historical tradition" involved in the issue of the removal for purely political reasons of administrative officers that are wholly executive, as opposed to "quasi-legislative" and "quasi-judicial" in nature, tailoring the textual meaning of the provisions of the law or the Constitution according to the "tradition" of the historical understanding of these words.[57] Just how he determined this "text and tradition" of the Constitution was not yet clear, but Scalia's use of the terms again planted the flag of a new jurisprudential exploration beyond the "original intent" theory of Robert Bork. And it was effective. Scalia's determined support for the administration's power to deal with budgetary policy had little economic effect, as the government's deficit spending continued unabated; however, it brought Scalia's name to the attention of the administration once again. Just five months later, the Supreme Court would use Scalia's analysis to overturn the Gramm-Rudman-Hollings Act by a 7–2 vote.

For four years Scalia had been the model of a hardworking, highly intellectual, conservative jurist on the D.C. Court of Appeals. Despite his nascent "text and tradition" decision-making approach, his work on this court evidenced no single jurisprudential principle or philosophy. Rather than building a rigid judicial technique into which he forced all of the cases to the exclusion of those other views, Scalia demonstrated a willingness to use a number of techniques to decide cases: precedential and statutory interpretation, textual analysis, public policy analysis, the early beginnings of his version of an "original meaning" philosophy, and even legislative history. Scalia was a uniquely intellectual and scholarly jurist, experienced in judicial problem solving as a result of his executive branch work, who was also a devoted conservative, constantly evolving in his search for a better decision-making technique. He also had the self-confidence to shape his own image even when in the minority, by speaking solely for himself in dissent. Of the sixty-four opinions he had issued by this time, he had dissented in eleven of them, or about 17 percent, well above the levels of other D.C. appellate judges.[58]

Scalia had evolved from his earlier "Ninopath" days, showing that he could work with his liberal colleagues. With only a few exceptions, he behaved as a team-playing jurist, who demonstrated an ability to point out in a civil manner what he saw as the failings and errors in his liberal colleagues' legal analyses. When he believed it to be necessary, though, he could still scold his liberal colleagues, displaying flashes of the partisan tactics that would become more evident during his later judicial career. Whether he behaved as the "Ninopath" or as a team player, Scalia had discovered on the Court of Appeals that it was, after all, "easy to be right."

CHAPTER 8

Terminology Is Destiny

When Antonin Scalia stood to speak to the attorney general's Conference on Economic Liberties in Washington, on Saturday, June 14, 1986, he knew something that the audience did not know. This might well be his final speech as a member of the federal Court of Appeals for the District of Columbia. For that reason, he was determined to make it memorable.

As Scalia spoke, he could be forgiven if his mind was elsewhere. Unknown to the general public, the search for the next appointee to the Supreme Court had been under way for quite a while. Chief Justice Warren Burger had decided on May 22 to retire at the end of the Court's term, in order to devote himself to heading the Bicentennial Commission for the Constitution. After meeting secretly with President Reagan's outgoing White House counsel, Fred Fielding, at the chief justice's home, Burger traveled to the White House on Tuesday, May 27, to tell the president. At the end of the meeting Burger tried to influence the selection of his own replacement by presenting the president with a memorandum containing his recommendations. Among the names were two conservative members of his court, Associate Justices William Rehnquist and Byron White, and two judges on the federal Circuit Court of Appeals for the District of Columbia, Robert Bork and Antonin Scalia.[1]

In anticipation of this opening, the National Italian American Bar Association had already been laying the groundwork for this appointment for a year. Richard K. Cacioppo, the president of the organization, wrote Reagan chief of staff Donald T. Regan that Scalia had "outstanding credentials" for the next appointment to the Supreme Court when a vacancy occurred.[2]

The day after Burger expressed his intention to retire, Regan and new White House counsel Peter Wallison, chatted at the end of the standard daily operations meeting to discuss the upcoming search for the chief justice's replacement. In looking at the suggested list of names from Burger, they both agreed that "a complete search for an appropriate candidate" should be undertaken and that the attorney general, Edwin Meese, should be brought into the process. In a meeting the following day, Thursday, May 29, Meese, Regan, and Wallison agreed that the goal was to find "candidates who would be certain followers of the President's philosophy of judicial restraint," or deferring to the political branches and avoiding legislating from the bench. Knowing that Bradford Reynolds, the assistant attorney general for the Civil Rights Division, had long been planning the administration's judicial appointment strategy, Meese suggested that Wallison meet with Reynolds. All three men hoped to have a list of candidates for the president to interview secretly by Monday, June 9, in order to avoid the premature leaking of Burger's retirement intentions to the press and risk diminishing their control over identifying the best candidate.[3]

Ever since Reagan's inauguration, the Justice Department had been developing and reviewing files of potential Supreme Court appointees in anticipation of an opening. A memorandum outlined the Justice Department's ideal justice, arguing that the perfect appointment to the Court must be:

> An intelligent conservative with a forceful but congenial personality and a vision of where the Court should go. He should have some federal judicial or academic experience (preferably both) so that his views are predictable and settled; some administrative experience in government is also desirable. He should be no younger than 40 but no older than 60 (and preferably 45–50), in good health, desirous of spending the rest of his life on the Supreme Court, and aware of what the job entails (here, again, judicial or academic experience is useful). Obviously, he should be scandal-free and have judicial temperament. It would be nice if he was a telegenic one-armed Armenian who gave good speeches, but that is not essential.[4]

Up until the final facetious line, this memo described Antonin Scalia perfectly. But Scalia was, for the moment, no better than second on the working list of potential appointees to the Supreme Court. When the stacks of files of appointment materials arrived on Wallison's desk, it became clear that the order of the list of potential names began with Robert H. Bork. Wallison and two lawyers on his staff, Alan Raul and Chris Cox, began the process of sifting through the files on six Court of Appeals judges—Bork,

Scalia, Patrick E. Higginbotham of the Fifth Circuit, Anthony Kennedy and J. Clifford Wallace of the Ninth Circuit, and Ralph Winter of the Second Circuit—as well as two sitting Supreme Court justices, Rehnquist and Sandra Day O'Connor. Raul and Cox were charged with reviewing the public records of all of these candidates, along with other possible nominees. By the end of May, they transmitted files on Rehnquist and O'Connor to the White House for a review by chief of staff Regan. It was a massive investigative review, and exceedingly well organized. In less than a week, the investigation began centering on four candidates—Rehnquist, O'Connor, Bork, and Scalia.

Analyzing the Rehnquist and O'Connor candidacies was easy because their work was so visible and the politics of such an appointment was so clear. They had been classmates at Stanford Law School, but each justice brought different strengths. Rehnquist was a brilliant, ultraconservative justice appointed by Richard Nixon in 1971 who liked to write solo dissents arguing that even his conservative colleagues should issue more right-wing reversals of Warren Court decisions than they did. O'Connor was a more moderate, pragmatic jurist, a conservative who was prone to compromising with the moderates and liberals on the Court, her strength being that she would become the first female chief justice on the Supreme Court.

The selection process seemed straightforward. The confirmation process for either justice would be smooth since each had already been confirmed for the Court once and Republicans controlled the Senate. The elevation of a sitting justice, though, would create another vacancy on the Court, so another Senate confirmation would be required. The Senate confirmation process for Bork and Scalia was likewise expected to be routine. Since the appointment of either man to replace Burger would be a trade of a conservative justice for a conservative appointee, the voting balance of the Court itself would not change. The choice was two-fold. Did the administration see an internal Supreme Court problem in elevating one justice to the center seat over the others, and if so, which justice? And, if that happened, which of the two Court of Appeals judges, Bork or Scalia, would be the best appointment to fill the newly created vacancy?

Wallison and Bradford Reynolds focused on elevating Rehnquist, thinking that his judicial and political views were more in line with the highly conservative president. Reynolds, however, "did not believe that it would be easy to get Justice Rehnquist to accept the position of Chief. He was of the view that Rehnquist was tired and probably would not want the added administrative burdens of the Chief Justice position."[5] Failing to get Rehnquist, the two men began to consider appointing the new chief from outside the Court. Their files made clear that Bork, who was then fifty-nine years old, and who had been mentioned for both Republican Supreme Court appointments since 1975, was the premier candidate.

The Department of Justice's memo on Bork described him as "the leading spokesman for an interpretavist [original intent] theory of constitutional law and judicial restraint for over the 20 years. . . . His judicial philosophy is that of the President's: interpretavism and strict construction. That is, the judicial branch should interfere with the policy choices made by the elected representatives at the state or federal level only when the majority [in Congress] seeks to infringe on those freedoms expressly enshrined in the Constitution." Bork understood, as did the administration, that for justices to "overrul[e] democratically sanctioned choices by creating rights not found in the constitutional text" would represent "an illegitimate—indeed, tyrannical—suppression of self government through an assumption of powers by the judiciary." The Justice Department was pleased that Bork had "demonstrated a healthy lack of respect for unprincipled precedent," code words for being willing to overturn the liberal Warren Court decisions from the 1960s and even moderate Burger Court opinions since 1970, and "would not hesitate to overturn constitutional aberrations such as [the 1973 abortion decision] *Roe v. Wade*." No one exceeded Bork's towering qualifications, the memo added, explaining that he "possesses monumental intellectual and scholarly credentials" and "is extremely eloquent and persuasive, both in print and in person, a talent that will serve him well in building a consensus supporting conservative principles on the Court."[6]

While Bork initially had the edge in the selection process, Scalia was not without his advantages. He was nine years younger than Bork, with some thinking that he was in much better health. In addition, in what appeared to be a close race, there was one clearly evident jurisprudential difference between the two men in the First Amendment freedom of press area. Bork's more pro-press opinion in the Court of Appeals for the District of Columbia *Ollman v. Evans* libel case did not meet with favor from an administration devoted to an "original intent" philosophy. One Justice Department memo argued that "Bork, after determining the precise libertarian value enshrined in general phrases such as freedom of speech, would give full force to this value, apparently even in specific contexts and ways that the Framers had not intended." This was, the memo argued, "[Bork's] only disturbing opinion on the appellate court." Scalia, however, "rightly criticized [Bork's] opinion as inappropriate 'sociological jurisprudence.'" However, the memo added that the opinion was not to be held against Bork, normally the leading advocate of "original intent" decision making, because "perhaps it is best viewed as an isolated misstep attributable to Bork's normally laudable devotion to granting absolute protection to political speech." Further, Bork, a former solicitor general, had "acknowledged scholarly credentials and pre-existing personal relationships with many of the justices [which] should lead to his automatic acceptance on the Court while others would need to go through at least a brief transition period."[7] Despite his absolutist pro-press opinion, the Justice Department memos seemed to lean in Bork's direction, with one describing him as "brilliant, and a real intellectual powerhouse."[8]

While Scalia was not on the top of the Supreme Court nomination list, he had achieved nearly the same level of support as Bork from the Reagan Justice Department. One memo began, Scalia "is also an articulate and devoted adherent to the interpretavist theory of adjudication."[9] The memo acknowledged the differences between Scalia's "textualism" decision-making approach and Bork's "original intent" theory: "In seeking to determine the breadth of rights contained in the constitutional text, Scalia would probably be more inclined than Bork to look at the language of the constitutional provision itself, as well as its history, to determine if it grants an affirmative mandate for the judiciary to inject itself into the legislative process." While "Scalia's natural belief in the majoritarian process," and "innate distrust of the judiciary's ability to implement, or even to discern, public policy or popular will," would very likely lead him to "leave undisturbed the challenged activity," Bork would likely rely on "a 'core' constitutional value," as determined through an analysis of Founding Era history and "the general theory of government reflected by the Constitution's overall structure," in making such judgments in favor of the right.

The memo described Scalia as "obviously a superb intellect and scholar who has produced an extraordinary impressive body of academic writings," who "reasons and writes with great insight and flair," and had "written probably the most important opinions of any appellate court judge during the last four years, without a single mistake." In sum, the memo concluded "more so than Bork, [Scalia] is generally respected as a superb technician on 'nuts and bolts' legal questions."[10] Coming as it did just four months earlier, Scalia's work in the *Synar* balanced budget case clearly worked to his advantage.

There were other personal differences between Scalia, the man whom the D.C. Court of Appeals law clerks called "The Ninopath," and the relatively even-tempered Bork. While Scalia could be just as personable and gregarious as Bork, another Justice Department memo warned that Scalia was "potentially prone to an occasional outburst of temper," and "it is conceivable that he might rub one of his colleagues the wrong way." Moreover, even though he was "an extremely articulate and persuasive advocate . . . unlike Bork, he would have to undergo a relatively brief 'get-acquainted' period on the Supreme Court." Contrary to the fifty-nine-year-old Bork, Scalia, then fifty years old, "smokes heavily, and drinks, [but] he should have a lengthy career on the Court." Once more in this memo the *Ollman* libel case seemed to represent the tie-breaker that indicated to some in the Justice Department that Scalia might be the more reliably conservative vote on the First Amendment as well as many other Bill of Rights cases.[11]

With the comparison between the two men a close one, it was at this point that the tumblers of fate began moving in Scalia's direction. A third influential Justice Department memo on Scalia was drafted by Lee Liberman Otis, Scalia's former student at the University of Chicago Law School who had helped found the Federalist Society and was now the special assistant to Attorney General Meese specializing in federal judicial selection. In analyzing the conservative nature of Scalia's judicial decision making "in light of the profile of [the administration's] ideal candidate," Otis wrote that Scalia "defers to the judgments of other institutions unless it is clear that the Constitution or federal statutes command otherwise." Her analysis of Scalia's Court of Appeals opinions showed that he sought "to interpret the Constitution; he understands that it is a written document, and that its meaning is tied to what its Framers intended." In that way, Scalia's legal values were ideal for Reagan's purposes, as his "philosophical compass points correctly— in favor of less government, in favor of free markets, in favor of traditional values." Otis's conclusion for her detailed, fourteen-page analysis of Scalia's federal Court of Appeals opinions could not have been more favorable. She described him as "the conservative judge the most to be reckoned with on the D.C. Circuit," and a man whose "engaging personality" will allow him to "persuade judges who do not start out in agreement with him to go along with him or at least make some concessions." Contrary to the negative assessment of Bork's decision in the *Ollman* libel case, Otis had nothing but praise for her former teacher's work on the Court of Appeals: "In my review of Scalia's writings as a judge I did not find a single opinion in which either the result reached or the ground of decision seemed problematic. . . . He has written many of the most important opinions written recently by any federal judge." [12]

Otis's summary had great influence on the appointment process. Even the most casual reading of these memos on Bork and Scalia made clear that if the president was inclined to make a selection for chief justice from among those not currently on the Supreme Court, he could not go wrong by choosing either man.

But there was much to separate them from the two candidates for chief already on the Court. This assessment was confirmed on Monday, June 9, when Regan, Meese, and Wallison met for around forty-five minutes with the president. Everyone in the room agreed that the challenge was to find a candidate who would continue to follow Reagan's judicial restraint philosophy even after their lifetime appointment to the Court made them independent of the White House. They also understood that the president was searching for a candidate with a "clearly articulated [conservative] philosophy," ruling out the more ideologically moderate O'Connor. Reagan sensed that the choice for chief should be a person who was already on the Court, and possibly recalling the suggestion of outgoing Chief Justice Burger, the president asked to speak to Rehnquist. Beyond that, the seventy-five-year-old president said that he was "intrigued" by Scalia because his comparatively youthful age would allow him "to serve on the Court for an extended period of time."

But that was not the determining factor. Wallison had been arguing that Robert Bork should be appointed to this vacancy, with Scalia coming next, "because the first nominee would be easier [to gain Senate confirmation] than the second, and Scalia would be a stronger candidate because he was Italian American." Upon hearing that, Reagan asked Wallison "whether Scalia was Italian American." When it was confirmed, Reagan announced that Scalia "was his choice." Years later, Wallison would say of the decision, "I believe Reagan wanted to nominate the first Italian American" to the Court. All other things being equal between Scalia and Bork, it was ironic that having argued so vehemently in print against affirmative action, he now became a de facto affirmative action choice for the Supreme Court. [13]

When the president and Justice Rehnquist met on June 12, Reagan got right to the point. He told Rehnquist that Burger would be resigning when the Court's current term ended, which "seemed to come as no surprise to Justice Rehnquist." Though the president had been prepped with a series of seven interview questions for Rehnquist, Reagan dispensed with those and told his visitor that he was the "unanimous choice of all of us" to replace Burger and become the sixteenth chief justice of the United States. When Reagan offered him the chance "to think about it," Rehnquist said there was no need for any time, as he "immediately said that he would be honored and accepted."[14] With the next order of business being the filling of Rehnquist's vacant seat, the president mentioned that Scalia and Bork were under active consideration. Rehnquist was noncommittal, saying only that "he had high regard for both of them." By the end of the day, Scalia had an appointment to meet with the president on June 16.

Scalia had known for a while that he was actively under consideration for a seat on the Supreme Court. The White House had been carefully vetting his forty-two-page biographical questionnaire, complete with financial statements, tax information, and discussions of his legal and judicial qualifications. With his speech to the attorney general's Conference on Economic Liberties on June 14, he hoped he might make one final impression upon the Washington legal elite before a nomination was made. Hoping to be appointed to the Court, but remembering his disappointment at missing out on the solicitor generalship in 1981, he had told no one but his wife about his upcoming White House meeting.[15]

Knowing that he was so close to the highest rung on his career ladder, Scalia wanted his upcoming speech to make an argument for his elevation to the Supreme Court. He chose not to give one of his speeches offering a high-level exploration of the almost metaphysical intersection of morality, law, and economics. Nor would he deliver his legislative history speech that had served him so well for the last year. Instead, he decided on an entirely new speech with a very different goal. Under the guise of presenting a lively, and even somewhat playful, intellectual discussion of legal jurisprudence, the subtext of this speech was devoted to explaining why his brand of judicial conservatism was better than that of Judge Bork. To do this, Scalia decided to begin the argument where he had left off in his legislative history speech by saying one should interpret laws according to their meaning as "conveyed to a citizen" at "the time the law was enacted." By crafting the speech this way, he could also explain how his decision-making theory was different, and even better, than Bork's "original intent" theory devoted to divining "what the framers were trying to accomplish."[16]

After briefly recapitulating his legislative history speech, Scalia posed a rhetorical question: "From what you say, Judge Scalia, I presume you disagree with Attorney General Meese concerning original intent as the correct criterion for interpreting the Constitution." Like the good professor he once was, Scalia praised the work of others, knowing that his audience would like Bork's and Meese's original intent theory here. Then, for the first time, he proposed a paradigmatic shift by suggesting his own theory of "original meaning." As he put it, the term "original intent" should be redefined to mean, "not 'original intent of the Framers' but 'original intent of the Constitution.'" For Scalia, the proper question to ask was, "What was the most plausible meaning of the words of the Constitution to the society that adopted it—regardless of what the Framers might secretly have intended?" Just how his proposal would overcome the major objection to Bork's original intent theory—how to determine such a meaning—was not made clear.

Scalia argued that his theory of divining the "public meaning" of the constitutional language at the time of its ratification enabled him to go beyond the work of original intent theorists like Bork: "This does not mean, of course, that the expressions of the Framers are irrelevant. To the contrary, they are strong indications of what the most knowledgeable people of the time understood the words to mean." For Scalia, the trump card that his original meaning approach represented the more accurate and useful interpretation was: "Even if you believe in original intent in the literal sense you must end up believing in original meaning, because it is perfectly clear that the original intent was that the Constitution would be interpreted according to its original meaning." Scalia then brought his speech back full circle by arguing that determining the original intent of the Framers required judges to perform the equivalent of the same legislative history he had debunked earlier, but applying it to the Constitutional Convention.

With that, he launched into a devastating legislative history–style critique of the inadequate evidence available to determine Bork's and Meese's original intent. First, he noted that the central body of interpretive evidence for original intent advocates such as Bork, the *Journal of the Convention,* which reproduced notes of the convention, was kept under seal until 1818, published only after editing by then Secretary of State John Quincy Adams, meaning that for nearly thirty years justices of the Supreme Court had no such basis for deciding cases. Indeed, determining this meaning was a moving target as a result of the subsequent publication of James Madison's *Notes on the Debates in the Federal Convention of 1787* in 1840, *Jonathan Elliot's Debates* in the several state conventions on the adoption of the Federal Constitution five years later, and Max Farrand's more comprehensive *The Records of the Federal Convention of 1787,* published in 1911. With all of this additional historical evidence on the period, by the logic of the original intent theory, Scalia argued, "Chief Justice Burger should know more about what the Constitution originally prescribed than [the nation's third] Chief Justice [John] Marshall."

After quoting extensively from the letters of Madison, who believed that the intent of the Framers could not be divined, and the Constitutional Convention debates, which "can have no authoritative character," Scalia said he agreed with Madison that "the only authoritative intentions were those of the people of the States, as expressed through the [state] Conventions which ratified the Constitution."

It was a wonderfully self-reinforcing theory, choosing to rely not on the arguments of the Federalists in the Constitutional Convention notes, but rather on the arguments of the states' rights Anti-Federalists in the state ratifying conventions, as collected in Herbert J. Storing's volumes, *The Complete Anti-Federalist.* "I suppose I ought to campaign to change the label from the Doctrine of Original Intent to the Doctrine of Original Meaning," Scalia said further. "As I often tell my law clerks, terminology is destiny." Knowing that the decision about the Court appointment was imminent, Scalia surely hoped that his terminology would direct his destiny to the Supreme Court.

It was a remarkable speech, as through humor, intellectual ability, and a deft reshaping of the issues, Scalia demonstrated a skill at shaping an audience's views on matters beyond just the subject of the speech itself. This was Scalia at his most ambitious, reaching for the top rung on the federal judicial ladder through a campaign-style speech. The fact that it also undercut a competitor for the Court appointment could almost be lost in the friendly, entertaining tone of the speech. Because of the timing of this speech, Bork and his allies had no real chance to respond to Scalia's argument.

On Monday, June 16, two days after Scalia's speech, the president and his advisers met with him at 3:00 p.m. Just as he had done with Rehnquist, the president "came right to the point" and, after explaining that Burger would be resigning to be replaced by Rehnquist, said that Scalia "was the choice of all of us as Justice Rehnquist's successor." When Scalia "expressed his gratitude," Reagan asked him if he "would like to serve if selected." Scalia accepted the offer, "saying that he would be honored." [17] Since the Republicans controlled the Senate and South Carolina's Strom Thurmond chaired the Judiciary Committee, everyone expected that both nominations would gain swift approval.

The day after meeting with Scalia, the president appeared in the White House briefing room along with Chief Justice Burger, Justice Rehnquist, and Judge Scalia to announce his two Supreme Court appointments to a press corps still unaware of Burger's decision to retire. After recounting the events leading to these appointments and praising both of his new appointees, the president said of Scalia: "His great personal energy, the force of his intellect, and the depth of his understanding of our Constitutional jurisprudence uniquely qualify him for elevation to our highest Court."[18]

After the announcement, Scalia was asked by the assembled members of the press to comment on his legal philosophy, whether the subject of the *Roe v. Wade* abortion case was a matter of discussion in the appointment process, whether he was a "tough judge," and the precise timing and nature of his selection process. However, on all of these substantive questions, the normally loquacious Scalia followed Rehnquist's lead before him by "defer[ring]" all of that discussion until the Senate Judiciary Committee hearing. When asked about his "personal thoughts" on the appointment, Scalia could not resist: "My personal thoughts are, for somebody who spent his whole professional life in the law, getting nominated to the Supreme Court is the culmination of a dream, of course. And I'm greatly honored that the President would have such confidence in me and hope that the Senate will do so as well. And I'll certainly do whatever I can to live up to it."[19] Later, Scalia added, "Your name being mentioned for a job like that is about, you know, that plus whatever a token on the New York subway now costs will get you into the New York subway. It's very much a matter of lightning striking."[20] This auspicious occasion could have been better only if his parents had lived to see it.[21]

On August 5, with his wife and nine children seated in the front row, Scalia began his Senate confirmation hearing. Rehnquist had already faced very tough questioning before being confirmed for the chief justiceship with an extraordinarily high thirty-three votes against him.[22] Scalia looked very much like a serious intellectual sitting at the hearing room's witness table as he rolled his pipe in his left hand. Judiciary Committee chairman Thurmond began by reading softball questions prepared by his staff. Knowing that the conservative Scalia would be questioned closely by the liberals on the panel as to whether he would overturn liberal Warren Court precedents, Thurmond gave him a chance to answer the question with respect to judicial review in general. "Do you agree that *Marbury* [*v. Madison*] requires the

President and the Congress to always adhere to the Court's interpretation of the Constitution?" Thurmond asked.[23]

Scalia took the opportunity to set the ground rules as to how far he would be willing to answer questions on specific cases. "As I say, *Marbury* v. *Madison* is one of the pillars of the Constitution. To the extent that you think a nominee would be so foolish, or so extreme as to kick over one of the pillars of the Constitution, I suppose you should not confirm him. But I do not think I should answer questions regarding any specific Supreme Court opinion, even one as fundamental as *Marbury* v. *Madison*. If you could conclude from anything I have written, or anything I have said, that I would ignore *Marbury* v. *Madison*, I would . . . be in trouble, without your asking me specifically my views on *Marbury* v. *Madison*." From that point on, as they reviewed a variety of legal topics, including the Fifth Amendment–related *Miranda v. Arizona* coerced confessions case, Thurmond many times offered Scalia the chance to duck the questions. But Scalia had no problems answering questions from the conservative chairman.

When the questioner was liberal senator Edward Kennedy of Massachusetts, though, Scalia developed a reticence to answer. This was especially true when Kennedy turned the discussion to the matter on everybody's mind for this appointment. "Judge Scalia, if you were confirmed, do you expect to overrule the *Roe v. Wade* [abortion] decision?"

For the first time, Scalia played for time in answering the questions, rocking back and forth in his chair, fingering the pipe on his desk, and stroking his hair, before saying. "Senator, I do not think it would be proper for me to answer that question," later adding, "I think I would be in a very bad position to adjudicate the case without being accused of having a less than impartial view of the matter."

Kennedy tried to move the discussion in a different direction, asking how Scalia would deal with the existing pro-abortion precedent. "I am interested in your own concept of *stare decisis*. Do you believe in it? What is it going to take to overrule an existing Supreme Court decision?"

After sparring for a few minutes on how much "weight" Scalia would afford existing precedent, with Scalia seeming to support the preservation of important precedents, such as *Marbury v. Madison,* the candidate said, "I assure you, I have no agenda. I am not going onto the Court with a list of things that I want to do. My only agenda is to be a good judge. I decide the cases brought before me. And I try to decide them according to the law as best as I can figure it out. But it is not a programmatic matter, as far as I am concerned." Throughout the verbal exchanges with Kennedy and others, Scalia appeared to be highly confident and in full command of his material, as if he were the teacher and the senators were his students.

During his turn, Senator Joseph Biden turned to the June 14 speech by Scalia in seeking to explore his version of "original meaning" jurisprudence and how he would be deciding cases. "I will be happy to explain the difference between original meaning and original intent. It is not worth it. It is not a big difference." It was an intriguing answer for the man who, by design, had argued just the opposite in his speech.

Scalia elaborated on his response to show that his theory did not call for what Senator Biden called a "living Constitution." "What I think is that the Constitution is obviously not meant to be evolvable so easily that in effect a court of nine judges can treat it as though it is a bring-along-with-me statute and fill it up with whatever content the current times seem to require. To a large degree, it is intended to be an insulation against the current times, against the passions of the moment that may cause individual liberties to be disregarded, and it has served that function valuably very often. So I would never use the phrase, living Constitution." Scalia saw a different kind of constitutional evolution. "Now, there is within that phrase, however, the notion that a certain amount of development of constitutional doctrine occurs, and I think there is room for that. I frankly—the strict original intentist, I think, would say that even such a clause as the cruel and unusual punishment clause would have to mean precisely the same thing today that it meant in 1789." Scalia, though, made clear that his theory at this point was in flux on Bill of Rights phrases such as "cruel and unusual punishment." "If lashing was fine then, lashing would be fine now. I am not sure I agree with that. I think that there are some provisions of the Constitution that may have a certain amount of evolutionary content within them. . . . I have not developed a full constitutional matrix. You are right, though, in suspecting me to be more inclined to the original meaning than I am to a phrase like 'living Constitution.'"

Throughout the hearing, in contrast to William Rehnquist, who slouched to the side in his witness chair and seemed to be annoyed by having to answer the committee members' questions, Scalia appeared to be an earnest, learned, highly confident legal scholar. Presenting a pleasant personality, Scalia responded as if he wanted to help the senators understand his views and predict his future decisions, while refusing to make their interpretation easy by providing any answers dealing with controversial cases and issues. For their part, the Judiciary Committee members, exhausted by the more contentious Rehnquist hearings, seemed already certain that they would be voting for Scalia's confirmation.

The two-day hearing progressed effortlessly, and the remainder of Scalia's confirmation process could not have gone any smoother. On August 14, the Judiciary Committee approved his nomination by a unanimous 18–0 vote. And, on September 17, the full Senate approved Scalia's nomination by an astonishing 98–0 vote, with only conservative Republicans Jake Garn and Barry Goldwater, who would surely have voted favorably, not present on the floor.

The nature of this appointment and confirmation process told Scalia much about his new place in the American judicial firmament. For the only child of an entire generation of his family, and a man who always saw himself as something of an underdog fighting to the top—succeeding at Xavier when Regis would not have him, succeeding at Georgetown when Princeton would not have him, succeeding in practicing law in Cleveland when others went to New York and Washington—the fact that he had reached the pinnacle of the federal judiciary and done so by receiving an unusual, unanimous confirmation by the Senate was affirmation to him of his own excellence.[24] Years later, at a dinner in his honor, when renowned judicial scholar Henry J. Abraham of the University of Virginia mentioned in his after-dinner toast in Scalia's honor that he "had been confirmed by a vote of the Senate judiciary committee of eighteen to nothing," before he could even complete the story Scalia's voice boomed out from the back of the room, "It was ninety-eight to nothing!" Scalia's reaction, repeated in speech after speech, made clear that he took great pride in this accomplishment.[25] Another source of great pride was that he had beaten out the older and initially more visible Robert Bork for the position, the man who had enjoyed all the advantages he had not, and who had been nearly everyone's longtime odds-on choice for the nomination. For the time being, until Bork received the Supreme Court nomination that everyone expected would come, Scalia would have the stage to himself, just as he liked it, serving as the only "originalist" on the Court. Once there, as he promised in his June 14 speech, he would stake his claim as the true leader of the conservative legal movement.

But in less than five months the voters would turn control of the Senate back to the Democrats. Just a year later, when the White House was unexpectedly presented with another vacancy on the Court as a result of the retirement of the centrist swing justice Lewis Powell, the confirmation of the more controversial Bork for the swing seat on the Court was politically still-born. Had Reagan reversed the order of his appointments, choosing Bork first and then Scalia, television news reporter Jan Crawford Greenburg per-suasively argues in her book *Supreme Conflict,* both Bork and Scalia would have been easily confirmed. This would have given the conservatives, and the advocates of original meaning, a solid ideological hold on the Court ma-jority for a generation, enabling these two towering conservative legal intel-lectuals to work side by side as they had on the Court of Appeals. When Bork failed to win Senate confirmation, the appointment to fill Powell's seat went to the more moderate and less predictable Ninth Circuit Court of Appeals judge Anthony Kennedy. With that, the direction of the Court would be left in the hands of more centrist judges, including Kennedy and O'Connor.[26]

Nine days after his Senate confirmation on September 26, Scalia and his family gathered at the White House for his swearing in as associate justice of the Supreme Court. Scalia and Rehnquist were greeted by the president in the Blue Room of the White House and escorted to the East Room for the ceremony. In his brief remarks, President Reagan said of William Rehnquist that he "believe[d] he will be a Chief Justice of historic stature." And of Scalia, the president said that on the Court of Appeals "he became known for his integrity and independence and for the force of his intellect." The com-bination of these two men on the Supreme Court, promised the president, would represent "a time of renewal in the great constitutional system that our forefathers gave us," creating a judiciary observant of "judicial restraint" that would "be confined within the boundaries of the written Constitution and laws."[27] Then outgoing chief justice Warren Burger administered the constitutional oath to Rehnquist, who later did the same for Scalia.

In his brief remarks, Scalia thanked the president for the appointment, promising that he would "do my best to live up to his confidence." Scalia added, "I have to thank my wife, Maureen, who's an extraordinary woman, and without whom I wouldn't be here; or if I were here, it wouldn't have been as much fun along the way."

The reaction to Scalia's appointment to the Court by the legal commu-nity could not have been more positive. Universally, lawyers and former colleagues on the right and the left of the political spectrum predicted that Scalia would be a "consensus builder" on the Supreme Court.[28] Based on his work on the Court of Appeals, and what they described as his pleasant public temperament and collegiality, one after another of them foresaw that, just as William Brennan had united the liberals on the Warren Court of the 1960s into a potent decision-making machine, Scalia would do the same in uniting the Court's conservative wing. Professor A. E. Dick Howard of the University of Virginia said, "He brings a powerful mind, absolutely first-class intellect. Further he brings a well formed judicial philosophy. And third, he brings collegiality, he brings a pleasing, witty, warm personality that I think will make him wear well with the other people on the Court."[29] Professor Geoffrey Stone, a former colleague of Scalia at the University of Chicago, said of him, "He has the personal skills, intelligence, patience and manner to work out compromises and find common ground."[30] Even a longtime liberal judicial opponent, former Court of Appeals colleague Abner Mikva, said of Scalia that he was "aware that you can't always have it your own way. . . . When he's in doubt, he'll look for a middle ground. . . . I think he'll be a good justice. He has an appropriate amount of humility. It won't go to his head."[31] Scalia's former student at Chicago Law School, now Court of Appeals judge Michael McConnell, said of him, "I will predict you will not see him running off and writing separate opinions merely because he takes exceptions with small issues or details. . . . He believes it is important to the country for the Court to get together and to speak with a single voice, to provide actual resolution to the issues."[32]

In making these predictions, however, all of these associates and friends proved to be incorrect. Having fulfilled all of his career ambitions, unrestrained by any need to play a subordinate role to other conservatives, and seeing no reason to be subservient to his new judicial colleagues, the justice who arrived at the Supreme Court would prove to be very different from the Court of Appeals judge who had begun that journey. Contrary to Judge McConnell's observation, on the highest federal court Scalia was indeed ready to serve on a court that spoke "with a single voice," so long as it was *his* voice.

CHAPTER 9

A Court of One

When the Supreme Court opened on the first Monday in October of 1986, its newest member, Antonin Scalia, had taken occupancy of the former chambers of retired Justice Potter Stewart. Scalia assumed his seat on the bench to the far left of Chief Justice Rehnquist's center chair, moving the next junior justice, Sandra Day O'Connor, over to the far right chair. He joined a balanced Court consisting of four conservatives, four liberals, and one swing justice, who determined the Court's holding on nearly every issue by moving back and forth between the two wings.

Leading the conservative wing was Chief Justice Rehnquist, a former member of Nixon's Office of Legal Counsel, who was beginning his tenure as chief justice at age sixty-two after serving as an associate justice for fifteen years. While an associate justice, he built a record of solo conservative dissents on an already conservative court and became known as the "Lone Ranger." (He was even given a doll of the character by his law clerks.) He was by far the most ideologically conservative member of the Court. Another of the Court's reliable conservatives was, ironically, a Democrat, sixty-nine-year-old Byron White, who had been appointed to the Court in 1962 by President Kennedy. He was a former NFL football star nicknamed "Whizzer White" for his slashing running style. White's political philosophy changed during his twenty-three years on the Court, and by 1986 he could be counted among the conservatives except for issues involving racial relations and the death penalty.[1]

The conservative with whom Scalia seemed ideologically to have the most in common was the youngest of the group, fifty-six-year-old Sandra Day O'Connor. Appointed by Ronald Reagan in 1981, she was the first woman to serve on the High Court. The daughter of Duncan, Arizona, cattle rancher Harry Day, a "harsh, demanding, unpredictable man," she was dispatched at age six, during the depths of the Great Depression, to live with her maternal grandmother and attend public schools in El Paso, Texas.[2] Later she attended the Radford School for Girls, eventually graduating from the El Paso public high school. In visits home to her family's ranch, she was treated like the cowboys and expected to make her contribution by riding a horse and helping herd cattle. Out of this experience she developed a fierce sense of frontier independence that served her well when she attended Stanford University, and later graduated in the 1952 Stanford Law School class, along with Rehnquist, whom she had briefly dated.

Despite her academic success, in the sexist world of the law, O'Connor could not find a job in a private law firm and was offered only a legal secretarial position. She turned to the public sector, working as a deputy attorney general in San Mateo County, California, and eventually moved to Arizona with her husband, John O'Connor, and opened her own law firm. There she became involved in Republican Party politics, and when there was an opening in the Arizona State Senate in 1965, she was appointed to fill it. She remained there for two more terms before becoming a judge—first on the Maricopa County Superior Court, then in 1979 on the Arizona Court of Appeals, the state's highest court.[3] A lifelong Republican, appointed by President Reagan to fulfill a 1980 presidential campaign promise, O'Connor had nearly always voted with the conservative justices during her five years on the Supreme Court.

In working with these conservatives, Scalia would find his place. Since he was, in effect, replacing the conservative vote of the retired Chief Justice Warren Burger, he was expected to give the conservative group a reliable vote, maintaining the status quo.

Opposing the conservatives on almost every issue were four liberals. Anchoring the liberal wing of the Court were its two oldest members. William Brennan, age eighty, a beloved, elfinlike liberal Catholic and natural political compromiser, was appointed from the New Jersey State Supreme Court to the Court in 1957 by President Dwight Eisenhower. Brennan became the playmaking lieutenant for Chief Justice Earl Warren—another Eisenhower appointee—on the liberal, activist Court of the 1960s. Brennan was known to walk around the Court waving five fingers in the air, saying, "Five. Five votes can do anything around here."[4] For the past sixteen years, Brennan had tried, with only limited success, to prevent the conservatives under Warren Burger from wiping out his legacy from the Warren Court.[5]

Joining Brennan on the left was the Court's first African American justice, the legendary seventy-eight-year-old Thurgood Marshall. A Howard Law School graduate who had successfully argued the *Brown v. Board of Education* school desegregation case before the Supreme Court in 1954, Marshall did almost as much for ending the Jim Crow "separate but equal" laws in the legal arena as the Reverend Martin Luther King Jr. did in the political arena.[6] Marshall was appointed to the Court in 1967 by President Johnson, and he largely served as Brennan's "wing man." With the exception of race relations and death penalty cases, he relied heavily on his law clerks for the drafting of his opinions.

The other two members of the liberal wing were both appointments by Republican presidents who turned out not to be the conservative jurists they were expected to become. Harry Blackmun, age seventy-eight, was a former judge on the Court of Appeals for the Eighth Circuit whom Nixon appointed in 1970 to fill the seat opened by the forced resignation of liberal Abe Fortas. The humble and empathetic Blackmun liked to refer to himself as "Ole Number Three," referring to his appointment to the Court after Nixon's first two nominees, Clement F. Haynsworth and G. Harrold Carswell, failed to be confirmed by the Democratically controlled Senate. But to others he was initially known by another nickname, the "Minnesota Twin," because ideologically he so closely mirrored the conservative decisions of fellow Minnesotan Chief Justice Burger, his close friend. By the early 1980s, however, Blackmun had become more liberal and eventually the Court's most reliable liberal voter.[7]

The final member of the liberal bloc, John Paul Stevens, then sixty-six, was initially seen as a moderate conservative when he was appointed in 1975 to replace ultraliberal William O. Douglas by President Ford. Stevens, the son of a prominent Chicago hotel owner who had lost his fortune and gone to jail for embezzlement before his conviction was reversed on appeal, was a World War II Navy veteran who had served in the code-breaking intelligence service. He later served with distinction on the Court of Appeals for the Seventh Circuit, distinguishing himself by leading the Greenburg Commission ethics investigation of two wayward judicial colleagues, resulting in both men leaving the court.[8] The combination of his father's legal experience and the ethics investigation of fellow jurists left Stevens with a powerful sense of fairness and appreciation for due process. After joining the Supreme Court, Stevens evolved into a staunchly liberal jurist.[9]

With four reliable votes on each side, the swing justice often determined which side would win. Lewis Powell, age seventy-nine, held that position in

1986. He was a World War II veteran who had worked on Operation Ultra intelligence program and was the only member of that Court to come from private law practice, in Richmond, Virginia. He had been the chairman of the Richmond School Board and overseen the integration of the Richmond schools after the *Brown* decision. With the Court ideologically locked into a 4–4 vote, it was left to Powell, fueled by his moderate conservatism, and practical common law wisdom and fairness, to cast the tie-breaking vote and shaping compromise Court judgments on almost every issue. It was said, "As Lewis Powell goes, so goes the Court." [10]

If Scalia came to the Court thinking that he might by the power of his considerable intellect and argumentative skills be able to change the minds of the senior justices in conference discussions, he was very quickly disabused of this notion. His good relations on the Court were undermined by his powerful ego, and his growing desire for public attention. Scalia discovered that the most junior jurist on the Supreme Court had little to no real influence in the decision-making process, and received little attention for his efforts. Having his swearing in come so near the start of the term, Scalia did not participate in the first meeting in which the members of the Court chose which appeals to hear early that term. When he did attend his first conference, Scalia discovered, "Not very much conferencing goes on. In fact, to call our discussion of a case a conference is really something of a misnomer. It's much more a statement of the views of each of the nine justices, after which the totals are added and the case is assigned [for the drafting of the opinion]." [11] Worse still for him, as the junior justice, he spoke and voted last, meaning that by the time he voiced his views, the outcome had almost always been determined. One of Scalia's law clerks, Lee Liberman Otis, who served with him on both the D.C. Court of Appeals and the Supreme Court, would later say that it was "different [for him] because people on the D.C. Circuit actually did talk over cases. . . . That was the biggest surprise—the Supreme Court justices didn't talk with one another about cases. . . . Three people [on an appeals court panel] can talk about something; nine people can't talk about something." [12] Scalia's sole assignment as the newest member of the Court was, by the institution's tradition, to replace Sandra Day O'Connor as the doorkeeper for the conference room where the justices met.

Far younger at age fifty than nearly all of his new colleagues, Scalia now needed to decide how he would begin his journey among them. Contrary to his June 14 speech just before his appointment to the Supreme Court, where he laid the foundations for his original meaning alternative to Robert Bork's intent of the Framers' theory, Scalia's earliest decisions on the Supreme Court, like his decisions on the federal Court of Appeals in the District of Columbia, did not follow this proposed single, central decision-making principle.[13] Instead, Scalia's decisions in those earliest terms were largely governed by his notion of textualism, to limit the discretion and power of a judge by basing one's decisions on a close reading of the text.

Universally predicted to become a man who would use his gregarious personality and his skilled argumentation to unite the frequently disparate forces of the conservatives on the Court, Scalia, instead, had a different plan. He was determined *not* to be like other freshman justices who served unobtrusively as apprentices to the more senior jurists, allying with an ideological mentor and hewing to a central bloc while learning the judicial craft through noncontroversial opinion writing.[14] These "Freshman Justices," as they were called by legal scholars, often journeyed through an initial bewilderment phase, learning their fantastically difficult new job before traversing through an acclimation period for several Court terms, in what became known as the "apprenticeship" process.[15] Only then was a new justice prepared to go beyond gravitating toward a centrist bloc to minimize the anxiety of the position by joining one of the two ideological cliques of the group.[16]

Scalia, though, hardly lacking in confidence, in his initial term decided to do the opposite. Instead of bonding with an older mentor, gravitating toward the center of the Court, and serving his apprenticeship period for several terms, Scalia aggressively signaled to his more senior colleagues from the first moment he arrived on the Court that in his mind he was their equal, if not superior.[17]

From his first appearance on the bench, Scalia sought to make an impression in oral argument. In the case of *Hodel v. Irving,* which dealt with a federal law limiting the ability of Native Americans to bequeath to their heirs small portions of their tribal land, he quickly made himself, in the words of journalist Stephen J. Adler, "the center of attention."[18] Ignoring the fact that he was one of nine justices questioning the attorneys, Scalia treated the oral argument as one of his law school classes, playing the role of the professor, grilling the attorneys as though they were his students. He prepped for each of these oral arguments as though he were arguing each case before the Court himself. Prior to every argument, Scalia had one of his law clerks draft a memo summarizing all of the issues in the case and suggesting how he should vote. Then before the formal Court appearance, the former college debater would argue the issues in the case with his clerk, sometimes for as much as an hour, to get a feel for how the upcoming discussion might develop.

The *Hodel* case explored the meaning of the federal Indian Land Consolidation Act of 1983, which prevented Native Americans from the Oglala Sioux tribe from passing very small portions of tribal land to their heirs upon their death, and instead having them revert to, or in legal terms *escheat*, back to the tribe. The question became whether this was a taking of property without just compensation in violation of the Fifth Amendment of the United States Constitution. One of the perplexing issues in this case was just who had standing, that is, how tribal members could demonstrate enough personal injury to justify their ability to sue. They were arguing a concept called "third party standing," that even though others, members of the previous generation, had suffered injury by having their ability to pass on their land stripped from them, the loss was now visited upon the next generation, who could not receive the property. The problem with this concept from their side was that the older generation members were now dead, seemingly negating legal standing in the case unless the Court agreed with the third party standing concept.

During Assistant U.S. Solicitor General Edwin Kneedler's presentation, legal reporters such as Stephen Adler were mesmerized by how Scalia made it clear that he was ready to insert himself into the discussion: "A roving courtroom camera would find something catlike about Scalia as he gets set to ask a question. He sits forward, deepens the furrow in his already furrowed brow, puts a hand on his forehead, then his chin, takes his glasses off and puts them in his mouth, puts them back on, opens his mouth, closes it, opens it again, and pounces."[19]

With nine members on the Court doing the interrogation, and each attorney having only thirty minutes to present his case, it had generally been the practice for each justice as a courtesy to limit himself to a single question, often with a follow-up or two. Scalia instead monopolized the Court's argument in his first appearance with ten questions and comments in a row, consuming four minutes and fifteen seconds, in making clear his skepticism about the third-party standing concept. While this performance by the newest junior justice thrilled the journalists in the audience, it failed to captivate the other members of the Court. Midway through Scalia's questioning, Lewis Powell leaned over and whispered to Justice Marshall, "Do you think he knows that the rest of us are here?"[20] The answer, they all soon learned, was that Scalia did not care. After a handful of questions from three colleagues, Scalia jumped back in, saying that he was "still hung up on the standing point," and proceeded to ask nine more questions in a row, consuming the rest of the attorneys' time. Scalia had signaled to his colleagues what he believed to be both the importance and the suspect nature of these seemingly routine standing questions relied on by the tribal members suing the government, by pressing the questions with the *government's* representative.[21] It appeared that he wanted to take control of the decision and make the case go his way.

As the months went by, Scalia's domination of the Court's oral argument did not abate. Later that term, Adler charted the number of questions in one eight-argument period and found that Scalia asked 126 questions, nearly one-third more than the next most active questioner, Byron White, double that of the new chief justice, and many more than the rest of the Court.[22] Court journalists were captivated by the "obvious joy [Scalia] gets from a good argument and the infectiousness of this enthusiasm." Scalia loved the job, telling his good friend Washington attorney Leonard Garment, while "roll[ing] his eyes heavenward in delight," that he was "truly blessed to have this [Court position] in addition to everything else in his life."[23] But he still had a lot to learn about life on a nine-person Court, even if he did not realize it.

Normally the chief justice finds an easy, straightforward case to be assigned for a new justice's maiden opinion. That Rehnquist would do, assigning Scalia to write the majority in *O'Connor v. United States,* a minor case dealing with an income tax question for the United States government employees and their spouses of the Panama Canal Commission, which took only twenty days to resolve.[24]

But Scalia chose not to be bound to the Court "apprenticeship" tradition. While he had not won his first oral argument in the *Hodel v. Irving* case by persuading his colleagues that the litigants had no standing, he was far from done. Justice John Paul Stevens was assigned by the chief to write an opinion seeking a majority to uphold a broad right of standing in *Hodel.* Scalia notified Stevens, "I think it is possible to find standing here under a more limited theory," that is, limiting the third-party standing concept. Serving notice that as far as he was concerned, his monthlong apprenticeship period on the Court was now over, Scalia continued: "I intend to try my hand at an opinion along these lines in the hope of persuading you [Stevens] and the rest of my colleagues."[25] With these words the most junior justice on the Court served notice that he was going to write his own opinion in an effort to steal the majority in *Hodel*.

What should have been a relatively routine case drifted along until February 20, 1987, when Scalia finally wrote his concurring opinion. After redrafting his argument, he gained the votes of the chief justice and Thurgood Marshall, and opened up the possibility that he could add Lewis Powell, who wrote on his draft: "I am persuaded by your fine concurring opinion. With a few changes, I think I can join you." [26] Scalia made Powell's requested change and was only one vote short of gaining a majority. [27]

But it was Sandra Day O'Connor who gained the majority by effecting "a compromise between Nino's approach and the approach in my dissent" while ruling in favor of the Native Americans seeking to be compensated for their lost inheritance. [28] O'Connor argued: "The regulation destroyed 'one of the most essential sticks in the bundle of rights that are commonly characterized as property—the right to exclude others.' . . . In one form or another, the right to pass on property—to one's family in particular—has been part of the Anglo-American legal system since feudal times." [29]

Scalia, however, refused to give in, writing both Rehnquist and Powell that he would "join enough of [O'Connor's] opinion to create a disposition for the Court," but would also "have a revised concurrence in your hands by the morning, which I hope you will both continue to be able to join." [30] In short, for the second time, he would seek to undermine a more senior colleague on this case. The gambit did not work. Scalia circulated a revised concurrence expressing his disagreement with O'Connor's interpretation of one of the precedents that she linked to the case, a 1979 case called *Andrus v. Allard*, in which the Court supported the "abrogation of the right to sell endangered eagles' parts" under an environmental protection law. But Scalia then went far beyond a simple disagreement with O'Connor's interpretation of precedent and the case's facts to attack O'Connor's work, saying that her draft "mistakes the object of the inquiry," "misidentifies the interest to be balanced," and represents "an approach which is to my knowledge unprecedented." [31]

Unimpressed by Scalia's analysis, Powell was also offended by the personal attack on O'Connor. Abandoning his normally reserved, gentlemanly demeanor, Powell scrawled, "I don't like this" on Scalia's draft. [32] He also wrote to Scalia that his own interpretation of the precedent was "closer to Sandra's than to yours," and he had been "worried about this for a week or more." Sensing that a rift was already growing between Scalia and Powell, Rehnquist felt compelled to insert himself as an intermediary between the two men. After Powell had spoken to him twice about the situation, the chief justice persuaded Scalia to make enough changes in his concurrence to keep Powell and Rehnquist in agreement with him.[33]

Scalia, though, was oblivious to his senior colleague's unease and still unwilling to concede to O'Connor. He wrote O'Connor that if she minimized the reference to the *Andrus* precedent that he interpreted differently, he would "be able to join most of the opinion for the Court." A frustrated O'Connor wrote to the rest of the Court that she "had hoped the redrafting in this case was finally at an end, but Nino has advised me that if I would return to where I began—with only a brief reference to *Andrus v. Allard*—he would be able to join most of the opinion for the Court." Scalia's combativeness and intransigence had turned a routine case that the Court should have handled in a month or so into a protracted six-month negotiation and opinion-drafting operation. An exasperated Powell scrawled on the memo in which O'Connor informed the Court that in the interest of harmony she had made the change demanded by Scalia, "An unhappy case for all of us!!"[34] Later, Powell, seemingly recording events for future historians, would write in an account of the case on the margin of Scalia's next draft that he "unhappily joined Nino because I had joined his full opinion earlier, and also because the C.J. [chief justice] hoped I'd stay with Nino."[35] Though Scalia in the end reduced the size of his concurrence to a paragraph, the damage to his relationship with Lewis Powell had been done. Other members of the Court could see that life was not going to be the same with Scalia as their colleague.

As the term went along, Scalia sought to carve out a leadership position over his conservative colleagues, but in doing so he annoyed them more than he influenced them. He continued to lose support from Powell. Powell's biographer John Jeffries writes of their relationship:

> While Powell admired Scalia's formidable intelligence and obvious ability, he found his intellectual ardor vaguely unsettling. Zest for theory and new ideas did not strike a responsive chord in a man who relied chiefly on experience. . . . Scalia's boundless energy and pugnaciousness, which his many friends admired, struck his quiet, self-deprecating older colleague as almost uncivil. . . . As one clerk who worked for both Justices put it: "Those two wouldn't agree on

whether the sky was blue." After a pause, he added: "On second thought, they would agree, but for different reasons."[36]

Seemingly unaware of the disharmony that he had already created with Powell, Scalia almost immediately resumed his uninvited tutorial of Justice O'Connor.[37] The case of *O'Connor v. Ortega* involved the search of the office and computer of a doctor, employed by a state hospital, who was accused of improprieties. In a controlling plurality opinion, O'Connor ruled that the doctor was protected against "unreasonable seizures" from his office under the Fourth Amendment because he had a "reasonable expectation of privacy."[38] O'Connor explained that while the privacy of a public employee's business office must be assessed "on a case-by-case basis," the decision rule to be used here was whether the office is "so open to fellow employees or the public that no expectation of privacy is reasonable."[39] Once again, Scalia disagreed and sought to express his unhappiness with his colleague's decision-making technique. In a concurrence, he objected to the vagueness of O'Connor's rule, arguing that "No clue is provided as to how open 'so open' must be; much less is it suggested how police officers are to gather the facts necessary for this refined inquiry." Then, taking dead aim at O'Connor, he added: "I would object to the formulation of a standard so devoid of content that it produces rather than eliminates uncertainty in this field."[40]

• • •

At the beginning of his tenure on the Court, Scalia sought to establish his textualism theory as the basis for his judicial decision-making theory. In a series of impressive dissents Scalia demonstrated his new theory of basing decisions on the dictionary definition of the Constitution's or statute's words. Here the Court's most junior justice demonstrated a dazzling ability to solve perplexing legal issues armed mainly with an out-of-date dictionary, demonstrating an etymologist's skill for determining word origins, and relying on his ability to parse semantics and grammar. In seeking to determine the meaning of the Constitution, and the Bill of Rights, which were ratified in 1788 and 1791 respectively, he turned to the American dictionary published closest to the time that the words were written, Noah Webster's *American Dictionary of the English Language*, published in 1828. This book, which is now reproduced for fundamentalist Christians by the Foundation for American Christian Education, is big enough and thick enough to double as a doorstop for a large church door. Measuring eight and a half inches by eleven inches and over two and a half inches thick, it contains the definitions of every word that Webster encountered in his travels around the United States, beginning in 1807.[41] Ignoring the gap in time between the drafting of the words he was analyzing and the dictionary's publication, Scalia argued that this tool enabled him to accurately determine the meaning of the words written by the Framers of the Constitution and the Bill of Rights.

Scalia demonstrated his textualism theory in a dissent for the case of *Edwards v. Aguillard*, a case that overturned Louisiana's Balanced Treatment for Creation-Science and Evolution-Science in Public School Instruction Act, passed in 1987. This law required the teaching of creationism—the theory that the earth was created as described in the biblical book of Genesis—in public school science classes wherever Darwin's theory of evolution by natural selection was taught. The law's challengers argued that creationism is a religious belief, and as such, teaching it in public schools violated the First Amendment's prohibition on establishment of religion. Writing for a seven-person majority, Justice William Brennan argued that the law violated the 1973 *Lemon v. Kurtzman* three-pronged test, requiring that any law suspected of connecting religion and government have a "secular purpose," have an effect that "neither advances nor inhibits religion," and not create an "excessive entanglement between church and state." The failure to meet any one of these standards would put the law in violation of the First Amendment's prohibition on establishment of religion. For the majority, the Louisiana creationism act was overturned because it violated both the purpose and effect prongs of the *Lemon* test: "The purpose of the Creationism Act was to restructure the science curriculum to conform with a particular religious viewpoint. . . . [And] the Creationism Act is designed either to promote the theory of creation science which embodies a particular religious tenet by requiring that creation science be taught whenever evolution is taught or to prohibit the teaching of a scientific theory disfavored by certain religious sects by forbidding the teaching of evolution when creation science is not also taught."[42]

While Scalia did not disagree with the religious source of this law, he relied on his textual interpretation of the First Amendment to support his goal of increasing the connection, or accommodation, between church and state. Arguing in favor of judicial "self-restraint" when confronted with a duly enacted bill of a state legislature, Scalia saw a "secular purpose" to the law. He argued that the ruling, which for him unfairly assumed unconstitutional motives impelling the state legislators "each of whom had sworn to support the Constitution," and came before the law was implemented, was too hasty. He said in his dissent, "Had requirements of the Balanced Treatment Act that are not apparent on its face been clarified by an interpretation of the Louisiana Supreme Court, or by the manner of its implementation, the Act might well be found unconstitutional; but the question of its constitutionality cannot rightly be disposed of on the gallop, by impugning the motives of its supporters."[43]

Then Scalia applied his textual analysis of the term "creation science" in the statute itself to conclude: "We can only guess at its meaning. We know that it forbids instruction in either 'creation-science' or 'evolution-science' without instruction in the other . . . but the parties are sharply divided over what creation science consists of." Arguing that both sides in the case can find "considerable support in the legislative history" of the law for their own version of the "intended meaning" of creationism, Scalia sided with the religious groups that the term "creation science" did not include religious overtones. " 'Creation science' is unquestionably a 'term of art' . . . and thus, under Louisiana law, is 'to be interpreted according to [its] received meaning and acceptation with the learned in the art, trade or profession to which [it] refer[s].' . . . [The] experts [in this case] insist that creation science is a strictly scientific concept that can be presented without religious reference. . . . At this point, then, we must assume that the Balanced Treatment Act does not require the presentation of religious doctrine."[44] For him, textualism trumped Brennan's analysis of legislative intent.

Launching a religious battle that would become a central focus for him for decades to come, Scalia also challenged the majority's use of the prevailing Establishment Clause test in *Lemon v. Kurtzman*, to rule that the law violated the separation of church and state. Scalia argued that the prong of the *Lemon* test that required that a law should have a secular purpose should be abandoned because it had "made such a maze of the Establishment Clause that even the most conscientious governmental officials can only guess what [legislative] motives will be held unconstitutional." No one, he argued, could determine what constituted an acceptable "secular purpose" of legislation. As for his future approach in the Establishment of Religion cases, Scalia announced, his goal was "abandoning Lemon's purpose test."[45] Scalia's disenchantment with the majority's use of each element of the three-pronged *Lemon* test to separate church and state under the Establishment Clause of the First Amendment grew by the term.

During his first term Scalia hinted that he might be ready to move beyond just looking at the dictionary definition of the Constitution's words to make his judgments. In the case of *Booth v. Maryland*, the Court overturned a death penalty sentence as a violation of the "cruel and unusual punishment" prohibition in the Eighth Amendment because the prosecutor had read a victim impact statement during the sentencing phase of the jury. For the five-person majority, led by Justice Lewis Powell, the danger was that the sentencing jury would hear evidence that had not been used in the trial and conviction phase. And so, Powell reasoned, to require this form of victim impact evidence in the penalty phase "would create the risk that a death sentence will be based on considerations that are constitutionally impermissible or totally irrelevant to the sentencing process."[46]

In dissent, Scalia could find no justification for Powell's decision in his copy of the U.S. Constitution, and seemed prepared to go beyond that document in deciding this case: "The principle upon which the Court's opinion rests—that the imposition of capital punishment is to be determined solely on the basis of moral guilt—does not exist, neither in the text of the Constitution, nor in the historic practices of our society, nor even in the opinions of this Court."[47] Since his textualism theory would not completely resolve this issue, Scalia indicated that he was also prepared to go beyond a dictionary reading of the Bill of Rights, in this case the Eighth Amendment, to determine "the historic practices of our society" in order to decide that victim impact statements should be allowed. Just how one did this, and where it might lead, would be left for another day.

As Scalia's first term on the Court ended in June 1987, with the nation fully involved in its Bicentennial celebration of the drafting of the Constitution, the Reagan Department of Justice began circulating a "Report to the Attorney General" dealing with the critical question of how to interpret that document. Titled "Original Meaning Jurisprudence: A Sourcebook," it explained through a summary report containing questions and answers outlining this interpretive theory, supplemented by a compilation of writings and speeches, how judges should be limited in their interpretation of the Constitution by adhering to the meaning of the document when it was first drafted and ratified. The report generated some legal intellectual fireworks between Justice William Brennan and Reagan attorney general Edwin Meese. Having watched Robert Bork develop his restrictive "intent of the Framers" judicial interpretive theory, limiting the reach of the Constitution to the meaning understood by its authors, on October 12, 1985, Brennan, one of the last remaining liberal Warren Court holdovers, argued in a "text and teaching symposium" at Georgetown University on behalf of what he called a "public reading of the text" that was "evolutionary" in meaning. The Court, he said, should allow the constitutional protections and guarantees to grow over time and through the generations. Brennan argued:

> We current Justices read the Constitution in the only way that we can: as Twentieth Century Americans. We look to the history to the time of framing and the intervening history of interpretation. But the ultimate question must be, what do the words of the text mean in our time. For the genius of the Constitution rests not in any static meaning it might have had in a world that is dead and gone, but in the adaptability of its great principles to cope with current problems and current needs. What the constitutional fundamentals meant to the wisdom of other times cannot be their measure to the vision of our time. Similarly, what those fundamentals mean for us, our descendants will learn, cannot be the measure to the vision of their time.[48]

A month later, in mid-November 1985, Attorney General Meese responded to Brennan by telling the District of Columbia Lawyers' Division of the Federalist Society that "the text and intention of the Constitution must be understood to constitute the banks within which constitutional interpretation must flow." Meese explained his means for constitutional interpretation in terms similar to Bork's intent of the Framers' process. "In the main a jurisprudence that seeks to be faithful to our Constitution—a jurisprudence of original intention, as I have called it—is not difficult to describe. Where the language of the Constitution is specific, it must be obeyed. Where there is a demonstrable consensus among the framers and ratifiers as to a principle stated or implied by the Constitution, it should be followed. Where there is ambiguity as to the precise meaning or reach of constitutional provision, it should be interpreted and applied in a manner so as to at least not contradict the text of the Constitution itself." What he argued as a "fidelity to the Constitution" was "not [a] jurisprudence of political results," but rather one that "seeks to de-politicize the law."[49]

Relying on this theory, in the 1987 *Bowers v. Hardwick* gay rights case, Justice Byron White argued that the Georgia anti-sodomy law at issue in the case should be upheld. In his view, there was no right protecting this behavior in the Constitution, the practice had historically been banned by the Christian religion, and similarly restrictive laws had been adopted in twenty-five other states. For White, it was a matter of following historical and societal norms:

> Proscriptions against that conduct have ancient roots. . . . Sodomy was a criminal offense at common law and was forbidden by the laws of the original 13 States when they ratified the Bill of Rights. In 1868, when the Fourteenth Amendment was ratified, all but 5 of the 37 States in the Union had criminal sodomy laws. In fact, until 1961, all 50 States outlawed sodomy, and today, 24 States and the District of Columbia continue to provide criminal penalties for sodomy performed in private and between consenting adults. Against this background, to claim that a right to engage in such conduct is "deeply rooted in this Nation's history and tradition" or "implicit in the concept of ordered liberty" is, at best, facetious.

In dissent, Justice Harry Blackmun argued that the case was not about a "right to commit sodomy" as White argued, but rather a "right to personal autonomy privacy." For him, the Due Process Clause of the Fourteenth Amendment protected "the right to choose for themselves how to conduct their intimate relationships" as part of the "right to be let alone."[50] It was this debate, between the intent of the Framer theorists, including textualists such as Scalia, and the living, evolving interpreters of the Constitution, such as Brennan and Blackmun, that would frame the jurisprudential arguments on the Court for decades to come. But after this case it would go on without Justice Powell, who, at age eighty, decided to retire for reasons of health at the end of the 1986–87 term.

The balance of the Supreme Court appeared about to shift definitively toward the conservative, historical interpretation side on June 23, 1987, when President Reagan announced that the nation's most visible conservative legal theorist, Robert Bork, Scalia's former colleague on the Court of Appeals for the District of Columbia, would replace the retiring swing justice. This appointment would provide Scalia with a reliable ally in his effort to turn judicial interpretation of the Constitution and the Bill of Rights back to the Framers' understanding of their meaning. But the appointment was put in immediate jeopardy when, less than an hour after the announcement of Bork's nomination, Senator Ted Kennedy went to the Senate floor to deliver a speech attacking Bork:

Robert Bork's America is a land in which women would be forced into back-alley abortions, blacks would sit at segregated lunch counters, rogue police could break down citizens' doors in midnight raids, schoolchildren could not be taught about evolution, writers and artists could be censored at the whim of the Government, and the doors of the Federal courts would be shut on the fingers of millions of citizens for whom the judiciary is—and is often the only—protector of the individual rights that are the heart of our democracy. America is a better and freer nation than Robert Bork thinks. Yet in the current delicate balance of the Supreme Court, his rigid ideology will tip the scales of justice against the kind of country America is and ought to be.[51]

The confirmation battle could not have gone worse for the Republicans, largely because of the timing. Reagan was now a much less powerful lame-duck president in the final two years of his presidency, dealing with the negative fallout from the revelations of the Iran-contra scandal. After the 1986 election, the Senate was controlled by the Democrats, meaning that the Senate Judiciary Committee was no longer led by conservative Strom Thurmond of South Carolina, but rather by liberal Senator Joe Biden of Delaware. A massive coalition of liberal interest groups on abortion, race relations, and women's rights led by Ralph Neas, called the People for the American Way, knew they would get an extended opposition hearing in the proceeding.[52] And for the first time, this confirmation battle would play out on national television, making it even more of a partisan-driven media circus.

The Reagan administration failed to prepare Bork adequately for the virulence of the questions that he would face from the Senate panel.[53] Bork, sporting a goatee that made him look more like an academic than a judicial candidate, was not prepared for the impact of his impenetrable, lengthy scholarly answers to simple Senate questions that did not play well on the nightly television news. Broadcasters covered Bork's lengthy analysis of the *Griswold v. Connecticut* case, which ruled unconstitutional laws limiting access to birth control, with a sound bite from Biden, who responded simply with, "But judge, police in the bedrooms!" The most damaging question, beyond whether he would "roll back" the rights of women and minorities, came when Bork was asked why he wanted to be on the Supreme Court. He answered that for him it would be "an intellectual feast." It was a response that dismayed and frightened many liberal senators.[54]

The hearings dragged on through the summer, and when the Senate finally voted on the nomination on October 23, Bork amassed only forty-two votes, while fifty-eight senators voted against the nomination. The vote was as much of a turning point for Scalia as it was for Bork. Scalia was now completely free of the intellectual shadow of Robert Bork. He and he alone would represent the original interpretation theory on the Supreme Court. Scalia was now a "Court of One" on the Court and in the legal conservative community. Bork would soon leave the Court of Appeals to write books, give speeches, and become a public intellectual. Scalia would decide cases, laying the groundwork for his own theory of interpreting the Constitution. He would write the text for judicial originalism, relegating Bork's work to its footnotes.

CHAPTER 10

Faint-Hearted Originalist

After Robert Bork failed to be confirmed for the Supreme Court, observers wondered whether Scalia would have a conservative ally on the Court. For a time it was not clear. The next person to be nominated by Reagan to fill Powell's seat was Douglas H. Ginsburg, also a Court of Appeals judge from the District of Columbia. Ginsburg was seen as a "stealth candidate," nominated because, after the well-known Bork's fate, the Reagan administration believed that a less known candidate would be more successful in the Senate confirmation process. The problem with the strategy, though, was that the less well known the candidate, the more imperfect the vetting process by the Justice Department that might expose fatal weaknesses endangering the likelihood of Senate confirmation. In this case, the Justice Department vetting process did not turn up allegations that Ginsburg had been at a party of law faculty and students at Harvard University where marijuana was being smoked. In the new partisan confirmation circus, this allegation was sufficient to force Ginsburg to withdraw his nomination.[1]

After two failures, the administration finally found a confirmable candidate in federal Ninth Circuit Court of Appeals Judge Anthony Kennedy, who, despite having published nearly 1,200 opinions, was almost unknown nationally. Like Judge Ginsburg, Kennedy was a stealth candidate, but this time with better results. When Kennedy raised neither ideological nor personal objections among the battle-weary senators, he received a unanimous 97–0 vote for his confirmation. He joined the court in February 1988.

The fifty-one-year-old Kennedy was the same age as Scalia, and had attended the same law school, but it was their differences that would define their relationship. Kennedy's father, Anthony, called "Bud" by acquaintances, made his living in his solo law practice as a trial lawyer and a lobbyist with the state government on behalf of the California liquor and tobacco industries.[2] Rather than growing up in Scalia's world of books, classes, and languages, Kennedy came to the dinner table to find the politically connected clients of his father, and he was urged to participate in the evening's political discussions.[3] Unlike Scalia's devoutly conservative Catholic immigrant father, Kennedy was raised by Catholic parents based in the more openly inclusive religious mores of Sacramento, California.[4] His early boyhood was spent not in a Catholic military prep school learning Latin, but being tutored in a legal and political home. As a teenager, Anthony traveled with his father throughout Northern California to serve as his law clerk, helping him by taking notes at the counsel's table during trial, and typing up legal documents for his father's cases late into the night. Through his father's political contacts, Anthony also served as the then youngest page boy in the California state legislature.[5]

Kennedy attended Stanford, and spent his final year at the London School of Economics. Academically talented enough to be admitted to Harvard Law School, unlike Scalia, who became an editor of the *Harvard Law Review* in the class ahead of him, Kennedy lacked the grades to make law review and graduated only *cum laude,* the lowest level of graduation honors. After graduation from Harvard, he went into private law practice in San Francisco for two years, but when his father suddenly died of a heart attack, he returned to Sacramento to take over his father's practice for several years before joining another private practice.[6] Kennedy married his childhood sweetheart and raised his family in his childhood home, continuing to be an active member in the neighborhood. He also taught constitutional law at McGeorge School of Law at the University of the Pacific, located near his home.[7]

Appointed to the Court of Appeals in 1975, at the age of thirty-eight, Kennedy served for twelve years, revealing a conservative ideology with libertarian instincts on social issues. Kennedy was less combative than Scalia and devoted to educating people about American civics. Even after a dozen years on the federal Court of Appeals it was not entirely clear which decision-making approach he would use once on the High Court. No one could be certain how much he might agree or disagree with the textualism approach being developed by Scalia.[8]

With the appointment of a new colleague, Scalia began in his second term on the Court to extend beyond his textualism theory in order to follow what he called the historical tradition of a legal concept. In time, he would call this expanded historical decision-making technique the issue's "text and tradition."[9] As Scalia had proposed in his June 14, 1986, speech right before his Supreme Court appointment, his historically based theory searched for the understanding that the American people had of constitutional phrases at the time of the ratification in the states of the Constitution or the Bill of Rights—what he called their "public meaning." Beginning with the definitions of the words as determined by the appropriate dictionary from as close to the period in which the words were written as possible, Scalia then turned to various concordances of the Constitution, a library shelf of indices, much like the biblical concordances used to interpret Scripture, organized by phrase in the Constitution as well as other early writings, such as letters, diaries, and various newspaper articles, that help to reveal the meaning of those words.[10] For Scalia, it helped that many of these concordances, such as Philip B. Kurland and Ralph Lerner's *The Founders' Constitution,* and, later on, Edwin Meese's *The Heritage Guide to the Constitution* were conservative in nature and often supported the judgment that he was seeking to reach.[11] Beyond this, Scalia looked for interpretive guidance to an understanding of basic English and Early American history.[12]

During his second term on the Court, the classic early example of how Scalia's text and tradition technique led him to reach a result that he may not have liked came in the 1988 case of *Coy v. Iowa,* involving a man accused of sexually assaulting two thirteen-year-old girls while they were camping in a tent. When the two girls testified against him in open court, a screen was put up between the witness stand and the defendant's table to avoid possible trauma to the girls from seeing him as they spoke. By preventing such a face-to-face situation, the defendant claimed the court was denying him the Sixth Amendment's "right . . . to be confronted with the witnesses against him," and in doing so the right to properly cross-examine the witnesses. Writing for the Court, Scalia defined the term "confrontation" to mean direct "line-of-sight" testimony, thus overturning the conviction. The term, he argued, comes "with a lineage that traces back to the beginnings of Western legal culture. There are indications that a right of confrontation existed under Roman law. The Roman governor Festus, discussing the proper treatment of his prisoner, Paul, stated: 'It is not the manner of the Romans to deliver any man up to die before the accused has met his accusers face to face, and has been given a chance to defend himself against the charges.'" Then he turned to Latin and the words of William Shakespeare: "Simply as a matter of Latin as well, since the word 'confront' ultimately derives from the prefix 'con-' (from 'contra' meaning 'against' or 'opposed') and the noun 'frons' (forehead), Shakespeare was thus describing the root meaning of confrontation when he had Richard the Second say: 'Then call them to our presence—face to face, and frowning brow to brow, ourselves will hear the accuser and the accused freely speak.'" Scalia concluded that "the irreducible literal meaning of the Clause [must be] a right to meet face to face all those who appear and give evidence at trial.'"[13]

In dissent, Harry Blackmun was unimpressed by this historical, linguistic, and literary tour de force in favor of a line-of-sight meaning to the confrontation of witnesses in the courtroom, labeling it as Scalia's "reliance on literature, anecdote, and dicta from opinions that a majority of this Court did not join." For Blackmun, the best evidence that confrontation meant only the opportunity to undertake a proper cross-examination of a witness lay in the works of legal scholars such as Northwestern's legendary law school dean John Henry Wigmore: "I find Dean Wigmore's statement infinitely more persuasive than . . . the words Shakespeare placed in the mouth of his Richard II concerning the best means of ascertaining the truth. . . . In fact, Wigmore considered it clear 'from the beginning of the hearsay rule [in the early 1700s] to the present day' that the right of confrontation is provided 'not for the idle purpose of gazing upon the witness, or of being gazed upon by him,' but, rather, to allow for cross-examination."[14] Thus Blackmun saw no prejudicial effect in allowing a court to place a screen between the defendant and the minor victims so long as it still allowed for their cross-examination.

Scalia, though, was never one to allow a colleague to have the final word, offering his own primer as to how to use his textualism theory: "The dissent finds Dean Wigmore more persuasive than . . . William Shakespeare. . . . Surely that must depend upon the proposition that they are cited for. . . . The dissent cites Wigmore for the proposition that confrontation 'was not a part of the common law's view of the confrontation requirement.' . . . To begin with, Wigmore said no such thing. What he said, precisely, was: 'There was never at common law any recognized right to an indispensable thing called confrontation as distinguished from cross-examination. There was a right to cross-examination as indispensable, and that right was involved in and secured by confrontation; it was the same right under different names.'"[15] For Scalia the purpose of the right of confrontation was to allow the defendant to have direct line-of-sight vision of his accuser(s) in order to assess credibility.[16] By using his historical approach to protect the defendant in this manner, Scalia reached the opposite result from his normal support for law and order.

Scalia also demonstrated his new "text and tradition" theory in a controversial death penalty case called *Thompson v. Oklahoma*. This case involved the imposition of a death sentence on a fifteen-year-old boy who was found guilty of a particularly brutal murder. The question before the justices was whether imposition of the death penalty on a minor constituted a violation of the Eighth Amendment's guarantee against "cruel and unusual punishment." Writing for a four-person plurality, Justice John Paul Stevens ruled that an imposition of this penalty on a minor was unconstitutional because "The authors of the Eighth Amendment drafted a categorical prohibition against the infliction of cruel and unusual punishments, but they made no attempt to define the contours of that category. They delegated that task to future generations of judges who have been guided by the 'evolving standards of decency that mark the progress of a maturing society.'"[17] Stevens ruled that based on "the work product of state legislatures and sentencing juries in certain types of cases," putting a defendant who was younger than sixteen to death constituted cruel and unusual punishment.

Scalia did not like the decision or the way Stevens reached it. Unable to find the "evolving standards of decency" test in his copy of the Constitution, he argued in dissent on the basis of history of British common law, as it was reported in "Blackstone's Commentaries on the Laws of England, published in 1769," that the acceptable age for imposing the death penalty was actually "widely accepted" to be lower. "At the time the Eighth Amendment was adopted," Scalia explained, "according to Blackstone, not only was 15 above the age . . . at which capital punishment could theoretically be imposed; it was even above the age (14) up to which there was a rebuttable presumption of incapacity to commit a capital (or any other) felony. . . . The historical practice in this country conformed with the common-law understanding that 15-year-olds were not categorically immune from commission of capital crimes."[18]

Scalia directly challenged his colleague's use of the more expansive and modern "evolving standards of decency" to rule here. "It is assuredly 'for us ultimately to judge' what the Eighth Amendment permits, but that means it is for us to judge whether certain punishments are forbidden because, despite what the current society thinks, they were forbidden under the original understanding of 'cruel and unusual' . . . or because they come within current understanding of what is 'cruel and unusual,' because of the 'evolving standards of decency' *of our national society*; but not because they are out of accord with the perceptions of decency, or of penology, or of mercy, entertained—or strongly entertained, or even held as an 'abiding conviction'—by a majority of the small and unrepresentative segment of our society that sits on this Court."[19] Scalia did not like that, rather than using the "original understanding" of the Founding Era society to decide this matter, it was done by a majority vote of the "personal consciences" of the nine justices.

Scalia was looking instead for a more stable, less changing standard. He failed to find a "national consensus" banning the death penalty for fifteen-year-olds, citing evidence that many death-penalty states and the federal government had no stated ban on the imposition of this penalty for minors. Counting also those nineteen states that had no minimum age for the imposition of the death penalty, he concluded: "A survey of state laws shows . . . that a majority of the States for which the issue exists (the rest do not have capital punishment) are of the view that death is not different insofar as the age of juvenile criminal responsibility is concerned. . . . Thus, what Oklahoma has done here is precisely what the majority of capital-punishment States would do."[20]

In a concurring opinion, O'Connor tried to find the middle ground between Stevens's "evolving standards of decency" and Scalia's "original understanding" tests to interpret the Eighth Amendment: "The plurality [Stevens] and dissent [Scalia] agree on two fundamental propositions: that there is some age below which a juvenile's crimes can never be constitutionally punished by death, and that our precedents require us to locate this age in light of the 'evolving standards of decency that mark the progress of a maturing society.' . . . I accept both principles. The disagreements between the plurality and the dissent rest on their different evaluations of the evidence available to us about the relevant social consensus."[21]

Believing that these two theories could not be further apart, Scalia devoted a good portion of his dissent to setting O'Connor straight.[22] He argued that the answer lay in government action: "I do not agree . . . that there is any doubt about the nonexistence of a national consensus. The concurrence produces the doubt only by arbitrarily refusing to believe that what the laws of the Federal Government and 19 States clearly provide for represents a 'considered judgment.'"[23] Scalia then made clear that he was unimpressed by O'Connor's effort to craft a compromise solution. "The concurrence's approach is a Solomonic solution to the problem of how to prevent execution in the present case while at the same time not holding that the execution of those under 16 when they commit murder is categorically unconstitutional. Solomon, however, was not subject to the constitutional constraints of the judicial department of a national government in a federal, democratic system."[24]

Scalia's vigorous dissent had an impact the following term, when two other death penalty cases, this time dealing with the sentences imposed on one sixteen- and one seventeen-year-old, came to the Court and the newest justice, Anthony Kennedy, as well as Justice O'Connor, joined his side, allowing him to write his dissent from the *Thompson v. Oklahoma* case into law.[25] To keep the majority together, though, Scalia followed O'Connor's earlier suggestion by deemphasizing his own textualism and historical tradition theories in favor of blending them with a watered-down version of the "evolving standards of decency" test, as indicated by the actions of state legislatures, to uphold the constitutionality of the death penalties for minors.[26]

Only in the end of the opinion, in dealing with the dissenters' call to leave this decision to the state legislatures, did Scalia make clear that his loyalty was not to the evolving standards of decency in future cases, but rather to his evolving approach. He offered for the first time what would become his most powerful attack against the living Constitution theory, that it substitutes the judgment of the justices for that of a democratic majority in American society: "By reaching a decision supported neither by constitutional text nor by the demonstrable current standards of our citizens, the dissent displays a failure to appreciate that 'those institutions which the Constitution is supposed to limit' include the Court itself."[27] Scalia's professed agreement with the evolving standards of decency advocates on the Court on the death penalty would continue only so long as their evolving standards reached the same result as his restrictive interpretation of the Constitution's guarantees using his text and tradition theory.[28]

• • •

By the end of the 1987–88 term Scalia had the opportunity to refine his theory in a case called *Morrison v. Olson*, dealing with the constitutionality of the independent counsel provisions of the Ethics in Government Act of 1978, under which the special prosecutor system was established. As part of the legacy of the Nixon Watergate scandal, Congress created a permanent mechanism for the appointment of independent investigative officers to ensure that the government's activities complied with the law. The case arising from this statute involved a congressional oversight investigation of the Environmental Protection Agency's Superfund for cleaning up toxic waste sites. When President Reagan, citing executive privilege, refused to produce documents requested by Congress, the latter cited the head of the EPA for contempt. Theodore Olson, the Office of Legal Counsel head who had advised the president in this process, was accused of giving untruthful information to the investigating committee. Since in accordance with the law the independent counsel, Alexia Morrison, was appointed by offices within the United States Court of Appeals for the District of Columbia Circuit after a request from the attorney general, the question became whether this process violated the constitutional requirement for the appointment of executive officers by the president and requiring the confirmation of the Senate. Morrison argued that these independent counsels were inter-branch appointees, required to properly regulate the presidency, and so their appointment did not interfere with the president's constitutional powers or violate the constitutional separation of powers.

Speaking for a seven-person majority, Chief Justice Rehnquist upheld the law, arguing that its appointment process "does not violate separation of powers principles by impermissibly interfering with the functions of the Executive Branch." As he argued: "The power to appoint inferior officers such as independent counsel is not in itself an 'executive' function in the constitutional sense."[29]

While the line between a "principal officer" and an "inferior officer" was "far from clear," Rehnquist argued for several reasons that this was a constitutionally permissible "inferior officer," saying that Morrison was "subject to removal by a higher Executive Branch official," in this case the attorney general; was "empowered . . . to perform only certain, limited duties," in this case "investigation and, if appropriate, prosecution for certain federal crimes"; occupied an office that was "limited in jurisdiction," as it was applicable only "to certain federal officials suspected of certain serious federal crimes"; and "limited in tenure." Morrison, the chief added, was "appointed essentially to accomplish a single task, and when that task is over the office is terminated," and thus was no different from the Watergate special prosecutor's office that was upheld in the *United States v. Nixon* case.[30] In the opinion of William Rehnquist, the former head of the Office of Legal Counsel for Richard Nixon, the presidency was not threatened, but rather bolstered by the independent counsel program.

Opposing this view in dissent was the former head of the Office of Legal Counsel for Gerald Ford, Antonin Scalia, whose time in that office had left him with a different view of executive power. Drawing from his difficult

experience during that period of weakened presidential power in the post–
Nixon resignation years, Scalia wrote a solo dissent opposing the independent counsel, using his historical tradition analysis to return the presidency
to a position of preeminence in the constitutional separation of powers system. Scalia began with a history lesson, citing the Massachusetts constitution
of 1780, drafted by John Adams, the Constitution, the Bill of Rights, and
the *Federalist Papers* to argue, "It is not possible to give to each department
an equal power of self-defense. In republican government, the legislative
authority necessarily predominates. . . . As the weight of the legislative authority requires that it should be . . . divided, the weakness of the executive
may require, on the other hand, that it should be fortified."[31]

Seeking to indicate his displeasure with the Court's work, Scalia offered
one of his trademark turns of phrase: "That is what this suit is about. Power.
The allocation of power among Congress, the President, and the courts
in such fashion as to preserve the equilibrium the Constitution sought to
establish—so that 'a gradual concentration of the several powers in the same
department' . . . can effectively be resisted. Frequently an issue of this sort
will come before the Court clad, so to speak, in sheep's clothing: the potential
of the asserted principle to effect important change in the equilibrium of
power is not immediately evident, and must be discerned by a careful and
perceptive analysis. But this wolf comes as a wolf."[32] As he read Scalia's draft,
Blackmun was dismayed, scrawling "Screams!" in the margin.[33]

In Scalia's opinion, in a separation of powers system the executive branch
should have total control over this kind of a prosecutorial appointment. For
him, a legislative act creating an independent counsel, appointed by another
government official, served to diminish the power of the president, thus violating the Constitution: "The Court points out that the President, through
his Attorney General, has at least some control. That concession is alone
enough to invalidate the statute, but I cannot refrain from pointing out that
the Court greatly exaggerates the extent of that 'some' Presidential control."
For Scalia, the attorney general's statutory power to remove an independent
counsel for "good cause" was "somewhat like referring to shackles as an effective means of locomotion."[34]

For Scalia, the Constitution was violated when *any* presidential power
was removed. "It is ultimately irrelevant how much the statute reduces
Presidential control. . . . It is not for us to determine, and we have never
presumed to determine, how much of the purely executive powers of government must be within the full control of the President. The Constitution

prescribes that they all are."[35] While Scalia's historical approach would not allow for a rewriting of the president's constitutional powers, he argued that the majority vote of the Court did. "What are the standards to determine how the balance is to be struck, that is, how much removal of Presidential power is too much? . . . Once we depart from the text of the Constitution, just where short of that do we stop? . . . Evidently, the governing standard is to be what might be called the unfettered wisdom of a majority of this Court, revealed to an obedient people on a case-by-case basis. This is not only not the government of laws that the Constitution established; it is not a government of laws at all."[36]

This case seemed to have revived the nightmare for Scalia of working as President Ford's legal counsel, with attacks on executive power coming from the press and congressional investigations. For him, relying more on political than legal analysis, the reduction in presidential power due to the independent counsel program "deeply wounds the President, by substantially reducing the President's ability to protect himself and his staff. That is the whole object of the law, of course, and I cannot imagine why the Court believes it does not succeed. Besides weakening the Presidency by reducing the zeal of his staff, it must also be obvious that the institution of the independent counsel enfeebles him more directly in his constant confrontations with Congress, by eroding his public support. Nothing is so politically effective as the ability to charge that one's opponent and his associates are not merely wrongheaded, naive, ineffective, but, in all probability, 'crooks.'"[37]

Scalia also could not fathom the Court's analysis that the independent counsel, empowered with investigating and perhaps even bringing charges against a sitting president, did not affect the presidency. "The Court essentially says to the President: 'Trust us. We will make sure that you are able to accomplish your constitutional role.' I think the Constitution gives the President—and the people—more protection than that."[38] For Scalia, rather than trusting these special prosecutors with so much discretion and so much power to be fair to the chief executive and the members of the executive branch, the solution had long ago been devised by the constitutional Founders: "When they established a single Chief Executive accountable to the people: the blame can be assigned to someone who can be punished."[39] The answer, he believed, was to vote the president out of office for malfeasance. The breadth and depth of Scalia's analysis was impressive, but not to Justice Blackmun, who wrote on his draft, "Without the screaming, it could have been said in about 10 pages."[40]

Scalia fought a valiant fight as the lone dissenter on behalf of preserving presidential power, but he lost the battle. Later, though, he won the war. After another special prosecutor, Kenneth Starr, led to the political impeachment, but not conviction, of President Bill Clinton in 1998 over perjury charges relating to his relationship with a White House intern, Congress saw the dangers to presidential power of this office and refused to reauthorize it. It was replaced with the U.S. Department of Justice's Office of Special Counsel. And in time, Clinton's successor, George W. Bush, would use many of Scalia's theories to restore the powers of the presidency, creating what he called the "unitary presidency" by uniting the exclusive executive with the unwritten inherent constitutional powers of the office.[41]

Scalia's admirers understood his contributions to this process. Former law clerk Stephen Calabresi, a founder of the Federalist Society, said in 2006 on the occasion of the twentieth anniversary of Scalia's appointment to the Supreme Court: "Justice Scalia has written many important opinions on the Court over the last 20 years, but there are several that stand out and deserve special mention. [One of] Justice Scalia's best opinions, in my view, [was] . . . his dissent in *Morrison v. Olson*, where the Court upheld the constitutionality of court-appointed special prosecutors. The Morrison dissent amusingly came to be hailed by liberals as prophetic during the Clinton impeachment proceedings and it helped lead to a situation where the political branches jointly decided to junk the special-prosecutor law in 1999."[42]

• • •

During his third term on the Court, Scalia further developed his decision-making theory beyond textualism. One opportunity to do so came in an establishment of religion case concerning taxing religious publications. In February 1989, a majority led by William Brennan used the *Lemon* test to remove a sales tax exemption by the state of Texas for a religious publication called the *Texas Monthly* because the tax exemption violated all three sections of the test. In response, Scalia launched a verbal barrage in dissent: "As a judicial demolition project, today's decision is impressive. The machinery employed by the opinions of Justice Brennan and Justice Blackmun is no more substantial than the antinomy that accommodation of religion may be required but not permitted, and the bold but unsupportable assertion . . . that government may not 'convey a message of endorsement of religion.' With this frail equipment, the Court topples an exemption for religious publications of a sort that expressly appears in the laws of at least 15 of the 45 States that have sales and use taxes."[43] In supporting religious tax exemptions, Scalia went further in outlining his theory for doing so: "I dissent because I find no basis in the text of the Constitution, the decisions of this Court, or the traditions of our people for disapproving this longstanding and widespread practice."[44] For him the fact that more than a dozen states had laws allowing such tax exemptions for religious groups was sufficient to uphold the Texas law because "religious tax exemptions of the type the Court invalidates today permeate the state and federal codes, and have done so for many years."[45]

Just where Scalia would now be looking for "traditions of our people" to guide his decision making, much like his earlier "historic practices of our society" test in the *Booth v. Maryland* death penalty case, was not yet clear. But for him, the majority's tests were much less clear: "Today's decision introduces a new strain of irrationality in our Religion Clause jurisprudence. . . . It is not right—it is not constitutionally healthy—that this Court should feel authorized to refashion anew our civil society's relationship with religion, adopting a theory of church and state that is contradicted by current practice, tradition, and even our own case law. I dissent."[46]

One of the consequences of Scalia's historically based theory was that from time to time he would, as he did in the *Coy v. Iowa* Confrontation Clause case, have to vote in ways he did not like. This was certainly the situation when the Court heard the appeal in *Texas v. Johnson*[47] of a political protester named Gregory Johnson, who burned an American flag outside the Republican National Convention in Dallas, Texas, in 1988 to protest against U.S. foreign policy. In an unusual alliance of justices for this case, Scalia joined the majority opinion written by his frequent opponent on such cases, Brennan, who argued that burning a United States flag was symbolic speech, meaning that it was "expressive conduct" protected by the First Amendment's freedom of speech provision. And for Brennan, the level of that protection was absolute: "If there is a bedrock principle underlying the First Amendment, it is that the government may not prohibit the expression of an idea simply because society finds the idea itself offensive or disagreeable. . . . We have not recognized an exception to this principle even where our flag has been involved."[48] In this case, Brennan argued that the state of Texas had no right to protect the United States flag, which was a federal responsibility. In providing the fifth vote for Brennan's majority, Scalia did not write an opinion in the case. Over the years, his approach would lead him to vote consistently for an expanded free speech protection.

Years later, Scalia would speak on the lecture circuit about how this case was the classic example of how his theory led him to do the kind of thing he did not want to do. "Trust me, I did not like to not put Mr. Johnson in jail," he would say. To Scalia, he was "bearded, scruffy, sandal-wearing. . . . But I was handcuffed. I couldn't help it. That's my understanding of the First Amendment. I can't do the nasty things I'd like to do."[49] The day after the decision was announced, Scalia was treated at breakfast to a rendition by his wife, Maureen, of "It's a Grand Old Flag." Scalia, by his own admission, "got a lot of heat from that opinion, really serious biting criticism from the quarter I normally don't get criticism from—that is to say from the right rather than the left." However, former President George H. W. Bush, himself a respected war veteran, sent a letter to Scalia's wife saying: "I know your husband has been getting a lot of criticism for his flag-burning decision. Tell him not to worry about it. He did the right thing."[50]

• • •

After witnessing firsthand for more than two months how far apart his decision-making technique was from that of his colleagues, Scalia decided to debate with them beyond the confines of the Court. He now had his answer to Joe Biden's questions during his Senate confirmation as to how he "view[ed] the interpretation of the Constitution," and who he would become as a justice. He was not going to become a Court politician. Unlike the predictions of many when he first came to the Court, he would not become an engaging judicial playmaker like Brennan, able to develop and direct voting coalitions for the conservatives. Having decided to act as a "Court of One," Scalia would judge cases, often in ways that allowed him to write largely for himself, while developing his textualism and historical tradition theories. To further that process, he developed stump speeches, just as he had described in that June 14, 1986, speech to the attorney general's Conference on Economic Liberties, and delivered them to a wide variety of audiences in order to educate Court observers and develop followers.

While he worked out the nature of his constitutional theory on the Court on a case-by-case and speech-by-speech basis, by September 1988 Scalia had also begun to develop, as he termed it during his answer to Biden, "a full constitutional matrix" for deciding cases. Scalia was ready to share that vision with the world on the lecture circuit. In a pair of speeches, he answered the question, "What was the most plausible meaning of the words of the Constitution to the society that adopted it—regardless of what the Framers might secretly have intended?"[51]

For Scalia, the search for what he now called the "public meaning" of the Constitution was not only entirely different from Bork's original intent theory, but it also went beyond his own dictionary-based textualism theory that had guided him on the Court of Appeals and during his first term. Scalia was going beyond parsing Noah Webster and semantics to some historical, analytical version of how the general public at that time understood those words.

Scalia presented the early version of what he now called his originalism theory in September 1988, in the William Howard Taft Constitutional Law Lecture at the University of Cincinnati. He titled the address "Originalism: The Lesser Evil," and it became the foundation for his jurisprudence for the rest of his career.[52] Given the venue, it was perhaps appropriate that Scalia explored the "originalist approach to constitutional decision-making" taken by Chief Justice Taft in the 1926 case *Myers v. United States*, which argued under the meaning of the constitutional separation of powers, as understood in 1789, that the president had unlimited power to remove purely executive officers. In noting that it took the chief justice three years to write a massive seventy-page opinion, while Scalia's Court had taken only a couple of months to draft the recent *Morrison v. Olson* decision on the constitutionality of the independent counsel law, Scalia compared the two decisions.

He began as he usually did in such speeches by presenting his opponents as straw men to be attacked. Here he directed his criticism toward those living, evolving constitutionalists, like William Brennan, whose "nonoriginalist opinions have almost always had the decency to lie, or at least to dissemble, about what they were doing—either ignoring strong evidence of original intent that contradicted the minimal recited evidence of an original intent congenial to the court's desires, or else not discussing original intent at all, speaking in terms of broad constitutional generalities with no pretense of historical support." Scalia argued that his living, evolving Constitution Court opponents offered nothing of substance to this discussion.

> You can't beat somebody with nobody. It is not enough to demonstrate that the other fellow's candidate (originalism) is no good; one must also agree upon another candidate to replace him. . . . As the name "nonoriginalism" suggests (and I know no other, more precise term by which this school of exegesis can be described), it represents agreement on nothing except what is the wrong approach. . . . Nonoriginalism, in other words, is a two-way street that handles traffic both to and from individual rights.

Scalia posed two common objections to his theory of originalism, both of which he believed his audience would come to see were easily answered. The first criticism addressed the difficulty in accurately determining such a "public meaning." "It is often exceedingly difficult to plumb the original understanding of an ancient text," he began. But, Scalia explained, what appeared to be a weakness of his theory was actually a strength:

> Properly done, the task requires the consideration of an enormous mass of material—in the case of the Constitution and its Amendments, for example, to mention only one element, the records of the ratifying debates in all the states. Even beyond that, it requires an evaluation of the reliability of that material—many of the reports of the ratifying debates, for example, are thought to be quite unreliable. And further still, it requires immersing oneself in the political and intellectual atmosphere of the time—somehow placing out of mind knowledge that we have which an earlier age did not, and putting on beliefs, attitudes, philosophies, prejudices and loyalties that are not those of our day.

Here he made clear that he was not Robert Bork, simply divining the original intent of the constitutional Framers, but rather an American historian, analyzing the people in the society of that day to glean their understanding of the text. In the end, Scalia conceded: "It is, in short, a task sometimes better suited to the historian than the lawyer." The fact that Chief Justice Taft had done this in *Myers* and Scalia had done the same in the *Morrison* independent counsel case indicated to him that the task was not impossible.

The second objection to the originalist theory gave Scalia a bit more pause. What should a true originalist judge decide in the face of long-standing Court precedents or modern practice that reached a different result? Scalia argued:

> In its undiluted form, at least, [originalism] is medicine that seems too strong to swallow. Thus, almost every originalist would adulterate it with the doctrine of *stare decisis*. . . . *Stare decisis* alone is not enough to prevent originalism from being what many would consider too bitter a pill. What if some state should enact a new law providing public lashing, or branding of the right hand, as punishment for certain criminal offenses? Even if it could be demonstrated un-

equivocally that these were not cruel and unusual measures in 1791, and even though no prior Supreme Court decision has specifically disapproved them, I doubt whether any federal judge—even among the many who consider themselves originalists—would sustain them against an eighth amendment challenge. . . . Any espousal of originalism as a practical theory of exegesis must somehow come to terms with that reality.

Thus, Scalia said that he would be a "faint-hearted originalist," finding a way based on precedent or some other source to temper his historical findings by upholding long-time precedents.

In the end, he argued, the main advantage in his originalist approach is that it will limit judges' discretion, thus keeping them within the bounds of the Constitution:

Originalism does not aggravate the principal weakness of the system, for it establishes a historical criterion that is conceptually quite separate from the preferences of the judge himself. And the principal defect of that approach—that historical research is always difficult and sometimes inconclusive—will, unlike nonoriginalism, lead to a more moderate rather than a more extreme result. The inevitable tendency of judges to think that the law is what they would like it to be will, I have no doubt, cause most errors in judicial historiography to be made in the direction of projecting upon the age of 1789 current, modern values—so that as applied, even as applied in the best of faith, originalism will (as the historical record shows) end up as something of a compromise.

Scalia wanted his audience to believe that interpreting laws and the Constitution was easy, if only judges would do it his way. There were, however, fundamental structural problems with Scalia's approach that he was not willing to discuss in this speech. The fundamental assumption of his historical approach was that the history from this period, and thus the meaning of these words, could be determined with certainty. With Federalists and Anti-Federalists offering differing views in state ratifying conventions on many issues in the constitutional debate, divining one "original meaning" of those words seemed an unlikely, if not impossible, task. Writing history is a matter of making choices about the value of such evidence as still exists or can be uncovered. How does one measure the differences between the meaning of the words of the Constitution in the ratification debates of South Carolina as opposed to those in Massachusetts? How does one weigh the varying interpretations among the Federalists as opposed to the Anti-Federalists? Assessing such evidence is all a matter of making choices, and the choices are determined by the individual judge.

But did Scalia have the right tools for the job? In determining the textual meaning of the Constitution (1787) and the Bill of Rights (1791) by relying on Webster's *American Dictionary of the English Language*, published in 1828, Scalia was opening himself up to the question of the chronological appropriateness of the published work.[53] Did the Western mob that would nearly destroy the White House during General Andrew Jackson's inauguration celebration in 1829 understand the meaning of words in a manner identical to that of the aristocratic gentlemen of the Virginia-Massachusetts power axis of Washington, Adams, and Jefferson four decades earlier?[54] For a theory that argued that the meaning of the Constitution was static, the choice of dictionary should not allow for *any* change at all in the meaning of the words.

One of the nation's preeminent Early American historians, Gordon Wood of Brown University, took issue with the originalists in an essay in *The New York Review of Books* published earlier in 1988. Titled "The Fundamentalists and the Constitution," Wood's argument was based on an address that he had given for the Virginia Commission on the Bicentennial of the United States Constitution. Wood was one of the first to draw the connection between the proponents of original intention such as Bork and Scalia, and the intellectual history of the political philosophical theories of Leo Strauss of the University of Chicago, who preached close reading of philosophical texts in order to find what he and his devoted intellectual disciples believed to be their hidden, or "true," meaning. Wood credited the legal philosophy of the Reagan administration and Justice Department, as well as much of the Bicentennial celebration itself, to the Strauss group: "Perhaps the most remarkable fact about the scholarship of the bicentennial celebrations is the extent to which that scholarship has been colored by the students and followers of Leo Strauss. . . . 'Straussians' are everywhere in government and academia, in both high and low places, in conferences, in symposiums, in books and journals."[55]

But Wood came not to praise Strauss but to bury him, and those in the American legal world who would follow his teachings. Speaking of the theory of original intention, Wood said:

So long as "original intention" is confined to jurisprudence and not taken literally, the theory may be a legitimate and useful legal fiction for controlling judicial discretion. But historically there can be no real "original intention" behind the document. Not only were there hundreds of Founders, including the Anti-Federalists, with a myriad of clashing contradictory intentions, but in the end all the Founders created something that no one of them ever intended. . . . Ideas can, and often do, become political philosophy, do transcend the particular intentions of their creators and become part of the public culture, become something larger and grander than their sources.

And since they become "larger and grander than their sources," concluded Wood, then contrary to the legal theories of men like Bork and Scalia, they will not be limited to a static, historical interpretation. Rather, the meaning of the document must evolve and grow over time:

"Historicism" is as restrictive as it is permissive, as conserving as it is liberating. Historians know that the meaning of the Constitution has changed and will continue to change. They also know that no one is free to give whatever meaning he or she wants to it. In our choice of interpretations we are limited by history and by the conventions, values, and meanings we have inherited. If anyone in our intellectual struggles violates too radically the accepted or inherited meanings of the culture, his ability to persuade others is lost.

Such criticism as Wood's, however, had no impact on Scalia.

The yet-unstated question was whether Scalia's approach was what the judges authorized by Article III were intended to do. Did the Framers really intend for later judges to turn back the clock to their period to interpret the Constitution? Should the words of the Constitution, which were the result of months of compromise among countless drafters, have as much value for judges as the values that underlay the words? At base, the question was whether the Constitution was meant to be static, frozen in time by the Founders' words, or evolving in order to extend to new times. This would become the partisan fault line on the Supreme Court toward the end of the twentieth century.

With this September 1988 speech, Scalia had formally made his claim to be the new intellectual leader of the constitutional fundamentalists—devoted in his judicial decision making exclusively to the words and culture of the Founding period of the Constitution. In praising the historical interpretive method, most of Scalia's speech described his method for doing originalist, textual analysis. Over time, though, he would change his views about his willingness to overturn existing precedents. Asked in 2008 at a Federalist Society meeting, "Why are you a 'faint-hearted originalist'?" Scalia responded with a chuckle:

> Oh my. I said that a long time ago. I said in the course of, I guess it was an argue piece that you, if you are an originalist, you would have to say that the 8th Amendment . . . does not prohibit the cutting off of the ear, or the notching of the ears, which is the way in the framing generation felons used to be identified. Criminals they would notch the ears, and they would inflict corporal punishment lashes and so forth. Now I suppose that I have to say that that is not unconstitutional and, if I had a case right in front of me, at that time, at least, I said, you know, I'm not sure, maybe I'm too faint-hearted to say that. But as I've gotten older and crankier. I mean, I don't like that stuff, but, and the more horrible you make the example, the less likely it is to occur. I'm not really worried that people are going to start notching ears. So, you know, it's just sort of an academic question invented to embarrass an originalist.[56]

By early 1989 Scalia was ready to expand on the explanation of his approach. In another speech, on February 14, 1989, at the Oliver Wendell Holmes Jr. Lecture at Harvard Law School, he explained how to do his originalist/textualist approach.[57] Entitled "The Rule of Law as a Law of Rules," the speech argued that the originalist technique would guide judges in finding clear, bright-line "cateogorical rules" that would help them reach results while also limiting their discretion. Scalia explored in this speech what he called "the dichotomy between general rules and personal discretion within the narrow context *of law that is made by the courts.*" It was the "general rules" produced by originalism and textualism that Scalia preferred. "The law grows and develops, the theory goes, not through the pronouncement of general principles, but case-by-case, deliberately, incrementally, one-step-at-a-time. . . . When I was in law school, I was a great enthusiast for this approach—an advocate of both writing and reading the 'holding' of a decision narrowly, thereby leaving greater discretion to future courts. Over the years, however—and not merely the years since I have been a judge—I have found myself drawn more and more to the opposite view."

While the dual advantages of this use of general rules were both "uniformity" and "predictability," Scalia most appreciated that "Only by announcing rules do we hedge ourselves in." At this point, Scalia argued for another advantage to this use of "categorical rules"—the protection of minority groups against oppression by majority will. With general rules supplementing the courage of judges, Scalia argued, "The chances that frail men and women will stand up to their unpleasant duty are greatly increased if they can stand behind the solid shield of a firm, clear principle enunciated in earlier cases." And Scalia had already lectured as to where these general rules could be found: "Even where a particular area is quite susceptible of clear and definite rules, we judges cannot create them out of whole cloth, but must find some basis for them in the text that Congress or the Constitution has provided. It is rare, however, that even the most vague and general text cannot be given some precise, principled content—and that is indeed the essence of the judicial craft."

Having already outlined his method of "textual exegesis," or "adher[ing] closely to the plain meaning of a text," in his Cincinnati speech, Scalia argued that this was far better than the living, evolving constitutionalism of liberals William Brennan and Thurgood Marshall. "It is, of course, *possible* to establish general rules, no matter what theory of interpretation or construction one employs. As one cynic has said, with five votes anything is possible. But when one does not have a solid textual anchor or an established social norm from which to derive the general rule, its pronouncement appears uncomfortably like legislation." Thus, Scalia urged "that the *Rule* of Law, the law of rules, be extended as far as the nature of the question allows; and that, to foster a correct attitude toward the matter, we appellate judges bear in mind that when we have finally reached the point where we can do no more than consult the totality of the circumstances, we are acting more as fact-finders than as expositors of the law." Beyond the general theory, just how to find the "law of rules" was not made clear.

In these two speeches, with their messages of devotion to textualism, determining historically the "plain meaning" of the text, the need for a bright-line "law of rules," and the theory of "faint-hearted originalism," Scalia articulated the basis for his theory for interpreting the Constitution. The speeches were his opening salvos in his war to control the debate over the Court's work. He was demarcating the terms by which legal issues would be discussed, but also clearly marking the ground on which the battle on the Court would be fought. Not only would he be defining the terms of the discussions in the Federalist Society which he had helped to found, and the conservative law review scholarship where he had once published, but, in a sort of legal laboratory, he would then demonstrate on the Supreme Court how these theories would work in deciding cases.

On April 6, 1989, Scalia gave a third speech, at the University of Georgia Law School, which would provide the framework for the constantly evolving constitutional interpretation stump speech that he would give scores of times throughout his career.[58] Here Scalia sounded like a religious scholar, arguing: "Unlike any other nation in the world, we consider ourselves bound together not by genealogy or by residence but quite genuinely by belief in certain principles and the most important of those principles are set forth in the Constitution of the United States. Such is the veneration we have for the document."[59] At the end of this speech, though, Scalia unwittingly laid the foundation for one of the most devastating long-term alterations of his new theory: "the Supreme Court cannot save this society from itself because over the long haul the Court is no more than the society itself. The compromises of principle, the misperceptions of liberty that are believed in the homes, learned in the schools, and taught in the universities will ultimately be the body of knowledge and belief that new justices bring with them to the bench." Indeed, as new justices joined the Court, schooled and believing in new readings of the meanings of the words in the Constitution, Scalia's very technique could be used against him to reach different results.

Besides educating the legal community to his new judicial approach, there was an unintended consequence to Scalia's talks. In making these speeches from the bench, Scalia behaved more like an academic than a Supreme Court justice, choosing to break the prevailing ethical norms of the Court against such extrajudicial speechmaking. This informal rule had been in existence since 1969, after the forced resignation of Justice Abe Fortas. Since that time, the Court had almost entirely abstained from extrajudicial activities in order to avoid controversy.[60] Within the Court, one reporter later wrote, the norm had become that "Secrecy is almost a religion at the Supreme Court and its justices rarely violate the tradition of silence about their decisions."[61] It would be a full decade before John Paul Stevens, as well as three other justices, in late 1979, would give a speech explaining the Court's recent, controversial freedom of the press decision dealing with the public's right of access to courtrooms for some early stages for criminal trials.[62]

Then Justice Harry Blackmun ignored the Court's informal vow of silence on Thanksgiving Day 1982 by giving a televised interview to reporter Daniel Schorr for CNN, followed by an interview in early 1983 with *New York Times* reporter John Jenkins for a Sunday magazine article, and an interview with Bill Moyers for his *In Search of the Constitution* series in 1987.[63] All of Blackmun's appearances were given with the intention of humanizing the jurist, who was then getting death threats over his majority opinion in the *Roe v. Wade* abortion decision, and of announcing his professional split from conservative Chief Justice Warren Burger while moving toward the liberal wing of the Court.[64]

But Scalia's extrajudicial appearances were different from Blackmun's. Unlike Blackmun, who was discussing his own work in retrospect to explain why analysts and observers should see him differently, Scalia was outlining the terms of how he would act in the future in the hopes that other conservatives would follow his lead. Scalia's speeches, exactly like the ones he made while serving on the federal Court of Appeals to speak on legislative history, now served to change the Court's tradition, and in time others would follow him. As a result, Scalia, after the Bork failed confirmation, began the process of politicizing the Court and launching the partisan warfare among the justices. In time, liberal jurists would begin to speak in response to Scalia and debate him in public, and in doing so rachet up the partisan nature of the Court, while also encouraging others to breach the vow of silence.

Scalia now saw his mission as leading the war to change the Supreme Court from the liberal activism of the Warren Court of the 1960s and the waffling moderate conservatism of the Burger Court in the 1970s and 1980s to the dedicated, unwavering conservative-oriented search for the original meaning of the Constitution after 1986. He just needed to persuade people in speeches and writing off the Court that textualism and originalism were the proper ways to decide cases.

But in launching this legal crusade, Scalia had already forgotten one thing. Just as no man is an island, no individual justice runs the Supreme Court. Scalia ignored the politics of his position, and in doing so risked the most precious thing in his quest—judicial votes.

CHAPTER 11

Losing the Middle

Having laid out his decision-making theory, Scalia had to choose which strategy to follow in ruling on cases—an unwavering pursuit of his textualist/originalist theory or a more political approach to secure a majority of Court votes. It was clear by now that the conservatives on the Court, if they chose to act in harmony, had a 5–4 majority, with the most moderate among them, Sandra Day O'Connor, determining just how far to the right they could go in their decisions. In the past three terms, O'Connor had voted with Scalia in about three out of every four cases.[1] Conservative Byron White, and the pragmatic conservative chief justice, William Rehnquist, were happy to sign off on her judgments, though both occasionally wished that she, and they, could go further to the right. The Court's newest conservative jurist, Anthony Kennedy, was a bit more conservative than O'Connor, agreeing with Scalia 84 percent of the time.[2] With his addition, the members of the conservative majority would decide how to hold together in opposition to the three liberals, William Brennan, Thurgood Marshall, and Harry Blackmun, and the increasingly liberal moderate John Paul Stevens.

Faced with the choice of moderating his views and tempering his rhetoric to fit with O'Connor's style of incremental case-by-case changes in the rules, or following an uncompromising ultraconservative approach, Scalia knew exactly how he would proceed. Determined as he was to make his new textualism and originalism theories the prevailing legal philosophy in an effort to be seen as the intellectual leader of the Court, Scalia decided to adopt a take-no-prisoners approach to his decision making. Inevitably, this meant that he would clash once again with O'Connor.

Scalia had collided with O'Connor at the end of the 1988–89 term in a case called *South Carolina v. Gathers*, a follow-up to the *Booth v. Maryland* case, decided two years earlier, opposing the use of a victim impact statement during the sentencing phase of a death penalty case. With Lewis Powell re-placed by the more conservative Anthony Kennedy, Scalia believed that he had a chance to overturn the *Booth* precedent, making it possible for a pros-ecutor to place information not admissible at trial before a sentencing jury. In the new case, the prosecutor had read to the jury from a religious document called the "Game Guy's Prayer" that the victim had been carrying and placed before them the victim's voter registration card, arguing that the defendant deserved to be put to death for killing such an upright and moral person. The question here was whether the death penalty applied by the lower court should be overturned because the information placed before the jury had nothing to do with the "circumstances of the crime."

While Scalia drafted his opinion in the hopes of mustering a majority, O'Connor, who had supported Scalia's dissent in *Booth* but was writing a limited exception to it in *Gathers*, sent him a note making an offer: "Dear Nino: If you can persuade three other members of the Court to agree with you to overrule *Booth,* I will withdraw my [opinion] in this case and join a judgment simply overruling it rather than trying to limit it."[3] The chances for Scalia's success improved when he received what seemed to be a support-ing note from Anthony Kennedy: "Dear Nino: As I indicated at Conference, the difficulties *Booth* is causing in lower courts, both state and federal, is such that sound judicial administration suggests it be overruled now rather than chipping at it bit by bit. I will join an opinion to overrule."[4] Tallying up the possible votes here, Blackmun had penciled on his copy of this note that the case's result would be "up to B.R.W.," Justice Byron White.[5]

Hoping to get White's vote for the liberals' side, Brennan circulated a short majority opinion limiting the application of the *Booth* precedent disal-lowing the use of the additional information at sentencing in a death penalty case, but not generally.[6] However, Brennan added, "There no evidence whatever that the defendant read anything that was printed on either the tract or the voter card. Indeed, it is extremely unlikely that he did so. . . . Under these circumstances, the content of the various papers the victim happened to be carrying when he was attacked was purely fortuitous and cannot provide any information relevant to the defendant's moral culpabil-ity."[7] Since this material did not relate to the "circumstances of the crime," a Brennan-led majority would not allow its use.

In case Scalia's effort failed, O'Connor circulated a draft opinion refusing to overturn *Booth* by arguing that this precedent did not apply in *Gathers.*[8] But Justice White accepted Brennan's language.

In dissent, Scalia complained that even though O'Connor eventually voted with him, her vacillation and inaction had cost him a majority to overturn the *Booth* opinion: "Two Terms ago, when we decided *Booth v. Maryland* . . . I was among four Members of the Court who believed that the decision imposed a restriction upon state and federal criminal procedures that has no basis in the Constitution. I continue to believe that *Booth* was wrongly decided, and my conviction that it does perceptible harm has been strengthened by subsequent writings pointing out the indefensible consequences of a rule that the specific harm visited upon society by a murderer may not be taken into account when the jury decides whether to impose the sentence of death."[9] Scalia was not at all impressed by O'Connor's unwillingness to allow the consideration of admirable "personal characteristics" of the victim, as opposed to the "particular injury caused to the victim's family and fellow citizens," in determining the merits of a death sentence, and he "would often find it impossible to tell which was which." Scalia renewed his appeal to overturn *Booth* on originalist grounds by looking at the early societal history of the Eighth Amendment's "cruel and unusual punishment" clause: "*Booth* has not even an arguable basis in the common-law background that led up to the Eighth Amendment, in any longstanding societal tradition, or in any evidence that present society, [or] through its laws or the actions of its juries."[10]

Scalia's frustration with what he saw as O'Connor's centrist vacillation bubbled over that month into another case dealing with a Missouri antiabortion law, *Webster v. Reproductive Health Services.* Challenging *Roe v. Wade*, Missouri passed a law in 1986 that, among its twenty restrictive provisions, contained a preamble that stated "the life of each human being begins at conception," and "unborn children have protectable interests in life, health, and well-being." If upheld, this law would effectively overturn Blackmun's delicate balance in *Roe* among the rights of the pregnant woman, the police powers of the state, and the growing fetus during various trimesters of a pregnancy. It would also undercut Blackmun's foundation for this shifting standard based on the concept that protected life begins at the point of viability outside the womb, which he posited was at the end of the twenty-fourth week of pregnancy. The Missouri law allowed the state to protect unborn children by requiring doctors performing abortions after the twentieth week of a pregnancy to first determine the viability of the fetus, and banned the use of public facilities, public employees, or public funds in performing these abortions. While this case would test the constitutionality of each of the provisions of this law, the real issue was whether there was a majority on the Court ready to overturn *Roe v. Wade*.

The case was argued on April 26 and, in the Court's conference two days later, the justices looked at the question from a variety of perspectives.[11] Scalia argued that the statement in the preamble that "the life of each human being begins at conception" was simply an acceptable expression of Catholic religious doctrine.[12] Kennedy, who would be one of the centrist judges on this case, argued that given the 1973 *Roe* pro-abortion ruling, this was "a pure stare deci[sis case]," meaning that he "would leave it alone." O'Connor argued that the preamble of the law should have "no substantive effect on a law." Meanwhile, Justice Stevens appeared to be on the fence about portions of the law, with his vote seemingly obtainable by the conservatives.[13]

Chief Justice Rehnquist, who sided with the conservatives, assigned the case to himself and wrote a first draft that sought, by upholding the law's requirement that a doctor determine the viability of the fetus, to overturn the *Roe* precedent. In this draft, Rehnquist tested the law as to whether it "reasonably furthers the state's interest in protecting human life." But it was clear from the rest of the opinion, upholding the "life begins at conception" and "determination of viability" language, that he was disassembling the trimester test system of *Roe*. Rehnquist objected to the legislative approach used by Blackmun in *Roe*:

> *Stare decisis* is a cornerstone of our legal system, but it has less power in constitutional cases, where, save for constitutional amendments, this Court is the only body able to make needed changes. . . . The rigid *Roe* framework is hardly consistent with the notion of a Constitution cast in general terms, as ours is, and usually speaking in general principles, as ours does. The key elements of the *Roe* framework—trimesters and viability—are not found in the text of the Constitution or in any place else one would expect to find a constitutional principle. Since the bounds of the inquiry are essentially indeterminate, the result has been a web of legal rules that have become increasingly intricate, resembling a code of regulations rather than a body of constitutional doctrine.[14]

Rehnquist's draft undercutting the *Roe* precedent lost Stevens's vote immediately as he wrote in a memo to the chief that "it is a little out of char-

acter for you to be adopting Missouri's version of the Holy Trinity doctrine."
Later on, Stevens explained: "Because the test really rejects *Roe v. Wade* in
its entirety, I would think that it would be much better for the Court, as an
institution, to do so forthrightly rather than indirectly with a bombshell first
introduced at the end of its opinion." He did not like the new test for preventing abortion at all, saying that "the same result could be accomplished
by requiring tests of the woman's knowledge of Shakespeare or American
history." In the end, Stevens argued, "As you know, I am not in favor of
overruling *Roe v. Wade*, but if the deed is to be done I would rather see the
Court give the case a decent burial instead of tossing it out the window of
a fast-moving caboose."[15] The Stevens memo caught the attention of the
chambers of Harry Blackmun, who was deeply worried about his precedent
being overturned. Law clerk Edward Lazarus wrote Blackmun that Stevens's memo "hits the nail right on the head" and "perhaps it will shake
the Chief up a bit." But more importantly, "perhaps it will set SOC [Sandra
Day O'Connor] to thinking. Those are strong words for a man as ordinarily
temperate as JPS [John Paul Stevens]."[16]

Indeed, securing O'Connor's vote was exactly what Stevens's memo did.
With the vast majority of women then in support of the right to legalized
abortion, O'Connor, who had initially seemed to be leaning toward the conservative anti-*Roe* wing and who was the only woman on the Court, did not
want to tip the balance in favor of overturning the ruling and eliminating
this right. While she deliberated for four weeks following the Court's conference discussion on *Webster*, she secretly sent a typescript of her proposed
draft concurrence supporting some abortions to Blackmun. Then, on June 23,
O'Connor circulated her concurrence to the rest of the Court in which she
supported much of the Missouri law but backed away from the chief's direct
assault on *Roe*. Instead of using Rehnquist's new "reasonably furthers the
state's interest in protecting human life" test, which focused on the protection
of the fetus, she took the perspective of the pregnant woman by using her own
"undue burden" test in abortion cases, asking whether the law placed a "substantial obstacle" in front of a woman deciding whether to have an abortion.

Using this rule, she could craft another Solomonic opinion agreeing with
both Court wings. For the conservatives, she argued: "It is clear to me that
requiring the performance of examinations and tests useful to determining
whether a fetus is viable, when viability is possible, and when it would not be
medically imprudent to do so, does not impose an undue burden on a woman's

abortion decision." While the viability test could be upheld, O'Connor then cast her lot with Blackmun and the liberals on the larger issue of the future of the *Roe* decision. "Unlike the Court, I do not understand these viability testing requirements to conflict with any of the Court's past decisions concerning state regulation of abortion. Therefore, there is no necessity to accept the State's invitation to re-examine the constitutional validity of *Roe v. Wade*."[17] Her opinion quickly picked up the support of Stevens and the other pro-*Roe* supporters, thus saving the precedent for another day. Conceding the loss of O'Connor's vote and thus being faced with a majority willing to uphold the *Roe* precedent, Rehnquist circulated a final version of his majority opinion on July 3, admitting, "This case therefore affords us no occasion to revisit the holding of *Roe*, . . . and we leave it undisturbed. To the extent indicated in our opinion, we would modify and narrow *Roe* and succeeding cases."[18]

The late loss of O'Connor's vote and an anti-*Roe* majority was too disappointing for Scalia to bear. Blackmun's clerk wrote on June 26, after O'Connor had circulated a redraft in which she backed away from Rehnquist's opinion, "As you know Justice O'Connor has recirculated. . . . Justice Scalia's clerk tells me that the expected 'Ninogram' will arrive this morning."[19] Reminiscent of his moniker as the "Ninopath" on the Court of Appeals, Scalia would now from time to time on the Supreme Court get so upset about an opinion or a turn of events from a colleague that he would draft a scorching opinion that attacked his colleague by name. But what he circulated later that day was more than just the usual "Ninogram." This was a "Ninofit."

Scalia devoted his entire concurring opinion to attacking O'Connor, using a level of *ad hominem* charges against her rarely seen on the Court, where civility and politeness of argumentation is the normal approach to minimize any offense being taken by life-tenured colleagues whom one may later seek as allies. Scalia opened with a general assault on what he viewed as O'Connor's temporizing in considering whether to overrule the *Roe* precedent: "The outcome of today's case will doubtless be heralded as a triumph of judicial statesmanship. It is not that, unless it is statesmanlike needlessly to prolong this Court's self-awarded sovereignty over a field where it has little proper business since the answers to most of the cruel questions posed are political and not juridical. . . . Justice O'Connor's assertion . . . that a 'fundamental rule of judicial restraint' requires us to avoid reconsidering *Roe*, cannot be taken seriously."[20] For Scalia, the Court "could not avoid deciding" the fate of this precedent as "The only choice available is whether . . . we should use *Roe v. Wade* as the benchmark, or something else."[21] After

showing how O'Connor on several occasions had reconsidered and overruled other precedents, Scalia argued, "It would be wrong, in any decision, to
ignore the reality that our policy not to 'formulate a rule of constitutional law
broader than is required by the precise facts' has a frequently applied good-
cause exception. But it seems particularly perverse to convert the policy into
an absolute in the present case, in order to place beyond reach the inexpress-
ibly 'broader-than-was-required-by-the-precise-facts' structure established
by *Roe v. Wade.*"[22]

Shifting to a broader focus, Scalia argued that the O'Connor decision
would have bad political results for the entire Court in the abortion field:

> Ordinarily, speaking no more broadly than is absolutely required
> avoids throwing settled law into confusion; doing so today preserves
> a chaos that is evident to anyone who can read and count. . . . We can
> now look forward to at least another Term with carts full of mail
> from the public, and streets full of demonstrators, urging us—their
> unelected and life-tenured judges who have been awarded those ex-
> traordinary, undemocratic characteristics precisely in order that we
> might follow the law despite the popular will—to follow the popular
> will. Indeed, I expect we can look forward to even more of that than
> before, given our indecisive decision today.[23]

It was later in the opinion, though, in a footnote discussing O'Connor's
use of the "undue burden" test, that Scalia attacked his colleague personally:
"To avoid the question of *Roe v. Wade*'s validity, with the attendant costs that
this will have for the Court and for the principles of self-governance, on the
basis of a standard that offers 'no guide but the Court's own discretion' . . .
merely adds to the irrationality of what we do today."[24] In response to her
other new test in this case asking whether "viability is possible" to trigger *Roe*'s protections for fetuses, he added, "Similarly irrational is the new
concept that Justice O'Connor introduces into the law in order to achieve
her result, the notion of a State's 'interest in potential life when viability is
possible.' . . . Since 'viability' means the mere possibility (not the certainty) of
survivability outside the womb, 'possible viability' must mean the possibility
of a possibility of survivability outside the womb. Perhaps our next opinion
will expand the third trimester into the second even further, by approving
state action designed to take account of 'the chance of possible viability.'"[25]
Scalia blamed O'Connor and his liberal colleagues for upholding the *Roe*

abortion ruling. "The result of our vote today is that we will not reconsider that prior opinion, even if most of the Justices think it is wrong, unless we have before us a statute that in fact contradicts it. . . . It thus appears that the mansion of constitutionalized abortion law, constructed overnight in *Roe v. Wade*, must be disassembled doorjamb by doorjamb, and never entirely brought down, no matter how wrong it may be."[26]

But any limitation on *Roe* was too much for the now eighty-year-old Harry Blackmun, who, fearing that his *Roe* precedent was indeed being "disassembled" bit by bit, and with the changing Court in jeopardy of one day totally overturning it, wrote in dissent:

> Never in my memory has a plurality announced a judgment of this Court that so foments disregard for the law and for our standing decisions. Nor in my memory has a plurality gone about its business in such a deceptive fashion. . . . The plurality opinion is filled with winks, and nods, and knowing glances to those who would do away with *Roe* explicitly. . . . The simple truth is that *Roe* would not survive the plurality's analysis, and that the plurality provides no substitute for *Roe*'s protective umbrella. I fear for the future. I fear for the liberty and equality of the millions of women who have lived and come of age in the 16 years since *Roe* was decided. I fear for the integrity of, and public esteem for, this Court. I dissent.[27]

• • •

The split between Scalia and O'Connor widened further in April 1990 in a case called *Employment Division of Oregon v. Smith*. The case involved a Native American, Alfred Smith, and an Anglo, Galen Black, who were fired for cause from their jobs as drug rehabilitation counselors in Oregon because they ingested peyote for sacramental purposes as members of the Native American Church. The two men were seeking their unemployment benefits, which they claimed were denied to them because they practiced their religion, even though its tenets violated the state's drug laws. For decades, the Court's decision rules in such cases were considered to be clear. In 1878 the Court had established the "secular regulation rule," in a Mormon polygamy case called *Reynolds v. United States*, positing that neutral laws, which generally applied to everyone, could still be enforced even though they might burden the religions of certain groups, because they were valid "secular regulations."[28]

In 1957, though, the Court changed that rule in a case called *Sherbert v. Verner*, involving government unemployment benefits that were denied by law to people because they had failed to make themselves available to work on Saturdays on the basis that it was forbidden by their religion. In this case Adell Sherbert, a textile mill operator in South Carolina and a Seventh Day Adventist, was denied unemployment benefits because her religion celebrated a Saturday Sabbath, meaning she could not make herself available for work on a Saturday, as the law required to receive the state payments. For William Brennan this state law violated free exercise of religion because it meant that "Governmental imposition of such a choice puts the same kind of burden upon the free exercise of religion as would a fine imposed against appellant for her Saturday worship."[29] Brennan argued that people should not be put in the position of having to make a choice between following their religious beliefs or not doing so in order to receive government benefits necessary to live.

The Court devised a new, higher-level protection of the free exercise of religion for such cases by using a strict scrutiny test to examine any state law that would have the effect of restricting it. To satisfy this test, "We must consider whether some compelling state interest enforced in the eligibility provisions of the South Carolina statute justifies the substantial infringement of appellant's First Amendment right."[30] This meant that the Court would examine the case using "the least restrictive means" test, by which the state had to prove that its regulation, without making any exceptions for affected groups, was the *only* means for achieving its aim, in this case to prevent fraudulent claims of religious reasons for receiving aid. Since there was no evidence of fraud by Sherbert here, but only her religious devotion, and no exception had been written into the law to adjust for adherence to religious beliefs, the state would not be able to prevail.

In the *Smith* peyote case, where a Native American man had been fired because of a state antidrug law and thus denied their free exercise of religion right to smoke peyote, the same result seemed preordained. Like Sherbert before them, they had been put in this situation of having to make a choice between their religion and being eligible for the government benefits necessary to support themselves. Despite the difference that the two men had been fired for cause and then denied benefits, as opposed to Sherbert, who was already unemployed and not making herself available for work on Saturdays, it was argued that an exception to the drug law should be granted to Smith and Black because peyote consumption was an indispensable part of their religion.

But that was not how Scalia and the Court's conservative majority saw it. In this case, decided by a 6–3 vote, Scalia saw a neutral, generally applicable state law dealing with drug use that he argued had only an incidental effect on religion. He and the conservatives wanted to return in such drug law cases to using the *Reynolds* "secular regulation rule." For Scalia, this was a general state law trying to control drugs rather than one negatively affecting the free exercise of religion.[31] Ever the "faint-hearted originalist" who did not want to overturn existing precedent, Scalia did allow for three exceptions that would still trigger the stricter least restrictive means test: cases that were exactly like the *Sherbert* case in denying government benefits despite a religiously inspired action; cases where the states passed their own laws protecting religions with a higher level of judicial scrutiny; and those cases that were "hybrids," raising the Free Exercise Clause issues in conjunction with one or more other constitutional issues, such as the 1972 *Wisconsin v. Yoder* case granting the Amish a religious exception to the compulsory public high school education law.[32] Scalia also left the door open for the federal courts or Congress to create other exceptions to the *Smith* ruling, allowing for "strict scrutiny" protection. Since the two men had arguably violated the state's drug laws and those laws were ruled not to be unconstitutional violations of a Native American's free exercise of religion, they could be denied their unemployment benefits.

Speaking in concurrence, Sandra Day O'Connor argued that by resorting to the more exacting least restrictive means test she would still find that the state could demonstrate its "compelling state interest" in "prohibiting possession of peyote by its citizens." She worried that "A law that makes criminal such an activity therefore triggers constitutional concern—and heightened judicial scrutiny—even if it does not target the particular religious conduct at issue." O'Connor did not like Scalia's "bright-line," general "law as rules" secular regulation rule test: "Our free speech cases similarly recognize that neutral regulations that affect free speech values are subject to a balancing, rather than categorical, approach. . . . The Court's parade of horribles . . . not only fails as a reason for discarding the compelling interest test, it instead demonstrates just the opposite: that courts have been quite capable of applying our free exercise jurisprudence to strike sensible balances between religious liberty and competing state interests."[33] As she would do in later cases, O'Connor would nearly always claim to be observing the compelling state interest test, but then find a sufficient government justification necessary to uphold the regulation.

Scalia was hardly ready to concede this point to the centrist justice whom he had dismissed so contemptuously in the *Webster* abortion case. Adding four footnotes to a second draft of his majority opinion answering O'Connor by name, Scalia said in one of them: "Justice O'Connor contends that the 'parade of horribles' in the text only 'demonstrates . . . that courts have been quite capable of . . . strik[ing] sensible balances between religious liberty and competing state interests.' . . . But the cases we cite have struck 'sensible balances' only because they have all applied the general laws, despite the claims for religious exemption. . . . It is a parade of horribles because it is horrible to contemplate that federal judges will regularly balance against the importance of general laws the significance of religious practice."[34]

Harry Blackmun, among other liberals, signed on to O'Connor's opinion continuing the use of the least restrictive means test, in part because his clerk had worked with the O'Connor clerk to produce her opinion. However, Blackmun and the liberals explained in a separate dissent that their use of the higher level test led them to conclude that the state had *not* shown a compelling state interest and so they argued that the Court should safeguard the religious rights by providing the unemployment benefits. O'Connor remained unconvinced by Scalia's approach, writing a note to Harry Blackmun on the bench when the case opinion was announced on April 17, 1990: "Harry: The Court took the wrong turn in the Free Exercise case in my view. It pains me. S."[35]

•   •   •

By the end of the 1989–90 term, Scalia undertook to "educate" both of the Court's moderate conservatives. Anthony Kennedy was now voting so closely to O'Connor that he also had to be considered a swing justice capable of turning a minority into a majority. A difference between the two centrists was that on occasion Kennedy had a very thin skin and needed to be treated by the other justices with some delicacy. No case made this clearer than an abortion rights case called *Ohio v. Akron Center for Reproductive Health*, dealing with a 1985 Ohio law requiring either parental consent or a judge's permission for a girl under the age of eighteen to receive an abortion. Speaking for a six-judge majority, Kennedy upheld the law, saying that it fulfilled the

more government deferential "rational basis" due process requirements of
the Fourteenth Amendment. Reflecting a good bit of paternalism toward the
litigant, Kennedy concluded in his opinion:

> A free and enlightened society may decide that each of its members
> should attain a clearer, more tolerant understanding of the profound
> philosophic choices confronted by a woman who is considering
> whether to seek an abortion. Her decision will embrace her own des-
> tiny and personal dignity, and the origins of the other human life that
> lie within the embryo. The State is entitled to assume that, for most
> of its people, the beginnings of that understanding will be within the
> family, society's most intimate association. It is both rational and fair
> for the State to conclude that, in most instances, the family will strive
> to give a lonely or even terrified minor advice that is both compas-
> sionate and mature. The statute in issue here is a rational way to fur-
> ther those ends.[36]

In a concurring opinion, Scalia reiterated in a single paragraph his desire
from the 1989 *Webster* case to overturn the 1973 *Roe v. Wade* decision:

> I continue to believe ... that the Constitution contains no right
> to abortion. It is not to be found in the longstanding traditions of
> our society, nor can it be logically deduced from the text of the
> Constitution—not, that is, without volunteering a judicial answer to
> the non-justiciable question of when human life begins. Leaving this
> matter to the political process is not only legally correct, it is prag-
> matically so. That alone—and not lawyerly dissection of federal ju-
> dicial precedents—can produce compromises satisfying a sufficient
> mass of the electorate that this deeply felt issue will cease distorting
> the remainder of our democratic process. The Court should end its
> disruptive intrusion into this field as soon as possible.[37]

What pleased Scalia about Kennedy's ruling disturbed the author of
the *Roe v. Wade* opinion, Harry Blackmun. He argued that in seeming to
preserve the constitutional rights of minors seeking abortions by allowing
them to circumvent obtaining their parents' permission, seeking instead the
permission of a sitting judge through a judicial bypass procedure, the state
of Ohio was actually making it much more difficult for them to make such

a choice. As he wrote in an early draft of his dissent: "Rather than create a judicial-bypass system that reflects the sensitivity necessary when dealing with a minor making this deeply intimate decision, Ohio has created a tortuous maze. Moreover, the State has failed utterly to show that it has any significant state interest in deliberately placing its pattern of obstacles in the path of the pregnant minor seeking to exercise her constitutional right to terminate a pregnancy."[38] In making this argument, Blackmun took particular issue with the broad "state paternalistic protectionist" tone toward minors that Kennedy had adopted for his plurality opinion. Blackmun argued this draft:

> A plurality then concludes . . . with hyperbole that can have but one purpose: to further incite an American press, public, and pulpit already inflamed by the pronouncement made by a plurality of this Court last Term in *Webster v. Reproductive Health Services.* . . . The plurality indulges in paternalistic comments about "profound philosophic choices"; the "[woman's] own destiny and personal dignity" . . . and the desired assumption that "in most cases" the woman will receive "guidance and understanding from a parent." . . . I have cautioned before that there is "another world 'out there'" that the Court "either chooses to ignore or fears to recognize." . . . It is the unfortunate denizens of that world, often frightened and forlorn, lacking the comfort of loving parental guidance and mature advice, who most need the constitutional protection that the Ohio Legislature set out to make as difficult as possible to obtain.[39]

The final version of Blackmun's opinion, though, had one significant change in this section. Blackmun's original first sentence described Kennedy's, and the plurality's, "hyperbole that can have but one purpose: to further incite an American press, public, and pulpit already inflamed by the pronouncement made by a plurality of this Court last Term in *Webster*."[40] Kennedy read this sentence as implying that he had *intended* to reach this political effect, leading him to take great offense at Blackmun's charge. Kennedy took the unusual step, on June 21, of penning a personal note to Blackmun complaining about the phrasing. "After much hesitation, I decided it best for our collegial relation and, I hope, mutual respect to tell you that I harbor deep resentment at your paragraph on page 17 in *Ohio v. Akron Center*," Kennedy began. He continued. "You say my hyperbole is to incite an inflamed public. To write with that purpose would be a violation of my judicial duty. I am still struggling with the whole abortion issue and thought it proper to convey this in what I wrote." Kennedy wanted to make sure that Blackmun understood just why he was so offended: "I do not question the depth of your compassion and understanding, but neither do I yield to the charge that my own is somehow a mask for some improper purpose." All of that said, Kennedy now hoped to change his colleague's mind. "In any event, though it is late in the term, I thought you would want to hear this; and perhaps it will prompt you to reconsider what is a most unfair attribution of motives not consonant with the conscientious discharge of my office."[41]

While Kennedy's note got Blackmun's attention, it did not persuade him to remove the sentence entirely. Instead, he chose to replace the single word "purpose" in the phrase "hyperbole that can have but one purpose" with the word "result."[42] But Kennedy would soon have reasons to be offended by another colleague's language.

• • •

At the end of the 1989–90 term, the Court revisited, in a case called *Maryland v. Craig*, the questions left over from the *Coy v. Iowa* Confrontation Clause case two years before. A six-year-old girl, who the state said was a victim of sexual assault by the operator of a kindergarten center, was permitted to testify on a one-way closed circuit television. Like the use of the protective screen to shield the young witnesses in the *Coy* case, the state of Maryland argued here that the televised testimony protected the sensitivities of the child. The defense argued, though, that the process did not permit them to confront and cross-examine the witness as safeguarded by the Sixth Amendment. The voting quickly became complicated, and for a time it looked like the Court might deadlock 4–4–1, with Blackmun remaining unaligned. At this point the very active law clerk network began formulating a deal. Harry Blackmun's law clerk, Martha Matthews, wrote her boss, "J. O'Connor's clerk called me today, with a query about whether you might be persuaded to change your vote. The voting in this case is quite complicated. . . . The CJ [chief justice] assigned the opinion to SOC [Sandra Day O'Connor]; AS [Antonin Scalia] will write separately. SOC is concerned that, as matters stand now, the case might come out 4–4–1, and not resolve the Confrontation Clause issue. Her clerk hopes that you might be persuaded to join SOC's opinion, because her reasoning is much closer to your views as indicated in *Coy*, than AS's would be."[43]

O'Connor gave Blackmun a preview of her opinion, making an exception to the Confrontation Clause for victims of child sexual abuse, but Blackmun's clerk was not completely persuaded that it squared with Blackmun's dissenting opinion in the *Coy* case defending the use of a screen to protect the juvenile witnesses. The problem, the clerk explained, was strategic in nature: "There is an obvious strategic reason to join J. O'Connor's opinion. If you don't, there probably will be no opinion of the Court, because J. Scalia's position [in favor of direct, face-to-face questioning], with which you strongly disagree, may also have four votes. It may be better, as a matter of policy, to have a decision holding that exceptions to confrontation in child abuse cases are permissible, at least under certain conditions—rather than, by adhering to your conference vote, leaving that basic issue unresolved." The clerk concluded: "I hope that you can find a way to join J. O'Connor's opinion, both because I think her view is right, and for the strategic reasons I have outlined." [44] On June 1, Blackmun wrote O'Connor that while he had difficulties in voting for her position in light of his dissent in the *Coy* case, "I certainly am closer to your views than I am to Nino's. Why don't you circulate your opinion and let the case get underway. I shall do my best to find a way to join you. I may write separately or I may not, depending on what an initial draft here looks like." [45]

After Blackmun later signaled his willingness to switch his vote to join O'Connor's majority opinion, she argued on behalf of an exception to the Confrontation Clause for child witnesses in sexual abuse cases: "That the face-to-face confrontation requirement is not absolute does not, of course, mean that it may easily be dispensed with. As we suggested in *Coy*, our precedents confirm that a defendant's right to confront accusatory witnesses may be satisfied absent a physical, face-to-face confrontation at trial only where denial of such confrontation is necessary to further an important public policy and only where the reliability of the testimony is otherwise assured." [46] O'Connor concluded: "We likewise conclude today that a State's interest in the physical and psychological well-being of child abuse victims may be sufficiently important to outweigh, at least in some cases, a defendant's right to face his or her accusers in court." [47] In the end, after having his clerk draft a concurring opinion to resolve his new position relative to the *Coy* case, Blackmun decided simply to sign O'Connor's majority opinion, choosing to follow his clerk's "alternative of joining J. O'Connor without writing at all, and letting the commentators try to figure it out." [48]

Frustrated again, Scalia once more unloaded in dissent on his favorite target. He began by accusing O'Connor of playing politics with the Constitution. "Seldom has this Court failed so conspicuously to sustain a categorical guarantee of the Constitution against the tide of prevailing current opinion."[49] Reminiscent of the *Webster* case, Scalia belittled O'Connor's interpretation of the Confrontation Clause as not requiring face-to-face confrontation of one's accusers in a trial:

> That is rather like saying "we cannot say that being tried before a jury is an indispensable element of the Sixth Amendment's guarantee of the right to jury trial." The Court makes the impossible plausible by recharacterizing the Confrontation Clause, so that confrontation (redesignated "face-to-face confrontation") becomes only one of many "elements of confrontation." . . . This reasoning abstracts from the right to its purposes, and then eliminates the right. It is wrong because the Confrontation Clause does not guarantee reliable evidence; it guarantees specific trial procedures that were thought to assure reliable evidence, undeniably among which was "face-to-face confrontation."[50]

Then Scalia also attacked O'Connor's process in reaching this judgment: "The Court supports its anti-textual conclusion by cobbling together scraps of dicta from various cases that have no bearing here."[51] And then he argued that the majority had lost sight of the real interests in these cases:

> The Court characterizes the State's interest which "outweigh[s]" the explicit text of the Constitution as an "interest in the physical and psychological well-being of child abuse victims" . . . [and] an "interest in protecting" such victims "from the emotional trauma of testifying." . . . That is not so. . . . Protection of the child's interest—as far as the Confrontation Clause is concerned—is entirely within Maryland's control. The State's interest here is in fact no more and no less than what the State's interest always is when it seeks to get a class of evidence admitted in criminal proceedings: more convictions of guilty defendants. That is not an unworthy interest, but it should not be dressed up as a humanitarian one.[52]

And so Scalia concluded: "The Court has convincingly proved that the Maryland procedure serves a valid interest, and gives the defendant virtually everything the Confrontation Clause guarantees (everything, that is, except confrontation). I am persuaded, therefore, that the Maryland procedure is virtually constitutional. Since it is not, however, actually constitutional I would affirm the judgment of the Maryland Court of Appeals reversing the judgment of conviction."[53]

Whatever satisfaction Scalia may have gotten from his renewed criticism of Justice O'Connor came at a heavy price. He lost yet another member of the center of the Court as an ally, Anthony Kennedy. The beginning of Kennedy's shift away from Scalia in this period became noticeable to the press. One legal commentator, Richard C. Reuben, noted in an article on Kennedy that "Scalia's combativeness, judicial extremism and penchant for the jugular in dissenting opinions had begun to undercut his effectiveness. The gentlemanly Kennedy was said by former clerks to be put off by Scalia's fanged personal attacks on O'Connor in abortion and child witness testimony cases . . . drawing him closer to O'Connor."[54]

A loss of alliance with either, or both, of the moderate jurists would have real consequences for the conservatives as the aging Court began to change again on July 20, 1990. William Brennan, having suffered a devastating stroke a month earlier, sent his letter of retirement to President George H. W. Bush. "This was a very difficult decision after almost 34 years of service on the Court," Brennan announced in a separate statement. "It is my hope that the Court during my years of service has built a legacy of interpreting the Constitution and Federal laws to make them responsive to the needs of the people whom they were intended to benefit and protect. This legacy can and will withstand the test of time."[55] On July 23, Bush took the advice of two prominent New Hampshire Republicans, Senator Warren Rudman and Bush's chief of staff, John Sununu, and selected a judge from the Court of Appeals for the First Circuit, David Hackett Souter, to fill the vacancy. The president cited Souter for his "keen intellect and highest ability," with an aide adding that Souter was "a conservative, but not an extra-chromosome conservative."[56]

Souter was, in fact, the diametric opposite in philosophy and temperament from Scalia. He was a quiet, learned, independent-minded judge who still lived in his childhood home—a farmhouse in tiny Weare, New Hampshire, near the state capital of Concord. According to *The Washington Post*, Souter was also "a catalogue of such Puritan virtues as humility, probity, thrift, and industry; a disciplined, self-reliant New Englander who is happiest collecting rare books, reading volumes of history or hiking the White

Mountains."[57] Souter had been on the Court of Appeals so briefly that William Brennan, who had been the supervisory justice for the First Circuit, did not know him. At the time, though, it seemed like a reliable conservative choice for Bush, with Court reporter Stuart Taylor writing for *The Washington Post*, "Surprise! Souter Won't Surprise Bush."[58] After a swift confirmation by the Senate, Souter joined the Court for the 1990–91 term.

· · ·

Learning no lessons from his failing relationships with O'Connor and Kennedy, Scalia made no effort to amend his ways during the following term. Instead, in two jury trial cases, he sent Kennedy a "Ninogram" similar to the one he sent O'Connor in the *Webster* case.[59] These cases were an extension of a 1986 case called *Batson v. Kentucky*, in which the Court considered whether it was constitutional for the state's attorney to remove all of the potential African American jurors from a trial by using peremptory challenges, that is, dismissal without stating a reason. The Court, speaking through Justice Lewis Powell, ruled that if the reasons for the removal of the jurors was "purposeful discrimination," and the state could not meet its burden to suggest "a neutral explanation for his action," then any conviction under this kind of racially imbalanced jury would be reversed.[60]

In the first of the new cases, *Powers v. Ohio*, a Caucasian defendant in a murder trial objected to the removal of all of the African American jurors using peremptory challenges. Speaking for the majority, Justice Kennedy wrote that objections could be raised under the Fourteenth Amendment Equal Protection Clause to such peremptory challenge removals from a jury regardless of whether the race of the defendant and the jurors was the same. For Kennedy, the harm was not just to the defendant, but also to the potential jurors. He began his opinion by offering a civics argument that such jurors would miss the opportunity for civil service: "Jury service is an exercise of responsible citizenship by all members of the community, including those who otherwise might not have the opportunity to contribute to our civic life." For him, discrimination in this area caused an unconstitutional level of harm: "Active discrimination by a prosecutor during this process condones violations of the United States Constitution within the very institution entrusted with its enforcement, and so invites cynicism respecting the jury's neutrality and its obligation to adhere to the law." In addition, Kennedy argued, the excluded jurors would feel the sting of discrimination: "Both the excluded juror and the criminal defendant have a common interest in eliminating racial discrimination from the courtroom. A venire-person excluded from jury service because of race suffers a profound personal humiliation heightened by its public character. The rejected juror may lose confidence in the court and its verdicts, as may the defendant if his or her objections cannot be heard." Kennedy sought to remedy this situation by permitting "legitimate and well-founded objections to the use of peremptory challenges as a mask for race prejudice."[61]

Scalia was not swayed by Kennedy's ode to civic duty and nondiscrimination and made his objections known in a dismissive, cutting dissent. He argued that invoking race was not a reason to limit the use of peremptory challenges: "Our jurisprudence contain[s] neither a case holding, nor even a dictum suggesting that a defendant could raise an equal protection challenge based upon the exclusion of a juror of another race; and our opinions contained a vast body of clear statement to the contrary." As for Kennedy's fear that "doubt" and "cynicism" would result from such racial exclusion, Scalia was thoroughly unimpressed, asking how it proved that the person had been "injured in fact":

> Today's opinion makes a mockery of that requirement. It does not even pretend that the peremptory challenges here have caused this defendant tangible injury and concrete harm—but rather (with careful selection of both adjectives and nouns) only a *"cognizable* injury," producing a "concrete *interest* in challenging the practice." . . . I have no doubt he now has a cognizable injury; the Court has made it true by saying so. And I have no doubt he has a concrete interest in challenging the practice at issue here; he would have a concrete interest in challenging a mispronunciation of one of the jurors' names, if that would overturn his conviction. But none of this has anything to do with injury in fact.[62]

Scalia later mocked Kennedy for his quixotic mission to remedy America's racial ills:

> Judging from the Court's opinion, we can expect further, wide-ranging use of the jailhouse key to combat discrimination. . . . To me, this makes no sense. Lofty aims do not justify every step intended to achieve them. Today's supposed blow against racism, while enormously self-satisfying, is unmeasured and misdirected. If for any rea-

son the State is unable to reconvict Powers for the double murder at issue here, later victims may pay the price for our extravagance.[63]

Two months later, when Kennedy and the majority in *Edmonson v. Leesville Concrete Co.* denied private litigants in civil trials the right to exclude jurors purely for racial reasons, Scalia took aim again. Scalia argued that the decision was "unfortunate in its consequences. . . . *Both* sides have peremptory challenges, and they are sometimes used to *assure* rather than to *prevent* a racially diverse jury."[64] But his main purpose in this short dissenting opinion was to attack Kennedy's majority opinion, saying: "Although today's decision neither follows the law nor produces desirable concrete results, it certainly has great symbolic value. To overhaul the doctrine of state action in this fashion, what a magnificent demonstration of this institution's uncompromising hostility to race-based judgments, even by private actors! The price of the demonstration is, alas, high, and much of it will be paid by the minority litigants who use our courts."[65]

O'Connor later denied, in an interview with ABC News's George Stephanopoulos, that the "very, very biting" language in Scalia's dissents against her ever affected her: "When you work in a small group of that size, you have to get along and so you're not going to let some harsh language and some dissenting opinion affect your personal relationship. You can't do that."[66] It was excellent public relations, but those who study the Court could chart the effect of Scalia's words by noting how many times O'Connor and Kennedy now voted apart from Scalia, most especially in key cases. Journalist Jeffrey Toobin reported that in a later case, after Chief Justice Rehnquist had read another biting dissent by Scalia against O'Connor, he sent a note to his junior colleague, "Nino, you're pissing off Sandra again. Stop it!"[67]

By the end of the 1991 term, the case vote statistics showed how severely Scalia had damaged his relations with O'Connor and Kennedy. In his first three terms, Kennedy voted with Scalia an average of about 84 percent of the time, and was so in sync with Scalia that his own law clerks quietly referred to him as "Nini," meaning "little Nino."[68] Kennedy's agreement score with Scalia dropped to 72.4 percent in the 1990 term and fell even more, to 62.3 percent in the 1991 term. But the real damage in Scalia's voting power came in his relationship with O'Connor. After voting with Scalia just under 80 percent of the time in the 1989 term, her agreement with him dropped to 68.9 percent in the 1990 term and then to 53.5 percent of the time in the 1991 term.[69]

• • •

The membership of the Supreme Court changed again at the end of the 1990–91 term when Justice Thurgood Marshall, visibly discouraged by the loss of his longtime ally William Brennan and by the unabated string of losses that term to the conservative wing's 5–4 vote majority, announced on June 27, 1991, that he would be retiring. Marshall was particularly dismayed by the Court's end-of-term decision reversing its earlier precedents and allowing the use of victim impact statements in criminal trials in *Payne v. Tennessee*. Responding to the reversal of the Court's earlier judgments in the 1987 *Booth v. Maryland* and 1989 *South Carolina v. Gathers*, and thus a victory for Scalia's earlier dissenting position, an anguished Marshall saw this change as evidence of a shifting ideological Court membership, rather than a reinterpretation of the Constitution: "Power, not reason, is the new currency of this court's decision-making. Neither the law nor the facts supporting [these cases] underwent any change in the last four years. Only the personnel of this Court did."[70] Marshall ensured that there would be an airing of his views two years later, when he posthumously allowed the Library of Congress to release his judicial papers for scholarly study immediately upon his death in May 1993, thus enabling critical studies to be made of the conservative justices with whom he served.

Given his second opportunity to make an appointment to the Court, on July 1, 1991, President Bush announced his nomination of Clarence Thomas, an African American Court of Appeals judge for the District of Columbia, who had been the head of the Equal Employment Opportunity Commission in the Reagan administration. Bush explained that he had selected Thomas, an avowed conservative who had been raised by his grandparents in rural Georgia, because he was "the best person at the right time."[71]

Part of Thomas's appeal was that he was an African American replacing the legendary Marshall—also an African American and the grandson of a slave. Since Thomas had been confirmed by the Senate for the D.C. Court of Appeals just sixteen months earlier, he was expected to be easily confirmed for this appointment. However, it was not to be. Thomas was subjected to a bitter two-part confirmation hearing, with the first questioning his competence, and the second delving into sexual harassment allegations by law professor Anita Hill, who had worked with him at the EEOC. In the end, Thomas was confirmed by the Senate on October 15, by a 52–48 margin, the closest positive Supreme Court confirmation vote in a hundred years.

The confirmation of the ultraconservative Thomas to replace the ultraliberal Marshall led Court watchers to expect a much more conservative court. It appeared that now with Thomas, the other reliable conservatives, White, Rehnquist, and Scalia, together with the anticipated conservative vote from David Souter, would not need O'Connor or Kennedy to turn the Court their way.

When the 1991–92 term opened, Scalia had a chance to lead this new conservative wing by demonstrating his libertarian instincts toward the First Amendment's guarantee of freedom of speech. In December 1991, the Court heard arguments on the controversial issue of "hate speech" in the case of *R.A.V. v. St. Paul.* Worried about anti-minority statements and abusive, harassing, symbolic speech by hate-mongering individuals and groups, the city council of St. Paul, Minnesota, had banned certain kinds of offensive and harassing speech. The St. Paul Bias-Motivated Crime Ordinance, passed in 1990, provided that "Whoever places on public or private property a symbol, object, appellation, characterization or graffiti, including, but not limited to, a burning cross or Nazi swastika, which one knows or has reasonable grounds to know arouses anger, alarm or resentment in others on the basis of race, color, creed, religion or gender commits disorderly conduct and shall be guilty of a misdemeanor."[72]

Several teenagers in St. Paul, one of whose initials were R.A.V., were arrested because they had assembled a crude cross of broken wooden chair legs and tape and burned it before dawn inside the fenced yard of an African American family who had moved into their neighborhood. The question here should have been whether the law was an unconstitutional "content-based regulation," targeting certain kinds of speech, and thus allowing the authorities to ban speech they did not like. Instead, the Court chose to duck this issue by ruling on the basis of statutory interpretation whether the language of the ordinance had been written narrowly enough, that is, whether it covered *only* speech that was harmful and no more.

The key precedent for the case came from 1942. In *Chaplinsky v. New Hampshire* the Court had created the "fighting words" exception, by which overly offensive speech that moves the listener immediately to consider fighting was unprotected by the First Amendment and could be banned. The Court proposed a "two-tier theory" of speech, the higher level being a fundamental right to be protected by the Court: "Freedom of speech and freedom of the press, which are protected by the First Amendment from infringement by Congress, are among the fundamental personal rights and liberties which are protected by the Fourteenth Amendment from invasion by state action." [73] In the *Chaplinsky* case, though, the "fighting words" speech came from a "lower level" that did not express protected ideas, and could be banned:

> There are certain well-defined and narrowly limited classes of speech, the prevention and punishment of which have never been thought to raise any Constitutional problem. These include the lewd and obscene, the profane, the libelous, and the insulting or "fighting" words—those which by their very utterance inflict injury or tend to incite an immediate breach of the peace. It has been well observed that such utterances are no essential part of any exposition of ideas, and are of such slight social value as a step to truth that any benefit that may be derived from them is clearly outweighed by the social interest in order and morality. [74]

A unanimous Court in *R.A.V.* agreed to overturn the St. Paul ordinance, but could not agree on the reasons for doing so. In technical legal terms, the Court could not agree whether this law unconstitutionally banned too much speech, that is, included protected speech in its definition, thus making it "overbroad" or "over-inclusive," or whether it did not ban enough hateful speech, leaving some unconstitutional speech still unregulated, meaning that the law was "under-broad" or "under-inclusive." While the Court agreed that the government could ban only illegal speech and no more or less, it could not agree exactly what constituted unconstitutional "hate speech." Did it also include offensive speech, or speech that hurt people's feelings in addition to threatening speech, or just speech that drove people to immediately considering fighting? The justices focused on how to define banned speech, rather than fashioning a majority directly on the question of whether the Court would allow the banning of harmful and unconstitutional speech at all.

Scalia had already shown his willingness to protect all speech, even that which he did not like, in the 1989 case of *Texas v. Johnson* concerning flag burning. In *R.A.V.*, he argued that the St. Paul ordinance was both "content-based regulation," banning types of speech that the city council did not like, and was "under-inclusive," failing to ban speech that could be deemed harmful because it did not communicate ideas with social worth. As he argued: "The ordinance applies only to 'fighting words' that insult, or provoke violence, 'on the basis of race, color, creed, religion or gender.' . . . Those who wish to use 'fighting words' in connection with other ideas—to express hostility, for example, on the basis of political affiliation, union membership, or homosexuality—are not covered. The First Amendment does not permit St. Paul to impose special prohibitions on those speakers who express views on disfavored subjects."[75] In arguing that the ordinance constituted "viewpoint discrimination," Scalia used one example of the problems of defining "fighting words" that seemed for him to be very close to home: "One could hold up a sign saying, for example, that all 'anti-Catholic bigots' are misbegotten; but not that all 'papists' are, for that would insult and provoke violence 'on the basis of religion.' St. Paul has no such authority to license one side of a debate to fight freestyle, while requiring the other to follow Marquis of Queensberry rules."[76] Scalia concluded: "Let there be no mistake about our belief that burning a cross in someone's front yard is reprehensible. But St. Paul has sufficient means at its disposal to prevent such behavior without adding the First Amendment to the fire."[77]

Several of Scalia's colleagues, including the other conservatives, sided with his result but did not agree with his reasons for doing so. In concurrence, conservative Byron White argued that Scalia's interpretation was "an arid, doctrinaire interpretation, driven by the frequently irresistible impulse of judges to tinker with the First Amendment. The decision is mischievous at best and will surely confuse the lower courts. I join the judgment, but not the folly of the opinion."[78] For his part, moderate John Paul Stevens argued that the ordinance "does not ban all 'hate speech,' nor does it ban, say, all cross burnings or all swastika displays." Instead, Stevens explained, "it only bans a subcategory of the already narrow category of fighting words. Such a limited ordinance leaves open and protected a vast range of expression on the subjects of racial, religious, and gender equality. . . . Petitioner is free to burn a cross to announce a rally or to express his views about racial supremacy, he may do so on private property or public land, at day or at night, so long as the burning is not so threatening and so directed at an individual as to 'by its very [execution] inflict injury.' Such a limited proscription scarcely offends the First Amendment."[79]

As in other cases during the previous three years, beyond the unanimous pro–free speech position the *R.A.V.* case should have been one in which Scalia, with his devotion to protecting free speech, should have been able to lead the conservative majority on the Rehnquist Court to a clear resolution of the issue. Instead, it demonstrated once again how difficult this was for him to do.

As the 1991–92 term ended, Scalia seemed oblivious to the widening gap between him and the centrist justices, O'Connor and Kennedy. But for them, the worst of Scalia's wrath was yet to come.

CHAPTER 12

The Evil Nino

The turning point in the relationship between Antonin Scalia and Anthony Kennedy came in an establishment of religion case at the end of the 1991–92 term. *Lee v. Weisman* concerned Providence, Rhode Island, inviting a rabbi to deliver a nonsectarian prayer at its public middle school graduation. The father of a middle school student, Deborah Weisman, asked the Court to issue a permanent injunction against such prayers, arguing that forcing non-believers to be confronted with a state-enforced religious exercise violated the First Amendment's Establishment of Religion Clause.

Three years earlier, the Court had decided a pair of religion cases reinterpreting the three-pronged *Lemon* test created in 1973. The test, which had been used to decide the *Edwards v. Aguillard* creationism case in 1987, was designed to allow for some accommodation by the state toward religion, but not to create so much of a connection as to establish a state-backed religion. Since that time, though, the Court's newest members began reinterpreting the standard to allow for a greater interconnection between church and state.

They had an impact in the 1989 case of *County of Allegheny v. American Civil Liberties Union*, which combined challenges to two religious displays in the city of Pittsburgh's public buildings. One of these displays was a nativity crèche in the lobby at the base of the grand staircase in the Allegheny County Courthouse. Donated by the Holy Name Society, the crèche contained a banner reading "Gloria in Excelsis Deo!" ("Glory to God in the Highest!").[1] The other display was an eighteen-foot Chanukah menorah placed by the Jewish Chabad Society outside the Pittsburgh City-County Building near a forty-five-foot-tall Christmas tree.

Five justices, led by Harry Blackmun, with a concurrence from Sandra Day O'Connor, used the *Lemon* test to rule that the display inside the courthouse building was an unconstitutional violation of the Freedom of

Religion Clause of the First Amendment because its principal effect was to advance religion, but allowed the menorah outside the building, because it did "not have an effect of endorsing religious faith."[2] Blackmun's language was drawn from O'Connor's "no [government] endorsement" of religion variation of the *Lemon* test that she had introduced in the 1984 *Lynch v. Donnelly,* ruling to allow a publicly supported nativity scene erected during the Christmas season in Pawtucket, Rhode Island. In this case, the display was allowed because the nativity scene was surrounded by other nonsectarian seasonal holiday symbols.

Kennedy objected in the *Allegheny* case to what he saw as Blackmun's anti-religion view: "The majority holds that the County of Allegheny violated the Establishment Clause by displaying a creche in the county courthouse, because the 'principal or primary effect' of the display is to advance religion within the meaning of *Lemon v. Kurtzman.* . . . This view of the Establishment Clause reflects an unjustified hostility toward religion, a hostility inconsistent with our history and our precedents, and I dissent from this holding." Then, taking a page from Scalia's playbook, Kennedy, normally a decorous colleague relying on civility in his communications, continued:

> Obsessive, implacable resistance to all but the most carefully scripted and secularized forms of accommodation requires this Court to act as a censor, issuing national decrees as to what is orthodox and what is not. What is orthodox, in this context, means what is secular; the only Christmas the State can acknowledge is one in which references to religion have been held to a minimum. The Court thus lends its assistance to an Orwellian rewriting of history as many understand it. I can conceive of no judicial function more antithetical to the First Amendment.[3]

Blackmun, also normally very diplomatic in his Court relations, gave as good as he got. He wrote of his colleague: "Although Justice Kennedy repeatedly accuses the Court of harboring a 'latent hostility' or 'callous indifference' toward religion . . . nothing could be further from the truth, and the accusations could be said to be as offensive as they are absurd. Justice Kennedy apparently has misperceived a respect for religious pluralism, a respect commanded by the Constitution, as hostility or indifference to religion. No misperception could be more antithetical to the values embodied in the Establishment Clause."[4] Then Blackmun got even more personal, adding:

"Although Justice Kennedy accuses the Court of 'an Orwellian rewriting of history' . . . perhaps it is Justice Kennedy himself who has slipped into a form of Orwellian newspeak when he equates the constitutional command of secular government with a prescribed orthodoxy. . . . This Court is ill equipped to sit as a national theology board, and I question both the wisdom and the constitutionality of its doing so."[5] Later, Blackmun would learn that his verbal shot at Kennedy had found its mark.

In the 1992 *Weisman* graduation prayer case, the fact that atheist and agnostic students and relatives were compelled to sit through a school-endorsed prayer in order to participate in a graduation exercise made a difference to Kennedy. This became clear in his questions during the oral argument of Charles J. Cooper, assistant attorney general for the Office of Legal Counsel, on November 6, 1991, where Kennedy indicated that he might see this case differently from the earlier Christmas display case:

> Justice Kennedy: Has there been a stipulation that there's no stigma to the student who absents him or herself from the graduation during the prayer?
> Mr. Cooper: No, Your Honor, there is no such—
> Justice Kennedy: I find it very difficult to accept the proposition that it is not a substantial imposition on a young graduate to say you have your choice of . . . I want to characterize it in a neutral way . . . hearing this prayer, or absenting yourself from the graduation. In our culture, a graduation is a key event in the young person's life. The family comes, aunts, uncles, brothers, sisters. And I think it's a very, very substantial burden on the person to say that he or she cannot . . . can elect not to go.[6]

The argument might have continued further had it not been interrupted by Scalia, who proceeded to dominate the remainder of the discussion.

In the conference discussion of the *Weisman* case, Kennedy originally voted with Scalia and the other pro–church-state accommodation conservatives, as he had in the earlier *Allegheny* case, to uphold the graduation prayer. As the centrist whose vote was most needed to solidify the majority here, he was assigned by the chief justice to write the opinion. By March 30, though, he had come to a different point of view. Kennedy wrote to Blackmun: "After writing to reverse in the high school graduation prayer case, my draft looked quite wrong. So I have written it to rule in favor of the objecting student, both at middle school and high school exercises. The Chief said to go ahead and circulate, and I thought as the senior member of those who voted for this result you should have brief advance notice." Then Kennedy went further, seeking to build a new diplomatic bridge to Blackmun by putting his changed view on this issue into a larger context: "After the barbs in . . . [*County of Allegheny v. ACLU*], many between the two of us, I thought it most important to write something that you and I and the others who voted this way can join. That is why this took me longer than it should have and, of course, I will be most attentive to your criticisms. Probable circulation is late this afternoon, but for now you might keep this memo between us." In light of the testy relations between them, this was welcome news to Blackmun, who well understood that the shifting of alliances on this balanced Court could have implications for many other issues, including his 1973 *Roe v. Wade* abortion decision.[7] Later that day Kennedy circulated his newly changed draft, indicating his switched vote against the school graduation prayer.[8]

When Kennedy switched, there were five justices in support of *Weisman*. By Court rules, with the chief justice in dissent, the duty fell to Blackmun as the senior justice in the new majority to assign the writer of the opinion. He assigned it to Kennedy in order to keep him in the majority. Kennedy's approach was to spin off his oral argument question to create his own version of the *Lemon* test, the "no coercion" test. In his view, this school graduation prayer coerced students to listen to religious views they do not hold: "Prayer exercises in public schools carry a particular risk of indirect coercion. The concern may not be limited to the context of schools, but it is most pronounced there. . . . What to most believers may seem nothing more than a reasonable request that the nonbeliever respect their religious practices, in a school context may appear to the nonbeliever or dissenter to be an attempt to employ the machinery of the State to enforce a religious orthodoxy."[9] By applying this new test to the circumstances in this case, where students might feel compelled to miss an important event in their lives, Kennedy decided that the school graduation prayer could not stand:

> Everyone knows that in our society and in our culture high school graduation is one of life's most significant occasions. A school rule which excuses attendance is beside the point. Attendance may not be required by official decree, yet it is apparent that a student is not free to absent herself from the graduation exercise in any real sense

of the term "voluntary," for absence would require forfeiture of those intangible benefits which have motivated the student through youth and all her high school years. Graduation is a time for family and those closest to the student to celebrate success and express mutual wishes of gratitude and respect, all to the end of impressing upon the young person the role that it is his or her right and duty to assume in the community and all of its diverse parts.[10]

As happy as Blackmun was with Kennedy's switched vote, Scalia was even more distressed. As was now his wont, he attacked Kennedy with gusto. Having signed Kennedy's opinion in the earlier *Allegheny* case, Scalia, driven by his theory of deciding based on historical American traditions, now parted company in a draft dissent circulated to the Court on June 18: "Three Terms ago, I joined an opinion recognizing that the Establishment Clause must be construed in light of the 'government policies of accommodation, acknowledgment, and support for religion [that] are an accepted part of our political and cultural heritage.' That opinion affirmed that 'the meaning of the Clause is to be determined by reference to historical practices and understandings.' . . . These views of course prevent me from joining today's opinion, which is conspicuously bereft of any reference to history." What Scalia did not like was Kennedy's substitution of Scalia's search for American traditions with a new social science–based test, as he argued: "In holding that the Establishment Clause prohibits invocations and benedictions at public school graduation ceremonies, the Court—with nary a mention that it is doing so—lays waste a tradition that is as old as public school graduation ceremonies themselves, and that is a component of an even more longstanding American tradition of nonsectarian prayer to God at public celebrations generally. As its instrument of destruction, the bulldozer of its social engineering, the Court invents a boundless, and boundlessly manipulable, test of psychological coercion." To Scalia, Kennedy had become a judicial chameleon, and he was now ready to make him pay the price. "Today's opinion shows more forcefully than volumes of argumentation why our Nation's protection, that fortress which is our Constitution, cannot possibly rest upon the changeable philosophical predilections of the Justices of this Court, but must have deep foundations in the historic practices of our people."[11]

Just as he had done with O'Connor in the *Webster* case, Scalia then lit into Kennedy personally, belittling his new test assessing the level of "coercion" of a religious exercise:

The Court presumably would separate graduation invocations and benedictions from other instances of public "preservation and transmission of religious beliefs" on the ground that they involve "psychological coercion." I find it a sufficient embarrassment that our Establishment Clause jurisprudence regarding holiday displays ... has come to "require scrutiny more commonly associated with interior decorators than with the judiciary." ... But interior decorating is a rock-hard science compared to psychology practiced by amateurs. A few citations of "research in psychology" that have no particular bearing upon the precise issue here ... cannot disguise the fact that the Court has gone beyond the realm where judges know what they are doing. The Court's argument that state officials have "coerced" students to take part in the invocation and benediction at graduation ceremonies is, not to put too fine a point on it, incoherent.[12]

Scalia's attack did not end there. After suggesting that overturning the Pledge of Allegiance, with its "Under God" provision being forced on unbelieving public school students, "ought to be the next project for the Court's bulldozer" using Kennedy's "no coercion" test, Scalia could not help adding an attack on the existing *Lemon* test that he so despised. He argued: "The Court today demonstrates the irrelevance of *Lemon* by essentially ignoring it ... and the interment of that case may be the one happy byproduct of the Court's otherwise lamentable decision. Unfortunately, however, the Court has replaced *Lemon* with its psycho-coercion test, which suffers the double disability of having no roots whatever in our people's historic practice, and being as infinitely expandable as the reasons for psychotherapy itself."[13] If Kennedy did not like what Blackmun said about his motives in the earlier *Akron* abortion case, he certainly could not be pleased by this personal challenge to his jurisprudential process.

Scalia's vigorous dissent, though, caught the attention of another justice in what was now becoming the three-justice centrist wing of the Court. The scholarly and unfailingly polite David Souter decided to show the rest of the Court how to deal with its outspoken right-wing historian. An independent-minded, moderate conservative, Souter was the only justice who did not have a computer on his desk, preferring to write to his colleagues in longhand. His notes often contained metaphorical phrases drawn from his native New England to describe Court actions. In his words, a wavering justice was "walking the fence," reducing the reach of an opinion became "trimming the sails," and combining two differing opinions into a compromise judgment was, in the parlance of New Hampshire's practice of boiling sap to get maple syrup, "sugaring off."

Having taken his seat on the Court in early October 1990, Souter had not yet spoken from the high bench on the religion issue. While the Court volleyed back and forth in its initial negotiations, Souter sent a note to Harry Blackmun, who, as the senior justice then in the dissent, was drafting what was expected to be the main statement for that side: "Because [the *Weisman* case] is the first one on the Establishment Clause since my arrival, I will write something to stake out my ground, and have begun working on it."[14]

Six weeks later, Souter sent Blackmun a handwritten note reading: "I will of course defer any circulation until I see yours, and probably will not have tried to put anything into final form before reading yours anyway. I'm thinking of your opinion as the flagship on our side, whatever else I may feel the need to say for personal reasons."[15] Four months later, on April 15, 1992, after Kennedy switched his vote, Souter sent Blackmun another note, saying: "Since this is my first Establishment case, I expect to follow my original plan of filing a separate opinion to show where I stand on some, though hardly on all, of the points on which such cases turn."[16] While it was clear that Souter would not be following Scalia, Thomas, White, and Rehnquist's "pro–state accommodation" of religion posture in the dissent, with the Court majority debating how to frame the opinion of the Court, Souter had a chance to declare his choice of test for dealing with establishment of religion cases. But Souter did much more than that. He wanted to demonstrate how to beat Scalia's historical originalism approach on its own terms.

Relying on Scalia's type of originalist inquiry to decide this case, Souter demonstrated how the same Founding Era historical evidence could be read to support the *opposite* conclusion from his conservative colleague. He used the historical "public meaning" of the First Amendment to argue that many of the Founders were Deists who did not favor organized religion and opposed the state Anglicanism of Great Britain. For them, the danger of the church and state accommodationist reading of this history, which Scalia was positing, was the possibility that a state might seek to impose a religious view on the people that they did not hold. The linchpin of this argument, Souter well knew, was that Thomas Jefferson and James Madison, who wrote the First Amendment, expressly sought to erect what they described as a "high wall of separation" between church and state and sought to allow people to freely exercise whatever religion, or lack of religion, they chose to protect the "freedom of thought," "freedom of choice," and the "freedom not to believe." In short, Souter argued that by maintaining this high wall of separation between church and state, the Founders protected the religious, the irreligious, and the nonreligious.[17]

Souter was embracing what would later become known as "progressive originalism," using textualism and originalism techniques to argue that the Constitution and the Bill of Rights expanded, rather than restricted, rights. Realizing that if Scalia remained unchallenged as the only interpreter of these Founding Era histories, he would always appear to have the winning argument, Souter knew that someone had to draw alternative conclusions from this material to interpret the meanings of these sources.

In a concurrence joined by Justices Stevens and O'Connor, Souter concluded that the Court "should stick to" its position to keep church and state separate "absent some compelling reason to discard it." And he did not find such a compelling reason in Scalia's originalist history: "Some have challenged this precedent by reading the Establishment Clause to permit 'nonpreferential' state promotion of religion. . . . I find in the history of the Clause's textual development a more powerful argument supporting the Court's [separation of church and state] jurisprudence."[18]

Souter argued that Scalia's accommodationist position, what he labeled the "non-preferentialist" position of supporting the connection between church and state, put the Court where it did not belong: "Simply by requiring the enquiry, nonpreferentialists invite the courts to engage in comparative theology. I can hardly imagine a subject less amenable to the competence of the federal judiciary, or more deliberately to be avoided where possible."[19] Souter then directly challenged Scalia's interpretation of Founding Era American history by examining the early work of Thomas Jefferson in this area: "By condemning such non-coercive state practices that, in 'recommending' the majority faith, demean religious dissenters 'in public opinion,' Jefferson necessarily condemned what, in modern terms, we call official endorsement of religion. He accordingly construed the Establishment Clause to forbid not simply state coercion, but also state endorsement, of religious belief and observance."[20] And in his review of the history of the official connection by the state with religion, even ones that are "ceremonial" or "symbolic" in nature, Souter saw the requirement for a level of neutrality, not the accommodation urged by Scalia: "When public school officials, armed with the State's authority, convey an endorsement of religion to their students, they strike near the core of the Establishment Clause. However 'ceremonial' their messages may be, they are flatly unconstitutional."[21] After Souter's historical review—one he would repeat in later cases—others on the Court learned how to challenge Scalia's historical effort on its own terms.

Kennedy's switch in the school graduation prayer case was the first signal that the ideological tectonic plates on the Court were shifting, but the earthquake was yet to be felt. Scalia's continual hostility toward O'Connor and Kennedy in his judicial opinions helped to drive the centrist justices away from the conservative bloc, potentially costing the Rehnquist conservatives control of the Court on other key issues. The public did not know, however, that the open hostility of Scalia's dissent toward Kennedy in the religion case was likely linked to what Kennedy had done to him behind the scenes nearly three weeks before. It had to do with the negotiations over another major case that had not yet been announced and was also laced with religious implications, this one dealing again with the right to abortion.

The case, *Planned Parenthood of Southeastern Pennsylvania v. Casey*, involved a Pennsylvania antiabortion statute that required that a woman seeking an abortion give "informed consent," a minor must get parental consent for an abortion, a married woman must notify her husband of her decision to get an abortion, and the facilities providing abortions must meet certain reporting requirements, all with an exception for "medical emergency." Essentially, this case would allow the Court to rerun the debate in the *Webster* abortion case three years earlier, this time with the two new justices, David Souter and Clarence Thomas. Since both men were considered conservatives who had replaced more liberal jurists, Souter for William Brennan and Thomas for Thurgood Marshall, it appeared that the conservative dissenters in *Webster*, Chief Justice Rehnquist, Scalia, and Kennedy, might now have the votes to overturn *Roe v. Wade*.

While there was no doubt that Thomas, an originalist who based his decisions on the "unalienable rights" listed in the Declaration of Independence of life, liberty, and the pursuit of happiness, would vote with the abortion opponents, Souter's vote was in question. Like centrist Sandra Day O'Connor, Souter was a proponent of *stare decisis*, preferring to let existing precedents stand if at all possible. Since the *Roe v. Wade* abortion precedent had been in force for nineteen years, this augured well for both of them to support it. With Harry Blackmun and John Paul Stevens being the only other solid pro-abortion votes, though, unless there was a change in the voting elsewhere, it was still likely that the *Roe* holding was in jeopardy. Once more, the controlling vote on this ideologically balanced Court was in Anthony Kennedy's hands.

After the initial Court votes were cast in conference on April 24, 1992, there were five votes in favor of overturning *Roe*: Rehnquist, White, Scalia, Thomas, and Kennedy. As in the *Webster* case, Chief Justice Rehnquist assigned the case to himself. Energized by his characteristic opinion-writing efficiency, by May 27 Rehnquist had produced a draft that would uphold all of the restrictive provisions of the Pennsylvania law, seriously limiting the *Roe* precedent, by using his version of the "rational basis" test under which the Court defers to a state's laws because a "rational person" would agree with them.

But Rehnquist went even further to attack the *Roe* precedent directly: "We believe that *Roe* was wrongly decided, and that it can and should be overruled consistently with our traditional approach to *stare decisis* in constitutional cases." Knowing that if all of the portions of the Pennsylvania abortion law remained in force it would make getting an abortion in that state much more difficult, if not impossible for some. Rehnquist nonetheless favored use of the rational basis test instead of a higher level of scrutiny, such as "compelling state interest," because, as he saw it, a right to abortion was not "a principle of justice so rooted in the traditions and conscience of our people as to be ranked as fundamental."[22] For him, the Due Process Clause of the Fourteenth Amendment did "not endorse any all-encompassing right of privacy," protecting the right to an abortion. In *Roe v. Wade*, the Court recognized a "guarantee of personal privacy" that "is broad enough to encompass a woman's decision whether or not to terminate her pregnancy.... We are now of the view that, in terming this right fundamental, the Court in *Roe* read the earlier opinions upon which it based its decision much too broadly. Unlike marriage, procreation, and contraception, abortion involves the purposeful termination of a potential life."[23]

Rehnquist's devastating assault on the *Roe* precedent, threatening to end the constitutional right to abortion, dismayed its author, Harry Blackmun. After reading Rehnquist's draft, he penciled "Wow!" and "Pretty Extreme!" on the first page of the document.[24] But Blackmun soon learned that he had an unexpected ally. Two days after the circulation of Rehnquist's draft majority opinion, Kennedy sent Blackmun another handwritten note, reminiscent of the one he had sent changing his view on the *Weisman* case two months earlier: "Dear Harry: I need to see you as soon as you have a few free moments. I want to tell you about some developments in Planned Parenthood v. Casey, and at least part of what I say should come as welcome news."[25]

When the two men met the following day, Blackmun learned that Kennedy, Souter, and O'Connor, "the 3," as Blackmun called them, or "the Troika," as they became known to others, had been working together in secret, drafting a plurality opinion supporting the *Roe* precedent on the basis of *stare decisis*. If the group held together, they would, when added to the pro-*Roe* liberals, Blackmun and Stevens, effectively steal the Court majority away from Rehnquist, White, Scalia, and Thomas.

Kennedy told Blackmun that they would argue in the first part of their opinion that on the basis of their definition of fundamental rights under the Liberty Clause of the Fourteenth Amendment's due process provision, "*Roe* was sound, though not the trimester system." The only part of the Pennsylvania law that would be overturned would be the spousal notification provision. In the next portion, Souter would argue that the essence of the *Roe* precedent should be upheld on their theory of *stare decisis*, because nothing in the intervening nineteen years had changed requiring its reversal. Then O'Connor would announce that the standard for abortion cases would now be her "undue burden" test, rather than *Roe*'s "compelling state interest" test. Blackmun, seeing the reduction in protection for women due to the substitution of the "undue burden" test for his more supportive "compelling state interest" test, regarded this as only a partial win. But it was enough of a win to preserve much of the abortion right under *Roe*.[26]

When Scalia heard rumors of Kennedy's possible defection but was still unaware that he had also lost Souter's vote, he decided to do something unusual, given his uncompromising style: he would try to lobby Kennedy to stay with the conservatives. Since the two men lived only blocks apart in McLean, Virginia, Scalia persuaded Kennedy to take a walk around their neighborhood and discuss the case. Neighbors seeing the two justices walking on the suburban streets could not have known that the future of abortion policy in America hung in the balance. Reporter Jan Crawford Greenburg recounted that while the confident Scalia left their meeting believing that he had secured Kennedy's vote, it was only because Kennedy "hadn't said a word about" his work with Souter and O'Connor or his note to and meeting with Blackmun. Twenty-four hours later, on June 3, Scalia would learn of his failure when O'Connor circulated the Troika's first draft of its plurality preserving the *Roe* case.[27]

The final version of the centrists' plurality opinion, which became the controlling judgment when it was joined by Stevens and Blackmun, was a masterpiece of judicial compromise. "Liberty finds no refuge in a jurisprudence of doubt. Yet 19 years after our holding that the Constitution protects a woman's right to terminate her pregnancy in its early stages . . . that definition of liberty is still questioned," the three justices began.[28] Determined to maintain the right of women to choose abortion, they argued that the right of personal autonomy privacy was a "fundamental right" requiring strict protection by the Court. "Our law affords constitutional protection to personal decisions relating to marriage, procreation, contraception, family relationships, child rearing, and education. . . . These matters, involving the most intimate and personal choices a person may make in a lifetime, choices central to personal dignity and autonomy, are central to the liberty protected by the Fourteenth Amendment."[29] But then a sentence sounding like Justice Kennedy's hyperbolic, broad language offered a libertarian vision of the nature of personal autonomy privacy right. "At the heart of liberty is the right to define one's own concept of existence, of meaning, of the universe, and of the mystery of human life. Beliefs about these matters could not define the attributes of personhood were they formed under compulsion of the State."[30] This sentence later became known as what Scalia and other critical conservatives would disparagingly call the opinion's "sweet-mystery-of-life passage" and would be used by the Court to expand personal autonomy privacy rights even further.[31]

The Troika then argued that the nineteen-year-old *Roe* precedent required respect under the concept of *stare decisis* and did not fit the characteristics of a precedent that should be overturned: "The very concept of the rule of law underlying our own Constitution requires such continuity over time that a respect for precedent is, by definition, indispensable. . . . At the other extreme, a different necessity would make itself felt if a prior judicial ruling should come to be seen so clearly as error that its enforcement was for that very reason doomed."[32] In their judgment, none of the usual reasons had developed calling for overturning the *Roe* precedent:

> The sum of the precedential enquiry to this point shows *Roe*'s underpinnings unweakened in any way affecting its central holding. While it has engendered disapproval, it has not been unworkable. An entire generation has come of age free to assume *Roe*'s concept of liberty in defining the capacity of women to act in society, and to make reproductive decisions; no erosion of principle going to liberty

or personal autonomy has left *Roe*'s central holding a doctrinal remnant; *Roe* portends no developments at odds with other precedent for the analysis of personal liberty; and no changes of fact have rendered viability more or less appropriate as the point at which the balance of interests tips. . . . To overrule prior law for no other reason than that would run counter to the view repeated in our cases, that a decision to overrule should rest on some special reason over and above the belief that a prior case was wrongly decided.[33]

On the other hand, overturning the case in response to changing public political pressure, or changing membership on the Court, would negatively affect the public legitimacy of the Court: "The country's loss of confidence in the Judiciary would be underscored by an equally certain and equally reasonable condemnation for another failing in overruling unnecessarily and under pressure."[34]

Having thus preserved the *Roe v. Wade* precedent, the Troika then changed the test for determining a woman's right to choose an abortion from the more individual rights protective "strict scrutiny" standard of *Roe* to a more states' regulation protective "undue burden" standard created by Sandra Day O'Connor. The "undue burden" test was explained this way:

A finding of an undue burden [which] is a shorthand for the conclusion that a state regulation has the purpose or effect of placing a substantial obstacle in the path of a woman seeking an abortion of a nonviable fetus. A statute with this purpose is invalid because the means chosen by the State to further the interest in potential life must be calculated to inform the woman's free choice, not hinder it. And a statute which, while furthering the interest in potential life or some other valid state interest, has the effect of placing a substantial obstacle in the path of a woman's choice cannot be considered a permissible means of serving its legitimate ends.[35]

Effectively, this would further limit the *Roe* decision, changing the test for abortion restriction laws, from the state having to prove that it had a "compelling state interest" to regulate the choice to receive an abortion, to the woman now having to prove the impact of the law on her right to choose an abortion, thus providing the state with a better chance of winning such cases. As a consequence, the three justices ruled: "We reject the trimester framework, which we do not consider to be part of the essential holding of *Roe*."[36]

The plurality opinion upset Blackmun, who considered his "strict scrutiny" test protecting a fundamental right to get an abortion and his trimester constitutional evaluation system—protecting a woman's unfettered right to choose an abortion during the first three months of a pregnancy, allowing the state to regulate the health and safety of the abortion procedure during the next three months, and permitting the state to ban abortions in order to protect a viable fetus in the final three months of the pregnancy—essential for evaluating the relative rights of the mother and the fetus and the state's powers to limit abortions. As unhappy as Blackmun was, though, by this change in the legal standard that now favored the state's regulatory interests over individual rights, and in doing so further limited the *Roe* decision, he was pleased with the overall preservation of the "right to choose an abortion" in *Roe*, against what had seemed at first to be a hostile Court majority. His legacy would remain.

Nevertheless, Blackmun circulated an opinion in this case concurring with portions of the plurality opinion that saved his *Roe* opinion, but then dissenting against the moderate justices' watering down of the "compelling state interest" to the lower level of "undue burden" test protecting the abortion choice, and also against Rehnquist and Scalia's use of the "rational basis" test to try to overturn the *Roe* precedent completely. Though the plurality had saved the shell of his *Roe* decision, Blackmun was troubled by the way they did it: "I remain steadfast in my belief that the right to reproductive choice is entitled to the full protection afforded by this Court before Webster. And I fear for the darkness as four Justices anxiously await the single vote necessary to extinguish the light. Make no mistake, the joint [plurality] opinion . . . is an act of personal courage and constitutional principle. . . . [F]ive Members of this Court today recognize that 'the Constitution protects a woman's right to terminate her pregnancy in its early stages.'"[37]

In considering all of the assaults by his colleagues on the *Roe* decision, Blackmun decided to put his faith in the political process in an unusual appeal within a judicial opinion by a member of the Court with the 1992 presidential election approaching:

> While there is much to be praised about our democracy, our country since its founding has recognized that there are certain fundamental liberties that are not to be left to the whims of an election. A woman's

right to reproductive choice is one of those fundamental liberties. Accordingly, that liberty need not seek refuge at the ballot box. In one sense, the Court's approach is worlds apart from that of THE CHIEF JUSTICE and JUSTICE SCALIA. And yet, in another sense, the distance between the two approaches is short—the distance is but a single vote. I am 83 years old. I cannot remain on this Court forever, and when I do step down, the confirmation process for my successor well may focus on the issue before us today. That, I regret, may be exactly where the choice between the two worlds will be made.[38]

All that was left, after Blackmun had circulated his impassioned opinion against the diminution of his protective test, was to await what his law clerk, Stephanie Dangle, called "the evil Nino" to circulate his response.[39]

Having already issued his dissenting salvo against Kennedy in the *Weisman* case on June 18, just five days later, on June 23, Scalia circulated another blistering opinion, in the *Casey* abortion case, that concurred in part and dissented in part. "I will not swell the United States Reports with repetition of what I have said before," Scalia began, "and applying the rational basis test, I would uphold the Pennsylvania statute in its entirety." Scalia then violated his promise by attacking each passage of the plurality opinion. First, he made it clear that he had no respect for O'Connor's "undue burden" test: "The joint opinion explains that a state regulation imposes an 'undue burden' if it 'has the purpose or effect of placing a substantial obstacle in the path of a woman seeking an abortion of a nonviable fetus.' . . . An obstacle is 'substantial,' we are told, if it is 'calculated[,] [not] to inform the woman's free choice, [but to] hinder it.' . . . Defining an 'undue burden' as an 'undue hindrance' (or a 'substantial obstacle') hardly 'clarifies' the test. Consciously or not, the joint opinion's verbal shell game will conceal raw judicial policy choices concerning what is 'appropriate' abortion legislation."[40]

Next, Scalia made clear how much this form of pro-abortion political activism ran counter to his own philosophy:

> The Imperial Judiciary lives. It is instructive to compare this Nietzschean vision of us unelected, life-tenured judges—leading a Volk who will be "tested by following," and whose very "belief in themselves" is mystically bound up in their "understanding" of a Court that "speaks before all others for their constitutional ideals"—with the somewhat more modest role envisioned for these lawyers by the

Founders. . . . Or, again, to compare this ecstasy of a Supreme Court in which there is, especially on controversial matters, no shadow of change or hint of alteration.[41]

Left unsaid, of course, was that Scalia had been behaving as a member of an "Imperial Judiciary," albeit on the conservative side, since 1986, and using his own version of that power was now seeking to overturn a nearly two-decades-old Court precedent.

Scalia's concern was that his "living Constitution" colleagues were not willing to follow what he viewed as the clear mandates of his text and tradition originalism theory:

In truth, I am as distressed as the Court is—and expressed my distress several years ago, see *Webster* . . . about the "political pressure" directed to the Court: the marches, the mail, the protests aimed at inducing us to change our opinions. How upsetting it is, that so many of our citizens (good people, not lawless ones, on both sides of this abortion issue, and on various sides of other issues as well) think that we Justices should properly take into account their views, as though we were engaged not in ascertaining an objective law but in determining some kind of social consensus. The Court would profit, I think, from giving less attention to the fact of this distressing phenomenon, and more attention to the cause of it. That cause permeates today's opinion: a new mode of constitutional adjudication that relies not upon text and traditional practice to determine the law, but upon what the Court calls "reasoned judgment" . . . which turns out to be nothing but philosophical predilection and moral intuition.[42]

Scalia made clear that he saw a link between the majority's political decision-making approach, as opposed to his text and tradition method, in both the *Weisman* and *Casey* decisions in causing damage to the Court:

As long as this Court thought (and the people thought) that we Justices were doing essentially lawyers' work up here—reading text and discerning our society's traditional understanding of that text—the public pretty much left us alone. Texts and traditions are facts to study, not convictions to demonstrate about. But if in reality our process of constitutional adjudication consists primarily of making value judgments; if we can ignore a long and clear tradition clarifying an ambiguous text, as we did, for example, five days ago in declaring unconstitutional invocations and benedictions at public high school graduation ceremonies, if, as I say, our pronouncement of constitutional law rests primarily on value judgments, then a free and intelligent people's attitude towards us can be expected to be (ought to be) quite different.[43]

For Scalia, the foundations of democracy should be left with the votes of the people, not the personal mores of the Supreme Court:

The people know that their value judgments are quite as good as those taught in any law school—maybe better. If, indeed, the "liberties" protected by the Constitution are, as the Court says, undefined and unbounded, then the people should demonstrate, to protest that we do not implement their values instead of ours. . . . Value judgments, after all, should be voted on, not dictated; and if our Constitution has somehow accidently [sic] committed them to the Supreme Court, at least we can have a sort of plebiscite each time a new nominee to that body is put forward. JUSTICE BLACKMUN not only regards this prospect with equanimity, he solicits it.[44]

Scalia's anguish here became pronounced as he concluded his assault on the Court's role in the abortion area:

By foreclosing all democratic outlet for the deep passions this issue arouses, by banishing the issue from the political forum that gives all participants, even the losers, the satisfaction of a fair hearing and an honest fight, by continuing the imposition of a rigid national rule instead of allowing for regional differences, the Court merely prolongs and intensifies the anguish. We should get out of this area, where we have no right to be, and where we do neither ourselves nor the country any good by remaining.[45]

With Kennedy's two switched votes both moving away from Scalia and toward O'Connor and Blackmun, the prospects of a united conservative majority seemed even more remote. By attacking both of the Court's centrists in his critical opinions, Scalia had, in one seven-day period, helped drive them away, costing the Rehnquist-led conservative bloc the control of the majority.

Kennedy seemed to relish his influential swing role on the Court, permitting a press interview just as the *Casey* opinion was about to be announced in open Court that resulted in an unusual biographical portrait.[46] Peering out of his office window at the antiabortion protest crowds gathered outside on June 29, 1992, as the Court was about to announce its decision, he captured the pressures that he felt serving on the Supreme Court at such moments, telling *California Lawyer* reporter Terry Carter, "Sometimes you don't know if you're Caesar about to cross the Rubicon, or Captain Queeg cutting your own tow line." Minutes later, as Court was about to open, Kennedy dramatically ended the interview, saying, "I need to brood. . . . I generally brood, as all of us do on the bench, just before we go on. It's a moment of quiet around here to search your soul and conscience."[47]

Everyone in the audience in the Supreme Court chamber waiting for the announcement of that decision could detect from the body language of the justices that Scalia and the centrist jurists who now controlled the Court were not in agreement. Terry Carter wrote that as Kennedy read from his majority opinion his expansive "mystery of human life" definition of "liberty," Scalia, sitting several seats away, "slump[ed] back, swallowed by his chair. His arms folded across his chest, and his lips pursed."[48] After the session was over, Kennedy appeared to refer to Scalia's decision-making approach in telling Carter:

> You don't know. I think any person who calls himself a philosopher is dangerous. History has its own way of unfolding, tripping you up or vindicating you. You're required to look into a crystal ball, but you don't see much there. The art is in the challenge. You cannot write just from the facts before you—that would be unhelpful. You cannot write with a broad brush, or you make a mistake. There must be some balance. . . . But only history can tell.[49]

Scalia would agree with the last sentence, but the two men were writing different history books.

• • •

Matters came to a head for Scalia at the end of the 1991–92 Court term. On top of the double disappointment of Kennedy's pivotal switched votes, another reversal came in the form of a meltdown caused by Harry Blackmun. The dispute between the two men arose in a minor case called *Lucas v. South Carolina Coastal Council*, dealing with the rights of landowners under the so-called Takings Clause of the Fifth Amendment of the Constitution. The case involved a man named David H. Lucas, who in 1992 purchased two beachfront building lots on a barrier island of South Carolina for just under a million dollars. The state then appeared to make them worthless by invoking the Beachfront Management Act, under which his land was declared by the state-run South Carolina Coastal Council to be a "critical area" in the "coastal zone" within which building would be banned because of possible beach erosion. Lucas argued that under the Takings Clause, reading "nor shall private property be taken for public use, without just compensation," the value of his property had been taken from him and that he should be paid "just compensation." South Carolina argued that as a matter of its state sovereignty under the "police powers" of the Tenth Amendment, by which the state is empowered to govern the health, safety, morals, and public welfare of its citizens, it owed nothing under eminent domain, because a state had the right to determine how its property should be developed.

Scalia was assigned by the chief justice to write an opinion for a seven-justice majority, ruling in favor of forcing the state to compensate the landowner for the taking. To do so, he turned to his originalism theory to determine the historical meaning of the Takings Clause and the historical tradition that would guide him in applying this provision to South Carolina. To assess whether Lucas had been harmed by the restriction on his property rights, Scalia examined the historical "bundle of rights" attached to the title of the property being purchased and concluded that the new owner should either be able to use the property as he saw fit or be compensated if the state denied him that right.[50] Scalia concluded that it was "unlikely that common-law principles would have prevented the erection of any habitable or productive improvements on petitioner's land; they rarely support prohibition of the essential use of land." As he saw it, "to win its case South Carolina must do more than proffer the legislature's declaration that the uses Lucas desires are inconsistent with the public interest. . . . South Carolina must identify background principles of nuisance and property law that prohibit the uses he now intends in the circumstances in which the property is presently found. Only on this showing can the State fairly claim that, in proscribing all such beneficial uses, the Beachfront Management Act is taking nothing."[51]

In writing his dissent, Blackmun's reservations about this case began with its facts. "There is something fishy about this case," Blackmun's law clerk, Molly McUsic, wrote him after her review of the case record. Having noted the growing history of land sales for these properties that had "been underwater in recent memory" and now for some unknown reason had sky-rocketed in value, McUsic wrote: "It seems strange to me that the property would be sold so many times in such a short period of time. Nobody built on the property. It looks like it was speculative churning to raise the price. The increases in appreciation (90% between 1985 and 1986 alone) are too much to be believed. It also seems very odd that someone who was in on the island's development from the start would wait to buy the last lots at the highest prices."[52] Blackmun was not ready to make new law, using any decision-making technique, for a case with such facts.

Blackmun's problems with this case extended to the language of Scalia's majority opinion. Upon reading the first draft, Blackmun evidently felt that he had endured enough of Scalia's dogmatic originalism that term, and so he decided to begin his dissent with a dramatic metaphor to signify that this case was not yet worth the Court's time and effort:

> Today the Court launches a missile to kill a mouse. . . . I protest not only the Court's decision, but each step taken to reach it. More fun-damentally, I question the Court's wisdom in issuing sweeping new rules to decide such a narrow case. . . . My fear is that the Court's new policies will spread beyond the narrow confines of the present case. For that reason, I, like the Court, will give far greater attention to this case than its narrow scope suggests—not because I can intercept the Court's missile, or save the targeted mouse, but because I hope perhaps to limit the collateral damage.[53]

In Blackmun's mind, this was not a case ripe for the Court's review be-cause the state's decision was not yet final and the property, far from losing all of its value, could still be used in many ways and thus still had worth: "Pe-titioner still can enjoy other attributes of ownership, such as the right to ex-clude others, 'one of the most essential sticks in the bundle of rights that are commonly characterized as property.' . . . Petitioner can picnic, swim, camp in a tent, or live on the property in a movable trailer. State courts frequently have recognized that land has economic value where the only residual eco-nomic uses are recreation or camping."[54]

Blackmun had no tolerance for Scalia's version of originalism, as his own reading of the history and tradition of the Takings Clause led him to believe that the Court should not be so ready to rule in Lucas's favor: "There is nothing magical in the reasoning of judges long dead. They determined a harm in the same way as state judges and legislatures do today. If judges in the 18th and 19th centuries can distinguish a harm from a benefit, why not judges in the 20th century, and if judges can, why not legislators?"[55]

Blackmun then challenged the intellectual merits of Scalia's historical originalist theory: "I find no clear and accepted 'historical compact' or 'understanding of our citizens' justifying the Court's new takings doctrine. Instead, the Court seems to treat history as a grab bag of principles, to be adopted where they support the Court's theory, and ignored where they do not."[56] The literary and metaphorical style of Blackmun's opinion seemed to be drawn from Scalia's own playbook, nothing more or less than Scalia had done to O'Connor in *Webster*, Kennedy in *Weisman*, or the Troika in *Casey*. This opinion, though, had been written by Blackmun against Scalia, and Scalia did not like it at all.

Although the liberal law clerk grapevine usually had few sources in the offices of the conservative justices, Blackmun's chambers learned that another round of Scalia verbal mortar shells was about to be launched. McUsic wrote Blackmun on June 25 after the dissent had been circulated: "Re: *Lucas*: I talked to Scalia's clerk. As himself read our dissent and got so angry, he has decided to extensively respond (and do so nastily). This is requiring a period of time. Thus he does not even think it will be around today."[57]

The verbal barrage arrived in the Court's chambers the next day, June 26, and it was the equal of anything the angry Scalia had circulated so far. Rather than rewrite his majority opinion at this late date, Scalia's draft contained seven new footnotes referring to Blackmun by name in answering, belittling, and attacking his dissenting analysis. In footnote three, he argued: "JUSTICE BLACKMUN finds it 'baffling' . . . that we grant standing here, whereas 'just a few days ago, in *Lujan v. Defenders of Wildlife* [an environmental case dealing with the Endangered Species Act] . . . we denied standing. . . . He has a point: The decisions are indeed very close in time, yet one grants standing and the other denies it. The distinction, however, rests in law rather than chronology." Later, after calling one of Blackmun's arguments a "strange suggestion," Scalia added in another note, "We will not attempt to respond to all of JUSTICE BLACKMUN's mistaken citation of case precedent." In an especially critical footnote, Scalia took particular issue with the "launching a missile to kill a mouse" image contained in the opening paragraph of Blackmun's dissent, recrafting the metaphor in his response by mixing it with some textualism and originalism analysis:

> After accusing us of "launching a missile to kill a mouse"... JUSTICE BLACKMUN expends a good deal of throw-weight of his own upon a noncombatant, arguing that our description of the "understanding" of land ownership that informs the Takings Clause is not supported by early American experience. That is largely true, but entirely irrelevant. The practices of the States prior to incorporation of the Takings and Just Compensation Clauses ... which, as JUSTICE BLACKMUN acknowledges, occasionally included outright physical appropriation of land without compensation ... were out of accord with any plausible interpretation of those provisions. JUSTICE BLACKMUN is correct that early constitutional theorists did not believe the Takings Clause embraced regulations of property at all ... but even he does not suggest (explicitly, at least) that we renounce the Court's contrary conclusion.... Since the text of the Clause can be read to encompass regulatory as well as physical deprivations (in contrast to the text originally proposed by Madison) ... we decline to do so as well.[58]

Apparently this footnote barrage did not satisfy Scalia, because after a night's reflection, he circulated yet another draft the following day, expanding his attack on Blackmun in three new footnotes.

After the 1991–92 term, it appeared that Scalia's consistent loss of the swing voters had destroyed his chance of leading the conservative bloc on the Rehnquist Court to a majority position for the foreseeable future. In just three Court terms Scalia had antagonized the Court's two centrist judges, Sandra Day O'Connor and Anthony Kennedy, and had failed to find common ground with the independent-minded, centrist David Souter, who was drifting to the ideological left. Without at least one of these three justices, the Rehnquist Court conservative wing could not win on major social issues such as abortion, religion, or the death penalty. Scalia had also crossed the Court's two other senior jurists, Blackmun and Stevens, to the point that these two justices were now writing opinions in ways that would provoke him. Even Rehnquist's increasingly pragmatic conservative views, along with his willingness to follow a laissez-faire approach in allowing O'Connor and Kennedy to take the Court's majority where it wanted to go, worked at cross-purposes with Scalia's desire to pitch the Court to the right.

Unlike in 1989, when Scalia responded to the loss of the centrist judge with a series of speeches on his new originalism theory, this time he decided to deal with his losses in *Weisman* and *Casey*, and his judicial meltdown in *Lucas*, by seeking to persuade others of the merits of his originalism theory within new cases. In so doing, however, he could not resist further attacking his centrist colleagues.

CHAPTER 13
Master of the Barbed Opinion

Having alienated Kennedy and O'Connor, Scalia was left for the next several terms doing the equivalent of judicial singing in the shower. He would write opinions that would repeat and refine his originalism and textualism, but he made no effort to attract new voices to his choir. In case after case, Scalia still behaved as a "Court of One," failing to lead the conservatives on the Court or forge a voting majority including them.[1]

But Scalia continued writing more attention-getting attacks. By now, he had worked out an efficient and highly effective system for writing his judicial opinions. The task of judging had changed from the era of Justice Louis Brandeis, who said in the early part of the twentieth century that "The reason why the public thinks so much of the justices is that they are almost the only people in Washington who do their own work." Now, nearly all of the Supreme Court justices in the 1990s relied on their law clerks to help draft their judicial opinions.[2] By his own admission, Scalia "almost never wr[o]te the first draft" of his opinion.[3] The reason, he explained, was simple: "That's why you have law clerks. Why should I spend my time, you know, reciting all of the facts and blah blah blah blah? I tell them, this is the arguments [*sic*] I want to make, and they recite the facts, [and] make the arguments." From there, the clerks frame a logical set of arguments in the justice's voice based on their conversations with him about the case: "[The clerk] pretty much knows what my thoughts are on the case because we've discussed it intensively before the conference that voted on the case, OK? But nonetheless, I will usually say, you know, this is—this is what I think the opinion ought to say and, you know, go off and write it that way." After the law clerk delivered the first draft, there was still a great deal for Scalia to do: "I take the opinion apart and put it back together. I don't think anybody claims to be unable to recognize a Scalia opinion." No one would deny this to be true.

From there, it became a process of negotiation as the draft bounced back and forth between the justice and the clerk. Once that editing process was concluded, Scalia put the draft through one final step before sending it around to the other justices seeking votes: "I go through the whole thing, and I send it back to the law clerk and say, have I cut out any muscle in your view? And sometimes the clerk says yet [sic] and I put something else in and then, you know, send it around, see if anybody salutes it." It was a process by which Scalia produced tightly argued opinions, filled with quotable phrases and memorable metaphors that ensured that his opinions would be noticed by the press, included in constitutional law casebooks, and studied in law school classes for generations to come.

One memorable example of this process came in a school religion case in the 1992–93 term in which Scalia had once again failed to persuade his colleagues to abandon their attachment to the prevailing *Lemon* three-prong test measuring the separation between church and state. The case was *Lamb's Chapel v. Center Moriches Union Free School District*, dealing with a Long Island public school district that would not allow an evangelical church to use school facilities to show films of lectures by conservative Christian author James Dobson. The Court majority, speaking through Byron White, held that the school district's decision violated the Free Speech Clause of the First Amendment because singling out this one religious group among many other groups who were permitted to use school facilities gave the appearance that this was not a "content neutral" action, but rather discrimination against this one viewpoint. The Court also found no violation of the Establishment of Religion Clause, ruling under the three-pronged *Lemon* test that "the challenged governmental action has a secular purpose, does not have the principal or primary effect of advancing or inhibiting religion, and does not foster an excessive entanglement with religion."[4]

For Scalia, it made no difference that a pro-religion argument was being presented by another member of the conservative wing; he wanted no part of the *Lemon* test. "As to the Court's invocation of the *Lemon* test: Like some ghoul in a late-night horror movie that repeatedly sits up in its grave and shuffles abroad, after being repeatedly killed and buried, *Lemon* stalks our Establishment Clause jurisprudence once again, frightening the little children and school attorneys of Center Moriches Union Free School District. Its most recent burial, only last Term, was, to be sure, not fully six feet under."[5] His belittling attack continued: "The secret of the *Lemon* test's survival, I think, is that it is so easy to kill. It is there to scare us (and our audience) when we wish it to do so, but we can command it to return to the tomb at will. . . . Such a docile and useful monster is worth keeping around, at least in a somnolent state, one never knows when one might need him."[6] Years later, when the legal publication *Green Bag* offered its subscribers a bobble-head figurine of Scalia, celebrating his dissents, he was portrayed standing with a howling wolf to his right, symbolizing the "actual wolf" instead of one in sheep's clothing as he described in the *Morrison v. Olson* independent counsel case, with his left hand spearing a large lemon with a red pencil bearing the name of the school district in the *Center Moriches* case, thus signifying his determination to end the *Lemon v. Kurtzman* test.

At the end of the 1992–93 term, Byron White retired from the Court. Though White was appointed to the Court by John F. Kennedy in 1962, during his thirty-one years on the Court he became a reliable conservative vote on all issues except race relations and death penalty issues. Rather than following the recent practice of timing his retirement to make the seat available to an appointing president most in line ideologically with his judicial viewpoint, White retired while Democratic president Bill Clinton was in office, thus returning the vacancy to the political party that had been in power when he was appointed. After a lengthy search process, Clinton narrowed the list of potential nominees down to two. The first was Court of Appeals for the District of Columbia judge Ruth Bader Ginsburg, the "Thurgood Marshall of the National Organization for Women (NOW)," comparing her work on behalf of women's rights with Marshall's work for civil rights for the Legal Defense Fund of the NAACP. Ginsburg had a compelling life story, having been as victimized by gender discrimination in her teaching career at Columbia Law School as Justice O'Connor had been early in her legal career. The other candidate was Stephen G. Breyer, the chief judge for the Court of Appeals for the First Circuit, who had won supporters on both sides of the political aisle in the Senate for his work under Senator Ted Kennedy of Massachusetts as chief counsel for the Senate Judiciary Committee. Unfortunately for Breyer, his efforts to be interviewed for the position were hampered by a bicycle accident that landed him in the hospital.[7]

Ginsburg received the appointment on June 14. "Throughout her life," said President Clinton, "she has repeatedly stood for the individual, the person less well-off, the outsider in society, and has given those people greater hope by telling them they have a place in our legal system."[8] Initially there was hope by the liberal community that because Ginsburg's liberal vote replaced the generally conservative vote of Byron White, the new appointment would move the Court to the left. Almost immediately, though, to the bewilderment and disappointment of the liberal movement, Ginsburg adopted a more moderate stance as a justice than she had shown in her work as a pro–women's rights attorney. Still, with two career-oriented women on the Court, women's rights supporters believed that they now had better prospects before that body.

By 1993–94, the public bickering in opinions among the justices became even more noticeable. Former deputy solicitor general Philip Allen Lacovara, in an article titled "Un-Courtly Manners," wrote, "Far too many divided opinions of the Court are afflicted with insinuations or outright accusations that the justice authoring a divergent opinion is not simply wrong but benighted, or disingenuous." He added, "recent opinions by the justices often are peppered with accusations that statements by colleagues are 'simplistic,' 'facile,' 'not rational,' 'misleading,' or 'just not true.'" After noting some of these tough exchanges, Lacovara wrote that the Court had "a schoolyard ring to it, just with better vocabulary."[9]

Lacovara made clear in his piece that the justice he believed was most responsible for the disintegration of the Court's relations was Antonin Scalia. Scalia was, in his words, the "Master of the Barbed Opinion," a man in a league by himself in his confrontational and at times hostile assaults on his colleagues. This was especially true, Lacovara noted, in Scalia's relationships with the swing justices in the middle of the Court: "The strained relationship between Justices Scalia and Sandra Day O'Connor, for instance, is now approaching an embarrassing intensity. Once expected to become jurisprudential allies, today they rarely say a civil word about one another in their opinions."[10] Lacovara saw almost a "Jekyll and Hyde" quality to Scalia's personality on the Court, saying, "It is particularly ironic that some of the harshest attacks on fellow justices emanate from the sharp pen of Justice Antonin Scalia—ironic because his official style differs so dramatically from the gregarious and witty person that his friends and associates know."[11] But, of course, those friends and associates were not the ones now frustrating Scalia's goals on the Court.

One case at the end of the 1993–94 term demonstrated Scalia's intense disagreements with the Court's moderate conservatives. The *Board of Education of Kiryas Joel Village School District v. Grumet* dealt with an upstate New York special village school district that had been created by the state legislature in 1989 to allow an ultra-Orthodox Satmar Hasidic Jewish sect that had emigrated from Eastern Europe to run its own public schools.

Speaking for a six-justice majority, centrist David Souter argued: "Because this unusual Act is tantamount to an allocation of political power on a religious criterion and neither presupposes nor requires governmental impartiality toward religion, we hold that it violates the prohibition against establishment [of religion]."[12] Bypassing the three-pronged *Lemon* test, the Court only evaluated whether a state "pursue[s] a course of 'neutrality' toward religion, favoring neither one religion over others nor religious adherents collectively over non-adherents."[13] While Souter and the majority conceded that "the Constitution allows the State to accommodate religious needs by alleviating special burdens," he added that "accommodation is not a principle without limits, and what petitioners seek is an adjustment to the Satmars' religiously grounded preferences that our cases do not countenance." The Court did not agree that "an otherwise unconstitutional delegation of political power to a religious group could be saved as a religious accommodation."[14]

In dissent, Scalia argued that state accommodation of religion was what the Founders intended in the First Amendment, and so it was what he was determined to provide. He began by characterizing Souter's majority opinion as a historically untethered example of judicial activism at its worst: "The Founding Fathers would be astonished to find that the Establishment Clause—which they designed 'to insure that no one powerful sect or combination of sects could use political or governmental power to punish dissenters' . . . has been employed to prohibit characteristically and admirably American accommodation of the religious practices (or more precisely, cultural peculiarities) of a tiny minority sect. I, however, am not surprised. Once this Court has abandoned text and history as guides, nothing prevents it from calling religious toleration the establishment of religion."[15] Then, as he had done so many times before with others, Scalia vigorously attacked his colleague's argumentation: "JUSTICE SOUTER's steamrolling of the difference between civil authority held by a church and civil authority held by members of a church is breathtaking. To accept it, one must believe that large portions of the civil authority exercised during most of our history were unconstitutional, and that much more of it than merely the Kiryas Joel school district is unconstitutional today. . . . It is preposterous to suggest that the civil institutions of these communities, separate from their churches, were constitutionally suspect."[16] For Scalia, "There is no evidence (indeed, no plausible suspicion) of the legislature's desire to favor the Satmar religion, as opposed to meeting distinctive secular needs or desires of citizens who happened to be Satmars. If there were, JUSTICE SOUTER would say so; instead, he must merely insinuate." [17]

By now, the genteel Souter had lost his patience with Scalia's continual lecturing, and he was ready to say so in his majority opinion:

> Justice Cardozo once cast the dissenter as "the gladiator making a last stand against the lions." . . . JUSTICE SCALIA's dissent is certainly the work of a gladiator, but he thrusts at lions of his own imagining. We do not disable a religiously homogeneous group from exercising political power conferred on it without regard to religion. . . . The reference line chosen for the Kiryas Joel Village School District was one purposely drawn to separate Satmars from non-Satmars. Nor do we impugn the motives of the New York Legislature . . . which no doubt intended to accommodate the Satmar community without violating the Establishment Clause; we simply refuse to ignore that the method it chose is one that aids a particular religious community, as such . . . rather than all groups similarly interested in separate schooling. [18]

That said, Souter once again made clear how little he thought of Scalia's historical originalist decision-making approach in the religion area:

> [T]he license [JUSTICE SCALIA] takes in suggesting that the Court holds the Satmar sect to be New York's established church . . . is only one symptom of his inability to accept the fact that this Court has long held that the First Amendment reaches more than classic, 18th-century establishments. . . . Our job, of course, would be easier if the dissent's position had prevailed with the Framers and with this Court over the years. An Establishment Clause diminished to the dimensions acceptable to JUSTICE SCALIA could be enforced by a few simple rules, and our docket would never see cases requiring the application of a principle like neutrality toward religion as well as among religious sects. But that would be as blind to history as to precedent. [19]

Unwilling to give Souter the last word, Scalia maintained the hope that a more religion accommodationist Supreme Court would make it possible for the Satmars, and by extension other minority religions, to find assistance from the government: "Contrary to the Court's suggestion . . . I do not think that the Establishment Clause prohibits formally established 'state' churches and nothing more. I have always believed, and all my opinions are consistent with the view, that the Establishment Clause prohibits the favoring of one religion over others. In this respect, it is the Court that attacks lions of straw."[20] He concluded: "The Court's decision today is astounding. . . . The Court casts aside, on the flimsiest of evidence, the strong presumption of validity that attaches to facially neutral laws, and invalidates the present accommodation because it does not trust New York to be as accommodating toward other religions (presumably those less powerful than the Satmar Hasidim) in the future."[21]

• • •

In early April 1994, Justice Harry Blackmun, then eighty-six years old, announced his intention to retire at the end of the Court term, giving the appointment of his replacement to President Clinton. It was the liberal justice's last bit of revenge in keeping his seat away from the Republican Party, whose leader at the time, Richard Nixon, had appointed him, and the conservative Court wing against whom he had battled for so long.[22] The new opening on the Court provided Judge Stephen Breyer another chance for an appointment. This time, he received the nomination on May 13, and was overwhelmingly confirmed by the Senate that summer. Breyer promised to have the expansive constitutional rights point of view, as well as the necessary intelligence and willingness to debate Scalia. The trade of Breyer's generally moderate-liberal vote for the ultraliberal vote of the retiring Harry Blackmun, though, would not change the overall ideological balance of the Court.

The newly constituted Court had a chance to rule on First Amendment free speech rights in the election process in April 1995 in the case of *McIntyre v. Ohio Elections Commission.*[23] This case dealt with an Ohio law banning the distribution of anonymous campaign literature that was applied to a woman named Margaret McIntyre, who had been distributing unsigned leaflets opposing a local school tax levy in Westerville, Ohio. There was no allegation of fraud, libel, falsity, or any pernicious effect on the election process. Writing for a seven-person majority, Justice Stevens upheld the right of anonymous free speech, saying:

The decision in favor of anonymity may be motivated by fear of economic or official retaliation, by concern about social ostracism, or merely by a desire to preserve as much of one's privacy as possible. . . . Accordingly, an author's decision to remain anonymous, like other decisions concerning omissions or additions to the content of a publication, is an aspect of the freedom of speech protected by the First Amendment.[24]

For the Court, a state law banning such anonymous electoral speech, which is neither false nor libelous, must be overturned because it "occupies the core of the protection afforded by the First Amendment."[25]

Stevens argued that while the law might have reason at times to ban anonymous speech "on the eve of an election, when the opportunity for reply is limited," the ban on all anonymous speech, such as Mrs. McIntyre's local leaflets, seemed to be overly broad: "Under our Constitution, anonymous pamphleteering is not a pernicious, fraudulent practice, but an honorable tradition of advocacy and of dissent. Anonymity is a shield from the tyranny of the majority." Since the state of Ohio had "not shown that its interest in preventing the misuse of anonymous election-related speech justifie[d] a prohibition of all uses of that speech" here, this "blunderbuss approach" of "indiscriminately outlawing a category of speech, based on its content, with no necessary relationship to the danger sought to be prevented" was ruled to be unacceptable.[26]

Normally a self-proclaimed champion of nearly unlimited free speech, Scalia used his originalism theory to argue in dissent that the Court had gone too far here in exercising its constitutional authority.[27] He decried that "the Court discovers a hitherto unknown right-to-be-unknown while engaging in electoral politics," even though "there is inadequate reason to believe . . . those of the society that begat the First Amendment or the Fourteenth" saw such a right.[28] Scalia searched through the Founding Era history and argued that "Evidence that anonymous electioneering was regarded as a constitutional right is sparse, and as far as I am aware evidence that it was *generally* regarded as such is nonexistent."[29] Unable to find a historical protection of anonymous electioneering, Scalia assumed a long-standing presumption of constitutionality for legislative restriction on such action: "I can imagine no reason why an anonymous leaflet is any more honorable, as a general matter, than an anonymous phone call or an anonymous letter. It facilitates wrong by eliminating accountability, which is ordinarily the very purpose of the anonymity. . . . To strike down the Ohio law in its general application—and similar laws of 49 other States and the Federal Government—on the ground that all anonymous communication is in our society traditionally sacrosanct, seems to me a distortion of the past that will lead to a coarsening of the future."[30] Scalia's position was curious for an originalist, given the anonymous political essays by the authors of the Federalist and anti-Federalist papers.

Life on the Court came apart again for Scalia at the end of the 1995–96 term. Having just turned sixty, and facing his tenth year on the Court, this was a personal and career turning point for him. For four years, the Court had been moving in two ways. Scalia was drifting to the right while the Court's moderates were shifting their center, with O'Connor and Kennedy drifting a bit toward the conservative coalition after the additions of Ginsburg and Breyer. As the Court trended to a 5–4 majority on the right, Scalia moved even further to the right by staking out even more extreme positions.

• • •

As tough as it had been for Scalia to deal with his colleagues on the Court, something else happened in early April that particularly unsettled him. On April 8, during Holy Week, *Time* magazine published an issue bearing a portrait of Jesus and the title "The Search for Jesus." The lead article was titled "The Gospel Truth?" and discussed what the authors called "The Jesus Seminar," a study of "the historical Jesus," and argued that "it will repeat the assertion, published by the 75-person, self-appointed Seminar three years ago, that close historical analysis of the Gospels exposes most of them as inauthentic; that, by inference, most Christians' picture of Christ may be radically misguided. That their Jesus, in fact, is an imaginative theological construct, into which have been woven traces of that enigmatic sage from Nazareth—traces that cry out for recognition and liberation from the firm grip of those whose faith overpowered their memories."[31] While the article concluded that the forces of religion were more than holding their own, the notion that religion was being questioned, coming on the top of the losses in the Court, seemed to disturb Scalia profoundly.

He decided to lash out against this anti-religion message in a public address in a unique setting. On April 9 he journeyed to Jackson, Mississippi, to speak at a prayer breakfast for 650 students and faculty at the Southern Baptist–affiliated Mississippi College School of Law's Christian Legal Society. The traditional, pre–Vatican II Catholic Scalia spoke from his pulpit. Quoting the Apostle Paul in I Corinthians, he said: "We are fools for Christ's sake, but you are wise in Christ; we are weak, but you are strong; you are honorable, but we are despised."[32] Scalia argued that America had become a society of the "worldly wise" who scorned the religious as "cretins," which he told the audience was derived from the French word for "Christians." Of this characterization, Scalia said: "To be honest about it, that is the view of Christians taken by modern society. Surely those who adhere to all or most of these traditional Christian beliefs are to be regarded as simpleminded."[33]

Scalia sounded on this occasion more like a parish priest than a Supreme Court justice, and a sarcastic one at that: "They just will not have anything to do with miracles. . . . The worldly wise do not believe in the resurrection of the dead. It is really quite absurd [to them]. . . . So everything from the Easter morning to the Ascension had to be made up by the groveling enthusiasts as part of their plan to get themselves martyred. The wise do not investigate such silliness. They 'do not believe.' One can be sophisticated and believe in God. Reason and intellect are not to be laid aside where matters of religion are concerned." Scalia went on to preach: "A general belief in God is one thing, [but] it is quite another matter to embrace the miracles of the Virgin birth of Christ, His raising the dead and His own ascension from the grave. Yet it is 'irrational' to reject miracles *a priori*. One can be sophisticated and believe in God. Reason and intellect are not to be laid aside where matters of religion are concerned. What is irrational to reject [is] . . . the possibility of miracles and the Resurrection of Jesus Christ, which is precisely what the worldly wise do." Scalia closed by quoting again from St. Paul in Corinthians, "We must pray for the courage to endure the scorn of the sophisticated world. 'We are fools for Christ's sake.'" Upon hearing that, the devoted audience of believers collectively rose to their feet to give their speaker a rousing standing ovation.

Coming as this address did from a sitting justice who routinely dealt with cases raising religion issues on the Court, it drew a sharp rebuke from the press. Colman McCarthy, a columnist for *The Washington Post*, wrote: "This was less a speech than an outburst. . . . By declaring himself and his prayer breakfast audience 'fools for Christ's sake,' Scalia can further advance his martyr complex when critics dissent from his opinion: scorn of his views equals bias against religion."[34] The *Post*'s Richard Cohen wrote that he found the comments "jarring," explaining: "I think this Supreme Court Justice is a cheap shot artist. . . . Whatever his intentions, he showed himself to be a man who misjudges the nature and the motives of those who insist on a constitutional wall between church and state. It seems his mind is made up on such matters and anyone who thinks Scalia will give First Amendment issues a fair and reasoned hearing is, it seems, proceeding in a way Scalia would appreciate: solely on faith."[35]

Criticism of Scalia came from religious leaders as well. James Dunn, the director of the Baptist Joint Committee in Washington, said: "This is becoming a modern myth: that religion is somehow persecuted in American life. It's a right-wing litmus test. If you don't say religion is being beat up on, then you aren't politically correct. Everyone is competing to see who can whine the loudest."[36] Barry Lynn of the group Americans United for Separation of Church and State said of the speech: "This clearly undermines public confidence in his objectivity regarding religious controversies."[37]

Unfazed, three weeks later, in early May, Scalia maintained his focus on religious issues, traveling to Rome to speak on a panel titled "Left, Right, and the Common Good" at the Gregorian Pontifical University. Scalia's topic was "The Common Christian Good," as he turned this issue into an ideological one: "The burden of my remarks is not that a government of the right is more Christ-like, only that there is no reason to believe that a government of the left is. To tell you the truth, I don't think Christ cares very much what sort of political system we live under. He certainly displayed very little interest in that subject during his time among us, as did his apostles. Accordingly, we should select our economic and political systems on the basis of what seems to produce the greatest material good for the greatest number, and leave theology out of it."[38] In the question and answer period, the issue turned to the role of religion in government in America when one of the audience members asked, "I want to ask you what is the proper behavior of the Christian in an active political commitment, both regarding poverty or regarding life. Earlier abortion was cited. I don't know, for example, what you would think about a Catholic official who signs a law allowing abortion, whether he should resign or not." With respect to the abortion issue, Scalia responded: "I do not like the phrase 'the active political commitment of a Christian.' I should have thought that it's obvious from what I have said that the commitment of a Christian reflects itself in his personal life and in his persuasion of others, not in his acting through the instrument of government. Now the debate in the United States over abortion and over *Roe v. Wade* is a totally different issue from whether the government should prohibit abortion if the people do not want it prohibited. What *Roe v. Wade* held was that even if the people want it prohibited, the states could not prohibit it, because the United States Constitution forbids them to prohibit it. That's a totally different issue from what you and I are talking about."

In a follow-up question, an audience member asked: "In looking for the best government, that Christ is not interested in the type of government that we choose and that the government that we should look for is the one that seeks the interest of the greatest majority. But I think that here also there is a problem because what do we do with the minority? I think that is a very crucial problem." Feeling at that point as if he was in the minority both on the Court and in his conservative religious views in America, Scalia responded:

> The whole theory of democracy, my dear fellow, is that the majority rules, that is the whole theory of it. You protect minorities only because the majority determines that there are certain minorities or certain minority positions that deserve protection. Thus in the United States Constitution we have removed from the majoritarian system of democracy the freedom of speech, the freedom of religion, and a few other freedoms that are named in the Bill of Rights. The whole purpose of that is that the people themselves, that is to say the majority, agree to the rights of the minority on those subjects—but not on other subjects. If you want minority rights on other subjects, you must persuade the majority that you desire those minority rights. Or else take up arms and conquer the majority.

To "take up arms and conquer the majority"—that was Scalia's continuing goal on the Supreme Court, forgetting that in raw numbers he had been part of a conservative majority since his appointment in 1986, but his own actions had split their votes for years. To his way of thinking, the force of his words and the power of his arguments were all he should need.

• • •

Scalia was alone on his ice floe in 1996 as he drifted away from the iceberg where the centrist justices now controlled the Court's majority. The matter came to a head almost like clockwork at the end of the 1995–96 term, in what had become one of his periodic "Ninofits." Reminiscent of the 1988–89 and 1991–92 terms, when the Court's majority moved away from Scalia's position, by the middle of May 1996, Scalia had already filed three dissents and would file eight more by the end of the term. Five of those cases dealt with topics important to him: gay rights, the Fourteenth Amendment's Due

Process Clause, women's rights, and two dealing with the First Amendment right of free speech. Each one of those losses was hard for him to accept.

The run of late-term dissents began on May 20, with the announcement of two cases in which the majority's interpretation of the Constitution differed dramatically from Scalia's. The first of those cases involved an issue that Scalia thought had been settled nine years before. In the 1987 case of *Bowers v. Hardwick*, through which the constitutionality of Georgia's anti-sodomy law for same-sex couples engaged in intimate relations was tested, the Court issued an opinion by conservative Byron White favoring state laws banning the practice on moral grounds.

Ironically, it was Anthony Kennedy, the successor to Lewis Powell, the man whose changed vote had tipped the opinion against gay rights, who would become the leading spokesperson on the Court for protecting the constitutional and privacy rights for gays and lesbians. The new case, *Romer v. Evans*, involved Amendment 2 to the Colorado constitution, which was passed by the voters in a statewide referendum in 1992 and designed to remove from the books state and local laws protecting gay rights.[39] The advocates for Amendment 2 argued that this would end special protections for this group, while gay rights opponents argued that it effectively removed legal protection for a class of people from the Colorado state constitution.

Speaking for a 6–3 majority, Kennedy was persuaded by a legal brief from Harvard professor Laurence Tribe that the Equal Protection Clause of the Constitution prevented states from denying gays the protection of the law. Beginning with the statement by Justice John Harlan in the late nineteenth century that the Constitution "neither knows nor tolerates classes among citizens," Kennedy argued that "those words now are understood to state a commitment to the law's neutrality where the rights of persons are at stake." For the majority this meant that the state constitutional amendment must be overturned because it did "more than repeal or rescind [existing state] provisions [protecting gays and lesbians]. It prohibits all legislative, executive or judicial action at any level of state or local government designed to protect [gays and lesbians]."[40] Kennedy complained about this amendment's "damage to civic life" by arguing "even if, as we doubt, homosexuals could find some safe harbor in laws of general application, we cannot accept the view that Amendment 2's prohibition on specific legal protections does no more than deprive homosexuals of special rights. To the contrary, the amendment imposes a special disability upon those persons alone. Homosexuals are forbidden the safeguards that others enjoy or may seek without constraint."[41] Kennedy stated that "Amendment 2 classifies homosexuals not to further a proper legislative end but to make them unequal to everyone else. This Colorado cannot do. A State cannot so deem a class of persons a stranger to its laws."[42]

This was too much for Scalia, who saw no rights for gays and lesbians in his copy of the Constitution, his interpretation of the Founding Era for the Constitution, or his public policy understanding of how the states must be permitted to operate. "The Court has mistaken a Kulturkampf for a fit of spite," he began, referring to the "culture struggle" of Protestant German chancellor Otto von Bismarck against the Catholic Church in his effort to exert governmental control over the Church following the 1870 Vatican Council's announcement of the doctrine of "papal infallibility."[43] Scalia argued that rather than simply expressing their anger over the wave of protective laws for gays, which would be an unconstitutional denial of equal protection based on class, the Colorado voters were articulating their changing cultural values. In his view, this amendment represented "a modest attempt by seemingly tolerant Coloradans to preserve traditional sexual mores against the efforts of a politically powerful minority to revise those mores through use of the laws." For him, this "objective, and the means chosen to achieve it, are not only unimpeachable under any constitutional doctrine hitherto pronounced . . . they have been specifically approved by the Congress of the United States and by this Court."[44]

For Scalia, with gay rights unmentioned in the Constitution, this was simply an expression of one state's democratic majority, and "this Court has no business imposing upon all Americans the resolution favored by the elite class from which the Members of this institution are selected, pronouncing that 'animosity' toward homosexuality . . . is evil."[45] For him, "the amendment prohibits special treatment of homosexuals, and nothing more." This being the case, he did not see a constitutional violation here, because:

> The only denial of equal treatment [that the Court] contends homosexuals have suffered is this: They may not obtain preferential treatment without amending the state constitution. That is to say, the principle underlying the Court's opinion is that one who is accorded equal treatment under the laws, but cannot as readily as others obtain preferential treatment under the laws, has been denied equal pro-

tection of the laws. If merely stating this alleged "equal protection" violation does not suffice to refute it, our constitutional jurisprudence has achieved terminal silliness.[46]

Having thus defined the amendment, Scalia used the lesser "rational basis" test to measure the reasonableness of the amendment. In his opinion, the state had sufficiently "reasonable" justifications, a desire to preserve its view of morality, for such an amendment denying legal protection to gays, meaning that "No principle set forth in the Constitution, nor even any imagined by this Court in the past 200 years, prohibits what Colorado has done here. But the case for Colorado is much stronger than that. What it has done is not only unprohibited, but eminently reasonable, with close, congressionally approved precedent in earlier constitutional practice." Also "reasonable" for Scalia was the moral choice being made by the majority of the state population here:

> The Court's opinion contains grim, disapproving hints that Coloradans have been guilty of "animus" or "animosity" toward homosexuality, as though that has been established as un-American. Of course it is our moral heritage that one should not hate any human being or class of human beings. But I had thought that one could consider certain conduct reprehensible—murder, for example, or polygamy, or cruelty to animals—and could exhibit even "animus" toward such conduct. Surely that is the only sort of "animus" at issue here: moral disapproval of homosexual conduct, the same sort of moral disapproval that produced the centuries-old criminal laws that we held constitutional in *Bowers*.[47]

Scalia's linkage here of gay rights to the crimes of "murder . . . polygamy, or cruelty to animals," picking up on Byron White's language in *Bowers v. Hardwick*, became a staple of his later speeches on the subject.[48] It would lead to charges by some, including gay congressman Barney Frank of Massachusetts, that he was a homophobe.[49]

For Scalia, the elitist majority of the Court was just imposing on the states what he viewed as the pro–gay rights posture of the legal community. Opening himself up to later charges of intemperate behavior and homophobia, he argued:

When the Court takes sides in the culture wars, it tends to be with the knights rather than the villeins [peasants]—and more specifically with the Templars, reflecting the views and values of the lawyer class from which the Court's Members are drawn. How that class feels about homosexuality will be evident to anyone who wishes to interview job applicants at virtually any of the Nation's law schools. The interviewer may refuse to offer a job because the applicant is a Republican; because he is an adulterer; because he went to the wrong prep school or belongs to the wrong country club; because he eats snails; because he is a womanizer; because she wears real-animal fur; or even because he hates the Chicago Cubs. But if the interviewer should wish not to be an associate or partner of an applicant because he disapproves of the applicant's homosexuality, then he will have violated the pledge which the Association of American Law Schools requires all its member schools to exact from job interviewers: "assurance of the employer's willingness" to hire homosexuals.[50]

• • •

The next loss for Scalia came in a case dealing with the question of an excessive damages ruling against car manufacturer BMW. The case, *BMW of North America v. Gore,* had an unusual set of facts that became a staple of Scalia's later speeches on constitutional decision making. Dr. Ira Gore Jr. had purchased a $41,000 black BMW only to discover that before his purchase the car had been repainted, presumably because of its exposure to acid rain. Believing that his car was now worth less, Gore sued for damages and was awarded $4,000 by the jury to compensate him for the reduced value in his car, and $2 million in punitive damages to punish BMW for not revealing the damage.[51]

For the Court, the question was whether this large punitive damages award by a state court "exceed[ed] the constitutional limit" in trying to impose a national policy on a corporation. Speaking for the Court, John Paul Stevens argued, "While we do not doubt that Congress has ample authority to enact such a [deceptive trade practices prohibition] policy for the entire Nation, it is clear that no single State could do so, or even impose its own policy choice on neighboring States. . . . We think it follows from these principles of state sovereignty and comity that a State may not impose economic sanctions on violators of its laws with the intent of changing the tort feasors' lawful conduct in other States."[52] Unwilling to create a "bright line" for determining what would be an "excessive penalty," but empowering a state to rule this way within its own borders, the Court sent the case back to the Alabama courts to determine the awarded damages.

For Scalia, in dissent, the question was the same as he had just argued in the *Romer v. Evans* gay rights case: just where in the Constitution was there a limitation on awarding "excessive damages"? Using his originalism tools, he sought to prove that his colleagues in the majority had gone far beyond their constitutional powers. "Today we see the latest manifestation of this Court's recent and increasingly insistent 'concern about punitive damages that run wild,'" Scalia wrote, adding, "Since the Constitution does not make that concern any of our business, the Court's activities in this area are an unjustified incursion into the province of state governments."[53] For Scalia, the Fourteenth Amendment due process claims granted to Mr. Gore by the majority had limits: "I do not regard the Fourteenth Amendment's Due Process Clause as a secret repository of substantive guarantees against 'unfairness'—neither the unfairness of an excessive civil compensatory award, nor the unfairness of an 'unreasonable' punitive award. What the Fourteenth Amendment's procedural guarantee assures is an opportunity to contest the reasonableness of a damages judgment in state court; but there is no federal guarantee a damages award actually *be* reasonable."[54]

Ever the originalist, Scalia believed that the Court's decision here strayed from the historical understanding of the Fourteenth Amendment, as he argued: "At the time of adoption of the Fourteenth Amendment, it was well understood that punitive damages represent the assessment by the jury, as the voice of the community, of the measure of punishment the defendant deserved. . . . Today's decision, though dressed up as a legal opinion, is really no more than a disagreement with the community's sense of indignation or outrage expressed in the punitive award of the Alabama jury, as reduced by the State Supreme Court."[55] Scalia could not find in his copy of the Constitution either the power for the state to negate what it believed to be an unreasonable damages award by a jury, or the power of his Court to allow it to do so. In his words, "If the Court is correct, it must be that every claim that a state jury's award of compensatory damages is 'unreasonable' (because not supported by the evidence) amounts to an assertion of constitutional injury. . . . That is a stupefying proposition."[56]

Later, Scalia would explain in his speeches that his actions in the two cases on May 20, 1996, disagreeing first with the Court's liberals in the *Romer* case, then the conservatives in the *BMW* case, proved that he was being fair and neutral: "I dissented in both cases because I say, 'A pox on both their houses.' It has nothing to do with what your policy preferences are; it has to do with what you think the Constitution is."[57]

• • •

At the end of the Court term, Scalia once again differed with the majority of the Court, this time including its two female justices, in *United States v. Virginia*, on the question of whether the single-sex admissions policy of the state's all-male military prep college, Virginia Military Institute (VMI), violated the Fourteenth Amendment's Equal Protection Clause. VMI was established in 1839 to train male citizen soldiers. It surprised no one when the two female justices who had been victimized by discrimination in the beginning of their legal careers, Sandra Day O'Connor and Ruth Bader Ginsburg, voted to require VMI to admit women. They were joined by John Paul Stevens, Stephen Breyer, and Anthony Kennedy. Speaking for the majority, Justice Ginsburg argued that discrimination on the basis of sex required "heightened review" to ensure the Fourteenth Amendment's equal protection guarantee was not violated without there being an "important governmental objective" for doing so. Virginia argued that "Single-sex education at VMI serves an 'important governmental objective,' leading the state to maintain that the exclusion of women is not only 'substantially related,' it is essential to that objective." But Ginsburg disagreed, arguing: "[T]he Commonwealth's great goal is not substantially advanced by women's categorical exclusion, in total disregard of their individual merit, from the Commonwealth's premier 'citizen-soldier' corps. Virginia . . . 'has fallen far short of establishing the "exceedingly persuasive justification"' . . . that must be the solid base for any gender-defined classification."[58]

The state argued that its parallel Virginia Women's Institute for Leadership at the all-women's Mary Baldwin College provided an equal form of college-level military training for young women in the state. Using the separate but unequal logic that the Court had employed in the 1954 *Brown v. Board of Education* case, Ginsburg argued that Virginia had not truly provided an equal military educational facility for women: "VMI, too, offers an educational opportunity no other Virginia institution provides, and the school's 'prestige'—associated with its success in developing 'citizen-soldiers'—is unequaled. Virginia has closed this facility to its daughters and, instead, has devised for them a 'parallel program,' with a faculty less impressively credentialed and less well paid, more limited course offerings, fewer opportunities for military training and for scientific specialization." This being the case, Ginsburg concluded, "Women seeking and fit for a VMI-quality education cannot be offered anything less, under the Commonwealth's obligation to afford them genuinely equal protection."[59]

In dissent, Scalia—who understood the tradition of "Virginia Gentlemen" from his years of teaching at the University of Virginia Law School and who had witnessed that school becoming a coed institution—reached into his originalism playbook for reviewing history, in seeking to preserve the tradition of the existence of a state-supported all-male military school. "Today the Court shuts down an institution that has served the people of the Commonwealth of Virginia with pride and distinction for over a century and a half. To achieve that desired result, it rejects (contrary to our established practice) the factual findings of two courts below, sweeps aside the precedents of this Court, and ignores the history of our people."[60] Scalia would leave such matters to the democratic voting process for determination of the best course of action, rather than leave it to the courts for their decision:

> The virtue of a democratic system with a First Amendment is that it readily enables the people, over time, to be persuaded that what they took for granted is not so, and to change their laws accordingly. . . . So to counterbalance the Court's criticism of our ancestors, let me say a word in their praise: They left us free to change. The same cannot be said of this most illiberal Court, which has embarked on a course of inscribing one after another of the current preferences of the society (and in some cases only the counter majoritarian preferences of the society's law-trained elite) into our Basic Law.[61]

For Scalia, Virginia's policy of an all-male military school was historically acceptable: "The tradition of having government-funded military schools for men is as well rooted in the traditions of this country as the tradition of sending only men into military combat. The people may decide to change the one tradition, like the other, through democratic processes; but the assertion that either tradition has been unconstitutional through the centuries is not law, but politics-smuggled-into-law."[62] And so, he vehemently objected: "Today . . . change is forced upon Virginia, and reversion to single-sex education is prohibited nationwide, not by democratic processes but by order of this Court. Even while bemoaning the sorry, bygone days of 'fixed notions' concerning women's education . . . the Court favors current notions so fixedly that it is willing to write them into the Constitution of the United States by application of custom-built 'tests.' This is not the interpretation of a Constitution, but the creation of one."[63]

As tough as these three consecutive losses were for Scalia, they were just the prelude for two final defeats that he was about to endure. Both cases explored the balance between First Amendment freedom of association rights and a vindictive city or county political patronage system. They followed up on a 1990 case called *Rutan v. Republican Party of Illinois*, dealing with the Chicago public employees' hiring and promotion policy as it was affected by the city's political patronage system. The Court's ruling that the First Amendment prevented the Illinois governor from refusing to hire based on political affiliation had vexed Scalia six years earlier. Nothing in his version of the First Amendment's freedoms of speech or association in that case had barred hiring and firing based on political patronage.[64] Now the question was whether independent contractors who worked for the city could be forced to support the governing party by the manipulation of their city contracts, or whether that was also a violation of the First Amendment's freedom of association.

In one case, the owner of a towing company who had been on a city's list of preferred operators refused to contribute to the reelection campaign of that administration, instead supporting its opponents. As a result, his company was removed from that list.[65] In the other case, an independent trash hauler had his contract ended by city officials whose administration he had criticized.[66] The question was whether the independent contractors who were benefiting from business with the city retained or forfeited their First Amendment right to associate with any political party they wished. The two centrist justices, O'Connor and Kennedy, both of whom had signed Scalia's pro–patronage dissent in *Rutan*, now abandoned him to provide a majority for an anti-patronage, pro–First Amendment, free association rights position.

In the *O'Hare Truck Service v. City of Northlake* case, Justice Kennedy spoke for the seven-justice majority in arguing that the First Amendment freedom of association rights of independent city contractors protected them from being excluded from city contractor lists based on their party affiliation: "Independent contractors, as well as public employees, are entitled to protest wrongful government interference with their rights of speech and association. . . . The absolute right to enforce a patronage scheme, insisted upon by respondents as a means of retaining control over independent contractors . . . has not been shown to be a necessary part of a legitimate political system in all instances. . . . We decline to draw a line excluding independent contractors from the First Amendment safe-guards of political association afforded to employees."[67]

In the other case, *Board of County Commissioners v. Umbehr*, dealing with the free speech rights of trash haulers in the face of political party vindictiveness, Justice O'Connor added weight to Kennedy's pro–First Amendment argument, saying, "Because the courts below assumed that Umbehr's termination (or nonrenewal) was in retaliation for his protected speech activities, and because they did not pass on the balance between the government's interests and the free speech interests at stake, our conclusion [is] that independent contractors do enjoy some First Amendment protection. . . . We recognize the right of independent government contractors not to be terminated for exercising their First Amendment rights."[68]

Having already lost so many key cases at the end of this term, Scalia seemed deeply affected by the reduced support for his earlier dissenting position because of the switched votes of the two centrist justices. He criticized both of them: "Taken together, today's [two] decisions . . . demonstrate why this Court's Constitution-making process can be called 'reasoned adjudication' only in the most formalistic sense."[69] Scalia saw these cases as unacceptable extensions of the anti-patronage, pro–First Amendment rights ruling in the *Rutan* case just six years earlier: "One would think it inconceivable that [the Court would extend] far beyond *Rutan* to the massive field of all government contracting. Yet amazingly, that is what the Court does in these two opinions—and by lopsided votes, at that. It is profoundly disturbing that the varying political practices across this vast country, from coast to coast, can be transformed overnight by an institution whose conviction of what the Constitution means is so fickle."[70]

By now, Scalia was again in near total despair. As he later explained to biographer Joan Biskupic, "Things were bad. We were losing all of the cases I cared about. At the end of the term . . . the hard ones, the important ones, always come then. Boom! Boom! Boom! Four of those in a row, and you're really down."[71] "The wins . . . The wins. Damn few," Scalia would lament to Biskupic.[72] So Scalia struck back by concluding his dissent in the political patronage cases with a stern comment on all of the Court's work that term with which he disagreed: "This Court has begun to make a habit of disclaiming the natural and foreseeable jurisprudential consequences of its path-breaking (i.e., Constitution-making) opinions. Each major step in the abridgment of the people's right to govern themselves is portrayed as extremely limited or indeed *sui juris.* . . . The people should not be deceived. While the present Court sits, a major, undemocratic restructuring of our national institutions and mores is constantly in progress."[73]

For Scalia, his colleagues were now operating under a different rule book, arrogating power to themselves that he did not believe the Founders had intended to grant to the Supreme Court. And, for him, the results of the use of that power were profoundly disturbing: "They say hard cases make bad law. The cases before the Court today set the blood boiling, with the arrogance that they seem to display on the part of elected officials. Shall the American System of Justice let insolent, petty-tyrant politicians get away with this? . . . Favoritism such as this happens all the time in American political life, and no one has ever thought that it violated—of all things—the First Amendment to the Constitution of the United States. The Court must be living in another world. Day by day, case by case, it is busy designing a Constitution for a country I do not recognize."[74]

Even retired colleagues on the Supreme Court who were opponents could see that it had been a difficult year for Scalia. Ever the gentleman, retired Justice Harry Blackmun sent Scalia a sympathetic note: "I know that this has not been an easy year for you. But it is over with, and next October one will be rejuvenated and a new chapter will unfold. As a group or individually, we cannot get discouraged. May the summer be a good one for you."[75] It was an act of kindness by Blackmun, and much appreciated. A clearly moved Scalia responded immediately with his own handwritten note:

> *Dear Harry:*
>
> *How kind of you to write the nice note you did! You are right that I am more discouraged this year than I have been at the end of any of my previous nine terms up here. I am beginning to repeat myself, and don't see much use in it any more.*
>
> *I hope I will feel better in the fall. A cheering note from an old colleague—and one whom, God knows, I was not always on the same side with—sure does help. Many thanks—and have a pleasant summer. Respectfully, Nino*[76]

But it was clear to Scalia, with all that had happened on the Court to him that term, that if he was going to stay on the Court he would need a new plan of attack. And, as it happened, it was already in motion.

CHAPTER 14

War of the Words

While he was losing votes at the end of the 1995–96 term, Scalia developed a new plan for "conquering the majority" and taking control of American constitutional law. Just as he did after his judicial losses in 1988–89, Scalia decided to create a new "war of the words" in early 1996, previewing a new stump speech at Valparaiso University in Indiana before later presenting it at Catholic University in Washington, D.C.[1] During the previous seven years Scalia had continued to give his early speeches outlining his theories of textualism and faint-hearted originalism, reprising them so frequently that the media largely stopped reporting on them after 1991. His new idea was to combine the two speeches into one, entitled "A Theory of Constitutional Interpretation," which would explain his decision-making technique in a more accessible way for a general audience.

The origins for this new speech came from his prestigious Tanner Lecture a year earlier at Princeton University's Center for Human Values. In a speech titled "Common-Law Courts in a Civil-Law System: The Role of U.S. Federal Courts in Interpreting the Constitution and Laws," which he later turned into a book, *A Matter of Interpretation*, Scalia explored what he called "the current neglected state of the science of construing legal texts" while also "offer[ing] a few suggestions for improvements."[2] The first three-fourths of his address offered a combination of a reworked version of his 1985–86 talk on legislative history, and his 1988 textualism speech, discussing how judges should interpret statutory texts, with the goal of ending judicial lawmaking, thus limiting the judiciary's power. He began by discussing the "common law lawmaking" system in which judges used a process of *stare decisis,* or respect for precedent, "to establish whether the case at hand falls within a principle that has already been decided."[3] The task here, he argued, was complicated by the fact that "Every issue of law resolved by a federal judge involves interpretation of text—the text of a regulation, or of a statute, or of the Constitution."[4] However, he added, the problem was that "We American judges have no intelligible theory of what we do most."[5] And discovering the goals of the legislature was not possible because such a quest ventured into determining the "legislative intent" that he had long criticized: "Government by unexpressed intent is similarly tyrannical. It is the *law* that governs, not the intent of the lawgiver."[6] So Scalia counseled the "abandonment" of the use of "legislative intent" as being "simply not compatible with democratic theory that laws mean whatever they ought to mean, and that unelected judges decide what that is." Instead, he urged the use of his textualism approach. "The text is the law, and it is the text that must be observed."[7] Scalia insisted that no one should call him a "strict constructionist," a popular theory that judges should *only* rely on a strict interpretation of the text itself. This theory was used by Nixon during his 1968 presidential campaign in promising to search for such Supreme Court candidates as a means of both limiting the Court and turning back the liberalism of the Warren Court. Under Scalia's textualism theory, "A text should not be construed strictly, and it should not be construed leniently; it should be construed reasonably, to contain all that it fairly means."[8]

Having discussed textual interpretation, Scalia now tapped into his June 1986 speech that he delivered just before his Supreme Court appointment in turning to his theme exploring "the distinctive problem of constitutional interpretation."[9] Returning to familiar ground, Scalia explained his interpretive theory this way: "What I look for in the Constitution is precisely what I look for in a statute: the original meaning of the text, not what the original draftsmen intended." In searching for "original meaning," rather than Robert Bork's "original intent," Scalia opposed those "evolving Constitution" judges who sought the current meaning of the words in what they saw as a "Living Constitution."[10] He opposed rulings based on "the evolving standards of decency that mark the progress of a maturing society," instead arguing, "It certainly cannot be said that a constitution naturally suggests changeability; to the contrary, its whole purpose is to prevent change—to embed certain rights in such a manner that future generations cannot readily take them away."[11] But in calling for an interpretation of statutes based on textualism, and an unchanging Constitution, Scalia still had not explained *how* to determine the meaning of the Constitution using his theory of originalism. It was because he had to interpret history for his judicial decision-making approach that scholars of Founding Era history took issue with him.

1

Italian immigrant Salvatore Eugene "Sam" Scalia, a professor of Romance languages, and his first-generation Italian American wife, schoolteacher Catherine Panaro Scalia.

2

1952

Xavier High School

Young "Nino" Scalia attended Xavier High School, a Roman Catholic military prep school in Manhattan where classical education and traditional Catholicism were accompanied by military-style discipline.

3

Lieutenant Colonel Antonin Scalia, one of the leaders of the elite Xavier Regiment, was described by his faculty adviser as "by far, the best in his class in every way."

4

Scalia (right) played Macbeth in a Xavier school play, which he described fifty-five years later as "probably the most significant thing I've done in my life." Later, billed as "Tony" Scalia, he would continue his acting career at Georgetown University.

6

The ornate Philodemic Room in Healy Hall at Georgetown University, the home of the school's champion-ship debate society, where the aggressively argumentative Nino Scalia spent much of his time.

5

Scalia (seated to the left of the podium), and his debate partner at Georgetown, Peter G. Schmidt (seated to Scalia's right), became one of the best collegiate debate teams in the nation, displaying forensic talents that would one day send their legal careers in very different directions.

After Scalia married Radcliffe graduate Maureen McCarthy in 1961, they expanded the Scalia clan by producing nine children. As Scalia explained, "We're just old-fashioned Catholics, you know, playing what used to be known as Vatican Roulette."

The reformist Second Vatican Council, convened by Pope John XXIII in October of 1962, dramatically liberalized the Catholic Church, but it had no effect on Scalia, who continued to follow the traditional, Latin-based Catholicism of his parents.

As general counsel for the Office of Telecommunications Policy in the Nixon admin-
istration in the early 1970s, Scalia won praise for his efforts in outmanuevering the
White House in a dispute over the renewal of the funding for the Public Broadcasting
System (PBS).

Like Scalia, others working in the besieged presidential administration of Gerald R. Ford (center) after the resignation of Richard M. Nixon, such as White House chief of staff Donald Rumsfeld (left) and deputy chief of staff Dick Cheney (right), were so scarred by this experience that later in their careers they devoted themselves to increasing the power of the presidency.

Court of Appeals judge for the District of Columbia Antonin Scalia (right), a lifelong opponent of affirmative action policies, edged out his better-known colleague Judge Robert H. Bork for the Supreme Court opening in 1986 because President Ronald Reagan wanted to appoint the first Italian American to the Court.

When Scalia was sworn in by retiring chief justice Warren Burger, many expected that he would become the uniting force for the conservative majority on the Court.

A year after Scalia's appointment to the Court, President Reagan nominated Court of Appeals judge for the District of Columbia Robert Bork (right) to fill the seat of Lewis Powell. Bork failed to be confirmed by the Democratic-led Senate after a highly political confirmation hearing.

Scalia quickly offended his more senior colleagues on the Rehnquist Court (shown here when he joined it in 1986) by his domination of the oral arguments and his aggressive efforts to control the writing of the Court's judicial opinions. Seated (left to right): Thurgood Marshall, William J. Brennan Jr., Chief Justice William H. Rehnquist, Byron R. White, and Harry A. Blackmun. Standing (left to right): Sandra Day O'Connor, Lewis F. Powell Jr., John Paul Stevens, and Antonin G. Scalia.

The Rehnquist Court, shown here as it existed between 1994 and 2005, was evenly balanced between four liberals and four conservatives with the moderate conservative justice Sandra Day O'Connor often casting the deciding vote, to the dismay of Scalia. Seated (left to right): Antonin G. Scalia, John Paul Stevens, Chief Justice William H. Rehnquist, Sandra Day O'Connor, and Anthony M. Kennedy. Standing (left to right): Ruth Bader Ginsburg, David H. Souter, Clarence Thomas, and Stephen G. Breyer.

Justice William Brennan's "living" evolutionary theory of interpreting the Constitution, in contrast to Scalia's originalism, was summed up by his axiom, "Five votes can do anything around here."

John Paul Stevens was appointed as a justice by President Ford in 1975 and expected to decide cases as a moderate conservative, but instead he became the Court's leading liberal in the twenty-first century, frequently engaging in ideological debates with Scalia in major decisions.

Sandra Day O'Connor, the first female justice on the Supreme Court, appointed in 1981 by President Reagan, continually drew the wrath of Scalia in judicial opinions because of her moderate votes limiting the reach of the conservative majority.

Anthony Kennedy was appointed to the Supreme Court in 1987 by President Reagan to fill the seat denied to Robert Bork. He was subjected to Scalia's wrath for his often unpredictably moderate decision making.

David Souter was appointed to the Supreme Court in 1990 by President George H. W. Bush, and frequently frustrated conservatives by his moderate decision making and "expansive rights" version of Scalia's originalism theory.

Clarence Thomas became an ultraconservative, natural-rights-oriented originalist who was so willing to overturn longtime precedents that Scalia said of him, "I am a textualist. I am an originalist, but I am not a nut."

Ruth Bader Ginsburg. Her moderate liberal, judicial-self-restraint approach occasionally irked Scalia, one of her closest friends on the Court.

Stephen Breyer's "active liberty" theory has made him the one justice who has been willing to debate Scalia off the Court, with great success, on originalism versus the living, evolving Constitution.

In many speeches and judicial opinions, Scalia has argued that demonstrations such as this one over the Supreme Court's controversial 1989 *Webster v. Reproductive Health Services* abortion rights decision, in which Scalia attacked Sandra Day O'Connor for upholding the 1973 pro-abortion *Roe v. Wade* decision, would be eliminated if the Court would just follow his originalism theory and remove itself from deciding abortion cases.

In 2010, the Roberts Court became known for several historic firsts, but its primary distinction is that after conservative Samuel Alito replaced Sandra Day O'Connor in 2006 it became one of the most conservative Supreme Courts in decades. Seated (left to right): Clarence Thomas, Antonin G. Scalia, Chief Justice John G. Roberts Jr., Anthony M. Kennedy, and Ruth Bader Ginsburg. Standing (left to right): Sonia Sotomayor, Stephen G. Breyer, Samuel A. Alito, and Elena Kagan.

In October 2005, just a month after failing to be appointed as chief justice to replace William Rehnquist, Scalia's "Dead Constitution Tour" of speechmaking and public appearances brought him to New York City's Columbus Day Parade as the grand marshal. To Scalia's left is Lawrence Auriana, then president of the Columbus Citizens' Foundation, which sponsored the parade.

Scalia's public visibility off the Court did not always result in the image he was seeking, as illustrated by the public's reaction to this gesture he made to a photographer and a reporter as he exited Boston's Cathedral of the Holy Cross in 2006 after attending a Red Mass for lawyers and judges.

CHURCH & STATE

After the first majority of Catholic justices in the history of the Supreme Court provided the five votes necessary to ban late-term abortions in the *Gonzales v. Carhart* case in 2007, Philadelphia cartoonist Tony Auth made clear why he thought this decision was rendered.

When Missouri senator Claire McCaskill tweeted a different photo of Scalia's unusual headwear at Barack Obama's second inaugural in January 2013, under the heading #Scaliaweirdhat, she did not realize that he was wearing a replica of the hat worn by the Catholic martyr St. Thomas More. The hat led others to wonder whether Scalia was just fending off the cold or sending a symbolic message about the next four years.

Love him or hate him, Antonin Gregory Scalia, shown here with Maureen, his wife of more than fifty years, as they entered the White House for a dinner honoring British prime minister David Cameron and his wife, Samantha, in 2012, is a brilliant, cantankerous, charismatic jurist, unlike any other in the nation's history, who has made the country think deeply about the role of the Supreme Court in American society.

One of the respondents to this essay was Brown University's Early American historian Gordon Wood, who argued that the "extraordinary degree of discretionary power that American judges now wield" that so concerned Scalia was, in fact, "the product of immense changes in our legal and judicial culture which have occurred over the past two hundred years, and these changes cannot be easily reversed." [12] Wood found Scalia's "remedy of textualism in interpretation . . . scarcely commensurate with the severity of the problem and may in fact be no solution at all," since it was "as permissive and as open to arbitrary judicial discretion and expansion as the use of legislative intent or other interpretive methods, if the text-minded judge is so inclined." [13] In other words, a textualist, in arguing for a limited judicial lawmaking power, could in fact be an activist and evolving judge just by expansively interpreting the words contained in the text. For Wood, the only means "to limit the judges' interpretive power" was "by changing the attitude of judges themselves." [14] Scalia responded that Wood's apparent acceptance of the historical evolution of "judicial rewriting of democratically adopted texts" created "willful judges who bend the law to their wishes. But acknowledging evil is one thing, and embracing it is something else." [15]

Having laid this intellectual foundation, Scalia wove all of these themes from his Princeton speech and subsequent book into a new, more accessible speech that he delivered at Valparaiso University's law school in late January 1996. While he was on campus to teach a short course and help judge the law school's annual moot court competition, Scalia spoke to over six hundred people on the topic "Today's Interpretation of Our Constitution," which contained many of the catchphrases he would make famous in the next phase of his speaking career. He once again attacked the notion of a living Constitution. Scalia insisted that the Constitution had a fixed meaning, at least in theory. As he saw it, "People must make decisions based on the law, not on opinions and feelings. However, the real problem with having a living constitution is that it leaves [its] interpretation up to the majority." [16] And so, for him, change in America's democracy should come not from a majority vote of the nine justices on the Court, but rather from the people: "If you want change, all you need is a ballot box and the legislature. Democracy means discussion, vote and then majority wins." [17]

In the fall of 1996, Scalia expanded on his theory at Catholic University. He introduced himself by saying: "I belong to a school, a small but hardy school, called 'textualists' or 'originalists.' That used to be 'constitutional orthodoxy' in the United States." That said, he launched into the clearest short explanation that he had given thus far of how his theory differed from the original intent theory of his former Court of Appeals colleague Robert Bork and Attorney General Edwin Meese:

> The theory of originalism treats a constitution like a statute, and gives it the meaning that its words were understood to bear at the time they were promulgated. You will sometimes hear it described as the theory of original intent. You will never hear me refer to original intent, because as I say I am first of all a textualist, and secondly an original-ist. If you are a textualist, you don't care about the intent, and I don't care if the framers of the Constitution had some secret meaning in mind when they adopted its words. I take the words as they were promulgated to the people of the United States, and what is the fairly understood meaning of those words.

Harkening back to his "The Rule of Law as a Law of Rules" speech searching for general decision-making rules, Scalia now offered his Golden Rule for decision making:

> The words are the law. I think that's what is meant by a government of laws, not of men. We are bound not by the intent of our legislators, but by the laws which they enacted, which are set forth in words, of course. As I say, until recently this was constitutional orthodoxy. Everyone at least said . . . that the Constitution was that anchor, that rock, that unchanging institution that forms the American polity. Im-mutability was regarded as its characteristic. What it meant when it was adopted it means today, and its meaning doesn't change just because we think that meaning is no longer adequate to our times.

His Constitution could be changed, Scalia explained, but by only one means: "That's why there's an amendment provision."[18]

There was little doubt that Scalia's comments about the living Constitu-tion were aimed at the Court's three steadfast liberals, John Paul Stevens, Ste-phen Breyer, and Ruth Bader Ginsburg, but he also took issue with the three living, evolving, constitutional moderates: David Souter, Anthony Kennedy, and Sandra Day O'Connor. On occasion, Scalia also took issue with his two conservative colleagues—William Rehnquist and Clarence Thomas—when they were willing to craft new decision rules. For him, the split on the Court was no longer an ideological one of liberal versus conservative because, as he explained, sometimes "conservatives are fully as prepared to create new rights under this evolutionist theory of the Constitution, as liberals are. . . . [I]t's not liberal/conservative. It's modernist versus the traditional view of the Constitution."

Scalia would allow changes to protect rights, but through means other than five Supreme Court votes: "What was the situation, before *Roe v. Wade*? If you wanted a right to an abortion, create that right the way a democratic society creates most rights. Pass a law. If you don't want it, pass a law against it." Coining a favorite argument for future speeches, Scalia asked: "If you want somebody who's in touch with what are the 'evolving standards of decency' that reflect a maturing society, ask the Congress. . . . What makes you think a committee of nine lawyers ought to tell where we're evolving to." And as far as he was concerned, sticking to the original meaning of the words in the Constitution was what lawyers were qualified to do: "It's lawyer's work. But if that is not what the Constitution is, if it is not a text, like a statute, which means what it meant when it was passed. If it is rather sort of an empty bottle that contains the aspirations of the society, just all sorts of wonderful aspirations, the precise content of which is quite indeterminate. No cruel and unusual punishment today, it may mean the death penalty is OK, tomorrow it won't. Due process of law, whatever that means. We're just in love with these abstractions, and the Supreme Court in the future shall decree for us what these abstractions mean." Scalia's Constitution was meant not to promote change, but to retard or even prevent it: "The whole purpose of the Constitution is to prevent a future society from doing what it wants to do. That's the whole purpose. . . . The only reason you need a Constitution is because some things you don't want the majority to be able to change. That's my most important function as a judge in this system. I have to tell the majority to take a hike. I tell them, 'I don't care what you want, but the Bill of Rights says you cannot do it.'"

In this new speech, as opposed to the two from 1988–89, there was less discussion of textualism and more discussion of originalism, applying a reading of an unchanging Constitution to modern legal issues. It became the staple of Scalia's public appearances for the next nine years, and would become the foundation for the rest of his public speaking career. With each new iteration, Scalia became less and less attached to the precise dictionary definition of the text, which by his own explanation limited his flexibility to interpret, and more and more reliant on originalism, which afforded him greater leeway in choosing which historical documents and historical interpretations of the American Founding period would best support his decisions. Just how this interpretive technique was different from examining legislative intent is not always clear to anyone but Scalia, but his new decision-making process afforded him more discretion and more latitude to interpret those words in a way that allowed him to reach the traditional, conservative result that he preferred.

Stanford constitutional historian Jack Rakove, agreeing with Gordon Wood, articulated the problems that he saw in Scalia's overall theory in his 1996 Pulitzer Prize–winning work, *Original Meanings: Politics and Ideas in the Making of the Constitution*. In his preface to the volume, Rakove argued that "originalism is vulnerable to two powerful criticisms. First, it is always in some fundamental sense anti-democratic, in that it seeks to subordinate the judgment of present generations to the wisdom of their distant (political) ancestors. Second, the real problems of reconstructing coherent intentions and understandings from the evidence of history raise serious questions about the capacity of originalist forays to yield the definitive conclusions that the advocates of this theory claim to find." With tongue firmly in cheek, however, Rakove was willing to concede to Scalia: "On the other hand, I happen to like originalist arguments when the weight of the evidence seems to support the constitutional outcomes I favor—and that may be as good a clue to the appeal of originalism as any other."[19]

In his opening chapter, "The Perils of Originalism," Rakove argued that basing any judgment on history that is not written with an eye toward being used as the basis for judging is uncertain because "Historians have little stake in ascertaining the original meaning of a clause for its own sake, or in attempting to freeze or distill its true, unadulterated meaning at some pristine moment of constitutional understanding. They can rest content with—even revel in—the ambiguities of the evidentiary record, recognizing that behind the textual brevity of any clause there once lay a spectrum of complex views and different shadings of opinions."[20] Rakove cited with favor another constitutional historian, Leonard Levy, who argued that "the Supreme Court's use of originalist evidence is best described as a mix of 'law office history' [citing only supportive history for their side by lawyers in their legal briefs] and justificatory rhetoric which offers little reason to think that this method of interpretation can provide faithful and accurate application of the original constitutional understandings its advocates promise."[21]

Rakove then explained why Scalia's call for an originalist approach was both too limited and unreliable. There were, he argued, "four sets of sources that can be brought to bear to solve problems or puzzles about the original meaning of the Constitution" that Scalia could use. Rakove explained that there are two "textual" sources from "explicit discussion of the Constitution": "the records of debates of the federal and state conventions of 1787 and 1788" and "the commentaries published during the campaign over its ratification." Beyond this written material, Rakove argued that two other sets of "contextual" sources existed that "may enable [historians]—when explicit commentary on particular points seems inadequate—to reconstruct a body of tacit assumptions and concerns that informed the way in which framers and ratifiers thought about the questions they were resolving." Those two contextual markers were "those broad notions of government that Americans had acquired through their absorption in the political theory of the Enlightenment," and "their perceptions of what might be called the public-policy issues of their day," which "were arguably as likely to influence their thinking as the maxims and axioms they found in Locke or Montesquieu or Blackstone."[22] For Rakove, all of these additional sources allowed one to determine the context of "the original meaning of the Constitution" drafted by "delegates [who] came to Philadelphia essentially uninstructed by their legislative constituents," and thus were "the internal deliberations of the [1787 Constitutional] Convention."[23] For Rakove, the contextual sources were not part of Scalia's theory, which for him rendered the justice's interpretation of the original meaning of the Constitution suspect.

Rakove explained the limits of Scalia's originalism theory this way: "Like any other historical effort to explain how texts emerge from contexts, the recovery of original meanings, intentions, and understandings is itself an act of interpretation—but one that can at least be bounded, though not perfected, by canons of scholarship." In short, for him, "its goal is (and should remain) elusive."[24] Rakove articulated what he saw as the limits of originalism: "It is one thing to rail against the evils of politically unaccountable judges enlarging constitutional rights beyond the ideas and purposes of their original adopters; another to explain why morally sustainable claims of equality should be held captive to the extraordinary obstacles of Article V or subject to the partial and incomplete understandings of 1789 or 1868."[25]

But Scalia nearly always chose not to grapple with the challenges posed to him by the nation's top historians. As the man sitting on the Supreme Court, wearing the judicial gown, his constitutional authority became the trump card in this discussion, allowing, for him, his theory to prevail.

• • •

Soon after unveiling his revised explanation of originalism in the Valparaiso and Catholic University speeches, Scalia was able to demonstrate in cases how his newly packaged theory worked. In 1997 he wrote the majority opinion in a federal handgun control case, *Printz v. United States*, which dealt with the federal Brady Handgun Violence Prevention Act, named for James Brady, press secretary to President Reagan, who was severely injured in the attempted assassination of the president. The question in the case was whether the federal government could mandate that state police do a background check on prospective buyers of handguns. Scalia's answer was a resounding no. The Court had faced another version of this federalism issue in 1992, ruling in *New York v. United States*, which concerned a federal law compelling states to store the low-level radioactive waste from their state, that "States are not mere political subdivisions of the United States. . . . The Federal Government may not compel the States to enact or administer a federal regulatory program. . . . It does not, however, authorize Congress simply to direct the States to provide for the disposal of the radioactive waste generated within their borders." [26] In the new gun control case, Scalia wrote for a majority including the three conservatives on the Court plus moderates O'Connor and Kennedy, saying, "We held in *New York* that Congress cannot compel the States to enact or enforce a federal regulatory program. Today we hold that Congress cannot circumvent that prohibition by conscripting the State's officers directly. The Federal Government may neither issue directives requiring the States to address particular problems, nor command the States' officers, or those of their political subdivisions, to administer or enforce a federal regulatory program." [27]

A ruling by Scalia on behalf of states' rights, as opposed to federal power, and one that supported gun rights, was no surprise. In addition to his belief in state sovereignty, he was a gun owner and a hunter who loved his Second Amendment rights. But the vigor with which he demonstrated the historical basis for his conclusions served as an object lesson in what his decision-making process was becoming. Scalia presented a complete analysis of the early Founding Era history of Congress dealing with the use of state officials to enforce federal laws to conclude that it could not be done: "Not only do the enactments of the early Congresses, as far as we are aware, contain no evidence of an assumption that the Federal Government may command the States' executive power in the absence of a particularized constitutional authorization, they contain some indication of precisely the opposite assumption."[28] Scalia then turned to several sections of the *Federalist Papers* that supported a strong central government and concluded: "None of these statements necessarily implies—what is the critical point here—that Congress could impose these responsibilities *without the consent of the States*. They appear to rest on the natural assumption that the States would consent to allowing their officials to assist the Federal Government."[29] Any reading of the history from this period, he argued, would show that the states would never willingly consent to become permanent, subordinate agents of the new national government.

While Scalia did concede that there were several early laws under which the federal executive branch could commandeer the states for assistance, those precedents for him did not extend to the present day: "To complete the historical record, we must note that there is not only an absence of executive-commandeering statutes in the early Congresses, but there is an absence of them in our later history as well, at least until very recent years." And this historical record did not change substantially for him in the late twentieth century, when the unfunded spending mandates of the federal government were pressed upon the states. "The Government points to a number of federal statutes enacted within the past few decades that require the participation of state or local officials in implementing federal regulatory schemes. . . . For deciding the issue before us here, they are of little relevance. . . . They are of such recent vintage that they are no more probative than the statute before us of a constitutional tradition that lends meaning to the text. Their persuasive force is far outweighed by almost two centuries of apparent congressional avoidance of the practice."[30]

Relying on his historical examination, Scalia vigorously opposed the idea of the growth of federal power at the expense of the sovereign states: "The Framers' experience under the Articles of Confederation had persuaded them that using the States as the instruments of federal governance was both ineffectual and provocative of federal-state conflict. . . . This separation of the two spheres is one of the Constitution's structural protections of liberty."[31] Scalia concluded based on this historical review that there should be more balance in the federal-state relationship than the Brady law required: "It is an essential attribute of the States' retained sovereignty that they remain independent and autonomous within their proper sphere of authority. . . . It is no more compatible with this independence and autonomy that their officers be 'dragooned' . . . into administering federal law, than it would be compatible with the independence and autonomy of the United States that its officers be impressed into service for the execution of state laws." [32]

Interestingly, in dissenting, the liberals on the Court accepted Scalia's changing agenda of providing historical evidence for constitutional analysis. They argued instead that Scalia's interpretation of the historical record was neither the only one nor the correct one. In assessing the Framers' vision of the system of federalism, Justice Stevens argued based on his own reading of the *Federalist Papers*: "The historical materials strongly suggest that the Founders intended to enhance the capacity of the federal government by empowering it—as a part of the new authority to make demands directly on individual citizens—to act through local officials." And he found the same view was once shared by the states: "More specifically, during the debates concerning the ratification of the Constitution, it was assumed that state agents would act as tax collectors for the federal government." [33]

For Stevens, it was this vision of a cooperative partnership between the federal and state governments in the implementation of laws that would work to the benefit of the states. Thus, Stevens argued that limiting the possibility of a cooperative enterprise would work to the disadvantage of the states, because by keeping the federal government from "enlist[ing] state officials in the implementation of its programs, the Court creates incentives for the National Government to aggrandize itself. In the name of states' rights, the majority would have the Federal Government create vast national bureaucracies to implement its policies. This is exactly the sort of thing that the early Federalists promised would not occur, in part as a result of the National Government's ability to rely on the magistracy of the states." [34] Stevens concluded that it should be left to Congress to determine how best to press into service the proper mixture of federal, state, and local agents into an administrative bureaucracy for the law. "If Congress believes that such a statute will benefit the people of the Nation, and serve the interests of cooperative federalism better than an enlarged federal bureaucracy, we should respect both its policy judgment and its appraisal of its constitutional power." [35]

This growing Court debate over the use of historical sources in determining the meaning of the Constitution continued the following term in the case of *Clinton v. New York* as the Court ruled in 1998 on the constitutionality of the presidential line-item veto power. The issue was whether the law allowing the president to veto a portion of appropriation legislation concerning a budget, a tax benefit, or a "new direct spending" provision was constitutional. Opponents argued that this process would violate the Presentment

Clause in Article I, Section 7, Clauses 2 and 3 of the Constitution, giving the president the power to receive from Congress, and either sign into law or veto an entire bill within ten days after its presentation from Congress. The Republican-controlled Congress, pursuing Speaker Newt Gingrich's "Contract with America," had passed the line-item veto in 1996, so that it would be available for use by the next president, who they hoped would be a Republican. To their dismay, Democrat Bill Clinton won reelection and exercised the first use of the power against two provisions of their legislation: a portion of the 1997 Balanced Budget Act requiring New York to repay Medicaid money to the federal government, and a part of the Taxpayer Relief Act of 1997 that provided a tax benefit to certain food processors.

Speaking for a six-justice majority, John Paul Stevens overturned the law, arguing that it was a violation of the Presentment Clause. Stevens wrote: "Although the Constitution expressly authorizes the President to play a role in the process of enacting statutes, it is silent on the subject of unilateral Presidential action that either repeals or amends parts of duly enacted statutes."[36] With the question becoming how one interpreted the silence of the Framers on this question of a line-item veto, Stevens adopted Scalia's originalism approach in examining how America's first president, George Washington, treated this question: "The procedures governing the enactment of statutes set forth in the text of Article I were the product of the great debates and compromises that produced the Constitution itself. Familiar historical materials provide abundant support for the conclusion that the power to enact statutes may only 'be exercised in accord with a single, finely wrought and exhaustively considered, procedure.' . . . Our first President understood the text of the Presentment Clause as requiring that he either 'approve all the parts of a Bill, or reject it in toto.'"[37] Since President Clinton had approved only parts of two congressional bills, Stevens ruled that it was not a constitutional exercise of his powers. Should a president be allowed to make such partial changes, Stevens explained, it would give him the "unilateral power to change the text of duly enacted statutes," thus making the executive branch effectively a legislative one as well.[38]

In dissent, Scalia, a longtime supporter of broad presidential power, approved of the line-item veto and saw the majority's decision as an unacceptable diminution of presidential powers. For him this partial veto power was no different from the inherent power of the president to "impound funds," that is, refuse to spend lawfully appropriated funds for reasons of economy: "Insofar as the degree of political, 'law-making' power conferred upon the Executive is concerned, there is not a dime's worth of difference between Congress's authorizing the President to *cancel* a spending item, and Congress's authorizing money to be spent on a particular item at the President's discretion. And the latter has been done since the Founding of the Nation."[39]

Scalia could not understand the Court's inability to see the semantical differences in legal language that made this "line item veto . . . no different from [the] impoundment power." As he saw it: "The short of the matter is this: Had the Line Item Veto Act authorized the President to 'decline to spend' any item of spending contained in the Balanced Budget Act of 1997, there is not the slightest doubt that authorization would have been constitutional. What the Line Item Veto Act does instead—authorizing the President to 'cancel' an item of spending—is technically different. But the technical difference does *not* relate to the technicalities of the Presentment Clause, which have been fully complied with; and the doctrine of unconstitutional delegation, which *is* at issue here, is preeminently *not* a doctrine of technicalities."[40] Though Scalia lost this battle, he had once again demonstrated the ease with which he could structure his originalism to reach the result he was certain was correct.

• • •

Scalia's dedicated efforts on behalf of his brand of originalism on the Court did not go unnoticed. In 1999, Texas governor and presidential candidate George W. Bush was being interviewed by NBC moderator Tim Russert for the Sunday interview show *Meet the Press*. After the two men discussed various political issues, the topic turned to the Supreme Court. "Would you want to know the views of a potential Supreme Court justice on abortion before they were appointed, not for a litmus test but just [to] know their views?" asked Russert. In response, Bush outlined the process that he would be using as president to choose members of the federal court, and specifically Supreme Court justices. "Well, let me tell you what I'd like to know. I'd like to know are we compatible from a philosophical perspective on a wide range of issues. But the most important view I want to know is are you a strict constructionist, Mr. Jurist? Will you strictly interpret the Constitution or will you use your bench as a way to legislate? That's the kind of judges I've named in the state of Texas. One of the—I've got a record on this. I've named four Supreme Court justices in our state. As you know, we elect judges in Texas. But when there's a vacancy, I name, and I do." Seeing an opening,

Russert tried to make some news by pressing Bush, asking, "Which Supreme Court justice do you really respect?"

"Well, that's—Anthony [*sic*] Scalia is one," responded Bush.

"He is someone who wants to overturn *Roe v. Wade*," offered Russert, hoping to reopen the earlier discussion of whether there would be a litmus test for Court appointments.

"Well, he's a—there's a lot of reasons why I like Judge Scalia. I tell you a guy who I—" Bush began before Russert interjected.

"So you'd want to know how a judge feels about abortion. You just wouldn't put him on the bench blindly."

"I want to know how a judge feels about a lot of issues. The most primary one is—"

"Including abortion?" asked Russert.

"The most primary issue—the most primary issue is will they strictly interpret the Constitution of the United States," Bush said.

Russert thought he had enough to press for a defining description of Bush's hoped-for Court appointments: "Will your judges and judge appointments to the Supreme Court be similar to Scalia in their temperament and judicial outlook?"

"Well, I don't think you're going to find many people to be actually similar to him. He's an unusual man. He's an intellect. The reason I like him so much is I got to know him here in Austin when he came down. He's witty, he's interesting, he's firm. There's a lot of reasons why I like Judge Scalia. And I like a lot of the other judges as well. I mean, it's kind of a harsh question to ask because it now pits me—some of whom are friends of mine. I mean, it's—and so, in all due respect, Judge Thomas."[41]

Reporter Warren Richey of *The Christian Science Monitor* picked up on Bush's statement to Russert. In an article titled "The Next Supreme Court Majority," he highlighted the importance of appointments to the Supreme Court in the 2000 election by pointing out "speculation among court watchers . . . that Chief Justice William Rehnquist may choose to step down should a Republican win the presidency in November."[42] He further noted that George W. Bush "has said he would seek out justices in the same mold as Antonin Scalia and Clarence Thomas, the two most conservative justices on the court." Richey's version of the story became the way the public perceived Bush's comments in the Russert interview. Later that same month, Richard Willing of *USA Today* cited the seventy-five-year-old Rehnquist as being among the "three justices [who] seem likely to retire soon."[43] This language continued throughout the campaign and could not have eluded either Scalia or Thomas.[44]

• • •

While the speculation and rumors kept circulating about the demise of *Roe v. Wade*, and the future of the chief justiceship, for the moment it did little to cheer Scalia. By March 2000, he entered another of his cyclical down periods in which he began to complain about his situation on the Court. Court reporter Kim Eisler wrote in *Washingtonian* magazine that the upcoming presidential election could shape Scalia's next career move:

> Scalia has been in a funk since failing to persuade his fellow justices to overturn *Roe v. Wade*—and thus allow states to set their own laws on abortion. . . . [He] has decided the November election is make-or-break time. If the Democrats win the White House, Scalia will resign. A Gore presidency would eliminate his chance of becoming Chief Justice and ensure that his jurisprudence will never be anything more than a footnote. If a Republican wins, Scalia would stay on. There's a good chance a new Republican president would name Scalia or Thomas as Chief Justice.[45]

Indeed, Democratic candidate Al Gore, clearly a living, evolving Constitution advocate like the liberal members on the Supreme Court, promised to "appoint justices to that court who understand, and reflect in their decisions, the philosophy that our Constitution is a living and breathing document . . . intended by our founders to be interpreted in the light of the constantly evolving experience of the American people."[46] True as the second part of this story might have been, it seemed hard to believe that if Gore won, Scalia would vacate his seat for the new Democratic president to fill with a liberal evolving Constitution judge. But, the report of Scalia's mere threat elevated the stakes of the election.

There was another matter said to be impelling Scalia to consider retirement. Eisler explained: "Also weighing on Scalia is money. . . . One year after they leave his chambers, Scalia's clerks will be earning far more than the father of nine—a disparity that is increasingly aggravating not only to Scalia but also to the other justices."[47] These rumors caught the attention of Washington columnist Robert Novak, who wrote his own version of the "Scalia-to-leave-the-Court" story in the *Chicago Sun-Times*:

Word has spread through the capital's legal circles that if Al Gore defeats George W. Bush for president, Supreme Court Justice Antonin Scalia may retire at age 64 after 14 years on the high court. Scalia, the Supreme Court's conservative anchor, was dissatisfied with his colleagues even before President Clinton named two liberals to the nine-judge court. He grumbled privately that only Justice Clarence Thomas joined him in interpreting the Constitution as it was written instead of as it is imagined. If Gore is elected with the prospect of naming still more liberals, Scalia's frustration could be too much, and he may call it a judicial career.[48]

The Court's decisions at the end of the 1999–2000 term gave Scalia no reason to want to stay. After three terms of unsuccessfully trying to win converts to his originalism theory, two of the end-of-term decisions announced in June eerily resembled the string of losses that Scalia suffered four years earlier at the end of the 1995–96 term.[49] Ironically, the first loss for Scalia came to a longtime conservative ally.

Dickerson v. United States involved the police's right to interrogate an accused armed bank robber named Charles Thomas Dickerson. The appellant was also charged with violating federal law by using a firearm in the commission of a bank robbery. The first time he was questioned by the FBI he was not given the warnings laid out in the 1966 *Miranda v. Arizona*, protecting a suspect's Fifth Amendment rights against compulsory self-incrimination. This case required that when a criminal suspect was taken into custody, before the police could interrogate him, they would have to recite a four-part warning explaining that the suspect "has the right to remain silent, and that anything he says will be used against him in court; he must be clearly informed that he has the right to consult with a lawyer and to have the lawyer with him during interrogation, and that, if he is indigent, a lawyer will be appointed to represent him."[50] The FBI relied instead on a law passed by Congress two years after the *Miranda* case, called the Omnibus Crime Control Act of 1968.[51] This law said that statements could be taken and used even without the *Miranda* warnings so long as the statement was offered by a suspect "voluntarily," based on a judge's interpretation of the "totality of circumstances" of the interrogation and taking of the statement.

Few expected Dickerson to win in a Supreme Court dominated by a conservative pro-police majority led by longtime *Miranda* critic Chief Justice Rehnquist. Twenty-six years earlier, then Associate Justice Rehnquist had written an anti-*Miranda* majority opinion in another case, *Michigan v. Tucker*,[52] holding that *Miranda* warnings were not based in the Fifth Amendment but were only "prophylactic rules" developed by the Court, and thus "not themselves rights protected by the [Fifth Amendment protection against self-incrimination in the] Constitution."[53] Now, over a quarter century later, everyone expected that the *Dickerson* case would provide the chief justice an opportunity to fulfill his goal by delivering the coup de grâce to the *Miranda* warnings, at least in federal cases. The *Dickerson* case showed, instead, that the 1970s Court's solo dissenting "Lone Ranger," as Rehnquist was then known, had turned into a pragmatic conservative chief justice who had been moderating his opinions in an unsuccessful effort to unite the conservative majority. By Court tradition, this positioning within the mainstream of the conservative wing allowed the chief justice to maintain his power to assign to writers the majority opinions in which he joined. In this Fifth Amendment case he tried to balance his views with those of his more independent-minded moderately conservative colleagues to achieve some measure of consensus and harmony on a Court that was largely directed by its swing justice, Sandra Day O'Connor.

Rather than importing his logic from the earlier *Tucker* case to overturn the *Miranda* opinion, Rehnquist unexpectedly wrote a majority opinion in which he upheld the precedent. A large part of the reason for his vote was his abhorrence of the idea of Congress passing a law using a simple majority vote to override a Court decision interpreting the Fifth Amendment, normally reversible only by a constitutional amendment or changed majority vote by the Court. As he argued, "Congress may not legislatively supersede our decisions interpreting and applying the Constitution."[54]

But Rehnquist went beyond the basic separation of powers issue, and in doing so also displayed how his thinking had evolved since his 1974 opinion. He now argued "that *Miranda* is constitutionally based," and added later that "*Miranda* has become embedded in routine police practice to the point where the warnings have become part of our national culture." Interestingly, here, Rehnquist bolstered his support for upholding the *Miranda* precedent by citing a Fifth Amendment dissent the year before by Scalia in which even the faint-hearted originalist had argued that when a judicial decision enjoys "wide acceptance in the legal culture," that is an "adequate reason not to overrule" it.[55]

In return, Scalia filled his dissent with references to Rehnquist's earlier anti-*Miranda* rule in *Michigan v. Tucker*, arguing, "Those to whom judicial decisions are an unconnected series of judgments that produce either favored or disfavored results will doubtless greet today's decision as a paragon of moderation, since it declines to overrule *Miranda v. Arizona*. Those who understand the judicial process will appreciate that today's decision is not a reaffirmation of *Miranda*, but a radical revision of the most significant element of *Miranda* (as of all cases): the rationale that gives it a permanent place in our jurisprudence." Picking up on Rehnquist's earlier argument in 1974, Scalia argued that the judicial imposition of these "prophylactic rules" on the police "is an immense and frightening antidemocratic power, and it does not exist," which to him places it in "the realm of power-judging." Scalia's reading of case law indicated that he saw no constitutional basis for the *Miranda* holding: "Any conclusion that a violation of the Miranda rules necessarily amounts to a violation of the privilege against compelled self-incrimination can claim no support in history, precedent, or common sense, and as a result would at least presumptively be worth reconsidering even at this late date." Indeed, over the years a series of Court decisions had cut back the *Miranda* protections to a mere shell of its early reach.[56]

As he did so often with his other colleagues, Scalia then chided the chief justice for his evolving opinion on this issue, pointing out that in *Tucker* he "rejected the true-to-*Marbury*, failure-to-warn-as-constitutional-violation interpretation of *Miranda*." Scalia wrote that he would rather not have the Court create such interrogation protections but instead reserve to the people, speaking through their legislature, "the ability to decide for themselves what protections (beyond those required by the Constitution) are reasonably affordable in the criminal investigatory process." In his mind, as a result of Rehnquist both ignoring the congressional act and seemingly conferring on *Miranda* a greater constitutional foundation, Scalia wrote:

> Today's judgment converts Miranda from a milestone of judicial overreaching into the very Cheops' Pyramid (or perhaps the Sphinx would be a better analogue) of judicial arrogance. In imposing its Court-made code upon the States, the original opinion at least asserted that it was demanded by the Constitution. . . . I believe we cannot allow to remain on the books even a celebrated decision—especially a celebrated decision—that has come to stand for the proposition that the Supreme Court has power to impose extraconstitutional constraints upon Congress and the States. This is not the system that was established by the Framers, or that would be established by any sane supporter of government by the people.[57]

When the Court returned to the equally controversial issue of abortion in the case of *Stenberg v. Carhart*, Scalia could see how far removed he still was from the majority. In 1999 the state of Nebraska passed a law banning a late term abortion procedure called "partial birth abortion," by which a fetus is partially delivered, then killed and removed from the woman's womb, even after the fetus would be considered viable. Nebraska's law allowed an exception only if such an abortion was "necessary to save the life of the mother whose life is endangered by a physical disorder, physical illness, or physical injury, including a life-endangering physical condition caused by or arising from the pregnancy itself." Speaking for a five-justice majority that included Sandra Day O'Connor, Justice Stephen Breyer relied on the 1992 *Planned Parenthood v. Casey* decision to argue that this state regulation placed an unconstitutional "undue burden" on the choice of women to secure an abortion, meaning that it had "the purpose or effect of placing a substantial obstacle in the path of a woman seeking an abortion of a nonviable fetus." The problem here was that this late term fetus was viable. However, the language of the law was sufficiently vague that it could be used to ban other types of abortions performed earlier in the gestation process when the fetus would be unlikely to be viable. Breyer concluded that this act must be held unconstitutional because: "Using this law some present prosecutors and future Attorneys General may choose to pursue physicians who use D&E [dilation and evacuation] procedures, the most commonly used method for performing pre-viability second trimester abortions. All those who perform abortion procedures using that method must fear prosecution, conviction, and imprisonment. The result is an undue burden upon a woman's right to make an abortion decision."[58]

Scalia argued forcefully in dissent that the right to choose a partial birth abortion was not one protected in the Constitution:

> I am optimistic enough to believe that, one day, *Stenberg v. Carhart* will be assigned its rightful place in the history of this Court's jurisprudence beside *Korematsu* and *Dred Scott*. The method of killing a human child—one cannot even accurately say an entirely unborn human child—proscribed by this statute is so horrible that the most clinical description of it evokes a shudder of revulsion. . . . The notion that the Constitution of the United States, designed, among other things, "to establish Justice, insure domestic Tranquility . . . and secure the Blessings of Liberty to ourselves and our Posterity," prohibits

the States from simply banning this visibly brutal means of eliminating our half-born posterity is quite simply absurd.[59]

For Scalia, this decision by the Court was an unacceptable extension of the 1992 *Planned Parenthood of Southeastern Pennsylvania v. Casey* abortion decision: "There is no cause for anyone who believes in *Casey* to feel betrayed by this outcome. It has been arrived at by precisely the process *Casey* promised—a democratic vote by nine lawyers, not on the question whether the text of the Constitution has anything to say about this subject (it obviously does not); nor even on the question (also appropriate for lawyers) whether the legal traditions of the American people would have sustained such a limitation upon abortion (they obviously would); but upon the pure policy question whether this limitation upon abortion is 'undue'—i.e., goes too far."[60] For Scalia, his colleagues in the majority were offering "their policy-judgment-couched-as-law," meaning that "those who believe that a 5-to-4 vote on a policy matter by unelected lawyers should not overcome the judgment of 30 state legislatures have a problem, not with the application of *Casey*, but with its existence. *Casey* must be overruled."[61]

Once more, Scalia pleaded fruitlessly with his colleagues to adopt instead his text and tradition originalist views to limit the imposition of what he saw as an undemocratic use of judicial power in the abortion area:

> Today's decision, that the Constitution of the United States prevents the prohibition of a horrible mode of abortion, will be greeted by a firestorm of criticism—as well it should. I cannot understand why those who acknowledge that, in the opening words of JUSTICE O'CONNOR's concurrence, "the issue of abortion is one of the most contentious and controversial in contemporary American society" . . . persist in the belief that this Court, armed with neither constitutional text nor accepted tradition, can resolve that contention and controversy rather than be consumed by it. If only for the sake of its own preservation, the Court should return this matter to the people— where the Constitution, by its silence on the subject, left it—and let them decide, State by State, whether this practice should be allowed. Casey must be overruled.[62]

Try as he might, despite his repeated mantra that in his opinion "Casey must be overruled," the votes on the Court for his side still were not there.

• • •

Each of Scalia's earlier dark periods, in 1989, 1992, and 1996, in which he found himself so at odds with the Court majority, had been followed by his either changing the explanation of his theoretical approach to deciding cases or threatening to leave the Court, or both. This new dark period was different, though, as the end of the year would bring with it additional evidence that he was no longer able to control his frustrations. Soon he became engaged in a controversial battle with a reporter, this time *Legal Times*'s Court reporter Tony Mauro. Following up on the *Washingtonian*'s report of Scalia's "frustration" over the justices' low salary compared to the multimillion-dollar advocates appearing before him and the high starting pay of his law clerks after their year of service, Mauro and reporter Sam Loewenberg reported on the front page of the *Legal Times* on September 18, 2000, on Congress's consideration of what was being called the "Keep Scalia on the Court" bill. According to the two reporters, "At chance meetings and cocktail parties with lawmakers, their staff, and federal judges, Supreme Court justices would complain early and often about the 1989 [Ethics Reform] law that barred federal judges from accepting honoraria for their public appearances [while being promised regular annual cost-of-living increases that often were not forthcoming]. Congressional staffers learned that Antonin Scalia, in particular, was angry about the loss of what he saw as legitimate extra income for underpaid judges."[63]

For someone like Scalia, who according to *The Washington Post* had earned an extra $37,000 on top of his salary of $110,000 for fourteen speeches and appearances in the year before this new regulation was passed, much more than anyone else on the Court that year, this was a significant loss of potential income.[64] Fortunately for him, Scalia still augmented his income through law seminar "teaching fees" of over $20,000 according to the *Star Tribune* of Minneapolis.[65] Still, according to Mauro and Loewenberg, the "honoraria ban was one of the several factors that caused him to muse aloud from time to time about leaving the Court."[66]

According to the story, the result was almost immediate: "To hear knowledgeable sources tell it, Scalia's frustration, as much as anything else, was the trigger for inclusion, deep in a Senate appropriations bill, of a now-public provision lifting the ban on honoraria for the judiciary." Accompanying the article was a photo of Scalia containing the caption "Banking on the Hill."

Within the story, a Court of Appeals judge was quoted as saying about the provision, "Scalia's the only one who talks about it, and I've heard him talk about it quite a bit." At the request of Senator Mitch McConnell (R.-Ky.), Chief Justice Rehnquist sent a letter supporting the removal of the ban, but everyone understood that such a measure would be more beneficial to highly visible jurists such as Scalia than to the relatively anonymous lower federal court judges. In truth, it was not even clear that such a ban was constitutional under the First Amendment, having already been lifted for federal executive workers by a federal judicial decision in 1993.[67] And were it ever to be challenged in federal court, the very same justices who were harmed by it would be ruling on its fate.

Regardless of whether any of this report was true, or whether all of it was just part of the Washington rumor mill, with members of Congress or their staff believing that it was so, Scalia now took great offense at Mauro and Loewenberg's story. The thin-skinned justice, who loved to attack everyone on and off the Court, responded venomously when he was the one portrayed in a critical light. On the same day that the story was published by *Legal Times*, one of its news affiliates, *The Recorder*, ran a letter of protest by Scalia. "It is not my practice to respond to erroneous reports in the media," he began, but the Mauro and Loewenberg article "is such a mean-spirited attack upon my personal integrity that I make an exception."[68] The article, he protested, "makes gossipy, titillating (and thus characteristically Mauronic) copy, but in fact the honorarium ban makes no difference to me." Scalia explained that "all of my outside earned income has come from teaching," adding that it is "not covered by that ban." Scalia argued that "contrary to the unattributed statements in the article . . . [he had] never suggested to anyone that I would leave the bench because of that limitation." Rather, he had only discussed the ban "twice—not to urge it but to say, in response to inquiry, that I thought it was a good idea." For him, "the article's allegations of my preoccupation with money are not only false; they are not even plausible."

Scalia then pointed out that in 1982 he had left law school teaching, where he could double his income through consulting and his nine children's college tuition would be paid by the University of Chicago as one of his perquisites, to join the federal judiciary, which offered neither of these benefits. "The notion that one who was so indifferent to financial gain when he joined the Court of Appeals with nine children still to send through college," Scalia concluded, "should contemplate resigning from the Supreme

Court for financial reasons now that the last child is in her junior year is on its face absurd. No reasonable person would believe it; and only someone intent on writing a slanted story would assert it."

Uncowed by this response, Tony Mauro replied, "It's quintessential Scalia; he loves to play with words." To another reporter, Mauro explained, "[Scalia] misread the article or overread it. I wasn't accusing him of being obsessed with money."[69]

Beyond the verbal bluster, it was clear that the portion of the article that Scalia really objected to was the allegation that he was considering leaving the Court for financial reasons. With others reporting that Scalia was threatening to leave the Court that year, could it be that he did not want people to think that it was finances that might be impelling this consideration? Or was he using such a threat, and now seemingly withdrawing it, as a means of lobbying for the chief justiceship should William Rehnquist retire if George W. Bush won the 2000 presidential election? If so, his calculations could not have included the controversy he and his fellow justices were about to encounter.

CHAPTER 15

Bush v. Gore

The turning point in Antonin Scalia's life on the Supreme Court, and indeed a turning point for the entire nation, began on the evening of November 7, 2000, the day of the presidential election between Democrat Al Gore and Republican George W. Bush. But it was Justice Sandra Day O'Connor who first felt its effects. O'Connor, a seventy-year-old cancer survivor, and her husband, John, were attending an election night party at a friend's house. Huddled around a small television, they awaited the release of the early East Coast returns. Polls closed at 7:00 P.M. in most of Florida except for the portion of its northwest panhandle in the Central Time Zone. By 7:45, the Associated Press, CNN, and soon the major networks declared that Gore had won Florida.[1]

"This is terrible," Justice O'Connor said after hearing the report. Without Florida, she knew, Bush had little chance of winning the election.[2] "Moments later," Evan Thomas and Michael Isikoff of *Newsweek* reported, "with an air of obvious disgust, [O'Connor] rose to get a plate of food, leaving it to her husband to explain her somewhat uncharacteristic outburst."[3] John O'Connor told her friends, "She's very disappointed because she was hoping to retire." He added that she would not want to leave the choice of her replacement to a Democrat in the White House. He did not mention one reason for her desire to retire was to spend more time with him, because he was suffering from Alzheimer's disease.[4]

As the election played out, however, the outcome of the Florida vote was not so easy to determine. While Gore had a half-million-vote lead in the national popular vote, neither candidate had the required 270 electoral votes. Each needed Florida's votes to win, and the winner of that state's twenty-five electoral votes was still in doubt. By 10:00 P.M., newscasters were calling it "too close to call," giving the Republicans new hope. At 2:18 A.M., the networks declared Bush the winner in Florida, and thus winner of the election. But with the larger counties still counting votes, Bush led Gore by only 629 votes at 3:26 A.M., putting the state once again in the "too close to call" category. An hour later, it was apparent that the election was so close that some counties would have to recount their votes, and pundits predicted lawsuits over the Florida election.[5]

By dawn, Bush's margin of victory in Florida was 1,784 votes, triggering an automatic machine recount. While many newspapers reported a Bush victory, without Florida's twenty-five votes he could claim only 246 electoral votes to Gore's 267. Having lost the eleven votes of his home state of Tennessee, Gore was still three votes short of victory.[6] So the nation waited.

Justice O'Connor, like most of America, found her conversation dominated by the stalemated election. The justice's brother, Alan Day, argued that the Supreme Court would soon be facing this issue, but O'Connor vigorously disagreed. "Oh no," O'Connor was reported as saying, "it could never go to the Supreme Court. That's a state matter." Then a few days later, during a dinner that O'Connor gave for her brother and some friends, she explained the reason for her certainty that this issue would never be resolved in her Court: "It's a mess and they [the members of the Florida government] need to straighten it out." In explaining her views, Alan Day recalled his sister's "general annoyance" over the course of the difficulties Florida faced in determining a winner of their presidential vote.[7] But the battle over the election was just beginning, and Justice O'Connor could not have known that the matter would literally end up on her desk.

The Constitution clearly places the power over organizing elections and counting the votes in Article I, Section 4: "The Times, Places and Manner of holding Elections for Senators and Representatives, shall be prescribed in each State by the Legislature thereof; but the Congress may at any time by Law make or alter such Regulations, except as to the Place of Chusing Senators." When it comes to presidential elections, Article II places the power to choose the winner in the hands of an electoral college staffed by delegates sent by state legislatures. According to Article II, Section 1, the only federal power here was: "The Congress may determine the Time of Chusing the electors, and the day on which they shall give their Votes; which Day shall be the same throughout the United States." The Twelfth Amendment changed the determination of the winner of the states' electoral votes from the state legislatures to the voters. With the Constitution clearly intending for the states to regulate elections in most situations, it is hard to imagine that the

Framers would have wanted the Supreme Court determining the will of the voting public.

But it had happened before. The Supreme Court intruded in the disputed presidential election of 1876 between Democrat Samuel Tilden and Republican Rutherford B. Hayes. That year's election also involved twenty disputed votes in four states, one of which was Florida. To win, Hayes needed all twenty votes. Following some shady political dealings, an electoral commission awarded Hayes all twenty Electoral College votes, and the presidency. The political fallout was extensive. The prestige of the Supreme Court, which had participated in the Electoral Commission, was diminished due to the perception of a partisan grab of the presidency by one Republican Party–oriented member of the Court, Joseph Bradley. In response, Title III, Section 5 of the U.S. Code, the Electoral Count Act of 1887 was passed, requiring states to make a final determination of their presidential vote at least six days before the meeting of the presidential electors. Then the votes entered a "safe harbor," during which the electors' votes could not be challenged before being counted at the meeting of the Electoral College.[8]

Rather than requesting a statewide recount of the votes in Florida, Gore requested a recount in only four heavily Democratic counties where he believed the Democratic vote was underreported: Miami-Dade, Palm Beach, Volusia, and Broward. Two clocks began ticking. First, Florida law required that all counties certify their vote counts within a week of the election, leaving little time for the recount. The state's Republican secretary of state, Katherine Harris, gave no indication that she would allow any extension, seeming eager to certify the election for Bush (on whose campaign she had worked). More importantly, due to the provisions enacted after the Hayes-Tilden election, the state vote had to be certified by December 12, six days before the electors were to meet on December 18. That gave Florida only thirty-five days to determine its Electoral College vote. As the recount proceeded, Bush's lead began to evaporate until on November 9, two days after the election, his margin stood at only 537 votes.[9]

On Saturday, November 11, the Bush reelection team filed suit in federal district court to end the hand recounts of the ballots, but the request was rejected. Meanwhile, acting under state law that required certification of the vote within seven days of the election, Katherine Harris ruled that manual recounting should be stopped, spurring a court challenge by Gore's legal team in Florida's state courts. On Thursday, November 16, the Florida Supreme Court ruled that the manual recounting of votes in three disputed counties, Palm Beach, Miami-Dade, and Broward, should resume and enjoined the certification of the election. On Sunday, November 19, conservative *New York Times* columnist William Safire, evincing an unusual mixture of acerbic reading of history and constitutional hope, summed up the crisis by saying to host Tim Russert on *Meet the Press*, "in moments like these, some nations turn to their generals, and we turn to our lawyers."[10] The Palm Beach County Canvassing Board filed suit against Harris, and on November 21, the Florida Supreme Court ruled unanimously that to protect the "right of suffrage," which is "the pre-eminent right contained in the [Florida] Declaration of Rights," a full manual recount of the three counties had to be completed beyond the formal deadlines and included in the final state voting tally. This meant that the certification date for the election had to be pushed back to November 26.[11]

Three days later, on November 24, the United States Supreme Court agreed to hear an appeal from Bush to the Florida Supreme Court decision, and the legal battle of *Bush v. Gore* was joined. On November 26, Harris refused to grant Palm Beach County more time to recount the votes and certified the victory for Bush. Immediately thereafter, Governor Jeb Bush—the candidate's brother—certified the twenty-five Republican electors to Congress, and sent the required "certificate of attainment" to the National Archives the following day.[12]

Once the fight came to his Court, Scalia knew the stakes. After months of rumored threats that he would resign if Gore won the election, and seeing firsthand the deteriorating condition of seventy-six-year-old Chief Justice William Rehnquist at the head of the Court's conference table, Scalia could surely sense that an opportunity for advancement might fall into his lap. Bush had said that he admired him, and if he were elected he might elevate Scalia to the center seat. But how could Scalia make that happen? His originalism and textualism would be of no use now, because, as Justice O'Connor had said, the language of the Constitution made this election a state matter, and there was no obvious federal role here. Nevertheless, Scalia wanted George W. Bush in the White House, and he was prepared to use his judicial resources to help put him there.

As the Court was preparing to hear the appeal of the Florida Supreme Court's extension of the certification period, Scalia's task seemed clear. He needed to persuade both O'Connor and Anthony Kennedy to join his side. Many in the Supreme Court building had heard about O'Connor's election night outburst. And according to David Margolick in *Vanity Fair*, when law clerks from several chambers gathered for dinner on November 29, one of O'Connor's law clerks told the others that her boss "thought the Florida Court was trying to steal the election and that they had to stop it." [13] As a result, O'Connor was emphatically against Gore, and her clerk believed that, in Margolick's account, she "was determined to overturn the Florida decision and was merely looking for the grounds." [14]

The Court found sufficient grounds on December 4, remanding the case to the Florida Supreme Court for clarification of its initial decision. In an unsigned, *per curiam* decision, the Court ruled: "As a general rule, this Court defers to a state court's interpretation of a state statute. But in the case of a law enacted by a state legislature applicable not only to elections to state offices, but also to the election of Presidential electors, the legislature is not acting solely under the authority given it by the people of the State, but by virtue of a direct grant of authority made under Art. II, § 1, cl. 2, of the United States Constitution." The Court was not willing to allow the Florida Supreme Court to preempt what the U.S. Supreme Court saw as the exclusive power of the state legislature to organize the election or to change the "safe harbor" provision for the election of the president in the U.S. Code that had been passed in response to the Hayes-Tilden contest. By asking for more clarification, the conservatives on the Court seemed to be stalling for time to run out the electoral clock.

As the hours went by, O'Connor's position hardened. That evening, when the subject of the case was raised at a party being attended by the O'Connors, the justice became "livid" and said, "You just don't know what those Gore people have been doing. They went into a nursing home and registered people they shouldn't have. It was outrageous." [15] While this sort of thing was commonly done by both parties, not to mention that it had nothing to do with the constitutional issues in this case, two points were now clear. More seemed to be going into the decision of this case than the facts and issues in the legal briefs, and O'Connor was in Bush's corner. This made the deciding vote in the case that of Anthony Kennedy. Whichever side controlled his vote would win.

The Florida Supreme Court never responded to the Supreme Court's request for clarification. Instead, on December 8, just four days before the electoral vote was to enter its "safe harbor," it ruled by a 4–3 vote that the manual recount of the "undercount" ballots in Miami-Dade County, which had registered no clear vote for president, be resumed. As it argued: "Through no fault of appellants, a lawfully commenced manual recount in Dade County was never completed and recounts that were completed were not counted. . . . Only by examining the contested ballots, which are evidence in the election contest, can a meaningful and final determination in this election contest be made. . . . [We] remand this cause for the circuit court to immediately tabulate by hand the approximate 9,000 Miami-Dade ballots, which the counting machine registered as non-votes, but which have never been manually reviewed."[16] But there was a problem with this order, as the Court was vague as to its execution: "In tabulating the ballots and in making a determination of what is a 'legal' vote, the standard to be employed is that established by the Legislature in our Election Code which is that the vote shall be counted as a 'legal' vote if there is 'clear indication of the intent of the voter.'" In short, there would be no single, clear standard offered for each county as to how to evaluate whether the incomplete piercing of the punch-card ballots registered a vote.

The manual recount resumed throughout the state, and the Bush team, fearful that a sufficient number of ballots would be found to put Gore into the lead, immediately appealed through Justice Kennedy to the Supreme Court in seeking to stay the order to recount, arguing that it would cause "irreparable harm to the nation." Everyone knew that whichever candidate had the lead in the vote tallies when the counting stopped had the advantage in any electoral appeal. With the case once again back in his bailiwick, Scalia sprang into action. "In a highly unusual move," Margolick reported in *Vanity Fair*, "Scalia urged his colleagues to grant the stay immediately, even before receiving Gore's response."[17] The reason, he argued to the other justices, was that he "was convinced that all the manual recounts were illegitimate . . . [and they] would cast 'a needless and unjustified cloud' over Bush's legitimacy."[18] Scalia's argument here had nothing to do with originalism or any other reading of the Constitution, but rather it had everything to do with his evaluation of the raw politics of the situation. In taking the lead pro-Bush election position on the Court, *The Washington Post* reported, "Whatever happens, history will record that no member of the court played a more pivotal role than Scalia." He became, they argued, "a driving force in the court's approach to the election."[19] Scalia argued that this was a mission being forced on the Supreme Court, telling the *Post* reporters: "We should not be a prominent institution in a democracy. . . . We are called in to correct mistakes. When you have to call us in, someone has screwed up; something has gone terribly wrong."[20]

By chance, the night before the oral argument dealing with the request for the stay stopping the recount of the votes in the Supreme Court, Justice John Paul Stevens "bumped into" Stephen Breyer and quite naturally the two men discussed the case. Neither justice thought that the application for a stay had a chance. Years later, Stevens recalled for Scott Pelley of *60 Minutes*, "I remember both of us saying to one another, well, I guess we're going to have to meet tomorrow on this but that'll take us about ten minutes because it had . . . obviously, no merit to it. Because in order to get a stay of—in—in any situation, the applicant has to prove irreparable injury and there just, obviously, wasn't any irreparable injury to allowing a recount to go through because the worst that happens is you get a more accurate count of the votes."[21]

But, to Stevens's and Breyer's surprise, and to Scalia's delight, the Court did not see it that way. Five members, including O'Connor and Kennedy, issued a four-sentence order granting an immediate stay stopping the recount at 2:45 P.M. on Saturday, December 9. They also ordered an expedited schedule for argumentation before them, with legal briefs to be filed the next day and an unusually long 90-minute full oral argument scheduled for Monday, December 11. Eighty-year-old Justice Stevens anchored a foursome of Breyer, Ruth Bader Ginsburg, and David Souter in arguing in dissent that the Court's power did not even extend to this case:

> To stop the counting of legal votes, the majority today departs from three venerable rules of judicial restraint that have guided the Court throughout its history. On questions of state law, we have consistently respected the opinions of the highest courts of the States. On questions whose resolution is committed at least in large measure to another branch of the Federal Government, we have construed our own jurisdiction narrowly and exercised it cautiously. On federal constitutional questions that were not fairly presented to the court whose judgment is being reviewed, we have prudently declined to express an opinion. The majority has acted unwisely.[22]

Anticipating the arguments in this case, Stevens also wrote in defense of democracy, "Time does not permit a full discussion of the merits. It is clear, however, that a stay should not be granted unless an applicant makes a substantial showing of a likelihood of irreparable harm. In this case, applicants have failed to carry that heavy burden. Counting every legally cast vote cannot constitute irreparable harm." To the contrary, he argued, "there is a danger that a stay may *cause* irreparable harm to the respondents—and, more importantly, the public at large," by effecting a delay in the proceedings that "would be tantamount to a decision on the merits in favor of the applicants." Picking up on the political language being used privately by Scalia, Stevens added: "Preventing the recount from being completed will inevitably cast a cloud on the legitimacy of the election."[23]

As always, Scalia was unwilling to let Stevens have either the advantage or the last word. In a dispute in which every minute mattered, Scalia first prevented the Court from releasing its opinion for another hour while he drafted his response to Stevens's argument. Then, in issuing a concurring opinion for the stay, Scalia tipped off where he thought the Court was headed: "Though it is not customary for the Court to issue an opinion in connection with its grant of a stay, I believe a brief response is necessary to JUSTICE STEVENS's dissent. I will not address the merits of the case, since they will shortly be before us in the petition for certiorari that we have granted. It suffices to say that the issuance of the stay suggests that a majority of the Court, while not deciding the issues presented, believe that the petitioner has a substantial probability of success." Scalia suggested a Fourteenth Amendment equal protection violation here, arguing that the varying recount voting standards from district to district in Florida might raise constitutional issues as to whether some groups of voters were being treated differently from others in the state.

Then Scalia turned to politics in answering Stevens's opinion calling for speed in continuing the recount, adding: "The issue is not, as the dissent puts it, whether 'counting every legally cast vote can constitute irreparable harm.' . . . The counting of votes that are of questionable legality does in my view threaten irreparable harm to petitioner, and to the country, by casting a cloud upon what he claims to be the legitimacy of his election. Count first, and rule upon legality afterwards, is not a recipe for producing election results that have the public acceptance democratic stability requires."[24] The political nature of Scalia's argument delighted the liberal law clerks who opposed him, with David Margolick quoting one of them as saying: "The Court had worked hard to claim a moral high ground, but at that moment [Scalia] pissed it away. . . . And there was a certain amount of glee. He'd made our case for us to the public about how crassly partisan the whole thing was."[25] But with the nation in electoral crisis mode, few were parsing these opinions closely enough to receive this message.

By the time the Supreme Court met in its conference on December 11, it was clear that the discussion in the oral arguments earlier that day about the lack of equal protection issues raised by the varying county-by-county standards for recounting ballots had had an impact on Anthony Kennedy.[26] He initially voted with the four liberals to send the case back to the Florida Supreme Court for clarification of the vote-counting standards while the manual recount continued.[27] This might have been due to the lobbying efforts of Breyer, who had discussed the case with his colleague from his chambers next door.[28] Over the years, Kennedy had shown an inclination in deciding difficult cases toward changing his mind, often in the direction of the last justice or law clerk who talked to him. Knowing this, Scalia was determined to be that person. Margolick reveals that about a half-hour after the conference ended, having spoken to both Scalia and his own clerks, Kennedy switched and joined the conservatives in favor of Bush's arguments. Margolick quotes one liberal jurist's law clerk as saying: "We assumed that his clerks were coordinating with Scalia's clerks and trying to push him to stay with the [conservative] majority." Another added, in describing the urgency felt by the clerks in the Kennedy chambers: "They knew the presidency would be decided in their chambers. . . . They would have fought tooth and nail—they would have put chains across the door—to keep him from changing his vote."[29]

With Kennedy now securely on board, Chief Justice Rehnquist set about organizing what for the Court would be an expedited one-day process of writing a draft of the majority opinion for the case overruling the Florida Supreme Court and ruling for George W. Bush.[30] But it soon became clear that Kennedy's vote would come at a much higher price, with the lofty, high-flown language on the case's equal protection issues in the final *per curiam* opinion sounding more like it was drafted by him rather than the pedantic, pragmatic chief justice. Here the conservative majority of the Court argued: "When the state legislature vests the right to vote for President in its people, the right to vote as the legislature has prescribed is fundamental; and one source of its fundamental nature lies in the equal weight accorded to each vote and the equal dignity owed to each voter."[31]

In reversing the Florida Supreme Court's ruling and stopping the recount permanently, the final version of the *per curiam* opinion focused more on the equal protection concerns of Kennedy than the jurisdictional concerns of Rehnquist: "The votes certified by the court included a partial total from one county, Miami-Dade. The Florida Supreme Court's decision thus gives no assurance that the recounts included in a final certification must be complete. . . . The press of time does not diminish the constitutional concern. A desire for speed is not a general excuse for ignoring equal protection guarantees."[32]

Seeking to deflect the anticipated criticism of this opinion, the *per curiam* made it appear as though there was more agreement on the Court about the winner of this case than really existed: "Seven Justices of the Court agree that there are constitutional problems with the recount ordered by the Florida Supreme Court that demand a remedy. . . . The only disagreement is as to the remedy."[33] This language, dealing only with the varying county vote recounting standards, caused great unhappiness among the liberal justices' law clerks, who believed that their bosses' dissenting views were being misrepresented. Now the Court's liberals would be seen as agreeing with the Bush position in favor of abandoning the recount on equal protection grounds, when in fact they argued that these problems created by the varying standards for recounting votes were not insurmountable, still affording the prospect of a valid and accurate vote count by December 18.[34]

The majority seemed untroubled by the fact that it was ignoring its usual preference for protecting states' rights as well as its professed abhorrence of using the Equal Protection Clause for dealing with voting issues. But the justices tried to limit the damage to their earlier precedents by adding a limiting caveat: "The recount process, in its features here described, is inconsistent with the minimum procedures necessary to protect the fundamental right of each voter in the special instance of a statewide recount under the authority of a single state judicial officer. Our consideration is limited to the present circumstances, for the problem of equal protection in election processes generally presents many complexities."[35] In other words, this precedent would not be used to decide future cases.

The opinion closed with what sounded again like Justice Kennedy trying to make it appear that the Court had reluctantly and agonizingly been forced, against its will, to choose a new president: "None are more conscious of the vital limits on judicial authority than are the members of this Court, and none stand more in admiration of the Constitution's design to leave the selection of the President to the people, through their legislatures, and to the political sphere. When contending parties invoke the process of the courts, however, it becomes our unsought responsibility to resolve the federal and constitutional issues the judicial system has been forced to confront."[36] Forced or not, just as in the 1877 Hayes-Tilden electoral commission, this decision had the effect of terminating the election recount, freezing the narrow Republican state victory, and awarding all of that state's twenty-five electoral votes as well as the presidency to George W. Bush. In so doing, the Court substituted its own 5–4 vote for the as yet unclear voice of the voters.

In a concurring opinion, the most conservative members of the Court, Rehnquist, Scalia, and Thomas, argued that a decision to overturn the ruling of the Florida Supreme Court could also be supported by Article II, setting out the standards for electing a president, and the U.S. Code, effectively trumping Article I, Section 4. As Rehnquist explained:

> In most cases, comity and respect for federalism compel us to defer to the decisions of state courts on issues of state law. . . . But there are a few exceptional cases in which the Constitution imposes a duty or confers a power on a particular branch of a State's government. This is one of them. Article II, § 1, cl. 2, provides that "each State shall appoint, in such Manner as the Legislature thereof may direct," electors for President and Vice President. Thus, the text of the election law itself, and not just its interpretation by the courts of the States, takes on independent significance. . . . If we are to respect the legislature's Article II powers, therefore, we must ensure that postelection state-court actions do not frustrate the legislative desire to attain the "safe harbor."[37]

On this deeply divided Court, the four liberals—Stevens, Breyer, Souter, and Ginsberg—each issued impassioned dissents contesting different parts of the conservatives' arguments. Two of them, Stevens and Breyer, saw great harm. For John Paul Stevens, this case represented more than just a turning point in the selection of a president: "Although we may never know with complete certainty the identity of the winner of this year's Presidential election, the identity of the loser is perfectly clear. It is the Nation's confidence in the judge as an impartial guardian of the rule of law."[38] An equally upset Stephen Breyer stood arm-in-arm with Stevens as he issued a stirring dissent connecting the political nature of the dispute with the limited nature of the judicial power that he saw to resolve it:

> In this highly politicized matter, the appearance of a split decision runs the risk of undermining the public's confidence in the Court itself. That confidence is a public treasure. It has been built slowly over many years, some of which were marked by a Civil War and the tragedy of segregation. It is a vitally necessary ingredient of any

successful effort to protect basic liberty and, indeed, the rule of law itself. . . . But we do risk a self-inflicted wound—a wound that may harm not just the Court, but the Nation. . . . What it does today, the Court should have left undone. I would repair the damage done as best we now can, by permitting the Florida recount to continue under uniform standards.[39]

With his controlling five votes in hand, Scalia did not appreciate the vigorous dissents by his liberal colleagues. Disagreement by the members of the Court on such a seminal issue in American democracy, he warned, would in his opinion "threaten irreparable harm" and "cas[t] a cloud upon what [George W. Bush] claims to be the legitimacy of his election." In a remarkable case of the pot calling the kettle black, Scalia, in a memo of his own, "complained about the tone of some of the dissents."[40] The nature of the language of the dissents also bothered Kennedy greatly, leading him to complain in a memo that his objecting colleagues were "trashing the Court."[41]

With the decision made, and the opinions written, it was left until the next day, December 13, for the drama of the justices announcing the 5–4 decision by reading portions of their opinions from the bench. Would the dissenters make a show of their anger about the decision? Would there be outbursts from the audience? But the nation would never know because, rather than announcing the landmark decision from the bench, as is the usual practice, the justices made their announcement of this opinion only by releasing their final written decision to the Supreme Court press. As Linda Greenhouse of *The New York Times* described it: "Today, after darkness fell and their work was done, the justices left the Supreme Court building individually from the underground garage, with no word to dozens of journalists from around the world who were waiting in the crowded pressroom for word as to when, or whether, a decision might come. By the time the pressroom staff passed out copies of the decision, the justices were gone."[42] The journalists were left standing in the cold outside the ornate marble court building, on live television, frantically flipping through the opinion, trying to be the first to instantly analyze and report the decision. Thanks to the votes of the five conservatives on the Supreme Court, and Scalia's successful efforts to secure Anthony Kennedy's vote, George W. Bush would be inaugurated on January 20, 2001.[43]

Scalia had been on the winning side in the most important case in his judicial career, and he had every reason to believe that he was responsible for winning the greatest judicial battle of his career. There was no need now for him to leave the Court, as staying on it would keep him in line for the chief justiceship.

Year after year, members of the Court would be asked about the case, and the unhappiness of the dissenters and the passion of their disagreement with the final judgment never dissipated. Some members of the majority in that case were unpersuaded by the criticism of its results. When reporter Jan Crawford Greenburg asked Justice Kennedy about the case for her book *Supreme Conflict*, he said that it was "A no-brainer! A state court deciding a federal constitutional issue about the presidential election? . . . Of course you take the case."[44] But this explains why he voted to take the case, not why he decided as he did.

Another member of the majority, Sandra Day O'Connor, initially defended the decision, but later seemed to develop second thoughts. Nearly four years after she retired from the Court, in January 2010, O'Connor was asked by CNN reporter Wolf Blitzer whether *Bush v. Gore* was "the right decision." O'Connor responded, "I don't know. It was a hard decision to make. But I do know this. There were at least three separate recounts of the votes, the ballots, in the four counties where it was challenged. In not one of the recounts would the decision have changed. So I don't worry about it."[45] Three years later, though, during an interview with the editorial board of the *Chicago Tribune*, O'Connor was again asked about *Bush v. Gore*. This time, she said, "[The Supreme Court] took the case and decided it at a time when it was still a big election issue. Maybe the court should have said, 'We're not going to take it, goodbye.' . . . Probably the Supreme Court added to the problem at the end of the day."[46]

Of all the Court members who ruled in *Bush v. Gore*, only one justice, when asked about the case in public appearances, has remained consistently dismissive toward its critics—Antonin Scalia. When he was asked about the case six years later, following one of his public speeches, an exasperated Scalia responded: "Oh God, get over it. This is an election ago now. And the newspapers that did, newspapers, not Republicans, that did a survey, painstaking survey of how it would have come out if they had counted the dimpled chads and what are they, the dangling chads, that the Democrats wanted, [found that] they would have lost anyway." Scalia then turned to the legal issues as he saw them:

Why did we reverse the case? . . . It was the Democrats who wanted the Courts to decide the question. They brought it into Court, so the question was ultimately whether the election of the President of the United States was going to be decided by the Florida Supreme Court or by the Supreme Court of the United States. That seems to me not a very hard question. There was no way in which we could have turned that case down. Now the basis on which we decided the case was the equal protection clause. And on that issue, the case was not even close. Seven of the nine justices agreed that what was being done in Florida—some counties counting dimpled chads, some counties counting dangling chads, there's another category of chads what are they, dimpled, dangling and something else—they were all doing it differently. Seven of the nine agreed that that violated the equal protection clause. A person's vote ought to count the same way in Florida.[47]

Court scholars knew that the eventual vote had been 5–4, not 7–2, as Scalia was now claiming, by counting a skewed interpretation of Breyer's and Souter's votes. So, he turned back to democratic and judicial federalism politics in concluding:

The only point on which we were in disagreement, the only point on which we were five to four, was whether having waited something like three weeks and looking like idiots—the greatest democracy in the world can't run an election, you know? And we couldn't have a transition team in Washington to take over from—should we give the Florida Court another two weeks to straighten it all out. That was the only point on which we disagreed and five of them said no, enough is enough, let's put an end to it, uh it's improper and can't be counted. And that was the case, not a hard case and not all those who were in the four were Democrats. And to fully appreciate the case you have to read the opinion of the Florida Supreme Court. There was indeed a politically motivated Court involved in this, but it wasn't mine.

This "Get over it" answer, that the Court, and he, had been correct in 2000, became Scalia's short, stock response on his lecture circuit to any question dealing with *Bush v. Gore*. It was an interesting response, that the public should accept the decision because it was long ago and we had moved on, for the man who used the opposite argument in attempting to persuade the Court to rely on a reading of Founding Era American history to seek to overturn much older precedents. Year after year, Scalia repeated variations of this story for every journalist, legal academic, and audience who continued to ask about his version of history.[48]

Contrary to the expectations of Scalia and the Court's majority, the dispute over this case did not die down, and its real impact on the Court's prestige became clear on January 13, 2001. That day, a full-page display ad appeared in *The New York Times*, blaring the headline, "554 Law Professors Say," in bold white letters on a black banner background. Below was another enlarged, boldface headline reading, "By stopping the vote count in Florida, the U.S. Supreme Court used its power to act as political partisans, not judges of a Court of law." The protest ad continued, "We are Professors of Law at 120 American law schools, from every part of our country, of different political beliefs. But we all agree that when a bare majority of the U.S. Supreme Court halted the recount of ballots under Florida law, the five justices were acting as political proponents for candidate Bush, not as judges." In the background of the ad were the names and schools of hundreds of prominent law professors.

The ad continued, echoing the argument of Justice John Paul Stevens: "It is Not the Job of a Federal Court to Stop Votes from Being Counted." From there, the ad continued, "By stopping the recount in the middle, the five justices acted to suppress the facts. Justice Scalia argued that the justices had to interfere even before the Supreme Court heard the Bush team's arguments because the recount might 'cast a cloud upon what [Bush] claims to be the legitimacy of his election.'"[49] The protest revealed just how much the Court's decision had affected its prestige and its image of nonpartisanship.

Scalia could take pride that the protest ad against *Bush v. Gore* singled him out as the leader of the five-person conservative vote. After this decision he, too, would change his approach to working on the Court. No longer would he be trying to perfect his originalism theory in different cases, searching for converts to his cause. By abandoning originalism in *Bush v. Gore*, he had gotten exactly what he wanted.[50] The success of this change in practice was not lost on him.

For Scalia, winning the battle of *Bush v. Gore* meant everything. The man who had endorsed him and his brand of originalism would be sitting in the White House. For the next four and possibly eight years President Bush, aided by legions of former and present members of the same Federalist Society that Scalia had helped to create and support over the years, some of them sitting in the Justice Department, would be sending conservative, possibly originalist-oriented jurists to the federal judiciary. Any vacancies on the Supreme Court would be filled with those who would tip the voting direction in Scalia's favor, and who might also follow his brand of textualism and originalism.

With enough changes on the Court, Scalia might even have the chance to lead the group. Now Scalia could concentrate on his next objective: positioning himself for the inevitable vacancy in the chief justiceship. To support his candidacy, he decided to reinvent himself yet again.

CHAPTER 16

Scalia vs. the Pope

Once he had helped secure the White House for George W. Bush, Scalia had reason to believe that if the chief justice retired in the next year or two, he would surely be a top candidate.[1] But he soon learned otherwise.

The irony was that his success in *Bush v. Gore* soon became an obstacle in any quest for the center chair. With the public backlash about the case, both Chief Justice Rehnquist and Sandra Day O'Connor realized that they could not retire during Bush's first term as president. The appearance that they had chosen the president who would be filling their seat would have once again put the Court in the crossfire of public outrage. Scalia had to bide his time, wait for Bush's hoped-for second term, and expand on the conservative, originalism dogma that had made him so admired by the new president.

• • •

More and more religion began to take center stage in Scalia's professional life. By this time, he was a member of the St. Catherine of Siena Church, a traditionalist congregation named for the patron saint of unborn children and located in Great Falls, Virginia, a comfortable suburb of Washington. With about four thousand parishioners, this church, established in 1979, offered a Solemn High Latin Mass on Sundays.[2] Performing this Latin Mass, known as the Tridentine Mass, required that the parish receive special permission from its bishop, called an indult. For a time, the only indult churches in the Diocese of Arlington, Virginia, to be granted such a privilege were St. Catherine's and St. Andrew's, located in Clifton, where Justice Clarence Thomas was a parishioner.

The various religious activities and clubs organized by St. Catherine of Siena offer clear evidence of the conservatism of the parish. The church choir sings classical Masses, Gregorian chants, and ancient anthems and motets.[3]

The church also openly acknowledges supporting a conservative evangelical religious group called Opus Dei, a devout, secret Catholic religious organization founded in 1928 by Josemaria Escriva, and described by some as the "elite guard of God."[4]

Followers of Opus Dei describe its mission as "spread[ing] through every sector of society a deep awareness of the universal call to sanctity and apostolate, and more specifically of the sanctifying value of ordinary work."[5] One church scholar, John L. Allen, the Vatican correspondent for the *National Catholic*, who has written the definitive book on the organization, argues that "Opus Dei members do frequently seem 'traditional' by contemporary standards, if only in the sense that they have clung to older prayers, practices, and disciplines in a time when many of those traditions were being understood in new ways or abandoned."[6] According to one critic, the organization's "main tenets are that God is an authoritarian and, therefore, Opus Dei adherents support dictatorial societies; that women stand behind men in life; that mass should be in Latin; and that God created a natural order of life in which the rich are rich and the poor are poor—and the divine order of inequality shouldn't be disrupted."[7]

Some churches do not advertise the presence of Opus Dei in their midst, listing meetings simply as "evenings of recollection." St. Catherine's, however, clearly lists the different Opus Dei meeting times for men and women.[8]

More evidence of Scalia's preference for the traditional Tridentine Latin Mass was his occasional workday attendance at the conservative Saint Mary Mother of God, known as "Old St. Mary's." Located on Fifth Street in a poor Chinese and African American, Washington, D.C., community, this magnificent church offered a "standing room only" Latin Mass at which legal notables including Scalia and Justice Clarence Thomas were described as "regular attendees."[9] While one should avoid reading too much into the views of an individual simply because of his or her association with a particular church, Scalia's public statements on religion, and publicly expressed views on various social issues, together with his associations with the traditional St. Catherine's and St. Mary's churches, confirmed his conservative religious philosophy.

Over the years, Scalia's ultra-conservative religious beliefs led some of his detractors to accuse him of being a member of Opus Dei.[10] They argued that if that were true, it would impair his "impartiality and even-handedness" because he would be a "Radical on the High Court," using his official position to do what he perceived to be the "work of God."[11] None of these sources offered convincing proof of such membership. Rather, the best authority on this question, John L. Allen Jr., who relied on his extensive Vatican contacts to uncover the worldwide lists of Opus Dei members, was unable to link Scalia to the organization's membership.[12]

Whether Scalia was a member of Opus Dei or not is beside the question, for his conservative religious views, his textualism and originalism legal theories, together with his judicial decisions and his public speeches, were all perfectly in harmony with it.

• • •

By worshipping and acting on his own in such a traditional way, Scalia demonstrated repeatedly on many subjects just how different his traditional Catholic views were from post–Vatican II views. One area in which he diverged was on the issue of the death penalty. In March 1995, Pope John Paul II, after surveying several hundred Catholic bishops around the world on the morality of abortion, murder, the death penalty, and the "right to die," issued his *Evangelium Vitae*, or "Gospel of Life," encyclical. While the pre–Vatican II Church had supported capital punishment as a method for protecting society, the pope signaled that he would now be following a more liberal interpretation of the sanctity of life, including a change in the Church's stance on the death penalty.

Seeking to explain the Church's position on the sanctity of human life, the pope declared that "there is evidence of a growing public opposition to the death penalty, even when such a penalty is seen as a kind of 'legitimate defence' on the part of society. Modern society in fact has the means of effectively suppressing crime by rendering criminals harmless without definitively denying them the chance to reform." [13] For the pope, the chance of rehabilitating the defendant, even in the face of a judicial system's efforts to avenge even the most horrific crimes, took precedence: "The nature and extent of the punishment must be carefully evaluated and decided upon, and ought not go to the extreme of executing the offender except in cases of absolute necessity: in other words, when it would not be possible otherwise to defend society. Today however, as a result of steady improvements in the organization of the penal system, such cases are very rare, if not practically non-existent." [14] In September 1997 the Catechism of the Catholic Church was changed to read, "the cases in which the execution of the offender is an absolute necessity 'are very rare, if not practically non-existent.' " [15]

Scalia, however, did not agree. These pronouncements by Pope John

Paul II became the catalyst for him to begin moving beyond his originalism theory to layer on top of it a social conservatism based in pre–Vatican II theology. Never one to avoid controversy, and knowing that there was strong support for the death penalty among conservatives in the United States, Scalia chose to indicate his continued support for this form of punishment. On January 25, 2002, on a panel titled "Religion, Politics, and the Death Penalty," at the Pew Forum hosted by the University of Chicago Divinity School, Scalia sharply disagreed with the Supreme Court's growing pattern of restrictions on the use of the death penalty, relying on the "evolving standards of decency that mark the progress of a maturing society." Opposing that living, evolving Constitution philosophy, Scalia said that he relied on what he called his adherence to the "enduring," or what other people called "dead" Constitution, in the form of his version of originalism. Scalia's metaphorical description of the "Founders' intent" for the Eighth Amendment soon became a familiar refrain: "For me . . . the constitutionality of the death penalty is not a difficult, soul-wrenching question. It was clearly permitted when the Eighth Amendment was adopted—not merely for murder, by the way, but for all felonies, including, for example, horse thieving, as anyone can verify by watching a western movie. And so it is clearly permitted today as far as the Constitution is concerned." [16]

Explaining that he was following the "traditional system" of justice dating back to Chief Justice John Marshall's era, Scalia disagreed with his former colleague Justice Harry Blackmun's announcement near the end of his career that he would "no longer tinker with the machinery of death," meaning that he opposed the death penalty. For Scalia, "the choice for the judge who believes the death penalty to be immoral is resignation rather than simply ignoring duly enacted constitutional laws and sabotaging the death penalty. He has, after all, taken an oath to apply those laws, and has been given no power to supplant them with rules of his own."

With that, Scalia unapologetically addressed the challenge of dealing with the issue of the death penalty as a justice with particular religious views:

> Being a Roman Catholic and being unable to jump out of my skin, I cannot discuss that issue without reference to Christian tradition and the church's magisterium. . . . This is not the Old Testament, I emphasize, but St. Paul. . . . The core of his message is that government, however you want to limit that concept, derives its moral au-

thority from God. It is the minister of God with powers to revenge, to execute wrath, including even wrath by the sword, which is unmistakably a reference to the death penalty. Paul, of course, did not believe that the individual possessed any such powers. . . . He said, "Dearly beloved, avenge not yourselves, but rather give place unto wrath, for it is written vengeance is mine, said the Lord." And in this world, Paul's world, the Lord repaid, did justice through his minister, the state. These passages from Romans [favoring the death penalty] represent, I think, the consensus of Western thought until quite recent times—not just of Christian or religious thought, but of secular thought regarding the powers of the state. That consensus has been upset . . . by the emergence of democracy.[17]

Scalia then proceeded to deliver nothing short of a sermon on what he viewed as the mistaken international democratic view opposing the use of the death penalty:

It is easy to see the hand of almighty God behind rulers whose forebears, deep in the mists of history, were mythically anointed by God or who at least obtained their thrones in awful and unpredictable battle whose outcome was determined by the Lord of Hosts; that is, the Lord of Armies. It is much more difficult to see the hand of God or of any higher moral authority behind the fools and rogues—as the losers would have it—whom we ourselves elect to do our own will. How can their power to avenge, to vindicate the public order be any greater than our own? So it is no accident, I think, that the modern view that the death penalty is immoral has centered in the West.

Scalia then addressed the difference between his views and those of his Church:

You will gather from what I have said that I do not agree with *Evangelium Vitae* and the new Catholic catechism—or the very latest version of the new Catholic catechism—that the death penalty can only be imposed to protect rather than avenge, and that since it is, in most modern societies, not necessary for the former purpose, it is wrong. . . . It seems to me that the encyclical either ignores or rejects the longstanding church teaching that retribution is a valid purpose; indeed, the principal purpose of government punishment.

Had he agreed with the modern, reform Catholic Church on the death penalty, Scalia explained, it would have affected his job. As he explained, "I do not find the death penalty immoral."

Earlier popes, Scalia reasoned, had supported the death penalty, and he now chose to follow those religious leaders rather than the current pope. As he expounded:

> So I am happy to learn from . . . other canonical experts—that the statement contained in *Evangelium Vitae*—assuming it means the worst—does not represent *ex cathedra* [infallible] teaching; that is, it need not be accepted by practicing Catholics, although they must give it thoughtful and respectful consideration. Indeed, it would be remarkable to think that it was an *ex cathedra* pronouncement, that a couple of paragraphs contained in an encyclical principally devoted not to capital punishment, but to abortion and euthanasia, were intended authoritatively to sweep aside two millennia of Christian teaching. . . . In any case, I have given this new position—if it is indeed that—thoughtful and respectful consideration, and have rejected it.

However, Scalia added, "That is not to say that I favor the death penalty. I am judicially and judiciously neutral on that point. It is only to say that I do not find the death penalty immoral. I am happy to have reached that conclusion because I like my job and would rather not resign."

Years later, Sam Harris, an advocate for a scientifically based and secular society, in his book *The End of Faith*, would quote at length from Scalia's remarks to warn "just how close we are to living in a theocracy." [18] Harris explained, "Scalia has found *legal* reasons to insist that the Supreme Court not leaven the religious dogmatism of the states, but he leaves little doubt that he looks to Saint Paul, and perhaps to the barbarous author of Leviticus, for guidance on these matters." [19]

To give his Pew Forum comments a wider audience, Scalia published a revised version of his remarks in the Catholic magazine *First Things* under the title "God's Justice and Ours." [20] As he did in his speech, he began his piece by trying to construct a verbal firewall between his role as a Catholic, his Catholic beliefs, and his role as a justice on this issue:

> Before proceeding to discuss the morality of capital punishment, I want to make clear that my views on the subject have nothing to do with how I vote in capital cases that come before the Supreme Court. That statement would not be true if I subscribed to the conventional fallacy that the Constitution is a "living document"—that is, a text that means from age to age whatever the society (or perhaps the Court) thinks it ought to mean. . . . But while my views on the morality of the death penalty have nothing to do with how I vote as a judge, they have a lot to do with whether I can or should be a judge at all.[21]

The fact that as a textualist/originalist he had voted in a manner consistent with his traditionalist religious views might lead people to believe otherwise. Content to be part of the state's "machinery of death," Scalia argued that he was more true to the Constitution than his liberal colleagues:

> This dilemma, of course, need not be confronted by a proponent of the "living Constitution," who believes that it means what it ought to mean. If the death penalty is (in his view) immoral, then it is (hey, presto!) automatically unconstitutional, and he can continue to sit while nullifying a sanction that has been imposed, with no suggestion of its unconstitutionality, since the beginning of the Republic. (You can see why the "living Constitution" has such attraction for us judges.)[22]

But what would happen if one day, as a Catholic on the Court, he was instructed by the pope and his Church to observe the new teachings opposing the death penalty? Scalia was glad he did not face that quandary:

> And I am happy because I do not think it would be a good thing if American Catholics running for legislative office had to oppose the death penalty (most of them would not be elected); if American Catholics running for Governor had to promise commutation of all death sentences (most of them would never reach the Governor's mansion); if American Catholics were ineligible to go on the bench in all juris-

dictions imposing the death penalty; or if American Catholics were subject to recusal when called for jury duty in capital cases.[23]

Sister Helen Prejean, the Catholic nun who wrote *Dead Man Walking* about her advocacy against the death penalty, later argued in a follow-up book, *The Death of Innocents*, that Scalia's interpretation of Chapter 13 of the Epistle of St. Paul to the Romans, upon which he based part of his Chicago remarks, "is indistinguishable from that of fundamentalist preachers, who use this passage to argue that 'God's wrath on evildoers' not only justifies the death penalty, it demands it."[24] She was referring here to an addition that Scalia had made to his *First Things* article that was not in his Chicago remarks: "All this, as I say, is most un-European, and helps explain why our people are more inclined to understand, as St. Paul did, that government carries the sword as 'the minister of God,' to 'execute wrath' upon the evildoer."[25] Accusing Scalia of using a process called "proof-texting" to selectively choose Bible passages and interpret them to prove one's point, Sister Prejean pointed out that the biblical term "wrath of the sword," relied upon by Scalia, does not refer to the state power to execute for crimes, but more likely, after careful analysis of ancient history and linguistic interpretation, to the Roman policy of "keep[ing] the peace" in times of "rebellion" and "riots."[26] For her, Scalia's "interpretation of Romans 13, driven by his polemical bent, provides a hint of what we can expect when he interprets constitutional text."[27] Of this interpretation of the Bible, Sister Prejean concludes:

> Forgive me, but I'm flabbergasted at the arrogance of a man who says "death is no big deal" when it's not his child who's being put to death or his father, or his wife, or himself—personal catastrophes that he can't imagine. I cannot recognize Scalia's God, much less worship such a God. Who can kneel in awe before the "Lord of Armies," a military God whose divine authority is recognizable not in democratic leaders, but in kings, of all people, so many of whom were venal, arrogant men who sacrificed thousands of lives in their petty wars?[28]

•   •   •

A month after the publication of his *First Things* article favoring the death penalty, Scalia got a chance to show how "his God," as Sister Prejean put it, directed him to act as a government agent of "the machinery of death." By using his originalism and textualism, he found a way to craft a very restricted interpretation of the meaning of the Eighth Amendment's "cruel and unusual punishment" clause. The case, *Atkins v. Virginia*, involved Daryl Renard Atkins, who had been convicted of kidnapping, armed robbery, and murder, and sentenced to death despite the fact that he was mentally challenged with an estimated IQ of 59. Relying on the "evolving standards of decency that mark the progress of a maturing society," Justice John Paul Stevens wrote for a six-person majority that putting mentally challenged defendants, who might not understand either the nature of their crime, the nature of the judicial proceedings, or the nature of their punishment, to death, had come to be seen in the United States as "cruel and unusual punishment."[29] In making this ruling the Court was reversing its holding in the *Penry v. Lynaugh* case just thirteen years earlier.[30] Citing the increasing number of state laws banning the practice, as well as national and worldwide public opinion opposing it, Stevens now declared "the execution of mentally retarded criminal[s]" to be a violation of the Eighth Amendment because it did not "measurably advance the deterrent or the retributive purpose of the death penalty."[31] Based on these factors, argued Stevens, the death penalty for mentally challenged defendants was an "excessive" penalty.

Scalia, however, wrote that he was limited by his pro–death penalty reading of the Eighth Amendment to what the people in the United States understood it to mean, as it applied to various felonies at the time, when it was being ratified in the states. This was an interpretation that squared perfectly with his traditional Catholic values. Using that standard, he argued that putting mildly mentally challenged defendants to death had not been seen in the Founding Era as either "cruel" or "unusual." In Scalia's words, "Only the severely or profoundly mentally retarded, commonly known as 'idiots,' enjoyed any special status under the law at that time. They, like lunatics, suffered a 'deficiency in will' rendering them unable to tell right from wrong. . . . Instead, they were often committed to civil confinement or made wards of the State, thereby preventing them from 'going loose, to the terror of the king's subjects.' "[32]

While Stevens had argued that the *trend* in states was to abolish this form of punishment for this kind of offender, Scalia pointed out that only eighteen states, well below half of their number in the country, had actually done so. As for Stevens's reliance on "world opinion" and professional organizations to justify the Court's decision, Scalia, offering his form of American exceptionalism, had no patience for it:

> But the Prize for the Court's Most Feeble Effort to fabricate "national consensus" must go to its appeal (deservedly relegated to a footnote) to the views of assorted professional and religious organizations, members of the so-called "world community," and respondents to opinion polls. . . . The views of professional and religious organizations and the results of opinion polls are irrelevant. Equally irrelevant are the practices of the "world community," whose notions of justice are (thankfully) not always those of our people. Where there is not first a settled consensus among our own people, the views of other nations, however enlightened the Justices of this Court may think them to be, cannot be imposed upon Americans through the Constitution.[33]

Following his highly visible disagreement with the pope and debate with his Court colleagues, Scalia became a much more public Catholic in his appearances off the Court. He revised and expanded his originalism speech to delve into more religious topics. But the results of the increasingly religious nature of three of these speeches caused controversy.

On January 12, 2003, he spoke before about 250 people at the annual outdoor Religious Freedom Day held by the Knights of Columbus, a Roman Catholic service organization, in Fredericksburg, Virginia. Scalia placed a wreath at a statue honoring Virginia's Statute for Religious Freedom, a religion protection law written by Thomas Jefferson that was the forerunner of the First Amendment's religious protection clauses. He also participated in a group prayer and sang "God Bless America" with the rest of the attendees. The "cold as blazes" day, as Mayor Bill Beck described it, was then warmed considerably by the fiery comments of the justice in opposition to the Court's living, evolving Constitution theories of his liberal colleagues. Scalia charged, "It is a Constitution that morphs while you look at it, like Plasticman." Instead, he argued for more accommodation between church and state, saying, "The Establishment Clause was once well-understood not to exclude God from the public forum and from public life," drawing examples from the symbolic religious phrases "In God We Trust" on our coins and the phrase beginning every Supreme Court session, "God save the United States and this honorable court."[34] In contrast, Scalia argued: "The new constitutional philosophy says if those who decide the law think it would be a good idea to get religion out of the public forum, then it will be exterminated from the public forum through judicial fiat."[35]

While delivering these pro-religious accommodation remarks, Scalia noticed two protest signs in the back of the audience reading, "Get Religion out of government," and "Freedom is measured by the distance between government and religion." Referring to those signs, he said, "I have no problem with the philosophy being adopted democratically. If the gentleman holding the sign would persuade all of you of that, then we could eliminate 'under God' from the Pledge of Allegiance. That could be democratically done."[36] "From what he said," Mayor Beck recalled, "it was clear that he thought anyone who did not want school children to say the Pledge of Allegiance with the words 'under God' in it deserved a spanking."[37]

The problem here was that Scalia had seemed to foreshadow how he would vote in a case then being appealed from the Ninth Circuit Court of Appeals by atheist Michael Newdow challenging the requirement that his daughter and other public school students be forced to say the words "Under God" in the Pledge of Allegiance. The appeals court had ruled that the use of the phrase was an unconstitutional violation of the First Amendment's Establishment of Religion Clause. When the government appealed, Newdow argued his own case before the Court, and filed a petition the following September requesting that Scalia recuse himself, stepping aside from the case under 28 U.S.C., Section 455(a), arguing that because of his statement in Fredericksburg, Scalia's "impartiality might reasonably be questioned." Even Scalia, who is loath to step aside because of his extrajudicial comments, was forced to agree.

This was a pivotal action, removing a certain religiously accommodationist vote by Scalia in favor of the conservative wing's goal of restoring the "Under God" language. So, instead of finding against Newdow, the Court ruled by a tie 4–4 vote that he lacked standing to bring suit, because as a divorced father who did not have custody over his daughter, he had no right to sue on her behalf. The tie vote left standing the Ninth Circuit Court of Appeals holding that the phrase "under God" in the pledge was unconstitutional, meaning that Newdow's victory remained in force for that region. But in 2010 the Ninth Circuit Court of Appeals, in another lawsuit brought by Newdow, upheld the "Under God" provision.[38]

The controversy about Scalia's extrajudicial appearances continued two months later when he was invited to appear on March 18, 2003, at the City Club of Cleveland, a city where he had once practiced law, to receive its annual Citadel of Free Speech award. The award is presented to "a distinguished American" who has made a significant contribution to "the preservation of the First Amendment." It was being awarded at the behest of attorney Richard Pogue, one of the partners in Scalia's old Jones Day law firm, because of the justice's pro–free speech support of flag burning in the *Texas v. Johnson* case in 1989. Scalia celebrated the First Amendment freedom award by insisting that all television and radio reporters be evicted from the luncheon.[39] He was unapologetic, wanting his speech on originalism to remain "fresh for those who have not seen it on TV."[40]

Scalia's renewed penchant for extrajudicial controversy continued on May 20, when he spoke to the Philadelphia Urban Family Council, an anti–gay rights group that was then challenging a Philadelphia city ordinance providing legal rights for gay partners. Scalia had been asked to give the keynote address at a $150 per plate fundraising dinner honoring anti–gay rights Catholic bishop Anthony Bevilacqua.[41] However, the Court was then considering the case of John Geddes Lawrence, who had been arrested in Texas for engaging in intimate behavior with another man and was charged with violating that state's anti-sodomy law.[42] Once more, questions arose as to whether Scalia's public appearance compromised his neutrality in deciding that case.[43]

By this point Scalia's extrajudicial speeches and conduct had ventured far beyond those of any other justice, including Abe Fortas, who was forced to resign from the Court, and William O. Douglas, who was threatened with impeachment four times. Unlike Fortas and Douglas, whose ethical questions also involved allegations of financial improprieties, Scalia's inflammatory comments and speeches involved cases pending before the Court, issues yet to come before the Court, and direct personal attacks on his judicial colleagues. And, unlike Fortas and Douglas, Scalia's controversial comments were made in the age of 24/7 partisan news shows and internet blogs. By taking these actions Scalia was politicizing the Supreme Court, making it fodder for partisan attack, and inflaming as well as fueling the opponents of the institution and its conservative majority.

•   •   •

In a matter of weeks Scalia's opponents on the Court would succeed in reversing the 1987 case of *Bowers v. Hardwick*. Justice Kennedy, who led the movement in favor of gay rights on the Court in the 1996 *Romer v. Evans* case, now wrote for a six-justice majority in *Lawrence v. Texas*. He began with a broad reading of personal autonomy privacy rights:

Liberty protects the person from unwarranted government intrusions into a dwelling or other private places. In our tradition the State is not omnipresent in the home. And there are other spheres of our lives and existence, outside the home, where the State should not be a dominant presence. Freedom extends beyond spatial bounds. Liberty presumes an autonomy of self that includes freedom of thought, belief, expression, and certain intimate conduct. The instant case involves liberty of the person both in its spatial and more transcendent dimensions.[44]

Using an expanded version of the rational basis test, by which the state can justify a law if a rational person would agree with its purpose, Kennedy instead argued that the state had no right to justify its laws by enforcing its own view of morality, as against gays, through its laws: "For centuries there have been powerful voices to condemn homosexual conduct as immoral. The condemnation has been shaped by religious beliefs, conceptions of right and acceptable behavior, and respect for the traditional family. . . . These considerations do not answer the question before us, however. The issue is whether the majority may use the power of the State to enforce these views on the whole society through operation of the criminal law. 'Our obligation is to define the liberty of all, not to mandate our own moral code.'"[45] That being the case, Kennedy found that basing such a restrictive law in morality, as was done in *Bowers v. Hardwick*, is a violation of equal protection: "When homosexual conduct is made criminal by the law of the State, that declaration in and of itself is an invitation to subject homosexual persons to discrimination both in the public and in the private spheres. The central holding of *Bowers* has been brought in question by this case, and it should be addressed. Its continuance as precedent demeans the lives of homosexual persons."[46]

For Kennedy, the *Bowers* case, and thus this law, should be reversed because the state of Texas had no power to impose its view of morality in violation of the personal right to privacy: "The petitioners are entitled to respect for their private lives. The State cannot demean their existence or control their destiny by making their private sexual conduct a crime. Their right to liberty under the Due Process Clause gives them the full right to engage in their conduct without intervention of the government. . . . The Texas statute furthers no legitimate state interest which can justify its intrusion into the personal and private life of the individual."[47]

Scalia was so angry about the Court's decision that he took the unusual step of reading his dissent from the bench.[48] He first mocked the overturning of a seventeen-year-old precedent in light of the plurality's (of which Kennedy was one member) failure to overturn the nineteen-year-old *Roe* abortion ruling in the 1992 *Casey* case based on the concept of *stare decisis*: "'Liberty finds no refuge in a jurisprudence of doubt.' . . . That was the Court's sententious response, barely more than a decade ago, to those seeking to overrule *Roe v. Wade.* The Court's response today, to those who have engaged in a 17-year crusade to overrule *Bowers v. Hardwick*, is very different. The need for stability and certainty presents no barrier."[49] Scalia could not figure out Kennedy's apparent use of the higher level of judicial scrutiny in deciding to strike down the Texas statute even though he professed to be using only the lower-level rational basis standard:

> Though there is discussion of "fundamental propositions" . . . and "fundamental decisions" . . . nowhere does the Court's opinion declare that homosexual sodomy is a "fundamental right" under the Due Process Clause; nor does it subject the Texas law to the standard of review that would be appropriate (strict scrutiny) if homosexual sodomy were a "fundamental right." . . . Instead the Court simply describes petitioners' conduct as "an exercise of their liberty"—which it undoubtedly is—and proceeds to apply an unheard-of form of rational-basis review that will have far-reaching implications beyond this case.[50]

At this point, Scalia picked up on the immorality and criminality arguments that Byron White made against gay rights in his 1987 *Bowers v. Hardwick* plurality opinion in asking what had changed:

> The Texas statute undeniably seeks to further the belief of its citizens that certain forms of sexual behavior are "immoral and unacceptable" . . . the same interest furthered by criminal laws against fornication, bigamy, adultery, adult incest, bestiality, and obscenity. *Bowers* held that this was a legitimate state interest. The Court today reaches the opposite conclusion. . . . This effectively decrees the end of all morals legislation. If, as the Court asserts, the promotion of majoritarian sexual morality is not even a legitimate state interest, none of the above-mentioned laws can survive rational-basis review.[51]

For Scalia, as he had argued in the 1996 Colorado anti–gay rights constitutional amendment, *Romer v. Evans*, this new ruling once again represented nothing more than what he viewed as the current pro–gay rights culture of the legal community: "Today's opinion is the product of a Court, which is the product of a law-profession culture, that has largely signed on to the so-called homosexual agenda, by which I mean the agenda promoted by some homosexual activists directed at eliminating the moral opprobrium that has traditionally attached to homosexual conduct."[52]

In concluding, Scalia played judicial psychic by pointing out that if everything that Kennedy said about the states not being able to regulate gay rights based on morality was true, then his argument also supported gay marriage:

> At the end of its opinion—after having laid waste the foundations of our rational-basis jurisprudence—the Court says that the present case "does not involve whether the government must give formal recognition to any relationship that homosexual persons seek to enter." . . . Do not believe it. . . . Today's opinion dismantles the structure of constitutional law that has permitted a distinction to be made between heterosexual and homosexual unions, insofar as formal recognition in marriage is concerned. . . . What justification could there possibly be for denying the benefits of marriage to homosexual couples exercising "the liberty protected by the Constitution." . . . This case "does not involve" the issue of homosexual marriage only if one entertains the belief that principle and logic have nothing to do with the decisions of this Court. Many will hope that, as the Court comfortingly assures us, this is so.[53]

Later events would prove Scalia's prediction to be correct.

• • •

Kennedy's decision in the *Lawrence* case worked on Scalia all summer long. In late October, apparently concerned that his dissent had failed to have the desired effect, Scalia increased the distance between them by delivering a caustic speech undermining Justice Kennedy's opinion in the *Lawrence* case to the Intercollegiate Studies Institute, a conservative educational organization. After reading from Kennedy's decision using what was described by one journalist as "a mocking tone," Scalia argued that the case "held to be a constitutional right what had been a criminal offense at the time of the founding and for nearly 200 years thereafter." Scalia made clear that this notion of the living, evolving Constitution offered by Kennedy and others had no boundaries: "Most of today's experts on the Constitution think the document written in Philadelphia in 1787 was simply an early attempt at the construction of what is called a liberal political order. . . . All that the person interpreting or applying that document has to do is to read up on the latest academic understanding of liberal political theory and interpolate these constitutional understandings into the constitutional text." [54] But it was clear that Anthony Kennedy was not, and would never be, in agreement.

While Scalia believed he was consistent with his earlier views, many saw in his work an increasing conservatism that baffled even his earlier law clerks. "When I worked for him, he had a set of principles, and those principles led to principled results, which were sometimes conservative and sometimes liberal," explained Lawrence Lessig, a Scalia clerk from 1990 to 1991. "I don't understand anymore how his jurisprudence follows from his principles." [55]

Scalia's new attack on Justice Kennedy and the Court in the gay rights area drew the wrath of *Slate* reporter Dahlia Lithwick, in a widely noticed column titled "Scaliapalooza." [56] Referring to his Intercollegiate Studies Institute speech, Lithwick asked of Scalia:

> Is this brilliant jurist losing his mind? Is he so frustrated by 17 years of failure to sway an allegedly conservative court to his side on social issues that he no longer cares who he offends or how biased he may appear? Has he become so swept up by the Coulter/Limbaugh/O'Reilly game of court-bashing that he cannot see how damaging it is when played by a justice? Or is he running for elected office? What possesses Justice Scalia to eschew the reclusive public life of many justices, or at least the blandly apolitical public lives of most, to play the role of benighted public intellectual and knight gallant in the culture wars?

Placing this new public attack in the context of Scalia's earlier talks, Lithwick charged that "the body of his speeches and addresses makes it clear that he appears anything but 'impartial' as is seemingly required by the law. One can predict his vote on most cases with great confidence." In examining all of these statements, Lithwick argued that these pronouncements sprang from Scalia's "feeling besieged and marginalized by the constitutional wall that's been erected between church and state—a wall that keeps the devout from practicing and proselytizing in the public square." And so, for her, Scalia's latest public "speaking tour" had a very clear goal. "Merely by virtue of his public role he is actually tearing down the wall between church and state every time he opens his mouth. Which is precisely what he wants."

Echoing Lithwick's critique of Scalia's extrajudicial behavior, Stephen Gillers, a New York University law professor with an expertise in judicial ethics, who said, "Since World War II, I think it's fair to say, the extrajudicial conduct of only three justices have [sic] become newsworthy in a harmful way: Fortas, Douglas, Scalia. . . . Scalia is calling undue attention to himself, by mixing it up publicly in a way we associate with players, not referees, which is what a judge is supposed to be."[57]

Ironically, in seeking to shape public opinion in favor of his view of religion through his opposition to his own church on the death penalty, incorporating his religious beliefs into his extrajudicial pronouncements, and making clear in court in case after case his devotion to traditional Catholic principles, Scalia had aroused public opposition and criticism of his behavior. But with Chief Justice William Rehnquist suffering the effects of age and thyroid cancer, Scalia was surely most concerned about the opinion of the person who would appoint the chief's successor.

CHAPTER 17

Quack, Quack

In early January 2004, Scalia once again became embroiled in a controversy because of his behavior off the Court. This time the incident, stemming from both his love of hunting and possibly also some future career ambition, would cause even greater damage to his public image.

As he did around the beginning of every year, Scalia accepted an invitation from his old friend Wallace Carline, a Louisiana-based owner of an oil services company operating in the Gulf of Mexico, to hunt for ducks from a large barge in a backwoods marsh near tiny Patterson, Louisiana. This time he asked for an additional invitation for another old friend, Vice President Dick Cheney, to join them.[1] Scalia, along with two members of his family, traveled south with the vice president on Air Force Two.

For Scalia, this trip made all the sense in the world. First, he loved to hunt all types of fowl and game, and frequently paired his speaking engagements with hunting trips. Second, he had known Cheney for thirty years, dating back to their work together trying to shore up the presidency in the administration of President Gerald Ford. But there was one other possible benefit from this invitation. It could not have escaped Scalia's thinking that should the aging William Rehnquist decide to step down from the chief justiceship, the most powerful vice president in recent memory, if not in history, might put in a good word as to who should be his replacement.

The problem was that on December 15, 2003, three weeks before the trip, the Supreme Court had agreed to hear the case of *Cheney v. United States District Court for the District of Columbia*.[2] This case involved a lawsuit filed by a number of organizations, including Judicial Watch, a conservative legal watchdog organization, and the Sierra Club, against the vice president under the Federal Advisory Committee Act (FACA), which calls for the release of information about government committees to the public. Their interest centered on the membership list and records of the National Energy Policy Development Group, otherwise known as the National Energy Task Force. The stated purpose of the group, which was headed by Cheney, was to provide energy recommendations to the president, but many wondered if the membership and agenda of the task force was also designed to further the nation's oil companies' corporate interests. "Before I die, I want to read the notes from Vice President Cheney's energy task force," wrote the iconoclastic former Chrysler corporation president Lee Iacocca in his book *Where Have All the Leaders Gone?* "Remember that one? Cheney convened his secret task force within ten days of taking office back in 2001. Who participated? What was discussed? What evidence was outlined? What options were studied?"[3]

Cheney and the White House refused to release any information to Congress about either the task force or its meetings, citing the "executive privilege" power under the "inherent powers" of the presidency implied in Article II of the Constitution, to keep information about presidential advisers and advice secret. Just the mention of the "executive privilege" power raised the specter of President Nixon, who had tried to use this power to hide his Oval Office Watergate tapes from the Senate and a federal judge. Instead, he was told by a unanimous Supreme Court in *United States v. Nixon* in 1974 that while the power existed, it could be used only for national security, military secrets, and to safeguard diplomatic relations with other countries. It could not be used to protect the personal interests of the president.[4]

Questions arose about whether Scalia should be hunting with a named litigant in a case then on his Court's appellate docket. Three years before, Scalia had made clear that he saw no connection between these outside pleasure trips and his work as a judge, even when they connected him with litigants or their representatives. In 2001, while visiting the University of Kansas to give a speech, he had agreed to go on a pheasant hunting trip with Kansas attorney general Stephen McAllister, who was also the University of Kansas School of Law dean; Bill Graves, the governor of Kansas; and Dick Bond, the recently retired State Senate president. He did so despite the fact that the Supreme Court had on its docket two cases considering a Kansas law that kept sex offenders confined in jail even after their prison sentence had been served, for which McAllister would be arguing.[5] Even though McAllister later chose not to go on the trip, Scalia appeared oblivious to any ethical issues raised by his plans.

When he was questioned later about the Kansas trip by the *Los Angeles*

Times, Scalia offered a technical explanation as to why he believed there was no ethical problem. For him, the issue was not whom he *hunted with,* but who *had invited him* on the trip and *when* that invitation was made:

> I was not the guest of Stephen McAllister, but of the University of Kansas Law School. The invitation, in fact, had come not from Stephen McAllister but from his predecessor as dean of the law school, Michael Hoeflich. That invitation was issued in December of 1999 and accepted (by phone) some time before October of 2000—long before the October and November, 2001, cases you refer to were on our docket. My travel expenses to Lawrence were reimbursed by the University of Kansas, not by the state. I flew with the governor and others on the governor's plane from Lawrence to Beloit and back, and promptly reimbursed the state of Kansas for the cost.

Scalia concluded from this set of facts:

> I do not think that spending time at a law school in which the counsel in pending cases was the dean could reasonably cause my impartiality to be questioned. Nor could spending time with the governor of a state that had matters before the court. Indeed, if the latter were so, Supreme Court justices would be permanently barred from social contact with all governors, since at any given point in time virtually all states have matters pending before us, either in accepted cases or in petitions for certiorari [requests for the Court to hear a case].[6]

Why Scalia did not cancel his trip, as the Kansas attorney general had done, when he realized that a potential conflict had developed, was not addressed.[7]

But Scalia was answering the wrong question in the Kansas episode. The real issue was not the circumstances surrounding his acceptance of the invitation, but rather why he did not decline to sit in this case once it reached the Supreme Court because he had socialized with people who were connected to the case. The standard here was not whether the justice believed that his impartiality could be reasonably questioned, but whether *others* could reasonably believe this to be true.

The source for Scalia's rebuttal to the press criticism came from the federal law that sets forward the ethical standards required of federal judges for consideration of whether to recuse themselves, or step down from hearing a case. Title 28 of the United States Code, Part I, Chapter 21, Section 455(a) reads: "Any justice, judge, or magistrate judge of the United States shall disqualify himself in any proceeding in which his impartiality might reasonably be questioned."[8] For this reason, Scalia had been careful to reimburse his hosts for the plane fare, the cost of the commercial ranch where they hunted, and any other costs that were incurred. But the larger issue was whether the perception of Scalia's possible bias in favor of his hunting companions in the upcoming cases meant that "his impartiality might reasonably be questioned."

The problem with determining whether recusal is in order is that, by history and tradition, the justices decide for themselves whether to step down from a case, and, if so, whether they will offer an explanation as to why. Like other members of the Supreme Court, Scalia served as his own judge and jury on the question of recusal. And with each new controversy he pushed the line of acceptability for him a little further. Every time he survived a controversy, he seemed to interpret that event as granting him permission to do it again—eventually moving him far beyond the point where many thought he had crossed ethical lines.

Having survived the Kansas recusal incident three years earlier, during the duck hunting episode in 2004, Scalia initially tried to laugh off the queries by the *Los Angeles Times* about his involvement with Vice President Cheney. He began his explanatory letter to Supreme Court reporter David Savage with a joke: "Even though the duck hunting was lousy (our host said that in 35 years of hunting on this lease he had never seen so few ducks), I did come back with a few ducks, which tasted swell." After acknowledging that Vice President Cheney was one of those hunters, Scalia used an extension of the argument he had made in his earlier trip to Kansas: "I do not think my impartiality could reasonably be questioned. Social contacts with high-level executive officials (including cabinet officers) have never been thought improper for judges who may have before them cases in which those people are involved in their official capacity, as opposed to their personal capacity." For him this was no different than attendance at a White House dinner or the "Vice President's annual Christmas party."[9] Missing in this analysis, though, were examples of social contacts with political figures while cases involving them directly were then on the Court's docket.

Critics were not persuaded. On February 23, 2004, a number of organizations led by Alan Morrison of the Public Citizen Litigation Group and including the Sierra Club filed a massive brief calling for Scalia's recusal from the case. The argument was that Scalia's trip with Cheney "has led to reasonable questions about the Justice's impartiality" and the trip was "not a typical social contact" between a justice and a member of the executive branch. Their thesis, based on a close reading of the national press, was that "Justice Scalia's impartiality has been so questioned: there has been an outpouring of public concern over this matter, and dozens of editorials by the nation's newspapers, from all around the country, have called on Justice Scalia to step down. Indeed, to our knowledge, there has not been a single editorial arguing against recusal." [10]

The brief further posited that the interaction between Scalia and Cheney was "not the typical social contact between justices and Executive branch officials" because of the nature of their host's line of work and the issue facing the Supreme Court in this case. It argued: "The central question of this litigation is whether energy industry participation in the Task Force and its sub-groups made them subject to FACA [Federal Advisory Committee Act]. Therefore, the fact that Justice Scalia's vacation was hosted by the president and owner of an oil industry services firm has increased public discomfort about an appearance of impropriety." [11]

Through an extraordinary twenty-one-page judicial memorandum issued on March 18, "prior to the final case decision," Scalia denied the recusal motion and explained why he had decided to remain on the Court to hear this case. The memorandum was typical Scalia, indignant because he was being challenged, relying on a technical reading of the rules as he perceived them, and interpreting the historical evidence most favorable to his point of view, to reach the result that he was seeking. After going into great detail to correct the record by accusing the brief of containing fourteen factual errors, Scalia argued that this was "not an intimate setting" between him and the vice president. As he explained:

> The group hunted that afternoon and Tuesday and Wednesday mornings; it fished (in two boats) Tuesday afternoon. All meals were in common. Sleeping was in rooms of two or three, except for the Vice President, who had his own quarters. Hunting was in two- or three-man blinds. As it turned out, I never hunted in the same blind with the Vice President. Nor was I alone with him at any time during the trip, except, perhaps, for instances so brief and unintentional that I would not recall them—walking to or from a boat, perhaps,

or going to or from dinner. Of course we said not a word about the present case. The Vice President left the camp Wednesday afternoon, about two days after our arrival. I stayed on to hunt (with my son and son-in-law) until late Friday morning, when the three of us returned to Washington on a commercial flight from New Orleans.[12]

Left unspoken was any mention of the several-hour trip down to Louisiana on Air Force Two and the fact that all of this contact might cause *others* to "reasonably question" his impartiality, which was the legal standard that made it necessary for him to write this unprecedented memo.

While Scalia conceded that he might have thought about stepping down if he were still on the Court of Appeals, where he could be replaced by another member of the judges from that circuit, on the Supreme Court "The consequence is different: The Court proceeds with eight Justices, raising the possibility that, by reason of a tie vote, it will find itself unable to resolve the significant legal issue presented by the case."[13] Others might say here that Scalia decided not to recuse himself because he did not want to risk causing a tie vote, like the one in the *Newdow* "under God" pledge of allegiance case, which would have worked against the vice president.

For Scalia, the charge could be boiled down to whether he should step aside from the case involving the vice president because "it would suggest I am a friend of his." It is here that Scalia got to the heart of the charge against him. Did the hunting episode at this time, with a case involving the vice president as one of the named litigants in the case, cross the lines of propriety? He was absolutely certain that it did not: "A rule that required Members of this Court to remove themselves from cases in which the official actions of friends were at issue would be utterly disabling. Many Justices have reached this Court precisely because they were friends of the incumbent President or other senior officials—and from the earliest days down to modern times Justices have had close personal relationships with the President and other officers of the Executive." He drew from examples throughout American history of justices who were friends with presidents to argue against what he termed the "no friends rule." Scalia then noted that if such a rule was followed, it would be impossible for the Court to function with "no fewer than 83 cases in which high-level federal Executive officers were named in their official capacity—more than 1 in every 10 federal civil cases then pending." Even a casual reader could see here that Scalia was drawing a false comparison in that neither he nor his colleagues had gone hunting with those eighty-three executive officers while their appeals were being considered by the Supreme Court.

For Scalia, the Sierra Club had simply not proved its case:

> When I learned that Sierra Club had filed a recusal motion in this case, I assumed that the motion would be replete with citations of legal authority, and would provide some instances of cases in which, because of activity similar to what occurred here, Justices have recused themselves or at least have been asked to do so. In fact, however, the motion cites only two Supreme Court cases assertedly relevant to the issue here discussed, and nine Court of Appeals cases. Not a single one of these even involves an official-action suit. And the motion gives not a single instance in which, under even remotely similar circumstances, a Justice has recused or been asked to recuse. Instead, the Argument section of the motion consists almost entirely of references to, and quotations from, newspaper editorials.[14]

While the Sierra Club brief had failed to prove its legal point, it did prove that Scalia had once again brought controversy to the Court. But the ethical standard was not one of "embarrassment to the institution" but rather whether the matter would "reasonably cause [Scalia's] impartiality to be questioned," and *who* would define what is reasonable. Few who knew Scalia's views or opinions would have expected him to vote against Republican vice president Cheney on this issue, or likely any other, given his support for executive branch power and his conservative views. No one, given Scalia's self-evident honesty in other ethical matters, as displayed by his careful yearly financial reports on outside income and the nature of his personal financial behavior, would suggest that he could, as he suggests, have his vote be bought, let alone so cheaply. And it surprised no one when he joined Anthony Kennedy's seven-justice majority opinion vacating the discovery order against the vice president "to produce information about" the energy task force.[15]

But by law the real judge of the "reasonableness" of his participation in this case here was not Scalia himself but rather the general public. How would they see him as a justice in this and other cases, and how would they view the overall institution in sitting cases when he had been hunting with an individual connected with a case pending before his Court? And how would the other litigants who were not personal friends of a member of the Supreme Court view their chances in the case? Even more importantly, Scalia's behavior raised the question of what else might be happening on the Court with other justices that might affect that institution's impartiality.

Once this question became focused on the political effect of such a controversy on the Court, it was clearer that Scalia's actions were certainly "reasonably" open to scrutiny. While Scalia had cited the history of the justices' extrajudicial friendships, and it was true that Louis Brandeis, Felix Frankfurter, Abe Fortas, and William O. Douglas, among others, had shaped the informal standard governing such friendships, the ones who sat or risked sitting on cases with their friends as litigants got in trouble for doing so. Brandeis and Frankfurter had risked scandal for the Court by their continued private political advising of President Franklin Roosevelt and members of his administration.[16] Later, connections by justices to litigants in cases had brought more scrutiny and scandal to the Court than Scalia either knew or wanted to admit. Fortas's continued political connection to President Lyndon Johnson even after his appointment to the Court had led to his inability to be confirmed as chief justice in 1968. When it was discovered that Fortas had a financial connection to a foundation funded by a financier whose appeal of an SEC conviction for stock market irregularities, perjury, and obstruction of justice was headed for the Supreme Court, the public scandal forced Fortas to resign from the Court.[17] William O. Douglas nearly faced the same fate in 1970 when his financial connection to a Las Vegas casino financier led to impeachment charges against him that were bottled up by the Democratic-controlled House Judiciary Committee.[18] But in all of this history, *none* of these justices had arranged for the same degree of socializing with an executive branch official, or anything like this incident, and then failed to recuse themselves after that person became involved in an appeal before the Court.

The duck hunting episode with Vice President Cheney was the most serious controversy dealing with extrajudicial activities linked to cases then before the Court since the ethical scandals facing Fortas and Douglas in 1969 and 1970, respectively. Among the most extrajudicially active justices in American history, Scalia was the target of more outside calls for recusals from cases because of his extrajudicial activities than all four of the other justices (Brandeis, Frankfurter, Fortas, and Douglas) added together.[19] Based on this history of the extrajudicial activities of Supreme Court justices, and the informal ethical standard governing them, there was considerable evidence that Scalia had "reasonably cause[d] his impartiality to be questioned."

Scalia could not see the problems posed by the duck hunting episode because for him it was just part of his usual conduct off the Court. By now, single-handedly, through his own actions and speeches off the bench, he had changed the code of conduct for extrajudicial behavior by justices on the Supreme Court.[20] Because of his voluminous off-the-bench speeches and appearances, Scalia had opened the door for all manner of extrajudicial behavior. His widely reported and frequently controversial public remarks had changed the conventional perception of the justices from lofty judicial figures to partisan political actors.

Scalia's practice of speaking off the Court and traveling to Europe to teach classes encouraged others on the Court to do the same. By 2004, extrapolating from the financial disclosure reports filed by members of the Supreme Court, Scalia made more speaking appearances, fifteen, than four of his colleagues—Breyer (twelve), Ginsburg (fourteen), Kennedy (eleven), and Thomas (seven).[21] Four years later, in 2008, Scalia's annual number of speaking appearances had doubled to thirty, and while the number of speeches and teaching seminars for Clarence Thomas (nine) and Ruth Bader Ginsburg (eighteen) had increased a little, both Stephen Breyer (twenty-three) and Anthony Kennedy (twenty) had roughly doubled their number of appearances.[22] The rules for extrajudicial appearances by members of the Court continued to change, as did the politicization of the institution, impelling the press and Court critics to comment on, and criticize, the justices.

The controversy did not affect Scalia's behavior, or attitude about it, in the least. In mid-February 2004 he accepted an invitation from Amherst College to give his now-standard originalism speech. He arrived to find protesters outside the building, with one of the many issues they raised being the Cheney National Energy Task Force controversy. He was questioned from the audience by a student reporter from *The Amherst Student*, Brian Stout, about "the inconsistency between his belief in maintaining the Court's integrity and his questionable decision to vacation with Mr. Cheney." After initially declining to respond, Scalia thought better of it, and answered, "There is no law against socializing with members of the executive branch when there are no personal claims against them. That's all I'm going to say for now. Quack, quack."[23] By referencing the Cheney duck hunting controversy so casually, he indicated how dismissive he was of those critics of his behavior.

Two years later, in a speech at the University of Connecticut, Scalia would say that his decision "not to allow [himself] to be chased off that case" was "the proudest thing I have done on the bench." In telling students that he would have stepped down if the case involved Cheney personally, rather than acting as he was in his official capacity, Scalia added, "For Pete's sake, if you can't trust your Supreme Court justice more than that, get a life."[24]

From then on, the Cheney duck hunting controversy became the primary touchstone of anyone criticizing Scalia's failure to recuse himself in cases.[25] Four years later, he received a "lifetime achievement" award from Georgetown Law School in the form of a wooden duck decoy reminiscent of this controversy, which he would later display on a table in his Court office, causing him to joke to a reporter that "Nothing is as funny as a duck."[26] Comedian Jay Leno, though, thought otherwise in joking on *The Tonight Show* about the "embarrassing moment" for the vice president in visiting the White House when security officials "made him empty his pockets and out fell Justice Antonin Scalia!"[27]

• • •

Scalia's extrajudicial public appearances continued to cause difficulties for him with the press. In April 2004, he traveled to the William Carey College and then Presbyterian Christian High School in Hattiesburg, Mississippi, to speak about the Constitution. The speech at William Carey College went well, but the events afterward did not. While the no recording policy was made explicit before Scalia spoke, the press was led to believe that it would have access to the justice during the reception that followed. Upon seeing the assembled reporters at the gathering, Scalia told the college president, Larry Kennedy, "Your press is going to be disappointed because I don't do interviews. I don't talk to the press." According to the U.S. marshal then protecting the justice, after Scalia noticed that his post-speech appearance was being filmed, he "looked like he got angry. He walked over, kind of threw his notebook down, said something to the president of the college." The film crew got the message and promptly turned off their cameras and left.[28]

Scalia's appearance later that day at the Presbyterian Christian High School went even worse. As always gun-shy about the press in the audience, Scalia had requested of his hosts that the speech not be recorded, but there was no such announcement in the room before the speech was delivered. The packed audience of students, faculty, local political officials, and religious leaders also included two local reporters, Denise Grones of the Associated Press and Antoinette Konz of the local *Hattiesburg American*, who were covering the event. As the crowd was being treated to an entertaining version of Scalia's originalism speech, the U.S. marshal protecting him noticed that the two reporters sitting in the front row were recording it. "You may wonder what makes our Constitution so special," said Scalia. "I am here to persuade you that our Constitution is something extraordinary, something to revere. . . . Our Constitution is not only what started this great nation, but is what continues to make us one great nation. There is no other nation that can identify with those principles." But apparently, for the U.S. marshal, those principles did not include the First Amendment's right of freedom of the press.

What happened next created so much controversy that it resulted in a lawsuit against the Marshals Service by the two reporters, a three-year investigation by the Department of Justice, a stack of sworn depositions, and a several-hundred-page report. (This report on what became known as "the Hattiesburg Incident" was later made public by a government watchdog site called the Government Attic.) According to these documents, the U.S. marshal approached Grones, the AP reporter, and demanded that she erase the material on her digital recorder. Feeling, by her own description, "kind of dumfounded," the journalist initially resisted, saying, "Well, if I stop my machine, I can't do my job."[29] Nevertheless, she showed the marshal how to do so, and the recorder was then wiped clean. Then the marshal turned to Antoinette Konz, the other reporter for the local *Hattiesburg American* newspaper, making the same request, and she complied reluctantly.[30]

In one of the rare instances of publicly acknowledging error, Scalia later wrote both of the reporters letters of apology.[31] He wrote that "the marshals were doing what they believed to be their job, and the fault was mine in not assuring that the ground rules had been clarified."[32] To Konz, he added, "I abhor as much as any American the prospect of a law enforcement officer's seizing a reporter's notes or recording. It has been the tradition of the American judiciary not to thrust themselves into the public eye. It may be that my efforts to pursue it are doomed to failure."[33] As gracious as this letter was, it was hard to agree that by this time that Scalia had truly tried, or could even believe that he had tried, "not to thrust [himself] into the public eye."

• • •

While Scalia battled with the press, and others, the Supreme Court's work continued. He wrote what *New York Times* Supreme Court reporter Linda

Greenhouse would later call "the highest achievement of his originalist jurisprudence" by further extending the protections of the Sixth Amendment's Confrontation Clause in a case called *Crawford v. Washington*.[34] Sixteen years before, in the 1988 case of *Coy v. Iowa*, Scalia had used his text and tradition historical decision-making process to rule that the Sixth Amendment's right guaranteeing "In all criminal prosecutions, the accused shall enjoy the right . . . to be confronted with the witnesses against him" meant that only "direct line-of-sight" trial questioning of two young girls in a sexual assault case would safeguard the defendant's right of cross-examination.

In the case of *Crawford v. Washington*, Michael Crawford was charged with assault for stabbing a man. At trial, he claimed that the stabbing was in self-defense because the victim had grabbed a weapon. Crawford's wife could not be compelled to testify at trial due to spousal privilege, but had told the police in a previously recorded interrogation that the victim had no weapon. The prosecution used the wife's recording at trial against Crawford, and he was convicted. Crawford appealed, saying that unless he waived the spousal privilege, he could not cross-examine his wife concerning her recorded statement, and was thus denied his Sixth Amendment right of confrontation.[35]

In a majority opinion agreeing with Crawford, Scalia presented a tour de force of originalist and textualist analysis, outlining a sweeping history of the right to confront witnesses against oneself dating from the time of the Roman legal system to English common law, including the treason trial of Sir Walter Raleigh, as well as a number of later libel and bill of attainder trials. He concluded that by 1791, when the Sixth Amendment was ratified, people understood that the Confrontation Clause guarantee required line-of-sight cross-examination of witnesses because English "courts were applying the cross-examination rule even to examinations by justices of the peace in felony cases," and "[m]any [state] declarations of rights adopted around the time of the Revolution guaranteed a right of confrontation."

Citing his copy of Webster's *American Dictionary of the English Language*, Scalia argued that "'testimony' . . . was then understood to be '[a] solemn declaration or affirmation made for the purpose of establishing or proving some fact.'" For Scalia, this right "applies to 'witnesses' against the accused—in other words, those who 'bear testimony.'" For him, the wife's statements taken by the police were "testimonial" in nature, and thus were subject to cross-examination.[36]

While under earlier precedent, the Court tested such statements by an "indicia of reliability" test that made them acceptable for use in a trial directly, Scalia saw this as an impermissible extension of the "testimonial statement" despite the "unavailability" of the witness to be properly cross-examined. Mining the originalist history, Scalia argued that the Framers would not permit the use of such a statement alone, whose reliability was open to question, without face-to-face testimony to test it.[37] With a unanimous vote of the Court backing him, direct line-of-sight cross-examination of witnesses who had provided such statements would still be required in criminal trials.

Later that Court term, Scalia had another chance to express his unwavering support for a powerful American presidency when the Supreme Court heard two cases dealing with the limits of executive power in the "War on Terror" under the 2002 Authorization for Use of Military Force (AUMF) law. The AUMF had given the president the power to "use all necessary and appropriate force" against "nations, organizations, or persons" that he determines "planned, authorized, committed, or aided" in the terrorist attacks on the World Trade Center and the Pentagon on September 11, 2001. Under this law, suspected terrorists and enemies who were captured on the battlefields could be declared "enemy combatants," imprisoned indefinitely, and denied any legal rights. Yaser Esam Hamdi, an American citizen who was taken prisoner in Afghanistan in 2001 and accused of fighting with the Taliban, was imprisoned in Virginia. In the case of *Hamdi v. Rumsfeld*, he petitioned for his constitutional right of habeas corpus, seeking the opportunity to challenge in federal court his designation as an enemy combatant and his lack of due process during his nearly three-year incarceration.

Six justices voted in Hamdi's favor, but the reasoning behind their votes differed. Justice Sandra Day O'Connor, speaking for a four-person plurality, reasserted that even in times of undeclared war the federal judicial system must have the authority to hold the executive branch accountable to the law. As she put it, "the threats to military operations posed by a basic system of independent review are not so weighty as to trump a citizen's core rights to challenge meaningfully the Government's case and to be heard by an impartial adjudicator."[38] O'Connor then went further, challenging the Bush administration's theory of a "unitary presidency" during the "War on Terror," under which the unwritten inherent and exclusive constitutional powers of the president expressed and implied in Article II of the Constitution were combined to create the equivalent of a dictatorship during times of war. O'Connor stated, "We have long since made clear that a state of war is not a blank check for the President when it comes to the rights of the Nation's citizens."[39] For the Court, this meant that even the habeas corpus rights of alleged enemy combatants must be preserved unless that right was suspended by Congress, because "it would turn our system of checks and balances on its head to suggest that a citizen could not make his way to court with a challenge to the factual basis for his detention by his Government, simply because the Executive opposes making available such a challenge. Absent suspension of the writ by Congress, a citizen detained as an enemy combatant is entitled to this process."[40] Hamdi, and other detained citizens, she was promising, would receive their day in federal court.

Based on his originalist understanding of an all-powerful chief executive during times of crisis, and his unwillingness to have the federal courts second-guess the military during wartime, Scalia argued in dissent in favor of a "blank check" on behalf of total presidential power. He conceded, "The very core of liberty secured by our Anglo-Saxon system of separated powers has been freedom from indefinite imprisonment at the will of the Executive." However, for him, Hamdi was a traitor who was working with the enemy in times of war, and thus was not afforded the same protections.[41] His historical review told Scalia that during such times of crisis the constitutional rules were different for enemy combatants: "Even if suspension of the writ [of habeas corpus] on the one hand, and committal for criminal charges on the other hand, have been the only *traditional* means of dealing with citizens who levied war against their own country, it is theoretically possible that the Constitution does not *require* a choice between these alternatives." Scalia's objection here was that his judicial colleagues had assumed too much power: "That suspension power is left in the Constitution to Congress. . . . But there is a world of difference between the people's representatives determining the need for that suspension (and prescribing the conditions for it), and this Court's doing so."[42]

Scalia did not like the Court's use of what he called its "Mr. Fix-it Mentality" and "Make Everything Come Out Right" technique against the president's constitutional powers during times of war. For him, "The problem with this approach is not only that it steps out of the Court's modest and limited role in a democratic society; but that by repeatedly doing what it thinks the political branches ought to do it encourages their lassitude and saps the vitality of government by the people."[43] In Scalia's world, whatever George Bush wanted to do in the "War on Terror" should not be second-guessed by his judicial colleagues: "I frankly do not know whether these tools are sufficient to meet the Government's security needs, including the need to obtain intelligence through interrogation. It is far beyond my competence, or the Court's competence, to determine that. But it is not beyond Congress's. If the situation demands it, the Executive can ask Congress to authorize suspension of the writ—which can be made subject to whatever conditions Congress deems appropriate, including even the procedural novelties invented by the plurality today."[44] All in all, Scalia drew a very different balance between liberty and security from his colleagues:

> Many think it not only inevitable but entirely proper that liberty give way to security in times of national crisis—that, at the extremes of military exigency, *inter arma silent leges* [in time of war, all the laws fall silent]. Whatever the general merits of the view that war silences law or modulates its voice, that view has no place in the interpretation and application of a Constitution designed precisely to confront war and, in a manner that accords with democratic principles, to accommodate it. Because the Court has proceeded to meet the current emergency in a manner the Constitution does not envision, I respectfully dissent.[45]

• • •

After battling against the journalistic attacks on his character, his extrajudicial comments, and his pointed judicial decisions in defense of the Confrontation Clause and the presidential wartime powers, Scalia was ready to return to the religious mission on the Court that he had launched three years earlier. He chose to do so at a meeting of several hundred at a Knights of Columbus centennial celebration in Baton Rouge, Lousiana, in January 2005.

Scalia's message began with the same one he had offered in the Catholic prayer breakfast in April 1996, when he gave his "We Are Fools for Christ's Sake" speech at the Mississippi College School of Law.[46] Nine years after that controversial speech, Scalia was so fully engaged in bringing his religious views into his speeches that he delivered a revised version of it in Baton Rouge. Arguing in the face of what he viewed as the lack of morality in the modern culture that there was nothing wrong with "traditional Christianity," Scalia told another group of devout Christians that they should not be afraid of being scorned by "educated circles" for behaving as "fools for Christ." Relying on his familiar sarcasm, Scalia mockingly explained: "To believe in traditional Christianity is something else. For the son of God to be born of a virgin? I mean, really. To believe that he rose from the dead and

bodily ascended into heaven? How utterly ridiculous. To believe in miracles? Or that those who obey God will rise from the dead and those who
do not will burn in hell? God assumed from the beginning that the wise
of the world would view Christians as fools . . . and he has not been disappointed."[47] These were pointed religious public remarks indeed for a sitting
Supreme Court justice.

Scalia told the Catholic service group that they had "no greater model"
for their traditional faith than the martyred St. Thomas More, lord chancellor of England, and the patron saint of lawyers. More defended his Roman
Catholic faith and the papacy against Henry VIII's claim to be head of the
Church in England—and paid for it with his life. Scalia referred to the conservative, traditional nature of his own Catholic faith, represented for him
by St. Thomas More, when he said, "I find it hard to understand people who
revere Thomas More but who themselves selectively oppose the teachings
of the pope." No one noticed, or said, that Scalia himself was doing exactly
that, with respect to the death penalty. Regardless, Scalia's traditional religious approach to life on the Court was made clear. "If I have brought any
message today, it is this: Have the courage to have your wisdom regarded as
stupidity. Be fools for Christ. And have the courage to suffer the contempt
of the sophisticated world."[48]

In preaching about the need for Christian religious observance from his
position on the nation's highest Court, Scalia was fulfilling the mission he
had set out for himself and his classmates at Georgetown in his valedictory
address fifty years earlier. He was also rejecting the view of presidential candidate John F. Kennedy, who, in 1960, called for a separation between church
and state. Scalia's answer was straightforward: his church and religion were
not to be set aside when he made decisions as a justice or spoke about issues
off the bench. It was becoming clear that he was ready to go further, perhaps voting for more state accommodation of religion from his seat on the
Supreme Court.

Later that 2004–5 term, Scalia took the opportunity to answer Sister
Prejean on the death penalty issue dealing with the constitutionality of
whether capital punishment is appropriate for juvenile offenders in the case
of *Roper v. Simmons*. In 1989, the same year that the Court had upheld the
death penalty for the mentally challenged, it had also upheld the constitutionality of the death penalty for juvenile offenders under the age of eighteen.[49] Now, just sixteen years later, thanks to a shift in the voting pattern
of swing justice Anthony Kennedy, the majority of the Court stood ready

to reexamine these decisions. In response to the publication of new social science data, the rejection of the death penalty in other countries, and the declining use of the death penalty for juveniles by the several states, those on the Court who believed in a living, evolving Constitution decided to rule in a different direction.

The case before them involved a seventeen-year-old murder defendant named Christopher Simmons, who, along with two other juveniles, had planned and carried out a burglary and brutal murder of a woman in the belief that they could "get away with it" because they were minors at the time. Instead, Simmons, who had since turned eighteen, was charged and convicted as an adult and sentenced to death. In his appeal, he claimed that the death penalty for minors was an unconstitutional "cruel and unusual punishment" under the Eighth Amendment.[50] In voting to save the juveniles from execution, Justice Kennedy wrote as though he was observing an expansive version of Scalia's text and tradition approach: "The prohibition against 'cruel and unusual punishments,' like other expansive language in the Constitution, must be interpreted according to its text, by considering history, tradition, and precedent, and with due regard for its purpose and function in the constitutional design." But then he hedged this originalism approach with his own "living constitution" theory: "To implement this framework we have established the propriety and affirmed the necessity of referring to 'the evolving standards of decency that mark the progress of a maturing society' to determine which punishments are so disproportionate as to be cruel and unusual."[51]

To find these "evolving standards of decency" in writing for a five-justice majority limiting the use of the death penalty, Kennedy examined the policies of states to divine the changing "national consensus," and of other countries, in order to determine the evolving view of the modern age of maturity to permit the imposition of the death penalty. In finding a national consensus against the death penalty for juveniles, he saw a parallel analysis to the *Atkins* case from three years before, overturning the death penalty for a mentally challenged defendant:

When *Atkins* was decided, 30 States prohibited the death penalty for the mentally retarded. This number comprised 12 that had abandoned the death penalty altogether, and 18 that maintained it but excluded the mentally retarded from its reach. By a similar calculation in this case, 30 States prohibit the juvenile death penalty, comprising 12 that have rejected the death penalty altogether and 18 that maintain it but, by express provision or judicial interpretation, exclude juveniles from its reach.[52]

In searching other legal systems, Kennedy found that countries that put minors to death were among the world's most repressive regimes: "Only seven countries other than the United States have executed juvenile offenders since 1990: Iran, Pakistan, Saudi Arabia, Yemen, Nigeria, the Democratic Republic of Congo, and China. Since then each of these countries has either abolished capital punishment for juveniles or made public disavowal of the practice. . . . In sum, it is fair to say that the United States now stands alone in a world that has turned its face against the juvenile death penalty."[53]

Writing in dissent, Scalia was so offended by Kennedy's philosophy, and what he viewed as its threat to originalism and rigid adherence to the text of the Constitution, that he dismantled the argument bit by bit, seeking not only to defeat but to belittle it. Scalia sneered at Kennedy's math in determining a "national consensus" against the juvenile death penalty. As he saw it, the twelve states that had no death penalty at all should not be counted. Only the thirty-eight states that still had a death penalty mattered in his calculations, and of them, twenty permitted the execution of juveniles. "Words have no meaning if the views of less than 50% of death penalty States can constitute a national consensus."[54] But even here, Kennedy's statistical process for determining the number of states barring the juvenile death penalty raised problems for Scalia.

Consulting States that bar the death penalty concerning the necessity of making an exception to the penalty for offenders under 18 is rather like including old-order Amishmen in a consumer-preference poll on the electric car. Of course they don't like it, but that sheds no light whatever on the point at issue. That 12 States favor no executions says something about consensus against the death penalty, but nothing—absolutely nothing—about consensus that offenders under 18 deserve special immunity from such a penalty. . . . The attempt by the Court to turn its remarkable minority consensus into a *faux* majority by counting Amishmen is an act of nomological desperation.[55]

In an argument that Scalia had made in speech after speech, he again criticized the notion of nine lawyers on the Court becoming the moral arbiters for society:

> The real force driving today's decision is . . . the Court's "own judgment" that murderers younger than 18 can never be as morally culpable as older counterparts. . . . But the Court having pronounced that the Eighth Amendment is an ever-changing reflection of "the evolving standards of decency" of our society, it makes no sense for the Justices then to prescribe those standards rather than discern them from the practices of our people. On the evolving-standards hypothesis, the only legitimate function of this Court is to identify a moral consensus of the American people. By what conceivable warrant can nine lawyers presume to be the authoritative conscience of the Nation?[56]

Arguing that judges lacked the capacity to make such decisions, Scalia attacked Kennedy's use of social science data on juvenile maturity:

> Today's opinion provides a perfect example of why judges are ill equipped to make the type of legislative judgments the Court insists on making here. To support its opinion that States should be prohibited from imposing the death penalty on anyone who committed murder before age 18, the Court looks to scientific and sociological studies, picking and choosing those that support its position. It never explains why those particular studies are methodologically sound; none was ever entered into evidence or tested in an adversarial proceeding.[57]

Returning to an all-purpose metaphor that he first introduced in his old anti-legislative history speech from 1985, Scalia concluded here: "In other words, all the Court has done today, to borrow from another context, is to look over the heads of the crowd and pick out its friends."[58]

Scalia closed by making clear that he and Kennedy, as well as the other living, evolving Constitution advocates on the Court, could not be further apart on this or other issues: "This is no way to run a legal system. . . . To allow lower courts to behave as we do, 'updating' the Eighth Amendment as needed, destroys stability and makes our case law an unreliable basis for the designing of laws by citizens and their representatives, and for action by public officials. The result will be to crown arbitrariness with chaos."[59]

Just as Thurgood Marshall had written in his valedictory opinion before he retired in 1991, Scalia made clear that what had changed in the sixteen years since the two contrary death penalty decisions was not the law, but the judicial politics in the form of a combination of the Court's shifting personnel and the changing view of one of the swing justices.

All of the controversies surrounding Scalia's behavior off the bench, and decisions on it, in this period had taken a toll on his public reputation. He liked to tell audiences how amusing it was that during the 2004 election season a fundraising letter for the Democratic Party accidentally came to his house in an envelope reading "Imagine Chief Justice Scalia."[60] Scalia's "Couldn't care less!" reaction, guaranteed to draw a laugh from any audience, came from the same part of his personality that led him to say "Quack, Quack" to the audience at Amherst College. But after George Bush's reelection, and observing the rapidly deteriorating health of eighty-year-old Chief Justice Rehnquist in early 2005, Scalia would find reason to be more attentive to his public image.

CHAPTER 18

The Charm Offensive

The Woodrow Wilson Center in Washington, D.C., was filled to capacity on March 14, 2005, with C-SPAN's cameras rolling, when Scalia addressed an audience of Library of Congress officials, members of the press, academics, and Washington insiders on the topic "Constitutional Interpretation." More interesting than his topic was the manner in which Scalia chose to deliver it. He had presented varying versions of this speech explaining his decision-making theories for nine years and never released a text. And until now he had allowed no cameras or recording equipment to capture his entire speech for public distribution. Thirteen months after the flak over this policy at the Citadel of Free Speech award dinner in Cleveland, it surprised many that he was now allowing his Smithsonian speech to be videotaped and streamed live around the world on C-SPAN's website. Within hours, a transcript of the address would be circulated on the internet, and days later copies of the video would be offered for sale by C-SPAN. One could only wonder why Scalia had so radically changed his relationship with the press. The answer to this question lay in its timing.

Justice Scalia's announced purpose for the address was to explain his jurisprudence to the American people. He began by admitting to the audience that he was out of step with many of his Supreme Court colleagues' vision of "the Living Constitution."[1] Relying on their interpretation of what they called the "evolving standards of decency," Scalia explained, liberals and even moderates on the current Court argued for expanding judicial power over legal rights, even to the point of creating them, saying they were already in the Constitution. Scalia offered his response to their vision in a matter of minutes.

His shortened version of the stock speech, containing all of his favorite arguments and turns of phrase, was Scalia, the public speaker, at his very best: eloquent, persuasive, and down-to-earth. He even simplified his description of himself. In 1989 he called himself a "textualist," basing his views on the dictionary definition of the words used by the Framers. By the 1996 version of the speech delivered at Catholic University and Valparaiso, he opened with the sentence, "I belong to a school, a small but hardy school, called 'textualists' or 'originalists,'" thus allowing himself to expand his interpretation beyond the strict dictionary definition to the historically based "public meaning" of the words. But in 2005 he said he was "one of a small number of judges, small number of anybody—judges, professors, lawyers—who are known as originalists. Our manner of interpreting the Constitution is to begin with the text and to give that text the meaning that it bore when it was adopted by the people."

Now totally an originalist, Scalia relied on his own understanding of history to discern what was in the minds of the Founding Era population in the states at the time of the ratification of the Constitution. Though Scalia would never admit it, this was a substantial shift in his interpretive technique. The difference for him between his early form of "textualism" and this new form of "originalism" came in the broader range of historical sources that he could consult to make his interpretations. As a "textualist," Scalia was limited in his interpretation of a constitutional phrase to the strict definition of his dictionary of choice. To interpret freedom of speech, equal protection of the laws, or cruel and unusual punishment, he was bound by the definitions of words such as speech, equal, protection, cruel, unusual, and/or punishment. But as an originalist, Scalia was free to search beyond the words, roaming in the histories of the culture and semantical understanding of the people from an earlier era. In so doing, he could anchor the country in the culture of the Founding Era, imposing late-eighteenth century ideas on early-twenty-first century culture, feeling free to ignore and dismiss the more than two centuries of cultural change that had occurred. By setting himself free to choose the sources, histories, and historians that he preferred, Scalia could shape the law according to his partisan ideological views, since *he* was the one reading the history.

It was no coincidence that this change came after his public transformation into a more Catholic justice just a few years before. The more free-floating originalism based in a reading of history, rather than pure semantics as required by textualism, squared much better with his reverence for early history and the tradition of his pre–Vatican II Catholic beliefs. This gave Scalia free rein to use his unique reading of history to implement his partisan conservative and religious policy preferences on issues. And if his Catholicism influenced his interpretation, he could disavow the influence of his religious views when they coincided with some historical precedent.

Using this new incarnation of his legal theory, Scalia could interpret the Constitution to be whatever he said it was. He could decide cases based on his judgments and interpretation, regardless of the opinions of professional historians on the meaning of constitutional phrases among the populace during the Early American period. Only he could grade his own historical interpretation of that society. Now, Scalia argued, "I have my rules that confine me. I know what I'm looking for. When I find it—the original meaning of the Constitution—I am handcuffed. If I believe that the First Amendment meant when it was adopted that you are entitled to burn the American flag, I have to come out that way even though I don't like to come out that way. When I find that the original meaning of the jury trial guarantee is that any additional time you spend in prison which depends upon a fact must depend upon a fact found by a jury—once I find that's what the jury trial guarantee means, I am handcuffed."

But Scalia was not the only originalist on the Court. Clarence Thomas had his own view of originalism, as had a handful of the other 107 justices in the history of the Supreme Court.[2] Law library shelves are filled with volumes in which renowned historians debate the historical meaning of constitutional phrases. Scalia, though, was so confident in his approach that he anointed himself the ultimate arbiter of the Founding Era's "public meaning" of the law and Constitution. His demeanor of unwavering certainty suggested that he believed reason and common sense should immediately lead everyone to adopt his position.

Upon finishing the speech, Scalia answered a series of questions from the audience, effortlessly dispatching all challenges. He thus provided more than ample demonstration of the same intelligence and skill with which he handled the Court's oral arguments, fencing with some of the best legal and political minds in the nation. The timing of this public display was no accident. Rumors had been floating around Washington since October 2004 that eighty-year-old Chief Justice Rehnquist's failing battle with anaplastic thyroid cancer might force him to retire at the end of the term. He had been absent for much of the Court term and struggled in January 2005 to swear in President George W. Bush for his second term. Watching Scalia's performance at the Wilson Center, one could not help but muse about the ease with which Scalia might handle challenging questions from senators on the Judiciary Committee should he be tapped to take the center seat.

Scalia knew that since 2000 President Bush had been promising to appoint justices "in the mold of Scalia and Thomas."[3] In addition, the previous December, Senate minority leader Democrat Harry Reid of Nevada had opened the door to his possible promotion to the chief justiceship when, after calling Justice Clarence Thomas "an embarrassment to the Supreme Court," he described Scalia to the press as "one smart guy." Reid went on to say, "I disagree with many of the results that he arrives at . . . [but] his reasons for arriving at those results are very hard to dispute." Adding that there would be no Democratic-led filibusters of nominees in the Senate unless they were seen to be "extreme" conservatives, Reid made clear that if Scalia were elevated to the chief justiceship, he would likely have clear sailing toward confirmation.[4]

In reporting on the Woodrow Wilson Center speech, the national press took notice of its potential connection to Scalia's possible elevation on the Court. *The Washington Post* noted: "Scalia, who has been mentioned as a possible chief justice nominee should Justice William Rehnquist retire, outlined his judicial philosophy of interpreting the Constitution according to its text, as understood at the time it was adopted."[5] Others saw the connection here as well. "Is Scalia Campaigning for Chief Justice?" asked Tom Curry of MSNBC.[6] *Washington Post* reporter Dana Milbank noted that Scalia was "showing his softer side . . . with possible sights on Chief Job."[7] A week later, *The New York Times* in an editorial titled "That Scalia Charm" launched a preemptive campaign against what it perceived to be Scalia's designs for the chief justiceship: "His approach would mean throwing out much of the nation's existing constitutional law, and depriving Americans of basic rights. Justice Scalia's campaign to be chief justice, if it is that, is a timely reminder of why he would be a disastrous choice for the job."[8]

This videotaped public appearance was not a one-time occurrence for Scalia that spring. Three weeks earlier, he had debated his liberal judicial colleague Stephen Breyer at American University on the use of "foreign judicial and legal sources" in the Supreme Court's decision-making process.[9] A little more than a month after the Wilson Center speech, Scalia participated in a roundtable on constitutional decision making with his colleagues Breyer and Sandra Day O'Connor, moderated by NBC's Tim Russert at the National Constitution Center.[10] Both of these performances were also videotaped and made available for sale by C-SPAN. Little wonder that by mid-May 2005, Scalia was being described by Warren Richey of *The Christian Science Monitor* as "the best known among the six or seven others said to be on Mr. Bush's shortlist" for the chief justiceship when Rehnquist retired.[11]

Despite what members of the press were calling his new "charm offensive" for the chief justiceship, Scalia's name had been surfacing as a possible successor to William Rehnquist for at least three years.[12] In a late 2002 piece titled "Could Scalia Be the Chief?" legal reporter Tony Mauro suggested:

> It has the mouth feel of Scalia's favorite lunch at A. V. Ristorante, anchovy pizza and Montepulciano wine: bold, unexpected, and, to some tastes, hard to swallow. But it is a mouthful that has been heard with increasing frequency since the November 5 [2002] elections, a rumor traced back to the highest echelons of conservative Republican thinking as a scenario that could follow the now-more-than-likely retirement of Chief Justice William Rehnquist next summer. The theory goes like this: The Republicans' conservative base delivered the party's successes in the midterm elections—including a majority in the Senate—and will now need to be honored and repaid.[13]

Mauro did add that this was not the most palatable prospect for some in the Court's Marble Palace: "Outside the Court, Scalia is known as a witty, sometimes gregarious man with an Old World charm and gentility. But inside, the prospect of Scalia as a possible chief justice was greeted with stunned silence by some who work there, signaling that Scalia is not the most popular justice among the nine."

But the prospect did not disappear in the intervening years. In early 2005 *Time* magazine said: "The guessing game is in full swing over which of the court's sitting Justices is most likely to replace [Rehnquist]. If he does not go outside for the job, President Bush will probably choose one of the court's two most stalwart conservatives, Antonin Scalia and Clarence Thomas. Scalia seems to have the edge."[14] But, *Time* added, this prospect had a downside for some: "The President and his advisers are worried that the tart-tongued Justice may not have the people skills to manage the court, build consensus among its nine members and represent the institution in public." This was not something, *Time* reported, that had escaped Scalia's attention. "That may explain why the famously dyspeptic Scalia has become a merry mainstay on the A-list Washington social circuit of late. . . . 'Lately, I've been running into Nino everywhere,' says a friend and fellow lawyer. 'He's showing that he actually can be charming and gregarious. It's a sign that he's really interested in the job.'"

Conservatives began leading the charge for their man. In a piece titled "Chief Justice Scalia?: Rehnquist Illness Sparks Rumors," *Church and State*, a publication dealing with the separation of religion and politics, reported: "Rumors are circulating in Washington that Supreme Court Justice Antonin Scalia may have his eye on a promotion—to chief justice."[15] *Washington Post* reporter Charles Lane wrote that "an informal 'Scalia boomlet' is under way—and Scalia may be leading it."[16] Scalia gave the appearance of distancing himself from the campaign. For the annual reunion of Rehnquist law clerks in mid-June 2005, with the chief so weak from his illness that he attended for only half an hour, Scalia sent a videotaped message "denying any ambitions to be chief justice himself, and joking that he would rather be Pope than Chief Justice."[17]

But after Scalia's appearance at the Woodrow Wilson Center no one was buying his disclaimers. The sixty-nine-year-old jurist was clearly educating the president of the United States that he should still be, in George Bush's own words during the 2000 presidential campaign, one of his "models of a Supreme Court justice."[18]

Uncertainty about his future was not an emotion familiar to Scalia. The five decades prior to his ascension to the Supreme Court had been characterized by almost entirely unimpeded career successes and so much good fortune that he seemed to be living a charmed life. But there had also been missteps such as the duck hunting episode. Scalia knew he needed to wipe away the effects of one public relations crisis after another in the last several years, all of his own making and each one more serious than the last. Since the 2000 presidential election, Scalia had been excessively outspoken and critical of his colleagues, with the result that, in an institution dependent upon consensus and civility among the justices to operate smoothly, as well as to implement the conservative agenda, Scalia had made himself a lightning rod for press and public criticism.

By the end of that year's Court term, some began to suspect that Scalia was tailoring his votes in certain key cases to appear more acceptable to administration and Senate conservatives. One such case, *Gonzales v. Raich*, dealt with whether the federal government could, by using the Controlled Substances Act of 1970, prevent California's Compassionate Use Act of 1996 from permitting the private cultivation and use of homegrown marijuana for medical purposes. The Court's four liberals under John Paul Stevens, together with Anthony Kennedy, ruled that the federal government's power over drug control, based in its constitutional power to regulate interstate commerce, could preempt states from eliminating penalties for drug use.[19] In making this decision, the majority relied on an obscure 1942 Commerce Clause case, *Wickard v. Filburn*.[20] In that case, the Court ruled that by setting quotas for crop production, the federal government could also regulate the "strictly local" production of wheat for personal use, because "it exerts a substantial economic effect on interstate commerce."[21]

In what appeared to some as a case of "strange judicial bedfellows," Scalia, who as the editor of *Regulation* magazine was a well-known advocate for government deregulation, also voted with the liberal wing. Based on his past decisions, he should have been expected to join his conservative colleagues' dissent under his usual states' rights theory that the interstate commerce power could not reach such purely intrastate activities. He argued that while individual cultivation and use of marijuana for medical purposes did not constitute interstate commerce, it did have a sufficient effect on such commerce to merit federal regulation. As Scalia explained: "The power to regulate interstate commerce extends not only to those regulations which aid, foster and protect the commerce, but embraces those which prohibit it. . . . Congress's authority to enact all of these prohibitions of intrastate controlled-substance activities depends only upon whether they are appropriate means of achieving the legitimate end of eradicating Schedule I substances from interstate commerce."[22] For Scalia, they were.

Had Scalia used his originalist philosophy as he explained it, and as he used it that term in an Oregon case denying the federal government's effort to use its drug laws to block that state's "Death with Dignity" law, it would surely have led him to consider limiting the ability of Congress's interstate commerce clause power to reach purely local and intrastate criminal offenses.[23] This view might well have placed him with Clarence Thomas's entertaining originalist dissent in the *Raich* case, in which he argued that if "Congress can regulate this under the Commerce Clause, then it can regulate virtually anything," including "quilting bees, clothes drives and potluck suppers throughout the 50 states."[24] For Thomas, this private growth and use of marijuana for medicinal purposes was beyond the reach of the federal government.

Some legal academic commentators could not help but wonder about the timing and reasons for Scalia's atypical Commerce Clause position. Referring to Scalia's earlier 1989 essay "The Rule of Law as a Law of Rules" praising the need to limit judicial discretion through the reliance on clear, rather than vague, decision-making rules, libertarian Mark Moller, of the Cato Institute, argued disapprovingly:

> Scalia's reading of the Commerce Clause . . . is pretty clear. It tells lower courts they should avoid inquiring whether regulated conduct "affects" "interstate commerce," when Congress targets that conduct as part of a detailed regulatory scheme. That's easy for courts to apply, because it guts the Commerce Clause like a fresh mackerel. . . . Scalia condemns judges who enact their preferences at the expense of the law as it has been declared. Perhaps it's time to look in the mirror.[25]

Others saw political motivation in Scalia's decision. George Mason University law professor David Bernstein said, "Scalia went off the reservation. . . . You want to say [Scalia] just looked at the law . . . but it's difficult. . . . I don't know a serious originalist who thinks *Wickard* was decided right."[26] It was reporter Ryan Grim who was able to use Bernstein's analysis to connect the dots between Scalia's willingness to abandon both his originalism and states' rights views to rule in favor of the federal government and the challenging political situation then confronting him:

> Antonin Scalia's dilemma was perhaps the trickiest of all. In the thick of his campaign for chief justice, he had to stick somewhere near his expressed principles, not piss off Republicans in Congress and the White House—and, of course, make sure there are no hippies smoking legal marijuana anywhere in his United States. "Scalia tends to be more interested in originalism when it fits into his Catholic social conservatism," says Bernstein, "or when he's using it to bludgeon the left." Not much of doctrinal interest should be culled from Scalia's decision, however, since his vote in the 6–3 decision didn't matter. Had Scalia dissented on principle, he would have been sending a signal that he wants to curb congressional power, never a good idea when you may soon need congressional confirmation. At the same time, he may have been trying to assuage the left, showing that he's not some nutball who wants to roll back the clock to 1789. With the filibuster alive to fight another day, every vote counts.[27]

No one could foresee that this story was only beginning. The true legacy of *Bush v. Gore*, putting George W. Bush in the White House and in a position to fill new vacancies on the Supreme Court, began when the Supreme Court's term ended in late June 2005. Justice Sandra Day O'Connor realized that, with her husband, John, deteriorating quickly from Alzheimer's, it was time for her to retire and return with him to their native Arizona.[28] Knowing that Rehnquist's health was deteriorating, and suspecting that he might also be considering retirement, O'Connor went to visit her old friend twice, in March and later in June, to ferret out his future plans. Given the Court's informal tradition against voluntarily creating two vacancies at the same time, O'Connor wondered if the chief was planning to retire. If so, she planned to remain on the Court for another year to ease the transition for a changing Court.[29] Perhaps she also speculated that if Rehnquist vacated the chief justice's chair on such a deeply divided Court, by delaying her retirement she might be elevated to the chief's seat partly because of her moderate role on the Court, and partly as a politically symbolic gesture of appointing the first female chief justice in American history. But if this was her thinking, she misjudged in two ways. Given her age of seventy-five, and moderate conservative philosophy, that appointment was not a likely one for President Bush.[30] And Rehnquist had other plans.

When O'Connor consulted the chief about the possibility of coordinating their departure plans, he made very clear that he did not intend to leave just yet. As O'Connor remembers, "We talked a bit. I was concerned about whether he had an intention to step down since his plans might have altered my own. It's hard for the nation to grapple with two [retirements] at once. He indicated that he didn't want to step down."[31] In both of their meetings, when the issue of retirement timing was raised, Rehnquist said, "We don't need two vacancies." When she pressed about his plans, Rehnquist told her, "I want to stay another year."[32] Realizing that it was her move first, O'Connor said: "Well, okay, I'll retire then."[33]

The nature of Rehnquist's motivations here cannot be determined. It was a strange move for the infirm chief, who had once voted with the Court in his early years on the bench to nullify the voting powers of the stroke-ravaged William O. Douglas.[34] It was equally strange for the man who in 1991 had seen up close the impact of the ailing and soon-to-retire Justice Thurgood Marshall on the work of the Court. It is also possible that he was in denial about his prognosis and held out hope for a remission that would allow him to remain for a while longer. Rehnquist's biographer, John Jenkins, speculates that he had the view that his life-tenured seat on the Court meant exactly that, tenure for life. Beyond this, Jenkins argues that Rehnquist's well-known dislike for the press, who had been camping at his house and pestering him about his retirement plans, may have played a role: "It was really all about him. In spite of all the media's health watch—or, perhaps, *to spite* it—he was going to hang on."[35] But one is also left to wonder whether Rehnquist, who was frustrated at O'Connor's moderate views for years, sought, by delaying his departure, to ensure that she would not dismantle what was left of his legacy after he was gone. Without O'Connor, he, or his eventual replacement as selected by President Bush, might be able to help swing the Court in a more conservative direction after all.

Whatever Rehnquist's reasons, Justice O'Connor announced on July 1, 2005, that she would retire from the Court upon the successful Senate confirmation of her successor, a move that would keep the Court at full strength in the event of any delay in the selection process. The news caught off guard those who had been planning for Rehnquist's departure, and the great "conventional wisdom" machinery of Washington set to work rounding up prospects for her replacement.[36] One of the most interesting articles was published in the editorial pages of the conservative *Weekly Standard*, under Fred Barnes's byline. Barnes asserted that President Bush could "win confirmation of almost any conceivable nominee for the High Court, screams of protest by Democrats and hostile media coverage notwithstanding," and that the president "has a promise to keep. Since he began running for the White House six years ago, he has declared endlessly his intention to select judges who interpret the law rather than create it—in a word, conservatives. On this, he has never equivocated." Barnes was now going to hold the president's feet to the fire:

> There's little ambiguity in this. Bush has promised to pick judges, including to the Supreme Court, who understand the role of judicial power and the limits that must be placed on it. There's a name for such people—conservatives. To pick someone for the Supreme Court who doesn't fit this description would amount to betrayal by the president of his most reliable supporters, the very people who have believed in him the most. We don't expect the president to break his promise—quite the contrary.[37]

Despite this pressure, the Bush administration sought to avoid being hemmed in, telling Dana Bash of CNN that "Mr. Bush didn't actually publicly pledge a Scalia or a [Clarence] Thomas[–like]" appointment to the Supreme Court. Later, on Fox News, Barnes agreed, saying: "Let me correct something . . . for this story about the president preferring Scalia and Clarence Thomas back in 1999. I asked this question to David Beckwith, who was in the press office of the Bush campaign, 'Who does the president really admire on the court?' And the answer came back Thomas and Scalia. There's never been a promise that he would actually nominate another Thomas and Scalia."[38]

Thanks to the continually diligent vetting process of the Federalist Society, whose founding advisers were Robert Bork and Antonin Scalia, and with whom both men still remained especially close, finding reliable conservatives proved to be no problem at all. Because of the excellence of one of the candidates on the list, choosing a replacement did not take long. The initial buzz revolved around replacing O'Connor with another woman, or perhaps creating a new Hispanic seat on the Court by appointing Office of Legal Counsel head Alberto Gonzales or Fifth Circuit Court of Appeals judge Emilio Garza. But less than three weeks later, influenced by a lobbying campaign led by deputy White House counsel David Leitch, President Bush selected Court of Appeals judge for the District of Columbia John Roberts.[39]

Roberts, a former law clerk to William Rehnquist, had served on the District of Columbia Circuit Court for two years, after he was initially blocked for confirmation for the seat by being denied a vote from the Democratic-led Senate Judiciary Committee. By all accounts, Roberts was a highly meritorious choice to fill this vacancy. He made his reputation heading the federal appellate division of the Washington law firm Hogan & Hartson, appearing before the Supreme Court in thirty-nine cases, winning twenty-five of them. His method of preparing for those arguments was to put down the key points in the case on a stack of file cards, memorize them, and then scramble their order to restudy them so as to stimulate the unpredictable nature of the justices' questioning.[40] The announcement of his appointment was made by President Bush on national television at 9:00 P.M. on July 19, 2005. During the ceremony, the Washington press corps was delighted by an impromptu exuberant dance by the appointee's young son, Jack, who Roberts later explained was doing his impression of the comic book character Spider-Man "shooting out his webs."[41]

With the Senate out of session, the Judiciary Committee's confirmation hearing would have to wait until everyone returned to Washington in the fall. By late summer it became clear that the highly qualified Roberts would have little trouble in securing confirmation. Seeking time to fill the vacancy before the Court opened its next session on the first Monday in October, Judiciary Committee chairman Republican Arlen Specter of Pennsylvania announced that the hearings would begin on September 6. With reporters noting that there was "no serious talk of a filibuster" by the Senate Democratic Caucus, Roberts's confirmation seemed to be all but a formality.[42] But while Roberts was preparing himself for the confirmation hearing, Rehnquist's health continued to decline.

Two natural disasters, one outside the Court and one inside it, dictated the events that followed. On August 29, Hurricane Katrina struck the Gulf Coast with the combined effects of flooding and windstorms devastating the New Orleans area and parts of the Mississippi coast. The dramatic television coverage, with tens of thousands of people stranded in sports arenas and elsewhere, people being rescued by helicopter right off their rooftops, and the incompetent executives of the Federal Emergency Management Agency paralyzed by inaction, overwhelmed news about Roberts's confirmation hearing. As the Bush administration's inability to handle the crisis became more evident, the president's popularity plummeted.

Just five days later, on the evening of Saturday, September 3, Chief Justice William Rehnquist's health took, in the understated words of the Court's spokesperson, a "precipitous decline" and he suddenly died.[43] For George Bush, the goal for finding a new Chief Justice became one of identifying the most confirmable candidate, one who could be approved before the opening of the Court's term in early October, and, if possible, one who would immediately improve the president's public image. As Peter Baker of *The Washington Post* wrote, "As they sift through names, White House advisers are weighing whether it would be better to announce a nominee quickly or to wait until after the situation in the Gulf Coast is better in hand and the Roberts confirmation process is finished. With his poll rating at an all-time low, gasoline prices at a longtime high, and U.S. troops suffering rising casualties in Iraq, Bush confronts a perilous point in his presidency."[44] Fortunately for the president, with Roberts's Senate confirmation hearings scheduled to begin on Monday, the solution was already at hand. Why not switch Roberts's appointment to fill Rehnquist's chief justice seat?

Jan Crawford Greenburg's *Supreme Conflict* reveals that despite intensive lobbying on his behalf over two years and his own "charm offensive,"

Scalia was never really considered for the position. The reasons, she reveals, were many. First, Bush faced a Court with at least three members interested in the position. Not just Scalia, but Clarence Thomas and Anthony Kennedy had also been positioning themselves, and possibly lobbying, for the appointment, making it impossible to appoint any of them without possibly losing the others' support for the new chief and the administration's position on key cases.[45] Beyond that, elevating someone from within the Court, thus opening up a vacancy for that associate justice seat, would mean that, with O'Connor's seat still to be filled, the weakened administration would have to secure *three*, rather than two, confirmations in the fractious, partisan Senate.[46] And, in Scalia's own case, one major strike against him was his age. As Greenburg reported, "Bush's advisers also thought the sixty-nine-year-old Scalia was too old. His moment had passed. He would serve as chief for eight or ten years, presumably, which meant they ran the risk that a Democrat would be in the White House and positioned to name his successor. Bush would not want to take that chance."[47] Left unexpressed by Greenburg, but surely also a negative factor, was the likelihood, given Scalia's recent controversial actions and the intense nature of the liberal opposition to his ultraconservative judicial decisions, of facing a protracted Senate battle, thus costing Bush too much political capital for his confirmation. Even Scalia's friends could see that his chances for elevation were slim. "Scalia has raised a lot of hackles," said Robert Bork. Compared with Roberts, "the campaign against him would have been much more hysterical."[48]

Even had he been confirmed, a Scalia Court might not have been what the Bush administration wanted for its conservative legal agenda. As Lorraine Woellert, a reporter for *BusinessWeek*, explained, "Compounding the problem with a Scalia nomination: his diplomacy on the court—or lack thereof. The pugnacious jurist might simply have pontificated his way out of the job. Almost no one on the high court has been spared his short temper and biting pen, which he has used frequently to criticize his colleagues." Stephen Hess, a former Ford administration official, said, "Bush had been told by the legal community that Scalia would not have been an effective Chief [Justice]." Stanton Anderson, executive vice president of the U.S. Chamber of Commerce, added, "Roberts' personality might be better for forging majorities." Based on all of this information, Woellert concluded that "Scalia was never on the short list."[49]

While Scalia had never been asked about the position, Clarence Thomas had been polled about his interest in the center seat months earlier, rejecting the inquiry because of his unwillingness to endure another contentious Senate confirmation battle.[50] Greenburg wrote that Scalia "had been ambivalent about the prospect of becoming chief justice from the beginning." Still, Greenburg adds, Scalia "found himself feeling surprisingly disappointed when it became evident that he wouldn't get the chance. It would've been nice if the White House had at least asked."[51] The truth was that Scalia's wounds in this battle were self-inflicted. Lorraine Woellert concluded: "For many movement conservatives, Scalia's thunderous orations and incendiary writings from the bench made him the ideal Chief Justice to press the campaign for limited government and traditional values. But in the end, the combative Scalia left the path open for Roberts, a man with seemingly no rough edges."[52]

Just two days after Rehnquist died, on early Monday morning, September 5, with the fallout from the botched Hurrican Katrina crisis management still swirling around him, Bush nominated John Roberts as Rehnquist's replacement, making him, at age fifty, the youngest chief justice nominee since John Marshall, who was forty-five when nominated in 1801. In making this nomination, the president made clear that there were two reasons for such a selection—Roberts's exceptional qualifications and his rapid confirmability: "I chose Judge Roberts from among the most distinguished jurists and attorneys in the country, because he possesses the intellect, experience and temperament to be an outstanding member of our nation's highest court. . . . He's a gentleman. He's a man of integrity and fairness. And throughout his life, he's inspired the respect and loyalty of others. He has built a record of excellence in achievement and a reputation for goodwill and decency towards others."[53] And Bush had no doubt that quick confirmation would be forthcoming: "It's in the interest of the court and the country to have a chief justice on the bench on the first full day of the fall term. The Senate is well along in the process of considering Judge Roberts' qualifications. They know his record and his fidelity to the law. I'm confident that the Senate can complete hearings and confirm him as chief justice within a month."[54]

For Bush, the selection of Rehnquist's former law clerk as his replacement was perfect: "It's fitting that a great chief justice be followed in office by a person who shared his deep reverence for the Constitution, his profound respect for the Supreme Court and his complete devotion to the cause of justice."[55] However, the appointment did not sit well with leading members of Bush's ultraconservative base. "We were hoping the President might elevate someone like Scalia," said Tony Perkins, president of the conservative Family Research Council.[56] To which conservative commentator Pat Buchanan added that Scalia "should have been Bush's choice." In Buchanan's view, "To pass over Scalia for Roberts is like passing over George Patton and giving command of the 3rd Army to a brilliant young staff officer from the Pentagon."[57]

Scalia seemed to make clear that he was not overly thrilled with being passed over either. While the rest of the Court attended Roberts's swearing in at the White House on September 29, Scalia was playing tennis in a posh resort in Bachelor Gulch, Colorado, where he was teaching a two-day Federalist Society legal education seminar on the separation of powers. Scalia told a reporter that he missed Roberts's swearing in because "I was out of town with a commitment that I could not break." ABC News investigator reporter Brian Ross began his report on the seminar by noting that "what some call fact-finding missions, others call junkets. Judges have their own name for them; they call them educational seminars held at fancy resorts, all expenses paid by somebody else."[58] Then, failing to discuss the ten-hour legal education course that Scalia taught, the reporter criticized his fly-fishing expedition and his "speaking and socializing with members of the group that paid the expenses for his trip," a number of whom practiced before the Supreme Court. He also took exception to Scalia's attendance at a cocktail party, "sponsored in part by the same lobbying and law firm where convicted lobbyist Jack Abramoff once worked," and working at an event associated with the conservative Federalist Society. Legal ethics expert Stephen Gillers of NYU Law School was quoted as saying, "He's using the prestige of his office to advance the interest of a group with a decided political/judicial profile. By having a Supreme Court justice at your group's fairly intimate, very posh event, you're lending the prestige of your office to that group. I mean, that's—everyone would like that. And that's why he shouldn't have gone."[59] In the end, though, Ross concluded that there was no allegation that this had affected any cases. "This is not about bribery or influence-peddling, but rather a question of appearance. . . . It's the appearance of justice that is threatened. And that's what's important."[60] But still, the impression was left that Scalia had chosen to be anywhere but the swearing in of the man now sitting in the seat for which he appeared to have been campaigning.

When it was all over, Scalia tried to brush aside the idea that he had been seeking the center seat. "I'm not even sure I wanted it, to tell you the truth," he told reporters at a Waldorf-Astoria dinner nearly two weeks later. But few believed this, as he later conceded, "The honor would have been wonderful."[61] Five years later, in an interview before the national convention of the Federalist Society in Washington, Scalia was asked by Jan Crawford[62] whether the reason for this reluctance was that he "would have felt pressure to build consensus on the Court" as the chief. Scalia responded, "That's always the problem, and that's why I'm glad I'm not chief justice." After saying that he had not been approached by President Bush, Scalia was asked if he would have accepted; he responded, "I don't know. . . . I wouldn't have liked it." But he admitted that "he would have considered the opportunity." Scalia added that he had noticed a moderating influence in William Rehnquist's opinions when he became chief justice. "He was a shin-kicker before he became chief justice. He wrote very sharp, combative dissents."[63] In his version of "take what the game will give you," a "shin-kicker" Scalia would now remain.

Free of his ambition for the chief justiceship and with no further career advancement possible at his age, Scalia immediately made it clear that he would continue to observe a looser view of the limits of his extrajudicial activities off the Court. On October 10, he traveled to New York City to lay a wreath in honor of Christopher Columbus and also serve as the grand marshal of the annual Columbus Day Parade, certainly not the normal activity for a sitting member of the Supreme Court. As Scalia walked near New York City mayor Michael Bloomberg down Fifth Avenue, liberal New Yorkers took the opportunity to tell the ultraconservative native-son jurist just what they thought of him and his work. "Gore should be president. . . . Gore should be president!," one man yelled insistently, adding, "We're having a nice five years since you stole the election!" A number of others shouted their unprintably derogatory comments in Italian.[64]

Scalia had no problem with the hecklers, but he made it plain that one breed of critics was not welcome around him—members of the press. When he arrived at the reviewing stand on 68th Street and saw the throng of reporters and photographers with their cameras waiting for him, Scalia protested to his security men, "Let's get some crowd control and get these people out. For Pete's sake, will you get out of the way of the parade?"[65] At other spots on the route, when he saw friendlier members of the Fourth Estate, reporters noticed that Scalia "mugged for cameras and gave unusual interviews."[66] On one such occasion, a photographer recorded one priceless image showing the beaming justice standing next to Lawrence Auriana, the president of the Columbus Citizens' Foundation, which sponsored the parade, in front of a fancy orange sports car on the parade route. Scalia was wearing a sash reading "Grand Marshal" over his suitcoat, with his foot on top of his host's, and surrounded by three deadly serious bodyguards in trench coats.[67]

Controversy continued for Scalia the following day, when he returned to Washington to give a speech at the annual conference of the American Council of Life Insurers. Though the press had been told that the event would be open to them, once again they were barred. On October 12, Associated Press Supreme Court reporter Gina Holland wrote of the anti-media activity: "The real Antonin Scalia seems to be back."[68] As opposed to the kinder, gentler jurist who earlier that year had been campaigning for the chief justiceship, Scalia was reverting to the media-bashing justice.

By Saturday, October 15, *The New York Times* decided to take issue on its editorial page with Scalia's penchant for engaging in extrajudicial behavior. In an editorial titled "Time to Ban Judicial Junkets," the piece criticized "posh multi-day indoctrination-vacations" such as the one that Scalia had just led at the Colorado resort, and urged a new commission charged with revising the American Bar Association's Model Code of Judicial Conduct to adopt "a bright-line rule forbidding judges from accepting such travel gifts." Citing Scalia's earlier duck hunting trip with Vice President Cheney, the *Times* concluded, "If commission members are truly concerned about faltering trust in the judiciary's fairness and integrity, they will act boldly against the lobbying of judges by private interests."[69]

But Scalia was not done yet. During this period, CNBC aired an extended interview that he had done with Maria Bartiromo, the so-called "money honey" for *The Wall Street Journal Report* television show. It was a strange performance in which the justice seemed to alternate between flirting with the attractive reporter and coyly pulling back in response to her questions. When asked about the changes on the Court, Scalia said, "I'm sick of these same old people. . . . I guess there hasn't been a change for 10 years, that's all. And it's refreshing to have some new faces." But for the departed Sandra Day O'Connor, with whom he had engaged in an epic battle over the abortion issue, and many others, for sixteen years, he had only kind words. "I'll miss Sandra Day O'Connor. . . . If there's anybody that has been the sort of the social glue of the Court, it's been Sandra." When asked about the confirmation process for the Supreme Court nominees, he said, "I wouldn't want to go through it today, I'll tell you that much. It has become politicized, but the reason it has become politicized is that for, oh, maybe 35 years, 40 years the Supreme Court has been making more and more political decisions that are not resolved by the Constitution at all."[70]

Supreme Court reporter Kim Eisler wrote of the performance:

The Bartiromo interview didn't create much news, but the buzz around the Supreme Court is that Scalia has a more "devil-may-care" attitude since John Roberts was named chief justice. To say that Scalia coveted the late chief justice William Rehnquist's job is an understatement. Scalia had assumed that after Rehnquist's death, there would be a period of time for Scalia's friends and advocates to persuade President Bush that he should be the new chief justice. Scalia was miffed when Bush quickly moved Roberts into the chief position before Scalia had a chance to make his case.[71]

• • •

Though he did not get the chief justiceship, that appointment and the one that would fill the vacancy left by the retiring Sandra Day O'Connor reflected the success of Scalia's and the conservative wing's victory in *Bush v. Gore*. The Republican president would choose two young justices to be added to the Court, thus tipping the institution clearly in favor of the conservatives. When this happened, Scalia could be in a position to lead the new conservative wing.

Rather than seizing this opportunity, less than six weeks after John Roberts's ascension to the Supreme Court, Scalia, realizing that he was beyond anyone's control as an associate justice for the remainder of his life, served notice that he intended to live his life on the Court any way that he chose, regardless of the prevailing historical and ethical norms.

CHAPTER 19

The Dead Constitution Tour

His charm offensive now over, for the first time Scalia knew what position he would hold for the rest of his professional life. As the composition of the Court continued to change, so would its ideological direction. With O'Connor's vacancy to fill, on October 3, 2005, President Bush selected White House counsel Harriet Miers, his former deputy White House chief of staff. The nomination ran into immediate trouble because of concerted opposition from conservatives. When the opposition grew, much of it on conservative internet blog sites, owing to the lack of certainty as to Miers's legal views, Bush withdrew the nomination on October 27.

Three days later, determined not to repeat the Miers debacle, Bush nominated a Federalist Society favorite, fifty-six-year-old Samuel Alito, who was then serving on the federal Court of Appeals for the Third Circuit. Alito's confirmation was not without incident. During the confirmation hearing, his fate briefly seemed to be in jeopardy when the Senate Judiciary Committee focused on a "Personal Qualifications Statement" Alito had filed in 1985, hoping to get a job as an assistant attorney general in the Reagan administration. It mentioned his membership for over a decade in the conservative Concerned Alumni of Princeton, or CAP, which opposed the admission of minorities and women to the school. This was interpreted by the Senate Democrats, including Richard "Dick" Durbin of Illinois, as an indication that Alito did "not evidence an open mind." The grilling was so severe that when conservative South Carolina Republican Lindsey Graham later tried to rehabilitate the candidate by asking, "Are you a bigot?," Alito's wife, Martha-Ann, began to cry.[1] Despite an attempted filibuster by Massachusetts senator John Kerry and opposition from the ACLU, Alito, the son of Italian immigrant schoolteachers from New Jersey, was confirmed by the Senate to become the second Italian American to serve on the U.S. Supreme Court on January 31, 2006. Alito's ethnic heritage, his conservative Catholic faith, and his ultraconservative political views initially seemed to be so similar to Scalia's that he was nicknamed "Scalito."

The jurisprudential and ideological comparison of the new justice to Scalia ultimately did not prove to be accurate, given Alito's lack of appreciation for the senior jurist's originalism theory.[2] However, the replacement of the conservative Alito for the more moderate swing justice, Sandra Day O'Connor, would soon tilt the Court more clearly to the conservative side. As it did, Justice Anthony Kennedy, who since 1994 had voted consistently to the conservative side of Sandra Day O'Connor, would become the new pivotal swing justice, determining with his vote the outcome in key cases.

For his part, still an associate justice, and with nothing to gain or lose, Scalia was free to be whoever he wanted to be, and behave any way he desired without worrying about the consequences.[3] He had something to say, and now there was no rule or person to prevent him from saying it. He was ready to go back to the only place where he had been able to control his own agenda and receive some personal and professional adulation and solace—a personal speaking tour. In the fall of 2005, Scalia embarked on a series of speeches and public appearances criticizing his living Constitution colleagues in what blogging pundits labeled his "Dead Constitution Tour."[4]

On October 21, just eleven days after the controversial television interview with Maria Bartiromo, Scalia made another appearance halfway around the world. At Trinity College in Melbourne, Australia, he gave the Sir John Young Oration for the prestigious Boston, Melbourne, Oxford Conversazioni on Culture and Society, an annual debate among academics and lawyers from the three countries about the meaning of politics and law. The topic that year was "Judicial Activism: Power Without Responsibility," with the question for the speaker and his respondent, Australian barrister Julian Burnside, being "From what does government derive the right to rule?" The title of Scalia's new speech said it all. No longer would this be just the "Constitutional Interpretation" speech he had given the year before. Now he titled his address: "Mullahs of the West: Judges as Authoritative Expositors of the Natural Law?"[5] With this title, he could link, and thus disparage, both extremist Muslims and activist, liberal jurists around the world, including his own liberal colleagues.

The theme of Scalia's new verbal crusade was that the living, evolving Constitutionalists were nothing but "judge moralists" who had created a "judicial hegemony" that was now spreading to other courts in the Western industrialized countries, such as the new European Union court. To him, their version of an evolving Constitution had led to a malleable, partisan policy–oriented, religious-type ideology that warped the meaning of the Constitution.

Scalia began with a provocative thesis: "In the first half of the last century, American political theory was obsessed with the expert. The key to effective government, it was thought, was to take the direction of government agencies out of the hands of the politicians, and to place it within the control of men experienced and knowledgeable within the various fields of government regulation." American policymakers, Scalia proposed, had become obsessed with the notion of a rule by experts, only to discover that there were "no right or wrong answers that experts can discover." Over time, he argued, in the United States, "and indeed throughout the world, belief in the expert has been replaced by belief in the judge-moralist." In trying to rule on social questions using natural law, these judges soon raised the question "who, in a democratic society, should have the power to determine the government's view of what the natural law is."

For him, the American and European societies and governments had become "addicted to abstract moralizing" by judges. As an example of this technique, he argued against a case that became a staple in his newly developed speech. The European Union Court of Human Rights, in the 1981 case *Dudgeon v. United Kingdom*, had overturned a nineteenth-century law allowing a conviction for "gross indecency" for any same-sex intimate behavior. The court overturned the law using Article 8 of the Council of Europe's Convention for the Protection of Human Rights and Fundamental Freedoms, protecting "the right to respect for . . . private and family life," because it banned consensual sexual acts.[6] Scalia's objection to this decision was that judges were overturning long-standing laws based solely on their own interpretation of morality and the meaning of privacy.

For Scalia, the proper process for the rejection of such laws should come from the people, not the courts. However, European judges, like those on his American Supreme Court, used their own evolving judicial interpretation of laws to uphold the rights of abortion, same-sex intimate behavior, and assisted suicide, to limit the application of the death penalty, and to ban single-sex military schools. "Until relatively recently the meaning of laws, including fundamental laws or constitutions, was thought to be static," said Scalia. But for him the living Constitution theory, by which some of his colleagues measured laws according to "the evolving standards of decency that mark the progress of a maturing society," led to new, but not necessarily better, judgments by people he viewed as no more qualified to make such decisions than the average person. "Judges have no greater capacity than the rest of us to determine what is moral," explained Scalia.[7]

It was ironic that Scalia, the man who put no stock or faith in the use of foreign sources in deciding American constitutional cases, was now imploring those foreign judges to reconsider their approach. He "question[ed] the propriety—indeed, the sanity—of having a value-laden decision . . . made for the entire society (and in the case of Europe, for a number of different societies) by unelected judges. There are no scientifically demonstrable 'right' answers to such questions, as opposed to answers that the particular society favors." The result, Scalia predicted, would be an increase in the partisanship of judicial nominations and the confirmation process for Supreme Court appointments. As he put it to the Australian audience, "If judges are routinely providing the society's definitive answers to moral questions on which there is ample room for debate—rather than merely determining the meaning, when enacted, of democratically adopted texts—then judges will be made politically accountable." In short, voters would soon "be looking for people who agree with [them] as to what the annually revised Constitution ought to say." Scalia concluded, "What I do want . . . is the selection of judges who view it as their role to abide by the texts that the people have adopted, and in the sense that the people [who adopted them] intended."

What Scalia did not explain in this newer speech was that by relying solely on his interpretation of Founding Era sources to determine the public meaning of the Constitution, he was just as activist as they were, imposing his own version of late-eighteenth-century-based judicial morality to restrict twenty-first-century rights. Sometimes, in certain individual rights cases, such as those dealing with the Confrontation Clause, and the free speech aspects of flag burning, he expanded rights through this process.

In the months that followed, Scalia continued to deliver more outspoken versions of his "Mullahs of the West" attack. Each speech became more strident and virulent, as did his answers to questions that followed. It was some of these off-the-cuff responses, rather than the speech itself, that were reported widely. In a speech delivered in Puerto Rico on February 13, 2006, at a meeting of the Federalist Society for Law and Public Policy Studies, Scalia was quoted as giving a new twist to one of his most familiar points by saying: "The argument of flexibility . . . goes something like this: The Constitution is over 200 years old and societies change. It has to change with society, like a living organism, or it will become brittle and break. But you would have to be an idiot to believe that."[8] Subsequent articles about the speech reported that Scalia thought all "non-originalists are idiots."[9] He later defended himself by claiming that he had been misquoted. He did not think people who believed in a living Constitution were idiotic; only the arguments supporting their view were.[10]

On March, 8, 2006, Scalia, then on the verge of turning seventy years old, spoke at Switzerland's only Roman Catholic university, the University of Fribourg in Geneva, as a result of an invitation by one of the school's law professors, Samantha Besson. More than a half century earlier, he had studied there for a year as part of Georgetown University's study abroad program. Now that he was back, he planned to offer his impromptu thoughts on the U.S. Constitution to a gathering of European students and faculty.[11] Undoubtedly expecting the gathering to draw little or no notice at home, he spoke freely.

The occasion began just after 5:00 P.M. with a short introduction by an earnest-looking Swiss junior professor, who explained in labored English how the school's bureaucracy had forced this impromptu address by their distinguished speaker to be moved into the stadium-seating auditorium rather than taking place in front of "the Fireplace," the school's traditional speaker forum. For Scalia, who thought that many of the students in the French-German bilingual school would not be adept enough at English to understand him, let alone be aware of the nuances of American law and politics, this was going to be a quick, routine appearance. Stepping to the podium with a bemused expression on his face, he began by saying to a round of laughter, "I didn't know I was here to give a speech. I assume that most of you are here to practice your English. So it doesn't matter what I say."[12]

But Scalia could not have been more wrong. Unbeknownst to him, Scalia was about to face every public speaker's nightmare: an audience that he had underestimated. The audience was filled with European students fluent in English, and sprinkled with distinguished English-speaking professors and graduate students, nearly all of whom were well versed in American politics. One was a law professor who had just spoken at Harvard, a couple more were senior professors with considerable international contacts, and at least one was a visiting American student. Almost to a person the audience members were angry about the Bush administration, America's foreign policy, and the conduct of the American wars in Iraq and Afghanistan as well as its overall "War on Terror." To this audience, Scalia was an ultraconservative

American justice who had helped to put Republican George W. Bush into the White House, and was as a result inextricably linked to that administration's policies. His visit represented their best chance to vent their anger about the course of American policy and politics.

In speaking, the senior jurist failed to be concerned about the two geeky-looking young men in the second row to his immediate right who were recording him on their handheld digital camera. As it turned out, they were recording the occasion for a small European broadcast service, called the Bureau Audiovisuel Francophone, or BAFWEB, thus making it possible for them to transmit their shaky video of Scalia's seemingly private remarks around the world two days later.[13] Like it or not, Scalia would be speaking to a much wider audience than the group sitting before him.

Blissfully unaware of the underlying tensions in the room and the certainty of the international distribution of his remarks, Scalia almost absent-mindedly rattled through a shortened version of his "Dead Constitution" speech. To the delight of his audience, he proclaimed, "The only good Constitution is a dead Constitution. The problem with a living Constitution in a word is that somebody has to decide how it grows and when it is that new rights are—you know—come forth. And that's an enormous responsibility in a democracy to place upon nine lawyers, or even thirty lawyers." Waving his finger in the air, Scalia added, "Why should it be up to me to decide whether there ought to be, and hence there is, because the Constitution is a living instrument, a right to suicide?" Now warming up to the day's topic, he began bouncing up and down, saying, "There never has been, for 200 years, nobody ever thought the Bill of Rights gave that—gave that right to people. Why should we . . . what did I learn at Harvard Law School that makes me more qualified to decide that profound moral question than Joe Six Pack. Joe Six Pack is the common man. It's the American name for the common man. Joe Six Pack knows just as much about whether there should be a right to suicide as I do."[14]

The pace of Scalia's opening remarks, all delivered without notes, was so confidently measured, and spoken with such an appearance of authority, that it made his eloquent address even more persuasive. "Some people think it is the living Constitution," said Scalia, characterizing the views of those jurists, adding:

> I don't know why, because they like lawyers, let's have lawyers decide everything. But judges are wonderful, they should decide whether

there is a right to abortion, a right to suicide, or death penalty. So when I do lecture I point out that the main problem with the "Living Constitution" is this, or to put it another way, the main virtue of my Constitution, which I will not call the "Dead Constitution," I will call it the "Enduring Constitution," the main benefit of the "Enduring Constitution" is that I have a criterion. When a case comes to me, I don't do whatever I feel like doing. I have a standard. The standard is what would the people at the time the Constitution was enacted have said.

In a handful of sentences Scalia had summed up his entire judicial philosophy and had offered a nutshell version of the hundreds of speeches on this issue that he had given over the last two decades.

To avoid losing his European audience's attention, Scalia then turned to the most controversial topic he could think of for them to consider. "So, the question comes up, is there a Constitutional right to homosexual conduct? Not a hard question for me." Waving his right hand in the air he said, "It's absolutely clear that nobody ever thought when the Bill of Rights was adopted, they gave a right to homosexual conduct. Homosexual conduct was criminal for 200 years in every state. Easy question." At this point, Scalia began sawing his open hands back and forth as though he was wiping dirt from his palms.

Scalia was now ready to drive home his final point about his role as a Supreme Court justice. "If you don't use my criterion, what is your criterion? And you know what?" he said, lowering his voice to a raspy whisper, "There isn't any other. I mean think about it, what can you possibly use, other than the understood meaning of the text when it was adopted? If you don't use that, if you say, 'Oh no, it changes, it grows,' okay fine. What criterion are you going to tell your judges to use as to when it changes? Are they going to take a public opinion poll?" For Scalia, the choice was clear: "You either use the original meaning of the text, the original understanding of the text, or else you tell your judges, 'Oh, wise judges, you went to Harvard Law School or Stanford Law School. You must be experts in all of these moral questions for the whole society. You decide it for us, five out of nine of you. Decide for the whole country, whether there can be abortion, or there must not be abortion. Whether there can be the death penalty or there must not be the death penalty.'"

In concluding, Scalia attacked "the Constitutional Courts of the world," by which he meant the European courts, as the "Mullahs of the West." Referring to his recent speech in Australia, he criticized those who "mak[e] moral judgments for the whole society on the basis of, you know, empty phrases or inspiring phrases such as 'the right of privacy.'" The audience could clearly see that Scalia included among these "Mullahs" his liberal colleagues on the U.S. Supreme Court. He argued: "I love the right of privacy, it's a wonderful phrase, but what does it mean? . . . You just ask these judges, 'do you think there should be a right to suicide?' I mean my reaction is 'Why ask me?' If the people elected me, I could vote for a law that permits it or doesn't permit it. I haven't been elected, I'm just a lawyer." [15]

With that, one of the world's most visible and outspoken jurists ended his less than fourteen minutes of informal remarks. In offering these comments, Scalia displayed both his brilliant, argumentative eloquence and his magnetlike attraction to controversy. Next, he opened the discussion up for questions, saying to considerable laughter: "I used to be a law professor. I used to get paid money for teaching this class. So if you're bored and falling asleep, it's not because I'm not experienced. It's just because I'm not good." [16]

Once the floor was thrown open, the early questions were respectful and tentative, and tied to the theme of his remarks. As he answered them, Scalia walked across the stage and adopted an aggressive debating posture, making clear he was prepared for more discussion.[17] He took a question from a student with very limited English skills, who asked about a newly passed South Dakota law that banned abortion: "When do you think that *Roe v. Wade* will be overturned by the Supreme Court?" Scalia appropriately demurred, saying that the issue might one day come before his Court. On the larger issue of the future of the *Roe* decision, though, Scalia added, "I have no idea . . . and no idea whether it will be. . . . There are still five justices on our court who voted in favor of *Roe v. Wade*. If I had to guess, I would say, 'not yet . . . maybe not ever, but certainly not yet.' The American dream is still to come." For his part, though, Scalia argued that he "could not find a legal right to abortion in the Constitution," adding, "It is not contained in the Constitution of the United States." Contrary to those on the Court following a living Constitution who supported the right of abortion, Scalia warned "it is an enormous responsibility, in a democracy, to entrust that to nine lawyers." [18]

After the discussion of *Roe v. Wade*, the direction of the questioning by the audience took an unexpectedly aggressive turn. About halfway up the auditorium a distinguished-looking gentleman launched into a rambling tirade about "president [George W. Bush, who] stands up and lies in front of the Congress because of going into Iraq . . . [and] President Clinton goes to Court in the Paula Jones case and he's lied in front of the Court." Explaining that he was not being "anti-American," the man wanted "to understand how the Americans think about this."

Scalia tried initially to deflect the nationalistic hostility with a joke, "Like using the budget of a French government to keep a mistress in Paris? Which everybody knows about, and there is not a scandal. The difference is in America, there is a scandal. In Paris, hey," Scalia gestured with his arms in a "who cares" motion to the laughter of the crowd. But humor did not work, as the questioner just kept on ranting with his list of grievances against American policy. "Is this a question, or a diatribe against—" Scalia asked. But before he could finish, he was cut off.

"My question is how do you see that?" said the man.

Scalia made clear by the exasperated expression on his face that he had heard enough. "The answer is that it is not so," he exhorted sharply. "The answer is that you have been reading too much of the anti-American left wing press in Europe, I mean it's as simple as that. For example, you come up and state as a matter of fact—" Before he could explain, he was cut off again. Scalia now realized from the aggressiveness of the questioner, and the rising chorus of supportive murmurs throughout the audience, that the tone of the gathering had changed in an ugly direction. No longer was he answering the respectful questions of a crowd in awe of his position on the Supreme Court. Instead he had become a lightning rod drawing verbal fire as a representative of the current administration. In moments, Scalia was literally backed against the wall in the face of a critical cacophony. But the pride of the Georgetown University Philodemic Society's debate team, and the U.S. Supreme Court was more than up to the task.

"I heard this on television, on CNN . . ." pressed the man.

Scalia had heard enough. Looking both aggrieved and offended, now gesturing his arms forcefully, he fired back:

> I listened to you and now you listen to me. You said that the President of the United States lied to the Congress about Iraq. . . . That's certainly not an established fact at all. It's a huge controversy about whether or not he believed, as the intelligence service of every country in the world believed, that weapons of mass destruction were possessed by Iraq. To come and state as a fact that the President lied about it, I mean if that's the body of fact on which you base your

question I mean it's no use answering it. And as for the morality of the American people, I would put it up against the morality of other people in the world. . . . Clinton got into a lot of trouble. He was almost impeached. He was almost impeached.[19]

Though he realized that the entire auditorium was now largely allied against him, Scalia never once looked like he was the least bit intimidated. The verbal fireworks continued when the next person to regain the floor said: "I'd like you maybe to comment in the same way for the case of CIA prison flights and prison transfer of terrorism suspects in Europe. . . . What do you think about it on a constitutional and judicial . . ."

"Easy answer," crackles Scalia, now ignoring the stricture against commenting on issues that might come on appeal to his Court. "The Constitution, if these are foreigners and the action is occurring abroad, they are not covered by the United States Constitution. Now whether it's a good idea or a bad idea, whether it should be done or shouldn't be done, is a different question. That's above my pay grade."

"No way," barked a heckler wearing a baseball cap embroidered with a St. Louis logo, abandoning all sense of courtesy and protocol for their distinguished visitor.

"We don't like Europeans in old St. Louis Rams baseball caps," Scalia tried to joke. "We have a policy against it." The joke fell flat, but Scalia had let them know that he just did not care what these unruly Europeans thought.

Moments later, a young woman joined the fray. "I just would like to say that honestly after listening to some of the things you've said, I am scared. Guantanamo Bay and all these examples, I think that the law should have the obligation to make a cut from politics, and not be the point of view of a person in your government, or a group of people in relevance to this moral point of view . . ."

"Having heard you, I am scared," responded Scalia. "A world in which these moral sentiments would be given full expression by unelected judges would scare the devil out of me. I have a Constitution that I live under. It's been adopted by my people. I have statutes that my people have democratically adopted. And my job is to give a fair interpretation to them. You want a world run by an oligarchy, that's fine, but it scares me."

"That's exactly the point," said the woman. "We have Geneva Rights, we have human rights in the convention, it's just like it's not . . ."

"What do they mean?" Scalia responded.

"They mean a lot."

"They mean almost anything," said the justice.

At this point the moderator lost control of the audience as random comments were shouted out from among the sea of new hands in the air. But Scalia stood his ground, clearly unwilling to concede any ground.

"If my brother or father . . . was not even proven guilty or not guilty . . ." continued the same woman.

With that comment, Scalia had had enough. Putting aside his role as a U.S. Supreme Court justice, and no longer answering as just an American defending his president and his country abroad, he adopted a different role—an intensely personal one. Speaking over the questioner's voice he began, "If he is captured by my army, on a battlefield, that is where he belongs," the justice spat out with considerable emotion while pointing his now empty Styrofoam cup at the woman. *"I had a son on that battlefield. And they were shooting at my son. And I am not about to give this man who was captured in a war, a full jury trial. I mean it's crazy."* [20] It was an understandable comment from a father whose son had been at risk on the battlefield from these suspects, but an unfortunate one for a justice who was about to decide a case called *Hamdan v. Rumsfeld* [21] dealing with that very issue. But he wasn't done yet.

"Well I think that what happened. Well I think that Guantanamo is a very, very sad error of the humanity [*sic*]," the woman concluded.

"I think that you're absolutely wrong," responded Scalia. "Guantanamo is sad. Guantanamo is a problem for only one reason. Not because people captured in a war are being held without trial. That happens all the time." When someone interrupted him yet again, the justice pleaded, "Please let me finish. The problem with Guantanamo, and I don't know how to solve this problem, is that there may be no end to this war. Other wars you have an army fighting under a leader, and when the leader lays his sword down, or is blown up in a bunker, the war is over. And the two countries make peace and the captured soldiers are returned home. Okay, who makes peace in this war? That's the problem, how long are you going to keep these people in Guantanamo? That's the problem that I worry about. And that is a serious moral problem if you like," he said, motioning to the other questioner on this point. "But, it is certainly not the problem, my goodness, that we are not giving people captured on the battlefield a civil trial." [22] For nearly an hour Scalia had responded to hostile questions about everything from *Roe v. Wade* to Guantanamo. Finally, the moderator tried to sum up the shattered pieces of what was intended to be a civilized conversation among academics, lawyers, and a sitting Supreme Court justice about American law and politics. All in all, it was a magnificent performance. Regardless of one's views of Scalia, or his interpretation of the issues, it was a stirring demonstration by one man arguing against a hundred angry Europeans in defense of his country, his president, his Court, his view of the law, and everything he believed and held dear, including a son in the army.

Just outside the auditorium, the two men who had been video-recording the performance from their seats in the second row asked Scalia on camera what he thought of the audience. "Oh, I thought it was a fine audience," the justice responded. "They asked some hostile questions, but I often provoke hostile questions. I guess I'm a provocative person."[23]

Two days after the speech, a story about it appeared on a website called LifeNews.com: "Speaking to a group of professors and students in Switzerland, pro-life Supreme Court Justice Antonin Scalia said the Supreme Court may never overturn the Roe v Wade decision."[24]

Soon another pro-life site, LifeSiteNews.com, picked up the report and provided a link to the BAFWEB video of the speech.[25] It would take nearly three weeks before the mainstream American press discovered the Internet video. When the press reported on the speech, Scalia would once again be embroiled in controversy. One newspaper criticized the speech as "Scalia's Ill-Chosen Words."[26] A report also appeared on *Newsweek*'s website on Sunday, March 26, later published as an article titled "Scalia Speaks His Mind." The article said that the justice had "dismissed the idea that the detainees [at Guantanamo] have rights under the U.S. Constitution or international conventions, adding that he was 'astounded' at the 'hypocritical' reaction in Europe to Gitmo." Professor Samantha Besson of Fribourg, who had invited Scalia to speak, was quoted as saying: "The comments provoked 'quite an uproar.'"[27] Shortly after these reports, the site and the video disappeared from the internet.[28]

Once more there were calls for him to step down from hearing the *Hamdam v. Rumsfeld* case, which dealt with presidential war powers and the legal rights of captured enemy combatants in the "War on Terror." "This is clearly grounds for recusal," said Michael Ratner of the liberal human rights group Center for Constitutional Rights, cofounded by defense attorney William Kunstler. New York University's legal ethics expert, Professor Stephen Gillers, added, "As these things mount, a legitimate question could be asked about whether he is compromising the credibility of the [Supreme] Court."[29] A CNN internet story titled "Report: Scalia Against Rights for Gitmo Detainees," added: "Ethics experts said the impression that Scalia had already made up his mind before the hearing should mean that he will voluntarily drop out of the proceedings."[30] Shortly thereafter, a group of retired U.S. military generals filed a formal court petition asking Scalia to recuse himself from the *Hamdan* case. The generals argued that Scalia's Fribourg comments "give rise to the unfortunate appearance that, even before briefing was complete, he had already made up his mind," and that it gave the appearance of "personal bias arising from his son's military service."[31]

While the argument was technically accurate in that Scalia's comments *did* preview his ultimate decision, the recusal petition from the generals showed a lack of appreciation for the context of these remarks and the nature of the situation that caused them. Even if one argues that in a perfect world *Justice* Scalia should not have said this, *Antonin* Scalia, the father of a soldier fighting in Iraq and an American under verbal assault at the time, felt he had every right to defend himself in that situation. If Scalia could be faulted, it would be for agreeing to speak to that group in the first place, for so badly misjudging the level of knowledge and mood of his audience, and for making comments that gave the appearance of bias.

This was the third time in four years that Scalia's comments or actions had led to calls for his recusal from a case. His "under God" comments on the Pledge of Allegiance case at a Knights of Columbus Religious Freedom Day rally in January 2003 had forced his recusal from that case. A year later, a recusal petition stemming from his duck hunting expedition with Vice President Dick Cheney in Louisiana failed to persuade him to step out of the case dealing with the vice president's Energy Task Force. Now, after Fribourg, Scalia was once more faced with the dictates of the federal judicial recusal rules that a judge "shall disqualify himself in any proceeding in which his impartiality might reasonably be questioned."[32] But no one really expected Scalia to recuse himself here.[33] And they were right.

After a full six months of speaking and appearing on his contentious "Dead Constitution Tour," Scalia hit bottom. On Sunday, March 26, 2006, Scalia had just left Boston's Catholic Cathedral of the Holy Cross, where, along with six hundred parishioners, including other prominent members of the legal profession, he had attended a Red Mass, a special Catholic Mass dating back to the Middle Ages and meant to bless and guide those who practice the legal profession. As he emerged, waiting for him were two reporters, Peter Smith, a Boston University professor and freelance photojournalist working for the Archdiocese of Boston's weekly newspaper, *The Pilot*; and Laurel Sweet, a reporter from the *Boston Herald*. Upon seeing Scalia, Sweet asked what he would say "to those people who objected to [his] taking part in such public religious ceremonies as the Red Mass [that he] had just attended."[34] Realizing that there was a camera pointed at him, Scalia glared at the lens for a moment, then simultaneously smirked and said, "You know what I say to those people?" With that, he flicked the fingers of his right hand backward from under his chin toward the reporter and photographer.

Just what Scalia said next, and meant by it, as he made the crude Italian gesture became a matter of dispute. According to Sweet, he said, "That's Sicilian. It's none of their business. This is my spiritual life. I shall lead it the way I like."[35] However, the photographer, Smith, recalled Scalia saying, "To my critics, I say, Vaffanculo." While this Italian slang word has many meanings, the most common one is "Fuck you." It was then that Scalia realized his error as he heard the clicking sound signifying that Smith's camera had captured his gesture. Sweet recalled later that a "jocular" Scalia added, "Don't publish that." The photographer later explained, "[Scalia] immediately knew he'd made a mistake, and said, 'You're not going to print that, are you?'" However, the image Smith had captured was just too good not to find its way into print.[36]

The *Boston Herald* decided to print Smith's photo on the front page along with the headline: "THE GESTURE: Obscene? You Be the Judge: The picture justice didn't want to get out." It was a new public relations low for Scalia. Whatever the actual meaning of his Italian chin-flipping gesture, no member of the distinguished United States Supreme Court had ever before been photographed making one.

As he had done before, in complaining about Tony Mauro's critical article on Congress's consideration of a judicial honorarium ban in 2000, Scalia tried to deal with the swirling controversy by sending a letter of protest to the editor of the *Herald*. He began by arguing that the story's claim that he had "made an obscene gesture—inside Holy Cross Cathedral (Boston, Massachusetts), no less," was "false," and so he was asking that the paper reprint his letter in full. In fact, the *Herald* had reported that he had made the gesture "leav[ing]" and "outside of" the cathedral, but that detail did not prevent Scalia from calling the reporter "an up-and-coming 'gotcha' star."[37] Scalia claimed that he "responded, jocularly" with his gesture, and upon "seeing that she did not understand, I said, 'That's Sicilian,' and explained its meaning—which was that I could not care less." Scalia made clear his sense of outrage over what he viewed as a faulty interpretation of his action: "How could your reporter leap to the conclusion (contrary to my explanation) that the gesture was obscene? Alas, the explanation is evident in the following line from her article: '"That's Sicilian," the Italian jurist said, interpreting for the "*Sopranos*" challenged.' From watching too many episodes of the *Sopranos*, your staff seems to have acquired the belief that any Sicilian gesture is obscene—especially when made by an 'Italian jurist.' (I am, by the way, an American jurist.)" When in doubt, the justice liked to turn the tables, this time accusing others of discrimination.

The overwhelming interpretation gleaned from the days-long debate in the press and the blogosphere was that it was an offensive gesture, and inappropriately used by a sitting member of the U.S. Supreme Court, especially while he was coming out of church.[38] While the publication of the photo caused the photographer to lose his job with the church, the controversy made clear once again that Scalia was the poster child for misbehavior and controversy on the United States Supreme Court.[39]

• • •

Only days after the controversial hand signal, the appeal of Salim Ahmed Hamdan was argued before the Court. In another "I couldn't care less" gesture, Scalia resisted the pressure to recuse himself after his comments in Fribourg and chose to hear the case along with his colleagues.

At issue was the portion of the 2002 Authorization for Use of Military Force (AUMF) that granted the president the authority "to use all necessary and appropriate force against those nations, organizations, or persons determined to have planned, authorized, committed or aided the September 11, 2001, al Qaeda terrorist attacks, or harbored such organizations or persons, in order to prevent any future acts of international terrorism against the United States by such nations, organizations or persons."[40] The Bush administration interpreted this congressional resolution to allow indefinite military detention of terrorism suspects without benefit of the protections in the Bill of Rights, and military tribunals to adjudicate such cases, should they ever come to trial.

Hamdan was a Yemeni citizen who had been Osama bin Laden's chauffeur and bodyguard. He was captured on a battlefield in Afghanistan, charged with being an enemy combatant against the United States, and detained at the U.S.-run Guantanamo Bay prison in Cuba. He was held there for over two years before being charged with one count of conspiracy to "commit . . . offenses triable by military commission." Hamdan's appeal claimed that he should not be tried in a military tribunal, but rather in civilian U.S. courts, with all of the rights guaranteed by the United States Constitution.[41]

A preliminary question in the appeal was whether the Supreme Court had jurisdiction. The question arose as the result of the Detainee Treatment Act of 2005 (DTA), passed on December 30, 2005, a law that was designed to compel the military to follow anti-torture guidelines when conducting interrogations. It also stated that "no court, justice, or judge shall have jurisdiction to hear or consider" the *habeas* application of a Guantanamo Bay detainee seeking to bring their case to federal civilian court. If that law was upheld, it would deny the Supreme Court the jurisdiction to hear habeas corpus appeals from Hamdan or prisoners like him in Guantanamo. The four liberals on the Court, together with Anthony Kennedy, in a 5–3 vote (with Roberts not participating), used legislative history to summarily dispose of that argument by saying that the Court had jurisdiction because Hamdan's case was already pending when the DTA was passed.

Moving to the merits of the case, Justice Stevens wrote for the Court that the government had failed to prove its "case for inclusion of conspiracy among those offenses cognizable by law-of-war military commission. . . . Because the charge does not support the commission's jurisdiction, the commission lacks the authority to try Hamdan."[42] The Court majority went on to rule that the president did not meet the requirements for setting up and operating military tribunals during times of armed conflict under the Uniform Code of Military Justice and the Geneva Conventions. After ruling that the Court was not "address[ing] the Government's power to detain [Hamdan] for the duration of active hostilities in order to prevent . . . harm," the majority concluded that "in undertaking to try Hamdan and subject him to criminal punishment, the Executive is bound to comply with the rule of law that prevails in this jurisdiction."[43] Thus, Hamdan might never get his day in court, but if he did, it would be in a civilian court.

Scalia disagreed. He did not even bother with the final disposition of the case because, he argued, the majority's decision on the issue of jurisdiction was "patently erroneous." His reading of the text of the statute denying the Supreme Court's jurisdiction was "unambiguous," leading him to heartily disapprove of the majority's "reliance on the legislative history of the DTA to buttress its implausible reading" that the cases could be reviewed. Once more, Scalia challenged the idea of deciding a case using congressional legislative history comprised of statements, often made by a single senator or representative on the chamber floor, as representative of the entire body with respect to the meaning of a law. As he argued: "Of course this observation, even if true, makes no difference unless one indulges the fantasy that Senate floor speeches are attended (like the Philippics of Demosthenes) by throngs of eager listeners, instead of being delivered (like Demosthenes' practice sessions on the beach) alone into a vast emptiness."[44] By allowing such pending habeas corpus petitions from Guantanamo to be heard in federal court, Scalia maintained, "The Court's interpretation transforms a provision abolishing jurisdiction over *all* Guantanamo-related habeas petitions into a provision that retains jurisdiction over cases sufficiently numerous to keep the courts busy for years to come."[45] Just as he promised in Fribourg months before, Scalia in his official capacity would do nothing on behalf of an enemy that he argued had been shooting at his son on the battlefield.

• • •

Shortly before the Court term ended in June, the new chief justice, John Roberts, made clear his vision for what he wanted his Court to become. Giving the Commencement Address at the Georgetown University Law Center graduation, Roberts argued that the Supreme Court gained more power and prestige from exercising its power by consensus rather than partisan division. Clearly referring to the polarized Court he had joined, Roberts argued that the Court gained more from unanimity in its decision making

> Because there are clear benefits to a greater degree of consensus on the Court. Unanimity, or near unanimity, promote clarity and guidance for the lawyers and for the lower Courts, trying to figure out what the Supreme Court meant. Perhaps most importantly, there are jurisprudential benefits. The broader the agreement among the justices, the more likely it is that the decision is on the narrowest possible ground. It's when the decision moves beyond what's necessary to decide the case that Justices tend to bail out. If it's not necessary to decide more to dispose of a case, in my view it is necessary *not* to decide more.

Drawing on his vast knowledge of the Court's history, Roberts turned to one of the institution's greats to argue that the Court should seek to avoid issuing decisions that it would later have to reverse. "In Felix Frankfurter's words, 'a narrow decision' helps insure that we quote 'not embarrass the future too much.' The rule of law is strengthened when there's greater coherence and agreement about what the law is." In order to promote "broad agreement" on the Court and avoid "embarrass[ing] the future too much," Roberts argued that his role as chief justice was clear:

> In my view the important point is that the key to achieving this broader consensus on a collective and collegial Court does not rest with any individual member, Chief Justice or not, but with the Court as a whole. It is the obligation of each member on the Court to be open to the considered views of the others. We are a collegial and collegiate Court, not simply because we act after voting but because we work together to function as a Court in deciding the cases, and in crafting the opinions.[46]

Scalia did not require a speech to respond. When asked by Jan Crawford Greenburg later that year about Roberts's plea for "more unanimity, more narrow opinions" on the Court, he responded:

> Lots of luck. Of course that's desirable and I think we work hard to achieve it. . . . We work hard, we work hard to do that. Beyond that, you know, you can get more agreement of course by deciding less. If you wanted to decide almost nothing at all, and decide the case on such a narrow ground that it will be of very little use to the bar in the future, you can get nine votes. So, it's really always a tradeoff between how helpful you want the opinion to read, do you want it to take on the big question that's really the source of the disagreement in the lower courts? If you do that, it's going to be harder to get a 9–0 vote. If you want to decide this case based on the little technicalities of this case, you'll decide this case but you won't help the bar at all. . . . I'd rather have a 5–4 or a 6–3 decision that gives that guidance than a 9–0 opinion that doesn't.[47]

Of course, the other reason for the sharply divided Court was the unwillingness by members of the ideologically polarized wings on the Court to compromise on any issue, large or small. And chief among those jurists driving a wedge between the two ideological sides was Antonin Scalia, who would still be going his own way, and brooking no compromise.

CHAPTER 20

Opus SCOTUS

Looking at his colleagues now sitting on either side of him on the Court bench in February 2006, Scalia, the second most senior justice after John Paul Stevens, could see how his professional life had changed. To his immediate right John Roberts sat in the chief justice's center seat, and the Court's newest member, Samuel Alito, sat to Scalia's far left. These two men possessed personalities and philosophies different from those of the justices they replaced.[1] One of them, Alito, was expected to turn some issues that had been tipped by O'Connor toward the liberal side into 5–4 votes for the conservatives.

The other key difference between the two justices, though, was that unlike O'Connor, an Episcopalian, Alito was a conservative Catholic like Scalia. With two other traditional Catholics on the Court, Clarence Thomas and John Roberts, the four justices held the potential to become a powerful religiously conservative voting bloc on social issues. And, even more importantly, together with Anthony Kennedy, for the first time in United States history, there was a majority of Catholics on the Court. None of this escaped the notice of newspaper reporters who filled their publications' pages with articles speculating about the newly emerging "Catholic majority" on the Court.[2]

Just how much religion might guide the votes of Scalia's new colleagues, and what was his potential for leading them, was a matter of simple math for him. Could he and Thomas, who always voted together on moral issues, find three other conservative Catholic votes to finally roll back the precedents on the death penalty, the right to abortion, the right to use contraceptives, and gay rights?

Thomas had reached the Court after a difficult personal struggle. Born in 1948 in the Jim Crow Deep South, Thomas was a teenager when the Vatican II reforms were instituted, and he developed a "love-hate-love" relationship with the Catholic Church. Thomas's tortured spiritual journey led him to become as religiously directed a justice as Scalia, and one of the most conservative jurists ever to serve on the United States Supreme Court.[3]

Thomas was seven years old when he and his younger brother, Myers, were given up by their mother to be raised by their strict Catholic grandparents: Myers "Daddy" and Christine "Aunt Tina" Anderson. Daddy raised the young boys to work hard and know their place in segregated Savannah, Georgia. Thomas with his grandparents attended St. Benedict the Moor, in Savannah, the oldest African American Catholic church in that state.[4] After enrolling in the segregated St. Benedict the Moor grammar school, he was taught by nuns who were strict enough for Daddy's liking, employing corporal punishment. There Thomas became an altar boy. His subsequent education was at conservative St. Pius X High School, the only Catholic high school in the area where African Americans were welcome. When Thomas decided that he would become a priest, he transferred to St. John Vianney Minor seminary in Savannah, where he was one of the first two African Americans to attend.[5]

At nineteen, Thomas entered the Immaculate Conception Seminary in northwest Missouri, but his time there was much briefer than expected. When pacifist civil rights leader Martin Luther King Jr. was shot in 1968, Thomas was horrified that some of his Caucasian classmates expressed the hope that the "son of a bitch died." Thomas not only left the seminary but, disenchanted by the Church's silence on the issues of segregation and discrimination, he began questioning his faith entirely. Abandoning his goal of becoming a priest, he enrolled in the Jesuit College of the Holy Cross in Worcester, Massachusetts.[6] By then Thomas had become, by his own admission, "an angry black man" strongly questioning the Church's views on racism. "During my second week on campus," Thomas later wrote, "I went to Mass for the first and last time at Holy Cross. I don't know why I bothered—probably habit, or guilt—but whatever the reason, I got up and walked out midway through the homily. It was all about Church dogma, not the social problem with which I was obsessed, and seemed to be hopelessly irrelevant."[7]

It would be thirteen years before Thomas would return to the Church. During his time away he joined and left the Black Power movement, became an ultraconservative, adopted Ayn Rand's libertarianism and "objectivism," and followed economist Thomas Sowell's lessons on self-reliance. After marrying his college sweetheart, Kathy Grace Ambush, he attended Yale Law School with the help of an affirmative action program. While there, he and his wife had a son, Jamal Adeen. Upon receiving his law degree, Thomas worked for Missouri attorney general John Danforth. Thereafter, he applied to work at top law firms, but he found that despite his high grades, he could not get a job, leading him to believe that potential employers assumed that he was not as good as his Caucasian Yale classmates. He came to despise affirmative action. "A law degree from Yale meant one thing for white graduates and another for blacks," he once said, adding that his diploma was only worth 15 cents. But not everyone saw him that way. Thomas took a job practicing corporate law at Monsanto in St. Louis, where he interacted well with his Caucasian co-workers. When Danforth was elected senator from Missouri, he offered Thomas a position on his staff in Washington, which Thomas accepted.[8]

By 1981 at age thirty-two, Thomas had lost his way spiritually. He resorted to bouts of heavy drinking and left his wife and son, followed by a divorce, before beginning his long, slow journey back to the Catholic Church. "I was so unhappy that I started going to church again. St. Joseph's on Capitol Hill was only a short walk from my new office . . . though I still couldn't bring myself to go to Sunday Mass. I wasn't yet ready to take that leap of faith."[9]

As one of the few conservative African Americans on Capitol Hill, Thomas was poised to ride the political wave of the incoming Reagan administration. In early 1982, he was named the chairman of the Equal Employment Opportunity Commission. Dealing with the death of both of his grandparents in 1983, and facing what he perceived to be daily attacks on him as a result of his conservative deregulation work in the EEOC, he reconsidered the direction of his life. As he wrote: "My troubles at EEOC had already driven me to my knees, and from there to daily prayer and meditation. Each morning I stopped at a Catholic church on my way to work and asked God for 'the wisdom to know what is right and the courage to do it.' . . . By running away from God, I had thrown away the most important part of my grandparents' legacy."[10]

It was Thomas's 1987 marriage to Virginia "Ginni" Lamp, a devout Methodist, and the support he received over the next few years from Danforth, himself a conservative Episcopal priest, that helped him take the next step. Both helped Thomas to survive his highly charged Supreme Court confirmation hearing following his 1991 nomination to succeed Thurgood Marshall. A partisan Democratic Judiciary Committee hoped to defeat the nomination, and when Thomas was accused of sexual harassment by law professor Anita Hill, the hearings became a televised spectacle. Despite strong feeling on both sides, Thomas was confirmed by the Senate by a vote of 52 in favor, 48 opposed—the closest confirmation in U.S. history. Subsequently, Thomas and his wife became parishioners at a charismatic Episcopal church, where, Thomas later recalled, "At long last, I had found peace." [11]

Thomas's spiritual journey had not yet ended. In the mid-1990s, he was guided back and formally reconciled to the more traditional form of Catholicism by a trio of conservative priests. Opus Dei priest Father C. John McCloskey of Washington led his process of rejoining the Church, aided by Father Paul Scalia, Justice Scalia's son, who "worked behind the scenes" to bring Thomas back to their faith. In addition, Thomas revealed that a Holy Cross classmate, Monsignor Peter Vaghi, then the conservative pastor of Washington's St. Patrick's Church, had been part of this process. [12] This interconnection of the conservative Catholic community in and around the nation's capital linking Justice Thomas and Justice Scalia led the press to take note of the proximity of their conservative religious views. Indeed, it was not uncommon to see the two men walking together to the Supreme Court building after attending Mass on Catholic holy days. [13]

Justice Thomas and his wife became parishioners at the traditionalist Catholic St. Andrew's Church in Clifton, Virginia, where the Tridentine Latin Mass was still celebrated. [14] Thomas made very clear the connection between his devout Catholic faith and his Court work, and his view of his critics in the press and inside the Beltway, by hanging in his Court office a copy of Cardinal Merry del Val's "Litany of Humility," seeking divine help in dealing with persecution. [15] Given the strong similarities in the religious views of Scalia and Thomas, and the place that their faith plays in each man's daily life, it is not hard to see the origins of the many points of agreement in their moral and legal philosophies.

When John Roberts joined the Court in October 2005, the national press took note that he seemed to share Scalia and Thomas's conservative Catholic views. [16] Senator Richard Durbin of Illinois was concerned about this, asking Roberts during a private pre-confirmation meeting what he would do if a divergence existed between his Catholic faith and the demands of the law. Roberts was, in the senator's words, "taken aback and paused for a long time before giving his reply," that he would probably have to recuse himself from the case. This delay in Robert's response concerned both the senator and some journalists. [17]

Like his other conservative colleagues, John Roberts is surrounded by a web of conservative Catholic figures and organizations in the Washington area. At the center of this web is his wife, attorney Jane Sullivan Roberts, who in 1995 joined the Feminists for Life, a group of conservative feminist Catholics who seek to ban abortion by concentrating more on "prevention than rhetoric." Almost immediately, she became a member of the organization's board and offered pro bono legal advice, not an inconsiderable gift from a partner in one of the District of Columbia's elite law firms.[18] Further evidence of Jane Sullivan Roberts's conservative religious views comes from her service on the traditional John Carroll Society's Board of Governors.[19] This organization is devoted to helping Catholic lawyers and politicians in the D.C. area "grow in their faith and inform them, from a Catholic standpoint . . . [and] encourage members to become more active in their particular professions, which, in turn . . . would benefit both the Church and the nation."[20]

Some draw further evidence of the Robertses' views from the fact that after marrying and settling in Maryland they followed the traditional, conservative Catholic pastor of their church—Monsignor Peter Vaghi (who had helped Clarence Thomas return to traditional Catholicism)—from parish to parish, ending up at the Church of the Little Flower in Bethesda, Maryland. While this church does not follow the Tridentine Latin Mass, Monsignor Vaghi's conservative Catholic philosophy has been well reported.[21] He has also served as chaplain for the John Carroll Society since 1987 and through it has created a pro bono legal program. Under Father Vaghi's spiritual leadership, the society has over 1,100 members who "embody the Church's understanding of an active laity as participants engaged in Christian fellowship, heightened prayer life, continued education in the faith, and charitable outreach."[22] There seemed little doubt, based on these personal connections, that when Scalia and Thomas searched for supportive Court votes on fundamentalist Catholic issues, Chief Justice Roberts would be a likely prospect. Realizing this, members of the press expressed concern that with the chief's most important power being the selection of the author of the Court's opinion when he is voting in the majority, Roberts might use this power to move the Court's opinions toward his religious views.[23]

Amassing a controlling majority of Catholic votes on the Court, though, required more allies. That is why Samuel Alito's joining the Court was so significant. Like his personality, which is subdued, during Alito's service as a Court of Appeals judge he observed his religious and moral beliefs in a quiet manner. Alito and his wife, Martha-Ann, were parishioners of Our Lady of the Blessed Sacrament in Roseland Park, New Jersey. They attended

Mass weekly, and his wife taught religious education classes in the parish, where their children were confirmed.[24] Through its stated goal to teach its parishioners how to incorporate Catholicism into their daily lives, the Alitos' New Jersey church's mission statement made clear that it was not the same kind of traditional conservative church as Scalia's St. Catherine's or Thomas's St. Andrew's.[25]

Alito, though, seemed closer to Scalia's and Thomas's conservative religious views personally. Some indication of Alito's traditional Catholic orientation to social issues became evident during his confirmation effort. After his Supreme Court appointment, his ninety-year-old mother, Rose Alito, was quoted as saying, "Of course, he's against abortion."[26] Alito provided support for this view in the form of a memo he wrote in 1985 when he was seeking a promotion in the Justice Department from his job in the Reagan administration solicitor general's office. There he stated that "I am particularly proud of my contributions in recent cases in which the government has argued in the Supreme Court that racial and ethnic quotas should not be allowed and that the Constitution does not protect a right to an abortion."[27]

Whether this statement was made in the hopes of securing a promotion two decades earlier, or whether it was an accurate reflection of his views and thus an indication of his decisions on the twenty-first century Court, was not clear. Those who worked with Alito in various political agencies, though, thought that it reflected his religious conservatism. Joshua Schwartz, a George Washington University Law School professor who worked with Alito in the solicitor general's office, said, "If you asked me to guess what Sam thought about abortion, it's probably the same thing his mother said. But obviously there is a real difference between what Sam Alito thinks is what's right and what's wrong and what does he think the law should be."[28] Beyond this, antiabortion groups drew comfort from Alito's opinion on the Third Circuit Court of Appeals in the landmark *Pennsylvania v. Casey* abortion case, where he was the only dissenter upholding the restrictive Pennsylvania abortion law.[29] Almost immediately after his appointment, some predicted that Alito would become the same kind of originalist as Scalia. That would not prove to be the case, but he did share Scalia's religious views.[30]

This left one more Catholic vote to secure on social issues, and it would be the most problematic. The fifth Catholic on the Court was Anthony Kennedy. When Kennedy was nominated by President Reagan in November 1987, the nature of his Catholic faith was not an issue. Now it became pivotal for the direction of the Court.

Despite being just four months younger than Scalia, and having been raised a Catholic in the pre-Vatican II reform era, Anthony Kennedy's religious views differed from those of the other traditional Catholics on the Court. Reporter Jeffrey Toobin, who observed Kennedy worshipping at Mass in Europe, described him as being "of pre–Vatican II vintage, who went to Mass every Sunday and prayed in the old-fashioned manner, hands clasped before him."[31] But when deciding social issues such as gay rights, Kennedy took a different position from the other Court Catholics.

Kennedy's home in the Land Park section of Sacramento, California, was near the offices of the Archdiocese of Sacramento, where he served as counsel before being appointed to the federal Court of Appeals for the Ninth Circuit.[32] When he attended church, Kennedy went to the Holy Spirit parish, which followed a more modern Catholic approach.[33]

Once in Washington, Kennedy found a Catholic church much like the one he'd left in Sacramento, St. Peter's on Capitol Hill. In addition, Kennedy and his wife went to Salzburg, Austria, every year, and worshipped at a church called Müllner Kirche. After attending Mass with Kennedy there, Toobin recounted that before the German-language Mass began, Kennedy whispered to him, "You won't understand a word, but I find with sermons that's not always a bad thing."[34]

Kennedy's more intellectual approach to his Catholicism allowed him to form his own interpretation of Scripture, rather than relying on a dogmatic pronouncement from the Church. He occasionally took a moderate stance on social issues, such as on the death penalty and gay rights, diverging from his more conservative Catholic colleagues. To Scalia's dismay, this vested considerable political power in Kennedy, allowing him to limit how far the other conservatives—the Catholics—on the Court could go on issues that raised religious dimensions.

The press took notice of Kennedy's pivotal role. In 1992, Richard Reuben from *California Lawyer* said of him, "Kennedy's conservatism was far different from the ideologically driven [Robert] Bork's. Born into Sacramento's upper class, Kennedy offered a pragmatic realism reflecting traditional small-town values." He added that Kennedy "appeared to back away from the judicial activism of Scalia and Rehnquist."[35]

By 1996, Court observer Jeffrey Rosen portrayed Kennedy in *The New Yorker* as "The Agonizer," struggling to deal with a divisive cultural issue in *Romer v. Evans*, a case challenging Colorado's state constitutional amendment restricting gay rights. "He has a self-dramatizing tendency," wrote

Rosen, "which leads him to worry about cases, both in public and in private, and to change his positions after casting his votes." Kennedy told Rosen, "It's easier to be a Rehnquist or a Scalia than a Kennedy."[36]

In 2007, Rosen reassessed Kennedy's work as the swing justice after the retirement of Justice O'Connor. In a *New Republic* article titled "Supreme Leader," and subtitled "The Arrogance of Justice Anthony Kennedy," Rosen argued, "Anthony Kennedy seems most at home when he is lecturing others about morality." Rosen made clear to his readers that he had lost patience with the equivocating process by which Kennedy reached a judicial result: "Kennedy makes a spot judgment about how the world should be, then expresses it as an ideal against which the world must be measured. The problem with Kennedy's snap judgments and sonorous aphorisms is that they often have little to do with reality."[37] Describing him as a jurist who "enjoys the sound of his own voice" and "who claims to worship democracy but, in fact, wants to short-circuit all our most important national debates through his jurisprudence—and then wishes his fellow citizens would applaud when he walks down the street," Rosen argued that Kennedy "has little interest in the views of real people in a real democracy."[38]

Jeffrey Toobin mirrored this intellectual path. In 2007, he praised Kennedy's use of foreign legal sources for writing liberal judicial opinions in an article for *The New Yorker.*[39] But one year later, Toobin came around to Rosen's point of view in his book *The Nine.* He wrote: "Kennedy relished his public role and sought out the opinions that would make the newspapers . . . always labor[ing] most closely on the sections of opinions that might be quoted in the *New York Times.*"[40] While Kennedy clearly relished his ability to tip the majority of the Court on major issues, the press and other commentators, both on the right and the left, did not. Four years later, in 2012, a cover story in *Time* magazine would label Kennedy as America's "uncertain" and "idiosyncratic" swing justice, whose "role . . . on the Supreme Court raises an even larger question. Is there something wrong with a democracy when one person holds so much sway over so many people?"[41]

• • •

This new Catholic majority on the Supreme Court had a chance to exert its influence in April 2007, when the Court faced its first major social issue since O'Connor's departure. After twenty-four years of refusing to carve out from *Roe v. Wade*'s abortion right a categorical ban on any type of abortion, the Court accepted for review the case of *Gonzales v. Carhart*, which challenged the constitutionality of a 2003 federal law banning any partial birth abortion "that is [not] necessary to save the life of a mother." This law was an effort by Congress to reverse the Court's 2000 decision in *Stenberg v. Carhart*, which overturned a nearly identical state partial birth abortion ban. A narrow 5-4 majority led by O'Connor overturned that state's law because its language was vague enough to ban other legal abortion procedures, meaning that it would create an "undue burden" on a woman who had chosen to seek an abortion.[42]

Kennedy had argued vigorously in dissent in that case, opposing partial birth abortion and supporting the Nebraska law, so his alliance with the conservatives in the 5-4 vote in *Gonzales v. Carhart*, and his writing the majority opinion upholding the federal law, was not a surprise. Influenced by a pro-life brief citing women who later came to regret their decision to abort, Kennedy diverted from his three judicial allies in the 1992 *Casey* decision by offering a completely new and seemingly paternalistic standard governing a woman's right to choose abortion:

> Whether to have an abortion requires a difficult and painful moral decision. While we find no reliable data to measure the phenomenon, it seems unexceptionable to conclude some women come to regret their choice to abort the infant life they once created and sustained. Severe depression and loss of esteem can follow. In a decision so fraught with emotional consequence some doctors may prefer not to disclose precise details of the means that will be used, confining themselves to the required statement of risks the procedure entails. . . . The State has an interest in ensuring so grave a choice is well informed.[43]

Given the expansiveness of this "so fraught with emotional consequence" language, it seemed inevitable that the conservative Catholic antiabortion groups would press the Court in future cases to further roll back *Roe v. Wade*. The central issue on that occasion would be how Kennedy, rather than Scalia, responded.

The possible link between the existing Catholic majority on the Court and the reversal in the abortion decision in the *Gonzales v. Carhart* case did not escape notice. A *Philadelphia Inquirer* political cartoonist, Tony Auth, satirized this religious shift in a panel he titled "Church & State," showing the five Catholic justices sitting on the bench wearing mitre hats and looking like a college of cardinals. While Auth portrayed Scalia bearing a wide smirk over this turn of events, it soon became clear that Scalia was not laughing about this message.[44]

The role of the new Catholic majority of the Court in overturning this law raised concerns for one former William Brennan law clerk, University of Chicago Law professor Geoffrey Stone. In a blog posting titled, "Our Faith-Based Justices," Stone noted:

> What, then, explains this decision? Here is a painfully awkward observation: All five justices in the majority in *Gonzales* are Catholic. The four justices who are either Protestant or Jewish all voted in accord with settled precedent. It is mortifying to have to point this out. But it is too obvious, and too telling, to ignore. Ultimately, the five justices in the majority all fell back on a common argument to justify their position. There is, they say, a compelling moral reason for the result in *Gonzales*. Because the [late term abortion procedure] seems to resemble infanticide it is "immoral" and may be prohibited even without a clear statutory exception to protect the health of the woman.

As Stone saw it, these jurists were basing their decisions on their Catholic religious beliefs:

> By making this judgment, these justices have failed to respect the fundamental difference between religious belief and morality. To be sure, this can be an elusive distinction, but in a society that values the separation of church and state, it is fundamental. The moral status of a fetus is a profoundly difficult and rationally unresolvable question. . . . It is not for the state—or for the justices of the Supreme Court—to resolve that question, and it is certainly not appropriate for the state or the justices to resolve it on the basis of one's personal religious faith. . . . As the Court observed fifteen years ago, "Some of us as individuals find abortion offensive to our most basic principles of morality, but that cannot control our decision. Our obligation is to define the liberty of all, not to mandate our own moral code." It is sad that Justices Roberts, Scalia, Kennedy, Thomas and Alito have chosen not to follow this example.[45]

Stone's posting stirred up a storm of controversy among conservatives in the legal academic community. But it also elicited an angry reaction from

Justice Scalia, who never liked his motives to be questioned, especially when those questions revolved around his religious views. Speaking to Court reporter Joan Biskupic, who was then researching a biography on him, Scalia said of Stone's blog:

> Now, he knows that that's a damn lie. . . . [Professor Stone] knows that Tony Kennedy is the fifth vote supporting *Roe v. Wade*. . . . And he knows what my judicial philosophy is and that I take neither side of that. . . . That really got me mad. . . . It got me so mad I will not appear at the University of Chicago until he is no longer on the faculty. . . . What made it so annoying was I had been very pleased and sort of proud that Americans didn't pay any attention to that. It isn't religion that divides us anymore. . . . It didn't bother anybody, but it has to bother this great liberal Geoff Stone.[46]

But Professor Stone was not alone, as the press had also been "pay[ing] attention." There had been articles by the press during the Roberts confirmation, and later during the Alito confirmation, noting the rising number of Catholics on the Court and later that a majority of the Court was now Catholic. And now the *Gonzales* case had shown the effect of that religious divide on the Court.[47] While it could not be proven for certain that religion dictated the Court majority's result in *Gonzales v. Carhart*, its potential influence could no longer be ignored.

By the fall of 2007, Scalia, perhaps seeking to defuse the growing sense of journalistic and public unease about the Catholic majority, agreed to deliver the keynote address for the second annual John F. Scarpa Conference on Law, Politics and Culture at Catholic Villanova University. His subject was "The Role of Catholic Faith in the Work of a Judge."[48] Upon seeing the overflow crowd, Scalia began by saying that he might be "a skunk in a garden party" in arguing "a minimalist view" of the announced topic. "There is no such thing as a 'Catholic Judge,'" he began. "The bottom line is that here Catholic faith seems to me to have little effect on my work as a judge. Just as there is no 'Catholic' way to cook a hamburger. I am really hard-pressed to tell you of a single decision or opinion of mine that would have come out differently if I were not Catholic." Scalia argued that his only religious connection to his work could be found in two Catholic axioms: "Be thou perfect as thy heavenly Father is perfect," and "Thou shalt not lie." Acting in line with these commandments, Scalia explained that he could not "re-characterize earlier cases to say what they should not say," leading him to follow precedent. Accordingly, since "the Constitution says nothing about abortion . . . I see no constitutional right to an abortion, just as I see nothing in there criminalizing or prohibiting abortion. . . . The reality is that the Constitution says nothing about abortion either way and the states are therefore allowed to permit it or to prohibit it."

He urged the largely Catholic audience not to root for any other outcome: "If it's proper for Catholic judges to do that, it's proper for atheistic judges, for secularistic judges, for judges opposed to all Christian and religious beliefs, to do the same thing. And, just between you and me, there are more of them than of us."[49] He added that he could "imagine that there are some cases I could not participate in as a Catholic and as a judge, but I just have not faced that situation yet." This was true, as his audience knew, because Scalia refused to observe the modern Church's views against the death penalty.[50]

But while Scalia did not see himself as a Catholic justice, some members of the Catholic legal theory community did. University of Notre Dame law professor Richard "Rick" Garnett, in the *Mirror of Justice* Catholic law blog, argued:

> To be a Catholic judge . . . is to be a judge in the way a Catholic, *like everyone else*, should be a judge: To take seriously one's obligation to decide impartially, to submit to the rule of law, rather than one's own preferences, and to have an appropriate humility about the task one is charged to perform. Obviously, this is not a *distinctively* Catholic way of judging—I'm not even saying that Catholics are more likely to judge in this way than others are—but it is, I think, the way a Catholic *should* judge. It's also the way Justice Scalia thinks he should judge and, I'm confident, he thinks this way (at least in part) because he is a Catholic.[51]

Villanova law professor Robert Miller responded, "A Catholic judge is not merely a Catholic who is a judge but someone who judges in a way different from other judges precisely because he is Catholic—and this is exactly what Scalia denies he does. There is not a peculiarly Catholic way of judging. And thus Justice Scalia is right when he says, 'There is no such thing as a Catholic judge.'"[52] To which UCLA law professor Stephen Bainbridge offered: "It seems to me Miller and Scalia are both missing something here. As Catholics, we have a moral obligation to avoid formal cooperation with evil. . . . As someone who is both a Catholic and a judge, Scalia is subject to those rules, even if he is otherwise correct that there is no such thing as a 'Catholic judge.'"[53]

Indeed, for Scalia, there were strong similarities between the literal reading of biblical text and the use of historical sources to interpret Scripture in the pre–Vatican II Catholic faith, and the historically based dictionary technique for interpreting the Constitution in his originalist/textualist legal philosophy.[54] Both religious leaders and originalist judges reveal the meaning of these sources while adopting a similar authoritarian relationship to the parishioners and lawyers before them, wrapped in their own sense of certainty. "Anyway, that's my view. And it happens to be correct," Scalia likes to say whenever his interpretation is challenged by others.[55] In sum, pre–Vatican II Catholicism and legal originalism/textualism are so parallel in their analytical approach that by using his originalism theory Scalia could accomplish as a judge all that his religion commanded without ever having to acknowledge using his faith in doing so.

• • •

The possible role of religion on the Supreme Court's decision making would continue to be debated. Two years later, after the appointment of Sonia Sotomayor, another Catholic, but one who was more modern in her decision making, Professor Geoffrey Stone once again noted the effect of the new religious divide on the work of the Court. In a blog post, he argued:

> The ten justices appointed since the 1973 decision in *Roe v. Wade* have cast a total of forty-five votes in cases involving the constitutional right to abortion. Twenty-two of those votes were cast in support of abortion rights (49%); twenty-three were cast to contract abortion rights (51%). . . . [T]he five Catholic justices cast only one vote in support of abortion rights (6%), and sixteen votes to contract abortion rights (94%). The five non-Catholic justices (two Jews and three Protestants) cast twenty-one votes in support of abortion rights (75%), and seven votes to constrict those rights (25%). That's a pretty considerable difference.[56]

Stone was willing to offer that "Perhaps the real explanation for this difference, however, is not religion, but judicial philosophy. That is, perhaps justices appointed by Republican presidents oppose abortion rights, whereas justices appointed by Democratic presidents support them." Thus, Stone concluded:

> Of course, none of this necessarily "proves" anything. The five Catholic justices appointed by Republican presidents since *Roe* often vote together on a range of issues having nothing to do with their religion. Moreover, it is certainly the case that not all Catholic justices oppose the constitutional right to abortion. . . . But *Gonzales* does raise interesting questions about whether and to what extent judges are and should be influenced by their religion, their ethnic background, their race, their life experiences, and their personal values.

He might have also mentioned the justices' gender, for among the males on the Court, only the Catholics consistently opposed abortion rights.

As encouraging as the result in the *Gonzales v. Carhart* case had been for the conservatives, it was not possible for Scalia to get through a summer break without, as had now become his norm, raising some controversy in his off-the-bench activities. During the Court's summer break, he appeared on a panel discussion in Ottawa, Canada, dealing with "terrorism, torture, and the law" at the "Administration of Justice and National Security" conference. The verbal fireworks began after the formal remarks by the members of the panel during the question and answer session when another conference participant, Canadian federal judge Richard Mosley, said, "Thankfully, security agencies in all our countries do not subscribe to the mantra, 'What would Jack Bauer do?'" referring to the hero of the popular American television show *24*.[57] Upon hearing that, Scalia launched into an unexpected defense of the rogue antiterrorism government agent. The justice, it turned out, was a big fan: "Jack Bauer saved Los Angeles! . . . He saved hundreds of thousands of lives!" At that point, Scalia asked: "Are you going to convict Jack Bauer? Say that criminal law is against him? Is any jury going to convict Jack Bauer? I don't think so! . . . So the question is really whether we believe in these absolutes. And ought we to believe in these absolutes." Once more, the justice seemed to cross an ethical line when he said, "I don't care about holding people. I really don't."

Unless the personnel on the Court changed, it would be left to the voters in the presidential election in 2008 to determine the future direction of the Court and Scalia's role on it.

CHAPTER 21

The Rock Star of One First Street

As the color of the leaves began to change in the autumn of 2007, law bloggers, the network of law school professors and lawyers posting on the internet, were the first to notice that the title of "leading conservative on the
Supreme Court" seemed to be shifting. Press reports on Scalia had slowed
to a trickle, while coverage of Clarence Thomas had exploded. One trigger for this change was the publication on October 1, 2007, of Thomas's
compelling autobiography, *My Grandfather's Son*, which had been the source
of considerable discussion since reporters learned that he had been paid a
reported $1.5 million for the book.[1] With its publication, the man who re-
mained almost entirely silent during Supreme Court oral arguments was
talking everywhere, publicizing his new book while journalists and critics
debated its merits.

My Grandfather's Son turned out to be remarkably candid and informa-
tive. The book presented a Horatio Alger success story of a desperately poor
African American boy on the fringes of the segregated society in America's
Deep South who rises to the top of his profession by means of his own intellect and relentless hard work. It also tells a story of personal redemption. For
a Supreme Court justice to have written such a revealing book was remarkable. But for the normally silent and reclusive Clarence Thomas to have
done so, and now be promoting it, became the law story of the year.

For those who failed at first to notice the book, they could not avoid his
whirlwind media tour beginning in late September. On September 27, he
did a rare hourlong radio interview with Rush Limbaugh, who asked questions so supportive that they made him seem like Thomas's publicist. Three
days later, on September 30, CBS TV aired Thomas's revealing two-segment
interview with Steve Kroft on *Sixty Minutes*.[2]

But with positive press for the new book growing, the next phase of the media tour began with a multi-part interview by ABC news legal corre-spondent Jan Crawford Greenburg.[3] In one of those reports for ABC News, Greenburg described Thomas as "one of the most complex, divisive figures in modern life" and "a really maligned and misunderstood justice."[4] Conser-vative TV talk show host Sean Hannity was equally supportive of the justice and his memoir when he interviewed Thomas for Fox News on October 7.[5] Then, after just a week, with the exception of a speech and book-signing at the conservative legal Federalist Society's 2007 National Lawyers Conven-tion and an occasional appearance at one of their regional meetings around the country to sign some books, the Thomas book tour was over.

Despite its brevity, the intense media blitz for the memoir was remark-ably successful. The book rose simultaneously to near the top of the sales charts for *The New York Times, Publishers Weekly,* the Associated Press, Amazon.com, and other national bestseller lists, to the point that even the critical articles about the tour served to help the publicity machine. Thomas's new media blitz also had a powerfully positive impact on the conservative movement's perception of him.

Thomas's success with the book meant that Scalia now faced the prospect of sharing the spotlight with the much younger and even more conservative Thomas. For years Scalia had been separating himself from Thomas's anti–*stare decisis* approach to decision making based on Thomas's form of origi-nalism derived from the Declaration of Independence. In an interview with National Public Radio, Scalia said: "You can't reinvent the wheel. You've got to accept the vast majority of prior decisions. . . . I do not argue that all of the mistakes made in the name of the so-called living constitution be ripped out. I just say, 'Let's cut it out. Go back to the good, old dead Constitution.'"[6] Speaking of Thomas's willingness to use his approach to overturn longtime precedents, Scalia added, "I am a textualist. I am an originalist, but I am not a nut."[7]

At seventy-one, and about to begin his twenty-first term on the Court in October 2007, Scalia was the second-longest-serving and second-oldest mem-ber, after liberal John Paul Stevens. Among the conservatives, Scalia's mortal-ity was evident to everyone. Anthony Kennedy was also seventy-one, with Thomas being just fifty-nine, Alito fifty-seven, and Chief Justice Roberts only fifty-two. The Court's two newest appointees had added a pair of conservative votes to the body, with neither man calling himself an originalist, so Scalia's new mission seemed to be solidifying his future legacy on the Court.

While Scalia saw nothing in Clarence Thomas's publicity barrage to compel any immediate alterations in year three of his "Dead Constitution Tour," in mid-March 2008 an unexpected event soon changed the political landscape. Six days after Senator John McCain had secured the presidential nomination for the Republican Party, conservative opinion leaders began turning their attention to the question of who would be the party's nominee for vice president. Knowing that McCain's history and reputation as an independent-minded maverick would not energize the party's conservative base, and with polls showing that moderate voters were shifting toward the Democratic Party, conservative opinion leader Bill Kristol, founder and editor of the conservative *Weekly Standard* magazine, wrote an op-ed piece for *The New York Times* entitled "McCain's Daunting Task." The article listed several names for consideration as vice presidential nominees.[8] Kristol's provocative list of "bold" and "unorthodox" vice presidential choices included Democrat-turned-Independent Connecticut senator Joe Lieberman and Iraq War commanders General David Petraeus and General Raymond Odierno. Then he counseled McCain to "persuade the most impressive conservative in public life, Clarence Thomas, to join the ticket." Putting aside the fact that Thomas was unlikely to accept such an offer and resign his life appointment to the Supreme Court, the comment had much larger ramifications for Scalia. Then seventy-two, the same age as McCain, by not being mentioned, even in passing, by Kristol, it seemed that the mantle of "conservative leader on the Court" was passing to Thomas.

Scalia needed a new media platform to restore his place in the conservative pantheon. In February 2008, Scalia traveled to London to address the London School of Economics and be interviewed on the BBC Radio 4 program *Law in Action*. Once more, his off-the-cuff remarks about current legal issues stirred controversy. After a lengthy conversation with host Clive Coleman on the topic of interpreting the Constitution using originalism, the discussion ventured into Scalia's views on the use of torture in the Bush administration's "War on Terrorism."

"Tell me about the issue of torture," Coleman began. "We know that cruel and unusual punishment is prohibited under the 8th Amendment. Does that mean that if the issue comes up before the Court it's a 'no brainer'?"[9] Scalia ignored the wisdom of avoiding such discussions and responded:

> Well a lot of people think it is, but I find that extraordinary. . . . Is it really so easy to determine that smacking someone in the face to find out where he has hidden the bomb that is about to blow up Los An-

geles is prohibited by the Constitution? Because smacking someone in the face would violate the 8th Amendment in a prison context. You can't go around smacking people about. Is it obvious that what can't be done for punishment can't be done to exact information that is crucial to the society? I think it's not at all an easy question to tell you the truth.

Clearly taken aback by his judicial guest's argument that governmental torture may *not* be "cruel and unusual punishment," Coleman responded: "It's a bizarre scenario because very likely you're going to have the one person who can give you the information and so if you use that as an excuse to permit torture, it seems perhaps that's a dangerous thing." But Scalia was unwilling to back off here, becoming even more graphic:

I don't even think something under the fingernails, [or] smacking him in the face, it would be absurd to say you couldn't do that. And once you acknowledge that we're into a different game. How close does the threat have to be? And how severe can the infliction of pain be? I don't think these are easy questions at all, in either direction, but I certainly know you can't come in smugly, and with great self-satisfaction and say, "Oh it's torture and therefore it's no good." You would not apply that in some real-life situations. It may not be a ticking bomb in Los Angeles but it may be where is this group that we know is plotting some very, uh, painful action against the United States. Where are they? What are they currently planning?

Scalia's remarks were reminiscent of his comments the previous summer in the Ottawa "Administration of Justice and National Security" conference in defense of the enhanced interrogation techniques of the television character Jack Bauer.[10] This time, though, his comments were no longer a discussion of a fictional television character. Rather, they were tied to issues that had already been considered and legislated by the United States Congress in the form of an anti-torture amendment sponsored by Senator John McCain, himself a victim of torture as a POW in the Vietnam War, which banned such action by military personnel in the Guantanamo prison. While President Bush's signing statement indicated some doubt whether he would enforce the law in question, Scalia's comments here could be seen as a preview of his likely vote should it be tested in court. If so, some might argue that Scalia should recuse himself from all such cases. His refusal to do so in the Cheney duck hunting espisode and following his War on Terror comments in Fribourg made clear that Scalia believed he had the right to speak as he wished off the Court without worrying about recusal.

Again, there was an outcry over Scalia's comments. "US Top Court's Scalia Defends Physical Interrogation," said Reuters.[11] "Scalia: Smacking Someone in the Face Could Be Justified," said the online *Wall Street Journal*.[12] In a separate report, the Associated Press added the incident to a growing list in a chart titled: "A Glance at Scalia Controversies."[13] The left-wing National Lawyers Guild called for Scalia to recuse himself from any cases that dealt with interrogation in the "War on Terror."[14]

Legal academics lined up for another round of Scalia bashing. On the *Mirror of Justice* Catholic legal theory blog, Notre Dame law professor Rick Garnett wrote, "I would rather Justice Scalia not amuse himself by being quite as candid and provocative as, it seems, he likes to be."[15] Legal ethics expert Steven Lubet of Northwestern Law School echoed these sentiments elsewhere: "It's extremely unusual for a justice to be so opinionated about a controversy that may well come before the court,"[16] George Washington University law professor Jonathan Turley viewed the behavior in a larger context, saying, "At times, Justice Scalia seems to follow Oscar Wilde's rule that the only way to be rid of temptation is to yield to it. . . . He is a brilliant jurist, even if you don't agree with his views. His greatest liability has always been a lack of self-control when it comes to public statements."[17] Later, Turley would write that Scalia had become the nation's "first real celebrity justice."[18]

Meanwhile, just four days before Scalia gave his "pro-torture" interview, the National Conference of Catholic Bishops had released an "Action Alert" to its followers to "URGE YOUR SENATORS TO EXPAND THE BAN ON TORTURE"—to get senators to sign on to an anti-torture provision in the Intelligence Authorization Act for FY 2008. The move was designed to close a loophole left from the McCain anti-torture amendment, that had been passed two years earlier, by extending it to cover U.S. intelligence agencies or their agents beyond the military at Guantanamo. The Conference's press release cited prevailing Church doctrine: "Torture is abhorrent in the eyes of the Church as it undermines and debases the dignity of both victims and perpetrators. Pope Benedict XVI said, 'I reiterate that the prohibition against torture cannot be contravened under any circumstance.' . . . We urge Senators to adopt this legislation as it is consistent with the Church's belief in human dignity and because it would allow the U.S. to regain the moral high ground and restore our credibility in the international community."[19] Indeed, the Catholic Catechism states: "Torture which uses physical or moral violence to extract confessions, punish the guilty, frighten opponents, or satisfy hatred is contrary to respect for the person and for human dignity."[20] The Church placed torture in the same category as kidnapping, hostage taking, terrorism, and "amputations, mutilations, and sterilizations performed on innocent people."

None of this seemed to bother Scalia, who had already made clear in the death penalty discussion five years earlier that he was free to disregard Church teaching that was not compulsory. Scalia argued again that this anti-torture policy was not issued by the pope *ex cathedra*, compelling followers to observe it, but rather was offered as a guide for the faithful. Congress passed the anti-torture amendment as part of the appropriation bill only to have President Bush veto the spending measure in March 2008 because of its inclusion.

By that time, though, Scalia was on to other more pressing personal business. He had a book of his own. *Making Your Case: The Art of Persuading Judges*, written with Bryan Garner, the *Black's Law Dictionary* editor-in-chief and expert on legal writing and legal argumentation, was about to be released. This book was a primer for attorneys and law students on oral and written appellate argumentation. Published by a legal academic publisher, Thomson West, this volume discussed 115 useful tips for legal advocates, ranging in length from one to several paragraphs, and organized into three sections, "General Principles of Argumentation," "Legal Reasoning," and "Oral Argument."[21]

Seeking to publicize his new work, Scalia began his book tour by making an appearance on the same program where Thomas had appeared, *60 Minutes*. There he was interviewed by Lesley Stahl, who served more as his cheerleader than the harder-edged Steve Kroft had been when he interviewed Thomas. Describing Scalia as "one of the most brilliant and combative justices ever to sit on the Court" and "one of the most prominent legal thinkers of his generation," Stahl explained that this interview was supposed to be about Scalia's new book but that after several discussions "our story grew" into "his first major television interview." So like Thomas, Scalia would receive an unusual two segments on the program, the first on the book and his views regarding constitutional theory and cases, and the second offering new details on his life story.[22]

Unlike the combative, pugnacious image that Thomas projected in his *60 Minutes* appearance, a smiling and eminently accessible Scalia so charmed Stahl that she described him as "a man so unpretentious and down-to-earth you could forget he sits on the Supreme Court." It was a masterful performance, giving no hint of the overbearing "Evil Nino" and "Ninopath" who bullied attorneys in oral argument, attacked judicial colleagues in his opinions, or scowled at critical members of the press and limited their access to his appearances. Rather, the *60 Minutes* viewers met the charming, charismatic, piano-playing "Tony" Scalia of his Georgetown University dramatic acting days. Standing in the hallway of his old elementary school, being "grilled" by Stahl about his claim that he had gotten straight As there, Scalia smiled and put his right hand in the air as if taking an oath while saying, "Would I lie? . . . If you can't trust me, who can you trust, right?"

Stahl would correctly say of Scalia, "What stands out is his sharp intelligence and street-fighter personality," adding that he possessed a "certainty and feistiness his fellow justices come up against every day." Stahl explored this with Scalia in asking, "What's interesting is how you appear in person and the image that you have. The writings are often combative and your friends say that you're charming and fun." To which Scalia responded, "I can be charming and combative at the same time. What's contradictory between the two? I love to argue. I've always loved to argue. And I love to point out the weaknesses of opposing arguments. It may well be that I'm something of a shin-kicker. It may well be that I'm something of a contrarian." Later in the program, he delighted Stahl when he said lightheartedly of his debates with colleagues, "I attack ideas, I don't attack people. Some very good people have some very bad ideas. And if you can't separate the two you've got to get another day job. You don't want to be a judge, at least not a judge on a multi-member panel." This denial of ever attacking his colleagues in an *ad hominem* manner would certainly come as a surprise to those who read his judicial opinions opposing Justices Sandra Day O'Connor and Anthony Kennedy. But the viewers of the *60 Minutes* interview saw Scalia at his charming best.[23]

Two days later, Scalia was the subject of a three-part interview on NPR with Nina Totenberg, where he told the reporter: "I'm not as much of a big loser as I used to be if you want to keep score. . . . You know, winning and losing, that's never been my objective. It's my hope that in the fullness of time, the majority of the court will come to see things as I do."[24] Contrary to the earlier claim by Bill Kristol, Totenberg said to Scalia that he was "so beloved by the political right that some conservatives dream[ed] of him as a vice presidential candidate with John McCain." A clearly pleased Scalia responded with a huge guffaw. "For one thing, Senator McCain's—one of the accomplishments he was proudest of was McCain-Feingold, campaign financing reform, and I thought the whole thing was unconstitutional. The court approved it but not with my blessing. So you know, when someone—what should I say—disparages what you think is your life's principal achievement, you're not likely to want him to be on your presidential ticket. Besides which, ask—come on. Ask my wife. I'd be a lousy politician. I might say what I thought. . . . And that's not what politicians should do."[25] In another appearance, Scalia told a group of high school students from Virginia that being on the Supreme Court was not the kind of life that he set out to lead. When asked what he liked least about being a justice, Scalia said, not at all convincingly, that he did not like "being a public figure, which I never set out to do."[26] But his behavior suggested otherwise.

The opening of Scalia's new publicity tour did not go unnoticed. Reporter Jim Oliphant of the *Chicago Tribune* posted on his website an entry titled "Justice Scalia Launches a Charm Offensive." He began: "There's Antonin Scalia chatting with Lesley Stahl on '60 Minutes.' There's Scalia speaking at length on National Public Radio. And there he is again, taking questions from high school students on C-SPAN. Picture Greta Garbo joining Facebook and you get the idea." For Oliphant, all of this new press attention was no coincidence: "Until now, the Supreme Court justice has been notoriously allergic to the press. But this apparently is a new day, and not just for Scalia, but for other members of the high court," a reference to the appearances by the normally reclusive Clarence Thomas in association with the publication of his autobiography.[27]

Following his *60 Minutes* interview, Scalia launched into what one legal blogger called "The Scalia Road Show," by reprising the same story line with some new highly quotable or autobiographical statement for every television and radio host who would have him.[28] On his show for MSNBC, Tim Russert tried to make some news by pressing on an issue that had been raised the previous fall: "You went to Villanova University in Philadelphia recently and said there's no such thing as a Catholic judge. You happen to be Catholic. Explain why there's no such thing as a Catholic judge." Scalia responded:

How does my religion have anything to do with what those words [in the Constitution] mean and what they were understood to mean by the people who ratified them? Obviously nothing at all. . . . Now,

I have to say that if you have a different judicial philosophy, if you believe that the Constitution changes—never mind what the people thought it meant when they ratified it—you think it changes, the so-called living Constitution. . . . Living and breathing. I would find it very hard to keep my own philosophy, which includes my religion, out of my decisions, because I'm asking myself, what should the Constitution mean? And that has to be informed by my own philosophy, my own theology.[29]

Russert pressed further, asking whether it was possible that there was a link between Scalia's religion and the type of philosophy that guided his decision making. "You describe yourself as an originalist," Russert began. "Which means?" Scalia responded: "Which means I give the Constitution its original meaning. And what it prohibited then it prohibits now. And what it permitted then it permit[s] now. So, you know, for example, the death penalty. If you're an originalist, the issue of whether the death penalty is unconstitutional is really a non-issue."

"Why?" asked Russert.

"Because it is—it was—it was the only penalty for a felony at the time the Constitution was adopted. Nobody ever thought that the Constitution branded the death penalty as cruel and unusual punishment. It just didn't," responded Scalia.

"Is it different for Catholic legislators when the church will say you should not be voting for abortion rights, or the church feels this way on the issue of stem-cell research or the death penalty than it is for a Catholic judge?" asked Russert.

To which Scalia conceded: "It may well be. I've always been happy that I'm a judge. And all I have to do is look at the law. What does it say? Tell the truth about what it says, and that's my job. It would be harder for me as a legislator."

But Russert did not ask the next question. If one is "legislating" from the bench with his conservative "originalist" philosophy, as many Scalia critics attack him for doing, could it not be said that the choice of "originalism," or the "return to the sources" of the Constitution, was in fact a product of his Catholic faith?[30]

While Thomas's book tour had lasted only a week, Scalia's was now well into its second month. He made the rounds of Federalist Society chapters around the country, signed books, and took the opportunity to expand on his personal narrative. Legal blogger David Lat, who attended one such session, wrote that Scalia was "the Rock Star of One First Street," referring to the D.C. address of the Supreme Court.[31]

After so many stops on this book tour, it was left to the incomparable PBS interviewer Charlie Rose to elicit the most revealing insight from Scalia.[32] After a lengthy conversation on Scalia's originalism, his decisions in key cases, the nature of the job on the Supreme Court, and life with his judicial colleagues, Rose took the discussion in a completely different direction, asking Scalia to name his favorite opera. After hemming and hawing a bit, Scalia said, "I like *Der Rosenkavalier*," a German comic opera by Richard Strauss that is based on a pair of French comedies by Louvet de Couvrai and Molière. Rose could not get Scalia to agree that this opera, or any other opera, was "his story" because, to him, most operas were "silly stories." Which Shakespearean character, then, Rose pressed, "resonates most with you?" At this point, Scalia grew a bit somber and, going beyond Shakespeare to all literature, said, "A character I would like to be—we were just talking before this session. . . . I would like to be Thomas More in *A Man for All Seasons*." Rose seized on the opening for a deeper understanding of the justice sitting before him, asking, "Why is that?"

The choices for Scalia were compelling: was it the legal courage or the determined religious posture of the patron saint of lawyers that most appealed to him? Did Scalia see himself as the lord chancellor for Henry VIII of England, acknowledged by many as the most accomplished legal mind of that time? Or did he see himself as the martyred religious zealot who had overseen the burning of so many at the stake for heresy and who was eventually accused of high treason? Scalia chose the latter view, responding: "Because he knew what he believed and he sacrificed everything, including his head, for what he believed." Then the justice offered an even more candid answer:

> That, plus the fact—you know, what *A Man for All Seasons* is about—
> he was a Catholic as I am. . . . And that's what he died for. But the
> play wasn't so much about a Catholic as it was about a lawyer. The
> man loved the law and saw the importance of the law, even to defend
> ideas that he didn't agree with. And it's a great play. And . . . my fa-
> vorite and if there's a character in—well, he is the character in litera-
> ture. He's the character in life that. . . . I would like to be as—which
> I'm not of course—as great as it would be, More.

Antonin Scalia aspired to be America's Sir Thomas More, a principled lawyer and a Catholic. He was willing to fight to the death for his originalism and textualism cause. In his own way, Scalia was "A Justice for All Seasons."

These comments made sense of something that C-SPAN's Brian Lamb had already uncovered in his televised interview with Scalia.[33] The two men were old friends, having worked together in 1971 in the Nixon administration's Office of Telecommunications Policy. At the end of their wide-ranging discussion about the new book, Lamb asked about the large oil portrait of Scalia by the renowned American portraitist Nelson Shanks then sitting on a tripod in the middle of one of the Supreme Court's conference rooms where they were filming. The justice was portrayed sitting at his desk and wearing his opened judicial gown over a blue shirt and red tie. Scalia explained, "That is a—it's a tradition at the court to have the law clerks of a justice commission a portrait which will be hung at the court when the justice dies or retires, and that portrait has to be made before he dies or retires, needless to say."

Lamb pressed: "What's there on the right where your hand—what's your hand on?"

To which Scalia responded: "My hand is on a kind—if you get real close, you can see the title, it's *The Federalist,* and above that is *Webster's Second International Dictionary.*" (Scalia does not like *Webster's Third International Dictionary,* which describes how people actually defined and spelled words as opposed to how they should do so as prescribed by the second edition.) Both of these volumes under his hand symbolized his "originalism" and "textualism" theories. But there was more, the justice explained: "And behind that is the wedding portrait of Maureen, and down at the bottom is a well-known portrait of Thomas More who's one of my heroes." So central was More to Scalia that artist Nelson Shanks had included, under the stack of books, the top of Hans Holbein's portrait of More, showing only More's head and shoulders.[34]

By mid-2008 some members of the press had grown unhappy with the Scalia road show. Court reporter Dahlia Lithwick of *Slate* and *Newsweek* wrote in a piece titled "Justice Scalia, Unplugged" that the justice "seems comfortable marinating in his own rightness."[35] Of Scalia's many media interviews, Lithwick said, "This is extraordinary exposure for Scalia, who has always been more comfortable lobbing his intellectual grenades in closed speeches, written opinions or inimitable comedic performances at the court's oral argument sessions." By now, this had become a conscious strategy for Scalia. As he explained to Brian Lamb in their interview:

> I've sort of come to the conclusion that that old common law tradition of judges not making public spectacles of themselves and hiding in the grass has just broken down. It's no use, I'm going to be a public spectacle whether I come out of the closet or not. . . . So if, you know, I am going to be a public figure, I guess the public may as well get their notion of me firsthand rather than filtered through people such as Brian Lamb. . . . At the urging of friends and family members, I've decided to be less reclusive.[36]

In doing so, Scalia either did not seem to be aware or did not want to admit that *he* had largely been responsible, through appearances such as this one, for the breakdown of "that old common law tradition of judges not making public spectacles of themselves and hiding in the grass."

Scalia did not discuss the significant financial benefits available to him, over and above his annual Supreme Court salary of between $194,000 and $213,900, for writing books and making public appearances.[37] In his annual financial disclosure forms, required by the Ethics in Government Act, Scalia reported that he had earned an additional $67,900 between 2004 and 2006 for teaching legal seminars and would receive another $121,900 for teaching such seminars between 2007 and 2011. During this latter period, when he was writing and publishing his book, he would receive an additional $310,000 in book advances and royalties.[38] Beyond the additional money, by shaping his public image this way, he continued to solidify the reputation that he had wrested away from Robert Bork in 1986—King of the Originalists. The cases then under consideration by the Court that term would offer him the chance to enhance his status.

CHAPTER 22

King of the Originalists

Three decisions announced by the Court in the spring of 2008 enabled Scalia to reestablish himself as the "King of the Originalists." The first of these decisions, *Baze v. Rees*, which was announced on April 16, challenged the use of a lethal injection consisting of a three-drug "cocktail," including a powerful paralytic called pancuronium bromide, as an alternative to electrocution in death penalty cases. Two death row inmates, Ralph Baze and Thomas Bowling, alleged that lethal injections caused so much pain for the paralyzed and dying inmate that they constituted cruel and unusual punishment in violation of the Eighth Amendment. Speaking for the seven-justice majority in upholding the lethal injection, Chief Justice Roberts noted that thirty-six states and the federal government used lethal injections to administer the death penalty. Acknowledging the existing test of whether the form of executing the death penalty was "objectively intolerable," the majority was still willing to allow it.[1]

Scalia and liberal John Paul Stevens dueled in separate concurring opinions over the originalism versus the living Constitution theories with respect to the constitutionality of the death penalty. On the lethal injection issue, Justice Stevens argued that the use of the paralytic drug was cruel and unusual punishment, because "it masks any outward sign of distress, [and thus] . . . creates a risk that the inmate will suffer excruciating pain before death occurs." He explained that since, "several states—including Kentucky—have enacted legislation prohibiting use of the drug in animal euthanasia. . . . It is unseemly—to say the least—that Kentucky may well kill petitioners using a drug that it would not permit to be used on their pets."[2]

Using his version of the evolving standards of decency test, Stevens concluded that if retribution is the stated justification for the death penalty, the decision to use the three-drug lethal cocktail to mask the pain of the injection was inconsistent with that goal: "[B]y requiring that an execution be relatively painless, we necessarily protect the inmate from enduring any punishment that is comparable to the suffering inflicted on his victim." This, for Stevens, "actually undermines the very premise on which public approval of the retribution rationale is based."[3]

In questioning the justification for the death penalty, Stevens was standing on the shoulders of five of his former judicial colleagues—Byron White, Lewis Powell, William Brennan, Thurgood Marshall, and most recently Harry Blackmun—all of whom had called for a total reexamination of the constitutionality of the death penalty.[4] Stevens was concerned about the harmful public policy implications here: "the danger of discriminatory application" of the death penalty, its "excessiveness" in use, "the risk of error in capital cases," and judicial "procedures that provide less protections to capital defendants than to ordinary offenders." Despite his wholehearted opposition to the death penalty and the use of the three-drug cocktail, Stevens decided for this case "to respect precedents that remain part of our law" and refused to overturn Kentucky's lethal injection law.[5]

While they agreed on the result in this case, Scalia dismissed Stevens's arguments for ending the use of this form of the death penalty or the death penalty itself. Stevens's approach, Scalia began, "is insupportable as an interpretation of the Constitution, which generally leaves it to democratically elected legislatures rather than courts to decide what makes a significant contribution to social or public purposes. Besides that more general proposition, the very text of the document recognizes that the death penalty is a permissible legislative choice."[6] As he had been doing in his public speeches for years, Scalia argued that the Eighth Amendment was never intended to ban the death penalty.[7]

Scalia was unmoved by what he termed his colleague's "astounding position" that the costs of the death penalty outweighed its benefits because its deterrence value could not be proven and did not satisfy its purpose of retribution. Scalia had little respect for any of Stevens's arguments:

> The experience of the state legislatures and the Congress—who retain the death penalty as a form of punishment—is dismissed as "the product of habit and inattention rather than an acceptable deliberative process." . . . The experience of social scientists whose studies indicate that the death penalty deters crime is relegated to a footnote. . . . The experience of fellow citizens who support the death penalty is de-

scribed, with only the most thinly veiled condemnation, as stemming from a "thirst for vengeance." . . . It is Justice Stevens' experience that reigns over all.[8]

To the contrary, Scalia, relying on his "enduring Constitution" to rule on this issue, reached what he argued was a higher truth—this should not be the role of judges: "I take no position on the desirability of the death penalty, except to say that its value is eminently debatable and the subject of deeply, indeed passionately, held views—which means, to me, that it is preeminently not a matter to be resolved here. And especially not when it is explicitly permitted by the Constitution."[9]

Nearly two months later, the Court ruled in the case of *Boumediene v. Bush* on the issue of whether alien enemy combatants captured on the battlefields of Iraq and Afghanistan and being detained in Guantanamo's prison had the constitutional right of habeas corpus. If a petition for habeas corpus were granted, it would enable those prisoners to remove their cases from the investigatory military commissions governed by military law, to be tried in federal civilian court, thus affording them American constitutional protections. At its core, this case, like the *Hamdan* case in 2006, called into question Congress's Authorization for Use of Military Force of 2001, including the powers to impose unlimited and secret detention. While these appeals were working their way to the Supreme Court for final resolution, Congress had tried to remove these and other anti-terrorism cases from the jurisdiction of the federal courts by passing the Detainee Treatment Act of 2005.

The real issue was the Suspension Clause in Article I, Section 9, Clause 2, of the Constitution, reading that only Congress has the right to suspend the writ of habeas corpus when during "Rebellion or Invasion the public Safety may require it." It was this provision that Abraham Lincoln had ignored during the Civil War, imposing his own order for martial law in Maryland and leading to the military arrest of a Southern-sympathizing soldier named John Merryman. Lincoln then refused to observe an order by Supreme Court Chief Justice Roger Brooke Taney to release the man, an action later ruled unconstitutional by the Court.[10] But that case dealt with an American citizen imprisoned in domestic territory, while *Boumediene* dealt with whether the Constitution applied to alien enemy combatants who were captured on the international field of battle and imprisoned indefinitely. Could Congress deny them the right to petition for habeas corpus?

Anthony Kennedy joined the Court's four liberals and wrote the majority opinion in favor of Lakhar Boumediene. After arguing that the Court did have sufficient jurisdiction to decide this case despite the Detainee Treatment Act, the majority ruled that the Defense Department did not possess the sole power to determine an enemy combatant's status and enforce the unlimited detention of suspects. Kennedy reviewed various Founding Era sources to demonstrate that such prisoners were protected by habeas corpus. Interpreting the same kinds of historical sources used by Scalia but reaching an opposite result, Kennedy wrote: "The Framers viewed freedom from unlawful restraint as a fundamental precept of liberty, and they understood the writ of habeas corpus as a vital instrument to secure that freedom. Experience taught, however, that the common-law writ all too often had been insufficient to guard against the abuse of monarchial power. That history counseled the necessity for specific language in the Constitution to secure the writ and ensure its place in our legal system."[11] Kennedy relied on his interpretation of this same history to explain the limits for suspending that right: "That the Framers considered the writ a vital instrument for the protection of individual liberty is evident from the care taken to specify the limited grounds for its suspension. . . . Surviving accounts of the ratification debates provide additional evidence that the Framers deemed the writ to be an essential mechanism in the separation-of-powers scheme." For him, there was "the need for structural barriers against arbitrary suspensions of the writ."[12]

Based on this historical understanding, Kennedy and the majority concluded that the habeas corpus rights extended to the alien enemy combatants in the *Boumediene* case and that they had not been lawfully suspended. Since, by treaty with Cuba, the area where the Guantanamo Bay prison was located was "under the complete and total control of . . . [the United States] Government," the Constitution and the federal judiciary had "full effect at Guantanamo Bay." Only if Congress suspended by law the writ of habeas corpus for those prisoners could they be denied judicial remedies. As a result, Kennedy ruled: "Petitioners, therefore, are entitled to the privilege of *habeas corpus* to challenge the legality of their detention."[13] As to the overall issue of the effect of this ruling on the president's powers in the nearly decade-long "War on Terror," Kennedy argued on behalf of the importance of judicial review: "Within the Constitution's separation-of-powers structure, few exercises of judicial power are as legitimate or as necessary as the responsibility to hear challenges to the authority of the Executive to imprison a person. Some of these petitioners have been in custody for six years with no definitive judicial determination as to the legality of their detention. Their access to the writ is a necessity to determine the lawfulness of their status, even if, in the end, they do not obtain the relief they seek."[14] For Kennedy, the key point was the vitality and applicability of the Constitution, even during crisis times: "The laws and Constitution are designed to survive, and remain in force, in extraordinary times. Liberty and security can be reconciled; and in our system they are reconciled within the framework of the law. The Framers decided that habeas corpus, a right of first importance, must be a part of that framework, a part of that law."[15]

Scalia, always an advocate for the broad use of presidential and national governmental power in dealing with threats, argued in dissent that "the writ of *habeas corpus* does not, and never has, run in favor of aliens abroad." Scalia took "judicial notice" that "America is at war with radical Islamists." That said, he became particularly brutal toward Kennedy, the man he had been attacking personally in judicial opinions for so many years: "The game of bait-and-switch that today's opinion plays upon the Nation's Commander in Chief will make the war harder on us. It will almost certainly cause more Americans to be killed."[16]

Scalia argued that by extending the habeas corpus rights to the enemy on the battlefield, federal judges might "impose a higher standard of proof (from foreign battlefields) than the current procedures require, [and] it would mean that the number of the enemy returned to combat will obviously increase."[17] In his view, what then transpired was not good for the safety of the 190,000 men and women fighting for America, and raised questions about the role of the judiciary: "What competence does the Court have to second-guess the judgment of Congress and the President on such a point? None whatever. But the Court blunders in nonetheless."[18] Thus, for Scalia, this "opinion makes unnervingly clear, how to handle enemy prisoners in this war will ultimately lie with the branch that knows least about the national security concerns that the subject entails."[19]

Seeing this "inflated notion of judicial supremacy" as an exercise of an "irrational and arrogant" Supreme Court, Scalia concluded, based on his interpretation of "the text and history of the Suspension Clause," that the majority had "no basis for our jurisdiction."[20] Instead, he added:

> Today the Court warps our Constitution in a way that goes beyond
> the narrow issue of the reach of the Suspension Clause. . . . It breaks
> a chain of precedent as old as the common law that prohibits judicial
> inquiry into detentions of aliens abroad absent statutory authoriza-

tion. And, most tragically, it sets our military commanders the impossible task of proving to a civilian court, under whatever standards this Court devises in the future, that evidence supports the confinement of each and every enemy prisoner. The Nation will live to regret what the Court has done today.[21]

After verbally beating up Kennedy once again, Scalia had no time to rest.

• • •

At that moment, Scalia was writing his judicial magnum opus, creating a textbook example of how to decide a constitutional law case using originalism. The case of *District of Columbia v. Heller* dealt with the District's Firearms Control Regulation Act of 1975, enacted in response to the soaring crime and murder rate in the nation's capital. The regulation prevented people from owning an unregistered handgun while also barring new handgun registrations. It also required that all lawfully owned guns have trigger locks on them. This, according to D.C. resident Dick Heller, violated the Second Amendment. Heller, a security guard, wanted to own a handgun for protection in his home and raised the issue of whether such a regulation by the District of Columbia, a federally governed region, violated the Second Amendment, which reads: "A well regulated Militia, being necessary to the security of a free State, the right of the people to keep and bear Arms, shall not be infringed."

The rich history of the Second Amendment dates back to the fears by the British in the seventeenth century that James II would disarm them, the need for arms by citizen militias, like the colonial Minutemen who fought the British during the Revolutionary War, and a proposal by James Madison from which the amendment's wording was taken.[22] Scalia, who was not only a conservative but a hunting enthusiast, sought a way through this case to strike down the D.C. regulation using originalist analysis. Standing in the way of this task, though, were an existing Supreme Court precedent and the rules of English grammar.

For the man who called himself a "faint-hearted originalist," arguing for two decades that he would try to avoid overturning long-standing precedents, the 1939 Second Amendment precedent, *United States v. Miller*, seemed to be squarely on point by upholding the power of the federal government to restrict the right to own guns.[23] The case involved Jack Miller, a bank robber and moonshiner, who was arrested and convicted of transporting an unregistered sawed-off double-barrel 12-gauge shotgun from Oklahoma to Arkansas in violation of the 1934 National Firearms Act (NFA). Since these sawed-off shotguns, along with machine guns, which were also covered by the law, were also the weapons of choice for bank robbers such as John Dillinger, Pretty Boy Floyd, and Bonnie and Clyde, not to mention the gunmen in the St. Valentine's Day Massacre that had spurred this law, Congress had limited the Second Amendment right "to keep and bear arms" by banning their interstate transportation.[24]

In writing a majority opinion upholding the law, ultraconservative Justice William McReynolds used what Scalia would later call originalism, citing the notes of the Constitutional Convention, the writings of British legal theorist William Blackstone, and early American and British history to argue that the "arms" borne by a person must relate to their use for general security in the "militia." As McReynolds explained, "Ordinarily when called for service these men were expected to appear bearing arms supplied by themselves and of the kind in common use at the time."[25] In short, he argued, since the military was not carrying sawed-off double-barrel 12-gauge shotguns into war, a citizen's ownership of them failed the militia-related use test, meaning that people in Oklahoma who were traveling to other states had no right to carry them either.[26]

None of this posed any problem for Scalia, who was by now adept in manipulating his originalist theory to reach the result that he sought. Scalia's version of grammar and history led him to interpret the Second Amendment much differently from his predecessor in writing for a five-justice majority in favor of *Heller*. First, he took issue with how McReynolds interpreted the structure of the words in the Second Amendment. As written, the Second Amendment has two parts. The initial clause reads, "A well-regulated Militia, being necessary to the security of a free State," describing a collective right, with the second phrase "the right of the people to keep and bear Arms, shall not be infringed," conveying an individual right. McReynolds had interpreted the first clause as modifying the second one, providing the reason for the right to own a gun. For him, the individual person's right to own a gun must be seen as a collective right dictated by the use of that weapon in the service of the militia.

Like all children of the 1950s, young Nino Scalia had learned at P.S. 13 in Queens and Xavier High School in Manhattan how to diagram a sentence. But having learned as a college debater at Georgetown the art of reinterpreting a proposition to favor the side he was defending, the task before Scalia was routine. In writing his majority, Scalia became the debater rather than the grammarian in seeking to make the introductory portion of the Second Amendment play a much different role than McReynolds thought.

Scalia began his opinion by explaining that he would be interpreting the Second Amendment based on how it "was written to be understood by the voters; [because] its words and phrases were used in their normal and ordinary meaning as distinguished from [their] technical meaning."[27] Knowing that Heller's Second Amendment gun rights could not be upheld if he limited his interpretation only to those weapons that would be used by "a well-regulated Militia, being necessary to the security of a free State," Scalia explained why, for him, this initial clause was not a limiting phrase to the right to keep and bear arms, but was there to "clarify" the rest of the sentence: "The Second Amendment is naturally divided into two parts: its prefatory clause and its operative clause. The former does not limit the latter grammatically, but rather announces a purpose." For support of this proposition, he cited an 1867 legal treatise, adding: "The Amendment could be re-phrased, 'Because a well regulated Militia is necessary to the security of a free State, the right of the people to keep and bear Arms shall not be infringed.'" Unexplained was how a rule presented in 1867 demonstrated Scalia's "public understanding" of a 1791 constitutional amendment.

He had not yet answered, nor would he answer, two questions: Did the general public in the Founding period also read this sentence as he did? And, did the people in the Founding Era understand that the purpose of the amendment was designed to protect their right to retain all weapons as opposed to those used in a state militia? Seeking to bolster his case, Scalia resorted not to history, but to logic:

> Logic demands that there be a link between the stated purpose and the command. The Second Amendment would be nonsensical if it read, "A well regulated Militia, being necessary to the security of a free State, the right of the people to petition for redress of griev-ances shall not be infringed." That requirement of logical connection may cause a prefatory clause to resolve an ambiguity in the operative clause. . . . But apart from that clarifying function, a prefatory clause does not limit or expand the scope of the operative clause.[28]

Having dispensed with the first part of the amendment, he turned to the second, what he called the "operative part." Here Scalia applied his textual and historical analysis to each portion of the "keep and bear arms" clause to argue that the arms ownership guarantee was a broad individual one, rather than a collective right: " 'Keep arms' was simply a common way of referring to possessing arms, for militiamen *and everyone else*. . . . It in no way connotes participation in a structured military organization. . . . These provisions demonstrate—again, in the most analogous linguistic context—that 'bear arms' was not limited to the carrying of arms in a militia."[29]

Scalia then argued that if the "right to bear arms" only "consist[ed] of the right to be a soldier or to wage war," then "the phrase 'keep and bear Arms' would be incoherent. The word 'Arms' would have two different meanings at once: 'weapons' (as the object of 'keep') and (as the object of 'bear') one-half of an idiom. It would be rather like saying 'He filled and kicked the bucket' to mean 'He filled the bucket and died.' Grotesque."[30] After examining the "textual elements" and "historical background" of the Second Amendment, Scalia argued that the operative clause protected only an individual's right to bear arms: "It has always been widely understood that the Second Amendment, like the First and Fourth Amendments, codified a *pre-existing* right. . . . There seems to us no doubt, on the basis of both text and history, that the Second Amendment conferred an individual right to keep and bear arms."[31]

Once he had finished his grammatical analysis, Scalia concluded on the basis of his reading of the state constitutions from the Founding period that "they secured an individual right to bear arms for defensive purposes."[32] For him, then, the Second Amendment was not safeguarding the existence of the group "militia" right, but rather the individual's "right to self-defense." In a kind of moving historical target, Scalia found his definition of the "right of self-defense" not in the Founding period but rather from the post–Civil War period. After acknowledging the gap in time from the ratification of the Second Amendment, he argued that as the American public "debated whether and how to secure constitutional rights for newly free slaves. . . . Those born and educated in the early 19th century faced a widespread effort to limit arms ownership by a large number of citizens; their understanding of the origins and continuing significance of the Amendment is instructive. Blacks were routinely disarmed by Southern States. . . . It was plainly the understanding in the post–Civil War Congress that the Second Amendment protected an individual right to use arms for self-defense."[33]

By recrafting the right to "keep and bear arms" into a "right to self-defense," Scalia was able to forge a majority by locking in the votes of the

Court's two libertarians, Clarence Thomas and Anthony Kennedy, both of whom saw this right as the essence of the Second Amendment's protection. Scalia did concede, though, that the Second Amendment did not confer an unlimited right, making it possible for a state to regulate this right: "Like most rights, the right secured by the Second Amendment is not unlimited. . . . Nothing in our opinion should be taken to cast doubt on longstanding prohibitions on the possession of firearms by felons and the mentally ill, or laws forbidding the carrying of firearms in sensitive places such as schools and government buildings, or laws imposing conditions and qualifications on the commercial sale of arms. We also recognize another important limitation on the right to keep and carry arms . . . [to] the sorts of weapons . . . 'in common use at the time.'"[34] So it was yet to be decided in battles between gun control advocates and the gun supporters, such as the National Rifle Association, whether there might be other types of arms that could be constitutionally excluded from the Second Amendment protection.

In dissent, Justice Stevens argued that there was "no indication that the Framers of the Amendment intended to enshrine the common-law right of self-defense in the Constitution."[35] For Stevens, the *Miller* precedent made gun ownership a collective security right because it was "both the most natural reading of the Amendment's text and the interpretation most faithful to the history of its adoption. . . . Indeed, a review of the drafting history of the Amendment demonstrates that its Framers *rejected* proposals that would have broadened its coverage to include such uses."[36]

Based on his own version of originalism, Stevens drew from his historical interpretation of the text of the amendment and its tradition to argue that "the Framers' single-minded focus in crafting the constitutional guarantee 'to keep and bear arms' was on military uses of firearms, which they viewed in the context of service in state militias."[37] He added that "so far as appears, no more than that was contemplated by its drafters or is encompassed within its terms. . . . Indeed, not a word in the constitutional text even arguably supports the Court's overwrought and novel description of the Second Amendment as 'elevat[ing] above all other interests' the right of law-abiding, responsible citizens to use arms in defense of hearth and home."[38] Stevens made clear in this opinion how little use he had for Scalia's pro-gun rights textual and originalist approach, mocking it in a footnote: "The Court's atomistic, word-by-word approach to construing the Amendment calls to mind the parable of the six blind men and the elephant. . . . In the parable, each blind man approaches a single elephant; touching a different part of the elephant's body in isolation, each concludes that he has learned its true nature. One touches the animal's leg, and concludes that the elephant is like a tree; another touches the trunk and decides that the elephant is like a snake; and so on. Each of them, of course, has fundamentally failed to grasp the nature of the creature."[39]

Hardly amused by this comparison, Scalia responded that "Justice Stevens flatly misreads the historical record." He said that Stevens "assumes from the prologue that the Amendment was designed to preserve the militia . . . (which we do not dispute), and then reviews some historical materials dealing with the nature of the militia, and in particular with the nature of the arms their members were expected to possess. . . . Not a word (*not a word*) about the history of the Second Amendment. This is the mighty rock upon which the dissent rests its case."[40]

With the announcement of the *Heller* opinion, Scalia had secured his claim as King of the Originalists. And he knew it, saying years later in an interview with National Public Radio Court reporter Nina Totenberg: "I think *Heller* is my legacy opinion insofar as it is the best example of the technique of constitutional interpretation, which I favor; that is to say, it is a good example of originalism, of going back and seeing what the meaning of the Second Amendment was at the time it was adopted. . . . I think it's the most complete originalist opinion that I've ever written."[41] Using his textual and historical analysis, he had held together a close majority of the Court in his battle against the living, evolving Constitutionalists. As a result, all of the commentary on the case would be on *his* opinion and *his* version of the originalism theory.

• • •

In the summer of 2008, the legal blogosphere was Scalia's domain once more as the internet filled with analysis of his *Heller* opinion. History professor Saul Cornell of Ohio State University wrote that "Scalia's interpretive principle might best be described as the Cheshire Cat Rule of Construction—now you see the preamble, now you don't. According to this approach, the preamble disappears during interpretation and only reappears if there is an ambiguity that needs to be resolved. While such a rule would be plausible if the Constitution had been written by Lewis Carroll, it seems hard to imagine the Founders embracing an Alice in Wonderland approach to constitutional interpretation." For Professor Cornell, this form of reading violated Scalia's own theory of originalism because it was "inconsistent with [British legal theorist William] Blackstone's primary injunction that one must consult the words, context, subject matter, effects, or spirit and reason of the law when seeking to discover the intent of the legislator."[42]

Another critical commentator was Stanford historian Jack Rakove, author of the 1996 Pulitzer Prize–winning *Original Meanings*. In commentary posted on Yale constitutional law professor Jack Balkin's legal blog, *Balkinization*, Rakove argued, "The Scalia opinion seems materially defective to me for several reasons. The most important . . . is its explicit disdain for the legislative history of the Amendment, whether that is described in terms of the Convention's framing of the Militia Clause, the public exchanges and ratification convention debates it sparked, or what we know of the progress of the Amendment itself through Congress. I understand that this position correlates with Scalia's general skepticism about legislative history in statutory construction, but that does not alleviate my concern." Rakove continued, "Scalia's version of originalism/textualism, as applied in this opinion, seems oblivious to the most important findings that historians from Edmund Morgan (writing on the Stamp Act) on through [Bernard] Bailyn, [Gordon S.] Wood, myself, and others have argued over the last half-century: that this was a deeply creative era in constitutionalism and political thought, and the idea that static definitions will capture the dynamism of what was going on cannot possibly be true."[43] For Rakove and the nation's other preeminent Founding Era historians, the meaning of the amendment had to evolve because a single "public meaning" of the ratification period could not reliably be determined given the available historical evidence.

Of these intellectual attacks against Scalia's *Heller* opinion, one of the most visible and telling came from conservative Court of Appeals judge for the Seventh Circuit Richard Posner, writing in *The New Republic*.[44] Posner sided with John Paul Stevens's version of Early American history in holding for the collective "militia-based" ownership of guns theory: "Since a militia, provided that it is well regulated, is a very good thing for a free state to have, the federal government must not be allowed to castrate it by forbidding the people of the United States to possess weapons. For then the militia would have no weapons, and an unarmed militia is an oxymoron." If the militia depends on armed citizens to exist, for Posner that version of the right to "keep and bear arms" must be safeguarded. As he put it, "Since the purpose of the Second Amendment, judging from its language and background, was to assure the effectiveness of state militias, an interpretation that undermined their effectiveness by preventing states from making efficient arrangements for the storage and distribution of military weapons would not make sense."

Using his own form of originalism to read the Second Amendment, Judge Posner turned to Blackstone in arguing for a "loose construction" or a broad, expansive reading of the right. "The purpose of the first clause of the amendment, the militia clause, is to narrow the right that the second clause confers on the 'people.'" Accordingly, Posner argued:

> The reigning theory of legislative interpretation in the eighteenth century was loose (or flexible, or nonliteral) construction. . . . Originalism without the interpretive theory that the Framers and the ratifiers of the Constitution expected the courts to use in construing constitutional provisions is *faux originalism.* True originalism licenses loose construction. And loose construction is especially appropriate for interpreting a constitutional provision ratified more than two centuries ago, dealing with a subject that has been transformed in the intervening period by social and technological change, including urbanization and a revolution in warfare and weaponry.

Indeed, Blackstone's "loose construction" statutory interpretive approach had been used by British judges since the first century after the Magna Carta was signed in 1215.[45]

Posner argued that Scalia's interpretation was "too dogmatic" because "the historical evidence is not as one-sided as his opinion suggests." For Posner, "it leaves the impression that all that divided the two wings of the Court was a disagreement over the historical record. That was playing into Scalia's hands." Just as Jack Rakove, drawing from fellow legal historian Leonard Levy, had argued about Scalia's historical technique twelve years earlier, Posner charged that

> The majority (and the dissent as well) was engaged in what is de-risively referred to—the derision is richly deserved—as "law office history." Lawyers are advocates for their clients, and judges are advocates for whichever side of the case they have decided to vote for. The judge sends his law clerks scurrying to the library and to the Web for bits and pieces of historical documentation. When the clerks are the numerous and able clerks of Supreme Court justices, enjoying the as-

sistance of the capable staffs of the Supreme Court library and the Library of Congress, and when dozens and sometimes hundreds of *amicus curiae* briefs have been filed, many bulked out with the fruits of their authors' own law-office historiography, it is a simple matter, especially for a skillful rhetorician such as Scalia, to write a plausible historical defense of his position.[46]

And so, Posner concluded, "The range of historical references in the majority opinion is breathtaking, but it is not evidence of disinterested historical inquiry. It is evidence of the ability of well-staffed courts to produce snow jobs."

Posner's "law office history" charge particularly stung Scalia, who would later admit, "That article stuck in my craw."[47] And, just as he had so many times before, he knew exactly how to respond.

CHAPTER 23

The Methodology of Originalism

A standing-room-only crowd of law students and faculty packed the Ames Courtroom at Harvard Law School in the fall of 2008 to hear Antonin Scalia deliver the inaugural Herbert W. Vaughan Lecture. His topic was "The Methodology of Originalism," and it would become his new stump speech. Three times before he had changed his basic originalism speech—in 1988–89, 1996, and 2005—but unlike the others, each of which followed his failure to control his colleagues' votes and the direction of the Court, this one came on the heels of his greatest judicial success to date. His majority opinion in the *Heller* case, though, had come at a cost, causing eminent historians and a leading conservative judge to criticize him. After a summer of thought and work he was prepared to answer those critics, and in doing so change the way he lectured about judicial decision making.

Scalia's various originalism speeches and law teaching stints had allowed him to travel for free, be seen by thousands of people, and earn tens of thousands of dollars beyond his salary. The only thing that varied from audience to audience was the questions following his remarks. However, even they were becoming so repetitive that the press coverage for his appearances had lessened over the years.

Now this new Harvard speech would allow him to renew his public persona. After being introduced by Harvard Law School dean Elena Kagan as "our nation's foremost proponent of textualism and formalism," Scalia used his speech to rebrand himself. His new argument would be simple, he began: since the English language wording of the Constitution is no different from the text of a statute, and lawyers were trained to interpret statutes, the lawyers who became judges were well qualified to interpret the nation's Founding charter. Scalia argued that his theory of using history to make decisions on the enduring original meaning of the Constitution was far superior to the ever-evolving, living Constitution theory of his colleagues. "Much as I love Harvard Law School, it didn't make me a moral philosopher," he told the group. Scalia argued from his work in the *Heller* case that judges had the capability to be good historians in making determinations as to whether the Second Amendment protected an individual "right of self-defense" rather than a collective, militia-oriented, right.

In this new speech, Scalia said that he was going to explain *how* his originalism process was undertaken and *why* he believed that judges rather than historians were uniquely qualified to understand the Constitution. "The Court had before it all the materials needed to determine the meaning of the Second Amendment at the time it was written. My burden as an originalist is not to show that originalism is perfect but merely to show that it beats the other available alternatives, and that is not difficult."[1]

Scalia argued that the task of the modern originalists "has become easier over time," both because of the increased number of legal historians on law school faculties and the increasing number of briefs submitted to the Court filled with historical analysis. Contrary to the dearth of historical briefing for the 1988 *Morrison v. Olson* independent counsel case, he explained, "the mass of briefing" in the *Heller* case "was nothing short of spectacular, filling over five volumes in the Supreme Court library," with one brief containing two hundred pages of historical material. In writing for the majority, Scalia argued: "The court had before it all the materials needed to determine the meaning of the Second Amendment at the time it was written. With these in hand, what method would be easier or more reliable than the originalist approach taken by the Court?"

As for other areas of personal rights, Scalia returned to his familiar theme of individual autonomy rights that were not in his Constitution: "In most cases, the originalist answer is entirely clear," he said. "Did any provision in the Constitution guarantee a right to abortion? No one thought so for almost two centuries." Scalia neglected to mention that for the same two centuries no one thought there was an individual right to bear arms, either. In saying the same about gay rights, the right to die, and the death penalty: "All of these questions pose enormous difficulty for non-originalists, who must agonize over what the modern Constitution ought to mean with each of these subjects, and then agonize again five or ten years later because times change." The benefit of his historical approach, Scalia argued, was: "Originalism does not invite the judge to make law what he thinks it should be. The historical evidence is sometimes indeterminate or subject to competing interpretation, but it's not infinitely malleable. . . . The honest originalist will sometimes, indeed often, reach a substantive result he does not personally favor." So, he concluded: "If ideological judging is the malady, the avowed application of such personal preferences will surely hasten the patient's demise, and the use of history is far closer to being the cure than it is to being the disease."

All went well as he delivered his address, but in the question and answer session Scalia was put on the defensive. He took a question from Harvard Law School's internationally known constitutional law professor Alan Dershowitz. Dershowitz began by noting Scalia's failure to use originalism to decide a 2003 Fifth Amendment self-incrimination case, *Chavez v. Martinez*. In this case, Scalia wrote a concurrence to an opinion written by Clarence Thomas that ruled that a confession by a paralyzed drug dealing suspect in a hospital bed, made without receiving his *Miranda* warnings, did not violate the Fifth Amendment when it was used in a criminal proceeding. Dershowitz argued there was "not a single word about history" even though "There is a long, long history on that, [and] debates on that during the framing," which would have led to the opposite result in the case. Dershowitz added that he "could cite 20 to 30 cases" in which Scalia "eschew[ed] history," and wondered why that was so for the man who constantly preached the values of originalism. Scalia deflected the challenge, saying to the audience's laughter, "I don't remember the details of that opinion, but what did Sarah Palin say? 'I'll get back to you on it.'" Try as Scalia might to dismiss the question, Dershowitz's charge was certainly a valid one.[2]

Before the year was out, another law review article critical of Scalia's *Heller* decision was published by conservative Court of Appeals judge J. Harvie Wilkinson III of the Fourth Circuit in Virginia.[3] Judge Wilkinson argued that in creating and protecting a new "right of self-defense" that could not be found in the wording of the Bill of Rights, Scalia was behaving more like Harry Blackmun, who had created a right of abortion in the Constitution in *Roe v. Wade*. As Wilkinson put it: "Both decisions share four major shortcomings: an absence of a commitment to textualism; a willingness to embark on a complex endeavor that will require fine-tuning over many years of litigation; a failure to respect legislative judgments; and a rejection of the principles of federalism."[4] And to do this, Wilkinson argued, Scalia used only his expansive theory of "originalism," while abandoning the more limiting conservative judicial techniques of "textualism; structuralism; federalism; historicism; and plain old modesty and restraint," which had also been missing in *Roe*.[5]

In making this argument, Judge Wilkinson, a friend of Scalia, had exposed one of the main weaknesses not only in the *Heller* case but in the entire originalist theoretical structure: "While *Heller* can be hailed as a triumph of originalism, it can just as easily be seen as the opposite—an exposé of original intent as a theory no less subject to judicial subjectivity and endless argumentation as any other."[6] As Wilkinson explained: "After decades of criticizing activist judges for this or that defalcation, conservatives have now committed many of the same sins. In *Heller*, the majority read an ambiguous constitutional provision as creating a substantive right that the Court had never acknowledged in the more than two hundred years since the amendment's enactment. The majority then used that same right to strike down a law passed by elected officials acting, rightly or wrongly, to preserve the safety of the citizenry."[7] In short, Wilkinson charged that the self-restraint jurisprudential theory outlined by Scalia in his writings and speeches had instead become in *Heller* an activist, result-oriented approach that allowed him to create rights not in the Constitution.

Despite the criticism from Posner and Wilkinson, both conservative federal Court of Appeals judges, Justice Scalia had finally found the perfect shorthand argument for his position. After arguing that American Founding Era historians could not be trusted to present the correct version of historical reality because they all disagree, Scalia said that the public should trust originalist judges to interpret the Constitution. This was true, Scalia argued, because: 1) lawyers are trained to read and interpret historical texts, 2) historians write differing interpretation of those texts, and so, 3) lawyers can weigh these interpretations to evaluate the historians. It was an elegantly simple position. Scalia, by his own admission not a trained historian, left open the question facing every academic—what do you do when other originalist-oriented scholars and judges, using the same interpretive approach but relying on different historical evidence, reach different conclusions?[8]

If Scalia's goal was to create a judiciary and professoriate dedicated to the unchanging interpretation of the "enduring" Constitution, he was destined to be disappointed. In time, the uncontrollable evolution of Scalia's originalist theory became evident. As the years went by new types of originalists, some of them arguing to expand rights to reach progressive liberal goals, appeared.[9] Beyond this, time and again, moderate swing justices such as Kennedy, along with liberal justices such as Stevens and Breyer, began to include "text" and "tradition" evidence as the foundation in their opinions for reaching more evolutionary constitutional results.[10]

Like other legal theories, originalism was becoming just another tool to reach whatever ideological result a judge preferred. But that was never Scalia's goal. For decades Scalia had been arguing for a static, restrictive form of interpretation. Now he was saying, *Trust me, Antonin Scalia, for the proper interpretation*. In short, Scalia was arguing that in law there was one single truth and only *he* knew it.

• • •

In the fall of 2008, Scalia was just one Court appointment away from his ideal of a perfect Supreme Court. All that was needed was one more Republican appointment of a conservative to the Court, replacing a liberal or even Anthony Kennedy, who had been slowing the pace of the conservative legal evolution. Scalia's hopes for the future of his Court were pinned on a conservative victory in the November election between Republican John McCain and Democrat Barack Obama.

The difference between the two presidential candidates regarding the future of the Supreme Court could not have been more pronounced. In his book *The Audacity of Hope*, Obama made clear what type of judge he would *not* be appointing: "Anyone like Justice Scalia looking to resolve our modern constitutional dispute through strict construction has one big problem. The founders themselves disagreed profoundly, vehemently, on the meaning of their masterpiece."[11] During the campaign, Obama told a Planned Parenthood conference about the future Supreme Court picks they could expect from him. "We need somebody who's got the heart, the empathy, to recognize what it's like to be a young teenage mom. The empathy to understand what it's like to be poor, or African-American, or gay, or disabled, or old. And that's the criterion by which I'm going to be selecting my judges."[12]

Advisers for Obama made clear that he would be appointing justices in the mold of Stephen Breyer and David Souter, justices chosen by presidents of different political parties. These justices were known as "judicial consequentialists," who assessed the policy results of their decision making. Douglas Kmiec, a law professor at Pepperdine University, then serving as a surrogate for Obama in discussing judicial appointment issues on the internet, explained: "These justices are individuals who tend to examine closely the consequences of legal decisions in terms of their effects on the larger society, as well as to examine a legal outcome in terms of the specifics of a particular record."[13]

In contrast, John McCain was seeking to appoint conservative "self-restraint" jurists who would oppose liberal "judicial activists." McCain's goal was to find a jurist who decided on behalf of conservative causes such as promoting states' rights, business interests, and police investigative powers over defendants' rights, as well as being dedicated to reversing the liberal decisions of the past. In a speech in 2008, McCain promised, "I will look for accomplished men and women with a proven record of excellence in the law, and a proven commitment to judicial restraint." As examples, he offered praise for George W. Bush's appointees, John Roberts and Samuel Alito, and former Chief Justice William Rehnquist.[14]

As the election season dragged on, it became clear that to win, McCain would need to mobilize the conservative political coalition that had propelled his party to success in 2004. But this self-described maverick was not popular with that segment of the party. Sensing the rising importance of the evangelical Protestant vote to his success, McCain would have to find a way to enlist their support. There was good reason to expect that the political price for their backing would be paid, among other places, in the one branch of government that most concerned religious conservatives—the federal judiciary.

The religious composition of the Supreme Court spoke volumes about their concerns. The five Catholics on the Court practiced a religion shared by 23.9 percent of the American population.[15] The two Mainline Protestant justices, Stevens and Souter, came from denominations representing around 18 percent of the American people. Two Jewish justices on the Court were drawn from only 2.3 percent of the American population. But the evangelical Protestants, whose 26.3 percent of the American population constituted the largest religious group at that time, were not represented at all on the Supreme Court.[16] With millions of evangelical voters who potentially could tip the balance in the election, as they had in 2004, McCain could be pressed by his evangelical Christian supporters to appoint one of their members to the Court if he won. That new person would almost certainly unite with the four conservative Catholics to form an interdenominational fundamentalist majority on cultural issues. If so, Scalia would finally have a majority voting with him on social and cultural issues.

As the political campaign unfolded, Jeffrey Rosen of *The New Republic* posted an internet article titled "McJustice," containing a provocative subhead, "Liberals' Long-Feared Judicial Apocalypse Is Nigh."[17] Rosen noted: "During every presidential campaign for the last two decades, liberals have predicted an apocalypse in the Supreme Court." But in the 2008 election, Rosen saw a difference: "This year, for the first time since the New Deal era, a single election really does have the power to transform the Court. . . . [An] Obama victory would maintain the current balance of the Court, while a McCain Court could create a solid conservative majority. . . . Voters who are hoping McCain will nominate relatively moderate judicial mavericks should think again." The thesis of this piece was direct: "Many prominent conservatives are confident that McCain, who has never cared much about the judiciary, would placate his conservative base by appointing activist movement conservatives." Rosen concluded: "Those who have long been too concerned about the future of the Supreme Court finally have reason to worry." The only question was, would the American voters choose that path?

On the eve of the election, this debate over the ideological future of the federal judiciary took a distinctly religious turn as Catholic legal community opinion leaders began splitting apart over the presidential candidates. Not surprising, many conservative Catholics argued vigorously against Obama and in favor of McCain. In "An Open Letter to Our Catholic Friends on Election Eve" on ProLifeBlogs.com, Edward Morrissey and Elizabeth Scalia (no relation to the justice) argued that "the foundation of our faith *and* of social justice: the sanctity of human life" compelled them to vote against Obama.[18] Other Catholics in the legal community, however, rather than voting reflexively against the pro-choice Obama, instead argued in his favor. Two prominent conservative Catholic legal scholars, Douglas Kmiec and Nicholas Cafardi, said that Obama deserved support because of his positions on moral issues such as ending the Iraq War, ending the use of torture in the "War on Terror," and alleviating poverty, while also seeking to preserve social justice. Voting for Obama, Cafardi wrote, was the "proper moral choice for this Catholic."[19]

By taking this stand as Catholics, Kmiec and Cafardi provided cover for those members of their faith who were considering campaigning for Obama, knowing that in some churches it might mean that they would be denied Communion by their conservative parish priest.[20] On November 4, a majority of Catholic voters, and voters in general, chose Obama. The press declared: "Obama Victory Ends GOP Hopes for a Much More Conservative Supreme Court."[21]

Scalia, though, saw a different reality. Speaking to the Federalist Society's National Lawyers Convention on November 22, 2008, he saw nothing but a bright future for his originalism cause. "As you heard, I was present at the birth [of this organization]," Scalia told a packed State Room in Washington, D.C.'s, Mayflower Hotel: "How have the fortunes of originalism fared in the times since the Federalist Society was founded, at a time when I was still a professor at the University of Chicago? . . . I used to be able to say with a good deal of truth, that one could fire a cannon loaded with grape-shot in the faculty lounge of any law school in the country and not strike an originalist. That's no longer true. . . . Originalism, which was once orthodoxy, at least has now been returned to the status of respectability."[22]

Six weeks later, though, the flaw in Scalia's optimistic vision of an inevitable original meaning federal court takeover was exposed when President Obama named Harvard Law School dean Elena Kagan, a progressive "living Constitution" advocate, as the solicitor general. Given Kagan's obvious legal talent, there was every reason to expect that this might not be her last administration appointment.

At seventy-two years of age, with a Democrat in the White House, Scalia was entering the winter of his life and his judicial career. He planned to continue his struggle to guide the conservative majority, but he had to be mindful of what kind of legal legacy he would leave behind. By this age, William O. Douglas was working on his two-volume memoir that would reshape his public image. Scalia's first chief, William Rehnquist, had partially rebranded himself as a respected writer of American history.[23] His arch-nemesis on the Court, Sandra Day O'Connor, was writing her early life memoirs.[24] What would Scalia do, what could he do, to build his legacy further during the Obama years?

• • •

In early May 2009, David Souter, who at age sixty-nine was the fourth youngest justice then on the Court, announced his retirement, to take effect at the end of the term. His retirement at this time gave Obama his first opportunity to make a nomination to the Court. The president's view of the proper appointee seemed clear, as he told C-SPAN, "What I want is not just ivory tower learning. I want somebody who has the intellectual firepower, but also a little bit of a common touch and has a practical sense of how the world works."[25] He also wanted a young candidate who might stay on the Court for decades.

Obama's choice to fill Souter's seat was a federal judge with seventeen years of experience on the Court of Appeals for the Second Circuit, Sonia Sotomayor. If confirmed, she would become the sixth Catholic on the Court, a fact not lost on Court watchers and commentators. It appeared, though, that she was a more modern Catholic with more liberal views on social issues than those currently serving on the bench. More important than her religion, however, was the fact that Sotomayor possessed both the empathy that Obama valued in a judge, and the experience on the bench to know how to use it. She became the first Hispanic appointment to the Court. Raised in New York City's housing projects, she called herself "Sonia from the Bronx," and faced discrimination while studying at Princeton University, where she said she felt like "a visitor landing in an alien country."[26] She became an activist in college and during her three years at Yale Law School lobbied for Latino faculty and courses.[27] She practiced both criminal and civil law, and worked for the Puerto Rican Legal Defense and Education Fund prior to her appointment to the federal bench. Since her more liberal views were similar to those of Souter, the ideological balance of the Court would not be altered by her addition. With nothing in her record to trigger the partisan circus that the Senate confirmation process had become, Sotomayor was easily confirmed by a 68–31 margin in August 2009. Because she was so likable and down-to-earth, Court watchers wondered whether she might become the Court's "next William Brennan," referring to the liberal Catholic who galvanized the liberals on the Court from 1957 through 1990.[28]

With six Catholics then on the Court, the issue of religion and the Court became a more sensitive one. An example came in the fall of 2009, when the case of *Salazar v. Buono* came before the Court. This dispute explored whether an eight-foot metal cross that had originally been erected by the Veterans of Foreign Wars (VFW) in 1934 at the top of Sunrise Rock in the Mojave Desert National Preserve in Southern California, and then replaced several times, represented a violation of the Establishment Clause of the First Amendment because the land was part of a national park. The case had its confusing points. The monument had been erected without governmental permits by private individuals in an effort to exempt it from constitutional prohibitions. It was intended as a war memorial, with a plaque placed near it reading: "The Cross, Erected in Memory of the Dead of All Wars." In the years that followed, though, the spot became the site of Easter morning religious services, making it harder to argue that it was a secular monument.

These factual issues became the basis for an interesting exchange between Justice Scalia and American Civil Liberties Union attorney Peter J. Eliasberg, who was challenging the constitutionality of the cross on public land. Eliasberg began by noting that the VFW's memorial did not, in fact, "honor all of the people who fought for America in World War I," but rather, "just Christians."

When he heard this, Scalia pounced from the bench:

JUSTICE SCALIA: The cross doesn't honor non-Christians who fought in the war? Is that—is that—

MR. ELIASBERG: I believe that's actually correct.

JUSTICE SCALIA: Where does it say that?

MR. ELIASBERG: It doesn't say that, but a cross is the predominant symbol of Christianity and it signifies that Jesus is the son of God and died to redeem mankind for our sins, and I believe that's why the Jewish war veterans—

JUSTICE SCALIA: It's erected as a war memorial. I assume it is erected in honor of all of the war dead. It's the—the cross is the—is the most common symbol of—of—of the resting place of the dead, and it doesn't seem to me—what would you have them erect? A cross—some conglomerate of a cross, a Star of David, and you know, a Moslem half moon and star?

MR. ELIASBERG: Well, Justice Scalia, if I may go to your first point. The cross is the most common symbol of the resting place of Christians. I have been in Jewish cemeteries. There is never a cross on a tombstone of a Jew. So it is the most common symbol to honor Christians.

The audience at that point laughed at the obvious correctness of the attorney's observation.

JUSTICE SCALIA: I don't think you can leap from that to the conclusion that the only war dead that that cross honors are the Christian war dead. I think that's an outrageous conclusion.

MR. ELIASBERG: Well, my—the point of my—point here is to say that there is a reason the Jewish war veterans came in and said we don't feel honored by this cross. This cross can't honor us because it is a religious symbol of another religion.

At this point Chief Justice Roberts rescued his senior colleague by changing the focus of the questioning to the wording on the plaque.[29]

Some in the legal community and the press had a field day with Scalia's self-evident insensitivity to the meaning of this religious symbol and the exclusion that it represented for people from other faiths. Professor Geoffrey Stone of the University of Chicago Law School, who had already clashed with Scalia over the possible effect of the Catholic majority on the Court's decision in the 2007 *Gonzales v. Carhart* partial birth abortion case, once again took him on. He posted the oral argument exchange in an internet *Huffington Post* blog entry entitled "Justice Scalia's Cross," describing it as "another example of Justice Scalia's proclivity to see constitutional issues through the lens of his own religious understandings and beliefs."[30]

A five-justice majority of the Court, speaking through Justice Kennedy, found no First Amendment Establishment of Religion violation with the memorial, arguing that this cross did not constitute governmental "endorsement" of religion, but rather was one of many acceptable religious symbols displayed for other reasons in this country: "Here, one Latin cross in the desert evokes far more than religion. It evokes thousands of small crosses in foreign fields marking the graves of Americans who fell in battles, battles whose tragedies are compounded if the fallen are forgotten."[31]

Despite the Sotomayor appointment, the Roberts Court continued to move in a more conservative direction. This became more evident on January 21, 2010, when the Court decided in a landmark case called *Citizens United v. Federal Election Commission* the constitutionality of the Bipartisan Campaign Reform Act of 2002 (BCRA), the so-called McCain-Feingold Campaign Reform law. This law was designed to regulate and limit the use of so-called soft money in an election, whereby lobbyists and political action committees could circumvent the legal limits on campaign donations by giving money to political parties instead of directly to candidates. Parties could use this soft money donated "for the good of the party" as long as they did not mention the names of candidates running for office. The law also limited the use of "issue advertisements," discussions by interest groups of controversial election issues, but not specific candidates, banning such ads thirty days before a primary election and sixty days before a general election. With O'Connor as the swing justice, the Court had narrowly, and repeatedly, upheld this law in the face of allegations that by regulating campaign money it limited free speech under the First Amendment.[32] But now Justice O'Connor was gone, and sitting in her seat was the much more conservative and pro–corporate free speech Samuel Alito.

The case that came to the Court in September 2010 involved a movie entitled *Hillary: The Movie*, which was released during the run-up to the 2008 Democratic presidential primary by a conservative nonprofit lobbying group called Citizens United. The movie was framed as a documentary, but in effect was more of an attack ad against Hillary Clinton's candidacy. The initial issue, then, was whether the movie would be subject to the restrictive issue ad requirements of the BCRA, or whether those limits violated protected speech under the First Amendment. The real issue, though, was whether it was constitutional to limit corporate free speech during political campaigns. This raised a 1990 precedent called *Austin v. Michigan Chamber of Commerce*, in which a Michigan campaign finance law, limiting the right of corporations to spend money from its general treasury to support political candidates during campaigns, was upheld under the First and the Fourteenth Amendments. According to an opinion authored by Justice Thurgood Marshall for a six-justice majority, "Corporate wealth can unfairly influence elections when it is deployed in the form of independent expenditures, just as it can when it assumes the guise of political contributions."[33]

In the opening lines of his powerful dissent in that case, Scalia defended the unlimited constitutional free speech right of corporations by citing the most provocative literary reference in his arsenal—George Orwell's *1984*: "'Attention all citizens. To assure the fairness of elections by preventing disproportionate expression of the views of any single powerful group, your Government has decided that the following associations of persons shall be prohibited from speaking or writing in support of any candidates. . . .' In permitting Michigan to make private corporations the first object of this Orwellian announcement, the Court today endorses the principle that too much speech is an evil that the democratic majority can proscribe." Scalia found this view to be undemocratic, "and incompatible with the absolutely central truth of the First Amendment: that government cannot be trusted to assure, through censorship, the 'fairness' of political debate."[34]

The *Austin v. Michigan Chamber of Commerce* case triggered Scalia's libertarian, "more speech is better" view of the First Amendment, leading him to seek the law's reversal. In doing so, he could not call upon the wisdom of the Founders, because, given their experience with businesses supported by the British Crown, such as the East India Company, whose cargo famously ended up in Boston Harbor, the Founders well understood that corporations were much different from living human beings and should not have the same speech rights. So Scalia turned instead to Alexis de Tocqueville, who wrote in his classic study, *Democracy in America*, first published in 1835:

"Governments . . . should not be the only active powers; associations ought, in democratic nations, to stand in lieu of those powerful private individuals whom the equality of conditions has swept away. . . . To eliminate voluntary associations—not only including powerful ones, but especially including powerful ones—from the public debate is either to augment the always dominant power of government or to impoverish the public debate."[35] Untroubled by the fact that Tocqueville was not speaking here of business corporations but of the plethora of citizen groups that he encountered in America, and the fact that during that time President Andrew Jackson was waging political war on corporations as being a threat to popular freedom, Scalia concluded: "It is entirely obvious that the object of the law we have approved today is not to prevent wrongdoing but to prevent speech."[36]

What the force of Scalia's dissent could not accomplish in 1990 toward protecting the rights of corporate free speech during an election, the changing ideological balance of the Court achieved two decades later. The Court ruled in *Citizens United v. Federal Election Commission* that corporations had the same free speech rights as living people to contribute to elections. Speaking for five members of the Court, Anthony Kennedy, who had also dissented in *Austin*, overturned that case and ruled that because of the First Amendment, corporate speech in the form of election campaign contributions could not be limited:

> The Government may commit a constitutional wrong when by law it identifies certain preferred speakers. By taking the right to speak from some and giving it to others, the Government deprives the disadvantaged person or class of the right to use speech to strive to establish worth, standing, and respect for the speaker's voice. The Government may not by these means deprive the public of the right and privilege to determine for itself what speech and speakers are worthy of consideration. The First Amendment protects speech and speaker, and the ideas that flow from each.[37]

Kennedy and the majority were following the long-held legal theory that corporations were the same as people under the law, though just where the idea originated that they were now "disadvantaged person[s] or [a] class" here was not made clear.[38] For them, "The corporate independent expenditures at issue in this case . . . would not interfere with governmental functions . . . [and] we find no basis for the proposition that, in the context of political speech, the Government may impose restrictions on certain disfavored speakers. Both history and logic lead us to this conclusion."[39]

Echoing Scalia's dissent in the *Austin* case, Kennedy and the majority argued that the government could not constitutionally "command where a person may get his or her information or what distrusted source he or she may not hear," because if it did so it would unlawfully "us[e] censorship to control thought." For the majority, "the First Amendment confirms the freedom to think for ourselves."[40] Unable to find a compelling interest by the government to limit the right of corporate speech in elections, Kennedy ruled that the limits on corporate campaign financing in the Bipartisan Campaign Reform Act should be overturned.[41] Since there would now be no limits on corporate speech, the majority saw no problem with a politically based, even if politically motivated, documentary, such as Citizens United's *Hillary: The Movie* being released during the primary election.[42] And the law's ban on issue ads close to an election was also overturned. It was here, though, that Justice Kennedy displayed what was later described by Arizona senator John McCain as his "naïveté" about politics, when he added: "[The government] reasons that corporate political speech can be banned to prevent corruption or its appearance . . . this Court now concludes that independent expenditures, including those made by corporations, do not give rise to corruption or the appearance of corruption. That speakers may have influence over or access to elected officials does not mean that those officials are corrupt. And the appearance of influence or access will not cause the electorate to lose faith in this democracy."[43] The continued public uproar over the *Citizens United* decision, and the vast sums donated by corporations to subsequent elections, suggest otherwise.[44]

In separate opinions, John Paul Stevens and Scalia dueled over the lessons to be drawn from the Founding period's history as to whether corporations should have an unlimited right of free speech to make campaign contributions in an election. Stevens began his combined concurring and dissenting opinion with a simple proposition, that corporations are different from human beings and should be treated as such by the law: "The conceit that corporations must be treated identically to natural persons in the political sphere is not only inaccurate but also inadequate to justify the Court's disposition of this case. In the context of election to public office, the distinction between corporate and human speakers is significant. Although they make enormous contributions to our society, corporations are not actually members of it. They cannot vote or run for office."[45] For Stevens, corporations might be treated as people in other areas of law, but they should not have the same full rights as people under the First Amendment.

Challenging Kennedy's lack of concern about corporate election campaign donations "giv[ing] rise to corruption," Stevens worried about the ability of large national and multinational corporations to warp elections: "The financial resources, legal structure, and instrumental orientation of corporations raise legitimate concerns about their role in the electoral process. Our lawmakers have a compelling constitutional basis, if not also a democratic duty, to take measures designed to guard against the potentially deleterious effects of corporate spending in local and national races. The majority's approach to corporate electioneering marks a dramatic break from our past."[46] Harking back to his plea in *Bush v. Gore* about the danger of the Court inserting itself into the political world, Stevens warned: "The Court's ruling threatens to undermine the integrity of elected institutions across the Nation . . . [and] I fear, do damage to this institution."[47]

Stevens then took a page from Scalia's playbook to explain why in his opinion the Founders never would have agreed that corporations had the same free speech rights as human beings. In a section titled the "Original Understandings" of the First Amendment, Stevens argued, using his version of originalism, that the majority's interpretation "has it exactly backwards." As he put it: "The Framers thus took it as a given that corporations could be comprehensively regulated in the service of the public welfare. Unlike our colleagues, they had little trouble distinguishing corporations from human beings, and when they constitutionalized the right to free speech in the First Amendment, it was the free speech of individual Americans that they had in mind. While individuals might join together to exercise their speech rights, business corporations, at least, were plainly not seen as facilitating such associational or expressive ends."[48] Stevens was unimpressed by Kennedy's use of the Framers to argue on behalf of the speech rights of corporations: "In fairness, our campaign finance jurisprudence has never attended very closely to the views of the Framers . . . whose political universe differed profoundly from that of today. We have long since held that corporations are covered by the First Amendment. . . . In light of the Court's effort to cast itself as guardian of ancient values, it pays to remember that nothing in our constitutional history dictates today's outcome. To the contrary, this history helps illuminate just how extraordinarily dissonant the decision is."[49]

To no one's surprise, Scalia in his concurring opinion took vigorous exception to Stevens's version of Founding Era history. Based on the text of the

First Amendment, Scalia argued that the protected speech rights were indistinguishable for everyone: "The Amendment is written in terms of 'speech,' not speakers. Its text offers no foothold for excluding any category of speaker, from single individuals to partnerships of individuals, to unincorporated associations of individuals, to incorporated associations of individuals—and the dissent offers no evidence about the original meaning of the text to support any such exclusion." Since that was so, Scalia continued, "A documentary film critical of a potential Presidential candidate is core political speech, and its nature as such does not change simply because it was funded by a corporation. . . . Indeed, to exclude or impede corporate speech is to muzzle the principal agents of the modern free economy. We should celebrate rather than condemn the addition of this speech to the public debate."[50]

Not everyone celebrated this ruling. As a result of this decision, so-called Super PACs would find a way to inject unlimited amounts of campaign donations by corporations, unions, large interest groups, the ultrarich, and even viewers of television comedian Stephen Colbert, into the elections, sometimes anonymously, so long as they did not coordinate their spending with the individual political candidates.

While Stevens read portions of his dissent from the bench, a most unusual move for him, observers in the courtroom noticed that the eighty-nine-year-old justice "looked weary."[51] As he delivered his brief statement "in sometimes halting fashion," Stevens had trouble pronouncing several common words and phrases, stumbling over "rejection," "Senate report," "Tillman Act," and "which observed." Sometimes, a reporter noticed, Stevens "would take a second or third run at the word, sometimes not."[52] Stevens later recalled the concern that he had at that moment: "When I announced my dissent in the *Citizens United* case . . . for the first time that I had ever done it, I had some trouble articulating what I wanted to say. . . . Which troubled me."[53]

Few knew that early in his tenure on the Court, Stevens had asked one of his law clerks, Stewart Baker, to draft a memo suggesting the optimal time for a justice to retire. Baker recommended that the best retirement age was roughly seventy-five. To ensure that he did not overstay his time on the Court, Stevens had also asked his then junior colleague David Souter to keep an eye on his mental acuity and let him know when he might be slipping enough to think about retiring. But with Souter now retired in New Hampshire, leaving him with no reliable outside check on his decision as to whether to leave, Stevens's struggles during his oral dissent from the bench caused him to consider retirement: "I thought, I should give some thought to the fact that I might not be able to, I might be changing in ways I had not recognized. . . . And as the year went by, I decided that it might be appropriate to do so."[54] Ten weeks later, on April 9, 2010, Stevens announced that he would be retiring at the end of that Court term. Before he did so, though, there were still some important decisions to announce.

• • •

In April 2010, Scalia ventured back to Charlottesville, where he had once taught in the University of Virginia's law school, to give a keynote address in honor of *emeritus* Professor Henry J. Abraham, one of the nation's preeminent Supreme Court scholars. Scalia took to the podium at the law school's Caplin Auditorium and delivered a slightly modified version of his "Methodology of Originalism" speech that he had given seventeen months earlier at Harvard Law School. This time, though, he added a new section at the end more directly responding to Judge Richard Posner's *New Republic* article charging that Scalia's originalism technique in the *Heller* case was just "law office history." Avoiding the use of Posner's name in the remarks by referring to him only as a "public intellectual" writing in a "bi-weekly magazine," Scalia took umbrage at the "law office history" charge, which he described as a claim that the Court was being "tendentious" in using "history slanted to advocate a point of view." "To equate chambers history with law office history is profoundly ignorant," Scalia said, arguing in response. "Judges are very capable of determining the weight of historical advocacy." Then, responding to Posner's claim that the professional historians sided with John Paul Stevens's dissent supporting only a collective militia-based right to own guns, Scalia chided, "Did [Posner] send out a survey form to them? Did he count the number of historians signing these briefs?" For Scalia, it was irrelevant how many professional historians sided with one litigant or the other, because "ultimately it is the judge's call," and, he added, "Figuring out the meaning of legal texts is judges' work." And this justice had made his call: "My own perception is that historians see the right to bear arms as beyond the military right, not limited to it." Scalia added that Posner was not correct in charging either that "the Supreme Court, in deciding constitutional cases, exercises a freewheeling discretion strongly flavored with ideology," or that "ideology drives decision in cases in which liberal and conservative values collide." Rather, Scalia concluded, originalism does not allow a judge to distort history because the Constitution is not "infinitely malleable."[55]

Later that evening, following a banquet honoring Scalia, he appeared at a small reception at the stately Boar's Head Inn in Charlottesville. After so many years of working on my biography of him, such a small gathering offered this author a rare opportunity to speak with the justice. This presented the chance to ask a lingering question.

It was then just weeks before the Court would announce its verdict in the follow-up case to Scalia's *Heller* gun control decision. The state-level version of that gun control case, *McDonald v. City of Chicago*, would explore whether the "right to keep and bear arms" that applied against the federal government should be incorporated into the Fourteenth Amendment's Due Process Clause and applied against state governments as well. Like the 2008 case, this one lent itself nicely to Scalia's originalism theory, but this time the question was whether the framers of the Civil War–era amendment had intended for the Second Amendment to apply to the states, and if so, whether it should be done through the Due Process Clause, or by resuscitating and using the Privileges or Immunities Clause that the Court had largely gutted in the 1873 *Slaughter-House Cases*.[56] There, the Court ruled that Louisiana's state legislature could back a single state-supported slaughterhouse monopoly in the face of complaints by other industry owners who said that this would take away their livelihood and thus deny them their "privileges or immunities" to make a living and run a business as guaranteed by the Fourteenth Amendment. For the Court, speaking through Justice Samuel Miller, this right protected only the privileges or immunities of United States citizenship, such as the rights to peaceable assembly, habeas corpus, and protection against piracy on the high seas, and not the rights of state citizenship. Since the right to make a living and run a business came under the state category, the slaughterhouse industry owners lost and the Privileges or Immunities Clause was effectively removed from the Constitution.

It was in anticipating an interesting battle between the two originalists on the Court, Scalia and Clarence Thomas, over how to interpret the Fourteenth Amendment in this case that I asked the justice about his evolving theory for decision making. Though he spoke and wrote about a "dead" and "eternal" Constitution and his inflexible, unchanging originalism theory for interpreting it, did he realize how much his own decision-making theory and approach had changed over the years? As I spoke, Scalia made very clear that he did not see it that way, looking a bit puzzled, scrunching up his face as if pained, and slowly shaking his head. As soon as the question was finished, he responded, "Why would I evolve? The meaning of the Constitution does not change."[57]

"What, then, do you see as the main difference between you and your originalism ally, Clarence Thomas?"

"Clarence has no trouble, if he doesn't like a precedent, in overturning it and sweeping it away. I don't do that," said Scalia.

"Would you ever change in your decision making, with historians always finding new evidence or changing their interpretations of existing evidence? What if it turned out that historians learned more from newly uncovered sources and changed their scholarship?"

"If someone brings me historical evidence that shows I was wrong in the past case, I would certainly write differently, saying 'on the basis of historical scholarship, I previously believed that this case interpretation was correct, but it turns out not to be true.' Then I would correct the holding."

"So that *would* allow you to evolve?"

"Yes."

At that point, another guest joined the conversation, mentioning the upcoming *McDonald v. Chicago* gun control case, but not by name, and asking: "What about the possible application of the Fourteenth Amendment's Privileges or Immunities Clause to protect the right to keep and bear arms? How would you have decided the *Slaughter-House Cases* in 1873?"

"I don't know how I would have decided. I probably would have agreed with them. Clarence would overturn this case if he did not agree with it. I wouldn't do that," said Scalia.

"Certainly it was a different Court composition, a different time, and they were closer in time to the Fourteenth Amendment ratification process," I pointed out.

"Yes," Scalia responded, adding, "I don't believe in legislative history, so I would *never* look at the *Congressional Globe* to see what the framers of the Fourteenth Amendment meant by the wording."

If Scalia was aware of how much he had evolved on and off the Court, he would not admit it. Nevertheless, any fair reading of his speeches and judicial opinions demonstrates clearly how the Court of Appeals judge, who had used a wide variety of decision-making theories, later became a strict textualist on the Supreme Court by the late 1980s, then evolved into a broader originalist by 1996, spoke as a Catholic on the Court in the early 2000s, became an even more partisan originalist by 2005, and was now casting himself as the judge of the historians. So while for Scalia the Constitution might not be living and evolving, he was. And as he changed, so did his interpretations, along with the type of sources he used.

More scholars of American history made clear that they were not persuaded by his unwavering claims of the intellectual correctness of his originalism theory. Historian Joseph J. Ellis, the author of the bestselling *Founding Brothers: The Revolutionary Generation*, dismissed Scalia's jurisprudence in a 2010 *Washington Post* column:

> The constitutional doctrine of original intent has always struck most historians of the founding era as rather bizarre. For they, more than most, know that the original framers of the Constitution harbored deep disagreements over the document's core provisions, that the debates in the state ratifying conventions further exposed the divisions of opinion on such seminal issues as federal vs. state jurisdiction, the powers of the executive branch, even whether there was—or should be—an ultimate arbiter of the purposefully ambiguous language of the document. Moreover, several of the most prominent Founders changed their minds in the ensuing years.

For Ellis, Scalia's use of history would not pass muster in the academic world.

> The doctrine of original intent rests on a set of implicit assumptions about the framers as a breed apart, momentarily allowed access to a set of timeless and transcendent truths. You don't have to believe that tongues of fire appeared over their heads during the debates. But the doctrine requires you to believe that the "miracle at Philadelphia" was a uniquely omniscient occasion when 55 mere mortals were permitted a glimpse of the eternal verities and then embalmed their insights in the document. Any professional historian proposing such an interpretation today would be laughed off the stage. That four sitting justices on the Supreme Court—Antonin Scalia, Clarence Thomas, John Roberts and Samuel Alito—claim to believe in it, or some version of it, is truly strange. We might call it the Immaculate Conception theory of jurisprudence.[58]

Ellis added, Thomas Jefferson argued that each new generation of Americans, then roughly every twenty years, was so different that the people should scrap the Constitution and rewrite it.[59]

But Scalia himself had already seen a flaw in his new argument about the qualifications of judges to read, interpret, and evaluate history in order to rule on the basis of it. More than two decades earlier, in first explaining his new theory in his "Originalism: The Lesser Evil" speech, Scalia had said of originalism:

> Its greatest defect, in my view, is the difficulty of applying it correctly. . . . What is true is that it is often exceedingly difficult to plumb the original understanding of an ancient text. Properly done, the task requires the consideration of an enormous mass of material. . . . And further still, it requires immersing oneself in the political and intellectual atmosphere of the time—somehow placing out of mind knowledge that we have which an earlier age did not, and putting on beliefs, attitudes, philosophies, prejudices and loyalties that are not those of our day. It is, in short, a task sometimes better suited to the historian than the lawyer.[60]

Scalia had come a long way from this warning that he had first offered in 1988. Whereas he once said lawyers can't do history, he had changed his view to, historians can't be trusted to do history, so leave it to the judges to evaluate them. Contrary to the nation's preeminent professional Founding Era historians like Jack Rakove, Leonard Levy, Gordon S. Wood, Pauline Maier, and Joseph Ellis, he now argued that the American people should trust the judges over the historians. And with "purposefully ambiguous language" to interpret, not just any judge would do. Scalia trusted only himself.

• • •

Not everyone who had served on the Court agreed. As the 2009–10 term began winding down to its closing month, with its most important decisions yet to be announced, criticism of Scalia's originalism theory came from a most unexpected quarter. David Souter delivered Harvard University's 359th college commencement address. Souter's discussion of what he called the "fair reading" jurisprudential model, his name for Scalia's and Thomas's originalism approach, represented his powerful answer to Scalia's 2008 Harvard Law School "Methodology of Originalism" speech.[61]

Souter, who had occasionally used originalism in cases such as the *Lee v. Weisman* public school prayer case, knew the difference between using the technique to restrict rights, as Scalia and Thomas did, and using it to expand rights, as he did. Souter began his address by defining the fair reading model as "deciding constitutional cases [in] . . . a straightforward exercise of reading fairly and viewing facts objectively." The problem, Souter explained, is that few provisions of the Constitution are this straightforward, with many of them being open-ended rights requiring more interpretation. "The Constitution has a good share of deliberately open-ended guarantees, like rights to due process of law, equal protection of the law, and freedom from unreasonable searches. These provisions cannot be applied like the requirement for 30-year-old senators; they call for more elaborate reasoning to show why very general language applies in some specific cases but not in others, and over time the various examples turn into rules that the Constitution does not mention."

Souter added his own critique of Scalia's originalism approach to that already offered by historians and other Supreme Court justices. "The fair reading model fails to account for what the Constitution actually says, and it fails just as badly to understand what judges have no choice but to do. The Constitution is a pantheon of values, and a lot of hard cases are hard because the Constitution gives no simple rule of decision for the cases in which one of the values is truly at odds with another." Souter argued that the vagueness of the Constitution requires the application of an evolving interpretation:

Not even . . . [the Constitution's] most uncompromising and unconditional language can resolve every potential tension of one provision with another, tension the Constitution's Framers left to be resolved another day; and another day after that, for our cases can give no answers that fit all conflicts, and no resolutions immune to rethinking when the significance of old facts may have changed in the changing world. These are reasons enough to show how egregiously it misses the point to think of judges in constitutional cases as just sitting there reading constitutional phrases fairly and looking at reported facts objectively to produce their judgments. Judges have to choose between the good things that the Constitution approves, and when they do, they have to choose, not on the basis of measurement, but of meaning.

For Souter, this judicial calculation of "meaning" is what the Scalia-Thomas technique misses: "The simplistic view of the Constitution devalues our aspirations, and attacks that our confidence [*sic*], and diminishes us. It is a view of judging that means to discourage our tenacity (our sometimes reluctant tenacity) to keep the constitutional promises the nation has made. . . . I have to believe that something deeper is involved, and that behind most dreams of a simpler Constitution there lies a basic human hunger for the certainty and control that the fair reading model seems to promise." For him, then, the fair reading originalist approach gave his former colleagues more "certainty and control" in reaching the case results that they wanted.

On the contrary, as opposed to the certainty and inflexibility of the originalist, Souter argued that "in an indeterminate world I cannot control, it is still possible to live fully in the trust that a way will be found leading through the uncertain future. And to me, the future of the Constitution as the Framers wrote it can be staked only upon that same trust." For him, the answer as to the best interpretation of the Constitution could be distilled from the overall vision of the Framers: "If we cannot share every intellectual assumption that formed the minds of those who framed the charter, we can still address the constitutional uncertainties the way they must have envisioned, by relying on reason, by respecting all the words the Framers wrote, by facing facts, and by seeking to understand their meaning for living people. That is how a judge lives in a state of trust, and I know of no other way to make good on the aspirations that tell us who we are, and who we mean to be, as the people of the United States."

Just as this attack was mounted from outside the originalists' camp, there was a new one emerging from inside it. Ever since the 2008 *Heller* case it had seemed that Scalia was the undisputed King of the Originalists on the Roberts Court. But in the most important case announced at the end of that 2009–10 term, Clarence Thomas once again laid claim to that title.

McDonald v. City of Chicago tested a gun control law in the aftermath of the *Heller* case. Just like Dick Heller in the District of Columbia case, Otis McDonald wanted to keep a handgun in his home to protect himself and his family. Citing the constitutional right of self-defense in *Heller*, he objected to a 2009 city ordinance in Chicago and Oak Park banning the home ownership of handguns in order to protect people "from the loss of property and injury or death from firearms."[62] The new issue he raised was whether the Second Amendment "right to keep and bear arms," which applied to the federal government, should also apply to the states through the Fourteenth

Amendment. And, if it did, should the Chicago gun control law, like the D.C. ordinance in the 2008 *Heller* case, be overturned?

Speaking for the Court's majority in ruling that the Second Amendment would be incorporated and applied to the states, Samuel Alito explained that the "due process [clause] protects those rights that are 'the very essence of a scheme of ordered liberty' and essential to 'a fair and enlightened system of justice.'" By incorporating what he termed the "essence" of the "right to keep and bear arms," Alito followed Scalia in the *Heller* case by extending the reach of the "core" of the Second Amendment as written by the Framers to the "right of self-defense." [63] Page after page of supportive historical analysis then followed in Alito's opinion, allowing him to conclude: "In sum, it is clear that the Framers and ratifiers of the Fourteenth Amendment counted the right to keep and bear arms among those fundamental rights necessary to our system of ordered liberty." [64] So, the Court applied the Second Amendment to the states and overturned the Chicago ordinance.

One critic of this substantive due process technique for incorporation was Clarence Thomas. Using his form of originalism to base his decisions on the meaning of the "unalienable rights" provision of the Declaration of Independence, protecting "life, liberty, and the pursuit of Happiness," Thomas believed that the notion of owning guns to protect and preserve one's own life and property fulfilled these goals. [65] He argued in a solo concurring opinion that the Court should abandon its use of the Fourteenth Amendment's Due Process Clause to apply the Bill of Rights to the states. As an alternative, Thomas offered a comprehensive historical review of the congressional debates over the creation of the Fourteenth Amendment, contemporaneous public speeches and newspaper articles, and other historical sources to argue that the Privileges or Immunities Clause was meant to protect fundamental rights against state restriction. [66] This allowed him to argue that for the Fourteenth Amendment's state "ratifying public" the "right to keep and bear arms was understood to be a privilege of American citizenship guaranteed by the Privileges or Immunities Clause." [67]

And just what was the right that states should now be protecting? Thomas argued that a primary purpose for protecting the right to keep and bear arms in the Privileges or Immunities Clause was to safeguard the right of the newly freed slaves, whose lives were often threatened, to own and carry guns for self-defense. Based on this history, Thomas concluded: "In my view, the record makes plain that the Framers of the Privileges or Immunities Clause and the ratifying-era public understood—just as the Framers of the Second Amendment did—that the right to keep and bear arms was essential to the preservation of liberty."[68] With this opinion Thomas had once again staked his claim as the Court's most disciplined originalist.

• • •

Thomas's opinion was largely overlooked by the press in favor of the judicial fireworks created by a final verbal battle between Scalia and John Paul Stevens. True to his statement at the University of Virginia, Scalia was unwilling to overturn the *Slaughter-House Cases* and rely on the Privileges or Immunities Clause of the Fourteenth Amendment to decide this case. Instead, in a concurrence, Scalia made clear that despite his doubts about the process of incorporating the Bill of Rights using the Fourteenth Amendment's Due Process Clause, he was still willing to sign on to Alito's majority upholding the "long established and narrowly limited" line of precedents holding this way. The purpose of his concurrence, Scalia wrote, was "only to respond to some aspects of Justice Stevens' dissent."[69]

And Scalia had understandable reasons for doing so, for in his valedictory dissenting opinion, Justice Stevens took issue with Scalia's entire originalism approach one final time. Nearly ninety years old, and about to conclude more than thirty-five years of service, the third-longest-serving justice in the Court's history, Stevens issued a ninety-eight-page dissent. Stevens relied solely on his interpretation of what he called the "liberty clause" of the Fourteenth Amendment, his name for the Due Process Clause itself, to decide whether it could be defined to include the Second Amendment's guarantee "to keep and bear arms," and then apply it to the states. As he did in *Heller*, Stevens argued that the Second Amendment protected the collective militia and "security" rights, meaning that only guns designed to protect the home should be applied to the states. Then, continuing his debate against Scalia's originalism theory from the *Citizens United* case earlier that term, Stevens argued, "The judge who would outsource the interpretation of liberty to historical sentiment has turned his back on a task the Constitution assigned to him and drained the document of its intended vitality."[70]

Stevens challenged Scalia's use of a historically derived fundamental rights approach to create rights such as "self-defense" that are not mentioned in the Constitution or the Fourteenth Amendment. The problem for Stevens in determining a right's "fundamental" qualities is that one person's gun ownership right could negatively affect another person's right to life and property. He argued: "First, firearms have a fundamentally ambivalent relationship to liberty. Just as they can help homeowners defend their families and property from intruders, they can help thugs and insurrectionists murder innocent victims. The threat that firearms will be misused is far from hypothetical, for gun crime has devastated many of our communities."[71] For Stevens, the Fourteenth Amendment's "liberty clause" alone had never been used to protect a right either of gun ownership or self-defense. "Despite the plethora of substantive due process cases that have been decided . . . I have found none that holds, states, or even suggests that the term 'liberty' encompasses either the common-law right of self-defense or a right to keep and bear arms. . . . It does not appear to be the case that the ability to own a handgun, or any particular type of firearm, is critical to leading a life of autonomy, dignity, or political equality."[72]

While Justice Alito praised Stevens's work here as an "eloquent opinion," Scalia threw judicial etiquette out the window. In an opinion reminiscent of his virulent attacks against O'Connor, Scalia criticized Stevens by name sixty-one times in the text and footnotes of his twenty-four-page concurrence. Scalia mocked Stevens's expansive interpretation of the Constitution as being "as valid as the Court's only in a two-dimensional world that conflates length and depth."[73]

As he had done many times before, Scalia attacked his colleague's reasoning ability personally, trying to persuade the reader that paying any attention to his opponent was not worth their time.

> JUSTICE STEVENS moves on to . . . his theory . . . that he would "esche[w] attempts to provide any all-purpose, top-down, totalizing theory of 'liberty.'" . . . The notion that the absence of a coherent theory of the Due Process Clause will somehow curtail judicial caprice is at war with reason. Indeterminacy means opportunity for courts to impose whatever rule they like; it is the problem, not the solution. The idea that interpretive pluralism would reduce courts' ability to impose their will on the ignorant masses is not merely naïve, but absurd. If there are no right answers, there are no wrong answers either.[74]

Scalia believed that reliance should be placed on the views of the voters, limited by the words of America's Founders. Arguing in conclusion, Scalia said, "JUSTICE STEVENS abhors a system in which 'majorities or powerful interest groups always get their way' . . . but replaces it with a system in which unelected and life-tenured judges always get their way. . . . It is JUSTICE STEVENS' approach, not the Court's, that puts democracy in peril."[75]

Just as his former colleagues William Brennan and Harry Blackmun had done near the end of their careers, Stevens directly challenged Scalia's ability to do his originalist historical analysis. "It is hardly a novel insight that history is not an objective science, and that its use can therefore 'point in any direction the judges favor,'" wrote Stevens. "Yet 21 years after the point was brought to his attention by Justice Brennan, JUSTICE SCALIA remains 'oblivious to the fact that [the concept of tradition] can be as malleable and elusive as "liberty" itself.' . . . Even when historical analysis is focused on a discrete proposition, such as the original public meaning of the Second Amendment, the evidence often points in different directions. The historian must choose which pieces to credit and which to discount, and then must try to assemble them into a coherent whole."[76]

Like Richard Posner and Jack Rakove before him, Stevens criticized Scalia's work as being nothing more than "law office history," employing "the malleability and elusiveness of history" to decide cases whichever way the judge preferred. In accusing Scalia of "conducting this rudderless, panoramic tour of American legal history," Stevens argued, "JUSTICE SCALIA's defense of his method, which holds out objectivity and restraint as its cardinal—and, it seems, only—virtue, is unsatisfying on its own terms. For a limitless number of subjective judgments may be smuggled into his historical analysis. Worse, they may be buried in the analysis. At least with my approach, the judge's cards are laid on the table for all to see, and to critique."[77] Using his own expansive interpretive approach, combined with some historical analysis, was more appropriate, Stevens argued. "My method seeks to synthesize dozens of cases on which the American people have relied for decades. JUSTICE SCALIA's method seeks to vaporize them. So I am left to wonder, which of us is more faithful to this Nation's constitutional history? And which of us is more faithful to the values and commitments of the American people, as they stand today?"[78]

Stevens closed his blistering dissent by firing one final verbal volley: "JUSTICE SCALIA's method invites not only bad history, but also bad constitutional law. . . . It makes little sense to give history dispositive weight in every case. . . . It is not the role of federal judges to be amateur historians. And it is not fidelity to the Constitution to ignore its use of deliberately capacious language, in an effort to transform foundational legal commitments into narrow rules of decision."[79] Contrary to Scalia's view that these answers should come from the voters in a democracy and the state legislatures, Stevens placed the responsibility for protecting liberties with an independent judiciary. "Under our constitutional scheme, I would have thought that a judicial approach to liberty claims such as the one I have outlined . . . has the capacity to improve, rather than '[im]peril' . . . our democracy. It all depends on judges exercising careful, reasoned judgment. As it always has, and as it always will."[80] And with that, John Paul Stevens hung up his judicial gown and retired, leaving the nation to wonder which judicial liberal would continue the constitutional battle with Scalia.

CHAPTER 24

Kennedy's Court

On May 10, 2010, President Obama furthered his legacy on the Supreme Court when he selected his liberal solicitor general, former Harvard Law School dean Elena Kagan, to replace the retiring Justice John Paul Stevens. Kagan, the president said, was "one of the nation's foremost legal minds," citing both her "openness to a broad array of viewpoints" and her "fair mindedness."[1]

Then only fifty years old, Kagan had developed the perfect résumé for the job. Like Justices Alito and Sotomayor a graduate of Princeton, she also held degrees from Oxford University and Harvard Law School. After serving as a law clerk for Justice Thurgood Marshall, she taught at the University of Chicago Law School and was White House counsel for President Bill Clinton. Clinton nominated her for a position on the D.C. Court of Appeals, but when the Republican-dominated Senate Judiciary Committee refused even to consider her nomination, Kagan returned to academia, teaching at Harvard Law. In 2003, she became the school's first female dean. After Obama named her solicitor general in January 2009, the Senate confirmed her appointment by a vote of 61–31.

Despite all of these career stops little was known about Kagan's personal or professional views. Following an uneventful Judiciary Committee appearance for her Supreme Court nomination, Kagan was confirmed by a partisan vote of 63–37. Her addition to the institution gave the Court its first majority of baby boomers, as well as a record three female members.[2] But with the liberal Kagan replacing the liberal Stevens, this appointment would not change the philosophical balance on the Court.[3]

Despite President Obama's two Supreme Court appointments, the Roberts Court was, in the words of *New York Times* reporter Adam Liptak, the "Most Conservative in Decades."[4] In a comprehensive article published on

Sunday, July 25, 2010, Liptak used four new sets of data to demonstrate that the Roberts Court was more conservative than the Burger and Rehnquist Courts, and even more conservative than the ultra-right-wing "Nine Old Men" who had driven President Franklin Roosevelt to propose his unsuccessful Court-packing plan of 1937. Of the six most conservative justices since 1937, four of them were currently serving on the Court, in Liptak's reckoning. In fact, Anthony Kennedy, whom some had called a moderate, was ranked by Liptak as the tenth most conservative justice in that time period. Moreover, Liptak argued, with the Court getting younger with each new appointment, it would not change ideologically for years to come: "The data show that only one recent replacement altered [the Court's] direction, that of Justice Samuel A. Alito Jr. for Justice Sandra Day O'Connor in 2006, pulling the Court to the right. There is no similar switch on the horizon. That means that Chief Justice Roberts, 55, is settling in for what is likely to be a very long tenure at the head of a court that seems to be entering a period of stability."[5] The only question seemed to be which of those conservatives would lead what was expected to be their stable majority.

The answer to that question appeared to be dictated by a small, but important, procedural change owing to John Paul Stevens's departure. Under the Court's informal rules, when the chief justice is in the majority on a case he or she assigns the writer of a majority opinion or writes the opinion himself, an important power shaping both the direction and tone of the ruling. However, when the chief is in dissent, the power to assign the majority opinion falls to the most senior justice in the majority in terms of years of service on the Court. The power to assign the majority opinion can depend on who is willing to be flexible enough to shape their opinion to command a majority. Benefiting from this shift in the opinion-assignment power in key cases from 1986 to 1989, William Brennan, the Court's most senior and liberal member, often stole majorities from Chief Justice William Rehnquist, the conservative "Lone Ranger" who refused to moderate his ideological views and join the majority. The result, on a Court dominated by conservatives, was several liberal decisions in cases dealing with issues such as flag burning laws and state abortion restrictions.

The same scenario now faced Rehnquist's former law clerk and current chief justice, John Roberts. With Stevens gone, Scalia was now the most senior justice on the Court by a few months over Kennedy. However, he was also likely to be in the same voting clique as the conservative chief and so would seldom be in a position to assign an opinion. This meant that any time Kennedy joined with the four liberals and not Roberts to form a majority, he, as the most senior justice in that majority, would have the power to assign the opinion. As a result of this rule, in cases where Kennedy's vote was in flux and Roberts was in disagreement, the chief could be left with three increasingly unpalatable options: assign a plum opinion to Kennedy to keep him with the conservative majority; vote with the four liberal justices rather than with the conservatives, in order to retain the power to assign the opinion; or watch Kennedy bolt to the liberal wing with the prospect that as the senior justice in the majority he might assign the writing of the opinion to himself.

All of this served to anoint Kennedy as the new "shadow chief" on the Court. By exercising his combined powers as the Court's swing justice, he could become the institution's most powerful member. Like it or not, Scalia now served not on the "Roberts Court," but on the "Kennedy Court," controlled by a colleague whom he had belittled in so many earlier cases.

Just before the 2010–11 Supreme Court opened, Scalia could not help creating some controversy once again. Speaking in September 2010 before four hundred law students in a ninety-minute question and answer forum called "Legally Speaking" at the University of California's Hastings College of Law in San Francisco, Scalia said of the Fourteenth Amendment's Equal Protection Clause, "Nobody thought it was directed against sex discrimination." Rather, he explained that its purpose was to outlaw racial discrimination. After conceding that bias against women "shouldn't exist," Scalia argued that the notion that such bias should be banned by the Constitution was "a modern invention." As Scalia said so many times to people who wanted to read rights into the Constitution, "If the current society wants to outlaw discrimination by sex, you have legislatures," adding that for him the same was true for the rights of gays and lesbians. Later speaking of another area of women's rights, the Court's abortion decisions, Scalia said that it "puts me in the position of being a legislator rather than a judge. . . . That's not law, and I won't do it."[6]

The comments went largely unnoticed until political satirist Stephen Colbert mentioned them on his Comedy Central cable show, *The Colbert Report*. Colbert, who plays a conservative pundit, began by saying of Scalia's originalism theory, "I've always said that a good Supreme Court justice is a constitutional scholar first, [and] a time-travelling mind reader second." Colbert continued:

As an originalist, Scalia argues that the idea that the Equal Protection clause of the Fourteenth Amendment protects women's rights is a "'modern invention" because in 1868 when it was written, "nobody thought it was directed against sex discrimination." Evidently, back then, women hadn't been invented yet. . . . So all Scalia is saying is that women aren't persons. Now, ladies, please, don't take it personally. Which you can't since Constitutionally, you're not persons. Scalia wants you to have rights. That's why this year, he joined the majority in the *Citizens United* ruling, which found that "Corporations are people, with constitutional rights." So ladies, all you have to do is incorporate.[7]

Scalia followed up his earlier remarks in an interview with University of California at Hastings Law professor Calvin Massey, which was published in the January 2011 issue of *California Lawyer*. Picking up on the same theme as his remarks at his school, Scalia said:

> The Constitution does not require discrimination on the basis of sex. The only issue is whether it prohibits it. It doesn't. Nobody ever thought that that's what it meant. Nobody ever voted for that. If the current society wants to outlaw discrimination by sex, hey we have things called legislatures, and they enact things called laws. You don't need a constitution to keep things up-to-date. All you need is a legislature and a ballot box. . . . Persuade your fellow citizens it's a good idea and pass a law. That's what democracy is all about. It's not about nine superannuated judges who have been there too long, imposing these demands on society.[8]

At this point *The New York Times* weighed in. In an editorial titled "There He Goes Again," the newspaper lambasted Scalia for his "antiquated view of women's rights," which it called "outlandish," "jarring," and "constricted." It was Scalia's whole jurisprudential philosophy that disturbed the editorial board:

> No less dismaying is his notion that women, gays and other emerging minorities should be left at the mercy of the prevailing political majority when it comes to ensuring fair treatment. It is an "original-

ist" approach wholly antithetical to the framers' understanding that vital questions of people's rights should not be left solely to the political process. It also disrespects the wording of the Equal Protection Clause, which is intentionally broad, and its purpose of ensuring a fairer society. Fortunately, Justice Scalia's views on women are not the law of the land.[9]

But Scalia continued fanning the flames by accepting a speaking invitation from one of those unprotected women, U.S. representative and Tea Party leader Michele Bachmann of Minnesota. With over sixty new Republican representatives joining the 112th Congress in January 2011, Bachmann invited Scalia to lecture all of the incoming members about the "Constitutional Separation of Powers." This group had announced that it would open the new session of Congress by reading the full Constitution, and would insist that every newly passed law contain an explanation of its foundation in that document.[10] His agreement to speak on this occasion dismayed even the conservative *Wall Street Journal*, which published in its law blog, "Controversy, thy name is Scalia."[11] Scalia was operating in what he liked to call his "shin-kicker" mode, bringing to mind the line in Arthur Miller's *Death of a Salesman*, "Attention, attention must be finally paid to such a person."

While attention *was* being paid now to Scalia, it was not always to his reputation's best advantage. This was made evident when he became embroiled in another controversy bringing his sense of judicial ethics into question. Common Cause, a public interest group investigating governmental and political campaign ethics, had discovered that four years earlier, in 2007, Scalia had spoken at a "political strategy and fund-raising" seminar organized by the billionaire industrialists and businessmen Charles and David Koch, and held at an exclusive desert resort in Indian Wells, California, near Palm Springs. The following year, Clarence Thomas appeared at the same seminar. Beyond the obvious problems presented by two Supreme Court justices appearing at a political strategy and fund-raising session for an upcoming election, neither justice had fully reported their involvement in this session in their annual federal financial disclosure forms, saying only that they had traveled to that region and been reimbursed by the Federalist Society for "transportation, food, and lodging." While Common Cause did not know the nature of the justices' messages, or even how much, if at all, either had interacted with the attendees, it was the secrecy of these appearances that fueled their protests.

In a letter to Attorney General Eric Holder Jr. calling for a Justice Department investigation into these appearances, Common Cause president and CEO Bob Edgar linked the appearances to the Court's later rulings in the 2010 *Citizens United* corporate speech case: "That appearance is heightened by the highly secretive nature of those meetings, which were closed to the public and the media. Neither Justice Thomas nor Justice Scalia listed their attendance on their disclosure forms, and the public has no way of knowing when the meetings took place in relation to the pendency of the *Citizens United* case, what issues were discussed or the extent of the Justices' involvement."[12]

Common Cause further argued in this letter that the organizers of the seminar were using the justices' names to entice other potential contributors to attend subsequent seminars, and doing so for political purposes. Relying on investigative work by a liberal blog site called *Think Progress*, Common Cause quoted from a brochure advertising a later session, "Understanding and Addressing Threats to American Free Enterprise and Prosperity," which stated: "This action-oriented program brings together top experts and leaders to discuss—and offer solutions to counter—the most critical threats to our free society. . . . Past meetings have featured such notable leaders as Supreme Court Justices Antonin Scalia and Clarence Thomas."[13]

Federalist Society president Eugene Meyer was quoted as saying that, despite the listings of his organization on the two justices' financial disclosure forms, the group had "no meetings of its own at the venue." But, Meyer added, the group "knew the justices were going to be out there," and that "the attendees would be interested in hearing what they had to say." The misleading expenses reimbursements report only served to create the appearance that the two justices were trying to conceal their attendance at the Koch brothers' sessions.[14]

Inferring from this new discovery that such an ultraconservative, and über-wealthy, gathering would almost certainly benefit from the *Citizens United v. Federal Election Commission* case, Common Cause argued in its letter to Holder that the Justice Department should investigate the ethical questions raised by Scalia and Thomas attending those sessions and then participating in the landmark 2010 decision.

On the issue of political activity by members of the Court, the Code of Judicial Conduct states that "A judge should not . . . make speeches for a political organization or candidate, or publicly endorse or oppose a candidate for public office; or solicit funds for, pay an assessment to, or make a contribution to a political organization or candidate, or attend or purchase a ticket for a dinner or other event sponsored by a political organization or candidate. . . . A judge should not engage in any other political activity."[15] But the federal Code of Judicial Conduct does not apply to Supreme Court justices. Just as in the case of Scalia's duck hunting trip with Vice President Cheney while the latter was a party to a case before the Court, Scalia and Thomas were their own stewards. Beyond that, on the separate issue of recusal from cases, which did apply to the Court, while a Supreme Court justice should "disqualify himself in any proceeding in which his impartiality might reasonably be questioned,"[16] the justices are not required to explain either their reasons for recusing, if they chose to do so, or their rationale for not recusing. Common Cause and the national press argued that in this case, where the Koch brothers and other seminar attendees might benefit from the *Citizens United* case's unlimited corporate campaign funding ruling, both Scalia's and Thomas's impartiality in this case "might reasonably be questioned."[17]

While Common Cause's letter to Attorney General Holder went nowhere, damage had been done to both justices' images on the issue of judicial ethics, and that of the Court as a whole. In February 2011, a group of over one hundred law professors sent a letter to the House and Senate judiciary committees requesting the passage of a law extending the federal Code of Judicial Conduct to the Supreme Court.[18] Then, in late May, Representative Chris Murphy, a Democrat from Connecticut, proposed legislation designed to extend the Code of Judicial Conduct to the Supreme Court and to require justices to explain both their reasons for recusals and, if challenged, their reasons for refusing to recuse, all of which was to be overseen by a panel of retired judges. To no one's surprise, that bill also went nowhere in the stalemated Congress.[19]

In November, *The New York Times* published a lengthy front-page investigative story detailing the financial connection between Justice Thomas and a wealthy real estate developer from Dallas, Harlan Crow. Crow had reportedly provided the initial half-million-dollar start-up donation for Thomas's wife Ginni's Tea Party–based lobbying organization Liberty Central, which was dedicated, among other policy objectives, to defeating the Obama health care reform law, the Patient Protection and Affordable Care Act of 2010.[20] In addition, it was reported that Crow had done a series of other substantial financial "favors" for Justice Thomas, including the financing of a wing for the Savannah library in Thomas's name, giving him a valuable Bible once owned by abolitionist Frederick Douglass, entertaining him on his private yacht and various other locations, reportedly making his private jet available to fly the justice to speaking engagements, and even donating money to re-store a Georgia cannery site where Thomas's grandmother had once worked and turning it into a museum. The accumulation of ethical questions deal-ing with the apparently unsupervised and unchecked private actions of the justices again renewed the public discussion of proposed changes in the rules governing such behavior.[21]

The issue became so heated by December 2011 that, in an unusual step, Chief Justice Roberts filed his annual "Year End Report on the Federal Judiciary"—usually devoted to topics such as the judiciary's heavy work-load, the large number of open federal court vacancies, and the lack of pay increases that Congress should remedy—with a discussion of the Court's in-ternal rules governing recusal decisions. These decisions, he explained, were much like the federal Code of Judicial Conduct but administered by indi-vidual justices according to their own, and the Court's, set of ethical norms. Roberts added that he had "complete confidence" in the decisions of his col-leagues, writing: "The Supreme Court does not sit in judgment of one of its own Members' decision whether to recuse in the course of deciding a case. They are jurists of exceptional integrity and experience whose character and fitness have been examined through a vigorous appointment and confirma-tion process. I know that they each give careful consideration to any recusal questions that arise." The chief justice went on to argue that as members of the highest court in the land, and arguably beyond the power of Congress to govern their ethics due to the constitutional separation of powers, Supreme Court justices were not like other members of the federal judiciary in recusal issues, because there was no one to replace them if they withdrew from a case. If an outside system was devised by which recusal decisions were made by one's colleagues, "it would create an undesirable situation in which the court could affect the outcome of a case by selecting who among its members may participate."[22] Persuasive as the chief justice can be, his argument boiled down to, "I know my colleagues and believe me when I say that they can be trusted to follow the ethics rules."

Roberts's argument did not prove to be the final word. In early Febru-ary 2012, five Democrats on the Senate Judiciary Committee sent a letter to Roberts asking him to explain any new code of conduct adopted by the Court to govern their outside income, and requesting that the Court agree to observe the federal Code of Judicial Conduct. On February 19, *The New York Times* published an editorial on the Court, "Trust and the Supreme Court," arguing that "the authority of the Supreme Court depends on the trust of the public. But in recent years, that trust has been undermined by controversies surrounding the court's lack of openness in how justices deal with ethics questions and in the court's continuing refusal to let oral arguments be televised."[23] The *Times* took note of the fact that since 2009, the Court's public approval rating in the Gallup Poll, a figure that usually hovered around 60 percent, had dropped to 46 percent.[24] By mid-June 2012, that number would drop further, to 44 percent.[25]

In early March 2012, the Alliance for Justice and other reform organizations delivered to the Supreme Court a petition containing 100,000 signatures, and a letter signed by 212 law professors, requesting that the justices voluntarily agree to abide by the federal Code of Judicial Conduct.[26] Nan Aron, the Alliance for Justice president, explained: "If there ever was a time for the Court to buttress public confidence in its propriety and objectivity, this is it. With so much at stake, there must be no hint of favoritism or bias. We can't afford to have any questions of integrity looming over the justices." When asked about Chief Justice John Roberts's "Year End Report on the Federal Judiciary," Aron added: "John Roberts is wrong. He is risking the trust of the American people. It's time to close the ethics loophole, once and for all. This simple voluntary act of adopting the Code would serve as an important signal to an increasingly skeptical public that the Court gets it. The time for accountability is now."[27] A week later *The New York Times* offered yet another editorial on the Court's ethics, "A Way Forward on Judicial Ethics," this time endorsing a proposal by legal ethics expert Stephen Gillers to govern judicial recusal decisions.[28]

For better or worse, through his twenty-five years of considerable extrajudicial speechmaking, interviews, and public appearances, along with his inflammatory and hyperbolic tone both on and off the Court, Scalia had done more than any other member of the Court to erase the self-enforced ban on extrajudicial actions dating back to the forced resignation of Justice Abe Fortas in 1969. While these activities provided Scalia with a platform from which to educate the general public about his legal theories, they came at a cost. He had removed himself from some cases, such as the *Newdow* "under God" Pledge of Allegiance case, and had been the subject of withering public criticism over recusal issues on cases involving Dick Cheney, the "War on Terror" (his comments in Fribourg), and torture (his pro-torture comments in Ottawa and London). After so many years of such behavior, this new Koch seminar controversy had almost become the norm for him and, as a result, for his colleagues. Each time he survived the criticism, Scalia seemed emboldened. The accumulation of these and other incidents had politicized the Supreme Court, and in so doing endangered its prestige.[29]

* * *

While Scalia survived again off the Court, in his work on the Court he could not have everything his own way. In February 2011, Justice Sonia Sotomayor wrote a majority opinion undercutting Scalia's longtime effort to extend the reach of the Sixth Amendment's Confrontation Clause in criminal cases. Repeatedly since his *Coy v. Iowa* decision in 1988 Scalia had used his textualism and originalism theories to establish that the Confrontation Clause's guarantee that criminal defendants "be confronted with the witnesses against him" required a direct line-of-sight questioning of opposing witnesses by the defendant in criminal trials, sentencing hearings, and cross-examination of those who made "testimonial statements" to the police later affecting the trial. In the 2011 case of *Michigan v. Bryant*, the Court explored whether an exception could be created to that rule, for statements that "enable[d] assistance to meeting an ongoing emergency," making them "non-testimonial," and thus not bound by the Sixth Amendment Confrontation Clause guarantee.[30] The greater the exception for such statements, the less Scalia's originalist guarantee of the Confrontation Clause would extend its protective umbrella.

The case had an odd set of facts. The Michigan police found a man named Anthony Covington dying in the parking lot of a gas station and claiming that he had been shot outside his home by a man named Richard Perry Bryant. Acting on this information, the police located and arrested Bryant, and charged him with second degree murder. During his trial, the dying man's statement was used against Bryant despite his lawyer's objections that it was "testimonial" and, under the Sixth Amendment, required the presence of the victim—now dead—in court to be "confronted" as a witness. The Court would have to decide whether a dying man's statement was "testimonial," ensuring the Sixth Amendment guarantee, or "non-testimonial," and thus usable in Court because it "enable[d] police assistance to meeting an ongoing emergency." Six members of the Court, led by Sotomayor, ruled for the latter position, that the "non-testimonial" statement did not require confrontation of the witness against the accused in trial.

For the majority, under the test established by the Court in an earlier precedent, this statement from a dying victim was reliable and so it did not require testing through cross-examination. The Court was persuaded that the "primary purpose of the interrogation," the "victim's physical state," and the "statements and actions of [the] interrogators," all indicated that there was an emergency that the police were trying to resolve. With a possible killer on the loose, the police were not seeking "testimonial" evidence but rather trying through their questioning of the dying man to discover who had done the shooting and where he might be located so he could be stopped. In a single sentence, Sotomayor attacked the heart of Scalia's historical originalism argument that all such situations require direct, line-of-sight cross-examination. "It hardly bears mention that the emergency situation in this case is readily distinguishable from the 'treasonous conspiracies of unknown scope, aimed at killing or overthrowing the king.'"[31] Instead, the Court ruled that Covington's statements could be admitted at Bryant's trial because they were not testimonial, and thus did not violate the Confrontation Clause.

Understandably unhappy over the partial burial of his earlier precedents and the attack on his historical analysis, Scalia launched a verbal broadside at the junior jurist:

> Today's tale—a story of five officers conducting successive examinations of a dying man with the primary purpose, not of obtaining and preserving his testimony regarding his killer, but of protecting him, them, and others from a murderer somewhere on the loose—is so transparently false that professing to believe it demeans this institution. But reaching a patently incorrect conclusion on the facts is a relatively benign judicial mischief; it affects, after all, only the case at hand. In its vain attempt to make the incredible plausible, however—or perhaps as an intended second goal—today's opinion distorts our Confrontation Clause jurisprudence and leaves it in a shambles. Instead of clarifying the law, the Court makes itself the obfuscator of last resort.[32]

One look at his *American Dictionary of the English Language* told Scalia that this statement was "testimonial" evidence because "At trial a witness 'bears testimony' by providing '[a] solemn declaration or affirmation . . . for the purpose of establishing or proving some fact.'"[33]

Using his originalist approach, Scalia argued that there was no doubt that his precedents should have protected the Sixth Amendment Confrontation Clause rights of the accused here: "Preventing the admission of 'weaker substitute[s] for live testimony at trial' such as this . . . is precisely what motivated the Framers to adopt the Confrontation Clause and . . . *Ex parte* examinations raise the same constitutional concerns whether they take place in a gas-station parking lot or in a police interrogation room." [34] For Scalia, there was no emergency here; rather, the "interrogating officers' purpose" was to build a case, making the statement "testimonial." "None—absolutely none—of their actions indicated that they perceived an imminent threat. They did not draw their weapons, and indeed did not immediately search the gas station for potential shooters. To the contrary, all five testified that they questioned Covington *before conducting any investigation at the scene.* Would this have made any sense if they feared the presence of a shooter? Most tellingly, none of the officers started his interrogation by asking what would have been the obvious first question if any hint of such a fear existed: Where is the shooter?" [35]

Scalia found no support in the Founding Era for the majority's approach: "The Framers could not have envisioned such a hollow constitutional guarantee. No framing-era confrontation case that I know of, neither here nor in England, took such an enfeebled view of the right to confrontation." And so, he concluded, "today's decision is not only a gross distortion of the facts. It is a gross distortion of the law—a revisionist narrative in which reliability continues to guide our Confrontation Clause jurisprudence, at least where emergencies and faux emergencies are concerned." [36] For Scalia, the defendant, Bryant, "has not received . . . the procedures that our Constitution requires. And what has been taken away from him has been taken away from us all." [37]

This judicial dispute in the *Bryant* case was quickly noted by one of the Court's keenest observers, Linda Greenhouse, formerly the Supreme Court reporter for *The New York Times*, then teaching at Yale Law School. Drawing from her reporting on Scalia's tenure on the Court for more than two decades, she argued that the fractured nature of his relationships on the Court was largely a problem of his own making. "One rough measure of how any Supreme Court term is going is to track the decibel level of Justice Antonin Scalia's dissenting opinion," she said. [38] After comparing the thrashing that Scalia had given Sotomayor in the Confrontation Clause case to his earlier attacks on Sandra Day O'Connor in the abortion cases, Greenhouse wrote, "I can't think of an example of one of Justice Scalia's bomb-throwing opinions ever enticing a wavering colleague to come over to his corner." Knowing that, she asked: "So the question raised by Justice Scalia's most recent intemperate display remains: what does this smart, rhetorically gifted man think his bullying accomplishes? It's a puzzle. But having raised the question, I will venture an answer. Antonin Scalia, approaching his 25th anniversary as a Supreme Court justice, has cast a long shadow but has accomplished surprisingly little. Nearly every time he has come close to achieving one of his jurisprudential goals, his colleagues have either hung back at the last minute or, feeling buyer's remorse, retreated at the next opportunity."

After a review of other Scalia judicial tantrums aimed at his colleagues, Greenhouse concluded: "While Justice Sotomayor's majority opinion [in *Michigan v. Bryant*] purported to accept *Crawford* as binding precedent, the opinion is suffused with an attitude of pragmatism. In the originalist cosmos of Antonin Scalia, pragmatism has no place. With the highest achievement of his originalist jurisprudence now in peril, fear as well as anger was palpable in his dissenting opinion as he suggested that the majority was not only wrong but was composed of hypocrites. . . . This Friday, March 11, is Justice Scalia's 75th birthday. It doesn't promise to be a happy one."

• • •

Both sides of Antonin Scalia, the brilliant and the undiplomatic, were evident a month later, as he completed his twenty-fifth year on the Court toward the end of the 2010–11 term. Scalia took the opportunity to lash out at the judicial colleague who seemed to be making his votes less relevant, Anthony Kennedy. In late May 2011, the Court ruled in the case of *Brown v. Plata*, concerning whether the conditions created by overcrowded prisons in California violated the inmates' Eighth Amendment protection against "cruel and unusual punishment." After it was proven that prisoners, due to overcrowding, were not receiving appropriate medical or mental health care, a special three-judge federal district court panel ordered the release of 38,000–46,000 prisoners to reduce the California prison population to 137.5 percent of capacity. The case came to the Supreme Court questioning whether the federal court's ordered release of prisoners violated the Prison Litigation Reform Act of 1995. A five-justice majority's response, speaking through Anthony Kennedy, was a resounding "No!"

Siding with the four liberal members on the Court, and with the chief justice in dissent, Kennedy assigned the majority opinion to himself and argued that reducing the prison population was the humane thing to do.[39] For Kennedy, who often cited "evolving standards of human decency," this "severe overcrowding in California's prison system," as well as the lack of adequate food and health care for the prisoners, was a violation of the Eighth Amendment.

Prisoners retain the essence of human dignity inherent in all persons. Respect for that dignity animates the Eighth Amendment prohibition against cruel and unusual punishment. . . . A prison's failure to provide sustenance for inmates "may actually produce physical 'torture or a lingering death.'" . . . Just as a prisoner may starve if not fed, he or she may suffer or die if not provided adequate medical care. A prison that deprives prisoners of basic sustenance, including adequate medical care, is incompatible with the concept of human dignity and has no place in civilized society.[40]

In an unusual move, to demonstrate the cruel and unusual nature of this institutionalized loss of human dignity, Kennedy included in his opinion three black-and-white photos showing the inhumane conditions in the prisons.[41]

In dissent, Scalia was offended both by the result in this case, "perhaps the most radical injunction issued by a court in our Nation's history," and the anti-originalist manner by which Kennedy reached that decision. For him, this was "a case whose proper outcome is so clearly indicated by tradition and common sense, that its decision ought to shape the law, rather than vice versa." Faced with the prospect of releasing "46,000 convicted felons," Scalia continued, one would expect the Court to "bend every effort to read the law in such a way as to avoid that outrageous result." Instead, the Court "violates the terms of the governing statute, ignores bedrock limitations on the power of Article III judges, and takes federal courts wildly beyond their institutional capacity."[42]

But then Scalia went beyond the legal arguments in an apparent effort to undercut the public's respect for Kennedy's decision. Reminiscent of the predictions of military doom in his earlier dissent against Kennedy in the *Boumediene* antiterrorism case, Scalia argued that this general release of prisoners due to overcrowding would pose a serious security threat to society: "It is also worth noting the peculiarity that the vast majority of inmates most generously rewarded by the release order—the 46,000 whose incarceration will be ended—do not form part of any aggrieved class even under the Court's expansive notion of constitutional violation. Most of them will not be prisoners with medical conditions or severe mental illness; and many will undoubtedly be fine physical specimens who have developed intimidating muscles pumping iron in the prison gym."[43] The fear-inducing nature of this message to the outside world could not be missed.

So upset was Scalia by Kennedy's ruling that, for only the second time that term, he dissented orally from the bench when the decision was announced. In what was described by the *Times*'s Adam Liptak as a "pungent and combative" style, Scalia read a statement from the bench about the "46,000 happy-go-lucky felons fortunate enough to be selected" for release, while Kennedy "looked straight ahead . . . his face frozen in a grim expression."[44]

Scalia was not yet finished with expressing his frustration toward Kennedy's new role on the Court that term. His next outburst came a month later in a case called *Sykes v. United States*, involving the interpretation of the Armed Career Criminal Act (ACCA), which required mandatory add-on sentences for persons who had been convicted of three "violent felonies." A man named Marcus Sykes faced an additional fifteen-year sentence for possessing a gun as a convicted felon because it was his third felony. Sykes argued that since one of the crimes for which he had been convicted, "knowingly or intentionally . . . fle[eing] from a law enforcement officer" by automobile, was in his view not a "violent crime," he should not receive additional punishment under the ACCA. Kennedy, speaking for an unusual bipartisan majority of three conservatives, Roberts, Alito, and Thomas, and two liberals, Breyer and Sotomayor, ruled that the defendant was still subject to the additional sentencing. Using a variety of statistical studies to prove the inherent danger of suspects fleeing from the police by car, Kennedy explained that the "Risk of violence is inherent to vehicle flight. . . . Flight from a law enforcement officer invites, even demands, pursuit. As that pursuit continues, the risk of an accident accumulates. And having chosen to flee, and thereby commit a crime, the perpetrator has all the more reason to seek to avoid capture."[45] For the Court, then, "Felony vehicle flight is a violent felony for purposes of ACCA."[46]

In dissent, Scalia ridiculed Kennedy's process of statutory contruction. After noting that this was the fourth time in as many years that the Court had reinterpreted this vaguely written law, Scalia wrote: "Insanity, it has been said, is doing the same thing over and over again, but expecting different results. Four times is enough. We should admit that ACCA's residual provision is a drafting failure and declare it void for vagueness."[47] For him, Kennedy had produced a "tutti-frutti opinion" composed of "untested judicial fact-finding masquerading as statutory interpretation."[48] As opposed to the results from his rigorous textual analytical approach, Scalia argued, "The Court's ever-evolving interpretation of the residual clause will keep defendants and judges guessing for years to come."[49] To Scalia, the results in this case came from the collaboration of incompetence in two branches of government: "Fuzzy, leave-the-details-to-be-sorted-out-by-the-courts legislation is attractive to the Congressman who wants credit for addressing a national problem but does not have the time (or perhaps the votes) to grapple with the nitty gritty. . . . Because the majority prefers to let vagueness reign, I respectfully dissent."[50]

. . .

The Jekyll and Hyde nature of Scalia's personality on the Court reappeared in the final days of the 2010–11 term in the form of his brilliant analysis of a perplexing freedom of speech issue. Scalia was at his very best as the originalist defender of the First Amendment's fundamental right of freedom of speech in a case called *Brown v. Entertainment Merchants Association*, dealing with a California law banning the sale or rental of "violent video games" to minors under the age of eighteen, and requiring warnings as to such violent content on their packaging. It would prove to be a technologically challenging case for a Court whose senior members, according to the institution's newest member, Elena Kagan, "haven't really gotten to email," and some of whom had to play the allegedly violent video games to better understand them. "It was kind of hilarious," Kagan recalled.[51]

During the oral argument for this case, Samuel Alito disassociated himself from originalism philosophy when considering whether governments could carve out an exception to the First Amendment to regulate violent video games. While the attorneys discussed the meaning of the First Amendment, Alito poked some gentle fun at Scalia when he said, "Well, I think what Justice Scalia wants to know is what James Madison thought about video games." Never one to be upstaged, Scalia responded, "No I want to know what James Madison thought about violence. Was there any indication that anybody thought, when the First Amendment was adopted, that there—there was an exception to it for—for speech regarding violence?"[52]

Scalia was tapped by the chief justice to write the majority opinion defending free speech in this case, and argued against carving an exception to allow the state to regulate violent video games sold to children. He began by saying, "Video games qualify for First Amendment protection. The Free Speech Clause exists principally to protect discourse on public matters, but we have long recognized that it is difficult to distinguish politics from entertainment, and dangerous to try."[53] Unsympathetic with the state's effort to equate violent video games to obscene speech, Scalia viewed this law as being "an impermissible content-based restriction on speech," regulating the games because of the ideas expressed rather than any dangers that they might pose. Scalia made clear that children were already exposed to violence in other forms of media: "Certainly the books we give children to read—or read to them when they are younger—contain no shortage of gore. Grimm's Fairy Tales, for example, are grim indeed. As her just deserts for trying to poison Snow White, the wicked queen is made to dance in red hot slippers 'till she fell dead on the floor, a sad example of envy and jealousy.' . . . Cinderella's evil stepsisters have their eyes pecked out by doves. . . . And Hansel and Gretel (children!) kill their captor by baking her in an oven." Classic literature such as *The Odyssey*, Dante's *Inferno*, and even William Golding's *Lord of the Flies*, he added, have long filled children's reading lists with violent scenes. Violence on children's television and cartoons only added to his argument. For Scalia, it made no difference to the Court that video games were interactive. "Like the protected books, plays and movies that preceded them, video games communicate ideas—and even social messages—through many familiar literary devices (such as characters, dialogue, plot and music) and through features distinctive to the medium (such as the player's interaction with the virtual world). That suffices to confer First Amendment protection."[54]

Because this was a fundamental free speech right, the state was required to demonstrate a "compelling state interest" for the law to stand, requiring that the drafting of the law be "closely tailored" to serve those interests. Scalia concluded that the Court had no place second-guessing the goals of the state's regulation, but the justices could assess the means that the legislature used to achieve those goals. The state's law was so broad that it was both underinclusive, because other violent images could reach children through other media, and overinclusive, because some parents and relatives would see the games as "a harmless pastime," and thus allow their viewing by minors. For Scalia, "Legislation such as this, which is neither fish nor fowl, cannot survive strict scrutiny."[55]

In dissent, the other originalist on the Court, Clarence Thomas, used the lessons that he drew from the Founding Era's history to reach a diametrically opposed version of what he called "the original public understanding of the First Amendment." Thomas offered an impressive review of family life and the role of parents in guiding children dating from the Puritan era through the Founding period. Based on this review he argued, "The historical evidence shows that the founding generation believed parents had absolute authority over their minor children and expected parents to use that authority to direct the proper development of their children. It would be absurd to suggest that such a society understood 'the freedom of speech' to include a right to speak to minors (or a corresponding right of minors to access speech) without going through the minors' parents."[56] Thomas concluded, "As a consequence, I do not believe that laws limiting such speech—for example, by requiring parental consent to speak to a minor—'abridg[e] the freedom of speech' within the original meaning of the First Amendment."[57]

Scalia received positive reviews for his video game opinion. Still, the three losses in the Confrontation Clause, the California prison release, and ACCA cases, each one with Anthony Kennedy in the majority, offered clear evidence that this was the "Kennedy Court" era. Faced with this new reality, Scalia did as he had done so many times before when he faced adversity. During the summer he prepared a new speech.

CHAPTER 25

Roberts' Rules of Order

As the new Court term was about to open in the fall of 2011, Antonin Scalia renewed his call for lowering what Thomas Jefferson and James Madison called the "high wall of separation" between church and state. Duquesne Law School dean Ken Gormley had invited Scalia to be the keynote speaker for the school's centennial celebration in September, and to speak on what it meant to be a Catholic law school. This gave him a chance to revisit the theme on which he had spoken four years earlier when he discussed the role of Catholicism in judging.

Appearing before a packed arena at the A. J. Palumbo Center, Scalia began by restating his message from Villanova Law School in 2007 disavowing that being a Catholic had affected his view of the law or his application of it as a justice. In arguing at Duquesne that "there is no such thing as Catholic law," Scalia said there might be "certain proposals [that] are contrary to what we call the Catholic point of view and others are affirmative of it."[1] For him, a Catholic law school could play a role in rectifying that condition: "One would expect its faculty and students and its graduates, to be of assistance in formulating legislative proposals that further the Catholic moral view, and opposing those that impede it. Not because that is part of their assignment, but because if it is a genuinely Catholic place, one would expect a higher proportion of its faculty, and student body to be interested in that enterprise, and to be encouraged in it, as would be the case in an American institution." Scalia was particularly impressed with what he viewed as the moral environment in which law could be learned at a Catholic institution. "It is possible, I would think, to have a law school that possesses a discernibly Catholic environment, by which I mean a religious faith and living the life and dedication which is in accordance with that faith are a part of the atmosphere of that place. This has nothing to do with making these students better lawyers, but everything to do with making them better men and women. Moral formation is a respectable goal for any educational institution, even a law school. But it is at the center of the law for a genuinely religious institution." What he sought was not the kind of "intelligent, well-educated society that gave birth to Naziism," but rather a "Catholic institution, even a law school, [established and operated] to create an atmosphere that enables moral formation, not just knowledge but moral formation." Returning to his theme from the Villanova Law School speech, though, he cautioned: "A university run by Catholics no more deserves to be called a Catholic university, than a supermarket owned by Catholics deserves to be called a Catholic supermarket. . . . The Catholic law school should be a place where it is clear though perhaps not spoken that the here and now is less important, when all is said and done, than the here-after. It should be a place that takes the law seriously, but not so seriously as to forget what the law is."

Six months later, Scalia continued his religion theme when he appeared as the keynote speaker at the annual "Living the Catholic Faith Conference" in Denver, Colorado, a two-day event of 3,500 devout Catholics. Scalia began his remarks before a standing room crowd by reprising portions of his basic "Christians as cretins" speech that he had used in his "being fools for Christ's sake" speech in Mississippi in 1996.[2] Scalia, as he had done before, proposed that the legacy of his hero, St. Thomas More, be considered as a "prime example" of "the Christian as cretin," because he "was not seeing with the eyes of men, but with the eyes of faith."[3] He continued, "My point is not that reason and intellect need to be laid aside. . . . A faith without a rational basis should be laid aside as false. . . . What is irrational is to reject *a priori* the possibility of miracles in general and the resurrection of Jesus Christ in particular."[4]

Little surprise, given these and other speeches on Catholicism and Christianity, as well as his pro-religion decisions on the Court, that when Boston University religion professor Stephen Prothero assembled a list of the dozen most influential Catholics in America, Scalia was second after Chief Justice John Roberts. Their four other Catholic Court colleagues were listed right behind them. Prothero explained that of these six, the most activist was Scalia, because "Justices are supposed to stick to interpreting the law rather than making it, especially if they adhere to the judicial philosophy of 'original intent,' but I'm not buying it. When it comes to 'judicial activism,' there are really only two kinds of judges: those who know they are acting and those who wrongly imagine they are not."[5]

• • •

When the Court considered that term the issue of the use of new technology to conduct a search and seizure under the Fourth Amendment, Scalia used the opportunity to demonstrate how his originalism theory should be applied. In January 2012, the Court announced its decision in *United States v. Jones*, a case involving a District of Columbia nightclub owner, Antoine Jones, who was convicted of "trafficking in narcotics" on the basis of information that the D.C. police and the FBI had gathered by placing an electronic GPS device inside the back right bumper of his wife's Jeep Grand Cherokee without benefit of a search warrant.[6] Using this device, the police tracked the car's movements for twenty-eight days, at one point even returning to replace the battery in the GPS device. Thanks in part to the two thousand pages of travel information that was compiled using the device, Jones was convicted.

Ironically, the Court's majority opinion for a Fourth Amendment case dealing with some of the most modern search technology was assigned by Chief Justice John Roberts to Scalia, who argued that the "public meaning" of the Constitution's Bill of Rights in 1791 should be used to decide the matter. Scalia had already shown in 2001 that his originalism interpretation of the Fourth Amendment did not allow for intrusive new search and seizure technology. *Kyllo v. United States* examined the use of a thermal imaging camera to determine that a suspect was using an upstairs room in his house as a greenhouse for growing marijuana. Scalia ruled that since the government was using technology "that is not in general public use," which allowed the authorities "to explore details of the home that would previously have been unknowable without physical intrusion," the Framers would have regarded it as a search covered by the Fourth Amendment and subject to the search warrant requirement.[7]

Could this theory be carried over to denying the authorities the power to place a tracking device on the undercarriage of a car parked on a public street? For Scalia and a unanimous Court, the answer was yes. Based on the historical rights of property and trespass, Scalia argued that the police had violated the Fourth Amendment by "physically occupy[ing] private property for the purpose of obtaining information." By ruling that this was an unacceptable "search" of an "effect," or the car, Scalia's historical reading required the use of a search warrant because "We have no doubt that such a physical intrusion would have been considered a 'search' within the meaning of the Fourth Amendment when it was adopted."[8] As his opinion proceeded, it became clear that Scalia's real objection was to the twenty-eight-day period in which the suspect was being tracked, making it more like the Colonial era "writs of assistance." Using such writs, the British were allowed to conduct general fishing-expedition searches of colonists' homes and papers. Had Jones been followed by teams of agents tailing the car and using "visual observation," or relying on "electronic means, without an accompanying trespass," the Court might have allowed it. But here they were unacceptably using technology that was attached within the bounds of Jones's property to gather information about his movements.

By arguing in this manner, Scalia lost a conservative ally. In a concurrence that read in part more like a dissent, Samuel Alito relied on existing Fourth Amendment search and seizure precedent rather than originalism theory to determine whether the suspect had a "reasonable expectation of privacy." For him, the question was not, as Scalia had suggested, one of "trespassing," or what "late-18th-century situations . . . are analogous to what took place in this case," meaning a determination of the "property based" nature of the majority's approach, but rather, how much privacy a "reasonable person" could expect in this situation. For him, the growing number of tracking devices for cars—EZ Pass, Onstar automobile aid services, and even the capacity to track the cell phones of drivers and passengers in cars—made such use of GPS to track cars more acceptable under the diminishing twenty-first-century "reasonable expectations of privacy" standard. And, Alito added, that standard would continue to be lowered: "The availability and use of these and other new devices will continue to shape the average person's expectations about the privacy of his or her daily movements."[9]

For Alito and three others on the Court, rather than using an originalism-based, anti-trespass rule to ban the use of GPS tracking entirely, "The best that we can do in this case is to apply existing Fourth Amendment doctrine and to ask whether the use of GPS tracking in a particular case involved a degree of intrusion that a reasonable person would not have anticipated." By using that as a rule, Alito envisioned a shifting standard based on the length of time of the search: "In this case, for four weeks, law enforcement agents tracked every movement that respondent made in the vehicle he was driving. We need not identify with precision the point at which the tracking of this vehicle became a search, for the line was surely crossed before the 4-week mark."[10]

To Scalia's dismay, Alito reserved the right to adjust his decision even more in favor of the police in future cases, depending on "whether prolonged

GPS monitoring in the context of investigations involving extraordinary offenses would similarly intrude on a constitutionally protected sphere of privacy."[11] While Alito did not define "extraordinary offenses" or explain how long he would allow such tracking based on the increasing severity of the crimes that were being investigated, it was clear that he subscribed to a shifting and diminishing right to privacy.

In many ways, Scalia had won a series of battles—originalism was the theory to which all of the justices reacted—but he was losing the war as the new generation of conservatives on the Court either adopted unique versions of the theory, as Clarence Thomas had done, or rejected Scalia's variation, as Alito and John Roberts seemed to be doing.

• • •

This case and others that term were dwarfed in the spring of 2012 when the Court heard arguments in three cases testing the constitutionality of the 2010 Patient Protection and Affordable Care Act, the landmark health care reform law often referred to as the ACA but more popularly known as Obamacare.[12] In the most controversial political case since the 2000 *Bush v. Gore*, and the biggest economic case since the 1937 Court-packing episode, the Roberts Court was facing a political crisis of its own making by accepting this case during an election year. Largely as a consequence of the public perception of its political decision making, and the controversies over the justices' off-the-bench activities, in a March 2012 Bloomberg News poll, 75 percent of the respondents believed that the Court's decision on the health care reform law test would be more "influenced" by "politics" than "based solely on legal merits."[13]

With the Court in a precipitous free fall in its public support, it faced a renewed attack from the legal academic community, the third such attack in just over a decade. Duke Law professor Paul D. Carrington headed another group of one hundred law school professors who were proposing a revolutionary "term limits" reform plan for the Supreme Court. Under this proposal, Congress would impose by law a fixed term of service for justices. A new justice would serve for a maximum of eighteen years, with a new member being appointed every two years, and the two most recently retired jurists serving in a sort of *emeritus* status, charged with sifting through appeals for the Court to hear and serving on cases in which the Court's membership was reduced because of recusals. This would maintain an ideological balance on the Court as each president would make two appointments per term of office. The proposal had zero chance of being passed by the partisan, stalemated Congress, but it did show how precarious the Court's political posture had become.[14]

It was in this shifting public relations landscape, with the presidential primaries already under way, that the Court considered the health care cases. Given the partisan lineup of the Court, the possibility now existed that five conservative justices appointed by Republican presidents could overturn the singular achievement of a first-term Democratic president and a Democratic-controlled Congress, with four liberal justices appointed by Democrats in dissent. If the Court divided like this, along partisan lines on such a controversial issue, it risked making the justices appear even more political than they were in *Bush v. Gore*. Regardless of how the Court ruled, disappointed partisans on either side would almost certainly attack the result.

It was just this kind of situation, possibly endangering the Court's public support, that Chief Justice John Roberts had said that he would seek to avoid in his Georgetown Law School graduation address in 2006. In his quest for achieving "a greater degree of consensus on the Court," Roberts had argued, he sought "unanimity, or near unanimity" among the justices, a "greater coherence and agreement about what the law is," to have "each member on the Court be open to the considered views of the other," and to have the justices "work together to function as a Court in deciding the cases, and in crafting the opinions."[15] Chief among these goals, though, was a final, unstated rule: "When in doubt: find a way to save the Court from partisan attack by voting to limit the reach of controversial decisions." These were Roberts' Rules of Order, and now the question was whether, and how, these rules might operate in the cases challenging the Obama administration's new health care law.

The three health care law cases coming before the Court raised several different issues. Did the Court have the constitutional power under the federal 1873 Anti-Injunction Act to hear a taxation case even though the taxes had not yet been imposed and collected? Did the federal government have the constitutional power under the interstate commerce clause and the federal taxing and spending power to pass such a massive health care reform law? Did the federal government have the power in opposition to the Tenth Amendment to compel the states to change and increase their Medicaid payments and serve more citizens? And, finally, if any portion of the law was ruled unconstitutional, was there a written, or implied, "severability clause" that would allow the rest of the law to stand?

Among all of these arguments, the key issue before the Court was the constitutionality of the law's controversial funding mechanism, the "individual mandate," or what the law called a "shared responsibility payment." This provision was based on a Massachusetts health care act passed, ironically, under Republican governor Mitt Romney, that compelled citizens' participation in the program by requiring them to either purchase health insurance or pay a penalty, which some regarded as a tax. Only with the full participation of everyone, including younger, healthier citizens, in the insurance pool would there be sufficient revenue to fund many aspects of the program, including the newly mandated coverage to customers with pre-existing conditions that made them more expensive to insure. Without the "individual mandate" funding mechanism, many believed the health care reform plan would be unsustainable.

During an extraordinary three days of oral argument from March 26 to March 28, the solicitor general, Donald B. Verrilli Jr., argued that congressional authority supporting the law came from Article I, Section 8 of the Constitution, granting Congress the power to regulate interstate commerce, and the power to tax and spend. The Necessary and Proper Clause, as it is known, further allowed the government to do whatever was necessary to regulate anything that "significantly affects" interstate commerce and the taxing powers. Since the health care industry comprises 17 percent of the American economy, the government argued that it "significantly affected" interstate commerce, and thus was subject to regulation under the Constitution.

But the constitutionality of the individual mandate was another matter. The government argued that, according to the 1942 *Wickard v. Filburn* case it was constitutional. In that case, a farmer named Roscoe Filburn claimed that wheat he grew in excess of government quotas prescribed by the Agricultural Adjustment Act of 1938 was for his own personal use and not subject to governmental regulation because it had never entered the stream of interstate commerce. The Court ruled otherwise, explaining that each loaf of bread Filburn baked and consumed was one that would not be bought in the market, thus affecting interstate commerce and subject to federal regulation.

By this logic, in the ACA cases the decision of a person *not* to buy into the health insurance plan could also be seen as affecting interstate commerce. Opponents of the health care reform act argued that the *Wickard* case did not apply where there is a conscious choice by people *not to participate* in the health care plan at all. In this interpretation, there was no commerce, so the Constitution could not govern it. Supporters of health care reform responded that the market for health care was unique because self-insured people inevitably participated in that market with the cost of any of their unpaid health care bills being paid through higher health care costs for the rest of society.

When the argument turned to the constitutionality of the individual mandate, on Tuesday, March 27, Scalia assumed his familiar aggressive argumentative posture. He made clear by the nature and tone of his questioning that he would not be supporting the health care program.

Early in that day's argument, the discussion turned to the requirement that everyone must participate in the plan, either by purchasing the contract or paying the penalty for not doing so. Justice Anthony Kennedy asked Solicitor General Donald Verrilli, "Can you create commerce in order to regulate it?"

The government's advocate responded, "That's not what's going on here, Justice Kennedy, and we're not seeking to defend the law on that basis. In this case, the—what is being regulated is the method of financing health—the purchase of health care. That itself is economic activity with substantial effects on interstate commerce."

With that, Scalia jumped in, asking, "So, any self-purchasing? . . . If I'm in any market at all, my failure to purchase something in that market subjects me to regulation?"

"No. That's not our position at all, Justice Scalia," responded Verrilli. "In the health care market—the health care market is characterized by the fact that aside from the few groups that Congress chose to exempt from the minimum coverage requirement—those who for religious reasons don't participate, those who are incarcerated, Indian tribes—virtually everybody else is either in that market or will be in that market, and the distinguishing feature of that is that they cannot—people cannot generally control when they enter that market or what they need when they enter that market."[16]

Seeking to better understand the power of the government to use law to shape commercial markets, various members of the Court turned to a series of hypotheticals. If the government can compel the purchase of health care insurance, Chief Justice Roberts began, what about compelling citizens to buy other products for their own welfare? "It seems to me, [that it] would be true, say, for the market in emergency services: police, fire, ambulance, roadside assistance, whatever. You don't know when you're going to need it; you're not sure that you will. But the same is true for health care. . . . So, can the government require you to buy a cell phone because that would facilitate responding when you need emergency services? You can just dial 911 no matter where you are?"

Throughout the argument, the solicitor general had trouble clearly articulating why the health care market was different: "No, Mr. Chief Justice. I think that's different. It's—we—I don't think we think of that as a market. This is a market. This is market regulation. And, in addition, you have a situation in this market not only where people enter involuntarily as to when they enter and won't be able to control what they need when they enter."[17]

Verrilli risked losing the pivotal fifth vote on this case when Anthony Kennedy asked, "I understand that we must presume laws are constitutional, but, even so, when you are changing the relation of the individual to the government in this, what we can stipulate is, I think, a unique way, do you not have a heavy burden of justification to show authorization under the Constitution?"

Verrilli tried to argue that the more governmentally deferential "reasonableness" interpretive test was appropriate here: "Congress has the authority under the commerce power and the necessary and proper power to ensure that people have insurance in advance of the point of sale because of the unique nature of this market, because this is a market in which . . . virtually everybody in society is in this market. And you've got to pay for the health care you get, the predominant way in which it's—in which it's paid for is insurance, and—and the respondents agree that Congress could require that you have insurance in order to get health care or forbid health care from being provided."[18]

In what would become one of the most talked-about exchanges in the three days of arguments, Scalia now seized on an opening for persuading Kennedy to join him in opposition to the law. Drawing from an example that had been floating in the newspapers the previous week, Scalia sought to show that using the solicitor general's logic the government could compel other kinds of purchases: "Could you define the market—everybody has to buy food sooner or later, so you define the market as food, therefore, everybody is in the market; therefore, you can make people buy broccoli."

Verrilli responded: "No, that's quite different. That's quite different. The food market, while it shares that trait that everybody's in it, it is not a market in which your participation is often unpredictable and often involuntary. It is not a market in which you often don't know before you go in what you need, and it is not a market in which, if you go in and—and seek to obtain a product or service, you will get it even if you can't pay for it."

Scalia interrupted at that point: "Is that a principled basis for distinguishing this from other situations? . . . It's a basis that explains why the government is doing this, but is it—is it a basis which shows that this is not going beyond what—what the—the system of enumerated powers allows the government to do?"

"Yes, for two reasons," responded Verrilli. "First, this—the test, as this Court has articulated it, is: Is Congress regulating economic activity with a substantial effect on interstate commerce? The way in which this statute satisfies the test is on the basis of the factors that I have identified."[19]

Moments later, Justice Kennedy asked the central question challenging the government's use of such an individual mandate to compel a purchase: "Well, then your question is whether or not there are any limits on the Commerce Clause. Can you identify for us some limits on the Commerce Clause?"

Verrilli tried to avoid the trap of arguing for an all-powerful government using its interstate commerce power to regulate every phase of American life: "Yes. The—the rationale purely under the Commerce Clause that we're advocating here would not justify forced purchases of commodities for the purpose of stimulating demand. We—the—it would not justify purchases of insurance for the purposes—in situations in which insurance doesn't serve as the method of payment for service."[20]

Later in the argument, Scalia tried to shape the day's narrative with the kind of anti-governmental regulation argument that others later would say he was lifting from the Tea Party political platform. "There was no doubt that what was being regulated was commerce. And here you're regulating somebody who isn't covered," Scalia said to Verrilli. "By the way, I don't agree with you that the relevant market here is health care. You're not regulating health care. You're regulating insurance. It's the insurance market that you're addressing and you're saying that some people who are not in it must be in it, and that's—that's different from regulating in any manner commerce that already exists out there."

The solicitor general responded: "Well, to the extent that we are looking at the comprehensive scheme, Justice Scalia, it is regulating commerce that already exists out there. And the means in which that regulation is made effective here, the minimum coverage provision, is a regulation of the way in which people participate, the method of their payment in the health care market. That is what it is."

Moments later, Scalia pressed on the image of an unlimited government, saying, "In addition to being necessary, it has to be proper. . . . And that's what all this questioning has been about. What—what is left? If the government can do this, what—what else can it not do?"[21]

Near the end of his argument, with Verrilli trying unsuccessfully to reserve the remainder of his time to argue, Scalia insisted on consuming it with what he thought was the winning argument for the day's debate: "You're saying that all the discussion we had earlier about how this is one big uniform scheme and the Commerce Clause, blah, blah, blah, it really doesn't matter. This is a tax and the Federal Government could simply have said, without all of the rest of this legislation, could simply have said, everybody who doesn't buy health insurance at a certain age will be taxed so much money, right?"

Upon hearing that, Verrilli thought *he* had the advantage in this verbal chess game: "It—it used its powers together to solve the problem of the market not—providing affordable coverage . . ."

"Yes, but you didn't need that," pressed Scalia, speaking over him. "You didn't need that. If it's a tax, it's only—raising money is enough."

"It is justifiable under its tax power," answered Verrilli.

With that, Scalia thought he had made his point, closing with a dismissively curt: "Okay. Extraordinary."[22] After the term ended, even Scalia's good friend on the Court Ruth Bader Ginsburg would gently tease him about closing his questioning of the solicitor general with the use of the sarcastic "Extraordinary."[23] But, Verrilli's "Plan B" argument, justifying the program's constitutionality by its power to tax, as opposed to its interstate commerce powers, would have more supporters than Scalia realized.

During day three of the six hours of argument, on Wednesday, March 28, the question turned to whether the remainder of the law could remain in force if one or more sections of it were ruled unconstitutional by the Court, using what is called a "severability clause." Scalia, however, was much less inclined to leave to Congress the job of legislating a repair to the law he seemed ready to overturn. In a question to former Bush administration solicitor general Paul Clement, one of his former law clerks, Scalia went far beyond the realm of the legal briefs in the case to ask about Congress's power to limit the effect of a possible Court overturn of the law: "[I]f we struck down nothing in this legislation but the—what's it called, the Cornhusker kickback, okay, we find that to violate the constitutional proscription of venality, okay? When we strike that down, it's clear that Congress would not have passed it without that. It was the means of getting the last necessary vote in the Senate. And you are telling us that the whole statute would fall because the Cornhusker kickback is bad. That can't be right."

Scalia got a hearty laugh in the courtroom, but he did so with a puzzling reference to a failed negotiating ploy by conservative Democrat Ben Nelson of Nebraska. After threatening to filibuster the bill because it did not contain some restrictions on federal funding for abortion, Nelson offered to trade his "yes" vote on the bill with Majority Leader Harry Reid in return for exempting his state's residents from increased Medicaid taxes. Nicknamed the "Cornhusker Kickback," the resulting public uproar over the deal caused Nelson to withdraw his request. Clement, though, played the question straight: "Well, Justice Scalia, I think it can be, which is the basic proposition, that it's congressional intent that governs. Now everybody on this Court has a slightly different way of divining legislative intent. And I would suggest the one common ground among every member of this Court, as I understand it, is you start with the text. Everybody can agree with that." [24] Everybody, that is, except for the critics of Scalia's questioning, who noted that this "Nebraska kickback" was never part of the final law's text.

Scalia's overtly partisan, and at times comedic, behavior during the oral arguments for this case raised serious questions for many. [25] Linda Greenhouse described Scalia's behavior in the oral arguments as "clownish" and "channeling the Tea Party from the bench." [26] By calling into question the Court's behavior in these arguments as "amateur economists" and "amateur political scientists," Greenhouse expressed the fear that the Court was drifting away from the "hypothetical Court" consisting of "justices [who] dispassionately go about applying law to the facts." *Slate*'s Matthew DeLuca asked, "Is Roger Ailes (of Fox News) clerking for Supreme Court Justice Antonin Scalia?" in a piece entitled "Did Scalia Parrot Fox News During Health Care Arguments?" [27] Even former Reagan administration solicitor general Charles Fried, a conservative, said that Scalia's "questions have been increasingly confrontational," and "he came across more like an advocate." Whatever one might say, commentators were talking about his arguments and his agenda.

• • •

By late June, while the country awaited the health care decision, Scalia found a way to remain in the spotlight. The occasion was the announcement of a decision on the constitutionality of an Arizona anti-immigration law called *Arizona v. United States*. Known as the Support Our Law Enforcement and

Safe Neighborhoods Act, the law was passed in 2010 by a state under siege from illegal immigrants flooding across its borders from Mexico because a stalemated Congress had not been able, or willing, to pass a comprehensive federal immigration law. With most of the federal immigration interdiction funds being spent in California and Texas, Arizona had crafted a law to "discourage and deter the unlawful entry and presence of aliens and economic activity by persons unlawfully present in the United States," through the use of "an official state policy of attrition through enforcement." Three of the law's provisions made nonregistration by aliens with the federal government a state misdemeanor, made the seeking of work by aliens a state misdemeanor, and empowered state police to make warrantless arrests of suspected aliens if the police had probable cause that an offense had been committed that would subject that person to removal from the United States. In perhaps the most controversial part of the law, state police were also empowered to ask for the immigration papers of any person based upon "reasonable suspicion" that the person might be an illegal alien. The reasonable suspicion standard, taken from Fourth Amendment search and seizure case law, is much lower than probable cause. As a result, this portion of the law permitted racial profiling by the police for any Hispanic they chose to challenge, and allowed for an indefinite detention of those arrestees in order to afford the police a chance to check their immigration status.

The issue in this case was whether the federal government's foreign policy powers under the Constitution gave it preemptive, and thus exclusive, powers over the states to legislate in this area. The majority opinion resolving the issue in favor of federal power was written by Anthony Kennedy, speaking for a bipartisan voting bloc consisting of Chief Justice John Roberts and three of the Court's liberals, Justices Breyer, Ginsburg, and Sotomayor. (Justice Kagan had recused herself because the issue had been before her as solicitor general.) The majority ruled that the Article I, Section 8 power of the federal government in foreign policy and immigration, together with the federal Supremacy Clause of Article IV of the Constitution, saying that the federal Constitution, laws, and treaties "shall be the supreme law of the land," precluded state governments from enacting their own immigration policy by using their sovereign powers under the Tenth Amendment to protect their citizens from outsiders.

The national nature of the policy questions here, and the difference in the powers of the two levels of government, made it necessary for the federal government to have the exclusive power to act. Kennedy and the majority ar-

gued that the "dynamic nature of relations with other countries requires the
Executive Branch to ensure that enforcement policies are consistent with this
Nation's foreign policy with respect to these and other realities."[28] Further,
they said, "Federal law makes a single sovereign responsible for maintaining a comprehensive and unified system to keep track of aliens within the
Nation's borders."[29] In this situation, contrary to the Arizona law, "Congress
made a deliberate choice not to impose criminal penalties on aliens who seek,
or engage in, unauthorized employment." The Arizona law "would interfere
with the careful balance struck by Congress with respect to unauthorized
employment of aliens." By allowing a warrantless arrest of suspected aliens
based on a crime that would make them removable, "This would allow the
State to achieve its own immigration policy. The result could be unnecessary
harassment of some aliens (for instance, a veteran, college student, or someone assisting with a criminal investigation) whom federal officials determine
should not be removed." In conclusion, Kennedy argued, "Decisions of this
nature touch on foreign relations and must be made with one voice."[30] This
ringing endorsement of total federal power in the immigration field ended
with a plea by the Court that Arizona not "pursue policies that undermine
federal law."

In dissent, Scalia turned Kennedy's argument on its head, arguing from
a states' rights philosophy to oppose the view of a preemptive, "exclusive"
federal power flowing under the Constitution to deal with immigration. Instead, he argued that "The United States is an indivisible 'Union of sovereign States.'" Blocking Arizona's immigration law, Scalia argued, "deprives
States of what most would consider the defining characteristic of sovereignty: the power to exclude from the sovereign's territory people who have
no right to be there." Because this was true, Scalia wrote that the "power to
exclude has long been recognized as inherent in [state] sovereignty." Using
this "power to exclude," Scalia explained, "in the first 100 years of the Republic, the States enacted numerous laws restricting the immigration of certain
classes of aliens, including convicted criminals, indigents, persons with con-
tagious diseases, and (in Southern States) freed blacks."[31]

Scalia did concede that the "primary responsibility for immigration
policy has shifted from the States to the Federal Government," and that
state legislation in this area could not act where it is "prohibited by a valid
federal law," or "conflict[s] with federal regulation." However, even after
allowing for the fact that the federal government was preeminent in the
foreign affairs area, Scalia added, "the Federal Government must live with

the inconvenient fact that it is a Union of independent States, who have their own sovereign powers. . . . Though it may upset foreign powers—and even when the Federal Government desperately wants to avoid upsetting foreign powers—the States have the right to protect their borders against foreign nationals."[32] Scalia concluded, "Arizona is *entitled* to have 'its own immigration policy'—including a more rigorous enforcement policy—so long as that does not conflict with federal law." For him, there was no reason why Arizona could not "make it a state crime for a removable alien (or any illegal alien, for that matter) to remain present" in that state.

For Scalia, this was a case of the state of Arizona exercising its own sovereign powers to protect its citizens and borders given the federal government's "willful blindness or deliberate inattention to the presence of removable aliens in Arizona." With the state believing that the "federal priorities are too lax" in the immigration field, "The State has the sovereign power to protect its borders more rigorously if it wishes, absent any valid federal prohibition. The Executive's policy choice of lax federal enforcement does not constitute such a prohibition."[33]

Had Scalia stopped there, the discussion of this case would have ended quickly. But instead, like Yellowstone Park's Old Faithful, he erupted once again from the bench, just as he had done so many times before when things were not going his way. The outburst came without warning, when the justices were announcing their decisions in this case from the bench by reading their shortened bench statements.

After Anthony Kennedy announced the Court's judgment in the case on Monday, June 25, Scalia followed by reading his unusually long eleven-minute oral dissent from the bench.[34] His text was drawn largely from the final four pages of his published dissent, in which he combined his ardent pro–states' rights view with a severe criticism of the federal government's lack of an immigration policy. The statement contained all of the highly quotable attacks in his full dissent designed to catch the attention of the Supreme Court press corps. He began by recasting the state-versus-federal sovereignty balance in the immigration area: "Of course there is no reason why the Federal Executive's need to allocate *its* scarce enforcement resources should disable Arizona from devoting *its* resources to illegal immigration in Arizona that in its view the Federal Executive has given short shrift." Scalia then attacked President Obama's recent executive order to suspend the deportation policy for the approximately 1.4 million illegal immigrants under the age of thirty, while they underwent background checks as a potential path to legal status. "The husbanding of scarce enforcement resources can hardly be the justification for this," Scalia said, "since the considerable administrative cost of conducting as many as 1.4 million background checks, and ruling on the biennial requests for dispensation that the nonenforcement program envisions, will necessarily be *deducted* from immigration enforcement."[35]

Scalia then went far beyond the record in the briefs for this case to add: "The President said at a news conference that the new program is 'the right thing to do' in light of Congress's failure to pass the Administration's proposed revision of the Immigration Act. Perhaps it is, though Arizona may not think so. But to say, as the Court does, that Arizona *contradicts federal law* by enforcing applications of the Immigration Act that the President declines to enforce boggles the mind."[36] As Scalia read his statement, Justice Elena Kagan "continued to look uneasy as [he] went on scolding Justice Kennedy." Just why a member of the high bench was critiquing a presidential policy that was not then before the Court boggled the mind of Court reporters such as *Slate*'s Dahlia Lithwick, who wrote that this was "Perhaps the first originalist reading of a presidential press conference."[37]

Scalia then turned to his originalist reading of the Constitutional Convention for support. A nation of states must have the power, he argued, to protect their own borders against "A Federal Government that does not want to enforce the immigration laws as written, and leaves the States' borders unprotected against immigrants whom those laws would exclude." That being the case, Scalia offered an interesting image from the Founding Era, asking:

> Would the States conceivably have entered into the Union if the Constitution itself contained the Court's holding? Today's judgment surely fails that test. At the Constitutional Convention of 1787, the delegates contended with "the jealousy of the states with regard to their sovereignty." . . . Now, imagine a provision . . . which included among the enumerated powers of Congress "To establish Limitations upon Immigration that will be exclusive and that will be enforced only to the extent the President deems appropriate." The delegates to the Grand Convention would have rushed to the exits from Independence Hall.[38]

Scalia ended by siding with the state's point of view here. "Arizona bears the brunt of the country's illegal immigration problem. Its citizens feel themselves under siege by large numbers of illegal immigrants who invade their property, strain their social services, and even place their lives in jeopardy. Federal officials have been unable to remedy the problem, and indeed have recently shown that they are unwilling to do so." For him, sovereign states had the power to fill in the gap left by a stalemated federal government. "Arizona has moved to protect its sovereignty—not in contradiction of federal law, but in complete compliance with it. The laws under challenge here do not extend or revise federal immigration restrictions, but merely enforce those restrictions more effectively. If securing its territory in this fashion is not within the power of Arizona, we should cease referring to it as a sovereign State."[39]

Former Clinton administration solicitor general Walter Dellinger later wrote in *Slate* that this was a very different Antonin Scalia from the one who had argued in his dissent to the 1988 *Morrison v. Olson* independent counsel case, and throughout the rest of his career, for near absolute executive power: "[Scalia] got one thing right in his bench statement in this week's immigration case. If securing its territory in this fashion is not within the power of Arizona, we should cease referring to it as a sovereign State. Motion seconded."[40] Indeed, Scalia's state-centered playbook now seemed to be drawn more from the failed Articles of Confederation, the nullification movement of the 1830s, and the state secession movement that launched the Civil War than from the modern Constitution.

Scalia's attack on President Obama's policies was also too much partisanship from the bench for some in the legal academy and the press to accept. Law professor Adam Winkler of UCLA wrote: "Scalia has finally jumped the shark. He claims to respect the founding fathers, but his dissent channels the opponents of the Constitution. . . . It's mind-boggling to see Scalia rail against the Executive's power to enforce the law. That is the core role of the president. He, not the state of Arizona, is the enforcer of our laws. Due to limited resources, every executive—state, federal, municipal—must make choices about how aggressively to enforce the law. . . . Scalia is an originalist: he has his own original view of the Constitution, ungrounded in history and steeped in conservative politics."[41]

Columnist E. J. Dionne of *The Washington Post*, in an article titled "Justice Scalia Needs to Resign from High Court," recalled the Cheney duck hunting episode and the Fribourg "War on Terror" speech, before saying of this harsh Arizona immigration case announcement: "It was a fine speech for a campaign gathering, the appropriate venue for a man so eager to brand the things he disagrees with as crazy or mind-boggling. Scalia should free himself to pursue his true vocation. We can then use his resignation as an occasion for a searching debate over just how political this Supreme Court has become."[42] The *Post* editorial board agreed, chastising "Scalia's Partisan Outbursts." After citing the "frivolity" in Scalia's oral argument questioning in the health care case, the editorial board concluded:

> Justice Scalia is nothing if not intelligent; his unpredictable approach to certain issues, especially free speech and criminal law, mark him as a less-than-doctrinaire conservative. . . . But his lapses of judicial temperament—bashing "a law-profession culture, that has largely signed on to the so-called homosexual agenda" in a written dissent, or offering views on this and that in sarcastic public speeches—detract from the dignity of his office. They endanger not only his jurisprudential legacy but the legitimacy of the high court.[43]

Perhaps the most stinging rebuke, though, came from one of the critics of his *Heller* gun control decision, Judge Richard Posner. He did not like that Scalia had sounded like a political candidate in criticizing a sitting president on public policy in an election year: "The nation is in the midst of a hard-fought presidential election campaign; the outcome is in doubt. Illegal immigration is a campaign issue. It wouldn't surprise me if Justice Scalia's opinion were quoted in campaign ads. The program that appalls Justice Scalia was announced almost two months after the oral argument in the *Arizona* case. It seems rather a belated development to figure in an opinion in the case."[44] Scalia, as always, was unfazed by criticism.

• • •

Scalia was saved from further journalistic skewering by the announcement three days later of the landmark health care case. On June 28, signaling his disappointment with the decision about to be revealed, Scalia entered the courtroom along with the rest of his colleagues precisely at 10:00 A.M., "look[ing] downward morosely, as if attending a wake," wrote one journalist, while his colleague Stephen Breyer entered bearing "a broad smile on his face."[45] After disposing of two other cases, and with the audience now silent, Chief Justice Roberts, described by one reporter as having bloodshot eyes and appearing very tired, began reading his majority opinion in the health care cases "in an oddly perfunctory, hurried tone, as if his main goal was to be done with it." As he read, Scalia's "sour look persisted."[46]

In writing his opinion, Roberts walked an intellectual tightrope, agreeing with the four liberals in upholding the law. On the first issue before them, whether the Anti-Injunction Act prevented the Court's decision because no tax had yet been collected, Roberts wrote that the law, which only applied to the nonpayment of taxes, did not come into play. He ruled: "Congress . . . chose to describe the 'shared responsibility payment' imposed on those who forgo health insurance not as a 'tax,' but as a 'penalty.' . . . There is no immediate reason to think that a statute applying to 'any tax' would apply to a 'penalty.'" And so, Roberts concluded, since the individual mandate was not a tax, the Court could rule on merits of the case because "The Anti-Injunction Act therefore does not apply to this suit."[47]

Roberts then explored whether the law, with its individual mandate, could be upheld on the basis of the federal interstate commerce power. Litigants had asked whether the federal government had the power to regulate the entire health care insurance industry under the interstate commerce power, plus the Necessary and Proper clause of Article I, Section 8, Clause 18. Carefully parsing his opinion on this issue, Roberts took a different approach from others in the majority, all of whom supported the government's power to regulate the health care industry. To the contrary, just as the four conservatives would argue in dissent, Roberts could find no acceptable argument to support the interstate commerce theory because "The individual mandate . . . does not regulate existing commercial activity. It instead compels individuals to *become* active in commerce by purchasing a product, on the ground that their failure to do so affects interstate commerce." For him, giving this power to the government "would open a new and potentially vast domain to congressional authority."[48] Roberts explained: "The Framers gave Congress the power to *regulate* commerce, not to *compel* it, and for over 200 years both our decisions and Congress's actions have reflected this understanding. There is no reason to depart from that understanding now."[49] Roberts concluded on this question: "The Commerce Clause is not a general license to regulate an individual from cradle to grave, simply because he will predictably engage in particular transactions. Any police power to regulate individuals as such, as opposed to their activities, remains vested in the States."[50] For him, "the proximity and degree of connection between the mandate and the subsequent commercial activity is too lacking to justify an exception of the sort urged by the Government."

Since he saw no delegated interstate commerce power justification, Roberts then dismissed the Necessary and Proper Clause argument as well. Misled by the way Roberts's opinion was structured, at this point in their live television analysis of the decision, reporters for both CNN and Fox News announced that the Obamacare law's individual mandate had been declared unconstitutional on interstate commerce clause grounds.[51] But the Chief Justice had a surprise for everyone as his opinion continued.

Roberts then switched sides again, and allied with the four liberals to uphold the overall health care law by adopting the solicitor general's "backup" argument, to "read the mandate not as ordering individuals to buy insurance, but rather as imposing a tax on those who do not buy that product." This allowed Roberts to rule that the federal government's taxing and spending power made the law constitutional. Having already ruled that the individual mandate was a penalty instead of a tax for the Anti-Injunction argument, the chief justice now turned his own argument on its head. Examining precedents and the nation's policy history, Roberts found that the use of this constitutional taxing power was "intended to affect individual conduct," and in so doing was "plainly designed to expand health insurance coverage," thus making the law constitutional. As Roberts put it, "taxes that seek to influence conduct are nothing new."[52] He concluded: "Congress's authority under the taxing power is limited to requiring an individual to pay money into the Federal Treasury, no more. . . . But imposition of a tax nonetheless leaves an individual with a lawful choice to do or not do a certain act, so long as he is willing to pay a tax levied on that choice."[53] And so, the law was upheld.

The conservatives did win one part of the case. On the issue of whether the federal government could withhold federal funds from states that failed to expand their Medicaid programs in line with the Affordable Care Act guidelines, Roberts, writing for a majority of seven justices, including the four conservatives and liberals Stephen Breyer and Elena Kagan, said it could not. "Permitting the Federal Government to force the States to implement a federal program," Roberts said, "would threaten the political accountability key to our federal system." The potential for states to lose all of their federal Medicaid funding as a penalty for noncompliance with the changes was, he explained, "coercive," and unconstitutionally designed to redirect state conduct. Roberts argued: "In this case, the financial 'inducement' Congress has chosen is much more than 'relatively mild encouragement'—it is a gun to the head." He added: "The threatened loss of over 10 percent of a State's overall budget . . . is economic dragooning that leaves the States with no real option but to acquiesce in the Medicaid expansion."[54]

Rather than following Scalia's lead and offering his opinion on the political wisdom of the law, Roberts left it to Congress to decide. "We do not consider whether the Act embodies sound policies. . . . Members of this Court are vested with the authority to interpret the law; we possess neither the expertise nor the prerogative to make policy judgments. Those decisions are entrusted to our Nation's elected leaders, who can be thrown out of office if the people disagree with them. It is not our job to protect the people from the consequences of their political choices."[55] The political future of the Affordable Care Act would be determined, he was saying, not by the Court but by Congress, as it would be reshaped by the voters in the 2012 election.

Roberts's Solomonic opinion giving each side a partial victory and a partial defeat surprised many beyond his conservative colleagues. By preventing a conservative majority from overturning President Obama's greatest legislative achievement, Roberts might have hoped to diminish some of the criticism of the Court as a partisan institution. Despite the narrowness of the voting margin, and the exotic nature of the argumentation, President Obama and the Democrats had all they needed to preserve the law.

With observers in the courtroom still trying to understand what had just occurred, Justice Kennedy read a dissenting opinion authored and, most unusually, signed by him and the three remaining conservative justices: Scalia, Thomas, and Alito. As Scalia had done days before in the Arizona immigration case, in considering whether government can compel "private conduct," the dissenters began by affirming their allegiance to the Tenth Amendment and state sovereignty, as opposed to the limited, delegated, federal powers: "Whatever may be the conceptual limits upon the Commerce Clause and upon the power to tax and spend, they cannot be such as will enable the Federal Government to regulate all private conduct and to compel the States to function as administrators of federal programs."[56] The four dissenters spoke in language and imagery that sounded like Scalia's in explaining that the federal government had no power to regulate private activity. For them, to argue that the failure to act "affects commerce and therefore can be federally regulated, is to make mere breathing in and out the basis for federal prescription and to extend federal power to virtually all human activity."[57] For more than forty pages, and without ever acknowledging it, the dissenters mirrored Roberts's argument in saying that the federal interstate commerce power would not support the individual mandate penalizing nonpurchase of federal health insurance.

When they turned to the taxing and spending power issue, having seen the majority duck the Anti-Injunction Act by saying that the law created a penalty rather than a tax that would have been covered, the dissenters put no stock in Roberts's subsequent characterization of the penalty as a tax for the constitutional purpose of upholding the law: "But we have never held— *never*—that a penalty imposed for violation of the law was so trivial as to be in effect a tax. We have never held that *any* exaction imposed for violation of the law is an exercise of Congress' taxing power—even when the statute *calls* it a tax, much less when (as here) the statute repeatedly calls it a penalty."[58] In one of the opinion's most persuasive sections, after pointing out that the law called the mandate a "penalty" eighteen times, and placed it in the "Operative core" of the law, rather than the "Revenue Provisions" section where a discussion of tax funding for the plan would normally be found, the dissenters concluded: "For all these reasons, to say that the Individual Mandate merely imposes a tax is not to interpret the statute but to rewrite it." The dissenters thus dismissed Solicitor General Verrilli's arguments and those of Chief Justice Roberts. "What the Government would have us believe in these cases is that the very same textual indications that show this is *not* a tax under the Anti-Injunction Act show that it *is* a tax under the Constitution. That carries verbal wizardry too far, deep into the forbidden land of the sophists."[59]

Not until two-thirds into the dissent did it become clear just how much the four conservatives were disagreeing with the chief justice and the majority. Having also rejected the law's "coercion" of the states to participate in the Medicaid expansion, as a "power and authority [that did] not rest with this Court," they argued: "The two pillars of the Act are the Individual Mandate and the expansion of coverage under Medicaid. In our view, both these central provisions of the Act—the Individual Mandate and Medicaid Expansion—are invalid."[60] Since for them the provisions of the law were not severable, that meant that the entire law should be overturned.[61] In a powerful conclusion that sounded very much as if it came from the libertarian-oriented Kennedy, the four dissenters concluded:

> The Framers considered structural [separation of powers] protections of freedom the most important ones, for which reason they alone were embodied in the original Constitution and not left to later amendment. The fragmentation of power produced by the structure of our Government is central to liberty, and when we destroy it, we

place liberty at peril. Today's decision should have vindicated, should have taught, this truth; instead, our judgment today has disregarded it. For the reasons here stated, we would find the Act invalid in its entirety.[62]

One was hard-pressed to find anyone in either the national press or among the internet Court commentators who had foreseen that it would be Chief Justice John Roberts who would join the liberals to save the ACA, and everyone scrambled to explain why.[63] While liberals praised the chief for his statesmanship and bipartisanship, conservatives alternated between complaining that Roberts had betrayed them and carefully parsing his opinion for signs that he had laid the groundwork for future restrictions on the Interstate Commerce Clause. Whatever the view of the majority opinion, Roberts had made clear by his clever positioning on the case that *he* was now leading the Supreme Court, not Anthony Kennedy.[64]

• • •

Three days after the announcement of the health care decision, CBS television reporter Jan Crawford, relying on leaks about the case from the normally tightly sealed Supreme Court building, broke a surprising story that "Chief Justice John Roberts initially sided with the Supreme Court's four conservative justices to strike down the heart of President Obama's health care reform law, the Affordable Care Act, but later changed his position and formed an alliance with liberals to uphold the bulk of the law. . . . Roberts then withstood a month-long, desperate campaign to bring him back to his original position, the sources said."[65] Crawford reported that after Roberts began writing the conservatives' majority opinion overturning the law, he became "wobbly" over his vote with that side, possibly after reading "countless news articles in May warning of damage to the court—and to Roberts' reputation—if the court were to strike down the mandate." One conservative member of the Court sought an explanation from Roberts for his decision in this case, but he "was unsatisfied with the response."[66]

But the battle was not done, Crawford reported, as Roberts "engaged in his own lobbying effort—trying to persuade at least Justice Kennedy to join his decision so the Court would appear more united in the case. There was a fair amount of give-and-take with Kennedy and other justices, the sources said. One justice, a source said, described it as 'arm-twisting.'" At

some point, Kennedy finally gave up on Roberts's vote, and the four dissenters "handed him their own message which, as one justice put it, essentially
translated into, 'You're on your own' and [they] were no longer even willing
to engage with him in debate."

Within a week, subsequent news reports and Twitter postings, relying
on other leaks from inside the Court building, speculated that Roberts had
authored both the majority opinion, and, depending on who was reporting,
anywhere from one-quarter to three-quarters of the published dissent when
it was initially a conservative majority opinion authored by him striking
down the law.[67] It seemed very likely that, following the example of Charles
Evans Hughes during the Court-packing crisis of 1937, who saved the independence of the Court by reversing his opinions in two cases and upholding
Roosevelt's New Deal legislation, Roberts had executed a second "switch in
time that saved Nine." *Time* magazine was so stunned by this turn of events
that just three weeks after its cover story had hailed the emergence of the
"Kennedy Court," the magazine's cover now read, "Roberts Rules."[68]

Whatever the truth about the Court's votes in this case and just how
the opinion was written, the flood of legal cyber chatter provided yet more
evidence that the health care law decision had placed the Court in a partisan
political cauldron. On July 18, a little over five weeks after the public opinion
polls for the Court had stood at a historically low 44 percent, the number
sank to 41 percent, with another equal number saying that they disapproved
of the Court's work.[69]

The announcement of the health care decision marked a turning point
for the Supreme Court. From all of the chief justice's rules that he had discussed in his Georgetown Law graduation speech, there was one more that
he had learned from watching the travails of his mentor, William Rehnquist:
the chief justice must take control of his Court. And in the health care case,
that he had done.

Roberts made it clear that in the future the Court could, and would, go
where his vote would take it—even as much as the vote of the swing justice. From then on, there would be two unpredictable voters on the Court.
Anthony Kennedy would continue to vote in line with his ideological perspective, occasionally abandoning his usual conservative views to vote as a
pro–individual rights libertarian on some social issues. John Roberts would
occasionally vote based on his jurisprudential perspective, choosing at times
to abandon his conservative philosophy in order to keep his activist conserva-

tive brethren from going too far to the right and taking his Court over a cliff. Meanwhile an aging and uncompromising Antonin Scalia, who later would say that the Affordable Care Act case was the "most wrenching decision" of his career, would become less and less influential on the Court's sidelines, casting predictably conservative votes and writing scorching dissents whenever either, or both, of these men dictated decisions by the Court that he did not like.[70]

CHAPTER 26

Reading Law

Immediately after the dramatic ending of the 2011–12 Court term, Chief Justice Roberts escaped to the island of Malta, where he would deliver a speech, while his colleagues traveled to various locales to teach law seminars and get some well-deserved rest. But as usual, in addition to teaching a summer law seminar at the Catholic St. Mary's University School of Law, in Innsbruck, Austria, for which he received $10,000, Scalia had a different plan.[1]

For the past three and a half years he had been working on what would become his new public script, one that would help him focus a more favorable spotlight back on him after the end-of-term controversy. Three weeks before the end of the term, without any prior publicity, Thomson West publishers announced that Scalia and Bryan Garner, his coauthor on the 2008 book, would be releasing a new book called *Reading Law: The Interpretation of Legal Texts*,[2] to be available the day after the term's final decision was announced.[3]

The 567-page book was the capstone of Scalia's extrajudicial writing and speaking career, pulling together all of the strands of his life and work. Its title harked back to Scalia's father, who described in his own writing the importance of analyzing texts literally this way: "Literalness is, for us, one of the chief merits of a translation. . . . Literalness, in a work which purports . . . to be a guide . . . is essential."[4] The book's organization, revolving around fifty-seven "Canons of Legal Interpretation," using the original Latin names of many as their titles, gave the appearance of a religious text. These were followed by thirteen examples of challenges to the canons called "Thirteen Falsities Exposed," to serve as warnings to those who might listen to whispers of the legal devil and stray from the correct path.

This was the first book of legal commentary by a sitting Supreme Court justice since Joseph Story's seminal two-volume *Commentaries on the Con-*

stitution of the United States, published in 1833.[5] With this book, Scalia had put himself in the same category of legal theorists on the bench as two of the titans from the early nineteenth century, Story and the legendary Chief Justice John Marshall, as well as the great legal philosophers of the twentieth century, Oliver Wendell Holmes and Benjamin Cardozo.[6] In offering a comprehensive theoretical contribution to the legal field, the book demonstrated Scalia's brilliance as a scholar and summed up everything he had learned in his long career. Coming when it did, this volume represented the product of the alter ego of his controversial public persona, offering the diametric opposite of his partisan outrage on the bench.

In the beginning of the book the authors described its purpose: "Our legal system must regain a mooring that it has lost: a generally agreed-on approach to the interpretation of legal texts."[7] The fifty-seven canons they discussed were designed to promote what the authors, mirroring the language of David Souter in his Harvard commencement speech, now called their "Fair Reading Method" for analyzing legal texts, which they defined as: "determining the application of a governing text to given facts on the basis of how a reasonable reader, fully competent in the language, would have understood the text at the time it was issued." Scalia wanted this model to unseat his longtime enemies, the proponents of the living, evolving Constitution, whom the book now called the *eisegetes*, a term most commonly applied to those interpreters of the Bible who "inser[ted their] own ideas into the text . . . enabling the introduction of all sorts of new material."[8] Whereas for the legal "Fair Readers," there can be only one original meaning of the text, for the *"eisegetes,* the possibilities are endless."[9] This work was designed to teach lawyers, judges, and the American reading public how to do what Scalia had been preaching about throughout his legal career, in the words of the lead epigraph to the book, which he took from medieval times, *"Verbis legis tenaciter inhaerendum,"* or, "Hold tight to the words of the law."

Scalia tried to indemnify himself from criticism for stretching the norms of his judicial position by writing this book by saying on the copyright page, "The views expressed in this book are those of the authors as legal commentators. Nothing in this book prejudges any case that might come before the United States Supreme Court." Seeking to build another firewall between his judicial role and his authorial role, at the end of the preface he wrote: "One final personal note: Your judicial author knows that there are some, and fears that there might be many, opinions that he has joined or written over the past 30 years that contradict what is written here—whether because of the demands of *stare decisis* or because wisdom has come late. Worse still, your judicial author does not swear that the opinions that he joins or writes in the future will comply with what is written here—whether because of *stare decisis,* because wisdom continues to come late, or because a judge must remain open to persuasion of counsel. Yet the prospect of 'gotchas' for past and future inconsistencies holds no fear." [10]

But there was one firewall that Scalia could not erect between the two sides of his professional personality—the serious legal scholar and the outspoken partisan judge, as he made clear in one comment about his judicial opponents: "The descent into social rancor over judicial decisions is largely traceable to nontextual means of interpretation, which erode society's confidence in a rule of law that evidently has no agreed-on meaning. . . . We seek to restore sound interpretive conventions." [11] In blaming only the living, evolving constitutionalists—the judicial colleagues whom he had once called idiots and the Mullahs of the West—for the nation's "descent into social rancor," Scalia accepted no blame and took no responsibility for contributing to this discord.

Reading Law was more than just a blueprint for decision making, it was a plan for reining in the judiciary: "Over the past 50 years especially, we have seen the judiciary incrementally take control of larger and larger swaths of territory that ought to be settled legislatively. It used to be said that judges do not 'make' law—they simply apply it. In the 20th century, the legal realists convinced everyone that judges do indeed make law." [12] For the authors, the cause of this judicial grab for power was the "notion that words can have no definite meaning," and those judges who do "believe in fidelity to text lack the interpretive tools necessary to that end." [13] In response, Scalia and Garner offered their textualism, or close reading, approach, defining their legal philosophy as "words mean what they conveyed to reasonable people at the time they were written." [14] "Everyone is a textualist," they argued, and in denying that this approach is meant to roll back rights, they added: "Textualism is not well designed to achieve ideological ends, relying as it does on the most objective criterion available: the accepted contextual meaning that the words had when the law was enacted." [15] Indeed, they argued that "if pure textualism were actually a technique for achieving ideological ends, your authors would be counted extraordinarily inept at it." Scalia and Garner explain that several sorts of cases, such as criminal sentencing, limits on the amount of punitive damages, imposing criminal punishment for "using a firearm," Confrontation Clause cases, and flag burning bans were cases in which Scalia reached results based on textualism that did not match his ideological philosophy on those issues.[16]

Embedded in the book were more scholarly versions of some of Scalia's greatest hits from over a quarter century of speaking and writing. They attacked "non-textualists," who "depar[t] from text in several ways," including the "purposivism" and "consequentialism" of Anthony Kennedy, Stephen Breyer, and John Paul Stevens. In their view, the purposivist "goes around or behind the words of the controlling text to achieve what he believes to be the provision's purpose,"[17] while a "consequentialist" construes laws "to produce sensible, desirable results, since that is surely what the legislature must have intended."[18] Consequentialists could also be called pragmatists, trying for a workable solution. All nontextual methods, Scalia and Garner argued, "invite[d] judges to say that the law is what they think it ought to be."[19]

Scalia and Garner's intent was to teach others how to find the "objective meaning" of the legal document.[20] The authors argued on behalf of the concept of originalism, which they called here "Fixed-Meaning," or the notion that "Words must be given the meaning they had when the text was adopted."[21] The book's theoretical section concluded with the argument that Scalia had made so many times before on the speechmaking circuit: "The conclusive argument in favor of originalism is a simple one: It is the only objective standard of interpretation even competing for acceptance. Non-originalism is not an interpretive theory—it is nothing more than a repudiation of originalism, leaving open the question: How does a judge determine when and how the meaning of a text has changed?"[22] "The choice is this," the authors argued. "Give text the meaning it bore when it was adopted, or else let every judge decide for himself what it should mean today."[23]

In the final section, the authors argued against "the false notion that the Living Constitution is an exception to the rule that legal texts must be given the meaning they bore when adopted."[24] They concluded with an attack on the metaphor of the "Living Constitution":

> The very name *Living Constitution* is misleading. It conveys the impression of a system designed to be flexible and adaptable. This quality is touted by the advocates of the system, who speak metaphorically of the Constitution as a "living organism" that must grow with society or else "become brittle and snap." It is not a living organism—any more than any other legal prescription is. And the notion that the advocates of the Living Constitution want to bring us flexibility and

openness to change is a fraud and a delusion. All one needs for flexibility and change is a ballot box and a legislature."[25]

For them, this was not the way that choice by democracy should operate: "Persuading five Justices is so much easier than persuading Congress or 50 state legislatures—and what the Justices enshrine in the Constitution lasts forever. In practice, the Living Constitution would better be called the Dead Democracy."[26]

As magnificent as this work was as a piece of legal scholarship, the tragedy for Antonin Scalia was that he had already become its author's worst publicity and marketing enemy. Because the book was timed to be released as the 2011-12 Supreme Court term closed, few noticed it initially in the deluge of highly critical commentary on Scalia's partisan dissent in the Arizona immigration case, and the reporting on the health care decision. In a cruel irony, there now seemed to be two public faces to Scalia: his Dr. Jekyll, the impressive legal scholar, who had written this magnificent book, and his Mr. Hyde, the controversial, highly partisan activist who had garnered so much negative publicity.

In one of the earliest reviews, *New York Times* online columnist and blogger Stanley Fish called it a "compulsively readable" book, adding, "The authors follow Horace's injunction to both teach and delight. In short, this is a wonderful book." However, in a lengthy blog post praising the lessons on writing, Fish argued that the work was "wrong in its main polemical thesis (it didn't have to have one)—the thesis that textualism is the one mode of legal interpretation that avoids subjectivity and the intrusion into the judicial realm of naked political preferences."[27] For illustration, he needed to look no further than the end of the previous Court term.

With this book now published, Scalia could devote his time to revising his stump speech for return visits to the various Federalist Society meetings, colleges and universities, and bar associations, to present his new version of "An Evening with Antonin Scalia." There Scalia would conclude a brief set of remarks followed by an always entertaining question and answer session, or sometimes just the latter, by sitting at a table to sign his *Reading Law* book for people expecting to put them on the shelf next to their signed copies of his first volume. Scalia would also make another round of news and interview shows, talking about his book, reflecting on his long Court career, and revealing more tidbits of his early life. In this way, he would be able to separate himself from the other conservative voters on this Court, and use his singular visibility to educate his colleagues, and America, about *his* view of the law and the Constitution.

Scalia had good reason to expect that he would benefit financially from this work, just as he had from his first book with Bryan Garner. The annual financial disclosure reports required by the Ethics in Government Act of 1978 and filed by members of the Supreme Court revealed that, having already received nearly $310,000 in royalties and advances from West Publishing between 2007 and 2011, a year later by the time of the first reporting date after the publication of *Reading Law*, Scalia had received an additional $63,991 in royalties.[28]

Just as he had done in 2008, Scalia began his national media book tour almost immediately. CNN interviewer Piers Morgan was invited to the Court on July 18 for his "exclusive" conversation with the justice. By appearing on such public news shows while his colleagues were away, Scalia offered himself as the unofficial public spokesman for the Court and its work in the 2011–12 term. Morgan made news by asking Scalia about his reaction to the reported John Roberts switch in the health care case. Was there any truth "that you and Justice Roberts have had a bit of a—a bit of a parting of the ways? You've gone from being best buddies to warring enemies?" Morgan asked.[29]

"Who told you that?" challenged Scalia. Morgan cited "credible sources" throughout the national press. Scalia responded, "You shouldn't believe what you read about the court in the newspapers, because the information has either been made up or given to the newspapers by somebody who is violating a confidence, which means that person is not reliable."

But Morgan was not done yet. "So you've had no falling out with Justice Roberts?"

To which Scalia responded, "I'm not going to talk about—no, I haven't had a falling out with Justice Roberts."

Later in the conversation, Morgan asked, "Do you think any of your colleagues act in . . . from a politically motivated manner?"

Forgetting the many times that his own critics had said that *he* had done so, Scalia responded, "Not a single one of them. . . . I don't think any of my colleagues, on any cases, vote the way they do for political reasons. They vote the way they do because they have their—their own—their own judicial philosophy. And they may have been selected by the Democrats because they have that Demo—that particular philosophy or they may have been selected by the Republicans because they have that particular judicial philosophy. But that is only to say that they are who they are. And they vote on the basis of what their own view of the law brings them to believe, not at all because—I mean to—the court is not at all a—a political institution. Not at all. I—I—not a single one of my colleagues . . ."

Morgan pressed further by asking, "When you see Justice Roberts—Chief Justice Roberts getting criticized for being political, for being partisan—But when—when you see that happening, do you . . . does it offend you that his integrity would be questioned like that?"

Scalia took the opportunity to offer his best critique of the argument that there was a "partisan divide" on the current Court with five Republicans voting against four Democrats. "It—it offends me that—that—that people point to the fact—and they didn't used to be able to when—when—when David Souter and John Paul Stevens were still on the court. They—they often voted with the appointees who were Democratic appointees, so that the 5–4 decisions was not always, you know, five Republicans appointees versus four Democratic. Now that they're off, it—it often does turn that way. But that had—that is not because they are voting their politics, not because they are voting for the Republicans or voting for the Democrats. It's because they have been selected by the Republicans or selected by the Democrats precisely because of their judicial philosophy. . . . I mean, that's what elections have been about for a long time."

Regardless of how "offended" Scalia might be about this partisan Court charge, this *was* the prevailing public image of the Court. And a big part of the reason for this image was his politicization of the Court and the issues before it on the lecture circuit and by his votes.

Just eleven days later, on Sunday, July 29, Scalia appeared on both Chris Wallace's *Fox News Sunday* show and Brian Lamb's C-SPAN *Q and A* to talk about his book. Wallace tried to generate some news by conducting the equivalent of a press conference with Scalia on the state of American constitutional law. After quoting back to Scalia Canon 38 of his book, "A statute should be interpreted in a way that avoids placing its constitutionality in doubt," Wallace said, "Didn't Justice Roberts do exactly what you say a good judge should do, try to find a way to avoid striking down the [health care] law?"[30]

But Scalia was not biting: "I don't think so. If you read the rest of the section, you would say, to find a way to find a meaning that the language will bear that will uphold the constitutionality. You don't interpret a penalty to be a pig. It can't be a pig. And what my dissent said in the . . . Affordable Care Act was simply that there is no way to regard this penalty as a tax. It simply doesn't bear that meaning. You cannot give—in order to save the constitutionality, you cannot give the text a meaning it will not bear."[31] Wallace chose not to mention that the dissent in that case had not been Scalia's, but rather that of the four conservatives.

When the issue turned to the familiar discussion of why Scalia argued against the right of abortion under the Constitution, the justice reiterated his old refrain. "No one ever thought that the American people ever voted to prohibit limitations on abortion. I mean, there is nothing in the Constitution that says that," Scalia argued.

Wallace responded, "What about the right to privacy that the court found in known [sic] 1965?"

"There is no right to privacy. No generalized right to privacy," responded Scalia.

Wallace was not persuaded, "Well, in the Griswold case, the court said there was."

Scalia made clear that William O. Douglas's pro-privacy judgment in the 1965 Griswold v. Connecticut anti-contraception case would not survive his scrutiny either: "Indeed it did, and that was—that was wrong."

The most newsworthy answer of the interview, though, came when Wallace gave Scalia a chance to respond to one of his conservative critics on the Seventh Circuit Court of Appeals, Richard Posner, who said that Scalia's dissent in the Arizona immigration case had "the air of a campaign speech." Scalia's response was particularly cutting: "He is a court of the appeals judge, isn't he? . . . He doesn't sit in judgment of my opinions as far as I'm concerned." Later, Scalia added, "When Richard Posner comes out with a statement like that, I should fire back a statement equally provocative."

As the interview came to a close, Wallace could not resist asking Scalia about any future retirement plans. "Does it go through your mind, if I retire, I'd like to see, since you talk about Republicans appointing one kind of justice and Democrats another, that you would want somebody who would adhere to your view, as in your book Reading Law?" Without hesitating, Scalia responded, "No, of course, I would not like to be replaced by someone who immediately sets about undoing everything that I've tried to do for 25 years, 26 years, sure. I mean, I shouldn't have to tell you that. Unless you think I'm a fool." Knowing that the loss of one conservative justice could end the hope of a conservative, if not an originalist-oriented, Court, Scalia was prepared to time his departure from the judicial battlefield when the person naming his successor was more sympathetic to his views than the current occupant of the White House.[32]

Seemingly unperturbed by Scalia's remarks on Wallace's program, Judge Richard Posner soon published a devastating 8,400-word review of Scalia's book in *The New Republic* titled: "The Incoherence of Antonin Scalia."[33] Posner began by attacking Scalia's view that "textualism" rendered a "passive," neutral, nonideological result: "[Scalia] is one of the most politically conservative Supreme Court justices of the modern era and the intellectual leader of the conservative justices on the Supreme Court. Yet the book claims that his judicial votes are generated by an 'objective' interpretive methodology, and that, since it is objective, ideology plays no role. It is true, as Scalia and Garner say, that statutory text is not inherently liberal or inherently conservative; it can be either, depending on who wrote it. Their premise is correct, but their conclusion does not follow: text as such may be politically neutral, but textualism is conservative." For Posner, the judicial interpreter brings a distinctly political point of view to this process: "The textual originalist demands that the legislature think through myriad hypothetical scenarios and provide for all of them explicitly rather than rely on courts to be sensible. In this way, textualism hobbles legislation—and thereby tilts toward 'small government' and away from 'big government,' which in modern America is a conservative preference."

In critiquing Scalia and Garner's arguments, Posner reprised a shortened version of his earlier "law office history" attack on Scalia's use of originalism. As illustrated in his argument against the *Heller* gun control case, he said, "Judges are not competent historians. Even real historiography is frequently indeterminate, as real historians acknowledge. To put to a judge a question that he cannot answer is to evoke 'motivated thinking,' the form of cognitive delusion that consists of credulously accepting the evidence that supports a preconception and of peremptorily rejecting the evidence that contradicts it." Posner concluded his review by writing, "Justice Scalia has called himself in print a 'faint-hearted originalist.' It seems he means the adjective at least as sincerely as he means the noun."

It was only a matter of time before Scalia responded. Stephen J. Adler, the editor-in-chief for his publisher, Thomson Reuters, asked Scalia in an internet marketing interview to respond to Posner's charge that he "actually resorts to legislative history in" writing the *Heller* opinion.[34] Scalia made the most of his opportunity:

Only—only in writing for a non-legal audience could he [Posner] have made that argument. Because any legal audience knows what legislative history is. It's the history of the enactment of the bill. It's the floor speeches. It's the prior drafts of committees. That's what legislative history is. It isn't the history of the times. It's not what people thought it meant immediately after its enactment. It's not what laws were—were continued in effect despite this. That—that is simply not legislative history. And and—and to say that I use legislative history in how—is—is simply, to put it bluntly, a lie. And—you can get away with it in the *New Republic* I suppose, but—but—but . . . not—not to a legal audience.[35]

As unseemly as it was to have a Supreme Court justice accuse a federal Court of Appeals judge of lying, for any reason, doing so against someone whose "offense" was to publish a critical review of a book seemed particularly unattractive.

Neither judge was willing to let the other have the final word. So, it was not surprising when Posner answered Scalia's charge days later in *The New Republic*: "Even if I accepted Scalia's narrow definition of 'legislative history' and applied it to his opinion in *Heller*, I would not be telling a 'lie.' For Justice Scalia *does* discuss the 'drafting history' (legislative history in its narrowest sense) of the Second Amendment. . . . So I would not have been lying, or even mistaken, had I said in my book review that in *Heller* Scalia 'actually resorts' to 'legislative history' in its narrowest sense ('drafting history'). But I did not say that."[36]

• • •

As the 2012 presidential campaign accelerated, Scalia's adversary on the issue of the effect of religion on the judiciary, Professor Geoffrey Stone of the University of Chicago Law School, posted an internet article titled "The Supreme Court and the 2012 Election," highlighting the importance of the outcome of this election for the future direction of the Court. The two presidential candidates, incumbent Democrat Barack Obama and challenger Republican Mitt Romney, he argued, could not have been further apart in the type of candidate they would nominate for any future Court vacancies: "What happens if Romney is elected and gets to replace, say, the oldest 'liberal' Justice (Ginsburg) or if Obama is elected and gets to replace the oldest 'conservative' Justice (Scalia)? In such circumstances, Romney would presumably nominate someone similar to the most recent Republican appointee (Alito), and Obama would likely nominate someone similar to the most recent Democratic nominee (Kagan)."[37] In examining eighteen of "the most important constitutional decisions since 2000," in which each ideological side had won only half of the cases, and using some counterfactual analysis to explore the effect of a different ideological membership on the Court, Stone argued that "given the current makeup of the Supreme Court a change in the ideology of only one Justice will have a profound impact on the course of constitutional law. . . . Had Kagan been on the Court in these years instead of Scalia, the moderate liberals would have won seventeen of the eighteen cases, and if Alito had been on the Court instead of Ginsburg, the conservatives would have won sixteen of the eighteen cases." Stone concluded, "The stakes in the . . . [2012] election for the future direction of the Supreme Court are, in short, . . . incredibly high."

There is little doubt that Scalia would have preferred the election of Mitt Romney, but Obama won the popular vote by a 51 to 47 percent margin and a vote of 332–206 in the Electoral College. For another four years, the White House, and thus, the choice of Supreme Court nominees, would be in Democratic hands. Scalia's only hope for his Court was that no member of the conservative majority would leave over the next four years, or that the filibuster-deploying Senate Republicans could prevent Obama from securing a liberal Court majority if one did.

Scalia continued on his normal path of lecturing on his new book, and preparing for cases in the 2012–13 Supreme Court term. He clearly relished being back in the limelight on his new *Reading Law* news interview book tour. Just as had happened during the publicity tour for his *Making Your Case* book in 2008, Scalia's most revealing conversation was with PBS's Charlie Rose in late November. After a long discussion of Scalia's legal views, and his "Fair Reading" method, Rose, as he so frequently does, asked the question that no one else had, in an effort to get to the foundation for the views and actions of his guest.

Wondering what Scalia would now do after the publication of his book, Rose turned to *Reading Law*, and said: "This is what you say in a final personal note at the conclusion of the preface, 'your judicial author,' that would be you, 'knows that there are some and fears that there may be many, opinions that he has joined or written over the past 30 years that contradict what is written here—whether because of the demands of *stare decisis,* or because wisdom has come late.' I love that idea. Wisdom has come late." Moments later, Rose asked: "I am intrigued by the word wisdom that came later. How has wisdom come later to you?"[38]

It was the kind of question framed to invite the interviewee's self-analysis, and it had not been asked of Scalia by anyone else. The justice's answer was revealing: "I was already pretty old, if age brings wisdom, when I came onto court. I was fifty years old. I had been thinking a lot about the Constitution, about interpreting statutes and I can't say that any of those fundamental views have changed, just as I don't think my colleagues' views have changed. And I don't try to persuade them about fundamental beliefs."

"I can't say that any of those fundamental views have changed." No one could have described Scalia any better.

But when he demonstrated that point during one of his public appearances, it did not turn out as he might have hoped. As part of his extended book tour, Scalia returned in mid-December 2012 to Princeton University to deliver the prestigious annual Herbert W. Vaughan Lecture. He began with the words, "The Constitution is dead. Dead. Dead. Dead." But the press said little about the remainder of the speech because of what happened afterward.

During the question and answer period that followed, with the Court having just accepted two gay marriage cases for review, a first-year student named Duncan Hosie stood to ask a question. Hosie was a member of the college's formidable debate team and was taking a freshman seminar on constitutional law taught by University provost Christopher Eisgruber, who had clerked for Justice John Paul Stevens. "Justice Scalia," Hosie began, "I'm gay, and as somebody who is gay . . . I think there is a fundamental difference between arguing the Constitution does not protect gay sex, which is a defensible and legitimate legal position I disagree with, and comparing gays to people who commit murder or engage in bestiality. Do you have any regret or shame for drawing these comparisons you did in your dissents? . . . Do you think it's necessary to draw these comparisons, to use this specific language, to make the point that the Constitution doesn't protect gay rights?"[39]

Scalia responded to this college student's challenge to the justice's comparison of state laws against gay rights to other morality-based criminal laws in the 2003 *Lawrence* vs. *Texas* case with what one reporter called "a note of something between sarcasm, condescension, and stubbornness"[40] "I don't think it's necessary, but I think it's effective," Scalia said. "It's a type of argument that I thought you would have known, which is called a reduction to the absurd. And to say that if we cannot have moral feelings against homosexuality, can we have it against murder, can we have it against these other things? Of course we can. I don't apologize for the things I raised. I'm not comparing homosexuality to murder. I'm comparing the principle that a society may not adopt moral sanctions, moral views, against certain conduct. I'm comparing that with respect to murder and that with respect to homosexuality." Then Scalia closed with, "It's a type of argument that I thought you would have known. . . . I'm surprised you aren't persuaded."[41] While both the questioner and the respondent received applause for their efforts, the press was not so kind to Scalia. A blogger for *The New Yorker* titled her critical post "The Animus of Antonin Scalia."[42]

• • •

By the end of the Court's 2012–13 term, attention was focused on the many controversial cases still pending before the Court. In addition to the gay marriage cases, the Court was still considering South Carolina's challenge to the 1965 Voting Rights Act and to an affirmative action admissions program at the University of Texas. As usual, the highly anticipated decisions would be announced at the end of the term. Until then, Scalia had a chance in a search and seizure case called *Maryland v. King* to demonstrate how his "Reading Law" interpretive method worked.

The *Maryland v. King* case offered a novel issue for the Court. Alonzo King was charged with first- and second-degree assault in 2009 after threatening people with a shotgun. Because King was arrested for a "serious crime," Maryland law, like that in twenty-seven other states, allowed a DNA cheek swab sample to be taken from him upon his incarceration, and sent to the FBI. There it was entered in the Combined DNA Index System (CODIS) database, where it could be analyzed for any connection to earlier unsolved crimes. King's sample was matched to an unsolved rape case from 2003, and he was charged and convicted for that offense as well. King argued that the taking of his DNA constituted an unconstitutional search and seizure in violation of the Fourth Amendment. So compelling was this issue that Justice Samuel Alito said of it in the case's oral argument: "I think this is perhaps the most important criminal procedure case that this Court has heard in decades."[43]

Kennedy, writing for an unusual five-person majority consisting of three of his conservative colleagues, Roberts, Alito, and Thomas, and liberal Stephen Breyer, upheld the search and use of the DNA evidence. The majority found the use of cheek swab for the DNA sample to be a "negligible" intrusion of an arrested suspect being held in custody and ruled that the defendant in prison had no "legitimate expectation of privacy," making this an acceptable warrantless search under the "traditional standards of reasonableness."[44] Also supporting the constitutionality of the search was its public policy purpose to keep the prison safe by properly identifying its prisoners, allowing officials to go beyond the use of just matching fingerprints and data collected about prisoners' physical features.[45] For Kennedy, the "unparalleled accuracy" of using the DNA sample made it much more helpful in this identification process. "The use of DNA for identification is no different than matching an arrestee's face to a wanted poster of a previously unidentified suspect; or matching tattoos to known gang symbols to reveal a criminal affiliation; or matching the arrestee's fingerprints to those recovered from a crime scene."[46] Kennedy added: "When officers make an arrest supported by probable cause to hold for a serious offense and they bring the suspect to the station to be detained in custody, taking and analyzing a cheek swab of the arrestee's DNA is, like fingerprinting and photographing, a legitimate police booking procedure that is reasonable under the Fourth Amendment."[47] This was a "special needs" exception to the search requirements of the Fourth Amendment, like drug testing of railroad workers and high school students, where the purposes of the search go beyond just solving crimes, and thus outweigh a person's privacy concerns. In all of this public policy analysis of the benefits of using DNA to catalogue prisoners, though, Kennedy avoided the central issue of whether that sample should be employed to match the suspect to any of the cold cases in the FBI's CODIS database.

Once more, Scalia wrote in dissent against Kennedy. Scalia's record to this point in the Fourth Amendment search and seizure area had been somewhat inconsistent. Earlier that term, he had written a majority opinion ruling that police bringing a drug dog onto the porch of a house to sniff whether marijuana was inside constituted an unacceptable search because it violated the owner's property rights, thus triggering the Fourth Amendment search warrant requirements.[48] Previously, though, he had allowed the police to kick open a door to search an apartment only three to four seconds after announcing themselves and approved general drug testing of high school student athletes.[49] In search cases involving new technology, however, he had leaned toward the side of the defendant. He had ruled against the use of a thermal image camera to search a house to determine whether marijuana was being grown there, and he had ruled that the placing of a GPS device underneath the frame of a car to track its travels for twenty-eight days was an unconstitutional violation of the ancient property trespass protections.[50]

When it came to the *Maryland v. King* case, though, Scalia vigorously defended the right of personal privacy, writing a pro–right of privacy dissent so compelling that it was the equal of the legendary dissents of Oliver Wendell Holmes and Louis Brandeis in the seminal 1928 *Olmstead v. United States* wiretapping case.[51] From the beginning, he disparaged Kennedy's majority opinion argument supporting the benefits of DNA searches to identify prisoners. "The Court's assertion that DNA is being taken, not to solve crimes, but to *identify* those in the State's custody, taxes the credulity of the credulous."[52] Offering a sweeping history of the Founding Era, Scalia examined the state of Virginia's Constitution and Declaration of Rights, the debates over the ratification of the United States Constitution, and the history of Madison's drafting of the Fourth Amendment to argue: "The Fourth Amendment's general prohibition of 'unreasonable' searches imports the same requirement of individualized suspicion."[53] In short, can you link the search to criminal behavior suspected of that particular suspect?

In challenging Kennedy's arguments that this was a "special needs" search, helping to identify prisoners rather than solving crimes and thus exempting it from the Fourth Amendment's protections, Scalia argued: "To put it another way, both the legitimacy of the Court's method and the correctness of its outcome hinge entirely on the truth of a single proposition: that the primary purpose of these DNA searches is something other than simply discovering evidence of criminal wrongdoing. . . . That proposition is wrong."[54] The effort to compare the DNA sample to the FBI cold case DNA database could be designed for only one purpose, and it was not to identify the prisoner:

> If identifying someone means finding out what unsolved crimes he
> has committed, then identification is indistinguishable from the or-
> dinary law-enforcement aims that have never been thought to justify
> a suspicionless search. Searching every lawfully stopped car, for ex-
> ample, might turn up information about unsolved crimes the driver
> had committed, but no one would say that such a search was aimed
> at "identifying" him, and no court would hold such a search lawful.
> I will therefore assume that the Court means that the DNA search
> at issue here was useful to "identify" [the defendant] in the normal
> sense of that word—in the sense that would identify the author of
> the *Introduction to the Principles of Morals and Legislation* as Jeremy
> Bentham.[55]

In a devastating section of his dissent, Scalia demonstrated that the purpose of the DNA search could *not* have been to identify the suspect because of the manner in which it was done, and the length of time it took to get that information. On the means for identifying a suspect, Scalia said: "King was not identified by his association with the sample; rather, the [FBI] sample was identified by its association with King. . . . King was who he was, and volumes of his biography could not make him any more or any less King. No minimally competent speaker of English would say, upon noticing a known arrestee's similarity 'to a wanted poster of a previously unidentified suspect' . . . that the *arrestee* had thereby been identified. It was the previously unidentified suspect who had been identified—just as, here, it was the previously unidentified rapist."[56] As for the time delay, he pointed out that the "DNA testing does not even begin until after arraignment and bail decisions are already made" and that "the samples sit in storage for months, and take weeks to test." Putting these together, Scalia concluded:

> What DNA adds—what makes it a valuable weapon in the law-enforcement arsenal—is the ability to solve unsolved crimes, by matching old crime-scene evidence against the profiles of people whose identities are already known. That is what was going on when King's DNA was taken, and we should not disguise the fact. Solving unsolved crimes is a noble objective, but it occupies a lower place in the American pantheon of noble objectives than the protection of our people from suspicionless law-enforcement searches. The Fourth Amendment must prevail.[57]

So powerful was this dissent by Scalia that constitutional scholar and privacy law expert Jeffrey Rosen wrote in an article for *The New Republic* titled "A Damning Dissent," that Scalia's *Maryland v. King* opinion was "not only one of his own best Fourth Amendment dissents, but one of the best Fourth Amendments dissents, ever."[58]

In writing this memorable dissent, Scalia had shown what he was capable of producing when he focused his considerable intellect, rather than his personal vitriol, on a problem. But that approach would not last.

CHAPTER 27

Grumpy Old Justice

With his twenty-seventh term on the Supreme Court slated to end the following week, Scalia did a most curious thing on the morning of Friday, June 21, 2013. Just as the Court was on the verge of announcing its decisions in the most important cases of that term, dealing with an affirmative action admissions program at the University of Texas, a restrictive voter ID law in Alabama, and two cases, dealing with one state and one federal law, involving the right of gays to marry and receive spousal benefits, Scalia was in Asheville, North Carolina, to speak to the North Carolina Bar Association. From the vast catalogue of speeches that he could have chosen to deliver that morning, he selected, by his own term, his "most provocative one": "Mullahs of the West: Judges as Moral Arbiters."

Just why, on the eve of the announcement of the gay marriage decisions, Scalia had dusted off and delivered this speech, one that he had not been reported as having given in four years, was not yet clear. In early 2006, his "Mullahs of the West" speech had been the staple of his "Dead Constitution Tour" following his failure to be named chief justice. After delivering the speech one more time, over three years later, in Warsaw, Poland, he had put it away.[1] So why was he once again arguing that his living, evolving Constitution colleagues such as Anthony Kennedy were "mullahs," or "judge moralists," who were unqualified to make moral decisions in cases? Some Court observers thought they had the answer. "Did Justice Scalia Just Telegraph his Decision on DOMA?" blogger Jean Ann Esselink asked about the upcoming gay marriage cases on *The New Civil Rights Movement* website.[2] But the headline was not quite right. Given his career-long opposition to gay rights, there was little doubt as to how Scalia would rule in these two potentially landmark gay marriage cases—*United States v. Windsor*, dealing with the constitutionality of the 1996 federal Defense of Marriage Act (DOMA), defining marriage for the purposes of receiving federal benefits as solely one between one man and one woman, and *Hollingsworth v. Perry*, dealing with the constitutionality of California's similarly restrictive Proposition 8 banning gay marriage. But by changing the focus of the question, the speech, and its timing, raised a central issue. Had Scalia revealed how the Court as a whole would be ruling on gay marriage the following week? Was he now lamenting that a majority of his colleagues had voted against him, and if so, was he using his extrajudicial forum to persuade the general public that his colleagues were wrong in supporting gay marriage? Or was he now cheering that his colleagues had changed their minds and were now voting with him, and explaining why they had come to that conclusion? Whatever the answer, the appearance concerned reporters, with Nathaniel Frank of *Slate* titling his column on the speech "Scalia the Mullah."[3]

Before the Court announced its gay marriage rulings, it had two other important cases to resolve. The first, *Fisher v. University of Texas*, examined the constitutionality of the affirmative action admissions program at the University of Texas, under which students could gain admission either by being in the top 10 percent of their high school graduating class, or by presenting some unique personal or talent factors, including consideration of race. An unsuccessful applicant, Abigail Fisher, complained that the program benefited students of color. While the Court's 7–1 majority, led by Anthony Kennedy, did not overturn the use of affirmative action in college admissions, citing the continuing need for diversity in the classroom to promote educational opportunity, it did send the case back to the lower federal court for a re-review with instructions making affirmative action admission programs harder to justify.[4] In response, Scalia made clear in a one-paragraph concurring opinion that he was ready to overturn affirmative action once and for all: "The Constitution proscribes government discrimination on the basis of race," he wrote, "and state-provided education is no exception."[5]

Next, the decision in *Shelby County v. Holder*, judging the state's restrictive voter ID law, brought the constitutionality of the 1965 Voting Rights Act into question. The act was designed to prevent nine Southern states that had historically discriminated against minority voters from changing their election laws in a way that would prevent minorities from voting. Any changes in the voting laws by those states had to receive a "pre-clearance" from the Department of Justice to certify that they did not discriminate against minority voters. Passed overwhelmingly in 1965, the law had been renewed four times by Congress by large margins, the last time in 2006.

Despite this congressional support for the law, in 2009 the Roberts Court had granted a municipal water district in northwest Austin, Texas, a statutory "bailout" from the pre-clearance process, ruling that "We are now a very different nation," and that the district's lack of recent history of voter discrimination made it unnecessary to trigger the Voting Rights Act's remedies.[6] The majority warned Congress that it needed more up-to-date evidence of discrimination against voters to justify the law's coverage formula, proving why some but not all states should have their sovereignty to legislate in this area overridden by the federal Department of Justice's pre-clearance voting rights enforcement.[7]

While Scalia did not write an opinion in this case, he had already made his views known during the oral arguments for the South Carolina case. In discussing with Solicitor General Donald Verrilli whether any changes to the Voting Rights Act should be left to Congress and not the Court, Scalia noted that the number of dissents in the Senate to the law had been declining with each renewal cycle until there were none in 2006. Scalia, abandoning for the moment his support for the democratic legislative will over the view of the courts, thought he knew the reason why: "I think it is attributable, very likely attributable, to a phenomenon that is called perpetuation of racial entitlement. It's been written about. Whenever a society adopts racial entitlements, it is very difficult to get out of them through the normal political processes. I don't think there is anything to be gained by any Senator to vote against continuation of this act. And I am fairly confident it will be reenacted in perpetuity unless—unless a court can say it does not comport with the Constitution."[8] What was seen by some as a racially insensitive comment brought "audible gasps in the Supreme Court's lawyers' lounge," wrote bloggers Nicole Flatow and Ian Millhiser, who added that it raised "concerns that [Scalia's] suspicion of the Act is rooted much more in racial resentment than in a general distrust of unanimous votes."[9]

With many states such as Texas and North Carolina standing ready to pass laws that would immediately restrict minority voting, the Court by a 5–4 margin in *Shelby County v. Holder* overturned the coverage formula in Section 5 of the Voting Rights Act. Alabama and the other Southern states covered by the act would no longer have to submit their voting law changes to the Department of Justice for pre-clearance.[10] Roberts invited Congress to redraft the state coverage formula in the voting rights law review procedure "based on current conditions," but everyone who followed politics understood that this would never happen in the partisan, stalemated Congress of

2013. For Chief Justice Roberts, who had made clear in other cases that he did not see a racial problem in the country, this was not a concern. "Our country has changed, and while any racial discrimination in voting is too much," he said, "Congress must ensure that the legislation it passes to remedy that problem speaks to current conditions." [11]

On the final day of the Court's 2012–13 term, Wednesday, June 26, ten years to the day since the Court's landmark pro–gay rights decision in *Lawrence v. Texas*, the justices announced their decisions regarding state and federal efforts to restrict marriage and the benefits of married couples solely to a union between a man and a woman. *Hollingsworth v. Perry* addressed the validity of the marriage of Kristin Perry and Sandra Stier performed in California during a six-month window when gay marriage was permitted as a result of a State Supreme Court decision. [12] The referendum known as Proposition 8 amended the California constitution to state that only heterosexual marriage would be valid in the state. The two women, along with their four sons, sought to overturn California's Proposition 8 and thus reestablish the legality of their marriage. [13]

Prop 8, as it was called, was challenged in federal court by an unusual partnership of attorneys Ted Olson and David Boies, the two opposing lawyers in the *Bush v. Gore* case in 2000. They were opposed by a citizens group that supported the law when the state of California refused to defend it in federal court. The proposition was ruled unconstitutional as a violation of the Constitution's Fourteenth Amendment Due Process and Equal Protection Clauses by federal District Court judge Vaughn Walker in August 2010, who then stayed the effect of his ruling until the case had been appealed. This decision was upheld by the Ninth Circuit Court of Appeals, which left the stay in force. When California's newly elected governor, Jerry Brown, and the state's attorney general, Kamala Harris, refused to appeal the decision, the group of private citizens who had been defending the law in the lower courts appealed this case to the Supreme Court.

To no one's surprise, given his long-standing opposition to gay rights, Scalia made very clear in the oral arguments for the *Perry* case, during an exchange with attorney Ted Olson on March 26, that he had no interest in constitutionally protecting the right for gays to marry.

"When did it become unconstitutional to exclude homosexual couples from marriage? 1791? 1868, when the Fourteenth Amendment was adopted?" Scalia asked Olson.

As skilled an advocate as anyone appearing before the Court, Olson responded, "When—may I answer this in the form of a rhetorical question? When did it become unconstitutional to prohibit interracial marriages? When did it become unconstitutional to assign children to separate schools?"

Scalia would not be put off. "It's an easy question, I think, for that one," he said. "At—at the time that the—the Equal Protection Clause was adopted. That's absolutely true. But don't give me a question to my question," he added, drawing laughter from the audience. "When do you think it became unconstitutional? Has it always been unconstitutional?" [14] After some back-and-forth, Scalia pressed again, asking, "Was it always unconstitutional?"

Olson replied, "It was constitutional [*sic*] when we—as a culture determined that sexual orientation is a characteristic of individuals that they cannot control." [15] By ruling for the gay couple, Olson was saying, the Court would signal that denial of rights due to sexual preference should be treated like discrimination against other "immutable" conditions such as race, and be judged by the most exacting "strict scrutiny" test, requiring governments to show that they had a "compelling state interest" to justify their discriminatory actions.

"When did that happen? . . . Well, how am I supposed to know how to decide a case, then . . . if you can't give me a date when the Constitution changes?" asked Scalia.

Olson saw his opening: "Because the case that's before you—in—the case that's before you today, California decided—the citizens of California decided, after the California Supreme Court decided that individuals had a right to get married irrespective of their sexual orientation in California and then the Californians decided in Proposition 8, wait a minute, we don't want those people to be able to get married." [16] The Court, he was saying, could make that change in this case.

Despite his hostility to treating same-sex marriage as a fundamental right, Scalia joined a five-person, bipartisan majority consisting of Justices Breyer, Ginsburg, and Kagan, speaking through Chief Justice Roberts, in refusing to grant the citizen group defenders of Proposition 8 standing in the case. [17] This type of case would have to wait for a later day, as Roberts explained: "We have never before upheld the standing of a private party to defend the constitutionality of a state statute when state officials have chosen not to. We decline to do so for the first time here." [18] In short, the citizens group did not have the authority to act in place of the state government officials who were refusing to enforce the proposition. This refusal to rule had the effect of leaving the pro–gay marriage District Court judgment in force, allowing Governor Brown to order that gay marriages once again be performed in California.

In the companion federal case, *United States v. Windsor*, the Court considered the status of Edith Windsor and her now deceased partner, Thea Spyer, who had married in Canada in 2007 when it was still not lawful to do so in New York, where they both lived. When Spyer died two years later, Windsor tried to claim the spousal exemption from the federal estate tax, but was prevented from doing so by the 1996 Defense of Marriage Act, which read in Section 3 that "the word 'marriage' means only a legal union between one man and one woman as husband and wife, and the word 'spouse' refers only to a person of the opposite sex who is a husband or a wife." Among more than one thousand federal laws and regulations that were interpreted as not recognizing gay marriage was the estate tax marriage exemption by the IRS that was being denied here. Under DOMA, Windsor paid more than $360,000 in estate taxes that she would not have owed if she had been considered a surviving spouse.

By the time her appeal of this decision was filed, President Obama had refused to allow his Justice Department to defend the law in court. So Congress's Bipartisan Legal Advisory Group (BLAG) arranged for former Bush administration solicitor general and accomplished Supreme Court advocate Paul Clement to defend the law. Two lower federal courts ruled in favor of Windsor, arguing that DOMA violated her constitutional rights under the Fifth Amendment's Due Process Clause.[19]

Advocates for gay marriage rejoiced as Justice Kennedy joined the four Court liberals in *United States v. Windsor* in overturning Section 3 of the law. Disposing of challenges to Windsor's standing and federalism questions, Kennedy concluded that the Court could and should decide this case. The heart of his opinion dealt with whether, under the Constitution, same-sex couples could "occupy the same status and dignity as that of a man and a woman in lawful marriage." If so, DOMA had to fall, because it had created an "unjust exclusion" of same-sex couples. For Kennedy, the mere linkage of the word "dignity" to this right, which he did nine times in this opinion, was an indication of how much he appeared to support the equal treatment of same-sex marriage.

Kennedy acknowledged that the determination of a lawful marriage was "within the authority and realm of the separate States," and the regulation of domestic relations was the "virtually exclusive province of the States." As a result, prior to this case the federal government had always "deferred to

state-law policy decisions with respect to domestic relations." DOMA, however, prevented gay couples even in states that recognized gay marriage from
being treated as married by the federal government. Thus the law rejected
"the long-established precept that the incidents, benefits, and obligations of
marriage are uniform for all married couples within each State." Kennedy
argued, though, that it was "unnecessary to decide whether this federal intrusion on state power is a violation of the Constitution because it disrupts
the federal balance." Instead, he said, "The State's power in defining the
marital relation is of central relevance in this case quite apart from principles
of federalism."[20]

He further found it highly significant that New York and, at that time,
eleven other states along with the District of Columbia, had legally recognized gay marriages: "Here the State's decision to give this class of persons
the right to marry conferred upon them a dignity and status of immense
import. When the State used its historic and essential authority to define the
marital relation in this way, its role and its power in making the decision
enhanced the recognition, dignity, and protection of the class in their own
community."[21] To the contrary, he added, "DOMA, because of its reach and
extent, departs from this history and tradition of reliance on state law to
define marriage."[22] This action by the federal government, he argued, created an "indignity" and "deprivation" that represented an unconstitutional
discrimination under the Fifth Amendment's Due Process Clause, which
under past interpretations also functioned like an Equal Protection Clause.[23]
DOMA, Kennedy argued, "writes inequality into the entire United States
Code" by "identify[ing] a subset of state-sanctioned marriages and mak[ing]
them unequal."[24] This meant that same-sex married couples would live in
two worlds, married in their states but unmarried under federal law. This,
for Kennedy, was unacceptable.[25]

Even more revealing, for future cases raising family issues from these
marriages, Kennedy added that these two tiers of marital recognition
harmed the children in these families: "It humiliates tens of thousands of
children now being raised by same-sex couples. The law in question makes
it even more difficult for the children to understand the integrity and close-
ness of their own family and its concord with other families in their community and in their daily lives." When all of these indignities were added to
the legal burdens imposed on these families as a result of the lack of federal
protection of their unions, Kennedy concluded that "the principal purpose
and the necessary effect" of DOMA "demean[s] those persons who are in a

lawful same-sex marriage."[26] Accordingly, Kennedy and the majority found DOMA to be an unconstitutional violation of the Fifth Amendment because it "singles out a class of persons deemed by a State entitled to recognition and protection to enhance their own liberty" and instead "imposes a disability on the class by refusing to acknowledge a status the State finds to be dignified and proper."[27]

In response, a clearly frustrated Scalia issued one of his sternest dissents ever. He began by noting that Kennedy had refused to use two clear ways to avoid deciding the constitutionality of federal laws against same-sex marriages—choosing not to rule that the parties lacked sufficient adverseness to create enough standing to justify making a decision, or deciding the case on the basis of federalism by ruling that the federal government had unconstitutionally exercised the states' police powers dealing with marriage licenses. Believing that the Court could have avoided the major issue in this case, Scalia blasted Kennedy for his use of judicial activism: "We have no power to decide this case. And even if we did, we have no power under the Constitution to invalidate this democratically adopted legislation. The Court's errors on both points spring forth from the same diseased root: an exalted conception of the role of this institution in America. The Court is eager—*hungry*—to tell everyone its view of the legal question at the heart of this case."[28] While he did have a point about how anxious Kennedy and the majority appeared to be to decide this issue *now*, Scalia's plea against the Court invalidating "democratically adopted legislation" mirrored the complaints by others that he and the majority had done exactly the same thing the day before in ruling against the similarly democratically adopted Voting Rights Act.

After devoting three-fifths of his opinion to arguing that there was no adverseness between the parties, and thus there was no case or controversy, Scalia argued that for the Supreme Court to decide the case was "jaw-dropping. It is an assertion of judicial supremacy over the people's Representatives in Congress and the Executive. It envisions a Supreme Court standing (or rather enthroned) at the apex of government, empowered to decide all constitutional questions, always and everywhere 'primary' in its role."[29] Scalia argued that Kennedy's decision was "just a desire to place this Court at the center of the Nation's life."[30] By arguing in this case dealing with a federal law defining marriage that the states had total power to define this relationship, while also making it clear that the government could not treat same-sex marriages differently, Scalia argued that Kennedy had left "the second, state-law shoe to be dropped later, (maybe next Term). But I am only guessing."[31]

Since the majority had gone beyond the standing issue, Scalia did the same in arguing that Kennedy had never made clear the legal standard by which he was now deciding this case. He did not think it fair that Kennedy overturned the law because, in his words, it was motivated by "a bare congressional desire to harm" couples in same-sex marriages.[32] This kind of approach, Scalia argued, led Kennedy to say that the government could not legislate based on morality, while also "maintain[ing] the illusion of the Act's supporters as unhinged members of a wild-eyed lynch mob."[33]

Scalia did not see Congress as being motivated by "animus" in enacting DOMA, but rather as offering "stabilizing prudence." For Scalia, by accusing Congress of demeaning same-sex couples through DOMA, Kennedy had misstated the purpose of this law: "To defend traditional marriage is not to condemn, demean, or humiliate those who would prefer other arrangements, any more than to defend the Constitution of the United States is to condemn, demean, or humiliate other constitutions. To hurl such accusations so casually demeans *this institution*."[34] Scalia viewed Kennedy's words as an attack by the majority on the motives of those members of Congress who had passed the law: "It is one thing for a society to elect change; it is another for a court of law to impose change by adjudging those who oppose it *hostes humani generis*, enemies of the human race."[35]

Even though Kennedy had said that this holding only applied to the federal rights of legally married same-sex couples, saying nothing about the constitutionality of gay marriage regulations in the states, Scalia believed that it was only a matter of time before that ruling came as well: "It takes real cheek for today's majority to assure us, as it is going out the door, that a constitutional requirement to give formal recognition to same-sex marriage is not at issue here—when what has preceded that assurance is a lecture on how superior the majority's moral judgment in favor of same-sex marriage is to the Congress's hateful moral judgment against it. I promise you this: The only thing that will 'confine' the Court's holding is its sense of what it can get away with."[36]

In assessing Kennedy's arguments against the Defense of Marriage Act, Scalia described them, in one of the most memorable phrases in any of his judicial opinions, as "a disappearing trail of its legalistic argle-bargle."[37] "Argle-bargle" is what grammarians call a "rhyming reduplication," like hocus-pocus, in this case using a version of an old Scottish phrase "argie-bargie," which has a variety of meanings ranging from a "lively discussion" to the more pejorative "mumbo-jumbo."[38] Just as Scalia had done in the 2003 *Lawrence v. Texas* gay rights case, correctly predicting that Kennedy's opinion would lead to support for gay marriage laws, now he predicted that the Court's arguments for federal recognition of gay marriage would lead to the same result in future cases dealing with state laws: "As far as this Court is concerned, no one should be fooled; it is just a matter of listening and waiting for the other shoe. By formally declaring anyone opposed to same-sex marriage an enemy of human decency, the majority arms well every challenger to a state law restricting marriage to its traditional definition."[39] Indeed, just six months later, two federal district court judges, one in Utah and one in Ohio, would "agree with" Scalia's predictive language in ruling that all or part, respectively, of these state laws banning gay marriages were unconstitutional.[40]

Rather than facing the prospect of a Kennedy-led Court majority one day deciding the fate of gay marriage, Scalia wanted to leave the decision over the future of gay marriage to the voting public: "Few public controversies touch an institution so central to the lives of so many, and few inspire such attendant passion by good people on all sides. Few public controversies will ever demonstrate so vividly the beauty of what our Framers gave us, a gift the Court pawns today to buy its stolen moment in the spotlight: a system of government that permits us to rule *ourselves*."[41] In a case of the pot calling the kettle black, Scalia accused Kennedy of lacking "judicial temperament" both because of the *ad hominem* nature of his argumentation and his failure to remove the Court from this debate. "In the majority's telling, this story is black-and-white: Hate your neighbor or come along with us. The truth is more complicated. It is hard to admit that one's political opponents are not monsters, especially in a struggle like this one, and the challenge in the end proves more than today's Court can handle. Too bad. . . . We might have covered ourselves with honor today, by promising all sides of this debate that it was theirs to settle and that we would respect their resolution. We might have let the People decide. But that the majority will not do."[42]

• • •

Even though he lost, Scalia's ideological war was not over. While his colleagues dispersed to varied locales for the summer, he once more embarked on his informal lecture circuit to offer his critique of the Court's decisions that term. Picking up where he left off in his North Carolina Bar Association speech, he journeyed to Snowmass Village, Colorado, to deliver once again his "Mullahs of the West" speech, this time to a meeting of the Utah State Bar Association.[43] But something went haywire during the appearance. Improvising a bit during the beginning of his speech, he made a reference to the "Holocaust" in Germany, a society he described as being, at that time, "the most advanced country in the world." When he added that activist German judges then had interpreted laws according to "the spirit of the age," or in German the *Zeitgeist*, and "g[o]t themselves and society into trouble," his comments were interpreted as an accusation that there was a link between activist judges and Naziism.[44] Some online commentators and reporters argued that Scalia was now approaching "Godwin's Law," which posited that inevitably "any online discussion will produce a comparison to Hitler or the Nazis."[45] A newspaper report of the speech in the *Aspen Times* quickly spread throughout the blogosphere. Liberal blogger Josh Marshall, posting on the *Talking Points Memo* site, said that the nation was now approaching "Peak Scalia."[46] Only after this online discussion had raged for a while did an emailer to the *Althouse* law blog site reveal that Scalia had actually made his comments about Naziism in responding to an earlier discussion in the conference about Germany, and that his real point had been that the teaching of "virtue" had been left out of Germany's formidable educational curriculum.[47] But by then, more damage to Scalia's reputation had been done.

Despite this controversy, Scalia was not finished with his extrajudicial commentary on the gay marriage decisions. Speaking in late August to an organizing event by the Federalist Society in Bozeman, Montana, he appeared to be referring to the gay marriage decisions when he said, "It's not up to the courts to invent new minorities that get special protections." Later, he added, "The court makes an amazing amount of decisions that ought to be made by the people."[48] Just as had happened as a result of his similar comment in September 2010 at the Hastings College of Law when he talked about the lack of protection by the Fourteenth Amendment for women's rights, this one received an equally hostile reaction. Scalia's critics pointed out that Kennedy had not "invented," but rather recognized, a gay minority, deserving of legal protection.[49] But Scalia, as always, was unfazed by any criticism of his remarks. For those critics, he had a new response, guaranteed to generate a laugh: "Can't scare me. I have life tenure."[50]

Considering all of Scalia's comments, *Slate*'s legal reporter, Dahlia Lithwick, saw a parallel between them and an interview by Justice Ruth Bader Ginsburg, who anguished liberal Court observers by telling *New York Times*

Supreme Court reporter Adam Liptak that she had no desire to time her departure from the Court to allow President Obama to fill her seat.[51] To Lithwick, Scalia and Ginsburg had become the "last two sitting justices who are so completely of another era," still hoping to achieve their goals even though their time was running out. Referring to a Jack Lemmon and Walter Matthau comedy, Lithwick said that Scalia and Ginsburg had become "Grumpy Old Justices."[52]

Scalia's grumpiness was on full display when he attracted the lion's share of attention on the eve of the opening of the Court's 2013–14 term when *New York* magazine published the transcript of his interview with reporter Jennifer Senior. Some of his comments were familiar to close observers of his speaking tours: he no longer considered himself a "faint-hearted originalist," he would continue to avoid the the State of the Union address, which he viewed as a "childish spectacle," and his refusal to recuse himself from the Cheney energy task force case was "maybe the only heroic opinion I ever issued."[53]

Elsewhere in the conversation, he decried the "coarseness of manners" as indicated by "the constant use of the F-word" in movies and on television. By his own account, he attended very few parties where liberals might be found, had ceased reading what he called the "shrilly, *shrilly* liberal" *Washington Post*, listened on the radio only to conservative Bill Bennett's talk show with its "good callers . . . they keep off stupid people," and when he sought to get outside the Beltway bubble, he hunted with avowed conservatives in Louisiana.[54] *Slate*'s Dahlia Lithwick observed from all of this Scalia's "remarkable isolation from anyone who doesn't agree with him."[55]

In one of the most discussed segments of Senior's interview, after a brief discussion of heaven and hell, Scalia ignored a question about his judicial opinion "drafting process" to say that he "even believe[s] in the Devil." After a testy back-and-forth with the reporter as to how the devil operated in modern society, Scalia confronted her: "You're looking at me as though I'm weird. My God! Are you so out of touch with most of America, most of which believes in the Devil? I mean, Jesus Christ believed in the Devil! It's in the Gospels! You travel in circles that are so, so removed from mainstream America that you are appalled that anybody would believe in the Devil! Most of mankind has believed in the Devil, for all of history. Many more intelligent people than you or me have believed in the Devil." Senior responded: "I hope you weren't sensing contempt from me. It wasn't your belief that surprised me so much as how boldly you expressed it." To which Scalia said, "I was offended by that. I really was."[56]

Senior would say later of her interview with the justice: "It's embarrassing, but the overlap between our worlds is almost nonexistent. It explains why the left and the right both responded so enthusiastically to this piece. Each side sees its own view affirmed. One sees a monster and the other sees a hero. It's extraordinary, actually. The [Bill] O'Reilly constituents think he's speaking sense; the Jon Stewart vote thinks virtually everything the guy says is nuts."[57]

Pressed once more by Senior about any retirement plans, Scalia admitted that while it was still not imminent, "I was worried lately about the fact that the job seems easier. . . . I still work hard. But it does seem easier than it used to. And that worried me. You know: Maybe I'm getting lazy. . . . But after due reflection, I've decided the reason it's getting easier is because so many of the cases that come before us present the issue of whether we should extend one of the opinions from the previous 27 years that I've been here, which I dissented from in the first place!"[58] Indeed, it would be Scalia's eight other colleagues, and not he, who would dictate the case results during the upcoming Court term.

• • •

Scalia's decisions and controversial comments throughout 2013 demonstrated the continuing dilemmas facing him as he moved through the latter stages of his career. As new cases come to the Supreme Court, Scalia will continue to use his originalism and textualism decision-making theories, his traditionalism as dictated by his religious beliefs, and his partisan conservatism, not always seeing how these are, at times, contradictory. However Scalia resolves these tensions, and others, there is one consideration that he will never ponder: should he change his views to accommodate those of his colleagues? It is inconceivable to believe that he will ever compromise his views in order to gain or retain the votes of his colleagues.

Scalia knows now that it will be either Anthony Kennedy, or at times Chief Justice John Roberts, who will dictate the results in the most controversial cases—not he. He knows also that it will be, with each passing term, the younger generation of judges who will have the votes to form majorities on cases. As such, the Court will be governed less by Scalia's originalism or textualism, and more by Kennedy's conservatism, libertarianism, and evolving constitutionalism, or by Chief Justice Roberts's tempering his conservatism with self-restraint to search for allies and achieve Court consensus. Until there are changes in the membership of the Court, it is these two men who will decide how conservative the Court will be, and how far each ruling will go. And through it all, Scalia will be a reliably conservative voter, lobbing written and verbal mortar shells from on and off the Court when he disagrees with his colleagues' results.

His status within the Court is something that Scalia himself pondered in his *New York* magazine interview: "You know, for all I know, 50 years from now I may be the Justice [A. George] Sutherland of the late-twentieth and early-21st century, who's regarded as: 'He was on the losing side of everything, an old fogey, the old view.' And I don't care. . . . There are those who think I am, I'm sure. I can see that happening as some of the justices in the early years of the New Deal are now painted as old fogies. It can happen."[59]

Despite his admitted role as a loner on a conservative Court, Scalia has every reason to believe that he is not done yet. He still has a role to serve as the continual stream of publicity that he gets from his extrajudicial comments and judicial opinions can attest. Scalia has molded the conversation on the Court, making originalism a theory that must be addressed. Through his solo dissents and provocative extrajudicial speeches, he has laid the groundwork for a future majority to follow his views. Toward this end, Scalia can, just as he has done throughout his career, continue his constitutional crusade as a "Court of One." Until the end of his time on the Supreme Court, indeed, until the end of his days on earth, Antonin Gregory Scalia will know that while the wins and losses in battles over future cases will come and go, his mission to give voice to his legal theory and political vision on the Court, and to America, will be his enduring legacy.

And one day, perhaps some of the law clerks he mentored, or some of the students he taught, or those he never knew but touched through his writings or his public appearances, will rise to the highest court in the land. There they might use his teachings to make his interpretations the law of the land, and in doing so, prevent the pride of the Scalias from being seen as an "old fogey" by legal historians and future generations of Americans. And whether he is still around to see it or not, through them his originalism will be resurrected—will come again—and he, and it, will live forever.

Or, perhaps not. . . .

ACKNOWLEDGMENTS

Traveling the intellectual road to produce this biography over the past eight years has been a wonderful and fascinating journey. There is no better professional life than that of a college liberal arts professor and writer of biography, and I am forever grateful to Professors Dean Alfange Jr. and Henry J. Abraham, along with Sheldon Goldman and Robert J. Harris, for setting me on that path.

When I was considering possible topics for this book, I knew I wanted to bring my previous biographies of twentieth-century justices—Louis D. Brandeis, Felix Frankfurter, Abe Fortas, and William O. Douglas—up to the present day. I was most grateful when my agent, John Wright, suggested writing a biography of Antonin Scalia, because, he said, Scalia was "the most interesting of all of the members of the current Court." John could not have been more right.

Like all scholars who build on the work of those researchers who came before them, I came to the Scalia project grateful for the existing body of fine biographical and analytical literature on him and his judicial decisions, as well as on the Supreme Court. I would like to thank all of those who previously wrote on Antonin Scalia, and on the Court, for their long-distance guidance, and my indebtedness to their work is indicated throughout the endnotes.

Much of the primary research material that serves as the foundation for this book is housed in the primary document collections in libraries around the country. Productive visits to those collections are not possible without the guidance of the skilled professional archivists who work there. I am indebted to the staff, especially Jeff Flannery, of the Manuscripts Division of the Library of Congress in Washington, D.C., with its treasure trove of material on Scalia in the papers of Justice Harry Blackmun and other justices as well as judges. Thanks also to the Archives Division of Georgetown University, with its revealing material on Scalia's college life, and especially Lynn Conway, who both guided me through that material and helped me obtain some wonderful photos of that period. I am also grateful to Deborah Ann

Cook, for her cite-checking assistance when I most needed it. The revealing archives of Justice Lewis F. Powell Jr., in the Washington and Lee Law School, would have remained a mystery to me had it not been for the kindness of archivist John N. Jacob in guiding me through them. I would also like to thank, among others, David Horrocks for his guidance in the Gerald R. Ford Presidential Library in Ann Arbor, Michigan, where I learned much that was not known about Scalia's formative work in the Office of Legal Counsel in the Ford administration. I benefited greatly from the staffs of the Richard M. Nixon Presidential Library, then in College Park, Maryland, and the National Archives, for their help in finding additional material. I extend my thanks also to the staff of the Ronald Reagan Presidential Library in Simi Valley, California, for their efforts in helping me gain access to the wonderful material in the Scalia and Rehnquist judicial appointment files, including the hitherto unexplored forty-two-page autobiographical Supreme Court Appointment Questionnaire, written by Scalia himself in 1986.

My best, and most revealing, source for this book on Antonin Scalia, though, has been Scalia himself. The justice likes to say in his public appearances that he does not like any of the books about the Supreme Court because they are not accurate. He explains that they are all based on interviews of individuals who work inside the Court building and thus are sworn to confidentiality. By breaking that oath, Scalia adds, they have proven themselves to be unreliable, and thus cannot be trusted to provide accurate information. In saying this, Scalia does not allow for other means of learning about the Court. By becoming an extremely active justice off the Court, and having thus changed the ethical boundaries of his position, he has left a long and wide trail of transcripts of speeches, public appearances, and news interviews, all of which are readily available in the digital age. When analyzed along with the documentary research, his large body of roughly eight hundred judicial opinions, and his writings on his legal theories, reveal a man who is unlike any who had emerged from other accounts. As much as possible, I have let Scalia speak for himself, answered by his critics and other scholars. And I am grateful to him for making that possible.

In the course of producing this book I have accumulated a great many personal debts, and while I cannot adequately repay all of these people, I am grateful for the opportunity to thank them. First, above all others, this volume would not have been possible without my wife and soulmate, Carol Lynn Wright. I am so blessed to be able to spend my life married to my best friend. Beyond this, I am so fortunate to be living with a highly talented fellow author and editor, and I have benefited so much from her insights, discerning editorial judgment, continuing wise counsel, and unflagging moral support during every stage of this work. Both of us have been blessed by the love and continual support of our two children, Emily and Geoffrey, not yet born when I first started writing, and now a writer and Broadway actor respectively. They both have always been so understanding of their father's fascination with searching out historical treasures and filling their house, and now their former rooms, with boxes of papers and documents that must be moved when they come home to visit. My children and my son-in-law Adam Glickman have, each in his or her own way and at different times, bolstered me in getting through some difficult periods finishing this book. I am continually amused by the ability of our rescue cats to shuffle those papers around, and am very grateful for the companionship of our rescue dog, Mr. Darcy, who stayed by my side as I edited chapter after chapter.

I am most grateful to my agent, John Wright, who has been a guiding, supportive force throughout this project, has always being available to counsel and cheer me on, and who carefully read through the manuscript, offering very useful suggestions. One of John's best pieces of advice was to guide me in signing with Simon & Schuster in order to work with my editor, Bob Bender. I cannot thank Bob enough for his patience, affording me the necessary time to work on the narrative, and for his continual support throughout the project. I have worked with some outstanding editors over the years, but Bob is the best of them. I am grateful for his superb and repeated line editing, which helped me to produce a much better paced and better written manuscript. The publishing team at Simon & Schuster has been first-rate, and chief among them has been copy editor Fred Chase, whose countless suggestions have saved me from many errors and misstatements and whose keen editing eye helped to further polish the final manuscript. I also benefited greatly from the discerning legal reading by Elisa Rivlin. Any errors that remain are my responsibility.

I benefited in my search for photos from the assistance of the following people. My primary thanks go to Steven Petteway of the Supreme Court Curator's Office, who was wonderfully helpful in collecting a huge body of excellent photos of Scalia and the entire Supreme Court. I am also grateful to Michael Pinckney of the Reagan Library photographic archives division and photographer David Anderson, the executor of the Stan Stearns photographic archives, for helping me locate, identify, and gain permission to use the very revealing portrait of Scalia in the Nixon administration. Thanks also to Ken Hafeli, the director of the photographic archives division of the Gerald R. Ford Presidential Library, and Joseph Gorski, the Vice President for Advancement at Xavier High School, in New York City, for helping me find other photos. I am also very grateful for Justice Scalia's permission to reproduce in this volume some of his family photographs, as well as for approving the use of other early photographs of his life that were located in other institutions.

I am truly grateful once again to the late Fred Morgan Kirby and his family and the Fred Morgan Kirby Foundation for supporting me so generously as the Fred Morgan Kirby Professor of Civil Rights at Lafayette College in Easton, Pennsylvania. I cannot sufficiently thank Helena Silverstein, Head of the Department of Government and Law at Lafayette College, for creating such a congenial work environment that has made it possible for me to concentrate on my work. Lafayette's fine provost, Wendy Hill, and her predecessor Tony Cummings, as well as Associate Provosts Mary J. S. Roth and John Meier have been very responsive to all of my requests for support throughout the project, and I am grateful for all of that assistance. My thanks go also to my colleagues in the Department of Government and Law and elsewhere throughout the Lafayette faculty for making my professional situation so pleasant and productive. The remarkably capable staffs in Lafayette's Skillman and Kirby Libraries, including Bob Duncan, Kandyce Fisher, Karen Haduck, Terese Heidenwolf, Ana Ramirez Luhrs, and Mercedes Sharpless, have, over the years, gone above and beyond in responding to all of my research and technical questions, while also helping me to locate difficult-to-find materials.

One of the true joys of teaching in a small liberal arts college like Lafayette College is having the opportunity to work with enterprising and creative students in the classroom and on one's research projects. It is a joy to thank all of them now for making my teaching career so rewarding, as well as for their contributions to this volume. The Mellon Foundation's "Community of Scholars" grant to Lafayette made it possible for three years for me to work with teams of students, including Lori Weaver, Amy Polizanno, Allison Ligorano, Brendan O'Regan, Colleen Sullivan, and Matt Gyory, to research and develop the early theoretical base for this book. Thanks also to the students in my biographical writing seminar, "Personality and Judicial Decision-Making," many of whose seminar papers are cited throughout this book, for their provocative questions and useful insights. And, thanks to the students in my Constitutional Law classes for their responses to my theories about Scalia's decision making, and to my students in my introductory American Government class for making me think even more deeply about the role of Scalia and the Supreme Court in American politics.

Thanks also are due to two dear friends. Larry Berman, my coauthor on our American government textbook *Approaching Democracy* and the Founding Dean of the Honors College at Georgia State, and Robert Harkavy, the emeritus Professor of Political Science at Penn State University, both of whom have been constant supporters throughout the writing of this volume.

As mentioned in my dedication page, my one true regret is that my beloved mother-in-law, Patricia Gebhard Wright, and my good friend and former department head, John T. McCartney, who guided me through my first nine years at Lafayette, did not live long enough to see this book completed. I am a better person for having known them. I am grateful, though, that my mother, Jean Hendrick Coe, will once again have an opportunity to show her friends what her son does for a living.

Finally, coming from a family with many members who never saw this happen, I would like to thank every one of the bearded members of the 2013 Boston Red Sox, the winners of the World Series, for giving this lifelong Sox fan the thrill of seeing his team win three World Championships in one lifetime.

It is my hope that all of these people will be as pleased to be associated with this book as I am thankful for their assistance in producing it.

Bruce Allen Murphy

Center Valley, Pennsylvania
February 15, 2014

SHORT TITLES USED IN NOTES

Biskupic, *American Original*: Joan Biskupic, *American Original: The Life and Constitution of Supreme Court Justice Antonin Scalia* (New York: Macmillan, 2009).

Blackmun Papers: The papers of Justice Harry Blackmun, Manuscripts Division, Library of Congress, Washington, D.C.

Charlie Rose interview, June 20, 2008: *Charlie Rose,* PBS, June 20, 2008, Lexis/Nexis.

Charlie Rose interview, November 27, 2012: *Charlie Rose,* PBS, November 27, 2012.

Tim Russert interview: *Tim Russert,* MSNBC, May 3, 2008, Lexis/Nexis.

Scalia = Antonin Scalia.

Scalia Justice Department Questionnaire: Antonin Scalia, 1986 Supreme Court Questionnaire, Peter J. Wallison Files, Ronald Reagan Presidential Library, Simi Valley, California.

Lesley Stahl interview, April 27, 2008: *60 Minutes,* CBS News, April 27, 2008.

Lesley Stahl interview, September 14, 2009: *60 Minutes,* CBS News, September 14, 2009.

Nina Totenberg interview: Interview with NPR's Nina Totenberg, Smithsonian Associates Interview, Lisner Auditorium, George Washington University, Washington, D.C., February 12, 2013, Lexis/Nexis.

Powell Papers: The papers of Justice Lewis F. Powell Jr., Washington and Lee University School of Law Archives, Lexington, Virginia. The Supreme Court papers are in Series 10.6. The collection has since been digitized and can be found on the web by year and case file name at http://law.wlu.edu/powellarchives/page.asp?pageid=1279.

NOTES

PROLOGUE: SCALIA IN WINTER

1. It was the second time that the reelected president took the oath that week, having done so the day before, on Sunday, as administered by Chief Justice John Roberts in the Blue Room of the White House, in order to fulfill the constitutional requirement that he be sworn into office by noon on January 20.
2. Joseph Straw and Dan Friedman, "Inauguration 2013 Notebook: What's Up with Justice Antonin Scalia's Hat?," New York *Daily News,* January 21, 2013, http://www .nydailynews.com/news/national/inauguration-notebook-scalia-odd-hat-designated -survivor-article-1.1244631. Information on the fabric: "The Secret Behind Justice Scalia's Hat," St. Thomas More Society, January 13, 2013, https://www.thomasmore society.org/2013/01/28/the-secret-behind-justice-scalias-hat/.
3. The tweets are taken from #Scaliaweirdhat, January 21, 2013, www.twitter.com, https:// twitter.com/search?q=Scaliaweirdhat&src=typd.
4. Goldman quoted in: Ernest Zuckerman, "Why Antonin Scalia Is Wearing That Hat to Inauguration," January 22, 2013, www.theatlanticwire.com.
5. Kevin Walsh, "About Justice Scalia's Headgear," *Walshlaw,* January 21, 2013, http:// walshslaw.wordpress.com/2013/01/21/about-justice-scalias-headgear/.
6. "The Secret Behind Justice Scalia's Hat," St. Thomas More Society.
7. Napp Nazworth, "Was Scalia's Hat a Birth Control Mandate Protest," January 23, 2013, http://www.christianpost.com/news/was-scalias-inauguration-hat-a-birth-control-man date-protest-88703/.
8. Matthew Schmitz, "First Thoughts," *First Things,* January 21, 2013, http://www.first things.com/blogs/firstthoughts/2013/01/21/scalia-wears-martyrs-cap-to-inauguration/.
9. For an account of Scalia's view on this speech, see Sam Baker, "Justice Scalia to Deliver Own Speech on State of the Union Night," *The Hill,* February 12, 2013, thehill .com/homenews/news/282571-justice-scalia-delivering-own-speech-during-state-of-the -union.
10. Scalia interview with NPR's Nina Totenberg, Smithsonian Associates Interview, Lisner Auditorium, George Washington University, Washington, D.C., February 12, 2013, Lexis/Nexis. Hereafter: Nina Totenberg interview.
11. Scalia interview with Charlie Rose, *Charlie Rose,* PBS, November 27, 2012, Lexis/Nexis transcript). Hereafter: Charlie Rose interview, November 27, 2012.

CHAPTER I: PRIDE OF THE SCALIAS

1. James Staab, *The Political Thought of Justice Antonin Scalia: A Hamiltonian on the Supreme Court* (Lanham, MD: Rowman & Littlefield, 2006), p. 1.

2. Scalia interview with Lesley Stahl, "Justice Scalia," *60 Minutes*, CBS News, April 27, 2008. Hereafter: Lesley Stahl interview.

3. The name is mentioned in the epigraph for S. Eugene Scalia, *Luigi Capuana and His Times* (New York: S. F. Vanni, 1952).

4. Steerage Passenger Manifest, "States Immigration Officer at the Port of Arrival," New York City, Ellis Island Passenger records, December 22, 1920, List 91, http://www.ellis island.org/search/viewTextManifest.asp?MID=08843433860891131616&FNM=SAL VATORE&LNM=SCALIA&PLNM=SCALIA&bSYR=1903&bEYR=1903&first_kind =1&last_kind=0&RF=1&pID=105267170046. For more see the article by Scalia's son, Eugene Scalia, response to Akiba Covitz, "Alito Is Not a Scalia Clone," TNR online, November 1, 2005, www.tnr.com.

5. Memoir of Professor Joseph F. DeSimone, October 2, 1989, Brooklyn College Archives. My thanks to Brooklyn College archivist Marianne La Batto for locating and providing this material. For the "deeply religious" comment, see Ruth Marcus and Susan Schmidt, "Scalia Tenacious After Staking Out a Position," *Washington Post*, June 22, 1986.

6. Ibid.

7. Scalia interview with Charlie Rose, *Charlie Rose*, PBS, June 20, 2008, Lexis/Nexis transcript. Hereafter: Charlie Rose interview, June 20, 2008.

8. This Scalia family material can be found on Ancestry.com at http://search.ancestry.com /iexec?htx=View&r=an&dbid=7488&iid=NYT715_2899-0983&fn=Salvatore&ln=Scalia &st=r&ssrc=pt_t1469813_p-1937247585_kpidz0q3d-1937247585z0q26pgz0q3d32768z0q 26pgPLz0q3dpid&pid=4024867058.

9. Ship Manifest for *Duca d'Aosta*, Port of New York passenger records, Ellis Island Foundation, www.ellisisland.org/search/viewTextManifest.asp?MID=168. See also S. Eugene Scalia response to Akiba Covitz, TNR online, November 1, 2009; and Antonin Scalia, "The Disease as Cure: In Order to Get Beyond Racism We Must First Take Account of Race," *Washington University Law Quarterly* (1979): 147–52.

10. Memoir of Joseph F. DeSimone.

11. Ibid.

12. Hanna Rosin, "The Partisan," *GQ*, May 2001, p. 202.

13. Giosuè Carducci biography, www.nobelprize.org, http://nobelprize.org/nobel_prizes /literature/laureates/1906/carducci-bio.html.

14. S. Eugene Scalia, *Carducci: His Critics and Translators in England and America, 1881–1932* (New York: S. F. Vanni, 1937).

15. Ibid., pp. 9–14, citing Francis Hueffer, "The Poets of Young Italy," *Fortnightly Review*, April 1881, 11.

16. S. Eugene Scalia, *Carducci*, pp. 14–15.

17. Ibid., p. 45.

18. Ibid., p. 71.

19. This literal reading style of interpretation, designed to capture more than just the words of the translation, but also its spirit, has once again become the subject of new scholarship in the translation field. See Daniel Weissbort and Astradur Eysteinsson, eds., *Translation—Theory and Practice: A Historical Reader* (Oxford: Oxford University Press, 2006); and Gillian Dow, "Uses of Translation: The Global Jane Austen," in Gillian Dow and Clare Hanson, eds., *Uses of Austen: Jane's Afterlives* (London: Palgrave Macmillan, 2012), pp. 154–75. With thanks to Ms. Dow for pointing out this parallel and suggesting these references.

20. S. Eugene Scalia, *Carducci*, p. 71.

21. Ibid., pp. 90, 94–95.
22. S. Eugene Scalia, *Luigi Capuana and His Times,* p. 250.
23. Franklin Fisher and Brian Kates, "They Judged Him Back Then," New York *Daily News,* June 19, 1986, p. 7.
24. Scalia interview with Stanley Pottinger, *Beyond Politics,* PLUM TV, July 2006.
25. Scalia interview with Lesley Stahl, *60 Minutes,* CBS News, September 14, 2009, CBS transcript. Hereafter: Lesley Stahl interview, September 14, 2009.
26. Ibid. See also Fisher and Kates, "They Judged Him Back Then."
27. Fisher and Kates, "They Judged Him Back Then," and Jennifer Senior, "In Conversation: Antonin Scalia," *New York,* Oct. 6, 2013.
28. Joan Biskupic, "Scalia, Long Shy of Media, Shows More Openness," *USA Today,* April 20, 2008.
29. Memoir of Joseph DeSimone.
30. Ibid.
31. Charlie Rose interview, June 20, 2008.
32. Dominick Carielli, *Sotto Voce: The Official Newsletter of the Center for Italian American Studies at Brooklyn College,* no. 1 (Fall 2009). See also Memoir of Joseph F. DeSimone.
33. Brooklyn College Bulletin, Division of Graduate Studies, "College Libraries, Centers, Institutes, and Special Studies," http://www.brooklyn.cuny.edu/bc/pubs/bulletin/2001/html/clcisf.htm. Carielli, *Sotto Voce.*
34. S. Eugene Scalia and Margherita Marchione, *Philip Mazzei: My Life and Wanderings* (Morristown, NJ: American Institute of Italian Studies, 1980).
35. Antonin Scalia, "The Limits of the Law," *New Jersey Law Bulletin,* April 30, 1987, p. 4.
36. Scalia interview with Brian Lamb, "Q and A Show," C-SPAN, May 4, 2008.
37. Scalia interview with Stanley Pottinger, "Beyond Politics."
38. In various speeches and http://www.wisequotes.net/quote/17331-bear-in-mind-that-brains-and-learning-like-muscle.html. A shorter version was presented to the National Italian American Federation, May 2004, quoted in Margaret Talbot, "Supreme Confidence," *New Yorker,* March 28, 2005, p. 43: "Brains are like muscles—you can hire them by the hour. . . . The only thing that's not for sale is character."
39. Scalia interview with Brian Lamb, May 4, 2008.
40. Charlie Rose interview, June 20, 2008.
41. Ibid.; Lesley Stahl interview, September 14, 2009; Scalia, "Supreme Court Justice Perspective," a talk in the West Conference Room of the Supreme Court Building to Thomas Jefferson High School, Fairfax County, Virginia, C-SPAN, April 9, 2008, Lexis/Nexis transcript.
42. Anthony Tommasini, "Justices Greet Diva: It's Ardor in the Court," *New York Times,* November 1, 2008.
43. Ibid.
44. Marcus and Schmidt, "Scalia Tenacious After Staking Out a Position."
45. "Antonin Scalia, Supreme Court Justice, b.1936," *New York,* March 31, 2013, http://nymag.com/news/features/childhood/antonin-scalia-2013-4/.
46. Ibid.
47. Scalia interview with Stanley Pottinger, *Beyond Politics.*
48. "Antonin Scalia, Supreme Court Justice, b.1936."
49. Lesley Stahl interview, September 14, 2009. They were consulting a copy of Scalia's report cards when speaking about this issue.

50. Originally the programs had been in the public schools, but changed to this because of the Supreme Court's decisions. See *Zorach and Clauson,* 343 U.S. 306 (1952).

51. Scalia keynote speech to Agudath Israel of America, June 2, 2008, http://www.jta .org/2008/06/02/news-opinion/the-telegraph/scalia-addresses-agudah.

52. The case was *Zorach v. Clauson,* in 1952, which overturned *McCollum v. Board of Education,* decided in 1948, in ruling through a majority opinion written by William O. Douglas that "released time" programs which were held outside public schools were not a violation of the Establishment of Religion Clause of the First Amendment.

53. Life as a Catholic is based on: Garry Wills, *Bare Ruined Choirs: Doubt, Prophecy, and Radical Religion* (Garden City, NY: Doubleday, 1971), Introduction, Chapters 1 and 2; Eugene Kennedy, *Tomorrow's Catholics, Yesterday's Church: The Two Cultures of American Catholicism* (St. Louis: Liquori, 1995); Jay P. Dolan, *In Search of an American Catholicism: A History of Religion and Culture in Tension* (New York: Oxford University Press, 2003), pp. 191–211, 238–59; Peter Steinfels, *A People Adrift: The Crisis of the Roman Catholic Church in America* (New York: Simon & Schuster, 2004), Introduction, Chapter 7; Donald Cozzens, *Faith That Dares to Speak* (Collegeville, MN: Liturgical Press, 2004), Chapter 5; Andrew Greeley, *The Catholic Revolution: New Wine, Old Wineskins, and the Second Vatican Council* (Berkeley: University of California Press, 2004), Introduction.

54. Wills, *Bare Ruined Choirs,* pp. 15, 1.

55. Ibid., p. 15.

56. Ibid., p. 18.

57. Ibid., p. 31.

58. Ibid., p. 16.

59. Ibid., pp. 17–18.

60. John W. O'Malley, *What Happened at Vatican II* (Cambridge: Belknap Press/Harvard University Press, 2008), p. 40 and Chapter 1.

61. Joan Biskupic, *American Original: The Life and Constitution of Supreme Court Justice Antonin Scalia* (New York: Macmillan, 2009), pp. 20–21.

62. Antonin Scalia, Justice Department Questionnaire for Judicial Appointment, 1986, Peter J. Wallison Files, Ronald Reagan Presidential Library Papers, Simi Valley, California. Hereafter: Scalia Justice Department Questionnaire.

63. Fisher and Kates, "They Judged Him Back Then," p. 7.

64. George Brennan Jr., *Excellence: Sons of Xavier Forever* (Bloomington, Indiana: 1st Books Library, 2003). Peter J. Reilly, "A Better Way to Celebrate Saint Patrick's Day," *Forbes,* March 16, 2012.

65. Ibid., p. 3.

66. Scalia, "Supreme Court Justice Perspective."

67. Clay Carey, "Scalia Champions Hunting and Conservation," Associated Press report of speech to National Wild Turkey Federation annual convention, February 26, 2006, www.gunandgame.com.

68. Margaret Talbot, "Supreme Confidence," *New Yorker,* March 28, 2005.

69. Fisher and Kates, "They Judged Him Back Then," p. 7.

70. Scalia keynote speech to Agudath of Israel.

71. Lesley Stahl interview, September 14, 2009; Scalia, "Supreme Court Justice Perspective."

72. Lesley Stahl, who examined his record for *60 Minutes.*

73. "Presenting," *Xavier Review,* November 7, 1952, p. 3. Also: interview with Xavier High School alumni director Joseph Gorski, February 3, 2010.

74. Marcus and Schmidt, "Scalia Tenacious After Staking Out a Position."

75. Sarah A. Knapp, "Justice Antonin Scalia, '53," in "National Leadership," *Xavier Alumni News*. Many thanks to alumni director Joseph Gorski for providing this information.

76. *Evening Parade,* Xavier High School yearbook, 1953, pp. 24–25.

77. Lesley Stahl interview, September 14, 2009; Scalia, "Supreme Court Justice Perspective"; Fisher and Kates, "They Judged Him Back Then," p. 7.

78. "Antonin Scalia, Supreme Court Justice, b.1936."

79. Scalia, "Supreme Court Justice Perspective."

80. Marcus and Schmidt, "Scalia Tenacious After Staking Out a Position."

81. Fisher and Kates, "They Judged Him Back Then," p. 7.

82. Ibid., p. 97.

83. Talbot, "Supreme Confidence."

84. Nina Totenberg interview.

85. "Girls Debate Boys on Election Issues," *New York Times,* October 20, 1952.

86. *Evening Parade,* p. 103.

87. Irvin Molotsky, "The Supreme Court: Man in the News: Judge with Tenacity and Charm: Antonin Scalia," *New York Times,* June 18, 1986.

88. "Presenting," *Xavier Review,* p. 3.

89. Knapp, "Justice Antonin Scalia, '53." Many thanks to Alumni Director Joseph Gorski for providing this further information.

90. The Scalia interview with Stanley Pottinger, *Beyond Politics,* contradicts the law review article on Scalia on the effect of his Italian background on his work. See also Peter Lauricella, "Chi lascia la via vecchia perla nuova perde e non sa quel che trova: The Italian-American Experience and Its Influence on the Judicial Philosophies of Justice Antonin Scalia, Judge Joseph Bellacosa, and Judge Vito Titone," *Albany Law Review* 60 (1997): 1701.

91. Scalia Justice Department Questionnaire.

92. Marcus and Schmidt, "Scalia Tenacious After Staking Out a Position."

CHAPTER 2: THE CHOSEN FEW

1. Georgetown University catalogue, 1954, p. 18.

2. See William Coleman Nevils, *Miniatures of Georgetown, 1634–1934: Tercentennial Causeries* (Washington, D.C.: Georgetown University Press, 1934), pp. 271–72; Georgetown University catalogue, 1954, p. 26, both in Georgetown University Archives, cross-checked with Georgetown website, www.georgetown.edu.

3. "Protecting Catholic Identity Important, Scalia Says." *The Hoya,* February 5, 2002, Georgetown University Archives, www.thehoya.com.

4. Garry Wills, *Bare Ruined Choirs: Doubt, Prophecy, and Radical Religion* (Garden City, NY: Doubleday, 1971), pp. 38–39.

5. Ibid., p. 48.

6. "History, Government Departments Now Divided," *The Hoya,* February 18, 1954; Georgetown University catalogue, 1954, 1955.

7. Tom Kaaelman, "Dr. Kerekes Dies; College Mourns Loss," *St. Joseph College Hawk,* October 10, 1969, Georgetown Archives.

8. Georgetown University catalogue, 1956, Georgetown University Archives.

9. Georgetown University catalogue, 1954, Georgetown University Archives.

10. Margaret Talbot, "Supreme Confidence," *New Yorker,* March 28, 2005.

11. J. Wm. Hunt, S.J., memo, "Debating at Georgetown University," 1956, Georgetown University Archives.

12. Ibid.; "Philodemic Oldest Society of College Debaters in U.S.," *The Hoya,* March 28, 1957, Georgetown University Archives; "G.U.'s Philodemic Society, First Debating Group in United States, Founded in 1830," *The Hoya,* March 17, 1955.

13. "Tourney Topic: Resolved U.S. Should Adopt a Policy of Free Trade," *The Hoya,* March 18, 1954, Georgetown University Archives. The description of debates is also based on the author's experience as a college debater and coach.

14. The author debated from 1969 to 1972 on the national debate circuit as a representative from the University of Massachusetts at Amherst, and his debate rounds with teams from Georgetown are among his most memorable.

15. Scalia entries in *Ye Domesday Booke,* Georgetown University yearbook, 1953 and 1954. Georgetown University Archives.

16. *Ye Domesday Book,* 1957. Georgetown University Archives.

17. Nancy Marz Better and Loren Feldman, "Wanted: The Park Avenue Swindler," *Australian Financial Review,* July 28, 1989; David Margolick, "A Lawyer Vanishes, Leaving a Trail of Fraud Charges," *New York Times,* May 12, 1989.

18. "Schmidt Awarded N.Y.U. Grant," *The Hoya,* May 16, 1957. Georgetown University Archives.

19. Margolick, "A Lawyer Vanishes, Leaving a Trail of Fraud Charges."

20. "Scalia Named White Prexy," *The Hoya,* April 8, 1954, Georgetown University Archives.

21. "Debate Groups Make Changes," *The Hoya,* October 14, 1954, Georgetown University Archives.

22. "Debate Teams to Compete at Vermont, Pa. Tourneys," *The Hoya,* November 18, 1954, Georgetown University Archives, and Hunt, "Debating at Georgetown University."

23. "G.U. Debaters Win 80% of Their Meets; Frost Post 93%," *The Hoya,* December 9, 1954, Georgetown University Archives.

24. Hunt, "Debating at Georgetown." Georgetown University Archives.

25. "Debaters Win at NYU; Post 3rd Tourney Victory," *The Hoya,* December 16, 1954, Georgetown University Archives.

26. David T. Boltz, "M and B's First Show: 4 Stars for Owens," *The Hoya,* December 12, 1954, p. 3, Georgetown University Archives.

27. Ibid., play program, November 4–5, 1954, Georgetown University Archives. "Scalia M & B Pres. Cast Announced," *The Hoya,* January 13, 1955, Georgetown University Archives. Dave Boltz, "M & B Play Festival; Loyola Takes First," *The Hoya,* February 24, 1955. Georgetown University Archives.

28. Arthur Ciervo, "Profiles: Antonin Scalia," *Georgetown Alumni Magazine,* 1976, Georgetown University Archives.

29. At the time the school was being run by the Dominicans because the Jesuits were "under political disfavor" in Switzerland. "Fribourg Contingent Rally Under Fr. McHugh," *The Hoya,* April 19, 1956, Georgetown University Archives.

30. "Fribourg Courses to Start in Fall," April 1, 1954, *The Hoya,* Georgetown University Archives.

31. "Hoyas at Fribourg Approve 'Junior Year Abroad' Plan," *The Hoya,* March 1, 1956; "Georgetown Juniors to Study at Fribourg, Tour Europe Next Year," *The Hoya,* May 12, 1955, Georgetown University Archives.

32. "Philodemic Society Team Captures NYU Tournament," *The Hoya,* December 6, 1956, Georgetown University Archives.

33. "Date Changed for Oral Exam in Philosophy," *The Hoya,* April 4, 1957, Georgetown University Archives.

34. "Debating Heads Mr. Hunt and Len Thornton Major Factors in Philodemic Accomplishments," *The Hoya,* March 13, 1958, Georgetown University Archives.

35. Scalia interview with Tim Russert, *Tim Russert,* MSNBC, May 3, 2008, Lexis/Nexis transcript. Hereafter Tim Russert interview.

36. Biskupic, *American Original,* p. 25.

37. Antonin G. Scalia, "Cohonguroton Address," *The Journal* 86, no. 1 (Autumn 1957), pp. 12–14.

38. "Journal Fall Issue on stands Nov. 12, with Cohonguroton," *The Hoya,* November 7, 1957, p. 1. Georgetown University Archives.

39. Anonymous interview with Georgetown University library official, January 22, 2008. According to this official, the material was removed at that time.

40. Scalia, "Cohonguroton Address," *The Journal,* p. 1.

41. Maya Noronha, "Protecting Catholic Identity Important, Scalia Says," *The Hoya,* February 5, 2002, Georgetown University Archives.

42. Lesley Stahl interview, April 27, 2008.

43. Charlie Rose interview, June 20, 2008.

44. Scalia, question and answer session with Thomas Jefferson High School students, C-SPAN, April 10, 2008.

45. Scalia interview with Brian Lamb, *Q and A Show,* C-SPAN, May 4, 2008. He told the same story in the Thomas Jefferson High School question and answer session.

46. Ibid.

47. "Schmidt Awarded N.Y.U. Grant," *The Hoya,* Georgetown University Archives.

48. Better and Feldman, "Wanted: The Park Avenue Swindler"; Margolick, "A Lawyer Vanishes, Leaving a Trail of Fraud Charges"; Deborah Rankin, "Personal Finance: When a Lawyer Steals Your Money," Business Day section, *New York Times,* April 30, 1989.

CHAPTER 3: THE HARVARD HIT PARADE OF THE 1950S

1. Oral History of Zona Hostetler, interviewer Joan Goldfrank, ABA Commission on Women in the Profession, "Women Trailblazers in the Law," October 18, 2008. Student numbers from Harvard Law School catalogue, 1957–58, Harvard Law School Archives, http://pds.lib.harvard.edu/pds/view/9045568?n=5308&imagesize=1200&jp2Res=.5.

2. Margaret Talbot, "Supreme Confidence," *New Yorker,* March 28, 2005, pp. 40–55.

3. Oral History of Zona Hostetler.

4. Ibid., Harvard Law School catalogue, 1957–58.

5. Harvard Law School catalogue, 1958–59, pp. 37–40.

6. Harvard Law School catalogue, 1957–58, p. 13.

7. Charles Tighe Oral History, June 5, 2002, William Madison Randall Library, University of North Carolina at Wilmington.

8. Polly J. Price, *Judge Richard S. Arnold: A Legacy of Justice on the Federal Bench* (Amherst, NY: Prometheus, 2009).

9. Harvard Law School Yearbook, 1958, pp. 162–63.

10. Stephen J. Adler, "Live Wire on the D.C. Circuit," *Legal Times,* June 23, 1986.

11. Ruth Marcus and Susan Schmidt, "Scalia Tenacious After Staking Out a Position," *Washington Post,* June 22, 1986.
12. Adler, "Live Wire on the D.C. Circuit."
13. Talbot, "Supreme Confidence," p. 46.
14. Harvard Law School yearbook, 1957–58, p. 174.
15. Harvard Law School yearbook, 1959–60, p. 173.
16. Peter B. Edelman, "Justice Scalia's Jurisprudence and the Good Society: Shades of Felix Frankfurter and the Harvard Hit Parade of the 1950s," *Cardozo Law Review* (1990–91): 1799.
17. William M. Wiecek, *The Birth of the Modern Constitution: The United States Supreme Court, 1941–1953,* History of the Supreme Court of the United States, Oliver Wendell Holmes Devise (Cambridge: Cambridge University Press, 2006), Vol. 12, pp. 446–63.
18. Ibid., p. 454.
19. Ibid., p. 451.
20. Harvard Law School catalogue, 1957–58, pp. 45–46.
21. Frank Michelman, "*Anastasoff* and Remembrance," *Arkansas Law Review* 58 (2005): 555.
22. Ibid.
23. Ibid., pp. 565–66.
24. Ibid., p. 574.
25. Ibid., p. 587.
26. Ibid., p. 588.
27. Ibid., p. 589.
28. For more on the *Brown v. Board of Education* case, see Richard Kluger, *Simple Justice: The History of Brown v. Board of Education and the History of Black America's Struggle for Equality* (New York: Vintage, 2004).
29. Michelman, "*Anastasoff* and Remembrance."
30. Quoted in: Talbot, "Supreme Confidence," p. 46.
31. Ibid.
32. Ibid.
33. Herbert Wechsler, "Toward Neutral Principles of Constitutional Law," *Harvard Law Review* 73, no. 1 (November 1959): 1–35. This is a footnoted copy of the speech as it was read. Scalia told Joan Biskupic, for her *American Original* biography (pp. 27–28), that he did not remember attending the lecture.
34. Edelman, "Justice Scalia's Jurisprudence and the Good Society," p. 1799ff.
35. Arthur Ciervo, "Profiles: Antonin Scalia," *Georgetown Alumni Magazine,* 1976, Georgetown Archives.
36. Lesley Stahl interview, April 27, 2008.
37. Ibid.
38. "Justice Scalia at Pepperdine," Los Angeles County Bar Blog, March 10, 2009, lacbablog.typepad.com.
39. Talbot, "Supreme Confidence," p. 46.
40. Ethan Bronner, "Bulldog Justice," *Washingtonian,* December 1990, p. 139; Adler, "Live Wire on the D.C. Circuit."
41. Scalia speech, Federalist Society meeting, October 15, 2012, www.fed-soc.org.
42. This section benefited greatly from the evidence and analysis in Michael Sean Winters, *Left at the Altar: How the Democrats Lost the Catholics and How the Catholics Can Save the Democrats* (New York: Basic Books, 2009).

43. Ibid., p. 78. Winters's analysis is based on 1960 campaign material in Box 1015, John F. Kennedy, Presidential Library and Museum, Boston.

44. John F. Kennedy, speech on his religion, September 12, 1960, http://www.npr.org/templates/story/story.php?storyId=16920600.

45. Ibid.

46. Winters, *Left at the Altar,* p. 70.

47. Ibid., p. 83.

48. Scalia speech, "The Role of Catholic Faith in the Work of a Judge," at the 2nd annual John F. Scarpa Conference on Law, Politics and Culture, Villanova University, October 16, 2007 (author's notes of speech). See also accounts of the speech: Mary Claire Dale, "Scalia Speaks at Villanova University," October 16, 2007, http://abclocal.go.com. Quote from David O'Reilly, "Scalia Opines on Faith and Justice," *Philadelphia Inquirer,* October 17, 2007, www.philly.com; and Jim McCaffrey, "Scalia Talks Catholic Values at Villanova Lecture," *Evening Bulletin* (Philadelphia), October 17, 2007, www.thebulletin.us.

49. "put aside" characterization from Rick Garnett, "Justice Scalia, a 'Catholic' Judge," *Mirror of Justice* blog, October 18, 2007, www.mirrorofjustice.blogs.com.

50. Scalia, "The Role of Catholic Faith in the Work of a Judge."

51. See John W. O'Malley, *What Happened at Vatican II* (Cambridge: Belknap Press/Harvard University Press, 2008), pp. 40–50.

52. Ibid., p. 52.

53. Adler, "Live Wire on the D.C. Circuit."

CHAPTER 4: BUILDING A RÉSUMÉ

1. E. R. Shipp, "Scalia's Midwest Colleagues Cite His Love of Debate, Poker and Piano," *New York Times,* July 26, 1986; Richard A. Brisbin, *Justice Antonin Scalia and the Conservative Revival* (Baltimore: Johns Hopkins University Press, 1997), p. 16.

2. Stephen J. Adler, "Live Wire on the D.C. Circuit," *Legal Times,* June 23, 1986, p. 89.

3. Scalia Justice Department Questionnaire.

4. Adler, "Live Wire on the D.C. Circuit," p. 89.

5. Ibid.

6. Shipp, "Scalia's Midwest Colleagues Cite His Love of Debate, Poker and Piano."

7. Paul Marcotte, "New Kid on the Block," *ABA Journal,* August 1, 1986.

8. Shipp, "Scalia's Midwest Colleagues Cite His Love of Debate, Poker and Piano."

9. Marcotte, "New Kid on the Block."

10. Shipp, "Scalia's Midwest Colleagues Cite His Love of Debate, Poker and Piano."

11. Regina McEnery, "James Courtney, former partner in Jones Day firm, Hanna Exec," *Cleveland Plain Dealer,* December 10, 2006.

12. Ibid.; Scalia Justice Department Questionnaire.

13. Scalia Justice Department Questionnaire.

14. Shipp, "Scalia's Midwest Colleagues Cite His Love of Debate, Poker and Piano."

15. Scalia Justice Department Questionnaire. The case being cited can be found at 355 F.2d 705 (1966).

16. Joan Biskupic, *American Original: The Life and Constitution of Supreme Court Justice Antonin Scalia* (New York: Macmillan, 2009), p. 37.

17. While women had not yet been admitted to the undergraduate school, there were a handful of women in the law school.

18. List of accredited law schools can be found at the American Bar Association, http://www.abanet.org/legaled/approvedlawschools/alpha.html.

19. Scalia, "Sovereign Immunity and Non-Statutory Review of Federal Administrative Action," *Michigan Law Review* 68 (1970): 867; Scalia and Graham Lilly, "Appellate Justice: A Crisis in Virginia," *Virginia Law Review* 57 (1971): 3; Scalia, "The Hearing Examiners Loan Program," *Duke Law Journal* (1971): 319; Scalia, "Don't Go Near the Water (A Proposal Concerning the FCC's Fairness Doctrine," *Federal Commercial Bar Journal,* 25 (1972): 111.

20. Scalia and Graham Lilly, "Appellate Justice: A Crisis in Virginia," p. 3.

21. Adler, "Live Wire on the D.C. Circuit," p. 89.

22. Scalia Justice Department Questionnaire. As Scalia later described the full range of his duties: "I was responsible for the legal matters of policy formation concerning such matters as the regulatory regimes that should govern commercial broadcasting, domestic satellites, specialized communications carriers, public television, land-mobile communications, telecomputers, and cable television (including copyright payments). My work involved almost exclusively federal and public international communications law."

23. See http://www.sectv.com/LV/our_founder.html.

24. One of the best general sources on the Cable Compromise of 1971 is a master's thesis by Harvey C. Jassem, "The Selling of the Compromise—1971 or Cable Television Goes to the City," Ohio State University, 1972; pp. 12–13.

25. *Fortnightly Corp. v. United Artists Television, Inc.,* 392 U.S. 390 (1968).

26. Sol Schildhause Oral History, Hauser Oral and Video Collection, the Cable Center, Penn State University, and Denver Colorado, http://www.cablecenter.org/cable-history/the-barco-library/hauser-oral-history-collection-cable-history.html.

27. Ibid.

28. Ibid.

29. Ibid.

30. Adler, "Live Wire on the D.C. Circuit," p. 89.

31. "The Cable and Satellite Carrier Compulsory Licenses: An Overview and Analysis," March 1992, Register of Copyrights, Washington, D.C.

32. Much of this story of CPB financing is based on a remarkable document presenting the summaries of over one thousand documents from that era on the question of Nixon and the CPB financing, released under a FOIA request: *The Nixon Administration Public Broadcasting Papers: A Summary, 1969–1974,* National Association of Educational Broadcasting, 1979. Hereinafter cited as Nixon Broadcasting Papers. This can also be found in a shorter version on the Internet as the Public Broadcasting Policy Base, PBPB, http://www.current.org/pbpb/nixon/nixon71.html.

33. Adler, "Live Wire on the D.C. Circuit," p. 89.

34. Ibid.

35. Scalia to Whitehead, "Memo to the President," June 4, 1971, Nixon Broadcasting Papers, pp. 29–30.

36. Ibid.

37. "Memorandum for the President," June 18, 1971, Nixon Broadcasting Papers, pp. 30–31.

38. Quoted in "Memorandum for the President," September 23, 1971, Nixon Broadcasting Papers, pp. 35–36.

39. Ibid., pp. 35–36.

40. Memorandum for the President, September 28, Nixon Broadcasting Papers, pp. 36–37.

41. Ibid., pp. 38–39.

42. Memorandum, Rose to Larry Higby, October 15, 1971, Nixon Broadcasting Papers, pp. 41–42.
43. Clay T. Whitehead speech to the National Association of Educational Broadcasters, October 20, 1971, Miami, Florida, Nixon Broadcasting Papers, p. 45.
44. Scalia to Whitehead, December 23, 1971, Nixon Broadcasting Papers, p. 52.
45. A.C.L.U. Report, 2/20/72, Nixon Broadcasting Papers, p. 57.
46. Adler, "Live Wire on the D.C. Circuit," p. 89.
47. Statement of Antonin Scalia, Associate Justice Supreme Court of the United States, Before the Subcommittee on Commercial and Administrative Law, Committee on the Judiciary, U.S. House of Representatives, hearing on the Reauthorization of the Administrative Conference of the United States, 108th Congress, Washington, D.C., May 20, 2004.
48. Ibid.
49. Scalia Justice Department Questionnaire.
50. Statement of Antonin Scalia, May 20, 2004.

CHAPTER 5: THE PRESIDENT'S LEGAL ADVISER

1. Jennifer Senior, "In Conversation: Antonin Scalia," *New York,* October 6, 2013, found at http:mymag/news/features/antonin-scalia-2013-10/.
2. "Robert G. Dixon, Jr. Dies," *Washington Post,* May 7, 1980.
3. Stephen J. Adler, "Live Wire on the D.C. Circuit," *Legal Times,* June 23, 1986.
4. Office of Legal Counsel, Department of Justice, http://www.usdoj.gov/olc/.
5. "Position Description," Office of Legal Counsel, February 2, 1962, White House Century Files, FG 17, Box 87, Ford Library.
6. Senior, "In Conversation: Antonin Scalia."
7. Scalia, "In Memoriam: Edward H. Levi," *University of Chicago Law Review* 67, no. 4 (2000): 983.
8. Letter, Gerald R. Ford to Attorney General [Saxbe], August 22, 1974, Philip Buchen Files, Box 32, Ford Library.
9. Memo, Scalia to Attorney General Saxbe, September 3, 1974, Philip Buchen Files, Box 32, Ford Library.
10. Ibid.
11. John M. Crewdson, "White House Says Tapes are Nixon's Own Property," *New York Times,* August 15, 1974.
12. Arthur Ciervo, "Profiles: Antonin Scalia," *Georgetown Alumni Magazine,* 1976, Georgetown University Archives.
13. Paul Marcotte, "New Kid on the Block," *ABA Journal,* August 1, 1986.
14. Letter, Attorney General William Saxbe to President Ford, September 6, 1974, Philip Buchen Files, Box 32, Ford Papers.
15. The materials were finally moved to the Nixon Library in Yorba Linda, California, in 2010.
16. Letter, Richard Nixon to Arthur F. Sampson, September 6, 1974, Philip Buchen Files, Box 32, Ford Library.
17. George Lardner, "Saxbe Not Told of Tape Deal," *Washington Post,* September 9, 1974.
18. "Congress Passes Nixon Tapes Bill," *New York Times,* December 10, 1974; "Ford Signs Bill on Nixon Papers," *New York Times,* December 20, 1974.
19. *Nixon v. Administrator of General Services,* 433 U.S. 425 (1977).
20. Ibid., p. 545.

21. Brandeis, *Other People's Money: And How the Bankers Use It* (New York: Frederick A. Stokes, 1933), p. 62.

22. Dan Lopez, Thomas Blanton, Meredith Fuchs, and Barbara Elias, "Veto Battle 30 Years Ago Set Freedom of Information Norms," *National Security Archive,* posted November 23, 2004, www.gwu.edu/~nsarchiv/.

23. Memo, by Mr. [John S.] Warner, "Subject: Veto Action on H.R. 1247," September 23, 1974, Office of General Counsel, CIA, FOIA release, "The Memory Hole" "Supreme Court Justice Scalia Fought Against the Freedom of Information Act," www.thememory hole.org/foi/scalia_foia.htm.

24. George Lardner Jr., "Cover-Up Trial Delay Barred," *Washington Post,* September 12, 1974.

25. Scalia to Phillip E. Areeda, September 24, 1974, Kenneth A. Lazarus Files, Box 25, Ford Library.

26. Ibid.

27. Memo, Scalia for John S. Warner, September 26, 1974, Office of General Counsel, CIA, FOIA release, "The Memory Hole" "Supreme Court Justice Scalia Fought Against the Freedom of Information Act," www.thememoryhole.org/foi/scalia_foia.htm.

28. Ford Veto Message, October 17, 1974, Blanton Briefing Book. Relying on Cole to Ford, September 25, 1974, Gerald R. Ford Library, cited in Blanton Briefing book.

29. Memorandum for the Record, "Subject: ICRC Revision of E.O. 11652 in Light of FOI," January 25, 1975, Office of General Counsel, CIA, FOIA release, "The Memory Hole" "Supreme Court Justice Scalia Fought Against the Freedom of Information Act," www .thememoryhole.org/foi/scalia_foia.htm.

30. Scalia to Areeda, February 13, 1975, with Blue Book foreword draft attached, and Areeda, Memorandum for the President, February 14, 1975, Kenneth A. Lazarus Papers, Box 25, Ford Library.

31. Kenneth A. Lazarus to Scalia, February 25, 1975, Kenneth A. Lazarus Papers, Box 25, Ford Library.

32. Scalia, Memorandum for the Honorable Philip W. Buchen, "Re: Applicability of the Freedom of Information Act to the White House Office," February 26, 1975, Kenneth A. Lazarus Papers, Box 25, Ford Library.

33. Ibid.

34. Scalia, "In Memoriam: Edward H. Levi," pp. 971ff.

35. Ibid.

36. Gerald K. Haines, "The Pike Committee and the CIA," http://bss.sfsu.edu/fischer/. John Prados, "Big Brother's History," May 25, 2006 found at www.tompaine.com. This section was aided considerably by the work of John Prados and other digital privacy experts, who laid the overall historical groundwork for my search of the Ford Library files on this question. L. Britt Snider, "Unlucky Shamrock: Recollections from the Church Committee's Investigation of NSA," *Studies in Intelligence* 43, no. 1, Winter 1999–2000, www.cia.gov/csi/studies; James G. Hudec, "Unlucky Shamrock—The View from the Other Side," found at www.cia.gov/library/; "Profile: Pike Committee," The Center for Grassroots Oversight, found at www.historycommons.org; also, Dubose and Bernstein, VICE book, pp. 35–38.

37. 418 U.S. 683 (1974).

38. Scalia to Philip W. Buchen, "Claim of Executive Privilege with Respect to Materials Subpoenaed by the Committee on Government Operations, House of Representatives," February 17, 1976, Presidential Handwriting Files, Box 31, Ford Library.

39. Many of these files remain classified, but this section is based on a review of the material by Ford Library archivist William H. McNitt, email communication with author, August 20, 2007.

40. Scalia speech, International Conference on the Administration of Justice and National Security in Democracies, Ottawa, Canada, June 12, 2007. Thanks to reporter Charlie Savage of *The New York Times* for providing a digital recording of this address. This speech is discussed in Savage's excellent *Takeover: The Return of the Imperial Presidency and the Subversion of American Democracy* (New York: Little, Brown, 2007). See also an account by Colin Freeze, "What Would Jack Bauer Do?," *Globe and Mail* (Canada), June 16, 2007.

41. Memo, Robert D. Murphy, Chairman, Intelligence Oversight Board, to President Ford, May 7, 1976, with memo attached, "CIA Program of Resettling Meo Tribesmen in Laos," Presidential Handwriting Files, Box 31, Ford Library.

42. Ibid.

43. Scalia, "Memorandum to the Attorney General, Re: Report to You from the Intelligence Oversight Board, dated May 13, 1976," May 27, 1976, FOIA release, Presidential Handwriting Files, Box 31, Ford Library.

44. Ford to George H. W. Bush, Director of Central Intelligence, July 10, 1976, Presidential Handwriting Files, Box 31, Ford Library.

45. Scalia speech, Ottawa, Canada.

46. Antonin Scalia, opening statement, Subcommittee on Intergovernmental Relations of the Committee on Government Operations of the United States Senate, considering Senate Bill 2170, October 23, 1975, reprinted in *Executive Privilege—Secrecy in Government,* Hearings before Subcommittee on Intergovernmental Relations of the Committee on Government Operations of the United States Senate, September 29 and October 23, 1975, pp. 96–125, at p. 125.

47. The Scalia and Muskie exchange is from ibid., pp. 71–89.

48. Buchen to Ford, February 3, 1976, Richard B. Cheney files, Box 5, cited also in Dubose and Bernstein, *Vice*, pp. 36–37; Philip Buchen, "Memo for the President," Subject: Chairman of the Federal Trade Commission, February 3, 1976, Richard B. Cheney files, 1974–77, Box 5, folder "Federal Trade Commission," Ford Library, cited in Dubose and Bernstein, *Vice*, pp. 36–37.

49. Scalia to Ford, January 14, 1976 [*sic*], WHCF FG 17–15/A, Scalia Name File, Ford Library; Ford to Scalia, January 18, 1977, WHCF, FG 17/A, Box 88, Ford Library.

CHAPTER 6: WILDFLOWERS AMONG THE WEEDS

1. The motto of the magazine is "competition of ideas is fundamental to a free society." William Niskanen, "A Retrospective," *Regulation,* Summer 2002, p. 4.

2. *Regulation,* July 8, 1977, p. 2.

3. Scalia Justice Department Questionnaire.

4. Ibid. The Scalias would have a ninth child in 1980, Margaret Jane.

5. Listing of courses in the University of Chicago Law School announcements, 1977–78, 1978–79, 1979–80, and 1981–82, University of Chicago Law School Archives. Thanks very much to D'Angelo Law Library reference librarian Todd Ito for his assistance in retrieving this information.

6. E. R. Shipp, "Scalia's Midwest Colleagues Cite His Love of Debate, Poker and Piano," *New York Times,* July 26, 1986.

7. For more, see Leo Strauss, *The City and the Man* (Chicago: University of Chicago Press, 1978); Leo Strauss, *Persecution and the Art of Writing* (Chicago: University of Chicago Press, 1988); and Leo Strauss and Joseph Cropsey, *History of Political Philosophy* (Chicago: University of Chicago Press, 1987).

8. Richard A. Epstein, "Foreordained for Chicago," Chicago Law School Centennial Essays, webcast-law.uchicago.edu/centennial/.

9. "Antonin Scalia and the Case of the Albemarle Pippins," August 10, 2006, Barbara, *Famosity,* http://famosity, Blogspot.com/2006.

10. Joan Biskupic, *American Original,* quoting Lee Liberman, p. 76.

11. "Antonin Scalia and the Case of the Albemarle Pippins."

12. Ibid.

13. Ibid.

14. Ibid.

15. Robert Bolt, *A Man for All Seasons,* quoted in story about the use of this passage by Scalia in Biskupic, *American Original,* pp. 66–67.

16. Biskupic, *American Original,* p. 67.

17. For more here, see Steven M. Teles, *The Rise of the Conservative Legal Movement* (Princeton: Princeton University Press, 2008), pp. 67–79.

18. Ibid., pp. 137–62. For a more recent history of the organization, see Michael Avery and Daniele McLaughlin, *The Federalist Society: How Conservatives Took the Law Back from the Liberals* (Nashville: Vanderbilt University Press, 2013).

19. Jerry Landay, "The Federalist Society: The Conservative Cabal That's Transforming American Law," *Washington Monthly,* March 2000; Owen M. Fiss, "What Is the Federalist Society?," *Harvard Journal of Law and Public Policy* 15, no. 1 (1992).

20. Steven Calabresi, speech Federalist Society 25th Anniversary Gala, November 15, 2007, http://www.fed-soc.org/publications/detail/25th-anniversary-gala-event-audiovideo.

21. Teles, *The Rise of the Conservative Legal Movement,* p. 141.

22. Program Federalist Society 25th Anniversary Gala, November 15, 2007, in *About Us,* Federalist Society video http://www.fed-soc.org/aboutus/. See also Landay, "The Federalist Society."

23. Calabresi speech, Federalist Society 25th Anniversary Gala.

24. Henry J. Abraham, *Justices, Presidents and Senators: A History of the U.S. Supreme Court Appointments from Washington to Bush II* (New York: Rowman & Littlefield Publishers, 2007), 5th ed., pp. 265–77.

25. The paperback was revised in 1993: Robert Bork, *The Antitrust Paradox: A Policy at War with Itself,* 2nd ed. (New York: Free Press, 1993).

26. Fiss, "What Is the Federalist Society?"

27. Teles, *Rise of the Conservative Legal Movement,* p. 142.

28. Samuel Alito speech, Federalist Society 25th Anniversary Gala, November 15, 2007.

29. Sidney Blumenthal, "Quest for Lasting Power," *Washington Post,* September 25, 1985.

30. Teles, *The Rise of the Conservative Legal Movement,* p. 142.

31. Landay, "The Federalist Society."

32. Federalist Society 25th Anniversary Gala.

33. Ibid.

34. Scalia, "Rulemaking as Politics," *Administrative Law Review* 334, no. 3 (1982): v–xi; Scalia, "Support Your Local Professor of Administrative Law," *Administrative Law Review* 34, no. 2 (1982); Scalia, "Separation of Functions: Obscurity Preserved," *Administrative Law Review* (Winter 1982): v.ff.

35. Scalia, "Two Wrongs Make a Right: The Judicialization of Standardless Rulemaking," *Regulation,* July 8, 1977, p. 40.

36. *Turner Broadcasting System v. FCC,* 512 U.S. 622 (1994).

37. Scalia, "The Legislative Veto: A False Remedy for System Overload," *Regulation,* November/December 1979, p. 19.

38. Scalia Justice Department Questionnaire.

39. *Immigration and Naturalization Service v. Chadha,* 462 U.S. 919 (1983).

40. Scalia, "The Freedom of Information Act Has No Clothes," *Regulation,* March/April, 1982, pp. 15–19.

41. Ibid., p. 15.

42. Ibid., p. 16.

43. Ibid., p. 19.

44. Ibid.

45. Scalia, "Testimony on the Constitutionality of Tuition Tax Credits," Washington, D.C., American Enterprise Institute, reprint No. 84, March 1978.

46. Ibid.

47. Scalia, "On Making It Look Easy by Doing It Wrong: A Critical View of the Justice Department," in Edward McGlynn Gaffney Jr., ed., *Private Schools and the Public Good: Policy Alternatives for the Eighties* (South Bend: University of Notre Dame Press, 1982).

48. 438 U.S. 265 (1978).

49. Scalia, "The Disease as Cure," *Washington University Law Quarterly* (1979): 154.

50. Ibid., p. 147.

51. Ibid., pp. 152–53.

52. Ibid., p. 152.

53. However, when the case was appealed before an *en banc* hearing the Justice Department was able to prevail, meaning that the evidence had to be provided to the SEC and could be transferred to the Justice Department. Scalia Justice Department Questionnaire.

54. Ibid.

55. This information was released as the result of a Freedom of Information search for the Antonin Scalia Name File, Ronald Reagan Presidential Library, Simi Valley, California.

56. Donald E. Santarelli to Edwin Meese, December 19, 1980; Frank D. Stella to Red Cavney, March 19, 1981, FOIA search Reagan Library.

57. Ethan Bronner, "Bulldog Justice," *Washingtonian,* December 1990, p. 245. For more on Scalia being upset about not getting the solicitor generalship, see Biskupic, *American Original,* pp. 72–74.

58. Cass Peterson, "Bork Reported in Line for D.C. Appellate Court," *Washington Post,* August 13, 1981.

59. Biskupic, *American Original,* p. 80.

CHAPTER 7: IT ISN'T EASY TO BE RIGHT

1. Laura A. Kiernan and Fred Barbash, "Appeals Judge Plans to Leave U.S. Court Here," *Washington Post,* April 2, 1982; Laura A. Kiernan, "Appeals Judge Robb Confirms His Plans," *Washington Post,* April 3, 1982.

2. Stephen J. Adler, "Live Wire on the D.C. Circuit," *Legal Times,* June 23, 1986, p. 91.

3. Ibid., pp. 10–11.

4. Ibid., p. 11. The panel had apparently not been impressed by Scalia's nineteen single-

spaced pages of explanations of all of the appellate court cases in which he had been involved. Scalia Justice Department Questionnaire.

5. Ibid.

6. Scalia to Judge Edward Allen Tamm, August 11, 1983, with attachment, Financial Disclosure Report, August 17, 1983, Peter J. Walliston Files, Reagan Library.

7. Confirmation of Federal Judges, Hearings Before the Committee on the Judiciary, United States Senate, 97th Congress, 2nd Session, Part 4, August 4, 1982, p. 91.

8. Ibid., pp. 91–92.

9. Ibid., p. 92.

10. Al Kamen and Laura Kiernan, "Metro," *Washington Post,* August 9, 1982.

11. Robert H. Bork Oral History, District of Columbia Court of Appeals Oral History, Manuscript Division, Library of Congress, Washington, D.C., pp. 3–4.

12. Ibid.

13. Patricia M. Wald Oral History, District of Columbia Court of Appeals Oral History, Manuscript Division, Library of Congress, Washington, D.C., pp. 195–96.

14. Ibid.

15. *Washington Post v. U.S. Department of State,* 685 F. 2d 698 (1982).

16. 31 U.S.C. § 67(f) (1) (Supp. IV 1980).

17. *Washington Post v. United States,* 685 F. 2d. 698, at 708 (1982) (Scalia, dissenting).

18. The cases are: *Community Nutrition v. Block; KCST-TV v. F.C.C.* 699 F.2d. 1185 (1983); *United States v. Richardson,* 702 F.2d. 1079 (1983); *Community for Creative Non-Violence v. Watt,* 703 F.2d. 586 (1983).

19. *Community for Creative Non-Violence v. Watt,* at 599.

20. Ibid., at 622 (Scalia, dissenting).

21. Ibid. Scalia paraphrased a sentence from the Saia loudspeaker protest case by one of his judicial heroes, Robert Jackson.

22. Ruth Marcus and Susan Schmidt, "Scalia Tenacious After Staking Out a Position," *Washington Post,* June 22, 1986.

23. Adler, "Live Wire on the D.C. Circuit," p. 5.

24. *Chaney v. Heckler,* 718 F.2d 1174 (1983) (Wright, majority).

25. Ibid., at 1197–98 (Scalia, dissenting).

26. Ibid., at 1198.

27. Adler, "Live Wire on the D.C. Circuit," p. 3.

28. Ibid., at 1198.

29. Marcus and Schmidt, "Scalia Tenacious After Staking Out a Position."

30. Ibid.

31. Alex Kozinski, "My Pizza with Nino," remarks at the Symposium for the Justisprudence of Justice Antonin Scalia, Benjamin N. Cardozo School of Law, October 28, 1990, *Cardozo Law Review* 12, 1991, p. 1583, at 1583–84.

32. Marcus and Schmidt, "Scalia Tenacious After Staking Out a Position." Marcus and Schmidt quote the Scalia phrase as "It isn't easy to be right," while Judge Kozinski describes it as "Nothing is easy." The two *Washington Post* reporters, though, quote the clerks who created the plaque.

33. *Ollman v. Evans,* 713 F.2d 838 (1983), at 839.

34. *Ollman v. Evans,* 750 F.2d 970 (1984), at 983.

35. Ibid., at 993.

36. Ibid., at 1036.

37. Ibid., at 1038–39.

38. Ibid., at 995–96.

39. Ibid., at 1039, footnote 2.

40. *In re The Reporters Committee for Freedom of the Press,* 773 F.2d 1325 (1985).

41. Ibid.

42. Address, Judge Antonin Scalia, before the Attorney General's Conference on Economic Liberties, Washington, D.C., June 14, 1986, Appendix C, *Original Meaning Jurisprudence: A Sourcebook, Report to the Attorney General,* Office of Legal Policy, U.S. Department of Justice, March 12, 1987, pp. 101–6.

43. Ironically, Scalia's "neutral principle" enabled him to reach an outcome that was the opposite of what Wechsler had been advocating. The irony, as Scalia would learn even later, is that others, following liberal rather than conservative goals, would be able to use his "neutral principle" of reliance on history to expand rather than contract constitutional rights in a process called "progressive originalism." See Robert Post and Reva Siegel, "Originalism as a Political Practice: The Right's Living Constitution," *Fordham Law Review* 75, no. 2, Article 5 (2006). One person's "neutral" originalist conservatism could become another person's equally "neutral" originalist liberalism.

44. Scalia, "The Use of Legislative History," speech delivered to the University of Chicago Law School, on file in University of Chicago Law School library, Hyde Park, Illinois. This is the actual reading copy of Scalia's speech, with the high points in it made clear because Scalia underlined the key sentences to punch up for his presentation.

45. Ibid. The quotation marks were added in Scalia's hand and are not in the original typed version.

46. Ibid.

47. It would be another ten months, in the fall of 1986, with conservative Douglas Ginsburg's appointment to the Court, and after Scalia had left it, that the Republicans finally took control of the circuit.

48. Robert H. Bork Oral History, District of Columbia Court of Appeals Oral History, Manuscripts Division, Library of Congress, Washington, D.C., pp. 8–9.

49. Dr. S. Eugene Scalia obituary, *New York Times,* January 7, 1986; Biskupic, *American Original,* p. 122. Confirmed by United States Social Security Index, thanks to Carol Wright for her confirming research on Ancestry.com.

50. For more, see Henry J. Abraham, *Justices, Presidents and Senators: A History of the U.S. Supreme Court Appointments from Washington to Bush II* (New York: Rowman & Littlefield, 2007), 5th ed.

51. *Immigration and Naturalization Service v. Chadha,* 462 U.S. 919 (1983).

52. Patricia M. Wald Oral History, p. 146.

53. Oliver Gasch Oral History, District of Columbia Court of Appeals Oral History, Manuscript Division, Library of Congress, Washington, D.C., p. 186.

54. Ibid.

55. Ibid., p. 188.

56. *Synar v. U.S.,* 626 F. Supp. 1374; (D.C. 1986), at 1403, February 7, 1986.

57. Ibid., at 1398–99.

58. While determining the correct dissent rate of Court of Appeals judges, there are indications that it is usually less that 10 percent of the time, at least on the D.C. Court of Appeals. Former D.C. Court of Appeals judge Harry T. Edwards, in "The Effects of Collegiality on Judicial Decision Making," *University of Pennsylvania Law Review* 151 (May 2003): 1639, note 65, using D.C. Court of Appeals statistics from 1986 to 2001, reported four sets of dissent rates in cases with published opinions varying from 7.8 per-

cent (2000), 8.9 percent (1999), 9.1 percent (1998), and also reporting an 11–13 percent rate from 1995 to 1997. On the other hand, Scott Gerber and Keeok Park found in their article "The Quixotic Search for Consensus on the U.S. Supreme Court: A Cross-Judicial Empirical Analysis of the Rehnquist Court Justices," *American Political Science Review* 91, no. 2 (1997): 390ff, *Academic OneFile,* August 21, 2010, that while justices from 1986 to 1994 dissent on the Supreme Court 21 percent of the time, those who served on the federal Court of Appeals, or in Sandra Day O'Connor's case, served on the Arizona State Supreme Court, dissented in only 2 percent of the cases. Thurgood Marshall dissented in 35 percent of the cases on the Supreme Court, but in only 3 percent of the time on the federal Court of Appeals. As for Scalia, of the 698 cases in which he wrote an opinion, from 1986 through the end of the 2009–10 term, he dissented in 201 of them, or 28.8 percent of the time.

CHAPTER 8: TERMINOLOGY IS DESTINY

1. "Memorandum for the File, Peter J. Wallison, Counsel to the President," August 29, 1986, Peter Wallison Files, Supreme Court/Rehnquist/Scalia, Notebook II, Folder 1 of 3, OX 14287, Reagan Library (Wallison Memoir); and "Remarks by the President, Chief Justice Warren Burger, Justice William Rehnquist and Judge Antonin Scalia," Peter Wallison files, Ronald Reagan Library (Wallison files). For additional accounts of this selection process, see David Yalof, *Pursuit of Justice: Presidential Politics and the Selection of Supreme Court Nominees* (Chicago: University of Chicago Press, 1999); and Jan Crawford Greenburg, *Supreme Conflict: The Inside Story of the Struggle for Control of the United States Supreme Court* (New York: Penguin, 2008).

2. Richard K. Cacioppo to Ronald Reagan, June 8, 1985, Scalia White House Alphabetical File, Reagan Library.

3. Wallison Memoir, August 29, 1986, Peter Wallison Files, Supreme Court/Rehnquist/Scalia, Notebook II, Folder 1 of 3, OX 14287, Reagan Library.

4. Untitled memo written by Roger Clegg, included in "Memorandum for the File, Peter J. Wallison, Counsel to the President," June 11, 1986, Peter Wallison Files, Supreme Court/Rehnquist/Scalia, Notebook II Folder 1 of 3, OX 14287, Reagan Library.

5. Wallison Memoir, August 29, 1986, Peter Wallison Files, Supreme Court/Rehnquist/Scalia, Notebook II Folder 1 of 3, OX 14287, Reagan Library.

6. "Materials Submitted by the Department of Justice," Supreme Court/Rehnquist/Scalia, Notebook II—Candidates [1 of 3], Peter J. Wallison files, Reagan Library.

7. Ibid.

8. Supreme Court—Robert Bork, Copy of Candidate Notebook, Rehnquist/Scalia, Arthur Culvahouse files [1 of 2], Reagan Library.

9. Untitled Scalia Appointment Memo, Supreme Court/Rehnquist/Scalia Notebook I—Candidates [3 of 4], Peter Wallison Files, Reagan Library.

10. Ibid.

11. Ibid.

12. Lee Liberman and staff Justice Department Attorneys, Untitled Scalia Memo, Supreme Court/Rehnquist/Scalia Notebook I—Candidates [3 of 4], Peter Wallison Files, Reagan Library.

13. Peter Wallison, *Ronald Reagan: The Power of Conviction and the Success of His Presidency,* (New York: Basic Books, 2004), p. 151, and Wallison email to author, October 29, 2013.

14. Wallison Memoir, August 29, 1986, Peter Wallison Files, Supreme Court/Rehnquist/ Scalia, Folder 1 of 3, OX 14287, Reagan Library.
15. Biskupic, *American Original,* p. 108.
16. Address, Judge Antonin Scalia, before the Attorney General's Conference on Economic Liberties, Washington, D.C., June 14, 1986, found in Appendix C, *Original Meaning Jurisprudence: A Sourcebook, Report to the Attorney General,* Office of Legal Policy, U.S. Department of Justice, March 12, 1987, pp. 101–6.
17. Wallison Memoir, August 29, 1986, Peter Wallison Files, Supreme Court/Rehnquist/ Scalia, Folder 3, Reagan Library.
18. "Remarks by the President, Chief Justice Warren Burger, Justice William Rehnquist and Judge Antonin Scalia," June 17, 1986, Alan Charles Raul Files, Supreme Court Nominations and Confirmations, Reagan Library.
19. Ibid.
20. ABC News transcript, September 26, 1986.
21. Dr. S. Eugene Scalia obituary, *New York Times,* January 7, 1986.
22. The Senate had been concerned about what some feared was Rehnquist's pattern of inclination toward bigotry, including his role in drafting an anti–*Brown v. Board of Education* 1954 case on school desegregation, his membership in an all-male club, and living in a house with a restrictive covenant against sale to African Americans. Really, though, there was unhappiness by the Senate liberals with the extremely conservative nature of Rehnquist's decision making on the Court, and their fear that he would lead the entire body in that direction as chief justice. For more on this, see John A. Jenkins, *The Partisan: The Life of William Rehnquist* (New York: PublicAffairs, 2012).
23. Nomination of Judge Antonin Scalia, Hearings Before the Committee on the Judiciary, United States Senate, 99th Congress, 2nd Session, August 5 and 6, 1986, Government Printing Office, Washington, D.C., 1987. The description of Scalia's appearance during the hearing comes from viewing a video of the hearing posted on the internet at the C-SPAN Video Library, Scalia Confirmation Hearing Day 1 and Day 2, found at http://www.c-spanvideo.org/program/150300-1 and at http://www.c-spanvideo.org/program/150300-2.
24. Thanks for this insight to my student Ed Daley in my "Personality and Judicial Politics" class at Lafayette College.
25. On other occasions, Scalia would tell audiences that he would not be confirmed by the Senate in the recent partisan-charged Washington atmosphere, and that he would not want to go through the process again. Debra Cassens Weiss, "Scalia Doubts He Would Win Confirmation Today," *ABA Journal,* July 29, 2010, http://www.abajournal.com/news/article/scalia_doubts_he_would_win_confirmation_if_vote_were_today/: "Scalia Wouldn't Want Confirmation Hearings Again," Fox News.com, October 10, 2005, http://www.foxnews.com/story/0,2933,171761,00.html.
26. For more, see Greenburg, *Supreme Conflict.*
27. "Swearing in of Chief Justice Rehnquist and Justice Antonin Scalia," September 26, 1986, Peter J. Wallison Files, Reagan Library.
28. Stephen J. Adler, "Live Wire on the D.C. Circuit," *Legal Times,* June 23, 1986.
29. ABC News transcript, September 26, 1986.
30. Ibid.
31. Ibid. See also Ted Gest, "Scalia: No Extremism Spoken Here," *U.S. News and World Report,* August 18, 1986.

32. E. R. Shipp, "Scalia's Midwest Colleagues Cite His Love of Debate, Poker and Piano," *New York Times,* July 26, 1986.

CHAPTER 9: A COURT OF ONE

1. For more, see Dennis Hutchinson, *The Man Who Was Once Whizzer White: A Portrait of Byron R. White* (New York: Free Press, 1998).

2. Joan Biskupic, *Sandra Day O'Connor: How the First Woman on the Supreme Court Became Its Most Influential Justice* (New York: Ecco-HarperCollins, 2005), p. 7.

3. Ibid. See also http://www.pbs.org/newshour/updates/law/jan-june07/oconnor.html.

4. Nat Hentoff, "The Constitutionalist," *New Yorker,* March 12, 1990, p. 45, http://www.newyorker.com/archive/1990/03/12/1990_03_12_045_TNY_CARDS_000353704.

5. For more, see Seth Stern and Stephen Wermeil, *Justice Brennan: Liberal Champion* (Boston: Houghton Mifflin, 2010).

6. See Richard Kluger, *Simple Justice: The History of Brown v. Board of Education and Black America's Struggle for Equality* (New York: Vintage, 2004); and Gilbert King, *Devil in the Grove: Thurgood Marshall, the Groveland Boys, and the Dawn of a New America* (New York: Harper, 2012).

7. Not much has yet been written on Justice Blackmun, but two excellent early books are: Linda Greenhouse, *Becoming Justice Blackmun: Harry Blackmun's Supreme Court Journey* (New York: Times Books, 2006), and Tinsley Yarbrough, *Harry A. Blackmun: Outsider Justice* (New York: Oxford University Press, 2008).

8. For more, see Kenneth A. Manaster, *Illinois Justice: The Scandal of 1969 and the Rise of John Paul Stevens* (Chicago: University of Chicago Press, 2001).

9. Bill Barnhart and Eugene Schlickman, *John Paul Stevens: An Independent Life* (Dekalb: Northern Illinois University Press, 2010); Robert J. Sickels, *John Paul Stevens and the Constitution: The Search for Balance* (University Park: Penn State University Press, 1988).

10. For more on Powell, see John C. Jeffries, *Justice Lewis F. Powell, Jr.: A Biography* (New York: Fordham University Press, 2001).

11. Linda Greenhouse, "Ruling Fixed Opinions," *New York Times,* February 22, 1988, p. A16.

12. Biskupic, *American Original,* p. 129.

13. In initially working with the conservative wing of this Court, Scalia, and his devoted conservative followers, fostered the image that his decision-making theory was called "originalism," interpreting the Constitution and the Bill of Rights according to the "public meaning" of the phrases in the minds of the people in the constitutional Founding Era, or at the time of the state ratification of those documents. We are led to believe that Scalia came to the Court with his theory fully formed and governed his decisions throughout his time there. But it is not so.

14. Interviews, biographies, and memoirs of justices have made clear, though, that the new job is so different from one's experience, no matter how brilliant the new justice, that it usually takes several years to adjust and learn the new tasks. Bruce Allen Murphy, *Fortas: The Rise and Ruin of a Supreme Court Justice* (New York: William Morrow, 1988); Bruce Allen Murphy, *Wild Bill: The Legend and Life of William O. Douglas* (New York: Random House, 2003); Harry Blackmun Oral History, Manuscript Division, Library of Congress, Washington, D.C.; William Brennan, "National Court of Appeals: Another Dissent," *University of Chicago Law Review* 40 (1983): 484ff. J. Woodford Howard, "Justice Murphy: The Freshman Years," *Vanderbilt Law Review* 18 (March 1965): 477ff. In

recent years, scholars have argued that the "freshman effect" literature is "either incorrect or time bound," with the Supreme Court "becom[ing] more individualistic," but still posit that "small group process remain influential and should not be discounted altogether." See Thea F. Rubin and Albert P. Melone, "Justice Antonin Scalia: A First Year Freshman Effect?," *Judicature* 72, no. 2 (August/September 1988): 98–102.

15. The "initial bewilderment" from Edward V. Heck and Melinda Gann Hall, "Bloc Voting and the Freshman Justice Revisited," *The Journal of Politics* 43 (1981): 853; "acclimation period" from Timothy M. Hagle, " 'Freshmen Effects' for Supreme Court Justices," *American Journal of Political Science* 37, no. 4 (November 1993): 1143. This literature spins from the seminal social psychological work on the early apprenticeship period of the Court by Eloise C. Snyder, "The Supreme Court as a Small Group," *Social Forces,* vol. 36 (March 1958), reprinted in Robert G. Scigliano (ed.), *The Courts: A Reader in the Judicial Process* (Boston: Little, Brown, 1962), pp. 232–38. See also Robert L. Dudley, "The Freshman Effect and Voting Alignments: A Re-Examination of Judicial Folklore," *American Politics Quarterly* 21, no. 3 (July 1993): 360–67.

16. Snyder, "The Supreme Court as a Small Group." While Heck and Hall do challenge Snyder's apprenticeship theory, they concede: "Freshman justices do indeed form close voting alliances with other justices during their first natural court [one in which the personnel do not change]." Heck and Hall, "Bloc Voting and the Freshman Justice Revisited"; Hagle, " 'Freshmen Effects' for Supreme Court Justices," 1143.

17. In this volume, I will be confirming, based on primary sources, the excellent "Scalia has no apprentice period" argument in the existing "freshman year." See Rubin and Melone, "Justice Antonin Scalia: A First Year Freshman Effect?" See also Michael Patrick King, "Justice Antonin Scalia: The First Term on the Supreme Court—1986–87," *Rutgers Law Review* 20, no. 1 (Fall 1988): 1–77; and Stephen J. Adler, "Scalia's Court," *American Lawyer Newspaper,* March 1987.

18. Adler, "Scalia's Court."

19. Ibid.

20. Jeffries, *Justice Lewis F. Powell, Jr.,* p. 534; quoted also in Margaret Talbot, "Supreme Confidence," *New Yorker,* March 28, 2005, http://www.newyorker.com/archive/2005/03/28/050328fa_fact_talbot.

21. Adler, "Scalia's Court."

22. Ibid.

23. Ibid.

24. *O'Connor v. United States,* November 4, 1986, 479 U.S. 27 (1986).

25. Scalia to Stevens, November 4, 1986, Lewis F. Powell Papers, Box 278, Washington and Lee Law School, Lexington, Virginia; *Hodel v. Irving* case file, ibid.

26. Powell to Scalia, February 26, 1987, *Hodel v. Irving,* Powell Papers, Box 278.

27. Rehnquist to Scalia, March 3, 1987, Scalia to Rehnquist, March 3, 1987, Powell to Scalia, March 4, 1987, Rehnquist to Scalia, March 4, 1987, *Hodel v. Irving*, Powell Papers, Box 278.

28. O'Connor to "The Conference," April 21, 1987, *Hodel v. Irving,* Powell Papers, Box 278.

29. *Hodel v. Irving,* 481 U.S. 704 (1987).

30. Scalia to Rehnquist and Powell, April 21, 1987, O'Connor, *Hodel v. Irving,* Powell Papers, Box 278.

31. Scalia, First Draft, *Hodel v. Irving,* April 1987, Powell Papers, Box 278.

32. Ibid.

33. Powell to Scalia, May 4, 1987, *Hodel v. Irving,* Powell Papers, Box 278.

34. Powell writing on O'Connor to "The Conference," May 5, 1987, *Hodel v. Irving*, Powell Papers, Box 278.
35. O'Connor draft, May 5, 1987, *Hodel v. Irving*, Powell Papers, Box 278.
36. Jeffries, *Justice Lewis F. Powell, Jr.*, pp. 534–35.
37. My analysis of this term and the next two was aided by excellent research by a student, Matt Gyory, who studied this question under a Mellon Foundation Community of Scholars grant, for which I thank both him and the Mellon Foundation. I also benefited from a student paper by Ed Daley for my senior seminar, "The Infancy of Justice Scalia."
38. *O'Connor v. Ortega*, 480 U.S. 709 (1987) at 712 (O'Connor, J., plurality).
39. Ibid., at 718.
40. Ibid., at 731 (Scalia, J., concurring). This type of clash with a colleague became the norm for Scalia as that year's most visible affirmative action case, *Johnson v. Transportation Agency*, led to another tangle, this time between him and the Court's senior liberal, William Brennan.
41. Harlow Giles Unger, *Noah Webster: The Life and Times of a Patriot* (New York: Wiley, 2000).
42. *Edwards v. Aguillard*, 428 U.S. 578, 593 (1987) (Brennan, J., majority).
43. Ibid., at 610 (Scalia, J., dissenting).
44. Ibid., at 611.
45. Ibid., at 639.
46. *Booth v. Maryland*, 482 U.S. 496, 502 (1987) (Powell, J., majority).
47. Ibid., at 520 (Scalia, J., dissenting).
48. Brennan, "The Constitution of the United States: Contemporary Ratification," Text and Teaching Symposium, Georgetown University, October 12, 1985, in *Original Meaning Jurisprudence: A Sourcebook, Report to the Attorney General,* U.S. Department of Justice, March 12, 1987. A year later, in a speech on the Fourteenth Amendment to the American Bar Association meeting at New York University Law School, Brennan would say that by using this "evolving reading" of the amendment by which the Bill of Rights could be extended to the states, "the Fourteenth Amendment should be summoned to the service of the protection of a broad range of civil rights and liberties." Only with this evolving tool could the Court fulfill what Brennan argued was its mission in America's democratic society: "Society's overriding concern today should continue to be, indeed must continue to be, providing freedom and equality, in a realistic and not merely formal sense, to all the people of this Nation." Here Brennan concluded in favor of "resisting cut-backs, particularly by the Supreme Court of the United States, of Fourteenth Amendment protection. One of the great strengths of our federal system is that it provides a double source of protection for the liberties of our citizens. Federalism is not served when the federal half of that protection is crippled." Brennan, "The Fourteenth Amendment," Address to the Section on Individual Rights and Responsibilities, American Bar Association, August 8, 1986, New York University Law School, found in "Original Meaning Jurisprudence: A Sourcebook," Report to the Attorney General, U.S. Department of Justice, March 12, 1987.
49. Address of Attorney General Edwin Meese III, D.C. Chapter of the Federalist Society Lawyers Division, November 15, 1985, in "Original Meaning Jurisprudence: A Sourcebook," Report to the Attorney General, U.S. Department of Justice, March 12, 1987).
50. *Bowers v. Hardwick*, 478 U.S. 186 (1987) (Blackmun, J., dissenting). For more on this issue, see Deb Price and Joyce Murdock, *Courting Justice: Gay Men and Lesbians v. the Supreme Court* (New York: Basic Books, 2002).

51. Senator Edward M. Kennedy, "Robert Bork's America," June 23, 1987, http://en .wikisource.org/wiki/Robert_Bork%27s_America.

52. See Ethan Bronner, *Battle for Justice: How the Bork Nomination Shook America* (New York: Union Square Press, 2007); Norman Vieira and Leonard Gross, *Supreme Court Appointments: Judge Bork and the Politicization of Senate Confirmations* (Carbondale: Southern Illinois University Press, 1998); and Mark Gitenstein, *Matters of Principle: An Insider's Account of America's Rejection of Robert Bork's Nomination for the Supreme Court* (New York: Simon & Schuster, 1992).

53. See Bronner, *Battle for Justice*; Vieira and Gross, *Supreme Court Appointments*; and Gitenstein, *Matters of Principle*.

54. See Linda Greenhouse, "Robert Bork's Tragedy," *New York Times,* January 9, 2013, found at opinionator.blogs.nytimes.com. Greenhouse argues persuasively that Bork was also hurt by an answer to Utah Republican senator Orrin Hatch's question about controversial cases beyond *Roe v. Wade,* in which Bork cites *Brown v. Board of Education* rather than *Dred Scott,* making it appear that he might be willing to overturn that school desegregation case as well.

CHAPTER 10: FAINT-HEARTED ORIGINALIST

1. Steven V. Roberts, "Douglas Ginsburg Withdraws Name as Supreme Court Nominee, Citing 'Marijuana Clamor,'" *New York Times,* November 8, 1987. Had Judge Ginsburg been confirmed to the Court, he would have been just as reliably conservative and historically oriented in his interpretation as Scalia. Moreover, he might have been just as influential in changing the conversation about conservative legal jurisprudence. Ginsburg later became a distinguished Court of Appeals judge, establishing himself as one of the founding proponents of the "Constitution-in-Exile" school, by which judges decided cases based on the conservative pre-1937 "Court-Packing Plan" philosophy of a pro-corporation, and pro–states' rights under the Tenth Amendment interpretation of the Constitution.

2. Jeffrey Toobin, *The Nine: Inside the Secret World of the Supreme Court* (New York: Doubleday, 2007), pp. 182–83.

3. Robert Reinhold, "Restrained Pragmatist: Anthony M. Kennedy," *New York Times* online, November 12, 1987.

4. For an excellent journalistic examination of the effect of Kennedy's upbringing in Sacramento, see Massimo Calabresi and David Von Drehle, "What Will Justice Kennedy Do?," *Time,* June 18, 2012, pp. 28–39.

5. Kennedy Interview, Academy of Achievement, New York, June 3, 2005, www.achieve ment.org.

6. Find Law for Professionals, http://supreme.lp.findlaw.com/supreme_court/justices /kennedy.html.

7. Reinhold, "Restrained Pragmatist: Anthony M. Kennedy." Kennedy is now the longest active member of the faculty at McGeorge School of Law and continues to teach a summer seminar to law students in Austria.

8. Helen J. Knowles, *The Tie Goes to Freedom: Justice Anthony M. Kennedy on Liberty* (New York: Rowman & Littlefield, 2009); Frank J. Colucci, *Justice Kennedy's Jurisprudence: The Full and Necessary Meaning of Liberty* (Lawrence: University Press of Kansas, 2009).

9. Scalia used this term so much that it became the title of a fine book about him by Ralph Rossum, *Antonin Scalia's Jurisprudence: Text and Tradition* (Lawrence: University Press of Kansas, 2006).

10. Scalia Speech to the American Enterprise Institute, "Outsourcing American Law," February 21, 2006. Another excellent source here is Thurston Greene's comprehensive *The Language of the Constitution* (New York: Greenwood, 1991), tracing every word in the Constitution in writings of any kind during the Early American period. As Scalia would explain to an attorney after his American Enterprise Institute speech as to how to gain this information: "Oh, well, there are concordances of the Constitution that will tell you where the various phrases in the Constitution come from and they will generally lead you into the cases that—that's the best I can do for a quick research job. I mean, there are obviously books on various subjects. But there are concordances. That's where I'd probably start."

11. Philip B. Kurland and Ralph Lerner, *The Founders' Constitution,* 5 vols. (Chicago: University of Chicago Press, 2000), online at http://press-pubs.uchicago.edu/founders/; Edwin Meese, Matthew Spalding, and David Forte, *The Heritage Guide to the Constitution* (Washington, D.C.: Regnery, 2005). In recent years liberal progressives have produced online a competing concordance: *Consource: The Constitutional Sources Project,* www.concource.org.

12. See Herbert J. Storing, *The Complete Anti-Federalist,* 3 vols. (Chicago: University of Chicago Press, 2007).

13. *Coy v. Iowa,* 487 U.S. 1012, 1020–21 (1988) (Scalia, J., majority).

14. Ibid., at 1029 (Blackmun, J., dissenting). Blackmun then explained in a footnote: "Interestingly, the precise quotation from Richard II the majority uses to explain the 'root meaning of confrontation' . . . is discussed in [Wigmore]. . . . That renowned and accepted authority describes the view of confrontation expressed by the words of Richard II as an 'earlier conception, still current in [Shakespeare's] day' which, by the time the *Bill of Rights* was ratified, had merged 'with the principle of cross-examination.'"

15. Ibid., at p. 1019 (Scalia, J., majority).

16. Ibid.

17. *Thompson v. Oklahoma,* 487 U.S. 815, 822–23 (1988) (Stevens, J., plurality).

18. Ibid., at 864 (Scalia, J., dissenting).

19. Ibid., at 873–74. Italics in original.

20. Ibid., at 867.

21. Ibid., at 848 (O'Connor J., concurring).

22. Ibid. (Scalia, J., dissenting).

23. Ibid., at 876.

24. Ibid., at 878.

25. See *Stanford v. Kentucky,* 492 U.S. 361 (1989), and *Penry v. Lynaugh,* 492 U.S. 302, 369–70 (1989).

26. *Stanford v. Kentucky,* 492 U.S. 361 (1989) (Scalia, J., majority), pp. 365–81.

27. Ibid., at 379.

28. *Roper v. Simmons,* 543 U.S. 551 (2005).

29. *Morrison v. Olson,* 487 U.S. 654, 696 (1988) (Rehnquist, C. J., majority).

30. Ibid., at 672–73.

31. Ibid., at 698 (Scalia, J., dissenting).

32. Ibid., at 699.

33. Harry Blackmun comment on Scalia *Morrison v. Olson* draft, *Morrison v. Olson* folder, Harry Blackmun Papers, Manuscripts Division, Library of Congress, Washington, D.C., Box 507.

34. *Morrison v. Olson,* at 706 (Scalia, J., dissenting).

35. Ibid., at 709.
36. Ibid., at 712.
37. Ibid., at 713.
38. Ibid., at 727.
39. Ibid., at 731.
40. Blackmun comment on Scalia *Morrison v. Olson* draft, Blackmun Papers, Box 507.
41. For more on the Bush theory of the "unitary presidency," see Charlie Savage, *Takeover: The Return of the Imperial Presidency and the Subversion of American Democracy* (Boston: Little, Brown, 2007).
42. Steven Calabresi speech at 20th anniversary of Antonin Scalia's service on the Supreme Court, Federalist Society, 2006, found at www.fed-soc.org.
43. *Texas Monthly, Inc. v. Bullock,* 489 U.S. 1, 23 (1989) (Scalia, J., dissenting).
44. Ibid., at 33.
45. Ibid., at 33.
46. Ibid., at 45.
47. *Texas v. Johnson,* 491 U.S. 397 (1989).
48. Ibid., p. 414.
49. An account of a speech by Scalia on "Catholicism and Justice" at John Carroll University in Cleveland, Ohio, found in an article, "Justice Scalia says rights excessive, Can be scaled down in wartime," March 21, 2003, at Kuro5hinhttp://www.kuro5hin.org/story/2003/3/21/35911/1828.
50. Nina Totenberg, "Justice Scalia, the Great Dissenter, Opens Up," April 28, 2010, www.npr.org.
51. Scalia address before the Attorney General's Conference on Economic Liberties, Washington, D.C., June 14, 1986, found in Appendix C, "Original Meaning Jurisprudence: A Sourcebook," *Report to the Attorney General,* Office of Legal Policy, U.S. Department of Justice, March 12, 1987, pp. 101–6.
52. Scalia speech, "Originalism: The Lesser Evil," in *University of Cincinnati Law Review* 57 (1989): 849ff.
53. Harlow Giles Unger, *Noah Webster: The Life and Times of a Patriot* (New York: Wiley, 2000).
54. See H. W. Brands, *Andrew Jackson: His Life and Times* (New York: Anchor, 2006); Jon Meacham, *American Lion: Andrew Jackson in the White House* (New York: Random House, 2009); and Gordon S. Wood, *Revolutionary Characters: What Made the Founders Different* (New York: Penguin, 2006). Wood's wonderful essay in the end of *Revolutionary Characters* makes clear how America changed with the increase in partisanship in the 1790s. Brands and Meacham make clear how the country changed again with the shift in the center of political gravity to the West and the increase in the voting franchise.
55. Gordon S. Wood, "The Fundamentalists and the Constitution," *New York Review of Books,* February 18, 1988, based on a speech and paper by the same name, delivered to the Virginia Commission on the Bicentennial of the United States Constitution, Center for Public Service, University of Virginia, 1987.
56. Scalia speech, Annual Convention of the Federalist Society, Washington, D.C., November 22, 2008, www.fed-soc.org.
57. Scalia speech, "The Rule of Law as a Law of Rules," in *University of Chicago Law Review* (Fall 1989): 1175ff. Italics and boldface in original.
58. I am indebted to my student, Jim Hlavenka, then a senior in my Judicial Biography seminar and now an attorney, for dating the speech.

59. Scalia speech, "Constitutional Interpretation," Sibley Lecture, University of Georgia Law School, 1989, www.ninoville.com.

60. Bruce Allen Murphy, *Fortas: The Rise and Ruin of a Supreme Court Justice* (New York: William Morrow, 1988); Bruce Allen Murphy, "Extrajudicial Activities," *Encyclopedia of the Supreme Court of the United States,* David S. Tanenhaus, ed. (New York: Thomson Gale, 2008).

61. Laura A. Kiernan, "Ruling on Press Shows High Court Confusion," *Washington Post,* September 17, 1979.

62. Morton Mintz, "Justice Says Press Too Afraid of Ruling," *Washington Post,* September 9, 1979. The speech was referring to *Gannett v. DePasquale,* 443 U.S. 368 (1979). Here, Justice Potter Stewart wrote that there was "no constitutional right . . . to attend public trials."

63. Daniel Schorr, "Justice Blackmun—The Harry I Knew," *Christian Science Monitor,* March 12, 1999; John A. Jenkins, "A Candid Talk with Justice Blackmun, *New York Times Magazine,* February 20, 1983; and Bill Moyers, *In Search of the Constitution,* Episode 2, "Mr. Justice Blackmun," www.amazon.com.

64. Schorr, "Justice Blackmun"; Jenkins, "A Candid Talk with Justice Blackmun"; Moyers, *In Search of the Constitution.* For more on the split between Blackmun and Burger, see Linda Greenhouse, *Becoming Justice Blackmun: Harry Blackmun's Supreme Court Journey* (New York: Times Books, 2005).

CHAPTER II: LOSING THE MIDDLE

1. 74.1 percent in the 1986 term, 78.1 percent in 1987, and 75.9 percent in 1988. *Harvard Law Review* annual summary statistics, for the 1986–87, 1987–88, and 1988–89 Supreme Court terms. *Harvard Law Review Annual Supreme Court Issues,* "The Statistics," *Harvard Law Review* 101 (November 1987): 362ff; 102 (November 1988): 143ff; 103 (November 1989): 394ff.

2. 83.1 percent in the 1987 term, and 85.0 percent in the 1988 term; figures from the *Harvard Law Review* annual Court statistics, November 1988 and November 1989.

3. O'Connor to Scalia, June 7, 1989, *South Carolina v. Gathers* File, Harry Blackmun Papers, Manuscript Division, Library of Congress, Washington, D.C., Box 533.

4. Kennedy to Scalia, June 7, 1989, *South Carolina v. Gathers* File, Blackmun Papers, Box 533.

5. Blackmun note on Kennedy note to Scalia, June 7, 1989, *South Carolina v. Gathers* File, Blackmun Papers, Box 533.

6. Brennan draft opinion in *South Carolina v. Gathers,* Blackmun Papers, Box 533.

7. *South Carolina v. Gathers,* 490 U.S. 805 (1989) (Brennan, J., majority).

8. O'Connor draft opinion in *South Carolina v. Gathers,* Blackmun Papers, Box 533.

9. Scalia first draft dissent in *South Carolina v. Gathers* circulated June 7, 1989, Blackmun Papers, Box 533.

10. Ibid.

11. *Webster v. Reproductive Health Services,* 492 U.S. 490 (1989), conference notes, Blackmun Papers, Box 536.

12. Ibid.

13. Ibid.

14. Rehnquist first draft opinion in *Webster v. Reproductive Health Services,* Blackmun Papers, Box 536.

15. Stevens to Rehnquist, May 30, 1989, Blackmun Papers, Box 536.
16. Memo, Eddie [Lazarus] to Blackmun, May 30, 1989, Blackmun Papers, Box 536.
17. Sandra Day O'Connor first draft opinion of *Webster,* June 23, 1989, Blackmun Papers, Box 536.
18. Rehnquist, final draft opinion of *Webster,* Blackmun Papers, Box 536.
19. Eddie [Lazarus] to Blackmun, June 26, 1989, Blackmun Papers, Box 536.
20. *Webster v. Reproductive Health Services,* 492 U.S. 490, 532 (1989) (Scalia, J., concurring).
21. Ibid., at 533.
22. Ibid., at 534.
23. Ibid., at 535.
24. Ibid., at 537.
25. Ibid.
26. Ibid.
27. Ibid., at 538 (Blackmun, J., dissenting).
28. *Reynolds v. United States,* 98 U.S. 145 (1878).
29. *Sherbert v. Verner,* 378 U.S. 393, 404 (1963) (Brennan, J., majority).
30. Ibid., at 406.
31. *Employment Division of Oregon v. Smith,* 494 U.S. 872, 879 (1990) (Scalia, J., majority).
32. Ibid., at 888.
33. Ibid., at 901 (O'Connor, J., concurring).
34. Ibid., at (Scalia, J., majority).
35. On the opinion negotiations, Blackmun clerk, "Martha" Matthews to Blackmun, March 13, 1990, Blackmun Papers, Box 546. On the Note, O'Connor to Blackmun, April 17, 1990, Blackmun Papers, Box 546.
36. *Ohio v. Akron Center for Reproductive Health,* 497 U.S. 502, 520 (1990) (Kennedy, J., plurality).
37. Ibid., at 520–21 (Scalia, J., concurring).
38. Blackmun dissent draft, *Ohio v Akron,* Blackmun Papers, Box 544.
39. Ibid.
40. Ibid.
41. Letter, Kennedy to Blackmun, June 21, 1990, Blackmun Papers, Box 544.
42. *Ohio v. Akron Center for Reproductive Health,* 497 U.S. 502, 541 (1990).
43. Martha [Matthews] to Blackmun, May 16, 1990, Blackmun Papers, Box 544.
44. Ibid.
45. Blackmun to O'Connor, June 1, 1990, Blackmun Papers, Box 544.
46. *Maryland v. Craig,* at 850 (O'Connor, J., majority); Blackmun to O'Connor, June 22, 1990, Blackmun Papers, Box 559.
47. *Maryland v. Craig,* at 853 (O'Connor, J., majority).
48. Martha to Blackmun, June 5, 1990, Blackmun Papers, Box 559.
49. *Maryland v. Craig,* at 861 (Scalia, J., dissenting).
50. Ibid., at 862.
51. Ibid., at 862–63.
52. Ibid., at 867.
53. Ibid., at 870.
54. Richard C. Reuben, "Man in the Middle," *California Lawyer,* October 1992, p. 38.
55. *New York Times,* July 21, 1990; Martin Tolchin, "Vacancy on the Court," *Washington Post,* July 22, 1990.
56. Ann Devroy, "President Selects Souter," *Washington Post,* July 24, 1990.

57. Ruth Marcus and Joe Pichirallo, "Seeking Out the Essential David Souter," *Washington Post,* September 9, 1990; Ruth Marcus and Joe Pichirallo, "Souter's Life in the Law," *Washington Post,* September 10, 1990.

58. Stuart Taylor, "Surprise! Souter Won't Surprise Bush," *Washington Post,* September 30, 1990.

59. Thanks to Reuben, "Man in the Middle," for suggesting these two cases as examples.

60. *Batson v. Kentucky,* 476 U.S. 79, 99 (1986) (Powell, J., majority).

61. *Powers v. Ohio,* 499 U.S. 400, 416 (1991) (Kennedy, J., majority).

62. Ibid., at 427 (Scalia, J., dissenting).

63. Ibid., at 439.

64. *Edmondson v. Leesville Concrete Co.,* 500 U.S. 614, 644 (1990) (Scalia, J., dissenting).

65. Ibid., at 645.

66. O'Connor and Stephen Breyer interview with George Stephanopoulos, *This Week,* July 6, 2003, ABC News transcript, Lexis/Nexis.

67. Jeffrey Toobin, *The Nine: Inside the Secret World of the Supreme Court* (New York: Doubleday, 2007), p. 129.

68. *Harvard Law Review* The Statistics; *Harvard Law Review* 102 (November, 1988): 143ff; 103 (November, 1989): 394ff; 104 (November, 1990): 359ff; 105 (November, 1991), 177ff; 106 (November, 1992): 163ff.; nickname from Terry Carter, "Crossing the Rubicon," *California Lawyer,* October 1992, p. 104.

69. Ibid. Kennedy's and O'Connor's agreement with Scalia scores between them averaged in the mid-80 percentile in their first three terms together (89.7 percent in the 1988 term, 83.2 percent in 1989, 84.6 percent in 1990), before dropping to a low of 63.2 percent in 1991.

70. *Payne v. Tennessee,* 501 U.S. 808, 844 (1991) (Marshall, J., dissenting).

71. John E. Yang and Sharon La Franiere, "Bush Picks Thomas for Supreme Court," *Washington Post,* July 2, 1991.

72. *R.A.V. v. City of St. Paul,* 506 U.S. 377 (1992).

73. *Chaplinsky v. New Hampshire,* 315 U.S. 568, 570–71 (1942) (Murphy, J., majority).

74. Ibid., at 572.

75. *R.A.V. v. City of St. Paul,* 506 U.S. 377, 391 (1992) (Scalia, J., majority).

76. Ibid., at 391–92.

77. Ibid., at 396.

78. Ibid., at 415 (White, J., concurring).

79. Ibid., at 436 (Stevens, J., concurring).

CHAPTER 12: THE EVIL NINO

1. *County of Allegheny v. American Civil Liberties Union; City of Pittsburgh v. ACLU; Chabad v. ACLU,* 492 U.S. 573, 621 (1989).

2. *County of Allegheny v. ACLU,* at pp. 620–21 (Blackmun, J., majority). Under O'Connor's "no endorsement" test in *Lynch v. Donnelly,* 465 U.S. 668 (1984), "Every government practice must be judged in its unique circumstances to determine whether it constitutes an endorsement or disapproval of religion." Symbolic religious displays will be acceptable if "they serve such secular purposes and because of their 'history and ubiquity,' such government acknowledgments of religion are not understood as conveying an endorsement of particular religious beliefs."

3. *County of Allegheny v. ACLU,* at 677 (Kennedy, J. concurring and dissenting).
4. Ibid., at 610 (Blackmun, J., majority).
5. Ibid., at 611.
6. Oral argument transcript, *Lee v. Weisman,* 505 U.S. 577 (1992), www.oyez.org, http://www.oyez.org/cases/1990–1999/1991/1991_90_1014.
7. Kennedy to Blackmun, March 30, 1992, Harry Blackmun Papers, Manuscripts Division, Box 586, Library of Congress, Washington, D.C.
8. Kennedy to Rehnquist, March 30, 1992, Blackmun Papers, Box 586.
9. *Lee v. Weisman,* 505 U.S. 577, 592 (1992) (Kennedy, J., majority).
10. Ibid., at 592.
11. Scalia, Draft Dissent to Conference, June 18, 1992, Blackmun Papers, Box 586. Wording also appears in *Lee v. Weisman,* 505 US 577 (1992), at 631–32.
12. Ibid., language in final opinion, p. 636.
13. Ibid., language in final opinion, p. 644.
14. Souter to Blackmun, November 18, 1991, and Conference Notes, November 8, 1991, Blackmun Papers, Box 586.
15. Souter to Blackmun, December 31, 1991, Blackmun Papers, Box 586.
16. Souter to Blackmun, April 15, 1991, Blackmun Papers, Box 586.
17. See Jon Meacham, *American Gospel: God, the Founding Fathers, and the Making of a Nation* (New York: Random House, 2007), passim.
18. *Lee v. Weisman,* 505 U.S. 577, 612 (1992) (Souter, J., concurring).
19. Ibid., at 616–17.
20. Ibid., at 629–30.
21. Ibid., at 631.
22. *Snyder v. Massachusetts,* 291 U.S. 97, 105 (1934); rule quoted in Rehnquist draft for *Planned Parenthood of Southeastern Pennsylvania v. Casey,* 505 U.S. 833 (1992), May 27, 1992, Blackmun comments, Blackmun Papers, Box 601.
23. Rehnquist draft, *Planned Parenthood,* Blackmun Papers, Box 601.
24. Ibid.
25. Kennedy to Blackmun, May 29, 1992, Blackmun Papers, Box 601.
26. Notes of meeting between Blackmun and Kennedy, March 30, 1992 [actually May 30], Blackmun Papers, Box 601.
27. Jan Crawford Greenburg, *Supreme Conflict: The Inside Story of the Struggle for Control of the United States Supreme Court* (New York: Penguin, 2008), pp. 155–56. Jeffrey Toobin, *The Nine,* p. 59, has a similar story.
28. *Planned Parenthood of Southeastern Pennsylvania v. Casey,* 505 U.S. 833, 844 (1992), (O'Connor, Souter, and Kennedy, J.'s, plurality).
29. Ibid., at 851.
30. Ibid. Kennedy's biographers would later cite this sentence as representing the heart of his judicial libertarian instincts. See Helen J. Knowles, *The Tie Goes to Freedom,* and Frank J. Colucci, *Justice Kennedy's Jurisprudence.*
31. *Lawrence v. Texas,* 539 U.S. 558, at 588. (2003) (Scalia, J., dissenting).
32. *Planned Parenthood,* at 854.
33. Ibid., at 864.
34. Ibid., at 868.
35. Ibid., at 877.
36. Ibid., at 878.

37. *Planned Parenthood of Southeastern Pennsylvania v. Casey,* 505 U.S. 833, 922–23 (1992) (Blackmun, J., concurring in part, dissenting in part).

38. Ibid., at 943.

39. Memo from Steff [Stephanie Dangle] to Blackmun, June 20, 1992, Blackmun Papers, Box 601.

40. *Planned Parenthood of Southeastern Pennsylvania v. Casey,* 505 U.S. 833, 987 (1992) (Scalia, J., dissenting).

41. Ibid., at 996.

42. Ibid., at 999.

43. Ibid., at 1000.

44. Ibid., at 1001.

45. Ibid., at 1002.

46. Terry Carter, "Crossing the Rubicon," *California Lawyer,* October 1992, pp. 9, 103.

47. Ibid.

48. Ibid., p. 104.

49. Ibid.

50. *Lucas v. South Carolina Coastal Council,* 505 U.S. 1003, 1027 (1992) (Scalia, J., majority).

51. Ibid., at 1031.

52. Molly [McUsic] to Blackmun, February 28, 1992, Blackmun Papers, Box 599.

53. *Lucas v. South Carolina Coastal Council,* 505 U.S. 1003, 1036 (1992) (Blackmun, J., dissenting).

54. Ibid., at 1044.

55. Ibid., at 1055.

56. Ibid., at 1060.

57. Molly [McUsic] to Blackmun, June 25, 1992, Blackmun Papers, Box 599.

58. Scalia draft dissent, *Lucas v. South Carolina Coastal Council,* Blackmun Papers, Box 599.

CHAPTER 13: MASTER OF THE BARBED OPINION

1. The research for this chapter was aided by the student papers of Charles Prutzman, "Justice Antonin Scalia, 1992–1994," and Todd Marschall, "Justice Antonin Scalia: Life Cycle Analysis: 1995–97 Terms," in my "Personality and Judicial Decision-Making" senior seminar course at Lafayette College.

2. Adam Liptak, "A Sign of the Court's Polarization: The Choice of Clerks," *New York Times,* September 6, 2010, http://www.nytimes.com/2010/09/07/us/politics/07clerks.html?pagewanted=all.

3. Nina Totenberg interview.

4. *Lamb's Chapel v. Center Moriches School District,* 508 U.S. 384, at 396 (1993) (White, J., majority).

5. Ibid., at 398 (Scalia, J., dissenting).

6. Ibid., at 399.

7. Ruth Marcus, "Judge Breyer May See Clinton Today," *Washington Post,* June 11, 1993.

8. Ruth Marcus, "Clinton's Unexpected Choice Is Women's Rights Pioneer," *Washington Post,* June 15, 1993.

9. Philip Allen Lacovara, "Un-Courtly Manners: Quarrelsome Justices Are No Longer a Model of Civility for Lawyers," *ABA Journal,* December 1994, p. 50.

10. Ibid., p. 52.

11. Ibid.

12. *Board of Education of Kiryas Joel Village School District v. Grumet,* 512 U.S. 687, 690 (1994) (Souter J., majority).

13. Ibid., at 696.

14. Ibid., at 706.

15. Ibid., at 732 (Scalia, J., dissenting).

16. Ibid., at 735–36.

17. Ibid., at 743.

18. Ibid., at 708 (Souter, J., majority).

19. Ibid., at 709.

20. Ibid., at 748 (Scalia, J., dissenting).

21. Ibid., at 752.

22. This view is bolstered by the fact that Blackmun quietly deposited a several-hundred-page oral history with the Library of Congress that was released just five years after his death, in 2004, when many of his colleagues were still on the bench dealing with the same issues that he had faced. (This new tradition of retiring so that the other party, in this case the Democrats, would get the appointment to keep the ideological balance on the Court more in tune with what the liberal retirees had supported was continued by David Souter in 2009, and John Paul Stevens in 2010.)

23. *McIntyre v. Ohio Elections Commission,* 514 U.S. 334 (1995).

24. Ibid., at 342 (Stevens, J., majority).

25. Ibid., at 346.

26. Ibid., at 357.

27. Ibid., at 371 (Scalia, J., dissenting).

28. Ibid.

29. Ibid., at 372.

30. Ibid., at 385. Scalia's anti–anonymous free speech position was a curious one for an originalist historian who was well aware of the fictitious names for anonymous speech used in the Founding Era by Thomas Paine, the authors of the *Federalist Papers,* the authors of the Anti-Federalist papers, and even the third chief justice of the United States Supreme Court, John Marshall, in defending the Court against attacks on the 1819 *McCulloch v. Maryland* state taxation of the national bank case. See Gerald Gunther, *John Marshall's Defense of McCulloch v. Maryland* (Palo Alto: Stanford University Press, 1970).

31. David Van Biem, Richard N. Ostling, Lisa H. Towle, et al., "The Gospel Truth?," *Time,* April 8, 1996, http://www.time.com/time/magazine/article/0,9171,984367,00.html #ixzz0v8DgjMwF.

32. I Corinthians 4:10, American King James Bible.

33. Though no text of the speech was released, quotes from the speech are taken from http://christianactionforisrael.org/isreport/fools.html. See also Eileen Loh, "Supreme Court Justice: Don't Be Afraid to Be a Christian," Associated Press, April 9, 1966; Tony Mauro, "Justice Scalia Says Religion, Reason Do Mix," *USA Today,* April 10, 1996; Joan Biskupic, "Scalia Makes the Case for Christianity," *Washington Post,* April 10, 1996; "We Are Fool's for Christ's Sake," Shalom Jerusalem Family, www.shalomeruslaem.com/heritage /heritage7.html/; and Rubel Shelly, "Fools for Christ's Sake," *Lovelines,* April 24, 1996.

34. Colman McCarthy, "Martyrs in Their Own Mind," *Washington Post,* April 23, 1996.

35. Richard Cohen, "Justice Scalia and the Worldly Wise," *Washington Post,* April 12, 1996.

36. Edd Doerr, "Scalia's Chutzpah," *Humanist,* July/August, 1996.

37. Quotes from the speech are taken from http://christianactionforisrael.org/isreport/fools .html.

38. Transcript of Scalia speech and question and answer session at Gregorian Pontifical University, June 13, 1996, Catholic News Service, http://www.catholicnews.com/data/stories/cns/960613.htm.

39. The Colorado amendment stated: "No Protected Status Based on Homosexual, Lesbian or Bisexual Orientation. Neither the State of Colorado, through any of its branches or departments, nor any of its agencies, political subdivisions, municipalities or school districts, shall enact, adopt or enforce any statute, regulation, ordinance or policy whereby homosexual, lesbian or bisexual orientation, conduct, practices or relationships shall constitute or otherwise be the basis of or entitle any person or class of persons to have or claim any minority status, quota preferences, protected status or claim of discrimination. This Section of the Constitution shall be in all respects self-executing."

40. *Romer v Evans,* 517 U.S. 620, 624 (1996) (Kennedy, J., majority).

41. Ibid., at 631.

42. Ibid., at 635–36.

43. Ibid., at 636 (Scalia, J., dissenting).

44. Ibid.

45. Ibid.

46. Ibid., at 638–39.

47. Ibid., at 644. Scalia's list of other state morality–based legislation is much longer; see the discussion of *Lawrence v. Texas* in chap. 16 and footnote 51.

48. Amy Davidson, "The Animus of Antonin Scalia," *New Yorker,* December 12, 2012, http://www.newyorker.com/online/blogs/comment/2012/12/the-moral-feelings-of-antonin-scalia.html.

49. Representative Barney Frank, "Why I Called Justice Scalia a Homophobe," *Huffington Post,* March 26, 2009, http://www.huffingtonpost.com/rep-barney-frank/why-i-called-justice-scal_b_179434.html.

50. *Romer v. Evans,* at 652 (Scalia, J., dissenting).

51. Scalia speech, "Constitutional Interpretation," Woodrow Wilson International Center for Scholars, Washington, D.C., March 14, 2005.

52. *BMW of North America v. Gore,* 517 U.S. 559, 572 (1996) (Stevens, J., majority).

53. Ibid., at 598 (Scalia, J., dissenting).

54. Ibid., at 599.

55. Ibid., at 600.

56. Ibid., at 607.

57. Scalia, "Constitutional Interpretation."

58. Ginsburg majority, *United States v. Virginia,* 518 U.S. 515, 545–46 (1996) (Ginsburg, J., majority).

59. Ibid., at 557.

60. Ibid., at 566 (Scalia, J., dissenting).

61. Ibid., at 567.

62. Ibid., at 569.

63. Ibid., at 570. Later, two of Scalia's law clerks, Steven G. Calabresi and Julia T. Rickert, used originalism theory to argue that the Constitution did protect women's rights here. See Calabresi and Rickert, "Originalism and Sex Discrimination," *Texas Law Review,* 90, no.1 (2011), p. 1ff.

64. *Rutan v. Republican Party of Illinois,* 497 U.S. 62 (1990).

65. *O'Hare Truck Service v. City of Northlake,* 518 U.S. 712 (1996).

66. *Board of County Commissioners v. Umbehr,* 518 U.S. 668 (1996).

67. *O'Hare Truck Service,* at pp. 723–24 (Kennedy, J., majority).

68. *Board of County Commissioners v. Umbehr,* at pp. 684–85 (O'Connor, J., majority).

69. Ibid., Scalia dissent *O'Hare* and *Umbehr,* p. 686.

70. Ibid., p. 687.

71. Biskupic, *American Original,* p. 220.

72. Ibid., p. 363.

73. *Board of County Commissioners,* at pp. 709–10 (Scalia, J., dissenting).

74. Ibid., at pp. 710–11.

75. Blackmun to Scalia, July 2, 1996, Blackmun Papers, Box 1408.

76. Scalia to Blackmun, July 2, 1996, Blackmun Papers, Box 1408.

CHAPTER 14: WAR OF THE WORDS

1. Chelsea Morse, "Constitutional Interpretation Undergoes Transformation," *Indiana Lawyer,* February 7, 1996; Scalia speech, "A Theory of Constitutional Interpretation," Catholic University of America, October 18, 1996, on *Ninoville* website, www.joink.com /homes/users/ninoville. My thanks to one of my senior seminar students, Jim Hlavenka, for dating this speech.

2. Antonin Scalia and Amy Guttman, *A Matter of Interpretation: Federal Courts and the Law* (Princeton: Princeton University Press, 1998), p. 3.

3. Ibid., p. 7.

4. Ibid., p. 13.

5. Ibid., p. 14.

6. Ibid., p. 17.

7. Ibid., p. 22.

8. Ibid., p. 23.

9. Ibid., p. 37.

10. Ibid., p. 38.

11. Ibid., p. 40.

12. Gordon S. Wood, "Comment," in ibid., p. 62.

13. Ibid., pp. 62–63.

14. Ibid., p. 63.

15. Scalia, *A Matter of Interpretation,* p. 131.

16. Morse, "Constitutional Interpretation Undergoes Transformation."

17. Philip Potempa, "Scalia Sees Misuse of Constitution," *South Bend Tribune,* January 24, 1996.

18. Scalia speech, "A Theory of Constitutional Interpretation."

19. Jack Rakove, *Original Meanings: Politics and Ideas in the Making of the Constitution* (New York: Vintage 1997), p. xv.

20. Ibid., pp. 9–10.

21. Ibid., p. 11.

22. Ibid., pp. 12–13.

23. Ibid., p. 13.

24. Ibid., pp. 21–22.

25. Ibid., pp. 367–68.

26. *New York v. United States,* 505 U.S. 144, 158 (1992) (O'Connor, J., majority).

27. *Printz v. United States,* 521 U.S. 898, 944–45 (1997) (Scalia, J., majority).

28. Ibid., at 909.

29. Ibid., at 910–11.
30. Ibid., at 916.
31. Ibid., at 936.
32. Ibid., at 940.
33. Ibid., at 946 (Stevens, J., dissenting).
34. Ibid., at 959–60.
35. Ibid., at 966.
36. *Clinton v. New York,* 524 U.S. 417, 439 (1998) (Stevens, J., majority).
37. Ibid., at 440.
38. Ibid., at 447.
39. Ibid., at 466 (Scalia, J., dissenting).
40. Ibid., at 469.
41. "Governor George W. Bush, Republican from Texas and a GOP Presidential Candidate, Talks About His Bid for the Presidency, Other Presidential Candidates and His Political Career," *Meet the Press,* NBC News transcript, November 21, 1999.
42. Warren Richey, "The Next Supreme Court Majority," *Christian Science Monitor,* January 20, 2000.
43. Richard Willing, "Abortion Case Could Put Campaign Spotlight on the Court," *USA Today,* January 17, 2000.
44. Frank J. Murray, "Election Could Reshape Court; Candidates Eager to Appoint Justices," *Washington Times,* October 16, 2000.
45. Kim Eisler, "Supreme Court's High Honor but Low Pay Could Send Justice Scalia Job Hunting," *Washingtonian,* March 2000.
46. Murray, "Election Could Reshape Court."
47. Eisler, "Supreme Court's High Honor but Low Pay Could Send Justice Scalia Job Hunting."
48. Robert Novak, "Scalia Hints He'll Quit High Court if Gore Wins," *Chicago Sun-Times,* April, 2, 2000.
49. There was a third loss for Scalia in that term as well. In *Troxel v. Granville* (530 U.S. 57 [2000]) the Court reviewed a case involving a request by grandparents in Washington State to be granted visitation rights to their granddaughters, the children of their son, who had committed suicide, and a woman to whom he was never married and who had denied the grandparents' visitation rights.

Justice O'Connor ruled that the reason the mother excluded the grandparents from visiting the children had more to do with a "mere disagreement" between the parties, and nothing to do with either any allegations that the mother was now an "unfit parent," or any other factors that would affect the "child's [*sic*] best interests." Since the lower court had incorrectly placed on the mother, who was "the fit custodial parent, the burden of disproving that visitation would be in the best interest of her daughters," O'Connor reversed that decision, saying that it was not the correct judicial standard here.

Speaking in dissent, Antonin Scalia returned to his originalism theory to propose a different resolution of the child visitation rights question. For him, then, the decision to assign those rights should be left to the political branches, as voted into office by the people, rather than be determined by the discretion of Supreme Court justices.
50. *Miranda v. Arizona,* 384 U.S. 436 (1966) (Warren, C. J., majority).
51. 18 United States Code, Section 3501.
52. *Michigan v. Tucker* 417, U.S. 433 (1974).
53. *Dickerson v. United States,* 530 U.S. 428 at 437–38 (2000) (Rehnquist, C. J., majority).

54. Ibid., at 437.

55. Ibid., at 443.

56. Ibid., at 424. The *Miranda* case has been cut back so extensively that it now offers much less protection, if any at all, to suspects. See *Rhode Island v. Innis,* 446 U.S. 291 (1980); *New York v. Quarles,* 467 U.S. 649 (1984); *Mary Berghuis, Warden v. Van Chester Thompkins,* 560 U.S. (2010); *J.D.B. v. North Carolina,* 564 U.S. _ (2011).

57. Ibid., p. 434 (Scalia, J., dissenting).

58. *Stenberg v. Carhart,* 530 U.S. 914, 945–46 (2000) (Breyer, J., majority).

59. Ibid., at 953 (Scalia, J., dissenting).

60. Ibid., at 954–55.

61. Ibid., at 955.

62. Ibid., at 956.

63. Tony Mauro and Sam Loewenberg, "Who Really Wants to Lift Ban on Fees?," *Legal Times,* September 18, 2000, www.nationallaw journal.com.

64. "Stevens Now a Millionaire, Supreme Court Filings Show," *Washington Post,* June 7, 1990.

65. "Judges Fail to Fully Comply with Financial Disclosure Rules," (Minneapolis) *Star Tribune,* 1994, http://www.google.com/search?q=Scalia+financial+disclosure&hl=en&client =firefox-a&hs=yAT&rls=org.mozilla:en-US:official&prmd=ivns&ei=_XEqTdPvEY=u8 Ab_1tjKAQ&start=10&sa=N.

66. Mauro and Loewenberg, "Who Really Wants to Lift Ban on Fees?"

67. "Ban Lifted on Speaking Fees for U.S. Workers," *New York Times,* March 31, 1993.

68. Scalia, "Text of Scalia's Letter on Reinstating Honoraria," *The Recorder,* September 18, 2000.

69. Frank J. Murray, "Irate Scalia Lashes Out at Resignation Rumors," *Washington Times,* October 3, 2000; Anne Gearan, "Supreme Court Justice Complains of 'Mean-Spirited Attack,'" Associated Press, October 2, 2000; "Scalia Strikes Back at Reporter," Newsmax.com, October 5, 2000; "Justice Scalia Tears into Newspaper, Denies His Needs Led Him to Back Pay Hike," SFGate.com, October 3, 2000.

CHAPTER 15: BUSH V. GORE

1. http://www.authentichistory.com/1993–2000/3-2000election/2-electionnight/index .html.

2. Evan Thomas and Michael Isikoff, "The Truth Behind the Pillars," *Newsweek,* December 25, 2000; Jeffrey Toobin, *Too Close to Call: The Thirty-Six-Day Battle to Decide the 2000 Election* (New York: Random House, 2002); Jeffrey Toobin, *The Nine: Inside the Secret World of the Supreme Court* (New York: Doubleday, 2007); Jess Bravin, "Supreme Interests: For Some Justices, the Bush-Gore Case Has a Personal Angle," *Wall Street Journal,* December 12, 2000.

3. Thomas and Isikoff, "The Truth Behind the Pillars."

4. Toobin, *Too Close to Call,* p. 249. A good collection of the articles about the case can be found in Richard K. Neumann Jr., "Conflicts of Interest in *Bush v. Gore*: Did Some Justices Vote Illegally?," *Georgetown Journal of Legal Ethics* 16 (Spring, 2003): 375–78.

5. http://www.authentichistory.com/1993–2000/3-2000election/2-electionnight/index .html.

6. Gore would eventually have one "faithless elector" from D.C. who refused to vote for him, putting his final count at 266.

7. Joan Biskupic, *Sandra Day O'Connor: How the First Woman on the Supreme Court Became Its Most Influential Justice* (New York: Ecco/HarperCollins, 2005), p. 303.

8. Bruce Allen Murphy, *The Brandeis/Frankfurter Connection: The Secret Political Activities of Two Supreme Court Justices* (New York: Oxford University Press, 1982). See also L. Anthony Sutin, "Presidential Election Law/The Recount," *Jurist Legal Intelligence,* December 14, 2000, http://jurist.law.pitt.edu/election/electionfaq.html. For my understanding of the complex law in *Bush v. Gore* I am indebted to Sutin, the former dean of Appalachian School of Law and expert in election law at Hogan & Hartson who worked in various Democratic Party campaigns and groups on this issue. Two years after writing this, Dean Sutin was tragically killed in a mass shooting at his law school.

9. For more on this timing, see the chronology of the recount and legal battle in Toobin, *Too Close to Call,* pp. xv–xix. As the recount proceeded in the various Florida counties, continuing reports surfaced of votes being lost because minority voters were denied access to the polls, and senior citizen voters in Palm Beach were baffled by the so-called butterfly ballot. As a result, thousands of voters in the county believed they had mistakenly voted for third-party conservative candidate Patrick Buchanan instead of, as they intended, the Democratic candidate, Al Gore. Perhaps because of this, Buchanan received far more votes than anticipated in the liberal county. Then came the question of whether votes could be counted even when a hole was not punched cleanly through the card. They also tried to interpret the meaning of ballots with "undervotes" for the presidential race, which the voting machine could not read and thus did not count, or where there was a missing vote on an otherwise completed ballot, and "overvotes," ballots that had more than one hole punched for a single office.

10. "Doris Kearns Goodwin and William Safire Discuss the Legal Battles in the Presidential Election," *Meet the Press,* NBC News, November 19, 2000.

11. *Palm Beach County Canvassing Board v. Katherine Harris,* 772 So. 2d 1220 (2000).

12. The process of vote count certification in Florida is outlined in Toobin, *Too Close to Call,* pp. 190–91.

13. David Margolick, "The Path to Florida," *Vanity Fair,* October 2000, p. 320.

14. Ibid.

15. Toobin, *Too Close to Call,* p. 248.

16. *Gore v. Harris,* 772 So. 2d 1243, December 8, 2000.

17. Margolick, "The Path to Florida," p. 322.

18. Ibid.

19. Bob Woodward and Charles Lane, "Scalia Takes a Leading Role in Case," *Washington Post,* December 11, 2000.

20. Ibid.

21. Stevens interview with Scott Pelley, *60 Minutes,* November 28, 2010. Stevens would add to his recollection of this encounter in his memoir, *Five Chiefs: A Supreme Court Memoir* (New York: Little, Brown, 2011): "We agreed that the application was frivolous. To secure a stay, a litigant must show that one is necessary to prevent a legally cognizable irreparable injury. Bush's attorneys had failed to make any such showing. . . . Justice Breyer expressed the same opinion, and we went our separate ways confidently assuming that the stay application would be denied when we met the next day" (pp. 198–99).

22. *Bush v. Gore* (Certiorari/Stay Application Order 531 U.S. 1046, 1047 December 9, 2000) (Stevens, J., dissenting).

23. Ibid., at 1047–48.

24. Ibid., at 1048–9 (Scalia, J., dissenting). On the timing of the opinion, see Margolick, "The Path to Florida," p. 355.

25. Margolick, "The Path to Florida," p. 355.

26. *Bush v. Gore,* Oral Argument, Oyez Project, http://www.oyez.org/print/58961.

27. Margolick, "The Path to Florida," p. 356.

28. Jan Crawford Greenburg, *Supreme Conflict: The Inside Story of the Struggle for Control of the United States Supreme Court* (New York: Penguin, 2008), pp. 174–77; and Margolick, "The Path to Florida," p. 356.

29. Margolick, "The Path to Florida," p. 356.

30. Ibid.

31. *Bush v. Gore,* 531 U.S. 98, 104 (2000) (*per curiam* opinion).

32. Ibid., at 108.

33. Ibid., at 111.

34. Margolick, "The Path to Florida," p. 357.

35. *Bush v. Gore,* at 109 (*per curiam* opinion).

36. Ibid., at 111 (*per curiam* opinion).

37. Ibid., at 114 (Rehnquist, C.J., concurring).

38. Ibid., at 129 (Stevens, J., dissenting).

39. Ibid., at 157–58 (Breyer, J., dissenting).

40. Margolick, "The Path to Florida," p. 357.

41. Toobin, *The Nine,* pp. 173–74; Toobin, *Too Close to Call,* p. 266; also cited in Margolick, "The Path to Florida," p. 357.

42. Linda Greenhouse, "Bush Prevails, by Single Vote, Justices End Recount, Blocking Gore After 5-Week Struggle," *New York Times,* December 13, 2000.

43. Less commonly known, though, is that in seizing for itself the duty of determining the outcome in this highly political question, the Court had circumvented another even more clear democratic process for determining the winner of the presidential election—one already established by law by Congress. According to Title III, Chapter 1, Section 15 of the United States Code, which deals with the counting of the Electoral College votes in presidential elections, the 2000 vote count should have been headed to the two chambers of the new, incoming 107th Congress for formal counting. The result would have been one of the most unusual events coming from an obscure dark corner of American politics that could be the subject of a good political novel. By federal law, the new Congress is required to convene on January 6 after the states' electors have met to count the Electoral College votes and certify the winner of the presidency. Had the Supreme Court not intervened, once Governor Jeb Bush certified the twenty-five Republican electors to Congress on Sunday, November 26, the two different slates of electors from Florida should have been submitted to Congress for counting. Title III, Chapter 1, Section 15 allows for objections in writing to be made to these state certifications, with the determination as to which slate will be counted left to a separate vote by both houses of Congress. Each house of the newly sworn in Congress is then instructed to "withdraw" and separately consider the various contesting Electoral College slates before casting votes choosing one of them. If both houses agree on a result, then that slate is counted. However, both houses of the new 107th Congress were not going to agree on this issue. At the time, there were 221 Republicans and 212 Democrats in the House, meaning that the Republican slate from Florida would have been chosen by that body. In the Senate, though, it was 50–50. By constitutional rule, it would be left to the president of the Sen-

ate, the sitting vice president, to cast the tie-breaking vote. Until January 20, that was Al Gore, whose vote would certainly have gone to the Democratic slate of electors that supported his election. Both houses of Congress would have been split on the determination of the assignment of the Florida Electoral College vote.

The federal vote-counting law had a solution for just this circumstance. With both houses of Congress splitting on the determination of the Florida Electoral College vote, Title III, Chapter 1, Section 15 is clear on who casts the tie-breaking vote: "If the two Houses shall disagree in respect of the counting of such votes, then, and in that case, the votes of the electors whose appointment shall have been certified by the executive of the State, under the seal thereof, shall be counted." In short, the governor of the disputed state, in this case Florida, would be the final determiner of which slate of electors from that state would be counted. *That* is why the result of the election would not have changed regardless of the Supreme Court's action. As the duly elected governor of Florida, even the most diehard Democrat would have to agree that, according to this federal law, Jeb Bush was empowered by Congress to settle the matter. By circumventing the voting process, disregarding the political question doctrine by which it should have avoided deciding this case, and ignoring states' rights issue involved here, while also deciding in favor of the Fourteenth Amendment Equal Protection Clause for a voting case, and limiting the precedential impact of this case as applying only to this case, the conservative majority had spared the nation the embarrassment of having Florida's governor, Jeb Bush, pick his own brother, George W. Bush, for the presidency.

For more, see L. Anthony Sutin, "Presidential Election Law/The Recount," *Jurist Legal Intelligence,* December 14, 2000, http://jurist.law.pitt.edu/election/electionfaq .html. And a reading of Title III, Chapter 1, Section 15 in the U.S. Code, Cornell University, Legal Information Institute, http://www.law.cornell.edu/uscode/html/uscode03 /usc_sec_03_00000015—000-.html. The process of certification in Florida is outlined in Toobin, *Too Close to Call,* pp. 190–91; Sutin suggests one more possible outcome: if somehow it was determined that Al Gore had actually won the popular vote, by Florida law the presidential electors, even members of the Republican electoral slate, were bound to vote for the winner of the popular election.

44. Greenburg, *Supreme Conflict,* p. 32.

45. Sandra Day O'Connor interview with Wolf Blitzer, *The Situation Room,* January 28, 2010. A few moments later, Blitzer asked, "So the right man was elected president?" "Well, the man who got the most votes," she responded. To Jan Crawford Greenburg, she added, "Could we have done a better job? Probably. But it wouldn't have changed the result." Greenburg, *Supreme Conflict,* p. 32.

46. Dahleen Glanton, "O'Connor Questions Court's Decision to Take Bush v. Gore," *Chicago Tribune,* April 27, 2013, www.chicagotribune.com. See also Rachel Weiner, "O'Connor: Maybe Supreme Court Shouldn't Have Taken Bush v. Gore," *Washington Post,* April 29, 2013, www.washingtonpost.com.

47. Scalia speech, University of Fribourg, Switzerland, March 8, 2006, www.bafweb.com, bureau audiovisuel francophone.

48. Interview with Antonin Scalia, by reporter Lesley Stahl, *60 Minutes,* CBS News, April 27, 2008; Scalia interview with Brian Lamb, "Q and A" program, May 4, 2008, C-SPAN, transcript found at http://www.q-and-a.org/Transcript/?ProgramID=1178; Interview with Scalia, *Charlie Rose Show,* PBS, June 20, 2008); Legally speaking, blog Calvin Massey, "The Originalist," January, 2011, found at http://www.callawyer.com /story.cfm?eid=913358&evid=1.

49. Display ad, "554 Law Professors Say," *New York Times,* January 13, 2001, funded by the liberal lobbying group People for the American Way.

50. See Robert Post and Reva Siegel, "Originalism as a Political Practice: The Right's Living Constitution," *Fordham Law Review* 75 (2006): 562; and Jack Balkin, *Balkinization,* October 10, 2004, http://balkin.blogspot.com/; both cited in Alan Dershowitz memo, "Scalia's Inconsistent Originalism, Reordered by Case Strength," December 4, 2008.

CHAPTER 16: SCALIA VS. THE POPE

1. This chapter benefited from the perspectives of several students who wrote seminar papers for my senior seminar course at Lafayette College: "Personality and Judicial Decision-Making," dealing with the impact of Scalia's Catholicism on his work on the Court; Allison Ligorano, "Italian Catholic Justices and Their Individual Differences in Judicial Decision-Making as a Result of Difference in Catholic Upbringing"; Lori Weaver, "Scalito or Alitist? The Future Evolutions of Justice Scalia and Justice Alito"; Amy Polizanno, "2002: A Catholic Justice Emerges"; Matt Soper, "Antonin Scalia: Originalist Martyr"; Katerina Mantell, "Antonin Scalia: A Catholic Justice: A Life Cycle Analysis." It also benefited from work done by four students—Allison Ligorano, Amy Polizzano, Lori Weaver, and Colleen Sullivan—under a Lafayette College Community of Scholars grant from the Mellon Foundation.

2. Molly Redden, "Rick Santorum's Virginia Church and *Opus Dei,*" *New Republic,* March 6, 2012, http://www.newrepublic.com/article/politics/101420/santorums-church -opus-dei#; Bill Broadway and David Cho, "Quiet Great Falls, Va., Parish Draws Famous, Demure Crowd," *Washington Post,* April 5, 2001, http://news.google.com /newspapers?nid=1774&dat=20010405&id=ElUhAAAAIBAJ&sjid=6YQFAAAAI BAJ&pg=6747,7664314; Michelle Boorstein, "Rare Latin Mass a Return to Ritual," *Washington Post,* June 4, 2006, http://www.washingtonpost.com/wp-dyn/content /article/2006/06/03/AR2006060300227.html.

3. "Music Schedule and Information," http://st-catherines.net.

4. Opus Dei began in 1928, when Spanish priest Josemaría Escrivá de Balaguer returned from a spiritual retreat in Madrid proclaiming that he received a vision from God to create this organization. He envisioned it as a conservative secular institute within the Catholic Church seeking to preserve its religious mission of a universal call to holiness. The best book on Opus Dei is John L. Allen, *Opus Dei: An Objective Look Behind the Myths and Reality of the Most Controversial Force in the Catholic Church* (New York: Doubleday, 2005). See also Robert Hutchison, *Their Kingdom Come: Inside the Secret World of Opus Dei* (New York: St. Martin's Press, 1998); and Michael Walsh, *Opus Dei: An Investigation into the Powerful, Secretive Society Within the Catholic Church* (San Francisco: Harper, 2004). Opus Dei lay members pursue their religious mission by observing Escrivá's admonition to practice "humility" and rely on discretion even to the point of secrecy. Members of the organization are forbidden to flaunt any evidence of their religion, or use the organization for personal or professional gain, that might separate them from other Catholics. Some believe that the most dedicated of its members practice self-sacrifice by sleeping on a board or the floor once a week, and commemorating the crucifixion of Jesus through "self-mortification," beating themselves with a cord whip called a "discipline" and wearing an uncomfortable hair shirt undergarment or even a spiked chain, called a "cilice," designed to break the skin of their upper thigh for a period of time each day in order to induce constant pain. Others see this organization as "the

elite guard of God," staffed by the most dedicated of the Catholic faith's followers, and criticize it as a secretive and conspiratorial cult.

Of the billion or so Catholics in the world, there are said to be fewer than ninety thousand Opus Dei members in the world, with three thousand or so in the United States. The everyday practice of Opus Dei members is to "strive for holiness in everyday life through strict adherence to the Roman Catholic Church's teachings, at work and at home." Members pray daily, and attend days of recollection, retreats, and workshops, which help them to strictly observe their devout faith. They also attend traditional Masses in Latin, and usually they are members of parishes that observe pre–Vatican II strictures.

5. "Jose Maria Escriva" website, found at http://www.escrivaworks.org/doc/opus_dei.htm.
6. Allen, *Opus Dei,* p. 4.
7. Mark Karlin, "Pope Francis Has Antonin 'Opus Dei' Scalia's Undies in a Bunch," December 20, 2013, Buzzflash.com, found at truth=out.org.
8. "Ministries and Organizations," St. Catherine of Siena Church website, http://st-catherines.net/organ.php; "Programs at Reston Study Center," Reston Study Center website, http://www.restonstudycenter.org. These spiritual activities are pursued at Longlea in the Blue Ridge Mountains of Virginia, and conducted by Opus Dei priests, who operate within the Prelature of the Catholic Church.
9. "Tridentine Travelogue: Old St. Mary's, Washington, D.C.," *Tridentine Community News,* June 17, 2007, http://www.detroitlatinmass.org/jospht/61707.pdf; Michelle Boorstein, "Rare Latin Mass a Return to Ritual," *Washington Post,* June 4, 2006.
10. See Mike Whitney, "Scalia and Opus Dei: Radicals on the High Court," *Counterpunch,* January 17–18, 2004, http://www.counterpunch.org/whitney01172004.html; Allen, *Opus Dei;* Hutchison, *Their Kingdom Come;* Walsh, *Opus Dei;* Frank Cocozzelli, "An Opus Focus on SCOTUS?," May 2, 2007, No. 26; May 5, 2007, No. 27; May 13, 2007, No. 28, www.streetprophets.com; "What One More 'Fundamentalist' US Supreme Court Justice Will Do to Constitutional Law in Our Country," *Time for Change's Journal,* February 18, 2008, http://journals.democraticunderground.com; Ron Grossman, "Catholics Scrutinize Enigmatic Opus Dei," *Chicago Tribune,* December 7, 2003; Sharon Clasen, "How Opus Dei Is Cult-Like," Opus Dei Awareness Network, and Alexander Cockburn and Jeffrey St. Clair, http://www.odan.org/tw_how_opus_dei_is_cult_like.htm; "Scalia and Opus Dei: Radicals on the High Court," *Counterpunch,* January 17/18, 2004, www.counterpunch.org/whitney; and Mark Karlin, "Pope Francis Has Antonin 'Opus Dei' Scalia's Undies in a Bunch."

Scalia is not alone in this regard, as others have speculated, though it has never been confirmed, that Clarence Thomas and the other conservative Catholics on the Supreme Court might also be members of the organization. Such criticism of highly visible Catholic public officials was also made against Democratic presidential candidate John F. Kennedy in 1960.

11. Whitney, "Scalia and Opus Dei."
12. Allen, *Opus Dei,* pp. 145, 278.
13. *Evangelium Vitae,* paragraph 27, March 25, 1995, http://www.vatican.va/holy_father/john_paul_ii/encyclicals/documents/hf_jp-ii_enc_25031995_evangelium-vitae_en.html.
14. Ibid., paragraph 56.
15. Catholic Catechism, p. 2267, cited in Sister Helen Prejean, *The Death of Innocents: An Eyewitness Account of Wrongful Execution* (New York: Vintage, 2006), p. 282. This section of the Catechism of the Catholic Church can be found in its Part III, Life in Christ,

Section II: The Ten Commandments, Chapter 2, "You Shall Love Your Neighbor as Yourself," Article 5, 5th Commandment, paragraph 2267.

16. Session 3, "Religion, Politics, and the Death Penalty," for the "A Call for Reckoning: Religion and the Death Penalty" conference transcript, January 25, 2002, thttp://features .pewforum.org/death-penalty/resources/transcript3.html.

17. See also Romans 13: 1–5. On the view of St. Paul (St. James Edition of the Bible): "Let every soul be subject unto the higher powers. For there is no power but of God: the powers that be are ordained of God. Whosoever therefore resisteth the power, resisteth the ordinance of God: and they that resist shall receive to themselves damnation. For rulers are not a terror to good works, but to the evil. Wilt thou then not be afraid of the power? Do that which is good, and thou shalt have praise of the same: for he is the minister of God to thee for good. But if thou do that which is evil, be afraid; for he beareth not the sword in vain: for he is the minister of God, a revenger to execute wrath upon him that doeth evil. Wherefore ye must needs be subject, not only for wrath, but also for conscience sake."

18. Sam Harris, *The End of Faith: Religion, Terror, and the Future of Reason* (New York: W. W. Norton, 2004), pp. 156–57.

19. Ibid., p. 158.

20. Antonin Scalia, "God's Justice and Ours," *First Things,* May 2002, pp. 17–21. Issue Archive found at www.firstthings.com.

21. Ibid.

22. Ibid.

23. Ibid.

24. Prejean, *The Death of Innocents,* p. 173. See also Sister Helen Prejean, *Dead Man Walking: An Eyewitness Account of the Death Penalty in the United States* (New York: Vintage, 1994).

25. Scalia, "God's Justice and Ones," pp. 17–21.

26. Prejean, *The Death of Innocents,* p. 176.

27. Ibid.

28. Ibid., pp. 178–79.

29. *Atkins v. Virginia,* 536 U.S. 304, at 312 (2002) (Stevens, J., majority).

30. *Penry v. Lynaugh,* 492 U.S. 302 (1989).

31. *Atkins v. Virginia,* at 321 (Stevens, J., majority).

32. Ibid., at 365 (Scalia, J., dissenting).

33. Ibid., at 370.

34. Kiran Krishnamurthy, "Scalia: Religion Has Its Place," *Richmond Times Dispatch,* January 13, 2003.

35. "Ethicists Don't See Scalia Sitting Out Most Church-State Cases," Associated Press, October 20, 2003, www.firstamendmencenter.org/news.aspz?id=122092.

36. Tony Mauro, "Scalia Recusal Revives Debate over Judicial Speech, Ethics," *Legal Times,* October 20, 2003, www.law.com, citing Gina Holland of the Associated Press.

37. Ibid.

38. *Elk Grove Unified School District v. Newdow,* 542 U.S. 1 (2004). See also "Federal Appeals Court in California Upholds 'Under God' in Pledge of Allegiance," March 11, 2010, http://www.foxnews.com/politics/2010/03/11/federal-appeals-court-california-upholds -god-pledge-allegiance.

39. David G. Savage, "Some 'Mystified' by Awards to Scalia for Free Speech," *Los Angeles Times,* March 18, 2003.

40. Ibid.

41. Years later, then Cardinal Bevilacqua was caught up in the charges over the Philadelphia Catholic Church's obstruction of justice in the parish priest pedophilia investigation, and was facing a court trial on this issue when he died in 2012. Robert Huber, "Catholics in Crisis: Sex and Deception in the Philadelphia Archdiocese," *Philadelphia,* July 2011, http://www.phillymag.com/articles/catholics-in-crisis-sex-and-deception-in -the-archdiocese-of-philadelphia/; MaryClaire Dale, "Philadelphia Priest Trial: Cardinal Anthony Bevilacqua Shredded List of Accused Priests' Names," *Huffington Post,* April 13, 2012, http://www.huffingtonpost.com/2012/04/13/philadelphia-priest-trial -anthony-bevilacqua-shredded-list_n_1423823.html; Matthew Archbold, "Was Cardinal Bevilacqua Murdered?," *National Catholic Register,* February 10, 2012, http://www .ncregister.com/blog/matthew-archbold/was-cardinal-bevilacqua-murdered.

42. *Lawrence v. Texas,* 539 U.S. 548 (2003).

43. "Scalia Speech Under Scrutiny," March 8, 2004, www.cbsnews.com.

44. Ibid., *Lawrence v. Texas,* at 562 (Kennedy, J., majority). See also *Bowers v. Hardwick,* 539 U.S. 558 (1987).

45. *Lawrence v. Texas,* 571 (Kennedy, J., majority).

46. Ibid., at 575.

47. Ibid., at p. 578.

48. Joan Biskupic, "Gay Sex Ban Struck Down," *USA Today,* June 27, 2003.

49. *Lawrence v. Texas,* at 586 (Scalia, J., dissenting).

50. Ibid., at 586.

51. Ibid., at 599. In another part of the opinion he cites: "State laws against bigamy, same-sex marriage, adult incest, prostitution, masturbation, adultery, fornication, bestiality, and obscenity . . ."

52. Ibid., at 602.

53. Ibid., at 604–5.

54. Anne Gearan, "Scalia Ridicules Court's Gay Sex Ruling," Associated Press Online, October 24, 2003.

55. Adam Liptak, "In Re Scalia the Outspoken v. Scalia the Reserved," *New York Times,* May 2, 2004.

56. Dahlia Lithwick, "Scaliapalooza," *Slate,* October 30, 2003.

57. Liptak, "In Re Scalia the Outspoken v. Scalia the Reserved."

CHAPTER 17: QUACK, QUACK

1. David Savage and Richard A. Serrano, "Scalia Was Cheney Hunt Trip Guest," *Los Angeles Times,* February 5, 2004. Background on this incident also benefited greatly from the account offered by Jeffrey Toobin, *The Nine: Inside the Secret World of the Supreme Court* (New York: Doubleday, 2007, pp. 201–4).

2. *Cheney v. United States District Court for the District of Columbia,* 542 U.S. 367 (2004).

3. Lee Iacocca, *Where Have All the Leaders Gone?* (New York: Scribner, 2007), p. 90.

4. *United States v. Nixon,* 418 U.S. 683 (1974).

5. See *Kansas v. Crane,* 534 U.S. 407 (2002).

6. David G. Savage and Richard A. Serrano, "Scalia Took Trip Set Up by Lawyer in Two Cases," *Los Angeles Times,* February 27, 2004.

7. See Scalia's statement attached to ibid.

8. U.S. Code, Title 28, Part I, Chapter 21, Section 455(a), at Cornell University Law School

site, www.la.cornell.edu; compared to ABA Model Code of Judicial Conduct, 2000 Edition, Center for Professional responsibility, www.abanet.org.

9. David Savage, "Trip with Cheney Puts Ethics Spotlight on Scalia," *Los Angeles Times,* January 17, 2004.

10. Appellate Court Brief for *Cheney v. United States District Court for the District of Columbia,* 542 U.S. 367 (2004), filed by Public Citizen Litigation and Sierra Club, 2004 WL 3741418 (U.S.), February 24, 2004, Lexis/Nexis, 003 U.S. Briefs 475; 2004 U.S. S. Ct. Briefs Lexis/Nexis 230, March 11, 2004. Internet version at http://newsandinsight .thomsonreuters.com/uploadedFiles/Reuters_Content/2012/12_-_December/sierraclub vcheney—recusalmotion.pdf.

11. Ibid.

12. The memo issued before the final case decision was Scalia, *Cheney v. United States District Court for the District of Columbia,* 541 U.S. 913 (2004).

13. Ibid.

14. Ibid. Scalia cited the examples of Justice Byron White's friendship with Attorney General Robert F. Kennedy, and Robert Jackson's socializing with President Franklin Roosevelt or members of the executive branch, both of whom still sat on cases involving those officials that were pending before the Court at that time. Scalia concluded: "The question, simply put, is whether someone who thought I could decide this case impartially despite my friendship with the Vice President would reasonably believe that I cannot decide it impartially because I went hunting with that friend and accepted an invitation to fly there with him on a Government plane. If it is reasonable to think that a Supreme Court Justice can be bought so cheap, the Nation is in deeper trouble than I had imagined. . . . If I could have done so in good conscience, I would have been pleased to demonstrate my integrity, and immediately silence the criticism, by getting off the case. Since I believe there is no basis for recusal, I cannot. The motion is denied."

15. *Cheney v. United States District Court for the District of Columbia,* 542 U.S. 367 (2004).

16. Bruce Allen Murphy, *The Brandeis/Frankfurter Connection: The Secret Political Activities of Two Supreme Court Justices* (New York: Oxford University Press, 1982). For the larger argument on the standard for judging extrajudicial activities, see Bruce Allen Murphy, "Extrajudicial Activities," in *Encyclopedia of the Supreme Court of the United States,* David S. Tanenhaus, ed. (New York: Macmillan Reference USA, 2008).

What is the standard by which one can "reasonably" question whether a justice's "impartiality [can or should] be questioned"? Extrajudicial, or off-the-bench, activities of Supreme Court justices can involve something as innocuous as giving a speech, being a member of any organization, or writing books and teaching classes. They can also include politically involved activities such as suggesting, lobbying for, or even drafting legislation or speeches by political figures. (For more, see Bruce Allen Murphy and David Levy, "Preserving the Progressive Spirit in a Conservative Time: The Joint Reform Efforts of Justice Louis D. Brandeis and Professor Felix Frankfurter, 1916–1933, *Michigan Law Review,* vol. 78, no. 8, August 1980.)

Because of the guiding ethical tradition established by the actions and mistakes made by justices in these decisions over the years, the range and extent of extrajudicial activities by Supreme Court justices has ebbed and flowed. Change in the standard governing them has only occurred when justices have created self-inflicted wounds for the Court by going too far in their political activity, becoming exposed and facing intense public criticism. In the nineteenth century, Justice John Catron and his colleague Robert C. Grier went too far after the 1856 presidential election when they leaked to newly elected president James Buchanan the Court's not yet announced decision in the slavery case, *Dred Scott v. Sandford,* which ruled the Missouri Compromise unconstitutional. This enabled Buchanan to predict in his inaugural address that the slavery issue would be "speedily and finally settled by the Supreme Court." The public uproar over this leak and connection between the members of the Court and the new president resulted in a new informal standard against such behavior. The tradition that Supreme Court justices do not run for president, or elected office, from the bench was established in 1916 when Justice Charles Evans Hughes was drafted by the Republican Party to run for president against Democrat Woodrow Wilson, and he resigned from the bench to do so. Hughes narrowly lost the election, owing to his inability to win California, and then was reappointed to the bench in 1930 as the Supreme Court's chief justice.

By the twentieth century, Justices Louis Brandeis and Felix Frankfurter developed a new, more secretive manner for advising the executive branch by engaging in political activities by proxy. After his Court appointment in 1916, Brandeis put thousands of dollars into a fund to support the progressive reform lobbying by Harvard Law professor Felix Frankfurter. In this manner, Brandeis hid his political involvement from public view by suggesting to Frankfurter the ideas for articles to be written in law reviews, policies such as federal unemployment insurance to be developed and promoted, political appointments to be sought, and even pieces of New Deal legislation to be drafted. While these activities did not become publicly known until years later, they instructed Frankfurter as to how he could operate politically after he was appointed to the Court in 1939. Despite his status as a justice he maintained his longtime advising relationship with his good friend President Roosevelt on an even wider range of issues than Brandeis had pursued. He suggested numerous appointments to the administration, proposed pieces of legislation, and personally visited the president to consult with him. (For more here, see Bruce Allen Murphy, *The Brandeis/Frankfurter Connection.*)

Because of Brandeis's and Frankfurter's example, Justice Abe Fortas, who was appointed to the Court in 1965, saw no reason to limit his extrajudicial work with his good friend President Johnson. Fortas helped to draft pieces of legislation, helped revise a State of the Union speech in the Oval Office, and even served as Johnson's secret emissary to the Dominican Republic during a 1965 coup. Fortas placed no limits in his discussions regarding political issues with President Johnson on the telephone, even including issues then under consideration by the Supreme Court. When all of these extrajudicial political activities were discovered, Senate conservatives were able to thwart Fortas's confirmation for chief justice in 1968 by beginning a filibuster. When William Lambert of *Life* magazine revealed a year later that Fortas had agreed to serve for an annual fee on a foundation dealing with civil rights for juveniles in Florida funded by Louis Wolfson, a man who had been convicted of stock irregularities and whose appeal was then in federal court, he was forced to resign from the Court. Because of the public uproar over this incident, Justice William Brennan resigned from one foundation, and William Douglas promised to resign from, but then remained on, a foundation funded by Albert Parvin, a man with Las Vegas connections. As a result of this connection, together with Douglas's flamboyant personal lifestyle and continual extrajudicial activity, he faced a very serious impeachment inquiry in 1970 that was only derailed by supportive liberal Democrats in Congress.

17. Bruce Allen Murphy, *Fortas: The Rise and Ruin of a Supreme Court Justice* (New York: William Morrow, 1988).

18. Bruce Allen Murphy, *Wild Bill: The Legend and Life of William O. Douglas* (New York: Random House, 2003).

19. The Cheney duck hunting episode became so controversial because it went even further than any of his other extrajudicial activities. Like Fortas's connection to President Johnson and Louis Wolfson, and Douglas's association with Albert Parvin, this hunting trip served as a sort of ethical trip wire, in that public criticism erupted when Scalia went a bit further than in the past. By constantly stretching those ethical boundaries, thus encouraging others on the Court to do the same, Scalia became his own best example of ethical overreach that could easily have been included in the Sierra Club's brief. The truth was that by now, no justice in the Court's entire history had ever generated more continuous negative public controversy and commentary over a nearly two-decade term of service as Antonin Scalia.

   In cases like this, it is preferable that the Supreme Court, which can set its own ethical standard, follow the earlier and somewhat broader standard of "avoiding the appearance of impropriety," even when it is demonstrably true that no impropriety has occurred. So here it seems reasonable to argue that it would have been better for Scalia's personal reputation, and the credibility of the institution on which he serves, if he had stepped aside from the *Cheney* case, even if it meant doing so after issuing his lengthy memo stating why he did not really need to do so. And it would have been wise to follow the same practice that law firms do in investigating to avoid potential conflicts of interest even in his personal recreational activities, such as hunting.

20. For more, see the discussion of the post–Abe Fortas extrajudicial era at the end of Chapter 10, "Faint-Hearted Originalist."

21. The reports are reproduced by the Center for Responsible Politics on OpenSecrets.org, http://www.opensecrets.org/pfds/candlook.php?CID=N99999918. The reports for 2004 and later are reproduced there, but only for justices who were serving on the Court in 2013.

22. Ibid.

23. Brian Stout, "Letter of Protest Was an Accurate Portrayal of the Scalia Lecture," *Amherst Student,* March 3, 2004; *Daily Kos,* February 11, 2004.

24. "Scalia: 'Proudest' Moment Was Staying on Cheney Case," Fox News, April 12, 2006, http://www.foxnews.com/story/0,2933,191525,00.html.

25. See Chapter 18, the Koch brothers seminar controversy in 2011. See also Nina Totenberg, "Bill Puts Ethics Spotlight on Supreme Court Justices," NPR, August 17, 2011, http://www.npr.org/2011/08/17/139646573/bill-puts-ethics-spotlight-on-supreme-court-justices.

26. Joan Biskupic, "Pen in Hand, Scalia Leaves His Mark on Ruling," *USA Today,* June 27, 2008.

27. David G. Savage, "Sierra Club Asks Scalia to Step Aside in Cheney Case," *Los Angeles Times,* February 24, 2004.

28. Tony Mauro, "Newly Disclosed Documents Shed More Light on Scalia's 'Hattiesburg Incident,'" *Legal Times,* December 14, 2007. See also U.S. Department of Justice U.S. Marshals Service Investigation of "the Hattiesburg Incident" of 07-April-2004 (OCR [searchable] version); FOIA release, governmentattic.org, at www.governmentattic.org.

29. Case Summary, U.S. Department of Justice U.S. Marshals Service Investigation of "the Hattiesburg Incident" of 07-April-2004.

30. Denise Grones, "Two Reporters Ordered to Erase Tapes While Covering Scalia Speech,"

Associated Press, March 7, 2004; Antoinette Konz, "Justice: Constitution 'Something Extraordinary,'" *Hattiesburg American,* April 8, 2004.

31. Adam Liptak, "Justice Contrite to Reporters; Marshal Destroyed Speech Recordings," *New York Times,* April 13, 2004.

32. U.S. Department of Justice U.S. Marshals Service Investigation of "the Hattiesburg Incident."

33. Adam Liptak, "In Re Scalia the Outspoken v. Scalia the Reserved," *New York Times,* May 2, 2004.

34. *Crawford v. Washington,* 541 U.S. 36 (2004). This comment comes from Linda Greenhouse, "Justice Scalia Objects," *New York Times,* March 9, 2011.

35. *Ohio v. Roberts,* 448 U.S., 56 at 66 (1980).

36. *Crawford v. Washington,* 541 U.S. 36, at 51 (2004) (Scalia, J., majority).

37. Ibid., at 67–68.

38. *Hamdi v. Rumsfeld,* 542 U.S. 507, at 535 (2004) (O'Connor, J., plurality).

39. Ibid., at 536.

40. Ibid., at 536–37.

41. Ibid., at 554–55 (Scalia, J., dissenting).

42. Ibid., at 573.

43. Ibid., at 576–77.

44. Ibid., at 577–78.

45. Ibid., at 579. To the surprise of many, the most liberal justice on the Court, John Paul Stevens, joined in Scalia's dissent. But they did not always agree on this subject. See *Rasul v. Bush,* 542 U.S. 466 (2004).

46. "We are Fool's for Christ's Sake," Shalom Jerusalem Family, www.shalomjerusalem .com/heritage/heritage7.html/. For more on the appearance at the Mississippi College School of Law in 1996, see Chapter 13, "Master of the Barbed Opinion."

47. "Justice Scalia: Be Fools for Christ," January 24, 2005, http://merecomments.typepad .com.

48. Ibid.; and James M. Wall, "Foolish Wisdom," www.religion-online.org.

49. *Penry v. Lynaugh,* 492 U.S. 302 (1989), and *Stanford v. Kentucky,* 492 U.S. 361 (1989).

50. *Roper v. Simmons,* 543 U.S. 551, at 555 (2005) (Kennedy, J., majority).

51. Ibid.

52. Ibid., at 564–65.

53. Ibid., at 575–76.

54. Ibid., at 608 (Scalia, J., dissenting).

55. Ibid., at 611.

56. Ibid.

57. Ibid.

58. Ibid., at 616–17.

59. Ibid., at 628–29.

60. Scalia speech, "Mullahs of the West: Judges as Authoritative Expositors of the Natural Law?," Trinity College, University of Melbourne, Australia, 2005.

CHAPTER 18: THE CHARM OFFENSIVE

1. Scalia speech, "Constitutional Interpretation." Remarks at the Woodrow Wilson Center for Scholars, Library of Congress, March 14, 2005, *Congressional Quarterly* transcript, Lexis/Nexis.

2. This was the number of justices as of 2005. That number has increased to 112, including Scalia, since then, as of June 2013. The list of other originalist-like justices is a matter of debate, but among the names being considered would be: Hugo Black, James Clark McReynolds, William Howard Taft, and Oliver Wendell Holmes.

3. Lorraine Woellert, "Why Not Scalia? The Pugnacious Darling of the Right Was Sidelined by Political Calculus," *BusinessWeek*, September 19, 2005.

4. Ibid.; Warren Richey, "One Scenario: Chief Justice Scalia?," *Christian Science Monitor*, May 13, 2005.

5. "Scalia Slams Juvenile Death Penalty Ruling," *Washington Post*, March 14, 2005 (referring to the recent *Roper v. Simmons* case).

6. Tom Curry, "Is Scalia Campaigning for Chief Justice?," MSNBC, March 14, 2005.

7. Dana Milbank, "Scalia Showing His Softer Side," *Washington Post*, March 15, 2005.

8. "That Scalia Charm," editorial, *New York Times*, March 21, 2005, p. A16.

9. Antonin Scalia and Stephen Breyer, Norman Dorsen Moderator, "Constitutional Relevance of Foreign Court Decisions," American University, February 27, 2005.

10. "Scalia, O'Connor, Breyer Conversation on the Court (with Tim Russert)," National Archives, Washington, D.C., April 22, 2005.

11. Richey, "One Scenario: Chief Justice Scalia?"

12. Carney and Cooper, "Justice Scalia: The Charm Offensive."

13. Tony Mauro, "Could Scalia Be the Chief?," *American Lawyer Media*, November 20, 2002, www.law.com.

14. Carney and Cooper, "Justice Scalia: The Charm Offensive."

15. Rob Boston, "Chief Justice Scalia?: Rehnquist Illness Sparks Rumors," *Church and State*, March 2005.

16. Charles Lane, "Former Clerks Pay Tribute to 'The Chief,'" *Washington Post*, June 18, 2005.

17. Ibid.

18. Jonathan Alter, "The Real Stakes in November," *Newsweek*, July 10, 2000; David Savage, "Supreme Stumpers: The Next President Could Reshape the Court and the Legal Arena," *ABA Journal*, October 2000.

19. *Gonzales v. Raich*, 545 U.S. 1 (2005).

20. *Wickard v. Filburn*, 317 U.S. 111 (1942).

21. Ibid., at 120, 125 (Jackson, J., majority).

22. *Gonzales v. Raich*, 545 U.S. 1 (2005), at 40 (Scalia, J., concurring).

23. For more on this case, see *Gonzales v. Oregon*, 546 U.S. 243 (2006).

24. *Gonzales v. Raich*, 545 U.S. 1 (2006), at 53 (Thomas, J., dissenting).

25. Mark Moller, "What Was Scalia Thinking?," *Reason.com*, June 14, 2005, www.cato.org.

26. Ryan Grim, "A Guide to *Gonzales v. Raich*," *Salon*, June 7, 2005, www.salon.com.

27. Ibid.

28. Debra Rosenberg, "Justice: Bench Player," *Newsweek*, February 12, 2007.

29. John Jenkins, *The Partisan: The Life of William Rehnquist* (New York: PublicAffairs, 2012), pp. 264–66.

30. Rosenberg, "Justice: Bench Player."

31. Ibid.

32. Jenkins, *The Partisan*, pp. 264–66.

33. Jan Crawford Greenburg, *Supreme* Conflict: *The Inside Story of the Struggle for Control of the United States Supreme Court* (New York: Penguin, 2008), p. 20.

34. Bruce Allen Murphy, *Wild Bill: The Legend and Life of William O. Douglas* (New York: Random House, 2003), Chapter 38.

35. Jenkins, *The Partisan,* p. 265.

36. Richard W. Stevenson, "O'Connor to Retire, Touching Off Battle over Court," *New York Times,* July 2, 2005.

37. Fred Barnes, "Judgment Day: What President Bush Needs to Keep in Mind with the Supreme Court," *Weekly Standard,* July 18, 2005.

38. "Did Bush Promise to Appoint a Justice like Scalia?," *Media Matters for America,* October 13, 2005, http://mediamatters.org/print/research/200510130005.

39. Tony Mauro, "Bush Got a Conservative Court, with Caveats," *Legal Times,* November 3, 2008.

40. Peter Baker and Jim VandeHei, "Bush Chooses Roberts for Court," *Washington Post,* July 20, 2005; Tony Mauro, "D.C. Circuit Gets on Supreme Court Short List," February 22, 2005, www.law.com.

41. "Roberts Says High Court Not About 'Political Preferences,'" ABC News, November 28, 2006 (a report of Roberts's appearance at the University of Miami to answer questions by Jan Crawford Greenburg).

42. Jesse Holland, "Sources: Roberts Confirmation Hearings to Begin on September 6," Associated Press, July 29, 2005.

43. Charles Lane, "Chief Justice Dies at Age 80," *Washington Post,* September 4, 2005.

44. Peter Baker, "Second Vacancy Triggers a Scramble," *Washington Post,* September 5, 2005.

45. Greenburg, *Supreme Conflict,* p. 240. On the Vinson appointment, see Murphy, *Wild Bill.* William O. Douglas, Hugo Black, Felix Frankfurter, and Robert Jackson all wanted to be chief justice.

46. The three confirmations would be for the chief justice's position, the replacement for the vacancy created by his elevation, and the replacement of the retiring Justice O'Connor.

47. Greenburg, *Supreme Conflict,* p. 240.

48. Lorraine Woellert, "Why Not Scalia?," *Business Week,* September 19, 2005.

49. Ibid.

50. Greenburg, *Supreme Conflict,* p. 240; Woellert, "Why Not Scalia?"

51. Greenburg, *Supreme Conflict,* p. 240.

52. Woellert, "Why Not Scalia?"

53. CBS news transcripts, September 5, 2005, Lexis/Nexis.

54. Ibid.

55. Ibid.

56. Woellert, "Why Not Scalia?"

57. Patrick J. Buchanan, "Stand Up to Them, Mr. President: Nominate Another Scalia," Human Events Online, September 9, 2005, www.humaneventsonline.com.

58. Cynthia McFadden and Brian Ross, "High Court, High Living; Power Trip," *Nightline,* ABC News transcript, January 23, 2006.

59. Ibid.

60. Ibid.

61. "Scalia: Didn't Expect to Be Chief Justice," CNN.com, October 10, 2005.

62. Following her divorce in 2009, Jan Crawford resumed using her maiden name. Any future references to her after this date will use this name. Citations to her work before that date will continue to refer to her married name.

63. For a report on the interview, see: Tony Mauro, "Scalia 'Wouldn't Have Liked' Being Chief Justice," November 19, 2010, blog, *Legal Times,* www.legaltimes.com.

64. "Scalia Puts Limits on Press at the Columbus Day Parade," *The Villager,* October 19–22, 2005, www.thevillager.com.
65. Ibid.
66. Gina Holland, "Supreme Court Notebook: Justice Scalia Goes Media Shy Again," Associated Press, October 12, 2005.
67. Corbis collection of photos on the Internet, www.corbisimages.com.
68. Holland, "Supreme Court Notebook: Justice Scalia Goes Media Shy Again."
69. "Time to Ban Judicial Junkets," editorial, *New York Times,* October 15, 2005.
70. Scalia interview with Maria Bartiromo, MSNBC transcript, October 10, 2005, Lexis/Nexis.
71. Kim Eisler, "Backbenched Scalia Speaks," *Washingtonian,* December 2005.

CHAPTER 19: THE DEAD CONSTITUTION TOUR

1. Liz Marlantes, "Alito Grilling Gets Too Intense for Some," ABCNews.com, January 11, 2005.
2. Robert Gordon, "Alito or Scalito?," *Slate,* November 1, 2005, http://www.slate.com /articles/news_and_politics/jurisprudence/2005/11/alito_or_scalito.html.
3. Scalia was now in the same phase of life as Justice William O. Douglas was in the late summer of 1960 when the much younger John F. Kennedy was nominated to run for the presidency on the Democratic ticket—a position that Douglas had been privately seeking for nearly two decades. Thus freed from the burden of this career ambition, the sixty-two-year-old Douglas went through his "Wild Bill" phase, becoming the icon of the liberals, and behaving personally however he wished. For more, see Bruce Allen Murphy, *Wild Bill: The Legend and Life of William O. Douglas* (New York: Random House, 2003), Chapter 30.
4. "American Idiot," February 15, 2006, www.SaveROE.com.
5. Scalia speech, "Mullahs of the West: Judges as Authoritative Expositors of the Natural Law?," Sir John Young Oration, Boston, Melbourne, Oxford Conversazioni on Culture and Society, Trinity College, University of Melbourne, Australia, 2005.
6. *Dudgeon v. United Kingdom* [1981] ECHR 5, (1982) 4 EHRR 149, IHRL 31 (ECHR 1981), 22nd October 1981, European Court of Human Rights [ECtHR].
7. Scalia speech, "Mullahs of the West."
8. Peter Lattman, "Scalia Assails Living Constitutionalists," *Wall Street Journal* online, February 11, 2006, http://blogs,wsj.com/law/); Jonathan Ewing, "Revisionist Liberals Are Idiots, Halfwits and Retards," Associated Press, February 14, 2006, http://myright mind.blogspot.com.
9. "Scalia: Non-Originalists Are Idiots," Associated Press, February 14, 2006, FoxNews .com. http://www.foxnews.com/story/0,2933,184815,00.html#ixzz1yGqgSYTp. See also Ewing, "Revisionist Liberals Are Idiots, Halfwits and Retards."
10. Antonin Scalia, Stephen Breyer, and Jan Crawford Greenburg, "A Conversation on the Constitution," Federalist Society, December 5, 2006, found at www.fed-soc.org.
11. All quotes here and below are taken from Steven Ertelt, "Supreme Court Justice Scalia: Roe Abortion Case May Never Be Reversed," March 10, 2006, Lifenews.com, http:// www.lifenews.com/nat2140.html.
12. Transcript of Scalia speech, University of Fribourg, Switzerland, March 8, 2006, Bureau Audiovisuel Francophone (BAFWEB), http://www.bafweb.com/60308scalia.wmv.

13. Terry Vanderheyden, "Justice Scalia on Roe v. Wade," Life Site News.com, http://www .lifeside.net/Idn/2006/mar/0631004.html; Tom Strode, "Supreme Court Not Ready to Reverse Roe, Scalia Says," March 13, 2006, www.bpnews.net.

14. Quotes that follow are from transcript of Scalia speech, University of Fribourg, March 8, 2006.

15. Ibid.

16. Ibid.

17. Ibid.

18. Ibid.

19. Ibid.

20. Ibid.

21. 548 U.S. 557 (2006).

22. Scalia Speech, University of Fribourg, March 8, 2006.

23. Ibid.

24. Ertelt, "Supreme Court Justice Scalia."

25. Vanderheyden, "Justice Scalia on *Roe v. Wade.*"

26. "Scalia's Ill-Chosen Words: Justice Crosses the Line—Again," *Philadelphia Inquirer,* March 31, 2006, Philly.com, http://articles.philly.com/2006-03-31/news/25415630_1_ military-tribunals-justice-antonin-scalia-activist-judges.

27. Michael Isikoff, "Supreme Court: Detainee's Rights—Scalia Speaks His Mind," MSNBC.com, April 3, 2006, www.msnbc.com; also found at http://www.thedailybeast .com/newsweek/2006/04/02/supreme-court-detainees-rights-scalia-speaks-his-mind .html.

28. Thanks to the timely notice by the antiabortion activist organizations, some Court watchers had already taped and transcribed the speech; and later on mirror sites of the speech would continue to pop up on search engines.

29. "Report: Scalia Criticizes Europe on Gitmo," *Washington Post,* March 26, 2006.

30. CNN report, "Report: Scalia Against Rights for Gitmo Detainees," March 27, 2008, http://www.cnn.com/2006/LAW/03/26/gu . . . eut/index.html.

31. Charles Lane, "Scalia's Recusal Sought in Key Detainee Case," *Washington Post,* March 28, 2006.

32. See 28 U.S.C. Sec. 455.

33. Dahlia Lithwick, "Courting Attention," *Washington Post,* April 9, 2006.

34. Marie Szaniszio, "Photographer: Herald Got It Right," *Boston Herald,* March 30, 2006. This version of the question is taken from Scalia's response, in the Scalia letter to the *Boston Herald* editorial board, March 29, 2006, *The Supreme Court* website, PBS.org. The *Herald*'s version was "how he responds to critics who might question his impartiality as a judge given his public worship."

35. Laurel J. Sweet, "Judicial Intemperance—Scalia Flips Messages to Doubting Thomases," *Boston Herald,* March 27, 2006.

36. Ibid.

37. Scalia letter to *Boston Herald* editorial board, March 29, 2006.

38. See, for example, Margery Eagan, "In a Flick of the Wrist, a Judge Can Say So Much," *Boston Herald,* March 28, 2006; "Justice Scalia Gives Obscene Gesture?," CBS News, March 27, 2006; Dahlia Lithwick, "How Do You Solve the Problem of Scalia?," Slate .com, March 30, 2006; and John in D.C., "Scalia Just Gave the Finger in Church Yester-day (Not Kidding)," Americablog.com; "An Update on Fingergate: Nino Is Still Cool," March 29, 2006, Wonkette.com.

39. Jessica Hesslam, "Church Fires Photographer over Scalia Picture," http://www .democraticunderground.com/discuss/duboard.php?az=view_all&address=102x 2201202.

40. P.L. 107-40 (2001). For more, see Richard F. Grimmett, "Authorization for the Use of Military Force in Response to the 9/11 Attacks (P.L. 107-40): Legislative History," *CRS for Congress,* January 4, 2006, http://www.law.umaryland.edu/marshall/crsreports/crs documents/RS22357_01042006.pdf.

41. For more, see http://scholar.google.com/scholar_case?case=1251834070131661299&q=ham dan+v.+rumsfeld&hl=en&as_sdt=2,39&as_vis=1. It cited App. to Pet. for Cert. 65a.

42. *Hamdan v. Rumsfeld,* 548 U.S. 557, at 611 (2006) (Stevens, J., majority).

43. Ibid., at 635.

44. Ibid., 665–66 (Scalia, J., dissenting).

45. Ibid., at 669.

46. John Roberts, Commencement Address, Georgetown University Law Center, May 26, 2006, http://www.law.georgetown.edu/webcast/assets/GL_2006523112710.mp3.

47. Antonin Scalia and Stephen Breyer, moderated by Jan Crawford Greenburg, "A Conversation on the Constitution," American Constitution Society and the Federalist Society joint session, Washington, D.C., December 5, 2006, http://www.fed-soc.org /publications/detail/a-conversation-on-the-constitution-with-supreme-court-justices -stephen-breyer-and-antonin-scalia-event-audio.

CHAPTER 20: OPUS SCOTUS

1. Thanks to Lori Weaver and Colleen Sullivan for their excellent research assistance on some of the material for this chapter done as part of a Mellon Foundation Community of Scholars research grant for Lafayette College.

2. See, for example, Alan Cooperman, "Court Could Tip to Catholic Majority," *Washington Post,* November 7, 2005; Lynette Clemetson, "Alito Could Be 5th Catholic on Supreme Court," *New York Times,* November 5, 2005; and Eric Black, "The High Court Could Be More Conservative—and More Catholic," *Minneapolis Star-Tribune,* November 1, 2005.

3. For the account of Thomas's journey, see Clarence Thomas, *My Grandfather's Son* (New York: HarperCollins, 2007).

4. School Restoration, St. Benedict the Moor Catholic Church, http://home.catholicweb .com/stbenedictthemoor/index. Even now, the church's website contains several links for "How to Be an African-American Catholic."

5. Clarence Thomas. *My Grandfather's Son,* pp. 1–30.

6. Ibid., pp. 42–44, 49.

7. Ibid., p. 51.

8. Ibid., pp. 99–100.

9. Ibid., p. 136; see also pp. 134–35.

10. Ibid., p. 184.

11. Ibid., pp. 189–90.

12. Frank Cocozzelli, "An Opus Focus on SCOTUS," *Talk to Action,* May 3, 2007, http:// www.talk2action.org/story/2007/5/5/10522/79375/; Terry Mattingly, "Justice's Son Answers a Higher Call," *Deseret News,* June 30, 2001; "The Religious Affiliation of Supreme Court Justice Clarence Thomas," www.adherents.com; "On Scalia and Thomas," *Newsweek,* March 9, 2001, cited in "Chief Justice Roberts and Opus Dei,"

PeakDemblogs, September 20, 2005, http://blog.peakdems.org/2005/09/chief-justice
-nominee-john-roberts-and.html.

A self-acknowledged Opus Dei leader, Father McCloskey had been the controversial chaplain at Princeton University, where his philosophies led him to clash with the school's faculty members and administration. Through a center that he established and ran between 1985 and 1990 near the university, Father McCloskey recruited financial and political elites to the Catholic Church. His traditionalist views included that Vatican II created a "generally unfortunate period for our country and our Church," and that college coeducation was a "failure" because of what he saw as the "particular needs of the complementary yet quite different sexes."

After leaving Princeton, McCloskey had moved to Washington, D.C., where he established and directed the Catholic Information Center on K Street, the heart of the lobbying industry in the District of Columbia. The Catholic Information Center, which McCloskey called D.C.'s "downtown center of evangelization" for Catholicism, was staffed by an Opus Dei cleric and featured a chapel and a bookstore that promoted McCloskey's traditional views. "A liberal Catholic is oxymoronic," McCloskey liked to tell reporters. "The definition of a person who disagrees with what the Catholic Church is teaching is called a Protestant."

Father McCloskey was reportedly singlehandedly responsible for converting several other high-level Washington notables to traditional Catholicism, many of them previously devoutly conservative and evangelical Protestants. Among these converts was Scalia's old colleague on the D.C. Court of Appeals, Robert Bork, former senator from and later governor of Kansas Sam Brownback, conservative television economics reporter Lawrence Kudlow, and the late conservative journalist Robert Novak. McCloskey also served as an adviser and inspiration to such other political figures such as former Pennsylvania senator and presidential candidate Rick Santorum. All of these people held religious views similar to those of Thomas. For more, see Julia Duin, "A Firm Voice, Fostering Faith," *CatholiCity,* http://www.catholicity.com/mccloskey/firm voice.html; Chris Suellentrop, "The Rev. John McCloskey: The Catholic Church's K Street Lobbyist," *Slate* August 9, 2002, www.slate.com; "Father John McCloskey," http://www.catholicity.com/mccloskey/ (Suellentrop, Chris, "The Rev. John McCloskey: The Catholic Church's K Street Lobbyist," *Slate,* http://www.slate.com/id/2069194). See also Rob Boston, *Breaking the Opus Dei Code*, and the chapter on Robert Hanssen titled "Of Spies and Saints: *Opus Dei* and Robert Hanssen," May 2006.

13. Rachel Zoll, "Alito Would Tip Court to Catholics: If Nominee's Confirmed, Members Would Hold Majority for 1st Time," *Indiana Star,* November 2, 2005.

14. Comments in a blog post by Reverend Franklyn McAfee, a priest within the Diocese of Arlington, www.Haloscan.com, http://www.haloscan.com/comments/stribe /158070305120960847.

Before Pope Benedict XVI decreed in September 2007 that the use of the Tridentine Mass could be expanded, St. Andrew's and Scalia's church, St. Catherine of Siena, were the only two churches in the Diocese of Arlington that were allowed to celebrate the traditional Latin Mass (Andrew Santella, "Bene, Vidi, Vici," *Slate,* July 7, 2007, slate. com. Haloscan.com). Like St. Catherine's, the conservative nature of St. Andrew's is indicated on their website announcing their groups and meetings (Bulletins, St. Andrew's Parish, accessed December 2, 2007, January 6, 2008, http://www.st-andrew.org/bulletins /previous/december).

15. Benjamin Schuman-Stoler, "Religion and the Supreme Court," September/October 2008, *Moment Magazine,* www.momentmag.com.

16. The other two Roman Catholic chief justices were Roger Brooke Taney and Edward Douglass White.

17. Christopher Hitchens, "Catholic Justice: Quit Tiptoeing Around John Roberts' Faith," *Slate,* http://www.slate.com/id/2123780/.

18. Hanna Rosin, "Nominee's Wife Is a Feminist After Her Own Heart," *Washington Post,* July 22, 2005.

19. Evan Thomas and Stuart Taylor Jr., "Judging Roberts," *Newsweek,* August 1, 2005. Leadership in the John Carroll Society: John Carroll Society website, http://www .johncarrollsociety.org/new_page_5.htm.

20. History of the Society: John Carroll Society website, http://www.johncarrollsociety.org /new_page_6.htm.

21. "Judge Roberts' Pastor, Msgr. Vaghi, on Tradition and Scripture," July 21, 2005, http:// richfreeman.blogspot.com; Julia Duin, "A Firm Voice, Fostering Faith," *CatholiCity*; http://www.catholicity.com/mccloskey/firmvoice.html.

22. "Is Judge Roberts Opus Dei?," *News from the Underground,* July 27, 2005, http://mark cripinmiller.blogspot.com/2005/07/is-judge-roberts-opus-dei.html.

23. Robin Toner, "Catholics and the Court," *New York Times,* August 7, 2005; Rosin, "Nominee's Wife Is a Feminist After Her Own Heart"; Richard Ostling, "Roberts Would Be Court's 4th Catholic," *Deseret News,* August 20, 2005; Patricia Zapor, "Nominee Would Be Fourth Catholic on Current Court," Catholic News Service, July 20, 2005, http:// www.catholicnews.com/data/stories/cns/0504186.htm.

   The chief justice also has a nominal role in arranging the discussion of the appeals to be considered for the Court in its conference discussions by creating a "discuss list" that will merit discussion by the Court in anticipation of a vote to consider the appeal, and a "dead list" of appeals that seem to have so little support that they will not even be discussed unless one justice votes to do so. However, it still takes a vote of four justices, with the chief's vote having no more weight than that of any of his colleagues, to accept an appeal for review.

24. Schuman-Stoler, "Religion and the Supreme Court."

25. Our Lady of the Blessed Sacrament website, homepage, http://www.olbs.org/, accessed December 1, 2007: "We, the people of Our Lady of the Blessed Sacrament Parish . . . form a Christian Community located in Roseland and made up of people from neighboring towns. Our mission is to give life and meaning to the reality of Christ and His message as proclaimed through the Gospel in an ever-changing world. As a community of faith we strive to provide: a life-giving worship that welcomes all people, a compassionate presence by reaching out to all those who are hurting, occasions for Christian love and bonding both within and beyond the confines of our Parish, and ongoing opportunities for experimental and intellectual growth into a mature faith life. We seek to accomplish this mission by challenging ourselves to respond according to our giftedness."

26. "Bush Court Pick Likely in for a Fight," MSNBC transcript, October 31, 2005.

27. Samuel A. Alito, attachment to PPO Non-Career Appointment Form (November 15, 1985), cited in "The Nomination of Samuel Alito: A Watershed Moment for Women," National Women's Law Center, December 15, 2005, http://www.nwlc.org/pdf/12-15 -05_AlitoReportExecutiveSummary.pdf.

28. "Alito's Abortion Stance Tough to Decipher," *USA Today,* November 26, 2005.

29. *Planned Parenthood of Pennsylvania v. Casey,* 505 U.S. 833 (1992).

30. Robert Gordon, "Alito or Scalito?," *Slate,* www.slate.com, November 1, 2005; Shannon P. Duffy, "The Mild Mannered Scalia," Law.com, March 3, 2003.

31. Jeffrey Toobin, *The Nine: Inside the Secret World of the Supreme Court* (New York: Doubleday, 2007), p. 53.

32. Eleanor Smeal, "A Crucial Coalition," *In These Times,* April 4, 2004, http://www.inthese times.com/article/726/a_crucial_coalition/.

33. Holy Spirit parish webpage, www.holyspiritparishsac.org.

34. Jeffrey Toobin, "Swing Shift: How Anthony Kennedy's Passion for Foreign Law Could Change the Supreme Court," *New Yorker,* September 12, 2005, p. 42.

35. Richard C. Reuben, "Man in the Middle," *California Lawyer,* October 1992, pp. 36–37.

36. Jeffrey Rosen, "The Agonizer," *New Yorker,* November 11, 1996.

37. Jeffrey Rosen, "Supreme Leader," *New Republic,* June 18, 2007, p. 19.

38. Ibid., pp. 20–22.

39. See Toobin, "Swing Shift."

40. Toobin, *The Nine,* p. 52.

41. Massimo Calabresi and David Von Drehle, "What Will Justice Kennedy Do?," *Time,* June 18, 2012, p. 39.

42. The Nebraska law lacked an exception for the health of the mother: *Stenberg v. Carhart,* 530 U.S. 913 (2000).

43. *Gonzales v. Carhart,* 550 U.S. 124 (2007) (Kennedy, J., majority).

44. Tony Auth cartoon, April 20, 2007, in Robert Miller, "The Auth Cartoon," *First Things,* April 26, 2007, www.firstthings.com.

45. Geoffrey R. Stone, "Our Faith-Based Justices," April 20, 2007, *Huffington Post,* www .huffingtonpost.com.

46. Biskupic, *American Original,* p. 204. Scalia later relented and returned to speak at the University of Chicago law school in February 2012.

47. See Cooperman, "Court Could Tip to Catholic Majority"; Clemetson, "Alito Could Be 5th Catholic on Current Supreme Court"; Toner, "Catholics and the Court"; Rosin, "Nominee's Wife Is a Feminist After Her Own Heart"; Ostling, "Roberts Would Be Court's 4th Catholic"; and Zapor, "Nominee Would Be Fourth Catholic on Current Court."

48. Scalia speech, "The Role of Catholic Faith in the Work of a Judge," 2nd Annual John F. Scarpa Conference on Law, Politics and Culture, Villanova University, October 16, 2007. These quotations are taken from the author's notes of the speech unless otherwise mentioned.

49. MaryClaire Dale, "Scalia Speaks at Villanova University," October 16, 2007, http://abc local.go.com.

50. David O'Reilly, "Scalia Opines on Faith and Justice," *Philadelphia Inquirer,* October 17, 2007, www.philly.com.

51. Rick Garnett, "Justice Scalia, a "Catholic" Judge," *Mirror of Justice,* October 18, 2007, www.mirrorofjustice.blogs.com.

52. Robert T. Miller, "Antonin Scalia Not a Catholic Judge," *First Things,* October 23, 2007.

53. "Is There Such a Thing as a Catholic Judge," *Business Associations,* October 23, 2007, www.businessassociationsblog.com.

54. This concept called "resourcement," or "return to the sources," comes from Father John O'Malley, *What Happened at Vatican II* (Cambridge: Belknap Press/Harvard University Press, 2008).

55. See Lesley Stahl interview, April 27, 2008. Also see Scalia speech, University of Fribourg, Switzerland, March 8, 2006, Bureau Audiovisuel Francophone (BAFWEB) http://www .bafweb.com/60308scalia.wmv.

56. Geoffrey R. Stone, "Justice Sotomayor, Justice Scalia and Our Six Catholic Justices," *Huffington Post,* August 28, 2009, www.huffingtonpost.com.

57. George Rush and Joanna Rush Molloy, "Scalia a Fan of '24' from the Gitmo," New York *Daily News,* June 26, 2007: Colin Freeze, "What Would Jack Bauer Do?," *Globe and Mail* (Canada), June 16, 2007. Scalia speech, International Conference on the Administration of Justice and National Security in Democracies, Ottawa, Canada, June 12, 2007 (transcript in author's possession).

CHAPTER 21: THE ROCK STAR OF ONE FIRST STREET

1. Clarence Thomas, *My Grandfather's Son: A Memoir* (New York: HarperCollins, 2007). And see David Kirkpatrick and Linda Greenhouse, "Memoir Deal Reported for Justice Thomas," *New York Times,* January 10, 2003.

2. Transcript, "The Justice Nobody Knows: Justice Clarence Thomas Discusses His Childhood, His Career, Anita Hill, and His Book," *60 Minutes,* CBS News Transcripts, September 30, 2007.

3. Carol Crawford Greenburg, *Supreme Conflict: The Inside Story of the Struggle for Control of the United States Supreme Court* (New York: Penguin Press, 2007).

4. "Tough Issues, Major Issues on the Agenda as the Supreme Court Opens," *ABC World News Sunday,* September 30, 2007.

5. Brian Stelter, "Clarence Thomas, Reality Star?," *New York Times,* October 1, 2007.

6. Nina Totenberg, "Scalia Vigorously Defends a 'Dead Constitution,'" *NPR,* Part 3, April 28, 2008, http://www.npr.org/templates/story/story.php?storyId=90011526.

7. Ibid. Scalia repeated this comment on other occasions. See Molly McDonough, "Scalia: I Am Not a Nut!," *ABA Journal,* April 8, 2008; and Jeffrey Toobin, *The Nine: Inside the Secret World of the Supreme Court* (New York: Doubleday, 2007), p. 103.

8. William Kristol, "McCain's Daunting Task," *New York Times,* March 10, 2008.

9. Scalia interview with Clive Coleman, *Law in Action,* BBC transcript, February 12, 2008.

10. George Bush and Joanna Rush Molloy, "Scalia a Fan of '24' from the Gitmo," *New York Daily News,* June 26, 2007; Colin Freeze, "What Would Jack Bauer Do?," *Globe and Mail,* June 16, 2007.

11. James Vicini, "US Top Court's Scalia Defends Physical Interrogation," Reuters, February 12, 2008.

12. Dan Slater, "Scalia: Smacking Someone in the Face Could Be Justified," *Wall Street Journal,* online, February 13, 2008.

13. "A Glance at Scalia Controversies," Associated Press, February 18, 2008.

14. "National Lawyers Guild Calls on Justice Antonin Scalia to Recuse Himself from Interrogation-Related Cases," Common Dreams Progressive Newswire, February 15, 2008.

15. Rick Garnett, "Scalia on 'Torture,' Cont'd," *Mirror of Justice* blog, February 13, 2008.

16. Joan Biskupic, "Scalia's Comments on Torture Latest Taste of Bluntness," *USA Today,* February 14, 2008.

17. Mark Sherman, "Scalia Weighs in Again on Controversy," FoxNews.com, February 13, 2008.

18. Jonathan Turley, "Scalia and the Rise of the Celebrity Justice: Should Justices Have a Political Base?," January 23, 2011, *Res Ipsa Logwiter,* found at jonathanturley.org. While Felix Frankfurter and William O. Douglas would disagree, it is true for the 24/7 internet, cable news era.

19. Action Alert, "URGE YOUR SENATORS TO EXPAND THE BAN ON TORTURE," February 7, 2008, Virginia Farris, Office of International Justice and Peace, http://www.harpers.org/media/image/blogs/misc/catholic-bishops-action.pdf, in Scott Horton, "Nino Scalia, Your Hairshirt Is Showing and Your Bishop Has a Message for You," February 12, 2008, www.harpers.org.

20. *Catholic Catechism,* no. 2297.

21. Antonin Scalia and Bryan Garner, *Making Your Case: The Art of Persuading People* (New York: Thomson, West, 2008).

22. Lesley Stahl interview, April 27, 2008.

23. Ibid.

24. Nina Totenberg, "Justice Scalia, the Great Dissenter, Opens Up," NPR, April 29, 2008.

25. Ibid.

26. Scalia, Question-and-Answer session with Thomas Jefferson High School students, C-SPAN, April 10, 2008.

27. Jim Oliphant, "Justice Scalia Launches a Charm Offensive," April 30, 2008, www.swamppolitics.com.

28. Ashby Jones, "The Scalia Road Show Talks Religion in Charlottesville," *Wall Street Journal Law Blog,* April 11, 2008, and Ashby Jones, "Next Stop on Nino's Book Tour," *Law Blog,* May 7, 2008.

29. Tim Russert interview, May 3, 2008.

30. Ibid.

31. David Lax, "ATL Field Trip: An Evening with Justice Scalia (Part 1), *Above the Law* blog, June 5, 2008 found at www.abovethelaw.com. See also "Underneath Their Robe," blog, October 26, 2004, and October 6, 2005, found at underneath their robes, blogs.com.

32. Charlie Rose interview, June 20, 2008.

33. Scalia interview, Brian Lamb, *Q and A Show,* C-SPAN, May 4, 2008, found at http://cspanvideo.org/program/AwithAn; http://www.cablecenter.org/education/library/oral HistoryDetails.cfm?id=132.

34. On Nelson Shanks and his artistic technique, see Steve Siegel, "I Chose to Go Directly to the Source," *Allentown Morning Call,* June 23, 2013, p. GO 1–2. One wonders why the artist did not use Webster's first *An American Dictionary of the English Language.*

35. Dahlia Lithwick, "Justice Scalia, Unplugged," *Newsweek,* May 19, 2008.

36. Scalia interview, Brian Lamb, *Q and A Show,* C-SPAN, May 4, 2008. In the course of that discussion, Lamb raised the issue of political satirist Jon Stewart's reaction on his popular *The Daily Show* to Scalia's *60 Minutes* interview discussion of the *Bush v. Gore* case (Scalia: "Gee, I really don't want to get into this. This is—get over it. It's so old by now"). To which Stewart said: "Really? It's so old? Because he's still . . . President, you know that? We're still at war. Gas is still $5.00 a gallon. So old by now, and yet it's still rattling around in the old noggin there. So the constitutional originalist on the Supreme Court doesn't want to revisit any Supreme Court decisions made before the year 2000. Dude, I am so getting a slave." Scalia, who confessed that he had seen Stewart's show "once, and that was enough," was not terribly amused when Lamb asked, "What's your reaction when you see it?" Scalia responded: "It's a free country. I thought it was childish. As for Bush versus Gore, it's still relevant. I mean, the President was re-elected after that, so,

you know, it's not as though blaming the war and everything else on the Supreme Court, that's just ridiculous."

37. Scalia's salary ranged between $194,000 and $213,900 during the period from 2004 to 2010. Salaries of Supreme Court Associate justices: 2004: $194,300; 2005: $199,200; 2006: $203,000; 2008: $208,100; 2009: $208,100; 2010: $213,900. "Salaries for Members of Congress, Supreme Court Justices and the President," http://www.ntu.org/on-capitol-hill /pay-and-perks/salaries-for-members-of.html; Robert Longley, "U.S. Supreme Court Retirement Benefits," About.com, US Government Info: A Full Salary for Life, http:// usgovinfo.about.com/od/uscourtsystem/a/scotusretire.htm.

38. See Supreme Court Annual Financial Reports, collected by Judicial Watch, http://www .judicialwatch.org/judge/scalia-antonin/; also at OpenSecrets.org, found at http://www .opensecrets.org/pdfs/candlook.php?txtName=scalia. Scalia reported in these forms that his annual compensation for teaching various law seminars was: 2004: $21,500; 2005: $21,900; 2006: $24,500; for a total of $67,900. Scalia reported in these forms that his annual compensation from West Publishing was: 2007: $33,000 (book advance); 2008: $98,716 (book advance and royalties); 2009: $121,535 (book advance and royalties); 2010: $37,797 (book royalties); 2011: $18,775 (book royalties); for a total of $309,823. He also reported that his annual compensation for outside teaching in law seminars between 2007 and 2011 was: 2007: $25,000; 2008: $25,500; 2009: $20,000; 2010: $24,500; 2011: $26,900; for a total of $121,900. As will be made clear in Chapter 26, it appears that in one or more of those years, likely 2008 and 2009, Scalia was also receiving as part of that figure the advances on a future book. Sandra Day O'Connor also wrote memoirs, though they were likely not nearly as lucrative as Justice Thomas's.

CHAPTER 22: KING OF THE ORIGINALISTS

1. *Baze v. Rees,* 553 U.S. 35, 50 (2008) (Roberts, C. J., majority).

2. Ibid., at 72–73 (Stevens, J., concurring).

3. Ibid., at p. 80.

4. The process began with Byron White, who led the Court's argument when it first declared that the death penalty was, in part, unconstitutional: "Justice White was exercising his own judgment in 1972 when he provided the decisive vote in *Furman,* the case that led to a nationwide reexamination of the death penalty. His conclusion that death amounted to 'cruel and unusual punishment in the constitutional sense' as well as the 'dictionary sense,' rested on both an uncontroversial legal premise and on a factual premise that he admittedly could not 'prove' on the basis of objective criteria. . . . As a matter of law, he correctly stated that the 'needless extinction of life with only marginal contributions to any discernible social or public purposes . . . would be patently excessive' and violative of the Eighth Amendment."

5. *Baze v. Rees,* at 66–87 (Stevens, J., concurring).

6. Ibid., at 87 (Scalia, J., concurring).

7. See chapters 10, 14, 18, and 21. His view here squares with his conservative Catholicism. See chapter 16.

8. Ibid., at 93.

9. Ibid., at 93.

10. For more on the case, see William Rehnquist, *All the Laws but One: Civil Liberties in Wartime* (New York: Vintage, 2000).

11. *Boumediene v. Bush,* 553 U.S. 723, 740 (2008) (Kennedy, J., majority).

12. Ibid., at 745.
13. Ibid., at 771.
14. Ibid., at 797.
15. Ibid., at 798.
16. Ibid., at 828 (Scalia, J., dissenting).
17. Ibid., at 829.
18. Ibid., 831.
19. Ibid.
20. Ibid., at 842–43.
21. Ibid., at 850.
22. For the reference to the Madison proposal, see Pauline Maier, *Ratification: The People Debate the Constitution, 1787–1788* (New York: Simon & Schuster, 2011), pp. 443–52.
23. *United States v. Miller,* 307 U.S. 174 (1939).
24. For more on this case, see Dr. Michael S. Brown, "The Strange Case of *United States v. Miller,*" *Enter Stage Right—A Journal of Modern Conservatism,* August 6, 2001. Thanks to National Rifle Association legal advocate Jon Goldstein for bringing this article and this argument to my attention. By the time the case came to the Supreme Court, Miller was dead—ironically of a losing battle with a handgun—so there was no argument on his side.
25. *United States v. Miller,* at 179 (McReynolds, J., majority).
26. In fact, the short-barreled shotgun was used by soldiers in the trenches in World War I, and by marines on naval ships. See Brown, "The Strange Case of *United States v. Miller.*"
27. *District of Columbia v. Heller,* 554 U.S. 570 (2008), 576–77 (Scalia, J., majority).
28. Ibid., at 577–78.
29. Ibid., at 585–86.
30. Ibid., at 586–87.
31. Ibid., at 592.
32. Ibid., at 602.
33. Ibid., at 614.
34. Ibid., at 646.
35. Ibid., at 637 (Stevens, J., dissenting).
36. Ibid., at 638–39.
37. Ibid., at 643.
38. Ibid., at 652.
39. Ibid., at 652, note 14.
40. Ibid., at 624 (Scalia, J., majority).
41. Nina Totenberg interview.
42. Saul Cornell, "The Second Amendment and the Right to Bear Arms After *D.C. v. Heller*: Heller, New Originalism, and Law Office History: 'Meet the New Boss, Same as the Old Boss,'" *UCLA Law Review* 56 (June 2009): 1107–8.
43. Jack Rakove, "Thoughts on Heller from a 'Real Historian,'" June 27, 2008, *Balkinization,* http://balkin.blogspot.com/2008/06/thoughts-on-heller-from-real-historian.html.
44. Richard A. Posner, "In Defense of Looseness," *New Republic,* August 27, 2008.
45. In so writing, Blackstone was being consistent with centuries of British judicial thinking and action on this matter. British legal historian Paul Brand of All Souls College at Oxford University writes that a loose, "extended interpretation" of statutes had been used by the British judiciary since the signing of the Magna Carta through the thirteenth and early fourteenth centuries. Judges did not hold themselves strictly to the words of a stat-

ute, but rather went beyond the words to look at the law's intent and primary purpose, while often deciding based on "who benefits." Far from being early originalists, then, these judges in the dawn of British law were behaving as "living, evolving" interpreters. Paul Brand, "The Judicial Interpretation of Legislation in Later Thirteenth and Early Fourteenth Century England," paper delivered at the 21st British Legal History Conference, July 9, 2013, Glasgow, Scotland. My thanks to Professor Brand for providing me with a copy of his paper.

46. For the reference to the earlier Rakove *Original Meanings* book, see "War of the Words" chapter infra.

47. The "stuck in my craw" speech: Scalia's Henry J. Abraham Speech, April 15, 2010, University of Virginia Law School, Charlottesville, Virginia, author's notes.

CHAPTER 23: THE METHODOLOGY OF ORIGINALISM

1. The account of this speech is based on two articles on the Harvard Law School website: "Scalia Defends the 'Methodology of Originalism,'" *Harvard Law Today,* November 2008; "In Inaugural Vaughan Lecture, Scalia Defends the 'Methodology of Originalism,'" *Spotlight at Harvard Law School,* October 3, 2008, www.law.harvard.edu.

2. Ibid., and Memo to Professor Alan Dershowitz, from his research assistants, December 4, 2008, "Scalia's Inconsistent Originalism, Reordered by Case Strength." Thanks to Professor Dershowitz for supplying the author with this memo. Other cases in which Scalia could have, but did not, use his originalism to decide: *Zelman v. Simmons-Harris* (2002), *Hudson v. Michigan* (2006), *Hamdan v. Rumsfeld* (2006), *Meredith v. Jefferson County* (2007), *Baze v. Rees* (2008), *United States v. Williams* (2008), *Kennedy v. Louisiana* (2008), *Davis v. F.E.C.* (2008), arguably *Boumediene v. Bush* (2008), *Pleasant Valley v. Summum* (2009), *Montejo v. Louisiana* (2009), and *Caperton v. A. T. Massey* (2009).

3. J. Harvie Wilkinson, "Of Guns, Abortions, and the Unraveling Rule of Law," *University of Virginia Law Review* 95, April 2009, 253. An excellent article on the conservative judges' attack on Scalia's *Heller* opinion can be found in Adam J. White, "Wilkinson and Posner Dissenting: Two Conservative Judges Challenge Judge Scalia," *Weekly Standard,* December 15, 2008.

4. Wilkinson, "Of Guns, Abortions, and the Unraveling Rule of Law," p. 254.

5. Ibid., p. 263.

6. Ibid., p. 256.

7. Ibid., pp. 264–65.

8. Scalia's argument has the same flaw as the classical American legal syllogism on which the power of judicial review is based, defining the final interpretive power of the Supreme Court over the political branches and the states for the Constitution. This argument was created by Chief Justice John Marshall based on Alexander Hamilton's position in *Federalist* 78. Marshall argued in *Marbury v. Madison* in creating the power of judicial review that: 1) judges interpret laws, 2) the Constitution is a fundamental law, and so 3) judges can interpret the Constitution to determine the validity of legislative laws. The problem for Marshall then, as it is for Scalia now, is who is doing the interpreting. Marshall did not live long enough to see this flaw. After his death in 1835, his successor, Chief Justice Roger Brooke Taney, a Jacksonian states' rights proponent in opposition to Marshall's nationalist posture, reached exactly the opposite views as the earlier Court simply by using a different, state-oriented interpretation of the Constitution.

9. Stanley Fish, "Politics in the Academy: The Same Old Song," "Opinionator," blog, *New*

York Times, February 6, 2012, www.nyt.com. Jack Balkin, *Living Originalism* (Cambridge: Belknap Press/Harvard University Press, 2011). Steven Calabresi and Julia T. Rickert, "Originalism and Sex Discrimination," *University of Texas Law Review* 90, no. 1 (2011): 1–101.

10. "Text of Justice David Souter's Speech," May 27, 2010, *Harvard Gazette,* http://news .harvard.edu/gazette/story/2010/05/text-of-justice-david-souters-speech/; Stephen Breyer, *Active Liberty: Interpreting Our Democratic Constitution First* (New York: Oxford University Press, 2008). See also *Roper v. Simmons,* 543 U.S. 551 (2005), *Lee v. Weisman,* 505 U.S. 577 (1992), *McCreary County v. ACLU of Kentucky* (545 U.S. 844 (2005), and *Van Orden v. Perry,* 545 U.S. 677 (2005).

11. Barack Obama, *The Audacity of Hope: Thoughts on Reclaiming the American Dream* (New York: Vintage, 2008), as quoted in Nina Totenberg, "Law School Past Shapes Obama's View on Justices," NPR, October 30, 2008, www.npr.org.

12. Justin Jouvenal, "Ten Picks for Obama's Supreme Court," *Salon,* November 19, 2008, www.salon.com.

13. Pete Winn, "Breyer, Souter Are Obama's Models for Supreme Court Choices, Advisor Says," CNSnews.com, October 31, 2008.

14. Tom Brune, "McCain Praises Bush Supreme Court Appointees," *Newsday,* May 6, 2008.

15. See the 2008 Pew Forum on Religious and Public Life, U.S. Religious Landscape Survey, 2008, http://www.pewforum.org/Topics/Religious-Affiliation/Unaffiliated/.

16. The remaining nearly 30 percent consists of those who are unaffiliated nonreligious (roughly 17 percent) and members of other religions.

17. Jeffrey Rosen, "McJustice," *New Republic,* November 5, 2008, www.tnr.com.

18. Edward Morrissey and Elizabeth Scalia, "An Open Letter to Our Catholic Friends on Election Eve," ProLifeBlogs.com, November 3, 2008. Scalia is a freelance writer and columnist for *InsideCatholic,* and the writer for the religious-oriented *The Anchoress* blog.

19. Douglas Kmiec, "Reaganites for Obama?," *Slate,* February 13, 2008, www.slate.com; Nicholas Cafardi, "I'm Catholic, Staunchly Anti-Abortion, and Support Obama," *National Catholic Reporter,* September 30, 2008, http://ncronline3.org/drupal/?q=print/2058.

20. Michael Paulson, "Priest: No Communion for Obama Voters," November 13, 2008, "Articles of Faith," blog, *Boston Globe* online.

21. Liz Halloran, "Obama Victory Ends GOP Hopes for a Much More Conservative Supreme Court," *U.S. News & World Report,* November 13, 2008.

22. Antonin Scalia speech, Annual Convention of the Federalist Society, Washington, D.C., November 22, 2008, www.fed-soc.org.

23. See William Rehnquist, *Grand Inquests: The Historic Impeachments of Justice Samuel Chase and President Andrew Johnson* (New York: Harper Perennial, 1999); William Rehnquist, *All the Laws but One: Civil Liberties in Wartime* (New York: Vintage, 2000); and William Rehnquist, *Centennial Crisis: The Disputed Election of 1876* (New York: Vintage, 2005).

24. See Sandra Day O'Connor and H. Alan Day, *Lazy B: Growing Up on a Cattle Ranch in the American Southwest* (New York: Random House, 2003); and Sandra Day O'Connor, *The Majesty of the Law: Reflections of a Supreme Court Justice* (New York: Random House, 2004).

25. Quoted in Jeffrey Toobin, "No More Mr. Nice Guy," *New Yorker,* May 25, 2009, pp. 42–51.

26. Jennifer Ludden and Linton Weeks, "Sotomayor: 'Always Looking over My Shoulder,'"

May 26, 2009, NPR. On the "Sonia from the Bronx" nickname, see Sonia Sotomayor interview with Scott Pelley, *60 Minutes,* CBS News, June 16, 2013. For more on Justice Sotomayor's background, see her memoir, *My Beloved World* (New York: Alfred A. Knopf, 2013).

27. Amy Goldstein and Alex MacGillis, "Sotomayor Was a Passionate but Civil Activist," *Washington Post,* June 1, 2009; David D. Kirkpatrick, "Judge's Mentor: Part Guide, Part Foil," *New York Times,* June 21, 2009.

28. Tony Mauro, "A Catholic Super-Majority on the Supreme Court," *The BLT: The Blog of Legal Times,* May 27, 2009.

29. *Salazar v. Buono,* Oral Argument, www.supremecourt.gov, October 7, 2009.

30. Geoffrey R. Stone, "Justice Scalia's Cross," *Huffington Post,* October 8, 2009, www.huff ingtonpost.com.

31. *Salazar v. Buono,* 559 U.S. 700 (2010) (Kennedy, J., majority).

32. *McConnell v. Federal Election Commission,* 540 U.S. 93 (2003).

33. *Austin v. Michigan Chamber of Commerce,* 494 U.S. 652, 660 (1990) (Marshall, J., majority).

34. Ibid., at 679 (Scalia, J., dissenting).

35. Ibid., at 693.

36. Ibid., at 687.

37. *Citizens United v. Federal Election Commission,* 558 U.S. 310, 340–41 (2010) (Kennedy, J., majority).

38. The source of this precedent is in dispute, but it goes back to the seminal Marshall Court case of *Trustees of Dartmouth College v. Woodward,* 17 U.S. 518 (1819).

39. *Citizens United v. Federal Election Commission,* at p. 341 (Kennedy, J., majority). See also Richard L. Hasen, "Super-Soft Money," *Slate,* October 25, 2011, www.slate.com. Whatever "history and logic" Kennedy saw here dismissing the prospect of corruption, it did not persuade the state of Montana, which in 2011 reinstated its ban on corporate campaign contributions to avoid corruption. The U.S. Supreme Court overturned this ban in June 2012. See "Supreme Court Ends Montana Ban on Corporate Political Spending," *Los Angeles Times,* June 25, 2012.

40. *Citizens United v. Federal Election Commission,* at 356 (Kennedy, J., majority).

41. Ibid., at 356–57.

42. Ibid.

43. Ibid., at 356. See also "Senator McCain Condemns Citizens United," *Salon,* March 18, 2012, www.salon.com; and Robert Barnes, "How Is the Roberts Court Unusual. A Law Professor Counts the Ways," *Washington Post,* March 4, 2012, www.washingtonpost.com; and see Benjamin H. Barton, "An Empirical Study of Supreme Court Pre-Appointment Experience," Social Science Research Network, February 24, 2012, www.ssrn.com.

44. See, for example, James Warren, "Richard Posner Bashes Citizens United Ruling," *Daily Beast,* July 14, 2012, http://www.thedailybeast.com/articles/2012/07/14/richard-posner -bashes-supreme-court-s-citizens-united-ruling.html; and Adam Skaggs, "Thanks Citizens United for This Campaign Finance Mess We're In," *The Atlantic,* July 27, 2012, http://www.theatlantic.com/politics/archive/2012/07/thanks-citizens-united-for-this -campaign-finance-mess-were-in/260389/.

45. *Citizens United v. Federal Election Commission,* at 394 (Stevens, J., dissenting).

46. Ibid., at 394.

47. Ibid., at 396.

48. Ibid., at 391–92.

49. Ibid., at 432.

50. Ibid., at 391–92 (Scalia, J., concurring).

51. Adam Liptak, "Justices, 5–4, Reject Corporate Spending Limit," *New York Times,* January 22, 2010, p. A1; Adam Liptak, "Stevens Era, Nearing End, Takes on an Edge," *New York Times,* January 26, 2010, p. A12. For more on this rare practice of oral dissents from the bench, see Christopher W. Schmidt and Carolyn Shapiro, "Oral Dissenting from the Supreme Court," *William and Mary Bill of Rights Journal* 19 (2010): 75–129.

52. Liptak, "Justices, 5–4, Reject Corporate Spending Limit."

53. Lark McCarthy interview with John Paul Stevens, "John Paul Stevens Discusses Longevity," *AARP The Magazine,* July 5, 2011, www.aarp.org.

54. Ibid.

55. Quotations and descriptions from author's notes of Scalia's Henry J. Abraham speech, April 15, 2010, University of Virginia Law School, Charlottesville, Virginia.

56. *The Slaughter-house Cases,* 83 U.S. 36 (1873).

57. Author conversation with Antonin Scalia, April 16, 2010, Boar's Head Inn, Charlottesville, Virginia.

58. Joseph J. Ellis, "Immaculate Misconception and the Supreme Court," *Washington Post,* May 7, 2010, p. A25. Ellis's arguments were subsequently bolstered by Founding Era scholar Pauline Maier of MIT in her seminal and magisterial book *Ratification,* which proves how widespread the disagreements were among people attending the various state ratification conventions as to the meaning of the Bill of Rights: Pauline Maier, *Ratification: Americans Debate the Constitution, 1787–1788* (New York: Simon & Schuster, 2010).

59. See letter from Thomas Jefferson to James Madison, September 6, 1789, in Philip B. Kurland and Ralph Lerner, *The Founders' Constitution,* University of Chicago Press online, http://press-pubs.uchicago.edu/founders/documents/v1ch2s23.html. Here Jefferson says, in part: "The question Whether one generation of men has a right to bind another, seems never to have been started either on this or our side of the water. Yet it is a question of such consequences as not only to merit decision, but place also, among the fundamental principles of every government. The course of reflection in which we are immersed here on the elementary principles of society has presented this question to my mind; and that no such obligation can be so transmitted I think very capable of proof.—I set out on this ground, which I suppose to be self-evident, *'that the earth belongs in usufruct to the living'*: that the dead have neither powers nor rights over it."

60. Scalia, "Originalism: The Lesser Evil," *University of Cincinnati Law Review* 57 (1989): 849ff.

61. Quotes from this speech come from "Text of Justice David Souter's Speech," May 27, 2010, *Harvard Gazette,* http://news.harvard.edu/gazette/story/2010/05/text-of-justice-david-souters-speech/. For more on the link between the terms "Fair Reading" and originalism, a link that Souter makes clear in his speech, see E. J. Dionne, Jr., "David Souter vs. the Antonin Scalias," *Washington Post,* June 3, 2010.

62. *McDonald v. City of Chicago,* 561 U.S. 3025 (2010).

63. *McDonald v. City of Chicago,* 130 U.S. 3020, 3036 (2010) (Alito, J., majority).

64. Ibid., at 3042.

65. Thomas had already made clear publicly his support for the Privileges or Immunities Clause as a means of protecting unenumerated individual rights and libertarianism. In 2007, speaking at the twenty-fifth anniversary of the founding of the Federalist Society, Thomas had said: "I attended a conference in 1988 at UVA, I think this organization was about 6 years old, and at that time, I had the opportunity to debate J. Harvie Wilkinson,

[now] Judge J. Harvie Wilkinson, about the privileges or immunities clause of the 14th Amendment. He was not too keen on it at the time, and I was very keen on it, and I remained very keen on it." Federalist Society 25th Anniversary Gala, Washington, D.C., November 15, 2007.

66. *McDonald v. City of Chicago,* at 3075 (Thomas, J., concurring).

67. Ibid., at 3077.

68. Ibid., at 3088.

69. Ibid., at 3050 (Scalia, J., concurring).

70. *McDonald v. City of Chicago,* at 3099 (Stevens, J., dissenting).

71. Ibid., at 3107.

72. Ibid., at 3108.

73. Ibid., at 3058 (Scalia, J., concurring). News accounts and blogs at the time questioned the vehemence of Scalia's attack. See, for example, Robert Barnes, "As Stevens Retires from Court, One Final Duel with Scalia," *Washington Post,* July 26, 2010.

74. *McDonald v. City of Chicago,* 3052–53 (Scalia, J., concurring).

75. Ibid., at 3058.

76. Ibid., at 3117 (Stevens, J., dissenting).

77. Ibid., at 3117–18.

78. Ibid., at 3118.

79. Ibid., at 3118–19.

80. Ibid., at 3119.

CHAPTER 24: KENNEDY'S COURT

1. Associated Press, May 10, 2010, http://www.msnbc.msn.com/id/36967616/.

2. Robert Barnes, "Supreme Court Opens with Three Women, Potential for Partisan Divide," *Washington Post,* October 2, 2010. Thanks also to my wife, Carol Wright, for pointing out both the baby boomer majority on the Court and, even more importantly, being the first person I know to see the real importance of the loss of Stevens from this Court.

3. Sheryl Kay Stolberg et al., "New Yorker Chose a Careful Path to Washington," *New York Times,* May 11, 2010; Amy Goldstein et al., "A History of Pragmatism over Partisanship," *Washington Post,* May 11, 2010; Carl Hulse, "Senate Confirms Kagan in Partisan Vote," *New York Times,* August 6, 2010.

4. Adam Liptak, "The Most Conservative Court in Decades, Under Roberts, Center of Gravity Has Edged to the Right," *New York Times,* July 25, 2010. at www.nytimes.com.

5. Ibid.

6. Bob Egelko, "Constitution Does Not Ban Sex Bias, Scalia Argues," *San Francisco Chronicle,* September 18, 2010.

7. Stephen Colbert, *The Colbert Report,* September 29, 2010, comedy central, at www.colbertnation.com.

8. "Legally Speaking: The Originalist," *California Lawyer,* January 2011.

9. "There He Goes Again," editorial, *New York Times,* January 4, 2011.

10. Eyder Peralta, "Justice Scalia Courts Controversy for Agreeing to Speak to Tea Party Caucus," at "The Two-Way: Breaking News from NPR," NPR online, at http://www.npr.org/blogs/thetwo-way/2011/01/05/132683456/justice-scalia-courts-controversy-for-agreeing-to-speak-at-tea-party-caucus, January 5, 2011.

11. "Critics Attack Scalia's Decision to Talk to New House Members," blog, *Wall Street Journal,* January 5, 2011.

12. Letter, Bob Edgar to Attorney General Eric Holder Jr., January 19, 2011, Common Cause, www.commoncause.org.

13. Ibid.

14. Quoted in Common Cause letter, Arn H. Pearson to Antonin Scalia, February 28, 2011, found at www.commoncause.org. The press reports included Kate Zernike, "Secretive Republican Donors Are Planning Ahead," *New York Times,* October 19, 2010. For more on the Koch brothers and politics, see Jane Mayer, "Covert Operations," *New Yorker,* August 30, 2010. In addition, the Common Cause letter argued that Justice Thomas should also have recused himself because his wife, Ginni's, conservative, Tea Party–linked associated lobbying organization, Liberty Central, would have benefited from the *Citizens United* decision.

15. "Code of Conduct for United States Judges," United States Courts, http://www.uscourts .gov/RulesAndPolicies/CodesOfConduct/CodeConductUnitedStatesJudges.aspx.

16. "Disqualification of Justice, Judge, or Magistrate Judge," 28 U.S.C. 455: "(a) Any justice, judge, or magistrate judge of the United States shall disqualify himself in any proceeding in which his impartiality might reasonably be questioned."

17. "Supreme Court Ethics," editorial, *Los Angeles Times,* May 25, 2011; "Common Cause Seeking Ethics Probe of Scalia and Thomas," *The BLT: The Blog of the Legal Times,* January 20, 2011.

Another source of the "reasonable questions" as to the impartiality of the justices stemmed from questions as to why the Federalist Society was compensating the justices for their expenses for the appearance, rather than the seminar organization itself. Some might interpret this failure to fully disclose the expenses reimbursement on their annual financial disclosure forms to be an effort by both parties to hide from public inspection the real reason for the trip to California, in order to avoid press and public scrutiny and criticism.

18. Bruce Allen Murphy, *Wild Bill: The Legend and Life of William O. Douglas* (New York: Random House, 2003), pp. 200–1. Such requests for corrective ethical legislation were not unprecedented. Similar inquiries were made in 1966 by members of Congress after revelations that Justice William Douglas had been taking money from an organization linked to interests in Las Vegas, but Chief Justice Earl Warren put it aside at the time when Douglas assured him that the matter had been handled.

19. R. Jeffrey Smith, "Professors Ask Congress for an Ethics Code for Supreme Court," *Washington Post,* February 23, 2011; "Supreme Court Ethics," editorial, *Los Angeles Times.*

20. Mike McIntyre, "Friendship of Justice and Magnate Puts Focus on Ethics," *New York Times,* June 18, 2011, www.nyt.com. See also Kenneth Vogel, Marin Cogan, and John Bresnahan, "Justice Thomas's Wife Now Lobbyist," *Politico,* February 4, 2011, www .politico.com. For more on the early reporting for this political donation, see Eric Lichtblau, "Justice Thomas's Wife Sets up a Conservative Lobbying Shop," *New York Times,* February 5, 2011; Reid J. Epstein, "Blog's Battle Over New York Times' Report on Justice Clarence Thomas," *Politico,* www.politico.com/news/stories/0611/57339.html; "Justice Thomas's Wife Now a Lobbyist," *Politico,* February 4, 2011, www.politico.com /news/stories/0211/48812_Page2.html; and Kenneth P. Vogel, "Secret Donors Make Thomas's Wife's Group a Tea Party Player," *Politico,* July 6, 2010, www.politico.com /news/stories/0710/39426.html.

21. "Cloud over the Court," editorial, *New York Times,* June 22, 2011.

22. Bill Mears, "Chief Justice Addresses Ethics and Recusal Questions in Year-End Report,"

CNN Justice, December 31, 2011, http://www.cnn.com/2011/12/31/justice/us-scotus-year-end-report/index.html.

23. "Trust and the Supreme Court," editorial, *New York Times,* February 19, 2012.

24. Jeffrey M. Jones, "Supreme Court Approval Rating Dips to 46%," October 3, 2011, Gallup Poll, http://www.gallup.com/poll/149906/Supreme-Court-Approval-Rating-Dips.aspx.

25. Adam Liptak and Allison Kopicki, "Approval Ratings for Justices Hits Just 44% in New Poll," *New York Times,* June 8, 2012.

26. "AFJ Joins Members of Congress, Concerned Groups, Law Professors, and 100,000 Americans in Calling for Ethics Reform at the Supreme Court," Alliance for Justice, March 6, 2012, www.afj.org/press/030712.html. The letter cited was dated March 5, 2012.

27. Ibid.

28. "A Way Forward on Judicial Ethics," editorial, *New York Times,* March 11, 2012.

29. For more on the concept of the "public judiciary," see Richard Davis, *Justices and Journalists: The U.S. Supreme Court and the Media* (London: Cambridge University Press, 2011).

30. In 2006, Scalia also wrote the opinion in *Davis v. Washington,* 547 U.S. 813 (2006), in which the Confrontation Clause cross-examination rights did not extend to a 911 call that was deemed to be "non-testimonial" because it was being used to report on an emergency.

31. *Michigan v. Bryant,* 131 U.S. 1143, 1164, note 17 (2011) (Sotomayor, J., majority).

32. Ibid., at 1168 (Scalia, J., dissenting).

33. Ibid.

34. Ibid., at 1171–72.

35. Ibid. Italics in original.

36. Ibid., at 1174.

37. Ibid., at 1176. While Scalia was certain that he had the best of the arguments, not even his conservative colleagues agreed. The only other dissenter was liberal Justice Ruth Bader Ginsburg. Elena Kagan did not participate in this case.

38. Linda Greenhouse, "Justice Scalia Objects," *New York Times,* March 9, 2011.

39. *Brown v. Plata,* 131 U.S. 1910 (2011).

40. Ibid., at 1928 (Kennedy, J., majority).

41. See Dahlia Lithwick, "Show, Don't Tell," *Slate,* May 23, 2011, www.slate.com.

42. *Brown v. Plata,* at 1950–51 (Scalia, J., dissenting).

43. Ibid., at 1952–53.

44. Adam Liptak, "Justices 5–4, Tell California to Cut Prisoner Population," *New York Times,* May 23, 2011.

45. *Sykes v. United States,* at 2274 (Kennedy, J., majority).

46. Ibid., at 2277.

47. Ibid., at 2284 (Scalia, J., dissenting).

48. Ibid., at 2285.

49. Ibid., at 2287.

50. Ibid., at 2288.

51. Will Oremus, "Elena Kagan Admits Supreme Court Justices Haven't Quite Figured Out Email Yet," *Slate*, August 20, 2013, www.slate.com, http://www.slate.com/blogs/future_tense/2013/08/20/elena_kagan_supreme_court_justices_haven_t_gotten_to_email_use_paper_memos.html.

52. *Schwarzenegger v. Entertainment Merchants Association*, November 2, 2010, Oral Argu-

ment, p. 17, Supreme Court website. After Jerry Brown was sworn into office as governor, this case became *Brown v. Entertainment Merchants Association.*

53. *Brown v. Entertainment Merchants Association,* 131 U.S. 2729, 2733 (2011) (Scalia, J., majority).
54. Ibid., at 2736–37. See also Adam Liptak, "Justices Reject Ban on Violent Video Games for Children," *New York Times,* June 27, 2011.
55. *Brown v. Entertainment Merchants Association,* at 2742 (Scalia, J., majority).
56. Ibid., at 2752 (Thomas, J., dissenting).
57. Ibid., at 2759.

CHAPTER 25: ROBERTS' RULES OF ORDER

1. Transcript of Scalia speech at Duquesne in author's possession, September 24, 2011.
2. Electa Draper, "Justice Scalia Tells Catholics to Brave the Scorn of Worldly People," *Denver Post,* March 6, 2012.
3. Hillary Senour, "Denver Conference Challenges Thousands to Live Catholic Faith," Catholic News Agency, March 5, 2012.
4. Draper, "Justice Scalia Tells Catholics to Brave the Scorn of Worldly People"; Debra Cassens Weiss, "At Catholic Conference, Scalia Talks About the Possibility of Miracles," *ABA Journal,* March 5, 2012.
5. Stephen Prothero, "My Take: America's 12 Most Influential Catholics," CNN Belief Blog, March 2, 2012.
6. *United States v. Jones,* 132 S.Ct. 945 (2012).
7. *Kyllo v. United States,* 533 U.S. 27, at 40 (2001) (Scalia, J., majority).
8. *United States v. Jones,* 132 S.Ct. 945 at 949 (2012) (Scalia, J., majority).
9. Ibid., at 963 (Alito, J., concurring).
10. Ibid., at 964.
11. Ibid.
12. The three cases were: *National Federation of Independent Business v. Sebelius; Department of Health and Human Services v. Florida;* and *Florida v. Department of Health and Human Services.*
13. Bloomberg National News poll, March 15, 2012, cited in Greg Stohr, "Scalia Turns Advocate Against Obama as Queries Criticized," *Bloomberg News,* May 15, 2012. A separate Gallup Poll found in mid-April 2012 that 50 percent of their respondents believed that the Court would decide the case based on their "partisan political views," while only four in ten expected that the decision would be made "on the basis of the law." Robert Barnes and Scott Clement, "Poll: More Americans Expect Supreme Court Health Care Decision to Be Political," *Washington Post,* April 11, 2012.
14. Paul D. Carrington, "Bring the Justices Back to Earth," *New York Times,* April 8, 2012.
15. John Roberts, Commencement Address, Georgetown University Law Center, May 26, 2006, http://www.law.georgetown.edu/webcast/assets/GL_2006523112710.mp3.
16. *Department of Health and Human Services v. Florida,* Oral Arguments, March 27, 2012, pp. 4–5, www.supremecourt.gov.
17. Ibid., at 4–7.
18. Ibid., at 11–12.
19. Ibid., at 12–14.
20. Ibid., at 16–17.
21. Ibid., at 22–29.

22. Ibid.

23. Later, this would become another one of the comments by Scalia that would nettle critics as being more evidence of his partisanship. Mark Sherman, "Scalia's Critics Fault Justice over Politics," Associated Press, July 5, 2012; David Lyle, "The Fox News Justice: Scalia Channels Right-Wing Talking Points in Health Care Arguments," Media Matters for America blog site, March 30, 2012, found at http://mediamatters.org/blog/2012/03/30/the-fox-news-justice-scalia-channels-right-wing/184261; and Bart Torvik, "Did Scalia Regurgitate Tea Party Talking Points During Oral Arguments," April 3, 2012, Gillette -Torvik Blog, found at http://gillette-torvik.blogspot.com/2012/04/did-scalia-regurgitate-tea-party.html.

24. All of these quotations below from the Transcript of the Oral Arguments of the Supreme Court in *Florida v. H.H.S.,* March 28, 2012, pp. 8–11, found at www.supremecourt.gov.

25. See, for example, Stohr, "Scalia Turns Advocate Against Obama as Queries Criticized," Matthew DeLuca, "Did Scalia Parrot Fox News During Health Care Arguments?," *Slate,* April 5, 2012, slate.com.

26. Linda Greenhouse, "Embarrass the Future?," *New York Times,* April 4, 2012.

27. DeLuca, "Did Scalia Parrot Fox News During Health Care Arguments?" See also Stohr, "Scalia Turns Advocate Against Obama as Queries Criticized."

28. *Arizona v. United States,* 132, S.Ct. 2492, at 2499 (Kennedy, J., majority).

29. Ibid., at 2502.

30. Ibid., at 2505–08.

31. Ibid., at 2511–12 (Scalia, J., dissenting).

32. Bill Mears, "Mexican National Executed in Texas," CNN, July 7, 2011, http://www.cnn.com/2011/CRIME/07/07/texas.mexican.execution/index.html.

33. *Arizona v. United States,* at 2516–17 (Scalia, J., dissenting).

34. Pete Williams, *NBC Nightly News,* June 25, 2012; Dahlia Lithwick, "What It Looks Like When Justices Tear into Each Other—From Close Up," *Slate,* June 25, 2012, slate.com.

35. *Arizona v. United States,* at 2521 (Scalia, J., dissenting). Scalia bench statement, *Arizona v. United States,* http://s3.documentcloud.org/documents/372493/scalia-statement.pdf. Scalia's bench statement consisted of extracts from his dissent in the case. (Herein after Scalia bench statement, *Arizona v. United States.*)

36. Ibid.

37. Lithwick, "What It Looks Like When Justices Tear into Each Other—From Close Up."

38. Scalia bench statement, *Arizona v. United States* and at *Arizona v. United States,* at 2522.

39. Ibid.

40. Walter Dellinger, "Perhaps Justice Scalia Is Reading from the Wrong Constitution," *Slate,* June 26, 2012, slate.com.

41. Quoted in Sahil Kapur, "Legal Scholar: 'Scalia Has Finally Jumped the Shark,'" *TPMLiveWire* blog, June 25, 2012, http://livewire.talkingpointsmemo.com/entry/legal-scholar-scalia-has-finally-jumped-shark.

42. E. J. Dionne, "Justice Scalia Needs to Resign from High Court," *Washington Post,* June 28, 2012.

43. "Scalia's Partisan Outbursts," editorial, *Washington Post,* June 28, 2012.

44. Judge Richard Posner, "Justice Scalia Is Upset About Immigration. But Where Is His Evidence?," "Supreme Court in Review," *Slate,* June 27, 2012, slate.com.

45. Tony Mauro, "Inside the Supreme Court on a Historic Morning," *The BLTG: Blog of the Legal Times,* June 28, 2012.

46. Ibid.

47. *National Federation of Independent Businesses v. Sebelius,* 132 U.S. 2566, at 2584 (2012) (Roberts, C.J., majority).
48. Ibid., at 2587.
49. Ibid., at 2589.
50. Ibid., at 2590–91.
51. Katherine Fung and Jack Murkinson, "Supreme Court Health Care Ruling: CNN, Fox News, Wrong on Individual Mandate," *Huffington Post,* June 28, 2012, http://www.huffingtonpost.com/2012/06/28/cnn-supreme-court-health-care-individual-mandate_n_1633950.html.
52. *National Federation of Independent Businesses v. Sebelius,* at 2596 (Roberts, C.J., majority).
53. Ibid., at 2600.
54. Ibid., at 2604–5.
55. Ibid., at 2579.
56. Ibid., at 2643 (Kennedy, J., dissenting).
57. Ibid.
58. Ibid., at 2651.
59. Ibid., at 2656.
60. Ibid., at 2668.
61. Ibid., at 2672.
62. Ibid., at 2676–77.
63. NBC News reporter Pete Williams reported that only once previously in his tenure as chief, early in his time on a minor mortgage case, had Roberts joined a majority opinion with four liberals. The group at that time was John Paul Stevens, Stephen Breyer, Ruth Bader Ginsburg, and David Souter. Interview with Pete Williams on Chris Matthews's *Hardball,* MSNBC, July 1, 2012.
64. This argument was made by Linda Greenhouse, "A Justice in Chief," *New York Times,* June 28, 2012; Adam Liptak, "Roberts Shows Deft Hand as Swing Vote on Health Care," *New York Times,* June 28, 2012.
65. Jan Crawford, "Roberts Switched Views to Uphold Health Care Law," CBS News, July 1, 2012. For more on this case, see Jeffrey Toobin, *The Oath: The Obama White House and the Supreme Court* (New York: Doubleday, 2012), pp. 263–98.
66. Crawford, "Roberts Switched Views to Uphold Health Care Law."
67. George Stephanopolous, *This Week,* ABC News, June 30, 2012; Paul Campos, "Roberts Wrote Both Obamacare Opinions," *Salon,* July 3, 2012, salon.com.
68. Massimo Calabresi and David Von Drehle, "What Will Justice Kennedy Do?," *Time,* June 18, 2012; David Von Drehle, "Roberts Rules," *Time,* July 10, 2012. Law professors posted in their blogs and on Twitter speculation that the decision by Roberts to switch may have been leaked to Washington's political leaders, such as Democratic Vermont senator Patrick Leahy, and the press, such as columnist George Will, while debating just who would have done so. See Orin Kerr, "Who Leaked?," *Volokh Conspiracy;* Stewart Baker, "Did the Supreme Court's Deliberations on Health Care Leak?," *Volokh Conspiracy,* July 1, 2012, and Ian Millhiser, "Supreme Court Springs a Leak: Leaks to Conservative Pundits May Have Started More than a Month Ago," *Think Progress,* July 1, 2012.

See also Campos, "Roberts Wrote Both Obamacare Opinions." From then on the blogs, such as *The Volokh Conspiracy,* contained debates over who knew what and when, and who was doing the leaking. See Orin Kerr, "So Now We Have Supreme Court Leaks Disagreeing with Other Supreme Court Leaks," *Volokh Conspiracy,* July 3, 2012;

and Ilya Somin, "Leaks, Counter-Leaks, and the Reason for Roberts' Switch," and "More on the Supreme Court Leaks," *Volokh Conspiracy,* July 4, 2012.

69. Adam Liptak and Alison Kopicki, "Public's Opinion of Supreme Court Drops After Health Care Decision," *New York Times,* July 18, 2012.

70. Scalia was answering a question here after a speech at the Federalist Society in Bozeman, Montana. Debra Cassens Weiss, "Scalia: SCOTUS Should Not 'Invent New Minorities,'" *ABA Journal,* September 20, 2013, www.abajournal.com.

CHAPTER 26: READING LAW

1. Amanda Frost, "What the Supreme Court Did This Summer," *Slate,* Slate.com, August 24, 2012, https://www.stmarytx.edu/?s=Antonin+Scalia&x=12&y=11. See also St. Mary's University website: https://www.stmarytx.edu/?s=Antonin+Scalia&x=12&y=11. On payment received, see Scalia, Financial Disclosure Statement, 2012, filed in 2013, *OpenSecrets* blog at OpenSecrets.org: Center for Responsive Politics, http://pfds.opensecrets.org/N99999921_2012.pdf.

2. Antonin Scalia and Bryan A. Garner, *Reading Law: The Interpretation of Legal Texts* (St. Paul, MN: Thomson/West, 2012). On the first publicity, see "Justice Antonin Scalia and Bryan A. Garner Release Book on the Interpretation of Legal Texts," Thomson Reuters, June 24, 2012.

3. See Tony Mauro, "In Second Book, Scalia, Garner Warn Judicial Decisions Leading to 'Descent into Social Rancor,'" *National Law Journal,* June 15, 2012; Richard Brust, "Scalia and Garner Release 567-Page Tome on Textualism," *ABA Journal.com,* June 19, 2012; and Adam Liptak, "Hints in New Scalia Book of Views on Health Law," *New York Times,* June 15, 2012

4. S. Eugene Scalia, *Carducci: His Critics and Translators in England and America, 1881–1932* (New York: S. F. Vanni, 1937), p. 90.

5. Joseph Story, *Commentaries on the Constitution of the United States,* 2 vols. (Boston: Little, Brown, 1858). While others, such as Felix Frankfurter, had written articles and given speeches on legal analysis, not since the early nineteenth century had a sitting Supreme Court justice written and published a book of legal commentary of such comprehensiveness. See Felix Frankfurter, "Some Reflections on the Reading of Statutes," *Columbia Law Review* 47 (1947): 527.

6. Marshall's legal commentary was done anonymously, and more briefly. See Gerald Gunther, ed., *John Marshall's Defense of McCulloch v. Maryland* (Palo Alto, CA: Stanford University Press, 1969).

7. Scalia and Garner, *Reading Law,* p. xxvii.

8. Ibid., p. 10.

9. Ibid.

10. Ibid., p. xxx.

11. Ibid., p. xxviii.

12. Ibid., p. 5.

13. Ibid., pp. 6–7.

14. Ibid., p. 16.

15. Ibid.

16. Ibid., p. 17.

17. Ibid., p. 18.

18. Ibid., p. 22.

19. Ibid.

20. Ibid., p. 30.

21. Ibid., p. 78.

22. Ibid., p. 89.

23. Ibid.

24. Ibid., p. 403.

25. Ibid., pp. 409–10.

26. Ibid., p. 410.

27. Stanley Fish, "Intention and Canons of Legal Interpretation," *New York Times,* July 16, 2012.

28. This earlier figure for the Thomson West Publishing payments likely included advances for writing both his *Making Your Case* and *Reading Law* books, in addition to his royalties on the former. For more on these payments, see Chapter 21. See Supreme Court Annual Financial Reports, collected by Judicial Watch, http://www.judicialwatch.org/judge /scalia-antonin/, and also found at the OpenSecrets.org website http://www.opensecrets .org/pfds/candlook.php?txtName=scalia. Scalia reported in these forms that his annual compensation from West Publishing was: 2007: $33,000 book advance; 2008: $98,716 (book advance and royalties); 2009: $121,535 (book advance and royalties); 2010: $37,797 (book royalties); 2011: $18,775 (book royalties). While the 2012 financial disclosure forms for the Supreme Court had not yet been posted as of this writing, the figure of $63,991 (some of which may included money for the first book as well) was reported in CNN: Bill Mears, "Sotomayor's Life Story Is Lucrative," CNN.com, June 7, 2013, http://politicalticker.blogs .cnn.com/2013/06/07/sotomayors-life-story-is-lucrative/?iref=allsearch. See also Jesse J. Holland, "From Robes to Riches: Supreme Court Justice Sonia Sotomayor Nets over Three Million from Memoir," *Washington Times,* June 7, 2013, http://www.washington times.com/news/2013/jun/7/sotomayor-gets-another-19-million-memoir/print/. While the remuneration to Scalia for these books is substantial, it pales in comparison to the more than million-dollar advance reported for Justice Thomas, and the $3.1 million to Justice Sotomayor for her memoir.

29. Piers Morgan interview, *Piers Morgan Tonight,* CNN, July 18, 2012.

30. Chris Wallace interview, *Fox News Sunday,* July 19, 2012.

31. Wallace did not point out that the dissent Scalia claimed sole credit for here was actually cowritten, and cosigned, by three other conservative colleagues.

32. This comment drew comment on the Internet from some who wondered about Scalia's "judicial temperament." See "Scalia's Surprising Admission," *Community* blog, July 31, 2012, at http://current.com/community/93858629_scalias-surprising-admission.htm.

33. Richard A. Posner, "The Incoherence of Antonin Scalia," *New Republic,* August 24, 2012, http://www.newrepublic.com/article/magazine/books-and-arts/106441/scalia-garner -reading-the-law-textual-originalism#.

Posner's critical review of Scalia's book reignited the verbal battle they had been engaged in since the *Heller* opinion. This verbal brushfire became a full-fledged conflagration as a result of online responses by Scalia's former law clerk Edward Whelan and his book's coauthor, Bryan A. Garner. In his "Bench Memos" blog for the *National Review Online,* Whelan posted a five-part response titled "Richard A. Posner's Badly Confused Attack on Scalia/Garner." Edward Whelan, "Richard A. Posner's Badly Confused Attack on Scalia/Garner," "Bench Memos," *National Review Online,* 5 parts, August 31, September 1, September 3, September 6, and September 7, 2012.

The postings, which would be supplemented by others on the topic over the next three weeks, began with the charge: "Posner's attack is remarkably slipshod and untrustworthy." After arguing that Posner had misinterpreted the book's arguments and committed a number of analytical errors in seeking to undermine the book's case analysis, Whelan concluded: "I have not attempted in these posts to provide an exhaustive account of Posner's errors. I have instead focused on those errors that show that his most incendiary charge—that Scalia and Garner have misrepresented the cases they cite—is false and that his review is untrustworthy and, indeed, incompetent." Ibid., Part 5, September 7, 2012.

Equally offended by the review, Bryan Garner launched his own verbal salvo on his blog "Law Prose," complaining about the "tendentious hostility" of Posner's review, and terming it "a high-profile literary rampage." Bryan Garner, "Law Prose," "Response to Richard A. Posner," September 5, 2012, http://www.lawprose.org/blog/?p=570.

But Posner was unimpressed, responding in the *New Republic*: "Bryan Garner's letter repeats criticisms by the *National Review* blogger Ed Whelan, a former Scalia law clerk who is the head of the Ethics and Public Policy Center, an extreme conservative think tank preoccupied with homosexuality (which Whelan believes is destroying the American family), abortion, embryonic stem cell research, and other affronts to conservative theology." Bryan A. Garner and Richard Posner, "How Nuanced Is Justice Scalia's Judicial Philosophy: An Exchange," *New Republic,* September 10, 2012. Midway through the piece, Posner bolstered his argument by offering what he characterized as another misuse of a case example, as evidence to him that the book is "riddled with inaccuracies, illustrating the adage that too many cooks spoil the broth." (Ibid.)

34. Terry Baynes, "Fanning Furor, Scalia Says Court of Appeals Judge Lied," Reuters, September 17, 2012; for earlier Stephen J. Adler article, see "Live Wire on the D.C. Circuit," *Legal Times,* June 23, 1986.

35. Quoted in Richard A. Posner, "Richard Posner Responds to Scalia's Accusation of Lying," *New Republic,* September 20, 2012, at www.tnr.com.

36. Ibid., in which Judge Posner responded to this accusation.

37. Geoffrey R. Stone, "The Supreme Court and the 2012 Election," *Huffington Post*, August 13, 2012, http://www.huffingtonpost.com/geoffrey-r-stone/the-supreme-court-and -the_b_1773347.html.

38. Charlie Rose interview, November 27, 2012.

39. Ushma Patel, "Scalia Favors 'Enduring,' Not Living, Constitution," December 11, 2012, Princeton University website, www.princeton.edu; Anna Mazarakis, "Challenging a Justice," December 12, 2012, *Daily Princetonian;* Caleb Kennedy, "Scalia Defends Gay Rights Position," December 11, 2012, *Daily Princetonian*; "Scalia Quizzed at N.J.'s Princeton on Gay Issue," *Bismarck Tribune,* December 11, 2012.

40. Amy Davidson, "The Animus of Antonin Scalia," December 12, 2012, www.newyorker .com.

41. Patel, "Scalia Favors 'Enduring,' Not Living, Constitution"; Mazarakis, "Challenging a Justice"; Kennedy, "Scalia Defends Gay Rights Position"; "Scalia Quizzed at N.J.'s Princeton on Gay Issue."

42. Davidson, "The Animus of Antonin Scalia."

43. Alito, *Maryland v. King,* Oral Argument, February 26, 2013, p. 35.

44. *Maryland v. King,* 186 L.Ed2d. 1 (2013), at 22–23.

45. Ibid., at 26–27.

46. Ibid., at 27–28.

47. Ibid., at 53.

48. *Florida v. Jardines*, 133 S.Ct. 1409 (2013).

49. *Michigan v. Hudson*, 547 U.S. 586 (2006); *Vernonia School District v. Acton*, 515 U.S. 646 (1995).

50. *Kyllo v. United States*, 533 U.S. 27 (2001); *United States v. Jones*, 32 S. Ct. 945 (2012).

51. *Olmstead v. United States*, 277 U.S. 438 (1928).

52. *Maryland v. King*, at 53 (Scalia, J., dissenting).

53. Ibid., at 56.

54. Ibid., at 57.

55. Ibid., at 59–60.

56. Ibid., at 67.

57. Ibid., at 78.

58. Jeffrey Rosen, "A Damning Dissent," *New Republic*, June 4, 2013, found at http://www .newrepublic.com/article/113375/supreme-court-dna-case-antonin-scalias-dissent -ages#.

CHAPTER 27: GRUMPY OLD JUSTICE

1. "N.C. Lawyers Listen as Justice Scalia Bemoans 'Moral Arbiter' on Eve of Gay Marriage Ruling," *Legal Monitor Worldwide*, June 22, 2013, Lexis/Nexis. Scalia described the Mullahs speech as his "most provocative one" to a New England School of Law banquet in 2006. Massachusetts Lawyers Weekly Staff, "Justice Scalia Delivers Speech to New England School of Law Banquet," *Massachusetts Lawyers Weekly*, March 27, 2006, Lexis/ Nexis.

   Scalia had shortened the title of the second Polish version of his speech from the more academic, Australian speech version, "Judges as Authoritative Expositors of the Natural Law," to the shorter and more eye-catching "Judges as Moral Arbiters." See both: Antonin Scalia, "Mullahs of the West: Judges as Authoritative Expositors of the Natural Law?," Sir John Young Oration, the Boston, Melbourne, Oxford Conversazioni on Culture and Society, Trinity College, University of Melbourne, 2005; and Antonin Scalia, "Mullahs of the West: Judges as Moral Arbiters," Rzecznik Praw Obywatelskich, August 24, 2009 (English translation).

2. Jean Ann Esselink, "Did Justice Scalia Just Telegraph His Decision on DOMA?," *The New Civil Rights Movement*, June 24, 2013, http://thenewcivilrightsmovement.com/did -justice-scalia-telegraph-his-decision-on-doma/legal-issues/2013/06/24/69455.

3. Nathaniel Frank, "Scalia the Mullah: The Justice's Misunderstanding of Morality, and How It Leads Him Astray in Cases About Homosexuality," *Slate*, June 25, 2013, slate .com, http://www.slate.com/articles/news_and_politics/jurisprudence/2013/06/scalia _and_gay_marriage_how_the_justice_misunderstands_morality.html.

4. *Fisher v. University of Texas*, 133 U.S. 2411 (2013). (Justice Kagan took no part in the decision.)

5. Ibid., at 2422 (Scalia, J., concurring).

6. *Northwest Austin Municipal Utility District No. 1 v. Holder*, 557 U.S. 193, 200 (2009).

7. Ibid. (Roberts, C. J., majority), at 211. "Perfect compliance with the Fifteenth Amendment's substantive command is not now—nor has it ever been—the yardstick for determining whether Congress has the power to employ broad prophylactic legislation to enforce that amendment. The burden remains with Congress to prove that the extreme circumstances warranting §5's enactment persist today. A record of scattered infringement of the right to vote is not a constitutionally acceptable substitute."

8. *Shelby County v. Holder,* Oral Argument, February 27, 2013, p. 47.

9. Nicole Flatow and Ian Millhiser, "Scalia: Voting Rights Act Is 'Perpetuation of Racial Entitlement,'" *Think Progress,* February 27, 2013, http://thinkprogress.org/justice /2013/02/27/1646891/scalia-voting-rights-act-is-perpetuation-of-racial-entitlement/. See also Spencer Overton, "Justice Scalia's Latest 'Racial Entitlement' Remark," *Huffington Post,* April 17, 2013, http://www.huffingtonpost.com/spencer-overton/justice-scalias -latest-ra_b_3103845.html; and "Scalia Calls Voting Rights Act 'Racial Entitlement,'" "Politics" blog, *SF Gate,* http://blog.sfgate.com/nov05election/2013/03/20/scalia-calls -voting-rights-act-racial-entitlement/.

10. *Shelby County v. Holder,* 133 U.S. 2612 (2013).

11. Ibid., at 2631 (Roberts, C. J., majority). For more on Roberts's view of the changes in race relations in this country, see *Parents Involved in Community Schools v. Seattle School District No. 1,* 551 U.S. 701 (2007), at 748, in which he said: "The way to stop discrimination on the basis of race is to stop discriminating on the basis of race."

12. Howard Mintz, "Kristin Perry and Sandy Stier, at the Center of Prop 8 Supreme Court Case," *San Jose Mercury News,* March 19, 2013, *Huffington Post,* http://www.huffington post.com/2013/03/19/kristin-perry-sandy-stier_n_2912223.html.

13. *In re Marriage Cases,* 43 Cal. 4th 757 (2008).

14. *Hollingsworth v. Perry,* Oral Arguments, March 26, 2013, pp. 38–39, www.supremecourt .gov.

15. Ibid., pp. 39–40.

16. Ibid.

17. *Hollingsworth v. Perry,* 133 S.Ct. 2652 (2013). Justice Kennedy wrote for an unusual group of three other dissenters—Justices Thomas, Sotomayor, and Alito—in being ready to grant standing and decide this case.

18. Ibid., at 2668 (Roberts, C. J., majority).

19. For the argument that the Fifth Amendment Due Process clause has equal protection aspects, see *Bolling v. Sharpe,* 349 U.S. 497 (1954).

20. *United States v. Windsor,* 133 S.Ct. 2675, at 2692 (Kennedy, J., majority).

21. Ibid.

22. Ibid.

23. Ibid.

24. Ibid., at 2694.

25. Ibid.

26. Ibid., at 2694–95.

27. Ibid., at 2695–96.

28. Ibid., at 2697–98 (Scalia, J., dissenting).

29. Ibid., at 2698.

30. Ibid., at 2703.

31. Ibid., at 2705.

32. Ibid., at 2707. Just as he had argued in the *Lawrence v. Texas* case, Scalia said here that he had trouble understanding which legal level of scrutiny Kennedy was using to decide the case.

33. Ibid., at 2707–8.

34. Ibid., at 2708.

35. Ibid. at 2709.

36. Ibid.

37. Ibid.

38. Rebecca Greenfield, "The Brouhaha Behind 'Argle Bargle': A Linguistic Explanation," *Atlantic Wire,* June 26, 2013, http://www.theatlanticwire.com/national/2013/06/brouhaha -behind-argle-bargle-linguistic-explanation/66630/.

39. Ibid. at 2710.

40. Federal District Court judge Robert Shelby struck down Utah's ban on gay marriages. The federal 10th Circuit Court of Appeals refused to overturn the decision immediately, allowing gay marriages to continue in that state. In Ohio, District Court judge Timothy Black ruled that despite that state's gay marriage ban, gay marriages performed in other states must be recognized for the purposes of creating a death certificate. In early January 2014, the United States Supreme Court put the gay marriages in Utah on hold, until the 10th Circuit could fully consider appeals from the district court cases. Then, the case would have to be appealed to the Supreme Court and accepted for review. For more, see Mark Joseph Stern, "Utah Judge 'Agrees with Scalia,' strikes down Gay Marriage Ban," *Slate.com,* December 20, 2013; Michael Muskal, "Federal Judge Backs Same-Sex Marriages in Utah; State to Appeal," *Los Angeles Times,* December 20, 2013; Vincent Bzdek, "Ohio's Ban on Gay Marriage Ruled Unconstitutional in Limited Case," *Washington Post,* December 23, 2013; Robert Barnes, "Scalia Finds His Predictions on Same-Sex Marriages Ruling Being Borne Out," *Washington Post,* December 29, 2013; Brett Logiurato, "Judge Completely Trolls Justice Scalia in Striking Down Utah's Gay Marriage Ban," *Business Insider,* December 20, 2013, found at Businessinsider.com; and Robert Barnes, "Supreme Court Blocks Gay Marriage," *Washington Post,* January 6, 2014. On February 13, 2014, a federal district court judge overturned Virginia's gay marriage ban. See Erik Eckholm, "Federal Judge Overturns Virginia's Same-Sex Marriage Ban," *New York Times,* February 14, 2014, at nyt.com.

41. *United States v. Windsor,* at 2710 (Scalia, J., dissenting).

42. Ibid., at 2711.

43. "Utah: Mullahs of the West: Judges as Moral Arbiters," Office of the Utah Lieutenant Governor, Plus Media Solutions, August 16, 2013.

44. According to the account in the Colorado *Aspen Times,* which was reposted elsewhere, "Scalia opened his talk with a reference to the Holocaust, which happened to occur in a society that was, at the time, 'the most advanced country in the world.' One of the many mistakes that Germany made in the 1930s was that judges began to interpret the law in ways that reflected 'the spirit of the age.' When judges accept this sort of moral authority, as Scalia claims they're doing now in the U.S., they get themselves and society into trouble"—Bob Ward, "In Snowmass Justice Scalia Says Judges Should Not Be Policymakers," *Aspen Times,* July 13, 2013. See also Steve Benen, "Scalia Reflects on 1930s Germany," *Maddow Blog,* July 22, 2013, http://maddowblog.msnbc.com /_news/2013/07/22/19616321-scalia-reflects-on-1930s-germany?lite; and Jillian Rayfield, "Scalia Reportedly Linked Judicial Activism to the Holocaust," *Salon,* July 21, 2013, salon.com, http://www.salon.com/2013/07/21/scalia_reportedly_linked_judicial_activ ism_to_the_holocaust/.

45. Abby Ohlheiser, "Report: Scalia Approaches Godwin's Law on Judicial Activism," *Atlantic Wire,* July 21, 2013, http://www.theatlanticwire.com/politics/2013/07/report-scalia -approaches-godwins-law-judicial-activism/67425. See also Elizabeth B. Wydra, "With Invocation of Nazi Germany, Scalia Loses Debate over Constitution," Constitutional Accountability Center, July 22, 2013, http://theusconstitution.org/text-history/2152 /invocation-nazi-germany-scalia-loses-debate-over-constitution.

46. Josh Marshall, "Peak Scalia," July 21, 2013, *Talking Points Memo,* http://talkingpoints memo.com/edblog/peak-scalia.

47. "Scalia Opened his talk with a reference to the Holocaust, which happened to occur in a society that was, at the time, 'the most advanced country in the world'": Althouse, blog site July 22, 2013, http://althouse.blogspot.com/2013/07/scalia-opened-his-talk-with -reference.html.

48. Matt Volz, "Scalia: Court Shouldn't 'Invent New Minorities,'" Associated Press, August 19, 2013, news.yahoo.com/scalia-court-shouldnt-invent-minorities-221932818 .html; Debra Cassens Weiss, "Scalia: SCOTUS Should Not 'Invent New Minorities,'" *ABA Journal: Law News Now,* August 20, 2013, http://www.abajournal.com/news/article /scalia_scotus_should_not_invent_new_minorities/; Lara Seligman, "Scalia: High Court Shouldn't 'Invent New Minorities That Get Special Protections,'" "The Hill's Blog Briefing Room," *The Hill,* August 20, 2013, http://thehill.com/blogs/blog-briefing -room/news/317773-scalia-scotus-shouldnt-invent-new-minorities.

49. Mark Joseph Stern, "Scalia Says Court Invented the Gay Minority. Women, He's on to You, Too," *Slate,* August 21, 2013, slate.com, http://www.slate.com/blogs/xx_factor /2013/08/20/antonin_scalia_to_supreme_court_don_t_invent_new_minorities_gay _people_and.html. See also Katelynn McBride, "Scalia: Inventing 'New Minorities' or Protecting Constitutional Rights?," National Constitution Center, *Yahoo News,* August 23, 2013, http://news.yahoo.com/scalia-inventing-minorities-protecting-constitutional -rights-095609174.html.

50. Scalia made this comment when he was told during the Q&A period after a speech at Tufts University that a reporter had gotten into line to ask a question. See Bridget Murphy, "Supreme Court Justice Scalia Speaks at Tufts," October 3, 2013, ABC News, http:// abcnews.go.com/US/wireStory/supreme-court-justice-scalia-speaks-tufts-20451490; O'Ryan Johnson, "Herald Can't Scare Scalia," *Boston Herald,* October 3, 2013, http:// bostonherald.com/news_opinion/local_coverage/2013/10/herald_can_t_scare_anto nin_scalia; "Justice Scalia Says Has Not Expressed View on Gay Marriage," *Reuters,* October 2, 2013, http://www.reuters.com/article/2013/10/02/us-usa-court-scalia-idUS BRE9911B820131002; and "The Coarsest, Meanest Prick in Washington Bemoans the 'Coarseness of the Culture,'" *Literary Chronicles,* October 7, 2013, http://library chronicles.blogspot.com/2013/10/the-coarsest-meanest-prick-in.html.

51. Adam Liptak, "Court Is 'One of Most Activist,' Ginsburg Says, Vowing to Stay," *New York Times,* August 24, 2013. Ginsburg called the Roberts Court "one of the most activist courts in history," but said there was no reason for her to leave soon because "There will be a president after this one, and I'm hopeful that that president will be a fine president." These comments anguished liberal observers of the Court, such as UCLA law professor Adam Winkler, who posted a string of eleven tweets over a several day period on the issue, including: "Hope Ginsburg lives to 120. But has pancreatic cancer (kills 95% w/in 5 yrs). She shld retire so Obama can replace" and "Ginsburg: this Court is most activist in years. Just wait til 6 conserve votes. Aint seen nothing yet." Adam Winkler Twitter posts, August 28, 2013, www.twitter.com. Some journalists were not supportive of such a view. See Emily Bazelon, "Stop Telling Ruth Bader Ginsburg to Retire: It's Counter-productive," *Slate,* December 18, 2013, at slate.com.

52. Dahlia Lithwick, "Grumpy Old Justices: Scalia and Ginsburg Are Really Disappointed in the Supreme Court. But Only One of Them Is Right to Be," *Slate,* August 26, 2013, slate.com, http://www.slate.com/articles/news_and_politics/jurisprudence/2013/08

/ginsburg_and_scalia_s_supreme_court_complaints_do_they_agree_about_what
.html.

53. Jennifer Senior, "In Conversation: Antonin Scalia," *New York,* October 6, 2013, http://
nymag.com/news/features/antonin-scalia-2013-10/#print.

54. Ibid., italics in original.

55. Dahlia Lithwick, "'No. No. Not That I Know Of': The Scalia Interview Reveals His
Remarkable Isolation from Anyone Who Doesn't Agree with Him," *Slate,* October 7,
2013, slate.com, http://www.slate.com/articles/news_and_politics/jurisprudence/2013/10
/scalia_interview_in_new_york_magazine_the_conservative_justice_reveals_his.html.
See also Tony Mauro, "Lawyer's Guide to Scalia's *New York* Interview," "Supreme Court
Insider," *National Law Journal,* October 8, 2013, http://www.law.com/jsp/nlj/PubArti
cleSCI.jsp?id=1202622672135&Lawyers_Guide_to_Scalias_New_York_interview.

56. Senior, "In Conversation: Antonin Scalia."

57. Lithwick, "'No. No. Not That I Know Of.'"

58. Senior, "In Conversation: Antonin Scalia."

59. Ibid.

SELECTED BIBLIOGRAPHY

UNPUBLISHED PRIMARY SOURCES

PAPERS AND ARCHIVAL COLLECTIONS

University of Chicago Law School Archives, University of Chicago, Hyde Park, Illinois
Gerald R. Ford Presidential Library, University of Michigan, Ann Arbor, Michigan
  Philip W. Buchen Files
  Richard Cheney Files
  Leo Cherne Files
  James M. Connor Files
  Department of Justice Files
  Kenneth A. Lazarus Files
  Attorney General Edward H. Levi Files
  Sarah C. Massengale Files
  National Security Files
  Office of Legal Counsel Files
  Richard D. Parsons Files
  Presidential Handwriting Files
  Barry Roth Files
  Antonin Scalia Name File
  Edward C. Schmultz Files
  William Seidman Files
  Robert M. Teeter Files
  White House Central Files
Special Collections, Georgetown University Archives, Washington, D.C.
Historical and Special Collections, Harvard Law School, Langdell Hall, Cambridge, Massachusetts
Manuscript Division, Thomas Jefferson Building, Library of Congress, Washington, D.C.
  Harry Blackmun Papers
  William J. Brennan Papers
  Thurgood Marshall Papers
  Judge J. Skelly Wright Papers
Attorney General Edward H. Levi Files, National Archives, Washington, D.C.
Richard M. Nixon Presidential Papers in Yorba Linda, California
  Antonin Scalia Name File
  Administrative Office of the U.S. Courts Files
  Office of Telecommunications Files
Lewis F. Powell Jr. Papers, Washington and Lee Law School, Lexington, Virginia

Ronald Reagan Presidential Library Papers, White House Office of Records Management, Simi Valley, California
    Carl Anderson Files
    Elizabeth Board Files
    Arthur B. Culvahouse Files
    Linus J. Kajelis Files
    Alan Charles Raul Files
    Antonin Scalia White House Alphabetical Files
    Antonin Scalia 1982 Court of Appeals Nomination Files
    Antonin Scalia 1986 Supreme Court Appointment Questionnaire (found in Peter J. Wallison Files, 1986)
    Supreme Court Nominations Rehnquist and Scalia Files
    Supreme Court/Rehnquist/Scalia Notebooks I and II Files—Candidates
    Supreme Court/Rehnquist/Scalia Press Clippings
    Supreme Court/Rehnquist/Scalia—General Selection Scenario
    Peter J. Wallison Files
    White House Subject Files

ORAL HISTORIES

Harry Blackmun Oral History, Manuscript Division, Thomas Jefferson Building, Library of Congress, Washington, D.C.
Oral Histories, Historical Society of the District of Columbia Circuit, Manuscript Division, Thomas Jefferson Building, Library of Congress, Washington, D.C.
    Robert H. Bork
    William B. Bryant
    Lloyd Cutler
    Oliver Gasch
    Gerhard Gesell
    David Ginsberg
    Abner J. Mikva
    Laurence H. Silberman
    Patricia M. Wald
Charles Tighe Oral History, William Madison Randall Library, University of North Carolina at Wilmington
Oral Histories Located in the Hauser Oral and Video Collection, the Cable Center Oral History Collection, Social and Cultural History, Penn State University, University Park, Pennsylvania, and Denver, Colorado
    Brian Lamb
    Sol Schildhause
    John Sie

SPEECHES AND PUBLIC APPEARANCES

Brennan, William. "The Constitution of the United States: Contemporary Ratification." Address for the Text and Teaching Symposium, Georgetown University, October 12, 1985, in *Original Meaning Jurisprudence: A Sourcebook,* Report to the Attorney General, U.S. Department of Justice, March 12, 1987.
———. "The Fourteenth Amendment." Address to the Section on Individual Rights and Responsibilities, American Bar Association, August 8, 1986, New York University Law

School, in *Original Meaning Jurisprudence: A Sourcebook*, Report to the Attorney General, U.S. Department of Justice, March 12, 1987.

Calabresi, Steven. Address, Federalist Society 25th Anniversary Gala, November 15, 2007.

Kennedy, Senator Edward M. "Robert Bork's America." Speech to the United States Senate, June 23, 1987, http://en.wikisource.org/wiki/Robert_Bork%27s_America.

Kozinski, Alex. "My Pizza with Nino." Remarks at the Symposium for the Jurisprudence of Justice Antonin Scalia, Benjamin N. Cardozo School of Law, October 28, 1990, *Cardozo Law Review* 12 (1990–91): 1583–84.

Meese, Attorney General Edwin III. D.C. Chapter of the Federalist Society Lawyers Division, November 15, 1985, in *Original Meaning Jurisprudence: A Sourcebook*, Report to the Attorney General, U.S. Department of Justice, March 12, 1987.

Roberts, John. Commencement Address. Georgetown University Law Center, May 26, 2006, http://www.law.georgetown.edu/webcast/assets/GL_2006523112710.mp3.

Scalia, Antonin G. "Cohonguroton Address." *The Journal* 86, no. 1 (Autumn 1957), pp. 12–14.

———. Speech, "The Use of Legislative History." Delivered between fall, 1985, and spring, 1986, at various law schools, presented to the University of Chicago Law School, University of Chicago Law School library, Hyde Park, Illinois.

———. Address, Attorney General's Conference on Economic Liberties, Washington, D.C., June 14, 1986, Appendix C, *Original Meaning Jurisprudence: A Sourcebook, Report to the Attorney General,* Office of Legal Policy, U.S. Department of Justice, March 12, 1987.

———. "Reflections on the Constitution," November 17, 1988, Kennedy Political Union, American University, Washington, D.C., C-SPAN video.

———. Speech, "Constitutional Interpretation." Sibley Lecture, University of Georgia Law School, May 1, 1989, www.ninoville.com.

———. "Originalism: The Lesser Evil," speech delivered September 16, 1988, in *University of Cincinnati Law Review* 57 (1988–89): 849ff.

———. "The Rule of Law as a Law of Rules," speech delivered on February 14, 1989, in *University of Chicago Law Review* 56 (Fall 1989): 1175ff.

———. "Francis Boyer Award Lecture." American Enterprise Institute, Washington, D.C., December 6, 1989.

———. Speech, Gregorian Pontifical University, June 13, 1996, Catholic News Service, http://www.catholicnews.com/data/stories/cns/960613.htm.

———. Address, "A Theory of Constitutional Interpretation." Catholic University of America, October 18, 1996, on *Ninoville* website, www.joink.com/homes/users/ninoville.

———. "Mullahs of the West: Judges as Authoritative Expositors of the Natural Law?" Sir John Young Oration, the Boston, Melbourne, Oxford Conversazioni on Culture and Society, Trinity College, University of Melbourne, October 2005.

———. Speech, "Constitutional Interpretation." Woodrow Wilson International Center for Scholars, Library of Congress, Washington, D.C., March 14, 2005, Lexis/Nexis.

———. Speech, "The Role of International Law." American Enterprise Institute, Washington, D.C., February 21, 2006, Lexis/Nexis.

———. Speech, University of Fribourg, Switzerland, March 8, 2006, Bureau Audiovisuel Francophone (BAFWEB), http://www.bafweb.com/60308scalia.wmv.

———. Speech, International Conference on the Administration of Justice and National Security in Democracies, Ottawa, Canada, June 12, 2007 (transcript in author's possession).

———. Speech, "The Role of Catholic Faith in the Work of a Judge." 2nd annual John F. Scarpa Conference on Law, Politics and Culture, Villanova University, October 16, 2007 (author's notes of speech).

————. Speech, Federalist Society 25th Anniversary Gala, Washington, D.C., November 15, 2007, www.fed-soc.org.

————. "Supreme Court Justice Perspective," a talk in the West Conference Room of the Supreme Court Building to Thomas Jefferson High School, Fairfax County Virginia, C-SPAN, April 9, 2008, Lexis/Nexis.

————. Speech, Annual Convention of the Federalist Society, Washington, D.C., November 22, 2008, www.fed-soc.org.

————. "Mullahs of the West: Judges as Moral Arbiters." Rzecznik Praw Obywatelskich, August 24, 2009 (English translation of Polish text), http://www.teoria.umk.pl/scalia.pdf.

————. "The Methodology of Originalism." Henry J. Abraham Speech, April 15, 2010, University of Virginia Law School, Charlottesville, Virginia (author's notes of speech).

————. Speech, Law School Centennial Speech. Duquesne University, September 24, 2011 (transcript in author's possession).

————. Address, Federalist Society meeting, October 15, 2012, www.fed-soc.org.

Souter, David. Commencement Speech, in "Text of Justice David Souter's Speech," May 27, 2010, *Harvard Gazette,* http://news.harvard.edu/gazette/story/2010/05/text-of-justice-david-souters-speech/.

JUSTICES' PUBLIC INTERVIEWS

Blackmun, Harry. Interview with Bill Moyers, "Justice Harry Blackmun on *Roe v. Wade,*" *In Search of the Constitution* (1987), billmoyers.com.

Kennedy, Anthony, Interview, Academy of Achievement, New York City, June 3, 2005, www.achievement.org.

O'Connor, Sandra Day. Interview with Wolf Blitzer, *The Situation Room,* CNN, January 28, 2010, Lexis/Nexis.

O'Connor, Sandra Day, and Stephen Breyer. Interview with George Stephanopolous, *This Week,* July 6, 2003, ABC News transcript, Lexis/Nexis.

Scalia, Antonin G. Interview by Maria Bartiromo, MSNBC, October 10, 2005, Lexis/Nexis.

————. Interview with BBC reporter Clive Coleman, *Law in Action,* BBC News, February 12, 2008 (author's notes of interview).

————. Interview with Brian Lamb, *Q and A Show,* C-SPAN, May 4, 2008, http://c-span video.org/program/AwithAn.

————. Interview with Brian Lamb, *Q and A Show,* C-SPAN, July 19, 2012, http://c-spanvideo.org/program/Antonin

————. Interview with Calvin Massey, "Legally speaking," blog, "The Originalist," January 2011, http://www.callawyer.com/story.cfm?eid=913358&evid=1.

————. Interview with Piers Morgan, *Piers Morgan Tonight,* CNN, July 18, 2012, Lexis/Nexis.

————. Interview with Stanley Pottinger, *Beyond Politics,* PLUM-TV, July 2006 (CD in author's possession).

————. Interview with Charlie Rose, *Charlie Rose,* PBS, June 20, 2008, Lexis/Nexis.

————. Interview with Charlie Rose, *Charlie Rose,* PBS, November 27, 2012, Lexis/Nexis.

————. Interview by Lesley Stahl, *60 Minutes,* CBS News. Originally broadcast April 27, 2008; replayed on September 14, 2008 online at "Justice Scalia on the Record," at http://www.cbsnews.com/8301-18560_162-4040290.html.

————. Interview with Tim Russert, MSNBC, May 3, 2008, Lexis/Nexis.

————. Interview with NPR's Nina Totenberg, Smithsonian Associates Interview, Lisner

Auditorium, George Washington University, Washington, D.C., February 12, 2013, Lexis/Nexis.

———. Interview with Chris Wallace. *Fox News Sunday*, July 19, 2012, Lexis/Nexis.

Scalia, Antonin, and Stephen Breyer. "Constitutional Relevance of Foreign Court Decisions," January 13, 2005, U.S. Association of Constitutional Law, Washington College of Law, American University, Washington, D.C., C-SPAN video.

Scalia, Antonin, and Stephen Breyer. "A Conversation on the Constitution," moderated by Jan Crawford Greenburg, American Constitution Society and the Federalist Society joint session, Washington, D.C., December 5, 2006, Lexis/Nexis.

Scalia, Antonin, and Bryan A. Garner. "Newsmakers: Conversation with the Authors: *Reading the Law*," by Reuters Publishers Editor-in-Chief Stephen J. Adler, September 17, 2012, http://www.youtube.com/watch?v=-hpAf6NhGuk.

Scalia, Antonin, Ruth Bader Ginsberg, et al. Panel discussion, "Separation of Powers in the Constitution," November 15, 1988, Washington, D.C., C-SPAN video.

Scalia, Antonin. Panel discussion, "Religion, Politics, and the Death Penalty," Session 3: "A Call for Reckoning: Religion and the Death Penalty," January 25, 2002, http://features .pewforum.org/death-penalty/resources/transcript3. html.

Scalia, Antonin, Sandra Day O'Connor, and Stephen Breyer. "Constitutional Conversation," moderated by Tim Russert, sponsored by the Aspen Institute and the National Archives, Washington, D.C., April 22, 2005, Lexis/Nexis.

Scalia, Antonin, and Nadine Strossen. "A Debate on the State of Civil Liberties," ACLU Membership Conference Debate, Washington, D.C., October 15, 2006, http://www .c-spanvideo.org/program/194843-1.

Senior, Jennifer. "In Conversation: Antonin Scalia," transcript of interview reprinted in *New York*, October 6, 2013, http://nymag.com/news/features/antonin-scalia-2013-10/#print.

Sotomayor, Sonia. Interview with Scott Pelley, *60 Minutes*, CBS News, June 16, 2013, Lexis/ Nexis.

Stevens, John Paul. Interview with Scott Pelley, *60 Minutes,* November 28, 2010, Lexis/Nexis.

———. Interview with Lark McCarthy, "John Paul Stevens Discusses Longevity," *AARP The Magazine*, July 5, 2011, www.aarp.org.

Thomas, Clarence. "The Justice Nobody Knows: Justice Clarence Thomas Discusses His Childhood, His Career, Anita Hill, and His Book," *60 Minutes*, September 30, 2007, CBS News, Lexis/Nexis.

BOOKS

Abraham, Henry J. *Justices, Presidents, and Senators: A History of the U.S. Supreme Court Appointments from Washington to Bush II*, 5th ed., Lanham, MD: Rowman & Littlefield, 2007.

Allen, John L. Jr. *All the Pope's Men: The Inside Story of How the Vatican Really Thinks*. New York: Doubleday, 2004.

———. *Opus Dei: An Objective Look Behind the Myths and Reality of the Most Controversial Force in the Catholic Church*. New York: Doubleday, 2005.

Avery, Michael, and Daniele McLaughlin. *The Federalist Society: How Conservatives Took the Law Back from the Liberals*. Nashville: Vanderbilt University Press, 2013.

Balkin, Jack. *Living Originalism*. Cambridge: Belknap Press/Harvard University Press, 2011.

Barnhart, Bill, and Eugene Schlickman. *John Paul Stevens: An Independent Life*. DeKalb: Northern Illinois University Press, 2010.

Belsky, Martin, ed. *The Rehnquist Court: A Retrospective*. New York: Oxford University Press, 2000.

Biskupic, Joan. *American Original: The Life and Constitution of Supreme Court Justice Antonin Scalia*. New York: Macmillan, 2009.

———. *Sandra Day O'Connor: How the First Woman on the Supreme Court Became Its Most Influential Justice*. New York: Ecco/HarperCollins, 2005.

Bokenkotter, Thomas. *A Concise History of the Catholic Church*. New York: Doubleday, 2006.

Boles, Donald E. *Mr. Justice Rehnquist, Judicial Activist: The Early Years*. Ames: Iowa State University Press, 1987.

Bork, Robert H. *The Antitrust Paradox: A Policy at War with Itself,* 2nd ed. New York: Free Press, 1993.

———. *Slouching Towards Gomorrah: Modern Liberalism and American Decline*. New York: Regan Books/HarperCollins, 1996.

———. *The Tempting of America: The Political Seduction of the Law*. New York: Free Press, 1990.

Bradley, Craig, ed. *The Rehnquist Legacy*. New York: Cambridge University Press, 2006.

Brennan, George Jr. *Excellence: Sons of Xavier Forever*. Bloomington, IN: 1st Books Library, 2003.

Breyer, Stephen. *Active Liberty: Interpreting Our Democratic Constitution First*. New York: Oxford University Press, 2008.

———. *Making Our Democracy Work: A Judge's View*. New York: Alfred A. Knopf, 2010.

Brinkley, Douglas. *Gerald R. Ford*. New York: Times Books, 2007.

Brisbin, Richard A. Jr. *Justice Antonin Scalia and the Conservative Revival*. Baltimore: Johns Hopkins University Press, 1997.

Bronner, Ethan. *Battle for Justice: How the Bork Nomination Shook America*. New York: Union Square Press, 2007.

Calabresi, Steven G. *Originalism: A Quarter Century of Debate*. Washington, D.C.: Regnery, 2007.

Cannon, James. *Time and Chance: Gerald Ford's Appointment with History*. Ann Arbor: University of Michigan Press, 1994.

Clark, Hunter R. *Justice Brennan: The Great Conciliator*. New York: Birch Lane, 1995.

Colucci, Frank J. *Justice Kennedy's Jurisprudence: The Full and Necessary Meaning of Liberty*. Lawrenceville: University Press of Kansas, 2009.

Coyle, Marcia. *The Roberts Court: The Struggle for the Constitution*. New York: Simon & Schuster, 2013.

Cozzens, Donald. *Faith That Dares to Speak*. Collegeville, MN: Liturgical Press, 2004.

Davis, Richard. *Justices and Journalists: The U.S. Supreme Court and the Media*. London: Cambridge University Press, 2011.

Davis, Sue. *Justice Rehnquist and the Constitution*. Princeton: Princeton University Press, 1987.

Dean, John W. *Conservatives Without Conscience*. New York: Viking, 2006.

———. *The Rehnquist Choice: The Untold Story of the Nixon Appointment That Redefined the Supreme Court*. New York: Free Press, 2002.

Dershowitz, Alan. *Supreme Injustice: How the High Court Hijacked Election 2000*. New York: Oxford University Press, 2001.

Devins, Neal, and Davison M. Douglas. *A Year in the Life of the Supreme Court*. Durham, NC: Duke University Press, 2004.

Dolan, Jay P. *In Search of an American Catholicism: A History of Religion and Culture in Tension*. New York: Oxford University Press, 2003.

Dubose, Lou, and Jake Bernstein. *Vice: Dick Cheney and the Hijacking of the American Presidency*. New York: Random House, 2006.

Eisler, Kim Isaac. *A Justice for All: William J. Brennan, Jr., and the Decisions That Transformed America.* New York: Simon & Schuster, 1995.

Foskett, Ken. *Judging Thomas: The Life and Times of Clarence Thomas.* New York: William Morrow, 2004.

Friedelbaum, Stanley H. *The Rehnquist Court: In Pursuit of Judicial Conservatism.* Westport, CT: Greenwood, 1994.

Gaffney, Edward McGlynn Jr., ed. *Private Schools and the Public Good: Policy Alternatives for the Eighties.* South Bend, IN: University of Notre Dame Press, 1982.

Gellman, Barton. *Angler: The Cheney Vice Presidency.* New York: Penguin, 2009.

Gerber, Scott Douglas. *First Principles: The Jurisprudence of Clarence Thomas.* New York: New York University Press, 1999.

Gillman, Howard. *The Votes That Counted: How the Court Decided the 2000 Presidential Election.* Hyde Park, IL: University of Chicago Press, 2001.

Gitenstein, Mark. *Matters of Principle: An Insider's Account of America's Rejection of Robert Bork's Nomination for the Supreme Court.* New York: Simon & Schuster, 1992.

Goldford, Dennis J. *The American Constitution and the Debate over Originalism.* New York: Cambridge University Press, 2005.

Goldman, Roger, with David Gallem. *Justice William J. Brennan, Jr.: Freedom First.* New York: Carroll & Graf, 1994.

Gordon, Mary. *Circling My Mother.* New York: Pantheon, 2007.

Gottlieb, Stephen. *Morality Imposed: The Rehnquist Court and Liberty in America.* New York: New York University Press, 2000.

Greeley, Andrew. *The Catholic Revolution: New Wine, Old Wineskins, and the Second Vatican Council.* Berkeley: University of California Press, 2004.

Greenburg, Jan Crawford. *Supreme Conflict: The Inside Story of the Struggle for Control of the United States Supreme Court.* New York: Penguin, 2008.

Greene, Thurston. *The Language of the Constitution.* New York: Greenwood, 1991.

Greenhouse, Linda. *Becoming Justice Blackmun: Harry Blackmun's Supreme Court Journey.* New York: Times Books, 2006.

Greenya, John. *Silent Justice: The Clarence Thomas Story.* Fort Lee, NJ: Barricade, 2001.

Grogan, John. *The Longest Trip Home: A Memoir.* New York: William Morrow, 2008.

Harris, Sam. *The End of Faith: Religion, Terror, and the Future of Reason.* New York: W. W. Norton, 2004.

Hayes, Stephen F. *Cheney: The Untold Story of America's Most Powerful and Controversial Vice President.* New York: HarperCollins, 2007.

Hudson, David L. Jr. *The Rehnquist Court: Understanding Its Impact and Legacy.* Westport, CT: Praeger, 2007.

Hutchinson, Dennis. *The Man Who Was Once Whizzer White: A Portrait of Byron R. White.* New York: Free Press, 1998.

Hutchison, Robert. *Their Kingdom Come: Inside the Secret World of Opus Dei.* New York: St. Martin's Press, 1998.

Irons, Peter. *Brennan vs. Rehnquist: The Battle for the Constitution.* New York: Alfred A. Knopf, 1994.

Jeffries, John C. *Justice Lewis F. Powell, Jr.: A Biography.* New York: Fordham University Press, 2001.

Jenkins, John A. *The Partisan: The Life of William Rehnquist.* New York: Public Affairs, 2012.

Kaplan, David A. *The Accidental President: How 413 Lawyers, 9 Supreme Court Justices,*

5,963,110 Floridians (Give or Take a Few) Landed George W. Bush in the White House. New York: William Morrow, 2001.

Keck, Thomas M. *The Most Activist Supreme Court in History: The Road to Modern Judicial Conservatism.* Hyde Park, IL: University of Chicago Press, 2004.

Kennedy, Eugene. *Tomorrow's Catholics, Yesterday's Church: The Two Cultures of American Catholicism.* St. Louis: Liguori, 1995.

King, Gilbert. *Devil in the Grove: Thurgood Marshall, the Groveland Boys, and the Dawn of a New America.* New York: Harper, 2012.

Kluger, Richard. *Simple Justice: The History of Brown v. Board of Education and the History of Black America's Struggle for Equality.* New York: Vintage, 2004.

Knowles, Helen J. *The Tie Goes to Freedom: Justice Anthony M. Kennedy on Liberty.* New York: Rowman & Littlefield, 2009.

Kurland, Philip B., and Ralph Lerner. *The Founders' Constitution.* 5 vols. Chicago: University of Chicago Press, 1986 (online at press-pubs.uchicago.edu).

Lazarus, Edward. *Closed Chambers: The First Eyewitness Account of the Epic Struggles Inside the Supreme Court.* New York: Crown, 1998.

Maier, Pauline. *Ratification: The People Debate the Constitution, 1787–1788.* New York: Simon & Schuster, 2011.

Maltz, Earl. *Rehnquist Justice: Understanding the Court Dynamic,* Lawrenceville: University Press of Kansas, 2003.

Manaster, Kenneth A. *Illinois Justice: The Scandal of 1969 and the Rise of John Paul Stevens.* Chicago: University of Chicago Press, 2001.

Mann, James. *The Rise of the Vulcans: The History of Bush's War Cabinet.* New York: Viking, 2004.

Meese, Edwin, Matthew Spalding, and David F. Forte. *The Heritage Guide to the Constitution.* Washington, D.C.: Regnery, 2005.

Merida, Kevin, and Michael A. Fletcher. *Supreme Discomfort: The Divided Soul of Clarence Thomas.* New York: Doubleday, 2007.

Montgomery, Bruce P. *Richard B. Cheney and the Rise of the Imperial Presidency.* New York: Praeger, 2009.

Morris, Jeffrey Brandon. *Calmly to Poise the Scales of Justice: A History of the Courts of the District of Columbia Circuit.* Durham, NC: Carolina Academic Press, 2001.

Murphy, Bruce Allen. *The Brandeis/Frankfurter Connection: The Secret Political Activities of Two Supreme Court Justices.* New York: Oxford University Press, 1982.

———. *Fortas: The Rise and Ruin of a Supreme Court Justice.* New York: William Morrow, 1988.

———. *Wild Bill: The Legend and Life of William O. Douglas.* New York: Random House, 2003.

Nevils, William Coleman. *Miniatures of Georgetown, 1634–1934.* Tercentennial Causeries, Washington, D.C.: Georgetown University Press, 1934.

Obermayer, Herman J. *Rehnquist: A Personal Portrait of the Distinguished Chief Justice of the United States.* New York: Threshold Editions/Simon & Schuster, 2009.

O'Connor, Sandra Day. *The Majesty of the Law: Reflections of a Supreme Court Justice.* New York: Random House, 2004.

O'Connor, Sandra Day, and H. Alan Day. *Lazy B: Growing Up on a Cattle Ranch in the American Southwest.* New York: Random House, 2003.

O'Malley, John W. *What Happened at Vatican II.* Cambridge: Belknap Press/Harvard University Press, 2008.

O'Neill, Jonathan. *Originalism in American Law and Politics: A Constitutional History.* Baltimore: Johns Hopkins University Press, 2007.

Owens, Erik C., et al. *Religion and the Death Penalty: A Call for Reckoning.* Grand Rapids, MI: William B. Eerdmans, 2004.

Perry, Michael J. *Morality, Politics and Law.* New York: Oxford University Press, 1990.

Posner, Judge Richard A. *How Judges Think.* Cambridge: Harvard University Press, 2008.

———. *Reflections on Judging.* Cambridge: Harvard University Press, 2013.

Prejean, Sister Helen. *Dead Man Walking: An Eyewitness Account of the Death Penalty in the United States.* New York: Vintage, 1994.

———. *The Death of Innocents: An Eyewitness Account of Wrongful Executions.* New York: Vintage, 2006.

Price, Deb, and Joyce Murdock. *Courting Justice: Gay Men and Lesbians v. the Supreme Court.* New York: Basic Books, 2002

Price, Polly J. *Judge Richard S. Arnold: A Legacy of Justice on the Federal Bench.* Amherst, NY: Prometheus, 2009.

Rakove, Jack. *Living Originalism.* Cambridge: Belknap Press/Harvard University Press, 2011.

———. *Original Meanings: Politics and Ideas in the Making of the Constitution.* New York: Vintage, 1997.

Rehnquist, William. *All the Laws but One: Civil Liberties in Wartime.* New York: Vintage, 2000.

———. *Centennial Crisis: The Disputed Election of 1876.* New York: Vintage, 2005.

———. *Grand Inquests: The Historic Impeachments of Justice Samuel Chase and President Andrew Johnson.* New York: Harper Perennial, 1999.

Richards, David A. J. *The Case for Gay Rights: From Bowers to Lawrence and Beyond.* Lawrenceville: University Press of Kansas, 2005.

Ring, Kevin A. *Scalia Dissents: Writings of the Supreme Court's Wittiest, Most Outspoken Justice.* Washington, D.C.: Regnery, 2004.

Robin, Corey. *The Reactionary Mind: Conservatism from Edmund Burke to Sarah Palin.* New York: Oxford University Press, 2001.

Rosen, Jeffrey. *The Supreme Court: The Personalities and Rivalries That Defined America.* New York: Times Books, 2006.

Rossum, Ralph. *Antonin Scalia's Jurisprudence: Text and Tradition.* Lawrenceville: University Press of Kansas, 2006.

Savage, Charlie. *Takeover: The Return of the Imperial Presidency and the Subversion of American Democracy.* New York: Little, Brown, 2007.

Scalia, Antonin, and Bryan Garner. *Making Your Case: The Art of Persuading Judges.* Rochester, NY: Thomson West, 2008.

———. *Reading Law: The Interpretation of Legal Texts.* Rochester, NY: Thomson West, 2012.

Scalia, Antonin, and Amy Guttman. *A Matter of Interpretation: Federal Courts and the Law.* Princeton: Princeton University Press, 1998.

Scalia, S. Eugene. *Carducci: His Critics and Translators in England and America, 1881–1932.* New York: S. F. Vanni, 1937.

———. *Luigi Capuana and His Times.* New York: S. F. Vanni, 1952.

Scalia, S. Eugene, and Margherita Marchione. *Philip Mazzei: My Life and Wanderings.* Morristown, NJ: American Institute of Italian Studies, 1980.

Scaperlanda, Michael A., and Teresa Stanton-Collett, eds. *Recovering Self-Evident Truths: Catholic Perspectives on American Law.* Washington, D.C.: Catholic University of America Press, 2007.

Schultz, David A., and Christopher E. Smith. *The Jurisprudential Vision of Justice Antonin Scalia*. London: Rowman & Littlefield, 1996.

Shannon, Elaine, and Ann Blackman. *The Spy Next Door: The Extraordinary Secret Life of Robert Philip Hanssen, the Most Damaging FBI Agent in U.S. History*. Boston: Little, Brown, 2002.

Sickels, Robert J. *John Paul Stevens and the Constitution: The Search for Balance*. University Park: Penn State University Press, 1988.

Simon, James F. *The Center Holds: The Power Struggle Inside the Rehnquist Court*. New York: Simon & Schuster, 1995.

Smith, Christopher, E. *Justice Antonin Scalia and the Supreme Court's Conservative Moment*. Westport, CT: Praeger, 1993.

Smolla, Rodney A., ed. *A Year in the Life of the Supreme Court*. Durham, NC: Duke University Press, 1995.

Sotomayor, Sonia. *My Beloved World*. New York: Alfred A. Knopf, 2013.

Staab, James. *The Political Thought of Justice Antonin Scalia: A Hamiltonian on the Supreme Court*. Lanham, MD: Rowman & Littlefield, 2006.

Steinfels, Peter. *A People Adrift: The Crisis of the Roman Catholic Church in America*. New York: Simon & Schuster, 2004.

Stern, Seth, and Stephen Wermeil. *Justice Brennan: Liberal Champion*. Boston: Houghton Mifflin, 2010.

Stevens, John Paul. *Five Chiefs: A Supreme Court Memoir*. New York: Little, Brown, 2011.

Storing, Herbert J. *The Complete Anti-Federalist*. 3 vols. Chicago: University of Chicago Press, 2007.

Strauss, Leo. *The City and the Man*. Chicago: University of Chicago Press, 1978.

———. *Persecution and the Art of Writing*. Chicago: University of Chicago Press, 1988.

Strauss, Leo, and Joseph Cropsey. *History of Political Philosophy*. Chicago: University of Chicago Press, 1987.

Sunstein, Cass. *One Case at a Time: Judicial Minimalism on the Supreme Court*. Cambridge: Harvard University Press, 2001.

———. *Radicals in Robes: Why Extreme Right-Wing Courts Are Wrong for America*. New York: Basic Books, 2006.

Teles, Steven M. *The Rise of the Conservative Legal Movement*. Princeton: Princeton University Press, 2008.

Thomas, Andrew Peyton. *Clarence Thomas: A Biography*. San Francisco: Encounter, 2001.

Thomas, Clarence. *My Grandfather's Son: A Memoir,* New York: HarperCollins, 2007.

Toobin, Jeffrey. *The Nine: Inside the Secret World of the Supreme Court*. New York: Doubleday, 2007.

———. *The Oath: The Obama White House and the Supreme Court*. New York: Doubleday, 2012.

———. *Too Close to Call, The Thirty-Six-Day Battle to Decide the 2000 Election*. New York: Random House, 2002.

Tushnet, Mark. *A Court Divided: The Rehnquist Court and the Future of Constitutional Law*. New York: W. W. Norton, 2006.

———. *In the Balance: Law and Politics on the Roberts Court*. New York: W. W. Norton, 2013.

Unger, Harlow Giles. *Noah Webster: The Life and Times of a Patriot*. New York: Wiley, 2000.

Urquhart, Gordon. *Opus Dei: The Pope's Right Arm in Europe*. Washington, D.C.: Catholics for a Free Choice, 1997.

Vidmar, John, OP. *The Catholic Church Through the Ages: A History.* New York: Paulist Press, 2005.

Vieira, Norman, and Leonard Gross. *Supreme Court Appointments: Judge Bork and the Politicization of Senate Confirmations.* Carbondale: Southern Illinois University Press, 1998.

Vise, David A. *The Bureau and the Mole.* New York: Atlantic Monthly Press, 2002.

Wallison, Peter J. *Ronald Reagan: The Power of Conviction and the Success of His Presidency.* New York: Basic Books, 2004.

Walsh, Michael. *Opus Dei: An Investigation into the Powerful, Secretive Society Within the Catholic Church.* San Francisco: Harper, 2004.

Webster, Noah, *An American Dictionary of the English Language* (1828 Facsimile Edition). Foundation for American Education, 1967.

Weizer, Paul I. *The Opinions of Justice Antonin Scalia: The Caustic Conservative.* New York: Peter Lang, 2004.

Werth, Barry. *31 Days: The Crisis that Gave Us the Government We Have Today.* New York: Doubleday, 2006.

Whittington, Keith E. *Textual Meaning, Constitutional Original Intent and Interpretation Judicial Review.* Lawrenceville: University Press of Kansas, 1999.

Wiecek, William M. *The Birth of the Modern Constitution: The United States Supreme Court, 1941–1953,* History of the Supreme Court of the United States, Oliver Wendell Holmes Devise, Vol. 12. Cambridge: Cambridge University Press, 2006.

Wilkinson, J. Harvie. *Cosmic Constitutional Theory: Why Americans Are Losing Their Inalienable Right to Self-Governance.* New York: Oxford University Press, 2012.

Wills, Garry. *Bare Ruined Choirs: Doubt, Prophecy, and Radical Religion.* Garden City, NY: Doubleday, 1971.

Winters, Michael Sean. *Left at the Altar: How the Democrats Lost the Catholics and How the Catholics Can Save the Democrats.* New York: Basic Books, 2009.

Wise, David. *Spy: The Inside Story of How the FBI's Robert Hanssen Betrayed America.* New York: Random House, 2002.

Yalof, David. *Pursuit of Justice: Presidential Politics and the Selection of Supreme Court Nominees.* Chicago: University of Chicago Press, 1999.

Yarbrough, Tinsley E. *David Hackett Souter: Traditional Republican on the Rehnquist Court.* New York: Oxford University Press, 2005.

———. *Harry A. Blackmun: The Outsider Justice.* New York: Oxford University Press, 2008.

———. *The Rehnquist Court and the Constitution.* New York: Oxford University Press, 2000.

Zelnick, Robert. *Swing Dance: Justice O'Connor and the Michigan Muddle.* Stanford, CA: Hoover Institution Press, 2004.

ARTICLES

"Antonin Scalia, Supreme Court Justice, b. 1936." *New York,* March 31, 2013, http://nymag.com/news/features/childhood/antonin-scalia-2013-4/.

Adler, Stephen J. "Live Wire on the D.C. Circuit." *Legal Times,* June 23, 1986, pp. 86–92.

Barnes, Fred. "What President Bush Needs to Keep in Mind with the Supreme Court." *Weekly Standard,* vol. 10, no. 41, July 18, 2005, weeklystandard.com.

Barnett, Randy. "Scalia's Infidelity: A Critique of Faint-Hearted Originalism." Social Science Research Network, posted on January 1, 2006, http://papers.ssrn.com/sol3/papers.cfm?abstract_id=880112.

Baynes, Terry. "Fanning Furor, Scalia Says Court of Appeals Judge Lied." Reuters, September 17, 2012.

Berger, Raoul. "Symposium on Civil Rights and Civil Liberties: 'Original Intention' in Historical Perspective." *George Washington Law Review* 54 (January–March 1986): 296ff.

Brennan, William. "National Court of Appeals: Another Dissent." *University of Chicago Law Review* 40 (1983): 484ff.

Brest, Paul. "The Misconceived Quest for Original Understanding." *Boston University Law Review* 60 (1980): 204ff.

Bronner, Ethan. "Bulldog Justice." *Washingtonian,* December 1990, pp. 137–39, 245–48.

Brown, Dr. Michael S. "The Strange Case of *United States v. Miller.*" *Enter Stage Right—A Journal of Modern Conservatism,* August 6, 2001, keepandbeararms.com.

Brust, Richard. "Scalia and Garner Release 567-Page Tome on Textualism." ABA Journal .com, June 19, 2012, abajournal.com.

Calabresi, Massimo, and David Von Drehle. "What Will Justice Kennedy Do?" *Time,* June 18, 2012, p. 39.

Calabresi, Steven G., and Julia T. Rickert. "Originalism and Sex Discrimination." *Texas Law Review* 90, no. 1 (2011): 1ff.

Carter, Terry. "Crossing the Rubicon." *California Lawyer,* October 1992, p. 104.

Cornell, Saul. "The Second Amendment and the Right to Bear Arms After *D.C. v. Heller*: Heller, New Originalism, and Law Office History: 'Meet the New Boss, Same as the Old Boss.'" *UCLA Law Review* 56 (June 2009): 1095–1108.

Davidson, Amy. "The Animus of Antonin Scalia." *New Yorker,* December 12, 2012, new yorker.com.

Dellinger, Walter. "Perhaps Justice Scalia Is Reading from the Wrong Constitution." *Slate,* June 26, 2012, slate.com.

Dow, Gillian. "Uses of Translation: The Global Jane Austen." In Gillian Dow and Clare Hanson, *Uses of Austen: Jane's Afterlives.* London: Palgrave Macmillan, 2012, pp. 154–75.

Dudley, Robert L. "The Freshman Effect and Voting Alignments: A Re-Examination of Judicial Folklore." *American Politics Quarterly* 21, no. 3 (July 1993): 360–67.

Duffy, Shannon P. "The Mild Mannered Scalia." Law.com, March 3, 2003.

Dworkin, Ronald. "Fidelity in Constitutional Theory: Fidelity as Integrity: The Arduous Virtue of Fidelity: Orignalism, Scalia, Tribe, and Nerve." *Fordham Law Review* 65 (March 1997): 1249ff.

Edelman, Peter. "Justice Scalia's Jurisprudence and the Good Society: Shades of Felix Frankfurter and the Harvard Hit Parade of the 1950s." *Cardozo Law Review* 12 (1990–91): 1799ff.

Edwards, Harry T. "The Effects of Collegiality on Judicial Decision Making." *University of Pennsylvania Law Review* 151 (May 2003): 1639, note 65.

Eisler, Kim. "Backbenched Scalia Speaks." *Washingtonian,* December 2005.

Eskridge, William N. Jr. "Textualism and Original Understanding: Should the Supreme Court Read the Federalist but Not Statutory Legislative History?" *George Washington University Law Review* 66 (June/August 1998): 1301ff.

Fisher, Daniel. "Justice's Skeptical of Justices All or Nothing Medicaid Arguments." *Forbes online Magazine,* March 28, 2012.

Fiss, Owen M. "What Is the Federalist Society?" *Harvard Journal of Law and Public Policy* 15, no. 1 (Winter 1992), pp. 5–10.

Frank, Nathaniel. "Scalia the Mullah: The Justice's Misunderstanding of Morality, and How It Leads Him Astray in Cases About Homosexuality." *Slate,* June 25, 2013, http://www .slate.com/articles/news_and_politics/jurisprudence/2013/06/scalia_and_gay_mar riage_how_the_justice_misund erstands_morality.html.

Frankfurter, Felix. "Some Reflections on the Reading of Statutes." *Columbia Law Review* 47 (1947): 527ff.

Garner, Bryan A., and Richard Posner. "How Nuanced Is Justice Scalia's Judicial Philosophy: An Exchange." *New Republic,* September 10, 2012.

Gerber, Scott, and Keeok Park. "The Quixotic Search for Consensus on the U.S. Supreme Court: A Cross-Judicial Empirical Analysis of the Rehnquist Court Justices." *American Political Science Review* 91, no. 2 (June 1997): 390ff.

Gordon, Robert. "Alito or Scalito?" *Slate,* November 1, 2005, www.slate.com.

Greenfield, Rebecca. "The Brouhaha Behind 'Argle Bargle': A Linguistic Explanation," *Atlantic Wire,* June 26, 2013, http://www.theatlanticwire.com/national/2013/06/brouhaha -behind-argle-bargle-linguistic-explanation/66630/.

Grim, Ryan. "A Guide to *Gonzales v. Raich.*" *Salon,* June 7, 2005, www.salon.com.

Hagle, Timothy M. "'Freshmen Effects' for Supreme Court Justices." *American Journal of Political Science* 37, no. 4 (November 1993): 1142–57.

Heck, Edward V., and Melinda Gann Hall. "Bloc Voting and the Freshman Justice Revisited." *The Journal of Politics* 43, no. 3 (1981): 852–60.

Hentoff, Nat. "The Constitutionalist." *New Yorker,* March 12, 1990, p. 45, http://www.new yorker.com/archive/1990/03/12/1990_03_12_045_TNY_CARDS_000353704.

Howard, J. Woodford. "Justice Murphy: The Freshman Years." *Vanderbilt Law Review* 18 (March 1965): 473–505.

Jenkins, John A. "A Candid Talk with Justice Blackmun." *New York Times Magazine,* February 20, 1983.

Kannar, George. "The Constitutional Catechism of Antonin Scalia." *Yale Law Journal* 99 (April 1990): 1297–1357.

King, Michael Patrick. "Justice Antonin Scalia: The First Term on the Supreme Court— 1986–87." *Rutgers Law Review* 20, no. 1 (Fall 1988): 1–77.

Kmiec, Douglas W. "Natural Law v. Natural Rights: What Are They? How Do They Differ?" *Harvard Journal of Law and Public Policy* 20 (Summer 1997): 627ff.

Lacovara, Philip Allen. "Un-Courtly Manners: Quarrelsome Justices Are No Longer a Model of Civility for Lawyers." *ABA Journal* (December 1994): 50–53.

Landay, Jerry. "The Federalist Society: The Conservative Cabal That's Transforming American Law." *Washington Monthly,* March 2000.

Lauricella, Peter. "Chi lascia la via vecchia perla nuova perde e non sa quel che trova: The Italian-American Experience and Its Influence on the Judicial Philosophies of Justice Antonin Scalia, Judge Joseph Bellacosa, and Judge Vito Titone." *Albany Law Review* 60, no. 5 (August 1997): 1701ff.

Lithwick, Dahlia. "Grumpy Old Justices: Scalia and Ginsburg Are Really Disappointed in the Supreme Court. But Only One of Them Is Right to Be." *Slate,* August 26, 2013, http://www.slate.com/articles/news_and_politics/jurisprudence/2013/08 /ginsburg_and_scalia_s_supreme_court_complaints_do_they_agree_about_what .html.

———. "'No. No. Not That I Know Of.': The Scalia Interview Reveals His Remarkable Isolation from Anyone Who Doesn't Agree with Him." *Slate,* October 7, 2013, http:// www.slate.com/articles/news_and_politics/jurisprudence/2013/10/scalia_interview_in _new_york_magazine_the_cons ervative_justice_reveals_his.html.

———. "Scaliapalooza." *Slate,* October 30, 2003.

———. "What It Looks Like When Justices Tear into Each Other—From Close Up." *Slate,* June 25, 2012.

Lupu, Ira C. "Textualism and Original Understanding: Time, the Supreme Court, and the Federalist." *George Washington Law Review* 66 (June/August 1998): 1324ff.

Manning, John F. "Textualism and Original Understanding: Textualism and the Role of the Federalist in Constitutional Adjudication." *George Washington Law Review* 66 (June/August 1998): 1337ff.

Marcotte, Paul. "New Kid on the Block." *ABA Journal,* August 1, 1986.

Margolick, David. "The Path to Florida." *Vanity Fair,* October 2000, pp. 310–77.

Mauro, Tony. "Could Scalia Be the Chief?" *American Lawyer Media,* November 20, 2002, www.law.com.

———. "In Second Book, Scalia, Garner Warn Judicial Decisions Leading to 'Descent into Social Rancor.'" *National Law Journal,* June 15, 2012.

———. "Lawyer's Guide to Scalia's *New York* Interview." "Supreme Court Insider," *National Law Journal,* October 8, 2013, http://www.law.com/jsp/nlj/PubArticleSCI .jsp?id=1202622672135&Lawyers_Guide_to_Scalias_New_York_interview.

———. "Scalia Recusal Revives Debate over Judicial Speech, Ethics." *Legal Times,* October 20, 2003, www.law.com.

McDonough, Molly. "Scalia: I Am Not a Nut!" *ABA Journal,* April 8, 2008.

Merrill, Thomas W. "Childress Lecture: The Making of the Second Rehnquist Court: A Preliminary Analysis." *St. Louis University Law Journal* 47 (Spring 2003): 569ff.

Michelman, Frank. "*Anastasoff* and Remembrance." *Arkansas Law Review* 58 (2005): 555ff.

Murphy, Bruce Allen. "Extrajudicial Activities." Encyclopedia of the Supreme Court of the United States, David S. Tanenhaus, ed., New York: Thomson Gale, 2008.

Neumann, Richard K. Jr. "Conflicts of Interest in Bush v. Gore: Did Some Justices Vote Illegally?" *Georgetown Journal of Legal Ethics* 16 (Spring 2003): 375–78.

Oremus, Will. "Elena Kagan Admits Supreme Court Justices Haven't Quite Figured Out Email Yet," *Slate,* August 20, 2013, http://www.slate.com/blogs/future_tense/2013/08/20 /elena_kagan_supreme_court_justices_haven_t_gotten_to_email_use_paper_memos.html.

Posner, Richard A. "The Incoherence of Antonin Scalia." *New Republic,* August 24, 2012.

———. "In Defense of Looseness." *New Republic,* August 27, 2008.

———. "Justice Scalia Is Upset About Immigration. But Where Is His Evidence?" "Supreme Court in Review," *Slate,* June 27, 2012.

———. "Richard Posner Responds to Scalia's Accusation of Lying." *New Republic,* September 20, 2012, www.tnr.com.

Post, Robert, and Reva Siegel. "Originalism as a Political Practice: The Right's Living Constitution." *Fordham Law Review* 75, no. 2, Articles 5 (2006): 545–74.

Powell, H. Jefferson. "The Original Understanding of Original Intent." *Harvard Law Review* 98 (March 1985): 885ff.

Rakove, Jack. "The Original Intention of Original Understanding." *Constitutional Commentary* 13 (Summer 1996): 159–86.

———. "Thoughts on Heller from a 'Real Historian.'" Balkinization, June 27, 2008, http:// balkin.blogspot.com/2008/06/thoughts-on-heller-from-real-historian.html.

Redden, Molly. "Rick Santorum's Virginia Church and *Opus Dei.*" *New Republic,* March 6, 2012, http://www.newrepublic.com/article/politics/101420/santorums-church -opus-dei#.

Reilly, Peter J. "A Better Way to Celebrate Saint Patrick's Day." *Forbes,* March 16, 2012, www .forbes.com.

Reuben, Richard C. "Man in the Middle." *California Lawyer,* October 1992, pp. 36–38.

Rosen, Jeffrey. "Annals of Law: The Agonizer." *New Yorker,* November 11, 1996, pp. 82ff.

————. "A Damning Dissent." *New Republic,* June 4, 2013, http://www.newrepublic.com /article/113375/supreme-court-dna-case-antonin-scalias-dissent-ages#.

————. "Supreme Leader." *New Republic,* June 18, 2007, pp. 19–22.

Rosenberg, Debra. "Justice: Bench Player." *Newsweek,* February 12, 2007.

Rubin, Thea F., and Albert P. Melone. "Justice Antonin Scalia: A First Year Freshman Effect?" *Judicature* 72, no 2 (August/September 1988): 98–102.

Savage, David. "Supreme Stumpers: The Next President Could Reshape the Court and the Legal Arena." *ABA Journal,* October 2000.

Scalia, Antonin, "The A.L.J. Fiasco—A Reprise." *University of Chicago Law Review* 47 (1979): 57–80.

————. "Back to Basics: Making Law Without Making Rules." *Regulation,* July/August 1981.

————. "Chairman's Message (Concerning Regulatory Reform Legislation)." *Administrative Law Review* 33 (Fall 1981).

————. "The Disease as Cure: In Order to Get Beyond Racism We Must First Take Account of Race." *Washington University Law Quarterly* (1979): 147–57.

————. "The Doctrine of Standing as an Essential Element of the Separation of Powers." *Suffolk University Law Review* 17 (March 1983): 881ff.

————. "Don't Go Near the Water (A Proposal Concerning the FCC's Fairness Doctrine)." *Federal Commercial Bar Journal* 25 (1972): 111–20.

————. "Economic Affairs as Human Affairs." *CATO Journal* 4, no. 3 (Winter 1985): 703–09.

————. "The First (and Last?) Published Opinion of the Intelligence Court." ABA Standing Committee, *Law and National Security Intelligence Report* 3, no. 12 (December 1981): 3–7.

————. "The Freedom of Information Act Has No Clothes." *Regulation* 6, no. 2 (March/ April 1982): 15–19.

————. "God's Justice and Ours." *First Things,* May 2002, pp. 17–21.

————. "Guadalajara! Regulation by Munificence." *Regulation,* March/April 1978.

————. "The Hearing Examiner Loan Program." *Duke Law Journal* (1971): 319–66.

————. "Historical Anomalies in Administrative Law." *Supreme Court Historical Society Review, 1985 Yearbook,* p. 103ff.

————. "In Memoriam: Edward H. Levi," *University of Chicago Law Review* 67, no. 4 (2000): 971–83.

————. "The Judges Are Coming." *Panhandle,* Spring 1980.

————. "The Judicialization of Standardless Rulemaking: Two Wrongs Make a Right." *Regulation,* July/August 1977.

————. "The Legislative Veto: A False Remedy for System Overload." *Regulation,* November/ December 1979, p. 19.

————. "The Limits of the Law." *New Jersey Law Bulletin,* April 30, 1987, p. 4.

————. "Morality, Pragmatism, and the Legal Order." *Harvard Journal of Law and Public Policy* 9 (1986): 123ff.

————. "1976 Bicentennial Institute—Oversight and Review of Agency Decisionmaking— The Legislative Veto." *Administrative Law Review* 28, no. 4 (1976): 569–742.

————. "A Note on the Benzene Case." *Regulation,* July/August 1980.

————. "On Making It Look Easy by Doing It Wrong: A Critical View of the Justice Department." In Edward McGlynn Gaffney Jr., ed., *Private Schools and the Public Good: Policy Alternatives for the Eighties.* South Bend, IN: University of Notre Dame Press, 1982.

————. "On Saving the Kingdom: Federal Trade Commission and Federal Communications Commission." *Regulation,* November/December 1980.

———. "Parties and the Nominating Process: The Legal Framework for Reform." *Common Sense* 4 (1981), pp. 40ff.

———. "Procedural Aspects of the Consumer Product Safety Act." *University of California Law Review* 20 (1973): 889–953.

———. "Regulation—The First Year: Regulatory Review and Management." *Regulation,* January/February 1982.

———. "Regulatory Reform—The Game Has Changed." *Regulation,* January/February 1981.

———. "Rulemaking as Politics." *Administrative Law Review* 34, no. 3 (1982): v–xi.

———. "Separation of Functions: Obscurity Preserved." *Administrative Law Review* 34 (Winter 1982).

———. "Sovereign Immunity and Non-Statutory Review of Federal Administrative Action: Some Conclusion from the Public-Lands Cases." *Michigan Law Review* 68 (1970): 867–974.

———. "Support Your Local Professor of Administrative Law." *Administrative Law Review* 34, no. 2 (1982), v–ix.

———. "The Two Faces of Federalism." *Harvard Journal of Law and Public Policy* 6 (1982): 19–22.

———. "Two Wrongs Make a Right: The Judicialization of Standardless Rulemaking." *Regulation* 1, no. 1 (July 8, 1977): 38–41.

———. "Vermont Yankee: The APA, the D.C. Circuit and the Supreme Court." *Supreme Court Law Review, 1978 Yearbook,* pp. 345–409.

Scalia, Antonin, and Graham C. Lilly. "Appellate Justice: A Crisis in Virginia." *Virginia Law Review* 57 (1971): 3–64.

Skaggs, Adam. "Thanks Citizens' United for This Campaign Finance Mess We're In." *The Atlantic,* July 27, 2012, http://www.theatlantic.com/politics/archive/2012/07/thanks-citizens-united-for-this-campaign-finance-mess-were-in/260389/.

Snider, L. Britt. "Unlucky Shamrock: Recollections from the Church Committee's Investigation of NSA." *Studies in Intelligence* 43, no. 1 (Winter 1999–2000), www.cia.gov/csi/studies.

Snyder, Eloise C. "The Supreme Court as a Small Group." *Social Forces* 36 (March 1958): 232–38, reprinted in Robert G. Scigliano, ed., *The Courts: A Reader in the Judicial Process* (Boston: Little, Brown, 1962).

Stern, Mark Joseph. "Scalia Says Court Invented the Gay Minority. Women, He's on to You, Too." *Slate,* August 21, 2013, http://www.slate.com/blogs/xx_factor/2013/08/20/antonin_scalia_to_supreme_court_don_t_invent_new_minorities_gay_people_and.html.

Stone, Geoffrey R. "Justice Sotomayor, Justice Scalia and Our Six Catholic Justices." *Huffington Post,* August 28, 2009, www.huffingtonpost.com.

———. "The Supreme Court and the 2012 Election." *Huffington Post,* August 13, 2012, http://www.huffingtonpost.com/geoffrey-r-stone/the-supreme-court-and-the_b_1773347.html.

Sutin, L. Anthony. "Presidential Election Law/The Recount." *Jurist Legal Intelligence,* December 14, 2000, http://jurist.law.pitt.edu/election/electionfaq.html.

Talbot, Margaret. "Supreme Confidence." *New Yorker,* March 28, 2005, pp. 40–55.

Toobin, Jeffrey. "Annals of Law: Swing Shift: How Anthony Kennedy's Passion for Foreign Law Could Change the Supreme Court." *New Yorker,* September 12, 2005.

Wechsler, Herbert. "Toward Neutral Principles of Constitutional Law." *Harvard Law Review* 73, no. 1 (November 1959): 1–35.

Weiss, Debra Cassens. "At Catholic Conference, Scalia Talks About the Possibility of Miracles." *ABA Journal,* March 5, 2012.

———. "Scalia Doubts He Would Win Confirmation Today." *ABA Journal,* July 29, 2010.

———. "Scalia: SCOTUS Should Not 'Invent New Minorities.'" *ABA Journal,* September 20, 2013, www.abajournal.com.

Wexler, Jay D. "Laugh Track." *The Green Bag* 9 (Autumn, 2005): 59–61.

Whelan, Edward. "Richard A. Posner's Badly Confused Attack on Scalia/Garner." "Bench Memos," *National Review Online,* 5 parts, August 31, September 1, September 3, September 6, September 7, 2012.

———. "Robert Reich's Reckless Attack on Thomas and Scalia." "Bench Memos," *National Review Online,* March 8, 2011.

White, Adam J. "Wilkinson and Posner Dissenting: Two Conservative Judges Challenge Judge Scalia." *Weekly Standard* 14, no. 13 (December 15, 2008).

Wilkinson, J. Harvie. "Of Guns, Abortions, and the Unraveling Rule of Law." *University of Virginia Law Review* 95, no. 2 (April 2009): 253ff.

Williams, Stephen F. "Textualism and Original Understanding: Restore Contact, Distorting Text: Legislative History and the Problem of Age." *George Washington Law Review* 66 (June/August 1998): 1366ff.

Woellert, Lorraine. "Why Not Scalia? The Pugnacious Darling of the Right Was Sidelined by Political Calculus." *Business Week,* September 19, 2005, p. 56.

Wood, Gordon S. "The Fundamentalists and the Constitution." *New York Review of Books,* February 18, 1988, found at www.nybooks.com.

GOVERNMENT HEARINGS AND PUBLICATIONS

Executive Privilege—Secrecy in Government, Hearings Before Subcommittee on Intergovernmental Relations of the Committee on Government Operations of the United States Senate, September 29 and October 23, 1975.

Guidelines on Constitutional Litigation, February 19, 1988, Office of Legal Policy, U.S. Department of Justice.

Antonin Scalia Testimony, November 20, 1975, U.S. Intelligence Agencies and Activities: Committee Proceedings, Proceedings of the Select Committee on Intelligence, House of Representatives, 94th Congress, 1st session, September 10–November 20, 1975, Part 4 Washington, D.C., U.S. Government Printing Office, 1976.

Original Meaning Jurisprudence: A Sourcebook, Report to the Attorney General, U.S. Department of Justice, March 12, 1987.

The Constitution in the Year 2000: Choices Ahead in Constitutional Interpretation, Office of Legal Policy: U.S. Department of Justice, Report to the Attorney General, 1988.

Antonin Scalia. Testimony on the Constitutionality of Tuition Tax Credits. Washington, D.C.: American Enterprise Institute, Reprint Number 84, March 1978.

Antonin Scalia testimony. Confirmation of Federal Judges, Hearings Before the Committee on the Judiciary, United States Senate, 97th Congress, 2nd Session, Part 4, August 4, 1982.

Nomination of Judge Antonin Scalia. Hearings Before the Committee on the Judiciary, United States Senate, 99th Congress, 2nd Session, August 5 and 6, 1986, Government Printing Office, Washington, D.C., 1987.

Statement of Antonin Scalia, Associate Justice Supreme Court of the United States, Before the Subcommittee on Commercial and Administrative Law, Committee on the Judiciary, U.S. House of Representatives, Hearing on the Reauthorization of the Administrative Conference of the United States, 108th Congress, Washington, D.C., May 20, 2004.

DISSERTATIONS, THESES, PAPERS, MEMOIRS

Barnett, Randy E. "Scalia's Infidelity: A Critique of Faint-Hearted Originalism." Posted February 1, 2006, Social Science Research Network, http://papers.ssrn.com/sol3/papers .cfm?abstract_id=880112.

Barton, Benjamin H. "An Empirical Study of Supreme Court Pre-Appointment Experience," February 24, 2012, Social Science Research Network, www.ssrn.com.

Brand, Paul. "The Judicial Interpretation of Legislation in Later Thirteenth and Early Fourteenth Century England." Paper delivered at 21st British Legal History Conference, July 9, 2013, Glasgow, Scotland.

Dershowitz, Alan, with Eric Nguyen and Brett Arnold. Memo, "Scalia's Inconsistent Originalism, Reordered by Case Strength," December 4, 2008, Harvard Law School, Cambridge, MA.

DeSimone, Joseph F. Memoir. Brooklyn College Archives, Brooklyn, New York.

Jassem, Harvey C. "The Selling of the Compromise—1971 or Cable Television Goes to the City." Master's thesis, Ohio State University, 1972.

————. The Nixon Administration Public Broadcasting Papers: A Summary, 1969–1974, National Association of Educational Broadcasting, 1979.

INTERNET ARCHIVAL RESOURCES

Dan Lopez, Thomas Blanton, Meredith Fuchs, and Barbara Elias. "Veto Battle 30 Years Ago Set Freedom of Information Norms." National Security Archive, posted November 23, 2004, www.gwu.edu/~nsarchiv/.

"Memo for Mr. [John S.] Warner, Subject: Veto Action on H.R. 12471," September 23, 1974. Office of General Counsel, CIA, FOIA release, "Supreme Court Justice Scalia Fought Against the Freedom of Information Act," "The Memory Hole," www.thememoryhole .org/foi/scalia_foia.htm.

John S. Warner. Memo, September 26, 1974, Office of General Counsel, CIA, FOIA release, "The Memory Hole" "Supreme Court Justice Scalia Fought Against the Freedom of Information Act," www.thememoryhole.org/foi/scalia_foia.htm.

U.S. Department of Justice U.S. Marshals Service Investigation of "the Hattiesburg Incident" of 07-April-2004 (OCR [searchable] version); FOIA release, governmentattic.org, www .governmentattic.org.

INDEX

CASE INDEX